Real Estate Taxation

A Practitioner's Guide

Third Edition

David F. Windish

CCH INCORPORATED
Chicago

Editorial Staff

Production: Diane McComb

This publication is designed to provide accurate and authoritative information in regard to the subject matter covered. It is sold with the understanding that the publisher is not engaged in rendering legal, accounting, or other professional service and that the author is not offering such advice in this publication. If legal advice or other expert assistance is required, the services of a competent professional person should be sought.

ISBN: 0-8080-0888-9

©2002, **CCH** INCORPORATED

4025 W. Peterson Ave.
Chicago, IL 60646-6085
1 800 248 3248
http://tax.cchgroup.com

No claim is made to original government works; however, within this Product or Publication, the following are subject to CCH's copyright: (1) the gathering, compilation, and arrangement of such government materials; (2) the magnetic translation and digital conversion of data, if applicable; (3) the historical, statutory and other notes and references; and (4) the commentary and other materials.

All Rights Reserved
Printed in the United States of America

To those who fill my days and nights,

and give me troubles and delights.

To my family, wife, and children . . . and dog.

Preface

The federal income tax impacts on real estate at every stage of its life cycle—acquisition, operation, and disposition. The essential structure of the major portion of *Real Estate Taxation—A Practitioner's Guide,* the first four parts, follows this life cycle and focuses on real estate used in business or held for the production of rental income. The remainder of the book is devoted to the tax consequences of the ownership of a personal residence and indirect ownership of real estate interests in the form of securities under federal law.

Part I looks at the acquisition of real property from a tax perspective, including the acquisition transaction itself, how the real estate is held, and how it is financed.

Parts II and III are concerned with the operational aspects of real estate. In the three chapters of Part II, the tax questions that arise from rental and leasing arrangements are explored. Tax deductions associated with real estate operation (including additional deductions to assist economically depressed areas and New York City following the terrorist attacks of September 11, 2001) and the limits placed on these deductions, the treatment of additions and improvements, and troubled real estate financings are the major topics in Part III. Also found in Part III is a chapter dealing with the tax questions and problems that arise in connection with the development, subdivision, and sale of real estate in the ordinary course of business—questions that are unique when compared to those involved in the one-time sale of business or investment property.

Part IV explores the last stage of the life cycle of real estate and examines the disposition of real estate through various taxable and nontaxable transactions. This third edition also includes a discussion of the reduced or zero tax rates for the sale of qualifying property in designated depressed areas.

Ownership of a personal residence is favored by the tax law. The owner of a home is given advantages not available to the occupant of a rented residential apartment or home. Part V explores these advantages, including deductions available to all homeowners, use of part of a residence for business, cooperative and condominium ownership, and the avoidance of federal income tax on the sale of a residence.

The final three chapters, which make up Part VI, take a brief look at ownership interests in real estate that are indirect and mass-marketed. These three types of interests—real estate limited partnerships, real estate investment trusts, and real estate mortgage investment conduits—offer participation in real estate through interests that are securities under federal securities laws.

David F. Windish

September 2002

About the Author

David F. Windish, J.D., LL.M. in taxation, is a tax attorney and consultant. He has served as an instructor of tax-advantaged investments at the New York Institute of Finance; an instructor of business law at the U.S. Merchant Marine Academy, Kings Point, N.Y.; and an adjunct professor at George Mason University, Fairfax, Va. He has also served as executive editor for Tax Analysts; managing editor for *Business Strategies,* published by **CCH INCORPORATED**; and senior editor for the Institute for Business Planning.

In addition to this book, Mr. Windish is the author of *Tax-Advantaged Investments* and *Investor's Guide to Limited Partnerships,* both published by the New York Institute of Finance. Through the Center for Video Education, he has authored continuing education courses dealing with real estate and closely held corporations. Those courses consist of readings, case studies, and videotape segments.

Mr. Windish is a graduate of Rutgers University Law School and the New York University School of Law, Graduate Division. He has been heard as a guest speaker at professional meetings and seminars and on popular radio programs.

Contents

A more detailed Contents starts on page xi.

Chapter   Page

Part I—Acquiring Ownership of Real Property

1	The Acquisition Transaction	5
2	Form of Ownership	39
3	Financing Real Estate	85

Part II—Rental and Leasing Arrangements

4	Payments Between Landlord and Tenant	143
5	Lease Acquisition and Disposition	163
6	Leasehold Improvements and Additions	181

Part III—Real Estate Operation

7	Operating Expenses and Taxes	203
8	Property Additions and Improvements	249
9	Depreciation	283
10	Development, Subdivision, and Sales in the Ordinary Course of Business	319
11	Passive Activity Loss Rules	339
12	Troubled Financings	387

Part IV—Disposition of Real Estate

13	Sales and Exchanges	425
14	Seller-Financed Sales	485
15	Casualty, Condemnation, and Demolition	521
16	Contributions and Gifts	553

Chapter		Page

Part V—Personal Residences

17	Deductions for Homeowners	579
18	Mixed-Use Residences	605
19	Cooperatives, Condominiums, and Associations	627
20	Sale of Residence	645

Part VI—Securitized Real Estate Investments

21	Real Estate Limited Partnerships	663
22	Real Estate Investment Trusts	677
23	Real Estate Mortgage Investment Conduits	679
	Case Table	683
	Index	689

Contents in Detail

Paragraph

Part I—Acquiring Ownership of Real Property

CHAPTER 1   THE ACQUISITION TRANSACTION

OVERVIEW OF CHAPTER	100
IMPORTANCE OF BASIS	101
Calculation of Basis	103
Property Acquired by Purchase	103.1
Property Constructed by or for the Owner	103.2
Property Acquired in an Exchange	103.3
Property Acquired on Exercise of an Option	103.4
Property Acquired by Gift	103.5
Property Acquired by Inheritance	103.6
Property Acquired from a Spouse or Former Spouse	103.7
Other Basis Rules	103.8
Mortgage and Basis	105
Contingent or Speculative Obligations	105.1
Borrowing Against Previously Owned Property	105.2
Artificially Inflated Purchase Price	105.3
PURCHASE OF REAL PROPERTY	111
Buying Expenses	115
Allocation of Costs	117
Land and Buildings	117.1
Land Improvements and Personal Property	117.2
Buildings and Personal Property	117.3
Real Estate as Part of a Going Business	117.4
Reporting Requirements	117.5
Apportionment of Real Property Taxes	119
Purchase from Foreign Person	121
CONSTRUCTION OF REAL PROPERTY	123
Capitalization of Construction Costs	127
Expenses Other Than Interest	127.1
Interest	127.2
Interest and Taxes on Pre-1987 Construction	131
Capitalization of Carrying Charges	135
LOW-INCOME HOUSING TAX CREDIT	139

Contents in Detail

		Paragraph
CHAPTER 2	**FORM OF OWNERSHIP**	
	OVERVIEW OF CHAPTER	200
	OWNERSHIP FOR TAX PURPOSES	201
	Use of Straw or Nominee Corporations	203
	Agency Relationship Requirement	205
	INDIVIDUAL AND JOINT OWNERSHIP	207
	Sole Individual Ownership	211
	Common and Joint Ownership	213
	Joint Ownership by Spouses	215
	Community Property	221
	PARTNERSHIPS	225
	Legal Characteristics	227
	General Partnerships	227.1
	Limited Partnerships	227.2
	Joint Ventures	227.3
	Syndicates	227.4
	Taxation of Partnerships	229
	Basis of Partnership Interest	229.1
	Contributions to Partnership	229.2
	Operation of Partnership	229.3
	Distributions	229.4
	Guaranteed Payments	229.5
	Elective Large Partnership Rules	229.7
	CORPORATIONS	231
	Legal Characteristics	233
	Taxation of Corporations	235
	Organization of Corporation	235.1
	Operation of Corporation	235.2
	Property Distributions and Liquidations	235.3
	LIMITED LIABILITY COMPANIES	237
	Entity Classification	237.1
	Partnership Conversion to LLC	237.2
	S CORPORATIONS	241
	Qualification as an S Corporation	243
	Income and Loss	247
	Built-In Gain	247.1
	S Corporation Losses	247.2

Contents in Detail

	Paragraph
OWNERSHIP IN TRUST	251
Tax Treatment of Trusts	253
Depreciation	255
Grantor Trusts	257
CHOICE OF THE OWNING ENTITY	261
Corporation or Partnership	263
S Corporation or Partnership	265
Comparison Chart of Business Entities	267

CHAPTER 3   FINANCING REAL ESTATE

	Paragraph
OVERVIEW OF CHAPTER	300
MORTGAGE FINANCING	301
Mortgage Costs	303
Borrower's Costs	303.1
Lender's Costs	303.2
Buy Downs and Similar Arrangements	305
Payoff of Mortgage	307
Prepayment Penalties	307.1
Payment Discounts	307.2
AT-RISK RULES	311
Taxpayers and Activities Subject to the Rules	313
Deductions Under the At-Risk Rules	315
Order of Deductions	315.1
Recapture of Prior Deductions	315.2
Determining Amount at Risk	317
Borrowed Amounts	317.1
Avoidance of At-Risk Rules	317.2
Computation of At-Risk Amount	317.3
Qualified Nonrecourse Financing	319
Financing from Related Person	319.1
Transfer of Property	319.2
INTEREST	321
Interest Income	323
Interest Deduction	325
Prepaid Interest	325.1
Investment Interest	325.2
Tracing Debt Proceeds	325.3

	Paragraph
Interest-Free and Below-Market Rate Loans ...	327
Gift Loans	327.1
Compensation Loans	327.2
Corporation-Shareholder Loans	327.3
Reporting Requirements	327.4
ORIGINAL ISSUE DISCOUNT AND IMPUTED INTEREST ON DEFERRED PAYMENT SALES	331
Imputed Interest	333
Unstated Interest	333.1
Land Sales Between Family Members	333.2
Original Issue Discount	335
Cash Method Accounting	335.1
Assumptions and Modifications of Debt Instruments	335.2
Interest Rates Under the Imputed Interest and OID Rules	337
Maximum Interest Rate	337.1
Installment Obligations	337.2
Variable Interest Rate Obligations	337.3
Contingent Interest	337.4
Excessive Interest	337.5
SALE-LEASEBACKS AND OTHER LEASE FINANCING	341
Straight Sale-Leaseback	343
Tax Benefits	343.1
Like-Kind Exchange and the Sale-Leaseback	343.2
Recognition of a Sale-Leaseback for Tax Purposes	345
Supreme Court Guidelines	345.1
IRS Guidelines	345.2
Variations on the Sale-Leaseback	347
Split Financing	347.1
Related Party Sale-Leasebacks	347.2
Equity Participation	347.3
Tax-Exempt Entity Leasing	347.4
Lease with Option as Conditional Sales Contract	349

Part II—Rental and Leasing Arrangements

		Paragraph
CHAPTER 4	**PAYMENTS BETWEEN LANDLORD AND TENANT**	
	OVERVIEW OF CHAPTER	400
	RENT	401
	Percentage Rents	403
	Payment of Lessor's Expenses	405
	Property Transactions	407
	Related Parties	409
	Intra-Family Leases	409.1
	Controlled Corporations	409.2
	Matching Lessee's Deduction to Lessor's Income	409.3
	TENANT'S RENT DEDUCTION	411
	Advance Rents	413
	Graduated Rents	415
	Decrease in Rents	415.1
	Increase in Rents	415.2
	LANDLORD'S RENT INCOME	421
	Advance Rents	423
	Assignments and Loans	425
	DEFERRED OR STEPPED RENTAL AGREEMENTS	431
	Section 467 Rental Agreements	433
	Constant Rental Accrual in Tax Avoidance Transactions	435
	Exemptions from Rental Agreement Rules	435.1
	Recapture in Leasebacks and Long-Term Agreements	435.2
	LEASES WITH PURCHASE OPTIONS	441
	Lease as Sales Contract	443
	Lease or Sale Distinguished	445
	DEPOSITS	451
	Lessee's Deduction	453
	Lessor's Income	455

Contents in Detail

		Paragraph
CHAPTER 5	**LEASE ACQUISITION AND DISPOSITION**	
	OVERVIEW OF CHAPTER	500
	LEASE ACQUISITION COSTS	501
	Classification of Payments as Lease Acquisition Costs	503
	Lessor's Costs	503.1
	Lessee's Costs	503.2
	Unsuccessful Lease Attempt	503.3
	Renewal Options	505
	Existing Improvements Costs	507
	LEASE CANCELLATION	511
	Payments by Lessee	513
	Lessee's Deduction	513.1
	Lessor's Income	513.2
	Payments by Lessor	515
	Lessor's Deduction	515.1
	Lessee's Income	515.2
	Unamortized Costs on Cancellation of Lease	517
	Modification of Lease	519
	SALE OF LEASE	521
CHAPTER 6	**LEASEHOLD IMPROVEMENTS AND ADDITIONS**	
	OVERVIEW OF CHAPTER	600
	IMPROVEMENTS AND ADDITIONS BY LESSOR	601
	Restoration or Maintenance by Lessee	603
	Improvements to Benefit a Particular Lessee	605
	Purchase of Property with Lessee Improvements	607
	IMPROVEMENTS AND ADDITIONS BY LESSEE	611
	Improvements as Rent	613
	Improvements as Capital Investment	615
	Pre-1987 Improvements	615.1
	Lease Termination	615.2
	INVESTMENT CREDIT	621
	Qualified Rehabilitations by Lessee	623

Contents in Detail

		Paragraph
Qualified Rehabilitations by Lessor		625
Election to Pass Credit to Lessee		625.1
Credit Split on Short-Term Lease Property		625.2

Part III—Real Estate Operation

CHAPTER 7   OPERATING EXPENSES AND TAXES

	Paragraph
OVERVIEW OF CHAPTER	700
TAX ACCOUNTING FOR REAL ESTATE	701
Accounting Period	703
Required Tax Years for Partnerships, S Corporations, and Personal Service Corporations	703.1
Election to Use Other Than a Required Year	703.2
Accounting Method	705
Cash Method	705.1
Accrual Method	705.2
Long-Term Construction Contracts	705.3
Controlling the Timing of Income and Expense	707
Deferring Income and Accelerating Deductions	707.1
Accelerating Income and Deferring Deductions	707.2
Related Party Transactions	709
Losses on Sales and Exchanges	709.1
Deductions for Expenses and Interest	709.2
Related Parties Defined	709.3
START-UP EXPENSES	711
Amortization of Expenses	713
Investigatory Expenses	713.1
Start-Up Expenses	713.2
Pre-Opening Expenses	713.3
Trade or Business Requirement	715
REAL ESTATE OPERATING EXPENSES	721
Repairs	723
Repair or Improvement	723.1
Replacement, Renovation, and Reconditioning	723.2
Removal of Architectural Barriers	723.3
Materials and Supplies	725

	Paragraph
Compensation	727
Real Estate Corporation Officers	727.1
Family Members as Employees	727.2
Independent Contractors and Employees	727.3
Licensed Real Estate Agents	727.4
Partners	727.5
Commissions and Fees	729
Real Estate Commissions	729.1
Kickbacks	729.2
Insurance	731
Advertising	733
Legal Expenses	735
Interest	737
REAL ESTATE TAXES	741
Real Property Taxes	743
Deduction of Real Property Taxes	743.1
Back Taxes Payments	743.2
Special Assessment and Local Benefit Taxes	745
Transfer Taxes	747
Impact Fees	749

CHAPTER 8 PROPERTY ADDITIONS AND IMPROVEMENTS

OVERVIEW OF CHAPTER	800
IMPROVEMENTS TO REAL ESTATE AS CAPITAL EXPENDITURES	801
Improvements to Land and Buildings	803
Replacements of Building Components	805
Abandonment of Improvement Plans	807
SPECIAL AMORTIZATION PROVISIONS	811
Pollution Control Facilities	813
Amortization Election Requirements	813.1
Limitation for Longer-Lived Facilities	813.2
Reforestation Expenses and Tax Credit	815
Soil and Water Conservation Expenditures	817
TAX CREDITS FOR BUILDING REHABILITATIONS	821
Rehabilitation of Older Commercial Buildings	823
Substantial Rehabilitation Test	823.1
Expenditures Incurred by Predecessor	823.2
The "Wall Test"	823.3

Contents in Detail

	Paragraph
Nonqualifying Expenditures	823.4
Basis Reduction by Credit Amount	823.5
Rehabilitations of Certified Historic Structures	825
Certification Requirements	825.1
Nonqualified Buildings Credit Allowance	825.2
Recapture of Rehabilitation Credits	827
LOW-INCOME HOUSING CREDIT	831
Overview of the Credit Process	831.1
Qualification for the Credit	833
Qualified Low-Income Building	833.1
Qualified Low-Income Housing Project	833.2
Calculation of the Low-Income Housing Credit	835
Applicable Credit Rates	835.1
Qualified Basis for Determination of Credit	835.2
Rehabilitation Expenditures	835.3
Compliance and Recapture Provisions	837
Increases in Tenant Income	837.1
Large Partnerships	837.2
Recapture Amount	837.3
Casualty Losses	837.4
RENEWAL COMMUNITIES AND NEW YORK LIBERTY ZONE	841
Commercial Revitalization Deduction	843
New York Liberty Zone	845

CHAPTER 9 DEPRECIATION

	Paragraph
OVERVIEW OF CHAPTER	900
MACRS DEPRECIATION SYSTEM	901
Computation of the Deduction	903
Recovery Periods	903.1
Straight-Line Method	903.2
Mid-Month Convention	903.3
Use of Optional Tables	903.4
Depreciation of Additions and Improvements	905
Land Improvements	905.1
Property Under Construction	905.2
ALTERNATIVE DEPRECIATION SYSTEM	911
Calculation of Alternative Depreciation	913
Election of Alternative Depreciation	913.1
Use of Optional Tables	913.2

	Paragraph
Real Property Subject to Alternative Depreciation	915
Tax-Exempt Use Property	915.1
Tax-Exempt Bond Financed Property	915.2
Alternative Minimum Tax	915.3
ACRS DEPRECIATION FOR PRE-1987 PROPERTY	921
Computation of Deduction	923
Straight-Line Election	923.1
ACRS Schedules	923.2
Additions and Improvements	925
Substantial Improvements as Separate Property	925.1
Qualification as Substantial Improvement	925.2
DEPRECIATION OF PRE-1981 PROPERTY	931
Calculation of Deduction for Real Property	933
Depreciation Methods	933.1
Change of Depreciation Methods	933.2
Anti-Churning Rules	935
Real Property Rules	935.1
Related Party Transfers	935.2
Tax-Free Transfers	935.3

CHAPTER 10 DEVELOPMENT, SUBDIVISION, AND SALES IN THE ORDINARY COURSE OF BUSINESS

OVERVIEW OF CHAPTER	1000
DEVELOPMENT COSTS	1001
Equitable Apportionment Rule	1003
Manner of Apportionment of Basis	1003.1
Methods of Apportionment of Basis	1003.2
Inclusion of Development Costs in Basis	1005
Development Improvements as Separate Interest	1005.1
Estimated Future Costs	1005.2
DEALER STATUS	1011
Characterization of Dealer Property	1013
Tests Applied for Classification of Property	1013.1
Subdivided Realty as Dealer Property	1013.2

Contents in Detail

	Paragraph
Tax Effects of Classification as a Dealer	1015
Dealer Installment Sales	1015.1
Dealer Sales of Timeshares and Residential Lots	1015.2
SUBDIVISION BY INVESTOR	1021
Qualification for Special Tax Treatment	1023
Holding Period Rules	1023.1
Improvements to Land Tracts	1023.2
Necessary Improvements to Property After 10 Years	1023.3
Calculation of the Amount and Character of Gain	1025
Five-Percent Rule	1025.1
Five-Year Rule	1025.2

CHAPTER 11   PASSIVE ACTIVITY LOSS RULES

	Paragraph
OVERVIEW OF CHAPTER	1100
GENERAL PROVISIONS	1103
Taxpayers Subject to the Rules	1105
Closely Held C Corporations	1105.1
Personal Service Corporations	1105.2
Activities Subject to the Rules	1107
Limited Partnership Interests	1107.1
Oil and Gas Property Working Interests	1107.2
Material Participation	1109
Material Participation by an Individual	1109.1
Material Participation by a Corporation	1109.2
IDENTIFICATION OF SEPARATE ACTIVITIES	1111
General Rule	1113
Limitations on Grouping	1115
Regrouping	1117
LIMITS ON RENTAL ACTIVITIES	1121
Rental Activity Defined	1123
Rentals Incidental to Nonrental Activities	1123.1
Property Provided to a Partnership, Joint Venture, or S Corporation	1123.2
Self-Rented Property	1125
Rental Incident to Development	1127
Rental of Nondepreciable Property	1129

Contents in Detail

	Paragraph
Active Participation in Rental Real Estate	1131
$25,000 Limit	1131.1
Filing Status	1131.2
Phase-Out of Deduction	1131.3
Real Property Business Exception	1133
Grouping Rental Real Estate Activities	1133.1
Limited Partnership Interests	1133.3
Coordination with Active Participation Exception	1133.5
TAX TREATMENT OF PASSIVE LOSSES AND CREDITS	1141
Computation of Deductible Loss	1143
Passive Activity Gross Income	1143.1
Passive Activity Deductions	1143.2
Partners and S Corporation Shareholders	1143.3
Closely Held Corporation's Passive Activity Loss	1145
Disallowed Losses	1147
Allocation of Disallowed Loss	1147.1
Allocation Within Loss Activities	1147.2
Carryover of Disallowed Deductions	1147.3
Disposition of a Passive Activity	1147.4
Passive Activity Credits	1149
Closely Held Corporation	1149.1
Carryover of Suspended Credit	1149.2
PUBLICLY TRADED PARTNERSHIPS	1151
Partnerships Subject to the Rule	1153
Partnerships Subject to Grandfather Rule	1157
Application of the Special Passive Activity Loss Rule	1159

CHAPTER 12 TROUBLED FINANCINGS

OVERVIEW OF CHAPTER	1200
SETTLEMENT OF DEBT AT DISCOUNT	1201
Tax Treatment of Debtor	1203
Solvent Debtor	1203.1
Insolvent or Bankrupt Debtor	1203.2
Qualified Real Property Business Debt	1203.3
Purchase-Money Mortgage Reduction	1203.5

Contents in Detail

	Paragraph
Tax Treatment of Creditor	1205
Loss on Discount	1205.1
Bad Debt Deduction	1205.2
Nonbusiness Bad Debts	1205.3
FORECLOSURE	**1211**
Tax Treatment of the Debtor	1213
Calculation of Gain or Loss	1213.1
Character of Gain or Loss	1213.2
Tax Treatment of the Creditor	1215
Foreclosure Expenses	1215.1
Purchase by Third Party	1215.2
Purchase by Mortgagee	1215.3
CONVEYANCE AND ABANDONMENT OF MORTGAGE	**1221**
Conveyance to Mortgagee	1223
Tax Treatment of Mortgagor	1223.1
Tax Treatment of Mortgagee	1223.2
Abandonment by Mortgagor	1225
REPOSSESSION OF SELLER-FINANCED PROPERTY	**1231**
Nonrecognition of Gain or Loss	1233
Prior Bad Debt Deductions	1233.1
Holding Period of Reacquired Property	1233.2
Basis of Reacquired Property	1233.3
Recognition of Gain	1235
Reacquisition Following Installment Sale	1235.1
Reacquisition Following Election Out of Installment Reporting	1235.2
Third-Party Mortgages	1235.3
Character of Gain	1235.4

Part IV—Disposition of Real Estate

CHAPTER 13   SALES AND EXCHANGES

OVERVIEW OF CHAPTER	1300
SALE OF REAL ESTATE	**1301**
Computation of Gain or Loss	1303
Adjusted Basis	1303.1
Amount Realized	1303.2
Disallowed Losses	1303.3
Sale Between Spouses and Former Spouses	1303.4

Contents in Detail

	Paragraph
Character of Gain or Loss	1305
Capital Gains and Losses	1305.1
Property Used in a Trade or Business: Section 1231 Assets	1305.2
Holding Period	1305.3
Depreciation Recapture	1307
Section 1245 Property Recapture	1307.1
Section 1250 Property Recapture	1307.2
Alternative Minimum Tax	1309
Basic Computation	1309.1
Small Business Exception	1309.2
Adjustments to Taxable Income	1309.3
Tax Preferences	1309.4
Optional 10-Year Writeoff	1309.5
Alternative Minimum Tax Credit	1309.6
TAX-FREE EXCHANGE OF PROPERTY	**1311**
Like-Kind Exchange Requirements	1313
Like-Kind Real Estate Defined	1313.1
Basis Rule	1313.2
Basis Allocation Among Multiple Properties	1313.3
Partially Tax-Free Exchanges	1315
Other Property or Money	1315.1
Mortgages and Other Liabilities	1315.2
Basis in Partially Tax-Free Exchanges	1315.3
Commissions and Other Expenses	1315.4
Multi-Party Exchanges	1317
Three-Way Exchange	1317.1
Four-Way Exchange	1317.2
REPORTING REQUIREMENTS	**1321**
Transactions Subject to Reporting	1323
Reporting Person	1323.1
Multiple Transferors	1323.2
Information Return and Statement	1325
Form and Content of Return	1325.1
Statement for Transferor	1325.2
Penalties	1327
REDUCED TAXES ON DEPRESSED AREA PROPERTY	**1331**
Rollover of Empowerment Zone Investment	1333
Renewal Community Capital Gain	1335
D.C. Zone Capital Gain	1337

Contents in Detail

		Paragraph
CHAPTER 14	**SELLER-FINANCED SALES**	
	OVERVIEW OF CHAPTER	1400
	INSTALLMENT SALES	1401
	Sales that Qualify as Installment Sales	1403
	Dealer Sales	1403.1
	Escrow Arrangements	1403.2
	Election Out of Installment Reporting	1403.3
	Reporting Installment Income	1405
	General Rules	1405.1
	Payments	1405.2
	Sale of Multiple Assets	1405.3
	Like-Kind Exchanges	1405.4
	Contingent Sales	1405.5
	Unstated Interest	1405.6
	Sales to Related Party	1407
	Sales of Depreciable Property	1407.1
	Resale by Related Purchaser	1407.2
	Interest on Deferred Tax	1409
	DISPOSITION OR PLEDGE OF INSTALLMENT OBLIGATIONS	1411
	Sale or Satisfaction at Less than Face Value	1413
	Exceptions to Rule for Recognition of Gain . .	1413.1
	Cancellation of Installment Obligations	1413.2
	Pledge of Installment Obligations	1415
	Repossession of Property	1417
CHAPTER 15	**CASUALTY, CONDEMNATION, AND DEMOLITION**	
	OVERVIEW OF CHAPTER	1500
	BUSINESS CASUALTY	1501
	Casualty Defined	1503
	Casualty Gains and Losses	1505
	Casualty Losses	1505.1
	Casualty Gains	1505.2
	Insurance and Other Reimbursements	1505.3
	Basis After Casualty	1505.4
	Disaster Area Losses	1507
	Method of Taking Earlier Deduction	1507.1
	Revocation of Election	1507.2
	CONDEMNATIONS	1511
	Condemnation Defined	1513

	Paragraph
Gain or Loss from Condemnation	1515
Determination of the Condemnation Award	1517
Severance Damages	1517.1
Special Assessments	1517.2
TAX-FREE REPLACEMENT OF PROPERTY	1519
Election to Postpone Gain	1521
Advantages and Disadvantages of the Election	1521.1
Method of Election	1521.2
Replacement Period	1521.3
Replacement Property	1523
Similar Property	1523.1
Required Replacement from Unrelated Person	1523.2
Special Rule for Condemned Property	1523.3
Presidentially Declared Disasters	1523.4
Outdoor Advertising Displays	1523.5
Acquisition of Corporate Control	1523.6
Basis of Replacement Property	1525
Replacement with Corporate Stock	1525.1
Direct Conversion to Replacement Property	1525.2
DEMOLITION AND ABANDONMENT	1531
Demolition	1535
Abandonment	1537
Abandonment of Land	1537.1
Abandonment of Improvements	1537.2

CHAPTER 16 — CONTRIBUTIONS AND GIFTS

OVERVIEW OF CHAPTER	1600
CHARITABLE GIFTS	1601
Valuation of Real Estate Gifts	1603
Types of Appraisals	1603.1
Required Appraisal	1603.2
Gifts with Mixed Motives	1605
Gifts of Appreciated Property	1607
Ordinary Income Property	1607.1
Capital Gain Property	1607.2
Mixed Property	1607.3
Gifts of Partial Interests	1609
Undivided Portion	1609.1
Remainder Interest	1609.2
Conservation Purposes	1609.3

	Paragraph
GIFTS AND CONTRIBUTIONS OF MORTGAGED PROPERTY	1615
Gifts to Family	1617
Charitable Gifts	1619
GIFTS OF LOSS PROPERTY	1625

Part V—Personal Residences

CHAPTER 17 DEDUCTIONS FOR HOMEOWNERS

	Paragraph
OVERVIEW OF CHAPTER	1700
MORTGAGE INTEREST	1701
Qualified Residence Interest	1703
Qualified Residence Defined	1703.1
Acquisition Indebtedness	1703.2
Home Equity Debt	1703.3
Pre-1987 Indebtedness	1703.4
Points	1705
Points Charged for Services	1705.1
Refinancing	1705.2
Special Mortgage Situations	1707
Redeemable Ground Rents	1707.1
Shared Appreciation Mortgage (SAM)	1707.2
Mortgage Interest Credit	1707.3
Housing Allowances and Assistance Payments	1707.4
Payment Penalties	1707.5
REAL ESTATE TAXES	1709
CASUALTY LOSSES	1711
Limitations	1713
Deductible for Losses	1713.1
Adjusted Gross Income Limitation	1713.2
Calculation of the Casualty Deduction	1715
Real Estate	1715.1
Personal Property	1715.2
Loss to Real and Personal Property	1715.3
Part Business and Part Personal-Use Property	1717
MOVING EXPENSES	1721
Qualification for the Deduction	1723
Distance	1723.1
Length of Employment	1723.2

		Paragraph
	Deductible Costs	1727
	Reimbursements	1727.2
	Foreign Moves	1727.3
	Armed Forces Members	1727.4
	DISTRICT OF COLUMBIA HOMEBUYER CREDIT	1731
CHAPTER 18	**MIXED-USE RESIDENCES**	
	OVERVIEW OF CHAPTER	1800
	BUSINESS USE OF HOME	1801
	Exclusive Use for Business Test	1803
	Exceptions to Exclusive Use Test	1803.1
	Principal Place of Business	1803.2
	Place to Meet Patients, Clients, or Customers	1803.3
	Separate Structures	1803.4
	Allocation of Deductions	1805
	Direct Expenses	1805.1
	Indirect Expenses	1805.2
	Limitation on Deductions	1807
	Determination of Gross Income from Business Use of Home	1807.1
	Order of Deductions	1807.2
	Use of Home as Day-Care Facility	1809
	Allocation Formula	1809.1
	Application of Formula	1809.2
	RENTAL OF PART OF HOME	1811
	Rental Income	1813
	Allocation of Expenses	1815
	RENTAL OF VACATION OR OTHER RESIDENCE	1821
	Dwelling Unit Classification	1823
	Use as a Residence	1823.1
	Personal Use	1823.2
	Determination of Income and Deductions	1825
	Rental for Less Than 15 Days	1825.1
	Rental for 15 Days or More	1825.2
	Other Limitations on Rental Losses	1827
	RESIDENCE CONVERTED TO INVESTMENT	1835

Contents in Detail

		Paragraph
CHAPTER 19	**COOPERATIVES, CONDOMINIUMS, AND ASSOCIATIONS**	
	OVERVIEW OF CHAPTER	1900
	COOPERATIVE HOUSING CORPORATIONS ..	1901
	Qualification as Cooperative Housing Corporation	1903
	One Class of Stock Requirement	1903.1
	Right of Occupancy	1903.2
	Distributions	1903.3
	Gross Income of Cooperative Housing Corporation	1903.4
	Deductions by Tenant-Stockholders	1905
	Interest and Taxes	1905.1
	Depreciation	1905.2
	CONDOMINIUMS	1909
	Tax Treatment of Unit Owner	1911
	Tax Treatment of Condominium Association ...	1913
	HOMEOWNERS ASSOCIATIONS.............	1915
	Qualification for Tax-Exempt Status..........	1917
	Association Property.....................	1917.1
	Use as Residences	1917.2
	Exempt Function Income..................	1917.3
	Expenditures...........................	1917.4
	Inurement	1917.5
	Taxation of Homeowners Association	1921
	Election of Exempt Status	1923
	Nonexempt Associations...................	1925
	Tax-Exempt Status......................	1925.1
	Cooperative Organization	1925.2
	Assessments...........................	1925.3
CHAPTER 20	**SALE OF RESIDENCE**	
	OVERVIEW OF CHAPTER	2000
	GAIN OR LOSS ON SALE OF RESIDENCE	2001
	Business or Rental Use	2003
	Residence Held for Gain...................	2005

	Paragraph
TAX EXCLUSION FOR PRINCIPAL RESIDENCE	2007
Qualification for Exclusion	2009
Joint Returns	2009.3
Special Situations	2009.5
TAX-FREE ROLLOVER OF GAIN	2011
Postponement of Tax Requirements	2013
Replacement Period	2013.3
Tax Treatment	2015
Gain on Old Residence	2015.1
Gain on New Residence and Basis	2015.2
Joint Ownership	2015.3
Partial Business Use	2017
EXCLUSION OF GAIN FOR TAXPAYER OVER 55	2021
Exclusion Amount and Qualification Requirements	2023
Ownership and Use Requirements	2023.1
Purchase of New Principal Residence	2023.2
Election and Revocation of Election	2025
Election of the Exclusion	2025.1
Revocation of the Election	2025.2

Part VI—Securitized Real Estate Investments

CHAPTER 21 REAL ESTATE LIMITED PARTNERSHIPS

OVERVIEW OF CHAPTER	2100
DEVELOPMENT OF LIMITED PARTNERSHIPS	2101
Limited Partnerships as Tax Shelters	2103
Real Estate Tax Shelters	2105
Real Estate Limited Partnerships	2107
TAX TREATMENT OF REAL ESTATE LIMITED PARTNERSHIPS	2111
Restrictions on Partnership-Generated Tax Losses	2113
At-Risk Rules	2113.1
Passive Loss Rule	2113.2
Limited Partnership Interests	2115

		Paragraph
	MASTER LIMITED PARTNERSHIPS	2121
	Origins of Master Limited Partnerships	2123
	Evolution and Growth of the MLP Concept	2125
	Impact of Tax Legislation on MLPs	2127
	Real Estate MLPs	2129
CHAPTER 22	**REAL ESTATE INVESTMENT TRUSTS**	
	OVERVIEW OF CHAPTER	2200
	TAX TREATMENT OF REITS	2201
	Management and Control...................	2205
	Liquidity and Marketability	2207
	INCOME RESTRICTIONS	2215
CHAPTER 23	**REAL ESTATE MORTGAGE INVESTMENT CONDUITS**	
	OVERVIEW OF CHAPTER	2300
	INVESTOR INTERESTS	2301
	TAX TREATMENT OF REMICS	2305
	Regular Interests	2309
	Residual Interests........................	2315
	Distributions...........................	2315.1
	Income and Basis	2315.2

Part I

Acquiring Ownership of Real Property

Introduction to Part I

Part I looks at the acquisition of real property from a tax perspective. Chapter 1 is concerned with the acquisition transaction itself. The acquisition puts into motion a host of tax provisions that will haunt the owner at every step of the property's life cycle. When a taxpayer acquires property, whether by purchase, construction, inheritance, or other means, the taxpayer must determine the tax basis for the property. It is this figure that determines many of the future tax consequences that will flow from the ownership of the property, including gain or loss on its eventual sale or disposition.

The vehicle that a taxpayer chooses to hold property also is a critical decision from a tax standpoint. If the real estate is business or investment property, individual or joint ownership, partnerships, limited liability companies, and corporations all have their advantages and disadvantages. The appropriate form of ownership and operation for real estate is explained in Chapter 2. Also, the very concept of ownership for federal tax purposes is explained so that taxpayers may assure themselves that the "right" person receives the tax benefits that flow from the ownership of real property.

Finally, a major concern in any real estate acquisition is how to finance the acquisition. Mortgage financing is common and raises tax questions for both the mortgagor and mortgagee. Is the interest paid by the mortgagor deductible for tax purposes? When is it deductible? When must the mortgagee include interest in income? Is there any hidden or unstated interest or original issue discount in the terms of the financing agreement? These questions, as well as many others, are explored in Chapter 3. Also explored in Chapter 3 are sale-leasebacks and other lease financing arrangements and the at-risk rules that limit deductions from property financed with nonrecourse financing.

Chapter 1

The Acquisition Transaction

¶ 100 OVERVIEW OF CHAPTER

The acquisition of real estate itself, whether for investment, business, or personal use, has few immediate tax consequences. For the most part, the cost of real property is a capital expenditure that produces no immediate tax liability or benefit. The acquisition, however, does put into motion a host of tax provisions that will haunt the owner at every step of the property's life cycle.

The structure of the acquisition transaction, that is, the deal struck between the buyer and seller, affects the tax consequences that will ultimately flow from the ownership of the real property. There are also many expenses related to the actual acquisition. Some of these will be considered part of the cost of the property and, accordingly, will have no immediate tax consequences. Others, however, will not be part of the acquisition cost of the property and may produce current tax deductions. Moreover, it is sometimes difficult to distinguish between the expenses that are part of the cost of the property and those related to the acquisition of the property, which, for tax purposes, are not part of the cost of the property. This is especially true when real property assets are constructed rather than purchased in a completed state.

Although money spent for real property generally produces no immediate tax effect, there is one case in which the actual cost of purchasing or constructing real property can produce a tax savings. The cost of low-income housing, under certain circumstances, is eligible for a tax credit.

These, then, are the topics of this first chapter: the cost of purchasing or constructing real property or otherwise determining the tax basis of property, the costs of acquiring the property which are not part of the tax basis of the property, and the tax credit for the purchase or construction of low-income housing.

¶ 101 IMPORTANCE OF BASIS

Knowing the basis of property is important for several reasons. It is the basis of property, adjusted for events that occur while the owner holds the property, that ultimately determines the amount of gain or loss on the disposition of the property.[1] This rule applies regardless of whether the real estate involved is used for business or personal purposes or is held for investment.

Example: A building with a current market value of $250,000 has an adjusted basis of $100,000. If the building is sold for its market value, the owner reports a gain of $150,000, that is, the difference between the amount realized on the sale and the basis of the property at the time of the sale.

The adjusted basis of property (original basis adjusted for events occurring while the property is held) also serves as the outside limit on the amount of any deduction in the event of the loss or destruction of the property.[2]

Example: A building with a current market value of $250,000 and an adjusted basis of $100,000 is destroyed by a hurricane. The maximum casualty loss that could be taken as a tax deduction is limited to $100,000. The amount of the actual deduction, of course, would depend on other factors, such as the amount of any insurance recovery and the type of property, that is, business or personal, involved.

In the case of real property that is used for business purposes or held for investment, basis is important for determining the amount of the annual depreciation deduction that may be permitted for the property.

¶ 103 Calculation of Basis

The original basis of any property depends on how the owner acquires that property. The original basis is then increased or decreased by events occurring while the owner holds the property. The most common adjustments to original basis in the case of real property are increases for additions and improvements and decreases for depreciation and casualty losses. The various adjustments to original basis are discussed throughout this book in connection with the transactions giving rise to those adjustments.

How to determine original basis is discussed in the following paragraphs which relate to various ways in which real property may be acquired.

¶ 103.1 *Property Acquired by Purchase*

When the owner acquires real property by purchase, the general basis rule of Code Sec. 1012 applies, that is, the original basis of the property is its cost. Cost, in addition to the cash paid by the buyer to

---

[1] Code Sec. 1011. [2] Code Sec. 165(b).

the seller, includes the amount of any mortgage given to secure payment of the balance of the purchase price and expenses directly related to the acquisition of the property such as commissions, legal fees, and title insurance premiums.

Cost does not include any amount for real property taxes that are treated as imposed on the purchaser under Code Sec. 164(d). Cost, however, does include real estate taxes that are treated as imposed on the seller but are assumed or paid by the buyer.

The acquisition of real property through purchase is considered in further detail at ¶ 111.

¶ 103.2 Property Constructed by or for the Owner

As with real property acquired by purchase, the general basis rule of Code Sec. 1012 (that the original basis of property is its cost) applies to property constructed by or for the owner.

Cost, in the case of constructed property, includes the cost of materials and contractors' charges. In addition, the cost basis of real estate may include many items incurred during the construction period that would be currently deductible expenses in other settings. Under Code Sec. 263A, all direct costs and the property's proper share of any indirect costs, including taxes, that are allocable to the property during its construction must be capitalized as part of the original basis of the property. This capitalization rule applies to property that will be used in a trade or business or activity conducted for profit. It does not apply to a personal residence constructed by or for its owner.

The acquisition of real property by construction is considered in further detail at ¶ 123.

¶ 103.3 Property Acquired in an Exchange

No gain or loss is recognized when property held for productive use in a trade or business or for investment is exchanged solely for property of like kind to be held either for productive use in a trade or business or for investment.[3] Under Code Sec. 1031(d), the basis of the old property given up in an exchange without recognition of gain or loss becomes the basis of the property received in the exchange.

The new property acquired in a "tax-free" exchange is said to have a "substitute basis" in that the basis of the old property is substituted for the basis of the new property. This substitute basis preserves the gain or loss that went unrecognized at the time of the exchange for later taxation when the acquired property is disposed of in a taxable transaction.

---

[3] Code Sec. 1031.

If an exchange of property is an uneven exchange, that is, if cash or other nonlike-kind property is included in the exchange, the substituted basis must be adjusted to reflect the gain or loss that is recognized. Like-kind exchanges and the complications involved are considered at ¶ 1311.

¶ 103.4 Property Acquired on Exercise of an Option

When real property is acquired through the exercise of an option on the property, the holder of the option adds the cost of the option to the price paid for the property at the time the holder exercises the option to determine the property's original basis. The holder of an option that allows it to lapse without exercising it is entitled to a loss deduction at that time.

¶ 103.5 Property Acquired by Gift

The basis of property acquired by gift is determined under Code Sec. 1015. The rule has undergone several changes over the years, and slightly different versions apply, depending on the date of the gift. Earlier versions of the rule remain important in case it is necessary to trace basis back through a series of transfers.

Current Rule

The basis of property acquired by gift generally is the basis the donor had in the property prior to the gift, adjusted for any gift tax paid on the transfer. The adjustment for the gift tax is the amount of gift tax attributable to the appreciation in value the property experienced while held by the donor. The appreciation is measured by the difference between the donor's basis and the fair market value of the property at the time of the gift. The adjustment for gift taxes, however, cannot be used to increase the donee's basis over the fair market value of the property at the time of the gift.

Example: The Donor has property with a basis of $100,000 and a fair market value of $250,000. On the transfer of this property to the donee, the Donor pays a gift tax in the amount of $50,000. The donee's basis for this property is $130,000, which reflects the Donor's basis of $100,000 increased by $30,000 of the gift tax, which is the amount of the gift tax attributable to the appreciation of the property while held by the Donor.

The $30,000 adjustment is determined from the ratio of the appreciation (fair market value less basis) to the total value of the gift. In this case the appreciation is $150,000 ($250,000 − $100,000), and this is 60 percent of the value of the gift. Accordingly, the amount of the gift tax adjustment is 60 percent of the total gift tax paid on the transfer.

The Acquisition Transaction

In the event that the donor's basis for the gift property exceeds the fair market value of the property at the time of the gift, a special rule limits the donee's basis to fair market value for purposes of determining any loss on the property on a later disposition by the donee.

Example: The Donor makes a gift of property with a fair market value of $250,000 and a basis of $100,000. Assuming no gift tax is paid on the transfer, the donee's basis for the property is $100,000.

If the figures were reversed and the property had a basis in the hands of the Donor of $250,000 but a value at the time of the gift of only $100,000, the donee's basis would be $250,000, unless use of that basis figure would produce a loss when the donee disposed of the property. For purposes of determining the amount of any loss realized by the donee on a disposition of the property, the basis would be $100,000, not $250,000.

Gifts Post-1958 and Pre-1977

The basis rule for gifts made after September 1, 1958, and before 1977, was the same as the current rule, except for the adjustment for gift taxes. The adjustment for gift taxes for gifts made during this period was the full amount of the tax, not just the portion attributable to appreciation.

Example: The Donor had property with a basis of $100,000 and a fair market value of $250,000 when the Donor made a gift of the property before 1977. On the transfer of this property to the donee, the Donor paid a gift tax in the amount of $50,000. The donee's basis for this property is $150,000, which reflects the Donor's basis of $100,000 increased by the $50,000 gift tax paid on the transfer.

(Note that the basis adjustment as applied to gifts made after September 1, 1958, applied to gifts made before September 2, 1958, if the donee held the gift property on September 2, 1958.)

Gifts Post-1920 and Pre-1958

The basis rule for gifts made after 1920 and before September 2, 1958, was the same as the current rule, except that there was no adjustment for gift taxes paid. The donee's basis for a gift was simply the donor's basis before the gift or, for purposes of determining loss, the fair market value of the property on the date of the gift if lower than the donor's basis.

Gifts Pre-1921

The basis of property acquired by gift before 1921 was the fair market value of the property at the time of the gift.

¶ 103.5

¶ 103.6 Property Acquired by Inheritance

Under Code Sec. 1014, the basis of property acquired from a decedent is generally the fair market value of the property on the date of the decedent's death. Under an election available to estates, the executor may elect to value estate property as of an alternate valuation date, which is generally six months after the decedent's death.[4] If this alternate valuation date is elected, the basis of property acquired from the decedent is its fair market value on the alternate valuation date.

There is also an election available to estates [5] which allows an executor to value certain real estate for estate tax purposes according to its use as farm property or in a trade or business, rather than at its fair market value. (Fair market value generally reflects the highest and best use of a particular parcel of real property.) If the executor elects this "special use" valuation, the basis of the property is its special use estate tax value rather than its fair market value.

Using the basis rules for gifts and for property acquired from a decedent, it might be possible to get an increased basis for appreciated property and avoid taxable gain by gifting the property to an elderly or terminally ill individual and then receiving back the property on the ultimate death of the donee. Making use of a deathbed-donee to get an increased basis for appreciated property, however, is blocked by Code Sec. 1014(e) if the donee dies within one year of the gift. In this case, the basis to the original donor who is receiving the property back from the donee-decedent is the adjusted basis of the property in the hands of the donee-decedent immediately before death. A similar rule applies if the estate of the donee-decedent sells the property and the original donor or spouse is entitled to the proceeds of the sale.

Effect of Estate Tax Repeal

The estate tax is scheduled to be repealed after 2009. Once the estate tax has been repealed, the rule that provides a fair market value basis for property acquired from a decedent will be replaced with a modified carryover basis rule. Recipients of property on a decedent's death will take a basis equal to the lesser of the decedent's adjusted basis or the property's fair market value on the date of the decedent's death. The executor will be allowed to step up the basis of assets owned by the decedent by up to a total of $1.3 million. In addition, the basis of property transferred to a surviving spouse can be stepped-up by an additional $3 million.

---

[4] Code Sec. 2032. [5] Code Sec. 2032A.

¶ 103.7 Property Acquired from a Spouse or Former Spouse

Anytime property is transferred from one spouse to another, or from one spouse to a former spouse incident to a divorce, the transfer is treated as a gift, and the transferee spouse's basis for the property is the adjusted basis the property had in the hands of the transferor spouse.[6] This special basis rule applies regardless of the actual form of the transfer, whether a true gift, a sale for consideration, or otherwise. This rule complements the provision that makes all such transfers tax-free events.[7]

The transfer of property from a spouse to a former spouse is considered incident to the divorce if the transfer takes place within one year after the date on which the marriage ends or is related to the cessation of the marriage.

¶ 103.8 Other Basis Rules

In addition to the basis rules discussed above, there are various basis rules throughout the Internal Revenue Code to cover special situations. These basis rules are covered at appropriate points throughout this volume. Notable among these special basis rules are those that determine basis following:

Sale of a taxpayer's principal residence before May 7, 1997 (or later in specified situations) and its replacement with a new residence (see ¶ 2011).

Foreclosure or repossession (see ¶ 1211 and 1231).

Casualty, condemnation, or other involuntary conversion (see ¶ 1501 and 1511).

Subdivision of a tract (see ¶ 1003).

Contribution to a partnership or corporation (see ¶ 229.2 and 235.1).

¶ 105 Mortgage and Basis

The original cost basis of property includes the amount of any mortgage given to secure payment of any portion of the purchase price. It does not matter whether the money is borrowed from a financial institution, other third-party lender, or from the seller of the property in the form of a purchase-money mortgage. Cost basis also includes the amount of any existing mortgage on the property. This rule applies whether the buyer actually assumes the existing mortgage or purchases the property subject to the mortgage without personally assuming the mortgage.

---

[6] Code Sec. 1041(b). [7] Code Sec. 1041(a).

(Note that basis does not include any principal amount that is recharacterized as interest under the imputed interest or original issue discount rules. Basis does include "interest" that is recharacterized as principal under these rules. The imputed interest and original issue discount rules are treated at ¶ 321 and 331.)

Example: The Buyer purchases real estate from the Seller for $250,000. The Buyer pays for the property by giving the Seller $50,000 cash and a purchase-money mortgage in the amount of $75,000. The Buyer also assumes an existing mortgage on the property in the amount of $125,000. The Buyer's original cost basis for this real estate is $250,000.

The other side of the coin, of course, is that the seller includes in the amount realized from the sale of property the amount of any mortgage debt the seller is relieved of on the sale, as well as the amount of any purchase-money mortgage the seller grants to the buyer.

Example: In the example above, the Buyer's basis is $250,000. By the same token, the amount the Seller has realized on the sale is $250,000—the $50,000 cash, the $125,000 mortgage obligation the Seller was relieved of when the Buyer assumed that mortgage in connection with the sale, and the $75,000 mortgage the Seller has taken back from the Buyer as part of the sale. The Seller's gain or loss is measured by the difference between the amount realized and the adjusted basis at the time of the sale.

This rule, which includes the amount of debt incurred to purchase property in the basis of the property for the buyer and the amount of debt discharged on the sale of property in the amount realized by the seller, can be traced back to the decision of the Supreme Court in *B.B. Crane.*[8]

Mrs. Crane inherited property from her husband. This property was valued for estate tax purposes at $262,000 and was subject to a $255,000 loan. At the time she inherited the property, there was $7,000 accrued interest due on the loan. In effect, the net value of Mrs. Crane's inheritance at the time of her husband's death was zero.

Mrs. Crane operated the property and claimed depreciation deductions for the property, but she never personally assumed the debt of $255,000. She ultimately sold the property and reported a taxable gain of $2,500, the net amount she received for the property. According to Mrs. Crane, all she inherited from her husband was her equity in the property, which was zero. All she sold when she sold the property was this equity. Therefore, her gain was only $2,500, the difference between

---

[8] S.Ct., 47-1 USTC ¶ 9217, 331 U.S. 1.

the zero "basis" for her equity and the $2,500 "realized" from the sale of this equity.

According to the IRS, however, Mrs. Crane sold real estate and not just her equity in the real estate. Her adjusted basis at the time of the sale was the estate tax value of the property reduced by the $25,000 in depreciation deductions claimed while she held the property, or $237,000. The amount she realized on the sale of the property was the $2,500 cash received plus the $255,000 principal amount due on the loan against the property, or $257,500. Her gain, therefore, was not the $2,500 she received for her "equity," but the difference between her adjusted basis of $237,000 and her amount realized of $257,500, or a taxable gain of $20,500. The Supreme Court agreed with the IRS, and that has been the rule for basis and amount realized ever since.

In most cases, it is the face amount of a mortgage or other debt that controls in determining the amount to include in basis or amount realized. Old debts or debts carrying a below-current-market rate of interest are not discounted to reflect this. The imputed interest and original issue discount rules discussed at ¶ 321 and 331, however, may convert a portion of nominal principal to interest when an inadequate rate of interest is provided in a purchase-money mortgage. Also, in potentially abusive situations, the principal amount of debt incurred to purchase property may be equated to the fair market value of the property (see ¶ 105.3).

Although original cost basis does include amounts borrowed to acquire property, there is no adjustment to basis as payments are made to reduce the debt. In other words, mortgage payments do not reduce or increase the basis of the mortgaged property.[9]

¶ 105.1 Contingent or Speculative Obligations

While the rule is that basis includes the amount of any mortgage given to obtain the property, there must be a reasonable likelihood that an amount will actually have to be paid on the mortgage. If payments on a mortgage are contingent on the happening of some event or events that are uncertain and speculative, no real obligation is created by the mortgage until the future contingency occurs. If payments are actually made on a contingent and speculative obligation, the amount of the payments is added to basis at that time.

See, for example, *S. Baron Est.*,[10] in which it was held that a recourse obligation was not treated as true debt because payment was too contingent. See also Rev. Rul. 80-235.[11]

---

[9] *Parker v. Delaney*, CA-1, 51-1 USTC ¶ 9112, 186 F.2d 455.

[10] CA-2, 86-2 USTC ¶ 9622, 798 F.2d 65.
[11] 1980-2 CB 229.

¶ 105.2 Borrowing Against Previously Owned Property

A taxpayer that borrows against property already owned does not increase basis for the new obligation, unless the loan is used to improve or make additions to the property (see ¶ 803). In the latter case, it is the cost of the additions or improvements that is added to basis, regardless of how they are financed, just as original basis is the cost of the property, regardless of how it is financed.

While borrowing against previously owned property does not affect basis, neither does it produce taxable income to the borrower. In general, borrowing is not a taxable transaction. When a mortgage is placed against property that is already owned, the borrower receives money, but the borrower has a corresponding obligation to repay that results in no benefit, at least as far as the tax law is concerned.[12]

¶ 105.3 Artificially Inflated Purchase Price

The use of debt to increase tax and financial benefits is a common and acceptable practice. In some cases, however, promoters have been known to artificially inflate basis (and claimed tax benefits) with liabilities incurred to purchase property at prices far in excess of the real value of the property. The IRS has waged a constant battle against this practice and has much case law on its side. When Congress passed the original issue discount rules in 1984, it made a direct attack on the use of debt to artificially inflate the basis of property in what are termed "potentially abusive situations."

In any potentially abusive situation, the principal amount of a debt instrument given to finance the purchase of property is considered to be the fair market value of the property reduced by the fair market value of any other consideration (such as a cash down payment) given for the property.[13] The effect of this rule when property is purchased with the use of debt in a potentially abusive situation is to limit the basis of the property to its fair market value regardless of the amount of the debt.

Potentially abusive situations include tax shelters, which are defined as partnerships, other entities, investment plans or arrangements, or any other plan or arrangement, if the principal purpose of the partnership, entity, plan, or arrangement is the avoidance or evasion of federal income tax. Other potentially abusive situations are those involving a recent sales transaction, nonrecourse financing, financing with a term in excess of the economic life of the property, or a debt instrument with clearly excessive interest.[14]

---

[12] See *James v. U.S.*, S.Ct., 61-1 USTC ¶ 9449, 366 U.S. 213.

[13] Code Sec. 1274(b)(3).

[14] See Reg. § 1.1274-3.

Example: The Taxpayer purchases real estate with a $1,000,000 down payment and a nonrecourse mortgage with a stated principal amount of $7,000,000. The fair market value at the time of the purchase is $7,000,000.

Since the transaction is a potentially abusive situation, the principal amount of the debt for tax purposes is treated as being $6,000,000, the fair market value of the property ($7,000,000) reduced by the amount of the down payment ($1,000,000). This means that the basis of the property for tax purposes is $7,000,000 ($1,000,000 down payment plus the imputed principal amount of the debt of $6,000,000), not the $8,000,000 the basis would be if the basis included the down payment plus the stated amount of the mortgage debt.

The fair market value limitation in potentially abusive situations applies whether or not adequate stated interest is provided under the normal original issue discount rules. Moreover, the fair market value rule does not affect case law that has developed in connection with artificially inflated or overstated basis. In situations not covered by the statute, the IRS may still attack the basis of property that has been artificially inflated with excessive mortgage or debt financing.

The decision in *D.L. Narver, Jr.*[15] illustrates the case law that developed before passage of Code Sec. 1274 to limit the use of inflated or "soft" mortgages to increase basis. *Narver* involved the purchase of a building, property, and an adjacent parking lot by Jack R. Young and Associates from the Sutherland Foundation for $650,000. Young immediately resold only the building to two partnerships that it controlled for $1,800,000 in nonrecourse debt and $180,000 in prepaid interest.

After the sale, the partnerships leased the building to a wholly owned subsidary of Young at a rental that exactly satisfied the partnerships' nonrecourse purchase obligation to Young. The partners, of course, took depreciation deductions based on the inflated $1,800,000 basis and interest deductions based on the nonrecourse $1,800,000 debt. (At the time, real estate was not subject to the at-risk rules.) The IRS challenged the partners' deductions and the Tax Court decided that in this situation, the partners actually had no equity in the building and were not building equity under the financing arrangement set up by Young. As a result, the partnerships had no basis in the building and there was nothing to depreciate.

---

[15] 75 TC 53, CCH Dec. 37,335, aff'd per curiam, CA-9, 82-1 USTC ¶ 9265, 670 F.2d 855.

¶ 105.3

In another case involving inflated mortgage financing, the Tax Court decided that there was no valid debt.[16] In this case, the promoter interposed a third party in the inflated mortgage sale. A limited partnership purchased properties from the Go Publishing Company for $1,000,000, which was 10 times the amount Go had paid to Cal-Am Corporation for the property. Cal-Am was controlled by the promoter and general partner of the limited partnership and had acquired the property for about $100,000 before its temporary sale to Go. When Go resold the property to the partnership, it accepted a minimum down payment and a nonrecourse mortgage for the balance.

See also *C.T. Franklin Est.*,[17] in which it was held that a nonrecourse debt did not represent a valid debt or actual investment in property and was not includible in the basis of the property for purposes of computing depreciation because the debt unreasonably exceeded the value of the property.

¶ 111 PURCHASE OF REAL PROPERTY

While it is easy to state the rule that the basis of purchased property is its cost, it is not always as easy to determine the exact cost figure for a specific property. Most, if not all, purchases of real estate assets involve more than a few incidental expenses. For the most part, these incidental or extra expenses are part of the cost of the property.

Once the purchaser settles on a specific cost figure, that figure must be allocated among the several assets that generally compose the "real estate package." The most obvious allocation in the case of business or investment property is, of course, the allocation of purchase price between depreciable improvements and nondepreciable land. Further allocation between various classes of depreciable assets also may be required.

¶ 115 Buying Expenses

The buyer of real estate has no choice in the treatment of expenditures made in connection with the purchase of real estate. Generally, any amounts paid out for new buildings or for permanent improvements or betterments made to increase the value of any property are not currently deductible expenses.[18] Rather, these expenses are capital expenditures that form part of the cost or basis of the property.

It does not matter whether these expenses are of the type normally born by the buyer in a real estate transaction or whether they are seller's expenses that are borne by the buyer under the terms of the purchase contract. It also does not matter that the type of expenditure

---

[16] *J.C. Beck*, 74 TC 1534, CCH Dec. 37,305, aff'd CA-9, 82-2 USTC ¶ 9427, 678 F.2d 818.

[17] CA-9, 76-2 USTC ¶ 9773, 544 F.2d 1045.

[18] Code Sec. 263; Reg. § 1.263(a)-1.

involved would not be a capital expenditure but would be currently deductible in other circumstances. The buyer must treat all expenses related to the acquisition of the property as additions to cost. For instance, a buyer who agrees to pay for repairs already contracted for by the seller is required to add the cost of the repairs to the cost of the property.[19]

Some of the more typical expenses related to the acquisition of property that the buyer includes in the cost are:

Appraisal fees	Improvements to the property
Attorneys' fees	Mortgage title insurance
Building line contest	Removing a cloud on title
Clearing and grading	Survey costs
Closing costs	Title abstract
Commissions	Title defense
Condemnation costs	Title determination
Credit investigations	Title insurance
Deed of correction to perfect title	Utility connection costs

Expenses for evaluating localities to determine the feasibility of selling residential property were capital expenditures and not currently deductible expenses for a taxpayer engaged in the business of acquiring residential properties for renovation and sale.[20] Similarly, the costs of exploration are part of the cost of property acquired or retained if property is acquired or retained based on the data obtained from geological and geophysical exploration.[21]

The proper treatment of points and other charges or expenses related to acquiring a mortgage on property, as distinguished from the acquisition of the property itself, is considered at ¶ 301.

¶ 117 Allocation of Costs

When only one asset is purchased in a single transaction, for example a vacant lot, the purchase price plus related acquisition expenses is the tax basis for the asset as discussed above. Most real estate purchases, however, involve more than the purchase of a single asset, even though purchase price is stated as a single lump sum. When more than one asset is purchased for a single sum, cost must be apportioned among the several assets acquired in order to determine the basis of each.

---

[19] *Wilensky & Sons Co.*, 7 BTA 693, CCH Dec. 2624.
[20] Rev. Rul. 74-104, 1974-1 CB 70.
[21] Rev. Rul. 77-188, 1977-1 CB 76; see also Rev. Rul. 83-105, 1983-2 CB 51.

¶ 117.1 Land and Buildings

The most common example of the purchase of multiple assets for a single lump sum is the purchase of land and a building. The buyer and seller usually negotiate the purchase price as if a single asset were involved. For tax purposes, however, the cost must be allocated between the separate assets, the land and the building, in all cases except the purchase of a personal residence. The portion of the total cost allocated to the building is subject to depreciation (see ¶ 901), but the cost of the land is not. A personal residence, since it is not held for business or investment use, is not subject to depreciation so the cost allocation is not required.

In most cases, the cost allocation is based upon the relative fair market values of the separate assets. Reg. § 1.167(a)-5 provides that when buildings and land are acquired for a lump sum, the basis of the buildings for depreciation cannot exceed an amount which bears the same proportion to the lump sum as the value of the depreciable buildings at the time of acquisition bears to the value of the entire property at that time. Similarly, the IRS has ruled that legal expenses, such as title search, verification of mortgage balance, and similar expenses, must be allocated between the land and improvements according to the fair market values of each at the time of the purchase.[22]

> *Example:* The Buyer purchases a commercial office building and the underlying land for $500,000 and incurs $50,000 in expenses directly related to the acquisition. The Buyer's basis for the land and building is $550,000, and this must be allocated between the nondepreciable land and the depreciable building. If the value of the land represents 25 percent of the total value, then the basis for the land would be $137,500 ($550,000 × 25%). The basis for the building would be $412,500 ($550,000 × 75%).

Relative Values

Although the rule requiring allocation of cost based on relative fair market values is a conceptually simple rule, its application to specific situations may be anything but simple. The real problem is determining relative values.

As a starting point, buyer and seller may negotiate the relative values of land and buildings and provide for the allocation in the purchase agreement. The IRS is likely to respect the allocation made by the parties if the negotiations are truly arm's-length and the buyer and seller have some adverse interest as to how the allocation is finally made. However, an allocation made by the parties under the contract

---

[22] Rev. Rul. 68-528, 1968-2 CB 331.

The Acquisition Transaction

of sale may be rejected if the allocation does not reflect the economic reality of the transaction.[23]

In some cases, the valuations placed on land and buildings for local real property tax purposes have been used as a guide for determining relative fair market values. Even though valuations for real estate taxes often may be too low to be used to determine the correct value of a real estate parcel, the valuations used by the local property tax assessor often do point to the relative value of the land and buildings located on the land.[24]

Relative values also have been established through appraisal by experts. Mortgage appraisals may be another source of information as to the relative values of land and buildings.[25]

In *S.A. Meiers*,[26] the Tax Court allocated the total purchase price of two condominium properties based upon the buildings' replacement costs at the time rather than the local property tax assessor's relative valuation of the land and buildings. In this particular case, the court felt replacement cost was the more accurate gauge of relative values. Replacement cost was also used in *Pensacola Greyhound Racing, Inc.*[27]

The capitalization of rentals method was used to allocate cost when the buildings included two houses that were rented to tenants.[28] And in *D.N. Marks*,[29] the court also used the capitalization of earnings method because the purchasers were investors. An income or capitalization of earnings approach reflects that investors generally purchase property for the income it is expected to produce.

Building Demolition

Cost is not allocated between land and buildings when the buildings will be demolished. Rather, the entire cost for the property is the basis for the land. This same rule applies to all demolitions, even when the demolition is of a building that has been owned for some time by the taxpayer. The cost of demolition and any loss sustained because of the demolition (usually, any remaining basis for the building) is added to the basis of the land on which the demolished structure was located.[30]

---

[23] See *D.N. Marks*, 49 TCM 1222, CCH Dec. 42,022(M), T.C. Memo. 1985-179.

[24] 2554-58 *Creston Corp.*, 40 TC 932, CCH Dec. 26,294; *Offshore Operations Trust*, 32 TCM 985, CCH Dec. 32,149(M), T.C. Memo. 1973-212.

[25] *L.R. Akers*, 40 TCM 574, CCH Dec. 37,044(M), T.C. Memo. 1980-238.

[26] 43 TCM 454, CCH Dec. 38,766(M), T.C. Memo. 1982-51.

[27] 32 TCM 1064, CCH Dec. 32,173(M), T.C. Memo. 1973-225.

[28] *P. Hurd*, 37 TCM 499, CCH Dec. 35,057(M), T.C. Memo. 1978-113.

[29] 49 TCM 1222, CCH Dec. 42,022(M), T.C. Memo. 1985-179.

[30] Code Sec. 280B.

¶ 117.1

Prior to 1984, costs and other losses incurred in connection with the demolition of buildings generally could be claimed as a current deduction unless the building and the land on which the structure was located were purchased with an intent to demolish the building. Only if the purchaser intended to demolish the building at the time of purchase were costs and other losses added to the basis of the land. Needless to say, this rule led to many contests between taxpayers and the IRS over whether an intent to demolish a building existed when the building was purchased. Such controversies ended with the passage of Code Sec. 280B.

¶ 117.2   Land Improvements and Personal Property

The division of real estate into land and buildings may be fairly obvious, but the purchase of real estate often involves more than the purchase of simply those two assets. The "bundle of assets" making up the real estate package may be further divided beyond land and buildings into land improvements and personal property. As with the allocation between land and buildings, these allocations should also be based on relative fair market values, with independent appraisals and costs analyses serving as the best means of establishing those relative values.

While the cost of land itself is not depreciable, various land improvements may be. Therefore, to take maximum advantage of available depreciation allowances, it is necessary to further allocate basis to those land improvements that qualify as depreciable. Generally, those land improvements that do not permanently improve the land but improve it only for use with a specific building are depreciable. As the IRS has put it, land improvement costs are depreciable if they are directly associated with buildings rather than inextricably associated with the land.[31]

In Rev. Rul 65-265, the IRS ruled that the cost of general grading of land is part of the cost basis of the land and is nondepreciable. The cost of digging and removing soil necessary for the proper setting of the buildings and paving of the roadways, however, is part of their cost and is depreciable. This ruling was further clarified by Rev. Rul. 68-193,[32] which allowed depreciation for certain grading costs for roads constructed to provide for movement of heavy materials between buildings when the grading would be abandoned or replaced with the buildings with which it was directly associated.

Landscaping consisting of perennial shrubbery and ornamental trees adjacent to buildings was considered a depreciable land improve-

---

[31] Rev. Rul. 65-265, 1965-2 CB 52.   [32] 1968-1 CB 79.

ment when replacement of the buildings would require replacement of the landscaping. On the other hand, the cost of general landscaping of the grounds around the same buildings was considered a general land improvement cost and part of the basis of the nondepreciable land.[33]

Rev. Proc. 87-56 [34] contains the class lives and recovery periods for computing depreciation deductions for various assets. Under this Revenue Procedure, land improvements include depreciable improvements such as sidewalks, roads, canals, waterways, drainage facilities, docks, bridges, fences, landscaping and shrubbery.

(Depreciation and related concepts are considered further in Chapter 9.)

¶ 117.3 Buildings and Personal Property

Just as land costs may be divided between land and land improvements to increase depreciation deductions, to the extent any portion of the cost of a building can be allocated to personal property, depreciation deductions may be increased. The cost of personal property may be recovered over much shorter periods than the cost of real property.[35] Making the allocation can be a troublesome undertaking. Nevertheless, the tax benefits that result usually make the effort worthwhile.

In order to allocate cost to those elements of the real estate package that may qualify as personal property it is necessary to identify those items. Historically, this was usually accomplished under the law as it developed for purposes of the investment credit, which, even though no longer available for most property, nevertheless provides a good starting point for cost allocation. The investment credit, when it was in effect, generally was available for "tangible personal property," but not for "buildings or their structural components."

In determining whether or not a particular item of property is tangible personal property for tax purposes, local law is not controlling. This means that an item of property may be personal property for tax purposes even though it is real property for purposes of local law.[36] Tangible personal property includes all property contained in or attached to a building other than structural components.

Structural components that are considered part of a building include walls, partitions, floors, and ceilings, as well as any permanent coverings for them such as paneling or tiling, windows and doors, all components of a central air conditioning or heating system, plumbing and plumbing fixtures such as sinks and bathtubs, electric wiring and lighting fixtures, chimneys, stairs, sprinkler systems, fire escapes, and

---

[33] Rev. Rul. 74-265, 1974-1 CB 56.
[34] 1987-2 CB 674.
[35] See ¶ 901.
[36] Reg. § 1.48-1(c).

other components relating to the operation or maintenance of the building.[37]

The IRS and the courts have, at times, applied a permanency test to determine whether assets attached to a structure are components of the building or are personal property. For instance, in *Minot Federal Savings & Loan Assn.*,[38] removable partitions that were not permanent and could be changed and moved without injury to the building were considered personal property.[39]

In an attempt to clarify existing law at the time, the Senate Finance Committee, in its report on the Revenue Act of 1978, included an extensive list of property associated with real estate that should be classified as personal property:

Beverage bars

Booths for seating

Carpeting

False balconies and other exterior ornamentation that have no more than an incidental relationship to the operation or maintenance of a building

Floor coverings that are not an integral part of the floor itself, such as tile installed in a manner so that it is readily removed (not cemented, mudded or otherwise permanently affixed to the floor)

Identity symbols that identify or relate to a particular retail establishment or restaurant and signs other than billboards

Movable and removable partitions

Ornamental fixtures, such as coats-of-arms, and depreciable artifacts

Pictures of scenery, persons, etc., that are attached to walls or suspended from the ceiling

Special lighting, including lighting to illuminate the exterior of a building or store, but not lighting to illuminate parking areas

Wall panel inserts designed to contain condiments or serve as framing for pictures of products

Despite this "clarification" of existing law, the distinction between structural components and personal property remains a troublesome one and one that is often a matter of dispute between taxpayers and the IRS. The following checklists contain some additional authorities on just what is a building or structural component and what is personal property for many assets associated with real estate.

Building Components

Canopies of concrete slab or steel frame over loading or storage docks which are integral parts of the walls [40]

Cinderblock walls, doors, rest rooms, plumbing, office partitions and electrical wiring in an underground storage facility [41]

Clean rooms within factory buildings [42]

Docks at a factory for loading and unloading materials [43]

---

[37] Reg. § 1.48-1(e)(2).
[38] CA-8, 71-1 USTC ¶ 9131, 435 F.2d 1368.
[39] See also Rev. Rul. 75-178, 1975-1 CB 9; *King Radio Corp. Inc.*, CA-10, 73-2 USTC ¶ 9766, 486 F.2d 1091; *J.E. Fleming*, 49 TCM 1134, CCH Dec. 42,005(M), T.C. Memo. 1985-165.
[40] Rev. Rul. 74-2, 1974-1 CB 10.
[41] Rev. Rul. 70-103, 1970-1 CB 6.
[42] Rev. Rul. 68-530, 1968-2 CB 37.
[43] Rev. Rul. 74-392, 1974-2 CB 10.

The Acquisition Transaction

Electrical distribution system servicing the overall electrical needs of the building [44]

Enclosed modular office structures installed within a factory [45]

Prefabricated, movable structure used as a restaurant [46]

Remote control operator houses as part of a ski-lift facility [47]

Structures housing machinery and equipment in breaker and fine-coal plants [48]

Wall partitions that could not be stored, reused in their entirety, or removed without minor damage to the structure [49]

Personal Property

Bank vault doors, night depository facilities and walk-up and drive-up teller's windows [50]

Chandeliers and hanging lanterns that were accessories to a restaurant business rather than components relating to the operation or maintenance of the buildings in which they were located [51]

Climate control system for processing cut roses in a greenhouse [52]

Compressor station structures of natural gas transmission company [53]

Electrical distribution system at large manufacturing complex except to the extent used to supply power for the overall operation and maintenance of buildings [54]

Fire extinguishers,[55] but a fire protection system that is designed to remain in place permanently is a structural component [56]

Individual room refrigeration units installed in a warehouse [57]

Merchandising huts that could be removed from their locations [58]

Raised floor built on existing floor to permit installation of wiring, ducts, and other services for computer equipment [59]

Removable partitions that are not permanent and can be changed and moved without injury to the building[60]

Wall-to-wall carpeting installed in the guest rooms, office space, bar areas and dining rooms of a motel [61]

¶ 117.4 Real Estate as Part of a Going Business

When real estate is purchased as part of a going business, basis for the real estate will be limited to fair market value. Under Code Sec. 1060, the purchase price of assets that constitute a trade or business must be allocated for tax purposes using the residual method to determine the amount allocable to goodwill and going concern value. Under the residual method, the purchase price for the business is allocated first to tangible assets and specific intangible assets, including covenants not to compete, to the extent of their fair market values, and any

---

[44] Rev. Rul. 70-160, 1970-1 CB 7.
[45] IRS Letter Ruling 8648005, April 21, 1986.
[46] *H.L. Tennyson*, DC Ida., 86-1 USTC ¶ 9147, 632 F.Supp 2.
[47] Rev. Rul. 69-169, 1969-1 CB 27.
[48] Rev. Rul. 68-50, 1968-1 CB 364.
[49] *Mallinckrodt, Inc.*, CA-8, 85-2 USTC ¶ 9841, 778 F.2d 402, aff'g per curiam 48 TCM 1290, CCH Dec. 41,536(M), T.C. Memo. 1984-537; *Dixie Manor Inc.*, CA-6, 81-1 USTC ¶ 9332.
[50] Rev. Rul. 65-79, 1965-1 CB 26.
[51] *Shoney's South, Inc.*, 48 TCM 768, CCH Dec. 41,398(M), T.C. Memo. 1984-413; but see also *L.A. Duaine*, 49 TCM 588, CCH Dec. 41,845(M), T.C. Memo. 1985-39.
[52] *Endres Floral Co.*, DC Ohio, 78-2 USTC ¶ 9614, 450 F.Supp. 16.

[53] Rev. Rul. 66-215, 1966-2 CB 11; but see also Rev. Rul. 86-15, 1986-1 CB 7.
[54] *Scott Paper Co.*, 74 TC 137, CCH Dec. 36,920.
[55] Rev. Rul 67-417, 1967-2 CB 49.
[56] Rev. Rul. 77-362, 1977-2 CB 8; see also *Ponderosa Mouldings, Inc.*, 53 TC 92, CCH Dec. 29,802, holding that a sprinkler system that was movable and could be transferred to another location at the risk of some damage to the system was not personal property.
[57] Rev. Rul. 81-240, 1981-2 CB 11.
[58] *Film N' Photos, Inc.*, 37 TCM 709, CCH Dec. 35,125(M), T.C. Memo. 1978-162.
[59] Rev. Rul. 74-391, 1974-2 CB 9.
[60] Rev. Rul. 75-178, 1975-1 CB 9.
[61] Rev. Rul. 67-349, 1967-2 CB 48.

excess is allocated to goodwill and going concern value.[62] The purpose of Code Sec. 1060 is to prevent amounts paid for goodwill or going concern value, which are amortizable over 15 years under Code Sec. 197, from being assigned to depreciable assets with shorter recovery periods, or for amounts paid for long-lived assets from being assigned to amortizable goodwill or going concern value.

A group of assets constitutes a trade or business under Code Sec. 1060 if their character is such that goodwill or going concern value could attach to the group under any circumstances. Factors considered in determining whether a group of assets constitutes a trade or business include (1) whether total consideration exceeds the aggregate book value of tangible and intangible assets (other than goodwill and going concern value) as shown on the books of the purchaser and (2) related transactions, including lease agreements, licenses, covenants not to compete, employment contracts, management contracts, or other similar agreements between the purchaser and seller in connection with the transfer.[63]

Example: The Purchaser acquires a going business that includes real estate, other tangible assets and goodwill for total consideration of $100,000. The Purchaser and the Seller allocate $80,000 of the purchase price to real estate, $10,000 to other tangible assets, and $10,000 to goodwill. If the real estate's fair market value were only $60,000 and not $80,000, Code Sec. 1060 would require that only $60,000 of the purchase price be allocated to the real estate and, assuming the fair market value of the other tangible assets was $10,000, $30,000 to goodwill. Similarly, if the fair market value of the real estate actually were $90,000 and the value of the other tangible assets was $10,000, there would be nothing left to allocate to amortizable goodwill.

¶ 117.5 Reporting Requirements

The purchaser and seller of a group of assets subject to Code Sec. 1060 must file asset acquisition statements on Form 8594 with their income tax returns for the taxable year that includes the purchase date.[64]

¶ 119 Apportionment of Real Property Taxes

When real property is sold, the buyer and seller usually, but not always, apportion the property taxes for the year between them. In any event, regardless of whether the parties make such an apportionment, Code Sec. 164(d) governs each party's deduction of current real prop-

---

[62] Reg. § 1.1060-1(c); Reg. § 1.338-6.
[63] Reg. § 1.1060-1(b).
[64] Temp. Reg. § 1.1060-1(h)T.

The Acquisition Transaction

erty taxes. This section allows a portion of the taxes for the real property tax year in which the property is sold to be deducted by the seller and a portion by the purchaser and limits the deductions to the portion of the taxes corresponding to the part of the real property tax year during which each owned the property.

When real property is sold, the portion of the real property tax allocable to that part of the real property tax year which ends on the day before the date of the sale is treated as a tax imposed on the seller, and the portion of the tax allocable to that part of the year which begins on the date of the sale is treated as imposed on the purchaser. This rule applies whether or not the seller and the purchaser apportion the tax.[65]

Example: The Purchaser buys real property from the Seller on June 30, 2002. The real property tax year at the location of the property is April 1 to March 31, and the property tax for the year ending March 31, 2003, is $1,460. Under Code Sec. 164(d), $360 of the real property tax is treated as imposed on the Seller (90/365 × $1,460), and $1,100 is treated as imposed on the Purchaser (275/365 × $1,460).

If the real property tax becomes a personal liability or a lien before the beginning of the real property tax year to which it relates, and the property is sold after the tax becomes a personal liability or lien, but before the related tax year begins, the seller may not deduct any amount of the real property tax and the purchaser may deduct the taxes for the taxable year in which they are paid or accrued by the purchaser according to the purchaser's method of accounting. Similarly, if the real property tax becomes a personal liability or lien after the end of the real property tax year to which it relates, and the property is sold before the tax becomes a personal liability or lien, but after the end of the related real property tax year, the purchaser may not deduct any amount of the real property tax and the seller may deduct the taxes for the taxable year in which they are paid or accrued by the seller according to the seller's method of accounting.

Example: The Seller sells real property to the Purchaser on November 15, 2002. The real property tax year at the location of the property is the calendar year and the tax becomes a lien on November 1 of the preceding calendar year. Under Code Sec. 164(d), the real property tax for the 2002 real property tax year, which became a lien on November 1, 2001, is apportioned between the Seller and the Purchaser. The entire real property tax for the 2003 real property tax year, which became a lien on November 1,

---

[65] Reg. § 1.164-6(b).

¶ 119

2002, may be deducted by the Purchaser when paid or accrued. No part of the 2003 real property tax may be deducted by the Seller even though the Seller owned the property when the 2003 tax became a lien.

A cash method seller may deduct the portion of taxes treated as imposed on the seller under Code Sec. 164(d) for the year of sale, whether or not they are actually paid in that year if the purchaser is liable for the real property tax or if the tax is not payable until after the date of sale. Alternatively, the seller may deduct the taxes for the year actually paid, if later than the year of sale.[66]

A cash method purchaser may deduct the portion of taxes treated as imposed on the purchaser under Code Sec. 164(d) for the year of sale, whether or not they are actually paid in that year if the seller is liable for the real property tax. Alternatively, the purchaser may deduct the taxes for the year actually paid, if later than the year of sale.[67]

Example: The Seller, a cash method taxpayer, sells real property to the Purchaser, also a cash method taxpayer, on May 30, 2002. The real property tax year where the property is located is the calendar year. The tax is a personal liability of the owner on June 30, but is not payable until February 28 of the following real property tax year. Under Code Sec. 164(d), 149/365 (January 1-May 29, 2002) of the real property tax payable on February 28, 2003, for the 2002 real property tax year is treated as imposed on the Seller and this portion may be deducted by the Seller for 2002 (the year of sale), whether or not actually paid that year or for the year the tax is actually paid. Also under Code Sec. 164(d), 216/365 (May 30-December 31, 2002) of the real property tax payable on February 28, 2003, for the 2002 real property tax year is treated as imposed on the Purchaser and may be deducted by the Purchaser for the taxable year in which the tax is actually paid.

If the real property tax is not a liability of any person, the person who holds the property at the time the tax becomes a lien on the property is considered liable for the tax.[68]

Example: The Seller, a cash method taxpayer, sells real property to the Purchaser, also a cash method taxpayer, on July 15, 2002. The real property tax year where the property is located is the calendar year and real property taxes are assessed and become a lien on June 30, but are not payable until September 1 of the current year. There is no personal liability for the real property taxes. Under Code Sec. 164(d)(1), 195/365 (January 1-July 14,

---

[66] See Reg. § 1.164-6(d)(1).
[67] See Reg. § 1.164-6(d)(2).
[68] See Reg. § 1.164-6(d)(3).

¶119

The Acquisition Transaction

2002) of the real property tax payable on September 1, 2002, for the 2002 real property tax year is treated as imposed on the Seller and this portion may be deducted by the Seller for the taxable year in which the sale occurs, whether or not actually paid or for the taxable year in which the tax is actually paid. Also under Code Sec. 164(d)(1), 170/365 (July 15-December 31, 2002) of the property tax is treated as imposed on the Purchaser and this portion may be deducted by the Purchaser for the taxable year in which the sale occurs, whether or not actually paid or for the taxable year in which the tax is actually paid.

For accrual method taxpayers who have not made the election to accrue property taxes under Code Sec. 461(c), the portion of any real property tax treated as imposed on the seller or purchaser under Code Sec. 164(d) which has not accrued as of the date of sale is treated as having accrued on the date of sale.[69]

Example: The Seller, an accrual method taxpayer who has not elected to accrue property taxes under Code Sec. 461(c), sells a parcel of real property to the Purchaser on June 30, 2003. The real property tax year where the property is located is the calendar year and the tax is assessed and becomes a lien on November 30 for the current year. There is no personal liability for the real property tax. Under Code Sec. 164(d), 180/365 of tax for the 2003 real property tax year is treated as imposed on the Seller and also is treated as accruing on June 30, 2003. The Purchaser, also an accrual method taxpayer who has not made the election under Code Sec. 461(c), accrues the share (185/365) of the real property tax on November 30, 2003.

Prior Deduction of Taxes

A taxpayer who, prior to the year of sale, has deducted an amount for real property taxes for the year of sale in excess of the portion of the tax treated as imposed on the taxpayer under Code Sec. 164(d) must include the excess in gross income for the taxable year of the sale.[70]

Reimbursements

If the seller pays real property taxes attributable to the year in which the sale occurs, the seller does not take into account in determining the amount realized from the sale any amount received as reimbursement for taxes which are treated under Code Sec. 164(d) as imposed on the purchaser. Similarly, in computing the cost basis under Code Sec. 1012, the purchaser does not take into account any amount paid to the seller as reimbursement for real property taxes which are

---

[69] Reg. § 1.164-6(d)(6).   [70] Reg. § 1.164-6(d)(5).

treated as imposed on the purchaser under Code Sec. 164(d). These rules apply whether or not the contract of sale calls for the purchaser to reimburse the seller for the taxes paid by the seller.[71]

On the other hand, if the purchaser pays an amount representing property taxes that are treated as imposed on the seller, that amount is taken into account both in determining the amount realized from the sale by the seller and in computing the purchaser's cost basis under Code Sec. 1012. It does not matter whether or not the contract of sale specifies that the sale price has been reduced by, or is in any way intended to reflect, the taxes allocable to the seller.[72]

Example: The contract of sale on a parcel of real property specifies a contract price of $50,000. The property tax for the year of sale on the parcel is $1,000, which is paid entirely by the Purchaser. Under Code Sec. 164(d), $250 of the property tax is treated as imposed on the Seller and $750 is treated as imposed on the Purchaser. The Purchaser's cost basis for this parcel is $50,250, regardless of the taxable year in which the Purchaser makes actual payment of the taxes. Similarly, the Seller realizes $50,250 from the sale of the parcel.

¶ 121 Purchase from Foreign Person

Code Sec. 1445 requires a purchaser or other transferee of a U.S. real property interest acquired from a foreign person to deduct and withhold a tax equal to 10 percent of the amount realized by the foreign person on the sale or other disposition. A purchaser or transferee who fails to withhold the required amount may be liable for the tax. There are several exemptions from the withholding requirement, the most important of which is the exemption for the purchase or acquisition, for $300,000 or less, of property for use as a personal residence by the transferee.

U.S. real property interests include any interest in real property located in the United States or the Virgin Islands and certain personal property, such as farm machinery, that is associated with the use of real property. Interests in mines, wells, or other natural deposits located in the United States are also considered U.S. real property interests.

An interest, other than as a creditor, in a domestic corporation may also be a U.S. real property interest. An interest in a corporation is not a real property interest if the corporation was not a U.S. real property holding corporation at any time during which the interest in the corporation was held, or during the five-year period ending on the

---

[71] Reg. § 1.1001-1(b)(1). [72] Reg. § 1.1001-1(b)(2).

date of disposition, if shorter. Also, if, on the date of disposition, the corporation did not hold any U.S. real property interests, and all U.S. real property interests held by the corporation at any time while the interest in the corporation was held, or during the five-year period ending on the date of disposition, if shorter, were disposed of in transactions in which the full amount of any gain was recognized, then an interest in the corporation is not a U.S. real property interest.

In addition to the exemption from withholding by the transferee for the purchase or acquisition of a personal residence for $300,000 or less, the other exemptions state that no withholding is required if:

1. The transferor furnishes to the transferee a certificate stating, under penalty of perjury, the transferor's U.S. taxpayer identification number and that the transferor is not a foreign person. (A foreign corporation that has elected to be treated as a domestic corporation under Code Sec. 897(i) may file a non-foreign affidavit.)

2. In the case of a disposition of any interest in any domestic corporation, the corporation furnishes to the transferee a certification stating under penalty of perjury that the interest is not a U.S. real property interest. The corporation may issue the statement only if it was not a U.S. real property holding corporation as defined in Code Sec. 897 at any time during the previous five years (or period interest was held, if shorter), or if the interests in the corporation ceased to be U.S. real property interests under Code Sec. 897(c)(1)(B).

3. The transferee receives a withholding certificate from the IRS. (Such a certificate also can reduce the amount of the required withholding. Either the transferee or the transferor may request a withholding certificate based on the transferor's maximum tax liability or an agreement to pay the tax.)

4. The disposition is of a share of a class of stock that is regularly traded on an established securities market.

The regulations under Code Sec. 1445 provide a detailed explanation of the withholding requirements, and Rev. Proc. 2000-35 [73] provides the procedures for obtaining a withholding certificate for exemption from the withholding requirement or for reduced withholding.

¶ 123 CONSTRUCTION OF REAL PROPERTY

The costs of constructing or improving buildings or other assets that have a useful life which extends beyond the end of the taxable

---

[73] 2000-35 IRB 211.

year are not currently deductible.[74] Rather, these expenditures, referred to as capital expenditures, become part of the basis of the constructed or improved property. These capitalized costs are recovered through depreciation or amortization [75] if the property is used in a business or investment activity. The capitalized costs of property not used for business or held for investment are recovered at the time the property is sold or otherwise disposed of when unrecovered basis is offset against the amount realized in computing gain or loss.

¶ 127 Capitalization of Construction Costs

It has long been clear that a taxpayer that constructs a building or other capital asset for its own use must capitalize all direct construction costs such as direct materials and labor. Also, depreciation on equipment used to construct the property may not be deducted currently but must be capitalized and added to the basis of the constructed property.[76] The tax treatment of many indirect expenses incurred in the construction of real property, however, was less certain.

In order to remove the uncertainty in this area, and to provide a single, comprehensive set of rules to govern the capitalization of costs, Congress enacted Code Sec. 263A. This section applies a single set of capitalization rules, the "uniform capitalization rules," to all costs incurred in manufacturing or constructing tangible property. The following discussion of these uniform capitalization rules is limited to their application to real estate. A comprehensive explanation of the uniform capitalization rules may be found in the regulations under Code Sec. 263A. Reg. 1.263A-0 contains an outline of those detailed regulations.

¶ 127.1 *Expenses Other Than Interest*

The uniform capitalization rules generally apply to real property built, constructed or improved by the taxpayer (or under contract for the taxpayer) for use in a trade or business or an activity conducted for profit. They also apply to real property acquired for resale which is not a capital asset and which is considered stock in trade or inventory property.[77] They do not apply to personal use property (such as a home constructed by a taxpayer for personal use). Also, the uniform capitalization rules do not apply to the development costs of oil and gas wells and other mineral property or to timber and ornamental trees and the real property underlying these trees.[78]

---

[74] Code Sec. 263.
[75] See ¶ 901.
[76] *Idaho Power Co.*, S.Ct., 74-2 USTC ¶ 9521, 418 U.S. 1, 94 S.Ct. 2757.
[77] Code Sec. 263A(b).
[78] Code Sec. 263A(c).

The Acquisition Transaction

The costs that must be capitalized as part of the construction cost of real property are the direct costs of the property and the property's share of those indirect costs, including taxes, that are allocable to the property.[79] Interest expense is subject to some special allocation rules and is discussed separately below.

Direct Costs

Direct costs that must be capitalized in connection with the construction of real property include direct material costs and direct labor costs.[80]

Direct material costs include the cost of the materials that become an integral part of the real property and the cost of the materials that are consumed in the ordinary course of constructing the real property.

Direct labor costs include the cost of labor that can be identified or associated with the construction of the real property. The elements of direct labor costs include items such as basic compensation, overtime, vacation and holiday pay, sick pay, shift differentials, payroll taxes, and payments to a supplemental unemployment benefit plan paid for employees engaged in direct labor.

Indirect Costs

Indirect costs that must be capitalized in connection with the construction of real property include all costs that directly benefit the construction or are incurred because of the construction, subject to a few exceptions mentioned below.[81] In some cases, indirect costs may directly benefit, or be incurred because of, the construction even though the same costs also benefit other activities. In these cases, a reasonable allocation is required to determine the portion of the costs which is allocable to the construction of the real property.

Examples of indirect costs that must be capitalized in connection with the construction of real property include amounts incurred for:

1. Repair of equipment or facilities;
2. Maintenance of equipment or facilities;
3. Utilities (heat, light, power, etc.) relating to equipment or facilities;
4. Rent of equipment, facilities, or land;
5. Indirect labor and contract supervisory wages, including basic compensation, overtime, vacation, holiday and sick pay, shift differentials, payroll taxes and contributions to supplemental unemployment benefit plans;

---

[79] Code Sec. 263A(a)(2).
[80] Reg. § 1.263A-1(e)(2).
[81] Reg. § 1.263A-1(e)(3).

¶ 127.1

6. Indirect materials and supplies;
7. Tools and equipment (if their cost is not otherwise capitalized);
8. Quality control and inspection;
9. Taxes otherwise allowable as a deduction (except state, local and foreign income taxes) that relate to labor, materials, supplies, equipment, land or facilities, other than property taxes that are added to and considered part of the cost of equipment or facilities;
10. Depreciation, amortization and cost recovery allowances on equipment and facilities;
11. Administrative costs, whether or not performed on a construction site, but not any cost of selling or return on capital;
12. Direct and indirect costs incurred by any administrative, service or support function to the extent allocable to the construction (allocation rules are contained in Reg. § 1.263A-1(g));
13. Compensation paid to officers attributable to services performed in connection with the construction;
14. Insurance, including insurance on machinery and equipment or on the construction activity itself;
15. Deductible contributions to employee benefit plans;
16. Rework labor, scrap, and spoilage; and
17. Bidding, engineering, and design expenses.

Noncapitalized Costs

Costs that do not have to be capitalized in connection with the construction of real property include amounts incurred for:
1. Research and development;
2. Marketing, selling or advertising;
3. Casualty and theft losses and other losses under Code Sec. 165;
4. Income taxes;
5. Depreciation, amortization and cost recovery allowances on equipment and facilities that are temporarily idle (assets are not temporarily idle on nonworking days, but an asset used in construction is idle when it is not enroute to or located at a jobsite);
6. Deductible contributions to pension or annuity plans that represent past service costs; and
7. Cost attributable to strikes.

¶ 127.1

¶ 127.2 *Interest*

Interest paid or incurred to finance the construction of certain real property must be capitalized under the uniform capitalization rules. The interest capitalization requirement generally applies to the same types of real property which are subject to the other capitalization requirements, except that interest on debt incurred or continued to finance the acquisition and holding of property for resale does not have to be capitalized. [82] Further, only interest costs paid or incurred during the construction period (see below) must be capitalized. [83]

Allocation of Interest

The amount of interest on debt that is incurred or continued to finance the construction of property is determined using the avoided cost method. It is based on the amount of interest expense that would have been avoided if the construction had not taken place and all construction expenditures were used to repay any indebtedness. [84]

Debt that can be specifically traced to the construction must first be allocated to that construction activity. If construction expenditures exceed the amount of debt specifically traced to the construction, other debt (if any) of the taxpayer is allocated to the construction activity. The interest rate applied to any additional debt allocated to the construction activity is the weighted average of the interest rates on the taxpayer's debts outstanding during the construction period, other than debt specifically traced to the construction. In other words, not only must interest on debt that directly finances the construction be capitalized, but also any interest on debt that could have been paid off by construction expenditures that are not directly financed.

If the construction is being performed by a contractor and the customer makes progress payments or advance payments to the contractor, interest on debt incurred or continued during the construction period to finance the payments made and the costs incurred by the customer must be capitalized by the customer. The contractor must capitalize interest costs for the property under construction to the extent that the construction expenditures incurred by the contractor exceed the accumulated payments received from the customer. [85]

Interest on debt incurred or continued to finance assets, such as construction equipment, that is used to construct the property must be capitalized to the extent it is paid or incurred during the construction period of the property. If assets are used to construct property and for

---

[82] Code Sec. 263A(f)(1)(B).
[83] Code Sec. 263A(f)(1)(A).
[84] Reg. § 1.263A-9(a).
[85] See Reg. § 1.263A-11(c).

other purposes, only the portion of the interest allocable to the construction activity must be capitalized. [86]

Construction Period

The uniform capitalization requirements apply to interest only to the extent paid or incurred during the construction period of the property. The IRS has provided guidance in the regulations. According to the IRS, the production period of real property generally begins when physical activity is first performed on the property and ends when all production activities reasonably expected are completed and the property is placed in service.[87]

Physical production activities include, for example,

1. Clearing, grading, or excavating of raw land;
2. Demolishing a building or gutting a standing building;
3. Constructing infrastructure such as roads, sewers, sidewalks, cables, and wiring;
4. Structural, mechanical, or electrical work on a building or other structure; or
5. Landscaping.[88]

On the other hand, planning and design, such as soil testing, preparing architectural blueprints or models, and obtaining building permits, and incidental repairs are not physical production activities.[89]

The production period must be determined for each "unit" of real property. A unit of real property includes any components that are functionally interdependent and an allocable share of any common feature even though the common feature does not meet the functional interdependence test. When the production period begins for any functionally interdependent component or any common feature of the unit, the production period begins for the entire unit of real property. The portion of land included in a unit of real property includes land on which real property, including a common feature, included in the unit is situated, land subject to setback restriction for the property, and any other contiguous portion of the tract other than land held for a purpose unrelated to the unit being produced.[90]

> **Example 1:** Taxpayer is constructing a high-rise office building with two wings. At the end of 2002, Wing 1, but not Wing 2, is placed in service. Also at the end of 2002, all production activities reasonably expected on Wing 1 are completed. Under Reg. § 1.263A-10(b)(1), Wing 1 and Wing 2 are separate units of prop-

---

[86] See Reg. § 1.263A-11(d).
[87] Reg. § 1.263A-12(c)(2) and Reg. § 1.263A-12(d)(1).
[88] Reg. § 1.263A-12(e)(2).
[89] Reg. § 1.263A-12(f).
[90] See Reg. § 1.263A-10(b)(1).

¶ 127.2

erty. The taxpayer may stop capitalizing interest on Wing 1 but not on Wing 2.

Example 2: Taxpayer is in the home construction business. He generally paints and finishes the interior of a house, but not until after a potential buyer is found. Because the taxpayer reasonably expects to undertake production activity—the painting and finishing—the production period of each house does not end until those activities are completed.

¶ 131 Interest and Taxes on Pre-1987 Construction

The uniform capitalization rules discussed at ¶ 127 generally do not apply to costs incurred before January 1, 1987. Also, they do not apply to costs incurred in connection with the construction of property if substantial construction occurred before March 1, 1986.

Prior to enactment of the uniform capitalization rules, former Code Sec. 189 required the capitalization of real property construction period interest and taxes.[91] Interest and taxes capitalized under former Code Sec. 189 were subject to 10-year amortization, that is, 10 percent of the capitalized amount could be deducted each year over a period of 10 years, beginning with the year the costs were incurred. If a building for which capitalized interest and taxes were incurred was not placed in service in the year the costs were incurred or the following year, the amortization deductions were suspended until the year the building was placed in service.

Real property construction period interest and taxes for former Code Sec. 189 are defined as interest paid or accrued on indebtedness incurred or continued to acquire, construct, or carry real property, and real property taxes, attributable to the construction period of the property and otherwise deductible for the taxable year in which paid or accrued.[92] The construction period for former Code Sec. 189 was essentially the same as the construction period for the interest capitalization requirement under the present uniform capitalization rules.

For buildings constructed before 1987, or those for which substantial construction occurred before March 1, 1986, even if construction extended beyond 1986, the 10-year amortization of construction period interest and taxes required by former Code Sec. 189 is the operable law. If property subject to the 10-year amortization provisions is sold or disposed of in a taxable transaction before the construction period interest and taxes are fully recovered, the unamortized amount is added to the seller's basis and, accordingly, reduces the taxable amount

---

[91] Former Code Sec. 189 was repealed by the Tax Reform Act of 1986 for costs subject to the uniform capitalization rules.

[92] Former Code Sec. 189(e)(1).

realized by the seller. For the year of sale, a deduction is allowed for a proportionate part of the amortization amount for the year.[93]

¶ 135 Capitalization of Carrying Charges

Certain taxes and carrying charges otherwise expressly deductible under the Internal Revenue Code may be capitalized and added to the basis of property under the election provided by Code Sec. 266. For the most part, current deductions provide a greater tax benefit than capitalization and, for this reason, the election is seldom utilized. Also, since enactment of the uniform capitalization rules, many more expenses must be capitalized and less are available as current deductions.

Note that Reg. § 1.263A-8 through Reg. § 1.263A-15 on the requirement to capitalize interest (see ¶ 127.2) apply before the application of the election to capitalize carrying charges under Code Sec. 266. After applying Reg. § 1.263A-8 through Reg. § 1.263A-15, a taxpayer may elect to capitalize interest under Code Sec. 266 for designated property within the meaning of Reg. § 1.263A-8(b), if a computation under any Internal Revenue Code provision is not materially distorted, including computations relating to the source of deductions.[94]

In any event, the election to capitalize otherwise deductible taxes and carrying charges relating to real property is available in the following cases.[95]

1. For unimproved and unproductive real property, annual taxes, interest on a mortgage, and other carrying charges. An election for these items relating to unimproved and unproductive real property is effective only for the year for which it is made.

2. For real property, whether improved or unimproved and whether productive or unproductive:

    a. Interest on a loan, but not theoretical interest of a taxpayer using his or her own funds,

    b. Taxes of the owner of the real property measured by compensation paid to the owner's employees,

    c. Taxes of the owner imposed on the purchase of materials, or on the storage, use, or other consumption of materials, and

    d. Other necessary expenditures.

For these items to be subject to the election, they must be paid or incurred for the development of the real property or for the construction of an improvement or additional improvement to

---

[93] Former Code Sec. 189(c)(2).
[94] Reg. § 1.266-1(a)(2).
[95] Reg. § 1.266-1(b).

the real property, up to the time the development or construction work is completed. An election for these items is effective until the development or construction is completed.

While taxes and carrying charges must be otherwise deductible to be subject to the election to capitalize costs under Code Sec. 266, not all deductible items are subject to the election. For instance, advertising expense on unproductive property and maintenance and upkeep costs attributable to improved and unimproved unproductive real property are not carrying charges subject to the election to capitalize.[96]

Taxes or carrying charges that only partially relate to property for which taxes or carrying charges may be capitalized may be allocated between the two types of property to determine the amount subject to the election.[97]

An election to capitalize otherwise deductible taxes and carrying charges is made by filing a statement listing the items that are being capitalized. This statement must be filed with the original tax return for the year for which the election is made.[98]

¶ 139 LOW-INCOME HOUSING TAX CREDIT

Over the years, Congress has provided various tax incentives to encourage the development and maintenance of low-income rental housing. These incentives have included special accelerated depreciation, five-year amortization of rehabilitation expenses, exemption from the capitalization requirement for construction period interest and taxes, and tax-exempt bond financing for multi-family rental properties.

In the Tax Reform Act of 1986, Congress repealed many of the existing tax incentives for low-income housing and enacted a tax credit that may be claimed by owners of residential property used for low-income housing.[99] The credit is available for the cost of new construction, the cost of rehabilitation, or the cost of acquiring existing buildings by purchase and their rehabilitation. Generally, only the cost of buildings attributable to low-income units qualifies for the credit. Cost attributable to residential units other than low-income units and cost attributable to land are not eligible for the credit.

The low-income housing credit is taken annually, generally for a period of ten years. New construction and rehabilitation expenditures for projects placed in service in 1987 are eligible for a credit equal to nine percent of the qualified cost each year for 10 years. The acquisition cost of existing projects and the cost of newly constructed projects

---

[96] Rev. Rul. 71-475, 1971-2, CB 304.
[97] Reg. § 266-1(e).
[98] Reg. § 1.266-1(c)(3).
[99] Code Sec. 42.

receiving other federal subsidies placed in service in 1987 are eligible for a credit equal to four percent of the qualified cost each year for 10 years. For buildings placed in service after 1987, the credit percentages are adjusted figures. The exact percentages are set in order to provide a total credit over the 10-year credit period equal to a present value of 70 percent of the qualified costs for new construction and rehabilitation, and 30 percent for other qualified costs.

The low-income housing credit is considered in further detail in ¶ 831.

Chapter 2

Form of Ownership

¶ 200 OVERVIEW OF CHAPTER

Most real estate acquisitions involve one buyer (or a husband and wife acting as one) using the buyer's own funds and a mortgage loan from a financial institution. If the real estate involved is a personal residence, the question of the optimum form of ownership does not arise, except, in the case of spouses, as to whether title should be in one spouse or they should own the property jointly. If the real estate is business or investment property, however, the choices available to the buyer increase. Should the real estate be owned and operated individually or through a corporation? If through a corporation, should it be a regular C corporation or an S corporation?

If, in connection with the acquisition of business or investment property, more than one individual buyer is involved, the number of choices for the owning entity increases again. Common or joint ownership is possible, as is the use of a C corporation or an S corporation. There is also the partnership form to consider and, if a partnership is chosen, whether a general partnership or limited partnership is appropriate. In most states, there is still another choice for the owning entity, a limited liability company, which may be treated as either a partnership or a corporation for federal tax purposes.

In some cases, the person who is to benefit from the property may not be a suitable owner, such as when the person is not capable of managing or dealing with the property for one reason or another. For example, a minor child might not be a suitable owner. In such cases, ownership in trust might be appropriate.

In any event, the form of ownership of real estate does have significant legal, financial, practical, and tax consequences. In this chapter, the appropriate form of ownership and operation for real estate is considered. Various forms of securitized real estate, that is, real estate ventures financed through a public offering, are considered at ¶ 2100 and 2200. Cooperatives and condominium ownership are considered at ¶ 1901 and 1909.

¶ 201 OWNERSHIP FOR TAX PURPOSES

It is generally the owner of real property who reports income from the property and who is entitled to the tax deductions, such as depreciation, generated by the property. But ownership for tax purposes, while it usually follows legal title, is not always the same as legal title. For example, an individual could deduct taxes paid on property even if the individual took title to the property in the names of a daughter and son-in-law for personal reasons and the record owners received no income and paid no expenses.[1] Similarly, it is the equitable owner, not the legal owner, who may deduct a loss on the foreclosure of property.[2]

The right to deduct depreciation does not depend on ownership of the legal title to property, but on the investment made in the property.[3] In *Gladdings Dry Goods Co.*, the test set is whether the taxpayer would suffer an economic loss as a result of a decrease in value of the property due to depreciation.[4]

In *Lazarus & Co.*,[5] the Supreme Court, citing *Gladdings Dry Goods Co.*, held that the test utilized to determine who is entitled to depreciation is who bears the burden of exhaustion of the capital investment. This test is usually applied by asking who has the "benefits and burdens of ownership." Factors the courts consider in answering this question include:

1. Whether legal title passes;
2. How the parties treat the transaction involved;
3. Whether an equity was acquired in the property;
4. Whether the contract creates a present obligation on the buyer of property to make payments;
5. Whether the right of possession is vested in the buyer;
6. Which party pays the property taxes;
7. Which party bears the risk of loss or damage to the property; and
8. Which party receives the profits from the operation and sale of the property.[6]

In the eyes of the IRS, it is apparently investment *plus* either possession or title that is controlling. Rev. Rul. 69-89[7] involved a company that entered into an executory contract for the purchase of

---

[1] *A.J. Gilbert*, 11 TCM 457, CCH Dec. 18,958(M).
[2] *S.J. Ritholz Est.*, 4 TCM 954, CCH Dec. 14,810(M).
[3] *Gladding Dry Goods Co.*, 2 BTA 336, CCH Dec. 642.
[4] *T.W. Blake, Jr.*, 20 TC 721, CCH Dec. 19,779, Acq. 1954-2 CB 3.
[5] S.Ct., 39-2 USTC ¶ 9743, 308 U.S. 252.
[6] *Grodt & McKay Realty, Inc.*, 77 TC 1221, CCH Dec. 38,472.
[7] 1969-1 CB 59.

land with a two-story building located in the state of Washington. Title to the property was retained by the seller until all payments called for by the contract were made by the purchaser. Under Washington law, the purchaser had no legal or equitable title or interest in the property under this contract, but the purchaser took possession of the property on the date of the contract and used the property for business purposes. The IRS ruled that the passing of title did not control who had the right to depreciation deductions for federal income tax purposes. According to the IRS, this situation is similar to the situation in which gain or loss on the sale of property arises at the time the deed passes or possession and the benefits and burdens of ownership are transferred to the buyer as a practical matter.

On the other hand, an investment without transfer of either title or possession may not be sufficient to produce ownership for tax purposes and allow the taxpayer making the investment to claim depreciation deductions.[8] In Rev. Rul. 68-431, the purchaser under a contract of sale made substantial improvements to some real estate before the seller was to surrender possession of the property and execute a land contract for the transfer of the property. The IRS ruled that the purchaser did not actually acquire the property and place it in service until the date possession of the property changed hands and the land contract was executed. The purchaser was not entitled to depreciation deductions until that time.

¶ 203 Use of Straw or Nominee Corporations

For real estate, it is often desireable that ownership be in some unincorporated form in order to take maximum advantage of the tax benefits available from the ownership of real estate. When real estate is owned by a corporation, the deductions are locked in the corporation, and income is subject to a possible double tax. Also, a distribution of appreciated property by a corporation, either in the normal course of business or in liquidation of the corporation, generally produces a double tax on the appreciation—once at the corporate level and again at the shareholder level.

On the other hand, there may be good financial or practical reasons for using a corporation as the owning entity for real estate. In some cases, mortgage lenders may demand that title to real estate be held by a corporation to avoid state usury limits that apply to unincorporated entities and individuals. Corporations may also shield the underlying owners from liability, either on the mortgage or from other activities conducted on or in connection with the particular real estate involved. Corporations can also preserve the shareholders' anonymity.

---

[8] Rev. Rul. 68-431, 1968-2 CB 99.

When the use of a corporation has been necessitated by non-tax factors, yet the tax benefits of not using the corporation were high, individuals often attempted to get the best of both worlds by using what have come to be known as "straw," "nominee," or sometimes "dummy" corporations. The essential idea of the straw corporation is to have the corporation serve its non-tax functions while having the existence of the corporation ignored for tax purposes.

(It should be noted that since the rules relating to S corporations, a form of business organization more fully explored at ¶ 241, were liberalized to permit the holding of passive investment assets, the S corporation may fill the need for an entity that provides the benefits of incorporation without the tax disadvantages and lessen the need for straw or nominee corporations in many situations. In any event, even when a nominee corporation is contemplated for holding real estate, it might be a good idea to elect S corporation status, if available, for the nominee in order to salvage some tax benefits in the event the corporation is treated as the taxpayer with respect to the real estate.)

As a general proposition, a corporation and its shareholders are treated as separate taxpayers. In an early case involving the question of the taxability of a straw corporation, the owner of real property transferred ownership to a corporation that the owner had organized at the request of, and for the protection of, the real property owner's creditors. On the eventual sale of the property, the taxpayer sought to have the corporation's existence ignored and the gain taxed to the shareholder in the shareholder's individual capacity. The Supreme Court,[9] however, ruled that the corporation's activities caused it to be taxable:

> The doctrine of corporate entity fills a useful purpose in business life. Whether the purpose be to gain an advantage under the law of the state of incorporation or to avoid or to comply with the demands of creditors or to serve the creator's personal or undisclosed convenience, so long as that purpose is the equivalent of business activity or is followed by the carrying on of business by the corporation, the corporation remains a separate taxable entity.

¶ 205 Agency Relationship Requirement

Since it is very difficult to benefit from a straw corporation that carries on no business activity whatsoever, this decision proved to be very troublesome to anyone seeking to have the existence of a corporation ignored for tax purposes. But actually ignoring the corporate existence proved not to be necessary in order to benefit from a nominee

---

[9] *Moline Properties, Inc.*, S.Ct., 43-1 USTC ¶ 9464, 319 U.S. 436.

corporation. Rather, it became a matter of shifting ownership for tax purposes away from the corporation and to the "beneficial owners" of the property. The corporation could be a valid taxable entity that held title to property and still not be taxable on the property if the corporation acted merely as the agent or nominal title holder on behalf of the true owner of the property.

This approach to the problem gained a boost from the Supreme Court decision in *National Carbide Corp.*[10] This case involved a corporation that organized several subsidiaries to act as agents for the parent in the sale of certain products. The subsidiaries maintained that they were mere collection agents for the parent and should not be taxed on profits that rightfully were taxable to the parent. While the Supreme Court did not agree in this case, it left the door open to the use of a corporate agent:

> What we have said does not foreclose a true corporate agent from handling the property and income of its owner-principal without being taxable therefor.

The Tax Court had occasion to examine the factors set out in *National Carbide Corp.* that would determine whether a true agency relationship existed in the context of a corporation formed to avoid state usury laws in *J.A. Roccaforte*.[11] The Tax Court, examining the following factors, found that a corporation formed by individual investors of a partnership engaged in the development of an apartment complex was a true corporate agent of its principals:

1. Whether the corporation operates in the name of and for the account of the principal;
2. Whether the principal is bound by the alleged corporate agent's acts;
3. Whether the alleged corporate agent transmits money it receives to the principal;
4. Whether the receipt of income is attributable to assets or employees of the principal;
5. Whether the alleged agent's relationship with the principal is based on its ownership and control by the principal; and
6. Whether the corporation's activities are consistent with the normal duties of an agent.

On appeal, however, the Fifth Circuit Court of Appeals reversed the Tax Court.[12] According to the Fifth Circuit, the Supreme Court decision in *National Carbide Corp.* holding that there is a possibility

---

[10] S.Ct., 49-1 USTC ¶ 9223, 336 U.S. 422.
[11] 77 TC 263, CCH Dec. 38,122.
[12] *J.A. Roccaforte, Jr.*, CA-5, 83-2 USTC ¶ 9452, 708 F.2d 986.

¶ 205

that an otherwise separate taxable corporate entity could, in some circumstances, qualify as a nontaxable agent of its principal set out two requirements that are mandatory: (1) the corporation's relations with its principal must not be dependent on the fact that it is owned by the principal, and (2) the corporation's business purpose must be the carrying on of the normal duties of an agent. Because the Tax Court found that the corporation's relations with the partners depended on their ownership and control of the corporation, the corporation was not a true nontaxable corporate agent.

While the Fourth Circuit adopted a similar position,[13] the Sixth Circuit refused to find such mandatory requirements and ruled that a valid agency is created when the attributes of an agency are present and the corporation conducts itself no differently than would an independent agent that had bargained with the principal at arm's length.[14] The split between the Circuits was resolved in favor of the Sixth Circuit position by the Supreme Court.[15]

In *Bollinger*, the Supreme Court ruled that a corporation that held record title to real property as agent for its shareholder was not the owner of the property for tax purposes. Rather, the shareholder, a partnership that developed and operated an apartment complex, was the true owner of the property. The corporation was formed to avoid Kentucky's usury law, and the corporation and the partnership entered into a written agreement that provided that the corporation would hold title to the apartment complex as the partnership's agent for the sole purpose of obtaining financing and would convey, assign, or encumber the property and disburse the proceeds only as directed by the partnership. The corporation had no obligation to maintain the property or assume any liability because of the execution of promissory notes or otherwise, and the partnerhsip agreed to indemnify and hold the corporation harmless from any liability it might sustain as its agent and nominee.

According to the Supreme Court, a true nontaxable corporate agent or nominee is created, and tax-avoiding manipulation adequately avoided, when:

1. There is a written agreement that states that the corporation is acting as agent for its shareholders with respect to the property at the time the property is acquired;
2. The corporation functions as an agent, and not as a principal, with respect to the property for all purposes; and

---

[13] *F.R. Ourisman*, CA-4, 85-1 USTC ¶ 9357, 760 F.2d 541.

[14] *J.C. Bollinger, Jr.*, CA-6, 86-2 USTC ¶ 9821, 807 F.2d 65.

[15] *J.C. Bollinger, Jr.*, S.Ct., 88-1 USTC ¶ 9233 485 U.S. 340, 108 S.Ct. 1173 (1988).

¶ 205

Form of Ownership

3. The corporation holds itself out as an agent, and not as a principal, in all dealings with third parties relating to the property.

The Supreme Court's *Bollinger* decision provides a clear safe harbor for the creation of a nominee corporation, without necessarily overturning the earlier tests based on *National Carbide Corp*. If the three criteria of *Bollinger* are followed though, a corporation dealing with real property is assured treatment as the true agent of its shareholders and the shareholders are assured treatment as the owners of the property for federal income tax purposes.

¶ 207   INDIVIDUAL AND JOINT OWNERSHIP

For tax purposes, the owner of real property can be only one of the following: an individual (proprietorship), a partnership, a corporation, or a trust or estate. This does not mean that if more than one person owns a particular parcel of real estate, the owners must form one of the available tax entities. As far as the tax law is concerned, two or more individuals together may own the same real estate and still be considered individual taxpayers with regard to that real estate. This section looks at the various ways individuals may own real estate without an intervening entity such as partnership, corporation or trust.

¶ 211   Sole Individual Ownership

An individual may acquire real estate in his or her own name and all tax consequences of the acquisition, operation and disposition of that real estate will fall directly on the individual. Income generated by the real estate will be added to the individual's other income and taxed accordingly. Deductions generated by the real estate, subject to various loss limitations such as the at-risk rules (see ¶ 311) and the passive loss rules (see ¶ 1105), will reduce the individual's income subject to tax.

As a practical matter, individual ownership is the simplest and least costly form of ownership. On the other hand, individual ownership also opens the door to allow all potential liabilities arising out of the ownership and operation of the property to fall directly on the owner. In most cases, the individual owner will guard against the damage an unexpected liability could cause through careful management of the property and liability insurance sufficient to protect the individual's assets.

Individual ownership is not the only route available when one person acquires property. The individual may form a corporation to take title to the property and, in the case of business or investment property, to manage and operate the property. A corporate entity, however, may not be a practical alternative for ownership of property unless the property is of fairly large value or is part of a business that would justify the added expense and administrative burdens of creating a new legal and tax entity. (The formation, operation, advantages and disadvantages of corporations are discussed at ¶ 231—235.)

¶ 213 Common and Joint Ownership

When two or more persons together own property, they may hold title as tenants in common or joint tenants. The distinction between the two forms of ownership is a legal one rather than a tax one. In either case, each owner owns an undivided interest in the entire property.

If the owners of property are tenants in common, each co-owner may deal with his or her interest as he or she pleases, that is, the co-owner may sell or encumber his or her interest and otherwise deal with it as his or her own property without the other co-owner's permission. The owner of an interest in real property as a tenant in common may bequeath the property to his or her heirs. As a practical matter, co-owners frequently limit their rights and arrange for the operation and management of the property in a separate contract or agreement.

The major difference between co-tenants and joint tenants is that, if the owners of property are joint tenants, each owner has a right of survivorship in the interest held by the other joint tenant. In other words, when one of two owners of property held as a joint tenancy dies, the surviving joint tenant automatically becomes the owner of the entire property. A joint tenant cannot bequeath his or her interest in the property and the joint tenant's interest does not pass to his or her heirs, unless they also happen to be surviving joint tenants. A joint tenant's interest in property on death remains out of the probate estate, while an interest as tenant in common is subject to probate.

While co-ownership may appear, at first glance, to be a form of partnership, it is not. Unlike partners, tenants in common or joint tenants cannot act on behalf of each other without authorization. Also, a co-owner is not liable for the contracts and debts of the other co-owner, even if the contracts or debts relate to the co-owned property. One partner, on the other hand, may bind all partners when that one partner is acting with respect to partnership business or property.

As long as co-owners do no more than hold the property and maintain, keep in repair, and rent or lease it, the status of the co-owners will not be challenged by the IRS. For example, if tenants in common of farm property lease it to a farmer for a cash rental or crop share, there is no partnership. Tenants in common, however, may be partners if they actively carry on a trade, business, financial operation, or venture and divide the profits from it. For example, a partnership exists if co-owners of an apartment building lease space and also provide services to the occupants either directly or through an agent.[16]

From a practical standpoint, there may be little tax difference in the final result in many cases regardless of whether property is held as co-tenants or in partnership. Of course, if a co-tenancy rises to the level of a partnership, the partnership entity then must file returns and make those tax elections relating to the property which must be made at the partnership, rather than individual, level.

In the usual case, each co-tenant merely reports the share of income from the property and deducts the share of expenses on his or her own tax return, just as if the co-tenant were the sole owner of the property. Should a co-tenant actually pay more than his or her share of expenses, however, an amount over and above his or her proportionate share may not be deducted. Rather, the excess payments are treated for tax purposes as loans to the other co-tenants when the co-tenant paying expenses on behalf of another co-tenant is legally entitled to reimbursement.[17]

¶ 215 Joint Ownership By Spouses

In most cases, the joint ownership of property by spouses, or ownership as tenants by the entirety, produces no special income tax consequences. As far as the joint ownership is concerned, the tax rules applied to spouses are the same as those applied to unrelated joint owners, except in the case of a sale or other transfer from one joint owner to the other.

If the spouses file a joint income tax return, then the joint ownership produces the same results as would individual ownership by one of the spouses, because each joint owner's share of the income and deductions from the property are combined on the joint return. On a sale of jointly owned property, each spouse reports his or her share of income or loss. On the death of a spouse, the surviving spouse receives a stepped-up basis for the interest acquired from the deceased spouse, but not for the interest already held by the surviving spouse. This can produce a tax disadvantage since the surviving spouse would receive a stepped-up basis for the entire property if the property were held solely by the deceased spouse and left to the surviving spouse by will.

On the sale or transfer of one spouse's interest to another, there is no gain or loss and the transfer is treated essentially as a gift. The

---

[16] Reg. § 301.7701-3(a); see also *L. Hahn*, 22 TC 212, CCH Dec. 20,300; *L.L.Powell*, 26 TCM 161, CCH Dec. 28,348(M), T.C. Memo. 1967-32.

[17] See *E.B. Boyd Est.*, 28 TC 564, CCH Dec. 22,410, involving tenants in common, and *J. Conte*,

42 TCM 1296, CCH Dec. 38,315(M), T.C. Memo. 1981-571, involving joint tenants.

transferee spouse takes the same basis for the interest received as the basis in the hands of the transferor spouse. This same rule applies on transfers incident to a divorce as well as on transfers between still married spouses.[18]

¶ 221 Community Property

Rights in and to real property are fixed by state law, but the federal tax treatment of income flowing from those rights is determined by federal law.[19] If the highest court of a state has made a determination as to ownership of a property interest, that decision controls in the federal courts for federal tax purposes. In the absence of a decision by the state's highest court, the federal courts must apply what they find the state law to be, after giving consideration to the decisions of lower state courts.[20]

There are eight community property states—Arizona, California, Idaho, Louisiana, Nevada, New Mexico, Texas, and Washington. Also, Wisconsin has enacted legislation creating community property rights in spouses. If spouses in a community property state file a joint income tax return, the distinction between separate income and deductions and community income and deductions has little significance. The distinction becomes important when husband and wife file separate returns.

It is the date of acquisition that controls the status of property in community property states. In all community property states, real property acquired before marriage is treated as the separate property of the spouse who owned the property prior to the marriage. Income from separate property, however, may be community income, taxable one-half to each spouse in some states.

The states that follow the "Texas" rule and treat income from separate property as community income are Idaho, Louisiana, and Texas. The other five community property states (Arizona, California, Nevada, New Mexico, and Washington) follow the "California" rule and treat income from separate property as separate income.

Deductions relating to the separate property of one spouse are equally divided between the husband and wife if the income from the property is community income taxable one-half to each spouse. This rule applies on a sale of the property as well, even though the entire gain is taxable to the spouse who owned the separate property.[21]

---

[18] Code Sec. 1041.

[19] *Poe v. H.G. Seaborn*, 2 USTC ¶ 611, S.Ct., 282 U.S. 101, 51 S.Ct. 58.

[20] *H.J. Bosch Est.*, 67-2 USTC ¶ 12,472, S.Ct., 387 U.S. 456.

[21] *L. Sanders*, CA-10, 55-2 USTC ¶ 9636, 225 F.2d 629, cert. denied 350 U.S. 967, 76 S.Ct. 435.

¶ 225 PARTNERSHIPS

When an individual lacks the ability or resources (including seller or third-party financing) to acquire and operate real property, a partnership is often the answer. A partnership allows two or more persons to acquire and operate property without all of the formalities associated with corporate formation and operation.

¶ 227 Legal Characteristics

A partnership is an association of two or more persons who join together as co-owners to carry on a business for profit. The partnership is a voluntary association and is formed by the agreement or contract among the partners who contribute capital or services to the partnership. It is their agreement or contract that controls the relationship among the partners, and the partners are free to mutually agree to alter or vary their agreement as they see fit, provided their agreement is not contrary to state law.

The partnership form of business organization is recognized by state laws on the subject. In most states, the laws are similar because of the adoption of the Uniform Partnership Act, which governs all partnerships, and the Uniform Limited Partnership Act (or Revised Uniform Limited Partnership Act), which provides additional legal guidelines for limited partnerships.

¶ 227.1 *General Partnerships*

The most important of the legal characteristics of a general partnership are those relating to the potential liability imposed on the partners and the ability of any one general partner to bind the others by his or her actions. The partnership is bound by the acts of any partner who is tending to partnership business. Outsiders to the partnership may rightfully assume that any one partner is acting for all when the partner conducts any partnership business.

This agency relationship among the partners means that any one partner can obligate all partners, and all partners are jointly and severally liable to third parties for the business acts of any partner. Also, partners are jointly and severally liable to third parties or outsiders for the acts of the employees and agents of the partnership. The joint and several liability imposed on general partners means that any one partner can be held responsible for the full amount of any third party claim against the partnership. While a partner who pays off a claim may have a right against other partners to seek contribution, the outsider is free to go after any one of the partners.

¶ 227.1

In addition to the agency relationship among the partners and the partners' potential for liability, other common characteristics that are associated with a general partnership include:

1. Management rights are vested in all general partners and all share equally in the right to conduct the business of the partnership.
2. Day-to-day operations of the partnership are controlled by a simple majority vote of the partners.
3. The partners are considered fiduciaries in their relationship with each other and are bound to look out for the interests of the partnership. A partner, either individually or through some other entity, cannot compete against the business of the partnership or interfere with the business of the partnership.
4. Partners must conserve and protect partnership capital. A partner may not transfer real estate, unless selling real estate is the partnership business and the transfer would be in the ordinary course of that business.

Keep in mind, of course, that the partnership is a creature of the agreement among the partners. Therefore, the partners may alter or change some of the usual characteristics of the general partnership if it suits their needs and is not contrary to state partnership law. For example, through agreement, partners may decide to give a larger voice in management to a partner who has contributed greater amounts of capital to the partnership, rather than allowing a simple majority vote of the partners to control.

¶ 227.2 *Limited Partnerships*

A limited partnership is essentially a general partnership in which one or more partners have their liability limited in much the same fashion as shareholders in a corporation. These special partners with limited liability are limited partners. To obtain the limited liability protection for its limited partners, a limited partnership must file and record a certificate of limited partnership with the state authorities. The filing puts all on notice of the limited nature of some partners' liability.

In every limited partnership, there must be at least one general partner who is responsible for the management of the partnership and who is personally liable for the obligations of the partnership. The rights and liabilities of the general partner of a limited partnership are essentially the same as those of a partner in a general partnership. Limited partners, however, are exempt from liability for partnership debts, obligations, and losses in excess of their capital contributions, as long as they do not participate in the management of the partnership.

¶ 227.2

The limited liability feature of limited partnerships makes them attractive as investment vehicles and popular vehicles for raising capital from outside investors. (Real estate limited partnerships, as securities and as vehicles for raising capital through public offerings or private placements, are given special consideration in Chapter 21.)

¶ 227.3   Joint Ventures

A joint venture is a partnership-like organization that is formed to carry out one project or transaction or a series of related transactions over a short period of time. It is this feature that primarily distinguishes a joint venture from a partnership, which is usually involved in the management and operation of an ongoing enterprise. Also, a joint venture, unlike a partnership, can be organized for social or recreational purposes and need not be organized for a profit-making activity.

In real estate, a joint venture may be formed for the subdivision and sale of a specific parcel of real estate. Also, a joint venture may be formed to construct a specific building, housing project, or industrial park. If the "partners" involved in the project are corporations, the corporations are more likely to form a joint venture than a partnership to carry out their joint goals.

For tax purposes, a joint venture, in most cases, will be treated as a partnership.

¶ 227.4   Syndicates

The term "syndicate" is a frequently used term in the real estate industry. When a real estate promoter uses the term, the promoter is most likely referring to the process of raising capital from investors, through either a public offering or private placement of participations or units.

In most cases, a syndicated real estate program will be organized as a partnership since this offers the most flexibility and freedom of operation for the promoter and tax advantages to the investors. There is no reason, however, why a real estate syndication may not refer to a venture organized as a corporation, or even some other arrangement, such as individual ownership of properties managed by the promoter or related party under an agency contract.

¶ 229   Taxation of Partnerships

Federal law, specifically the Internal Revenue Code as interpreted by the federal courts and the Internal Revenue Service, determines whether or not an entity is a partnership for tax purposes. The Internal Revenue Code definition of a partnership is very broad and includes "a syndicate, group, pool, joint venture, or other unincorporated organization, through or by means of which any business, financial operation, or

¶ 229

venture is carried on, and which is not, within the meaning of this title [the Internal Revenue Code], a trust or estate or a corporation." [22] For the most part, general partnerships and limited partnerships are treated alike for tax purposes. Also, joint ventures and similar arrangements are partnerships for tax purposes. (See the discussion of entity classification at ¶ 237.1.)

As a general rule, partnerships are not taxpayers, but rather serve as conduits through which business or investment results are passed to the partners. While a partnership does file a tax return, it pays no income taxes. Each individual partner must report his or her share of partnership results on the individual tax return and the final tax liability depends on the partner's other income and deductions as well as the share of partnership income and deductions. Note that partnership distributions are not required to trigger a tax liability on the part of the individual partners.

The following discussion is not meant to be a complete explanation of the partnership tax rules. Rather, the purpose is to merely highlight the critical areas that affect real estate that is owned and operated in partnership form.

¶ 229.1   Basis of Partnership Interest

Every partner must know the tax basis for his or her interest in the partnership. It is the basis of a partnership interest that is used to determine the:

1. Amount of gain or loss realized by a partner on the sale of the interest;
2. Tax consequences at the time a partnership or partnership's interest is liquidated;
3. Primary limit on the amount of losses from the partnership that a partner can take as a tax deduction;
4. Amount of the distributions from the partnership that the partner can receive without taxes in addition to those that arise on the pass-through of partnership income.

The ownership of a partnership interest is separate from ownership of property by the partnership. When a partnership acquires real estate, the partnership's basis is determined under the rules discussed at ¶ 103. If the partnership acquires real estate as a result of a capital contribution by a partner, however, the partnership's basis is the same as the basis of the property in the hands of the contributing partner at the time of the contribution.[23] Each partner's basis for the interest in

---

[22] Code Sec. 7701(a)(2).   [23] Code Sec. 723.

the partnership is determined according to how the partnership interest is acquired.[24]

The basis of a partnership interest acquired by a contribution of money or property to the partnership is the amount of money contributed plus the adjusted basis to the partner at the time of the contribution of any other property. If a partner realizes taxable income as a result of acquiring the interest in the partnership, that income is an addition to the partner's basis. If the partner contributes property, which is subject to a mortgage or liability, the partner's basis is reduced by the amount of the debt assumed by the other partners as a result of the contribution (the assumption of debt by a partnership is treated as a distribution of money to the partner whose debt is assumed and a contribution of money by the other partners, which in turn increases their bases).[25]

> *Example:* The New Partner acquires a 20 percent interest in a real estate partnership by contributing a parcel of real estate to the partnership. At the time of the contribution, the parcel had a fair market value of $100,000 and an adjusted basis to the New Partner of $40,000 and was subject to a mortgage in the amount of $20,000. The New Partner's basis for the 20 percent interest in the partnership is $24,000. This represents the New Partner's adjusted basis in the contributed property ($40,000) less the portion of the mortgage debt assumed by the other partners (80% × $20,000 = $16,000).

A partner who acquires an interest in a partnership other than by contributing money, property, or services to the partnership determines the basis under the rules applicable to the manner in which the interest is acquired (these are the basis rules discussed at ¶ 103). For instance, a partner who purchases an interest from another partner has a "cost basis" for the interest; an interest acquired by gift has the donor's basis, adjusted for gift taxes paid; an interest acquired from a decedent has a basis equal to its value on the date of the decedent's death; and so forth.[26]

The original tax basis of a partner's interest in a partnership must be adjusted for events that occur after the acquisition of the interest.[27] These adjustments are required to preserve the conduit nature of the partnership.

The original basis of a partner's interest is increased by the partner's share of taxable income and tax-exempt income of the partnership. The original basis is decreased by the partner's share of

---

[24] Code Sec. 705(a).
[25] Code Sec. 722 and Reg. § 1.722-1.
[26] Code Sec. 742 and Reg. § 1.742-1.
[27] Code Sec. 705.

¶ 229.1

partnership distributions, partnership losses, partnership expenditures that are not deductible in computing taxable income or loss and that are not capital expenditures, and the depletion deduction for oil and gas wells.

¶ 229.2 Contributions to Partnership

The general rule of Code Sec. 721 is that no gain or loss is recognized by the partners or the partnership on the contribution of money or property to the partnership in exchange for a partnership interest. When real estate or services are contributed to a partnership, however, there are a number of exceptions to the general rule that can cause problems or an unexpected tax liability. Problems also may arise for existing partners when a new partner is admitted to an existing partnership if the admission of the new partner results in a decrease of the existing partners' shares of partnership liabilities and ordinary income items.

Mortgaged Property

A partner's basis for the partnership includes the adjusted basis in contributed property at the time of its contribution to the partnership reduced by any liabilities assumed by the other partners as a result of the contribution. As noted above, the reduction in the contributing partner's share of liabilities is treated as a distribution of money to the partner by the partnership.[28] As the example above illustrates, there is no problem as long as the liabilities assumed do not exceed the adjusted basis of the property. If liabilities assumed by the other partners exceed the adjusted basis, however, the contributing partner realizes income to the extent that the liabilities assumed by the other partners exceed the contributing partner's adjusted basis in the contributed property.

> *Example:* The New Partner acquires a 20 percent interest in a real estate partnership by contributing a parcel of real estate to the partnership. At the time of the contribution, the parcel had a fair market value of $100,000 and an adjusted basis to the New Partner of $40,000 and was subject to a mortgage in the amount of $60,000. The New Partner's basis for the 20 percent interest in the partnership is zero. This represents the New Partner's adjusted basis in the contributed property ($40,000) less the portion of the mortgage debt assumed by the other partners (80% × $60,000 = $48,000). The New Partner's basis is zero because a partner's tax basis for a partnership interest is never reduced below zero.

---

[28] Code Sec. 752(b).

The portion of the mortgage assumed by the other partners ($48,000) is treated as a distribution of money to the New Partner. Of this amount, $40,000 was used to reduce the New Partner's basis to zero. The remaining $8,000, the excess of the mortgage assumed by the other partners over the New Partner's adjusted basis for the contributed property, is treated as a taxable gain to the New Partner.

Built-In Gain or Loss

At one time, a partner could contribute property to a partnership and shift a portion of the tax loss or gain that the partner would otherwise realize on the property to the other partners. Now, however, Code Sec. 704(c)(1) requires that gain and loss on property contributed to a partnership be shared among the partners in a way that takes into account any difference between the basis of the property to the partnership and its fair market value at the time of the contribution. This means that a contributing partner is taxed on any "built-in gain" on contributed property when that gain is realized by the partnership. Also, a "built-in tax loss" on contributed property cannot benefit partners other than the contributing partner.

Example: Two equal partners form a partnership. Partner A contributes real estate worth $100,000, but that has a basis of $50,000. Partner B contributes $100,000 cash. The basis to the partnership for the real estate is $50,000.

Under the usual partnership rules, if the partnership sold the real estate for its market value of $100,000, the partnership would have a $50,000 taxable gain that would be shared equally by A and B. A would have shifted $25,000 of taxable gain to B. Under Code Sec. 704(c)(1), however, A must report the entire $50,000 gain recognized by the partnership. If the partnership sells the real estate for more than $100,000, any gain in excess of the $50,000 "built-in gain" would be shared equally by the equal partners.

Also under Code Sec. 704(c)(1), gain or loss must be recognized by a partner who contributes property to a partnership if the partnership later distributes that property to the other partners within seven years (five years for property contributed to the partnership before June 9, 1997, or subject to a binding contract on June 8, 1997) of the contribution. No gain or loss is recognized, however, if the contributed property is redistributed to the contributing partner. The measure of the gain or loss recognized is the amount the contributing partner would have had to recognize had the property been sold by the partnership at its fair market value, that is, the difference between the partner's basis in the property and its fair market value at the time of the contribution (see

¶ 229.2

the example above). An exception applies under Code Sec. 704(c)(2) if the distribution is related to a distribution of like-kind property to the contributing partner (like-kind property is determined under the Code Sec. 1031 rules, as discussed at ¶ 1313). Appropriate basis adjustments are made to reflect any gain or loss recognized.

Disguised Sales

The "disguised sale" rule of Code Sec. 707(a)(2) is intended to prevent partners and partnerships from characterizing a sale or exchange of property as a contribution to the partnership followed by a distribution from the partnership in order to avoid or defer tax. Generally, if a partner transfers money or other property to a partnership and there is a related transfer of money or other property by the partnership to that partner or to another partner, then the transactions are outside the partnership rules and are treated as a sale between the partner and the partnership or the two partners, depending on the actual transfers involved.

Example: The New Partner contributes real estate worth $50,000 with a basis of $30,000 to a partnership in exchange for a 20 percent interest in the partnership. As part of the deal, the partnership distributes $30,000 cash to the New Partner. In this case, the related transactions may be viewed as a sale of the real estate by the New Partner to the partnership rather than as a tax-free contribution of property to the partnership followed by a tax-free distribution of cash (an amount not in excess of the New Partner's basis in the partnership) to the New Partner.

If the related distribution of cash were made to existing partners rather than to the New Partner, the transaction could be viewed as a sale of a partnership interest by the existing partners to the New Partner.

Admission of New Partners

The admission of a new partner to a partnership may also trigger a tax to existing partners if the new partner assumes a share of partnership liability and is credited with a portion of any ordinary income items of the partnership that have not yet been realized.[29] The reduction of the existing partners' share of partnership liability is treated as a cash distribution to them. To the extent that the existing partners' share of "unrealized receivables" is also reduced, the deemed cash distribution triggers an immediate tax. The problem may be avoided when unrealized receivables are present, if the new partner does not assume a share of existing partnership liabilities. If there are no

---

[29] Rev. Rul. 84-102, 1984-2 CB 119.

unrealized ordinary income items (receivables, depreciation recapture, substantially appreciated inventory, etc.), the problem usually does not arise, since the deemed cash distribution triggered by the new partner's assumption of liabilities merely serves to reduce the bases of the partnership interests of the existing partners.

Services

The contribution of services to a partnership in exchange for an interest in the partnership is outside the usual nonrecognition rule of Code Sec. 721. The partner contributing services realizes compensation income equal to the value of the partnership interest received for the services.[30] The value of the partnership interest received by the service partner generally is considered equal to the value of the services performed.[31]

¶ 229.3   Operation of Partnership

A partnership, although generally not a taxable entity, must still compute its taxable income in a fashion similar to the way in which an individual computes his taxable income. The tax consequences of the income or loss are then passed on to the partners who must take into account every separate item of income, loss, deduction, or credit that enters into the computation of taxable income. Each partner, in effect, treats his or her share of each partnership item as if the partner had received the share directly from the source of the item to the partnership.

Special Allocations

In some cases, a partnership agreement may give certain partners or classes of partners shares of certain items of income or loss that are greater or less than the shares they would receive under the general profit and loss sharing ratio of the partnership. This might occur as partners adjust their agreement to take into account their individual positions and strive to reach a bargain acceptable to all. In the heyday of tax shelters, special allocations of "tax losses" were common to attract investors.

The allocation of specific partnership items in a ratio that does not conform to the general profit and loss sharing ratio is called a special allocation. In order for a special allocation to be respected for tax purposes, the special allocation must have "substantial economic effect." [32] If a special allocation lacks substantial economic effect, the tax

---

[30] S. Diamond, CA-7, 74-1 USTC ¶ 9306, 492 F.2d 286.
[31] Hensel Phelps Construction Co., CA-10, 83-1 USTC ¶ 9270, 703 F.2d 485.
[32] Code Sec. 704(b).

law ignores the allocation called for by the partnership agreement and makes an allocation that conforms to the normal profit and loss sharing ratio.

Regulations issued by the IRS in an attempt to define "substantial economic effect" run on for page after page.[33] In the simplest of terms, a special allocation has substantial economic effect if the allocation affects the capital accounts of the partners as well as the tax consequences to the partners. Since a partner's capital account reflects the partner's adjusted investment in the partnership, adjustment of capital accounts because of a special allocation means that the special allocation must ultimately affect the partner's share of the economic income or loss of the partnership and thus have substantial economic effect apart from the tax consequences.

Organization and Syndication Costs

In computing the taxable income of a partnership, organization and syndication costs are not currently deductible.[34] Rather, the actual costs of organizing a partnership must be charged to a capital account and deducted over a period of at least 60 months. The costs of syndicating a partnership, however, are not deductible at all. Nondeductible syndication costs include all the expenses involved in selling partnership interests to investors and include:

1. Brokerage fees;
2. Registration fees;
3. Legal fees of the underwriter or placement agent and the issuer for securities advice and tax advice pertaining to the adequacy of tax disclosures in the prospectus or placement memorandum;
4. Accounting fees for the preparation of representations included in the offering materials; and
5. Printing costs of the prospectus, placement memorandum, and any other other material for promoting and selling partnership interests.

Allocations for Services

In order to avoid the restrictions on deductions for organization and syndication costs, some partnerships would allocate partnership income to a general partner who would pay these costs. Instead of paying these costs directly, or providing a reimbursement for these costs to the paying partner out of invested funds, the partnership agreement would allocate a share of partnership income to the paying

---

[33] Reg. § 1.704-1 and Temp. Reg. § 1.704-1T. [34] Code Sec. 709.

partner (a form of special allocation). The effect, as far as the other partners were concerned, was the equivalent of a deduction since their shares of partnership income would be reduced by the special allocation.

Code Sec. 707(a)(2) was a direct response to this type of tax trickery. The IRS now may treat allocations of partnership income made for property or services provided to the partnership as payments by the partnership for the property or services. This power goes beyond special allocations for organization and syndication costs and extends to all income allocations for property or services of any kind.

Example: In an attempt to avoid the requirement that requires capitalization of construction costs, a partnership agreement may provide a special allocation of partnership income to a partner who provides architectural services to a partnership in connection with the construction of a commercial office building by the partnership. Under Code Sec. 707(a)(2), the IRS may treat the income allocation as payment for the architectural services by the partnership. If this is done, the amount of specially allocated income will become part of the capitalized cost of the building which may be recovered only through depreciation deductions.

¶ 229.4 *Distributions*

The general rule is that gain is recognized by a partner from a partnership distribution only to the extent that there is a distribution of money in excess of the partner's basis in the partnership.[35] (But see the discussion of built-in gains and losses on contributions at ¶ 229.2.) A loss can be recognized only on a distribution that liquidates the partner's entire interest in the partnership.[36] If property is distributed, there is no immediate gain or loss, but the partner's basis for the property is the same as the partnership's basis before the distribution, but not more than the partner's basis in the partnership interest reduced by any cash distributed.[37]

It is the mechanism of the basis adjustment by which the conduit nature of the partnership is preserved. Income is taxed to partners as earned by the partnership and basis is increased. Money already taxed when earned is not subject to tax when distributed, but reduces basis. Taxing distributions only when they exceed a partner's adjusted basis for the partnership interest assures that a partner is not being taxed on the capital investment or on income for which the partner has already paid a tax.

---

[35] Code Sec. 731(a).
[36] Code Sec. 731(b).
[37] Code Sec. 732.

¶ 229.5 Guaranteed Payments

Sometimes, partners or a class of partners may be guaranteed a minimum return based on the amount of their capital contribution regardless of the income of the partnership. The same arrangement may be made for a partner who contributed services, that is, the "working partner" may be guaranteed a minimum amount for services regardless of the income of the partnership.

These guaranteed payments that are made without regard to partnership income are ordinary income to the recipient partners and, if otherwise deductible, are deductible in computing a partnership's taxable income.[38] In effect, guaranteed payments for the use of a partner's capital are in the nature of interest and are treated as such for tax purposes. Similarly, guaranteed payments in exchange for services are in the nature of wages or salary and are treated as such for federal income tax purposes.

229.7 Elective Large Partnership Rules

The Taxpayer Relief Act of 1997 introduced several special provisions to simplify tax reporting for electing large partnerships and their partners. Electing large partnerships are partnerships with 100 or more partners in the preceding tax year that elect to have Code Secs. 771 through 777 apply. Service partnerships, however, such as accounting and law firms, and partnerships that primarily buy or sell commodities or related financial products, are not eligible to make the election. Special rules in Code Sec. 776 apply to oil and gas partnerships.

The large partnership rules are effective for tax years beginning after 1997. The general effect of the election is to reduce the items the partnership must report separately to its partners. For instance, income or loss from all passive activities of the partnership are combined into a single activity; all tax preferences are combined into a single line item; and capital gains and losses are netted at the partnership level and short-term capital gains in excess of short-term capital losses are added to ordinary income rather than reported separately.

Electing large partnerships also are subject to simplified audit rules contained in Code Secs. 6240—6255. For instance, an electing large partnership generally may report audit adjustments as additional distributive share items in the year the adjustment is imposed, rather than the year to which the adjusted item relates. Alternatively, the partnership may elect to pay the tax at the entity level, on behalf of the partners, rather than flowing the adjustment through to the partners.

---

[38] Code Sec. 707(c).

Partners in an electing large partnership are not allowed to treat a partnership item differently on their returns than the way it was treated by the partnership. The partnership must provide Schedules K-1 to the partners no later than March 15 of the year after the close of the partnership tax year.

¶ 231 CORPORATIONS

Corporations may hold real estate as investment property or engage in the active conduct of a trade or business involving real estate. Corporations also may own real estate assets, such as plants, warehouses, farmlands, etc., which are necessary for their primary business operations. For income and tax purposes, corporations are separate entities apart from their shareholders. Corporations are also "legal persons," that is, as a matter of law, corporations also are separate entities apart from their shareholders.

¶ 233 Legal Characteristics

One reason why individuals may consider a corporation as the owning entity for real estate is that the corporation can insulate its shareholders from potential liabilities arising out of the ownership and operation of the real estate. As a general rule, a corporation's shareholders cannot be held personally liable for the debts, obligations, or any other liability that may attach to the corporation. Also, the assets within the corporation generally cannot be reached by creditors of the individual shareholders. A shareholder's interest in the corporation can be subject to claims against the shareholder, but those with such claims generally cannot touch the assets within the corporation.

The insulation from liability provided by a corporation, however, is not absolute. There are many instances in which the courts have "pierced the corporate veil" in order to reach shareholders. This is most likely to occur in the case of controlling shareholders in closely held corporations. It may also occur when shareholders themselves disregard the separate identity of the corporation and fail to follow corporate formalities.

Another reason individuals may consider the corporation as an owning entity for real estate is that the shares of stock representing ownership of the corporation are freely transferable and transfers of stock do not affect the corporate entity. All shareholders may sell their stock so that there is a complete change in corporate ownership, yet the "legal person" of the corporation remains undisturbed. Its business continues and its contracts and legal obligations are unaffected.

Corporate management is also removed from the shareholders, although shareholders do retain ultimate control over the corporation.

It is the shareholders who elect the board of directors who are charged with the management of the day-to-day affairs of the business. In small corporations, those with few shareholders, the shareholders and the board may be the same persons. Nevertheless, it is those who own or control a majority of the corporation's stock who control the corporation and the board. In many cases, a minority interest in a corporation gives the minority shareholder virtually no say in corporate affairs. (Compare this to the partnership, in which each general partner, regardless of the partner's interest, has an equal say in management.)

Of course, all of the factors discussed above are general in nature. They are not all true for all corporations at all times. For instance, preferred stock and other classes of voting and nonvoting stock can alter the rights and obligations of shareholders. Also, shareholder agreements, stock restrictions, and various forms of indemnity and hold-harmless agreements may be used to affect the relative power of shareholders within a given corporation and to limit a shareholder's otherwise unrestricted right to sell or transfer shares of stock in the corporation.

¶ 235 Taxation of Corporations

Corporations are taxpayers separate and apart from the shareholders who own the corporation. This is the critical tax difference between partnerships and corporations. There is, however, a type of corporation that has many of the tax features of partnership operation, the "S" corporation. The special tax features of S corporations are discussed at ¶ 241. The following discussion relates to regular or "C" corporations. (The letter designation is taken from the subchapter of the Internal Revenue Code that contains the tax rules relating to each of the two types of corporations.) The discussion is, by no means, an attempt to fully explain the tax rules applicable to corporations. The purpose is simply to call attention to those areas that may have special significance for a real estate corporation.

¶ 235.1 *Organization of Corporation*

In most cases, a real estate corporation may be formed without a current tax. Code Sec. 351 provides that the transfer of money or property to a corporation is tax free if two conditions are met. First, the transfer must be made solely in exchange for stock of the corporation. Second, the transferors as a group must be in control of the corporation after the transfer. Control, in this case, means 80 percent of the total combined voting power of all classes of stock entitled to vote and at least 80 percent of each class of nonvoting stock.[39] Note that this tax-

---

[39] Code Sec. 368(c).

free transfer of money or property to a corporation may take place at any time, not just when the corporation is organized. The control group (or sole shareholder if there is only one shareholder) may transfer money or property to the corporation at any time and take advantage of Code Sec. 351.

Any potential tax that is avoided because of a Code Sec. 351 transfer, however, is not forgiven. The basis rules preserve any gain for future tax. The basis of the property transferred to the corporation has the same basis for the corporation as it had in the hands of the shareholders before the transfer.[40] Similarly, basis of stock received by the shareholders is the same as the basis of the property they transferred.[41]

While most incorporations can be accomplished on a tax-free basis, there are some potential problem areas that may create a tax liability when individuals set up a real estate corporation.

Transfer of Services

In some cases, individuals may contribute their services to the corporation in exchange for stock. The performance of services for stock is outside of the nonrecognition provision of Code Sec. 351. What's more, if individuals performing services in exchange for stock receive more than 20 percent of the corporation's stock, the entire incorporation becomes taxable because the 80 percent control requirement will not have been met by the other shareholders. In such a case, individuals transferring appreciated property to the corporation will be taxed on the appreciation.[42] The basis of the property to the corporation, as well as the shareholders' basis for the stock received, will be adjusted to reflect the taxable nature of the transaction by increasing basis for the amount of gain recognized.

Mortgaged Property

When mortgaged property is transferred to a corporation in a transaction subject to Code Sec. 351, the mortgage generally has no effect on the tax-free nature of the transaction. This rule, however, is subject to two important exceptions that apply to any liability transferred to or assumed by the corporation in the transaction.

1. If there is no business purpose for the assumption of the debt by the corporation but rather the only purpose of effecting the transaction is tax avoidance, the entire amount of the debt assumed is treated as a payment of money to the transferor.[43]

---

[40] Code Sec. 362.
[41] Code Sec. 358.
[42] See, for example, *W.A. James*, 53 TC 63, CCH Dec. 29,799.
[43] Code Sec. 357(b).

This causes the transferor to recognize and be taxed on gain to the extent of this deemed payment of money. Basis is adjusted to reflect the amount of gain recognized.

2. If the liabilities transferred to the corporation exceed the basis of the property transferred, then gain is recognized by the transferor to the extent of the excess.[44] Again, basis on both sides of the transaction is adjusted to reflect the amount of gain recognized. There is an exception to exclude from this rule liabilities that are in the nature of trade accounts payable.

Taxable Incorporation

In some cases, incorporators may want the incorporation to be taxable in order to increase the basis of property in the hands of the corporation to its fair market value at the time of incorporation. This may allow for increased depreciation deductions by the corporation or lower amounts of income to be reported by the corporation at some later time. Of course, this is only desirable when it is thought that the future tax benefits to the corporation outweigh the current tax cost to the shareholders.

If a taxable incorporation is desired, however, it is sometimes very difficult to achieve. Code Sec. 351 nonrecognition is not elective. Anytime there is a transfer to a controlled corporation that meets the terms of the statute, Code Sec. 351 controls. Avoiding this section is usually a matter of having more than 20 percent of the corporation's stock issued to individuals who do not transfer money or property to the corporation.

Partnership Incorporation

Sometimes, it may be desirable to incorporate an existing partnership. When this is the case, the incorporation may be accomplished in any one of three ways:

1. The partnership transfers its assets to the new corporation in exchange for stock and then the partnership liquidates and distributes the stock to the partners;
2. The partnership liquidates and distributes assets to the partners who then transfer the assets to the corporation in exchange for stock; or
3. The partners transfer their partnership interest to the corporation in exchange for stock.

Regardless of how the incorporation of the partnership is accomplished, as long as the incorporation meets the requirements of Code Sec. 351, the incorporation is tax free. There are, however, other tax

---

[44] Code Sec. 357(c).

¶ 235.1

implications, depending on the method chosen. Rev. Rul. 84-111 [45] discusses these tax implications for the corporation and its shareholders.

Organization Costs

The costs associated with organizing a corporation are not currently deductible. Under Code Sec. 248, however, a corporation may elect to amortize these costs over a period of 60 months, beginning with the month in which the corporation begins business. Organizational costs subject to 60-month amortization include expenses such as:

1. Accounting services necessary to get the corporation up and running;
2. Fees and other costs paid to the state in order to incorporate;
3. Legal services for drafting the corporate charter and by-laws, the minutes of the organizational meeting, and the terms of the stock certificate; and
4. Temporary directors and organizational meetings of directors and shareholders.

"Syndication" costs, that is, commissions, professional fees and printing costs, and other expenses associated with issuing stock or securities, are not considered organization costs eligible for 60-month amortization.

¶ 235.2 *Operation of Corporation*

A C corporation reports income, takes deductions and credits, and pays taxes in much the same fashion as an individual taxpayer but under a different rate schedule. Corporate taxes are assessed at the following rates: 15 percent on the first $50,000 of taxable income; 25 percent on the next $25,000; and 34 percent on income in excess of $75,000.[46] Corporations that have taxable income in excess of $100,000 lose the benefit of all or some of the lower rate brackets. An additional five percent tax is imposed on corporate income in excess of $100,000 up to $335,000. This means that corporations with $335,000 or more of taxable income are paying a flat tax of 34 percent on their income.

A tax rate of 35 percent applies to corporations with taxable incomes over $10,000,000. Corporations with taxable incomes of over $15,000,000 pay an additional 3 percent on the excess, up to a maximum additional tax of $100,000.

After-tax corporate earnings paid out to shareholders can be subject to tax again, as dividends. This additional layer of taxation may increase the tax on income from an incorporated real estate venture.

---

[45] 1984-2 CB 88.   [46] Code Sec. 11.

For instance, if a corporation has $100,000 of pre-tax earnings, it pays a tax of $21,000. If the corporation distributes the after-tax balance of $79,000 as a dividend to a shareholder in the 31 percent individual tax bracket, the shareholder ends up with only $54,510 out of the original $100,000 in pre-tax earnings. The same pre-tax earnings realized directly by the individual or through a partnership would be reduced only by $31,000, to $69,000, by taxes.

The double tax detriment of corporate operation, however, may not really exist for many corporations. Most closely held corporations pay out little or none of their earnings as dividends. There are other ways to take money out of a corporation. Salary payments, if reasonable in amount, are deductible as an expense by the corporation, and so are not subject to the double tax. Corporate-provided fringe benefits also eliminate the double tax and, in some cases, may be tax free to the recipients as well.

If earnings are to be retained for operations or additional investment by the corporation, the double tax problem also may be minimal. Corporate tax rates on lower levels of income are lower than top individual tax rates and this means that high tax-bracket individuals may be able to use a corporation as a tax shelter. At $50,000 of taxable income, a corporation moves into the 25 percent tax bracket, but a single individual is already in the 27 percent bracket at $27,950 (inflation adjustment for 2002). The lower tax rates applied to the lower levels of income mean that more after-tax dollars may be left for reinvestment by the corporation than if an individual earned the income directly. Shareholders, however, must be aware of two penalty taxes that may be imposed when corporations retain income—the personal holding company tax and the accumulated earnings tax. These penalty taxes have no counterpart for individuals or partnerships.

Personal Holding Company Tax

A personal holding company is subject to a penalty tax at the highest rate applied to single filers (38.6 percent for 2002) on all *undistributed* personal holding company income. The tax [47] is intended to prevent taxpayers from using a corporation to hold passive investments so that the income from the investments is taxed at the lower corporate tax rates rather than the higher individual rates. A corporation is a personal holding company if five or fewer shareholders own more than 50 percent in value of the corporation's outstanding stock at any time during the last half of the taxable year (ownership is based on actual ownership and constructive ownership rules contained in the

---

[47] Code Secs. 541—547.

¶ 235.2

statute), and 60 percent of the corporation's adjusted ordinary gross income for the year is personal holding company income.

Personal holding company income includes such income items as dividends, interest, annuities, and royalties. In connection with real estate, rents are generally personal holding company income. However, an exception applies to what might be considered operating real estate corporations. Rents are not personal holding company income if rents are at least 50 percent of adjusted ordinary gross income and certain other requirements are met. Therefore, a corporation deriving most of its income from real estate generally will not be subject to this tax, but the tax may be a problem if the corporation holds other investment assets or temporarily invests funds in non-real estate assets.

Accumulated Earnings Tax

The accumulated earnings tax [48] is a penalty tax assessed on the earnings accumulated during the year that are in excess of the reasonable needs of the business. The tax is intended to prevent corporations from accumulating earnings rather than paying out dividends that would be taxed to the shareholders. Most corporations are allowed to accumulate $250,000 without question. Above this amount, accumulations must be justified by reasonable business needs. The tax is applied to excess accumulations for the year at the highest rate applied to single filers (38.6 percent for 2002).

As a practical matter, no corporation should be hit with this tax. The tax is usually imposed when shareholders ignore or are unaware of the tax and fail to make specific plans for the use of accumulated earnings.

¶ 235.3 Property Distributions and Liquidations

If a corporation sells appreciated property and distributes the proceeds to its shareholders, there is a double tax problem. This double tax is not avoided if the corporation distributes the appreciated property to shareholders or liquidates and distributes the property.

If a corporation distributes property to a shareholder and the fair market value of that property exceeds the adjusted basis of the property to the corporation, the corporation is taxed on the difference as if it had sold the property to the distributee at its fair market value.[49] If the property is subject to a liability, or the shareholder assumes a liability of the corporation in connection with the distribution, the amount of the liability is considered to be the minimum fair market value for the purpose of applying this rule. If the distribution represents a distribution of corporate earnings, that is, if it is considered a

---

[48] Code Secs. 531—537.

[49] Code Sec. 311(b).

dividend for tax purposes, the shareholder is also taxed on the value of the property received.

A similar rule taxes a corporation that distributes appreciated property in liquidation.[50] Shareholders treat distributions in complete liquidation of the corporation as payment in exchange for their stock.[51]

Note how these rules differ significantly from the partnership rules which do not impose an immediate tax on property distributions to partners but use the basis mechanism to preserve the potential gain on property for tax at a later time. It is these rules that may be the greatest detriment to the use of a C corporation as the owning entity for real estate.

¶ 237 LIMITED LIABILITY COMPANIES

Virtually all of the states have enacted laws providing for the formation of limited liability companies (LLCs). LLCs offer their members a flexible business entity that may be tailored and adopted to an endless number of business and investment situations. As a result of the advantages they offer, LLCs have become increasingly popular and often are the entity of choice when compared to partnerships. Many of the features that make LLCs attractive distinguish them from more traditional general and limited partnerships, although LLCs typically are structured to be classified as partnerships for federal income tax purposes.

Although local law varies as to the requirements for establishing an LLC, the common thread is that none of the members of an LLC are liable for the debts and obligations of the LLC beyond their contributions to the LLC, absent an express assumption of liability by a member if authorized under the applicable LLC statute. In addition, under local law LLCs frequently are managed by elected or designated "managers," who may be members of the LLC. When an LLC does not have managers, all members of the LLC ordinarily have rights, duties and obligations. If an LLC has elected or designated managers, who may or may not be members of the LLC, the managers ordinarily have many of the rights, duties and obligations that would otherwise be held by the members in an LLC without managers.

In short, LLCs offer the tax advantages of a partnership combined with the limited liability of a corporation.

¶ 237.1 Entity Classification

The ability to obtain the benefits of partnership taxation for LLCs received a big boost when the IRS adopted new regulations under Code

---

[50] Code Sec. 336.   [51] Code Sec. 331.

Sec. 7701 for classifying entities as partnerships or corporations (the "check-the-box" regulations). The previous regulations for classifying business organizations as associations taxable as corporations or as partnerships were based on the historical differences under local law between partnerships and corporations. The new regulations replaced those rules with a much simpler approach that generally is elective.

The first step in the classification process is to determine whether there is a separate entity for federal tax purposes.[52] The regulations explain that certain joint undertakings that are not entities under local law nonetheless may be separate entities for federal tax purposes, but not all entities formed under local law are recognized as separate entities for federal tax purposes. Whether an organization is treated as an entity for federal tax purposes is a matter of federal tax law, and does not affect the rights and obligations of its owners under local law. For instance, if a domestic limited liability company with a single individual owner is disregarded as an entity separate from its owner under Reg. § 301.7701-3, its individual owner is subject to federal income tax as if the company's business was operated as a sole proprietorship.

Business entities that are classified as corporations for federal tax purposes include corporations denominated as such under applicable law, as well as associations, joint-stock companies, insurance companies, organizations that conduct banking activities, organizations wholly owned by a State, and organizations that are taxable as corporations under a provision other than Code Sec. 7701(a)(3).[53]

Any business entity that is not required to be treated as a corporation for federal tax purposes (referred to in the regulation as an eligible entity) may choose its classification under the rules of Reg. § 301.7701-3. Those rules provide that an eligible entity with at least two members can be classified as either a partnership or an association, and that an eligible entity with a single member can be classified as an association or can be disregarded as an entity separate from its owner.

In order to provide most eligible entities with the classification they would choose without requiring them to file an election, the regulations provide default classification rules that aim to match taxpayers' expectations (and thus reduce the number of elections that will be needed). The regulations adopt a passthrough default for domestic entities, under which a newly formed eligible entity will be classified as a partnership if it has at least two members, or will be disregarded as an entity separate from its owner if it has a single owner.

---

[52] Reg. § 1.301.7701-1.   [53] Reg. § 1.301.7701-2.

¶ 237.1

An eligible entity may affirmatively elect its classification. The regulations require that the election be signed by each member of the entity or any officer, manager, or member of the entity who is authorized to make the election and who represents to having such authorization under penalties of perjury. An election will not be accepted unless it includes all of the required information, including the entity's taxpayer identifying number.

¶ 237.2 Partnership Conversion to LLC

The IRS has applied the same rule to the conversion of an interest in a domestic partnership into an interest in a domestic limited liability company[54] as it has to the conversion of a general partnership into a limited partnership.[55] The conversion does not cause a termination of the partnership under Code Sec. 708, and does not cause the tax year of the partnership to close as to all or any of the partners under Code Sec. 706. The IRS also says that because the conversion does not cause a partnership termination, the resulting LLC does not have to obtain a new taxpayer identification number. The tax consequences are the same regardless of whether the resulting LLC is formed in the same state as the converting partnership or in a different state.

¶ 241 S CORPORATIONS

The S corporation is a creature of the federal tax law. For all purposes other than tax purposes, the S corporation is treated just as any other corporation. The corporation has a separate legal existence and its shareholders have the usual corporate shield against liability. For tax purposes, however, the treatment of S corporations is similar to the treatment of partnerships—*similar but not identical.* For state income tax purposes, many states recognize S corporation status and provide treatment under state law that is similar to the federal treatment.

S corporation status must be elected by all the shareholders of the corporation. If elected, each shareholder reports his or her share of corporate income, loss, deductions and credits on his or her own tax return, whether or not the corporation actually distributes income.[56] This pass-through of tax items to the shareholders is similar to the pass-through of partnership items to partners.

¶ 243 Qualification as an S Corporation

For a corporation to become an S corporation, the shareholders of the corporation must unanimously consent to the election filed by the

---

[54] Rev. Rul. 95-37, 1995-17 IRB 10.
[55] Rev. Rul. 84-52, 1984-1 CB 157, and Rev. Rul. 86-101, 1986-2 CB 94.
[56] Code Sec. 1366.

corporation.[57] The election must be filed with the IRS in the year before or by the 15th day of the third month of the year for which the election is to be effective.[58] To be eligible to elect S corporation status, the corporation must meet the following requirements contained in Code Sec. 1361:

1. The corporation must have no more than 75 shareholders.
2. All shareholders must be individuals or certain qualifying trusts or estates.
3. No shareholder can be a nonresident alien.
4. The corporation must have only one class of stock.

The election terminates if the corporation fails to meet these requirements at any time.[59] Shareholders of an S corporation may terminate the election voluntarily by filing a notice of revocation with the IRS. This election to terminate requires the consent of shareholders who together own more than one-half of the shares of stock of the corporation.[60]

S corporation status also may be terminated if the corporation has passive investment income and accumulated earnings.[61] If more than 25 percent of the S corporation's gross receipts for three years are from passive investment income and there are accumulated earnings, the S corporation election terminates. Prior to the termination, the passive investment income is taxed at the corporate level.[62] Passive investment income for this rule includes rents. Also included are the gross receipts from the sale of capital assets, but, for assets other than stocks and securities, only gain is included in measuring gross receipts from passive investment income.

¶ 247 Income and Loss

The income of an S corporation is divided among shareholders according to their stock ownership.[63] This income is taxed to the shareholders whether or not there is an actual distribution to the shareholders. (Just as with a partnership, the basis mechanism assures that shareholders will pay but a single tax on S corporation income. A shareholder's basis is increased by the share of income passed through from the corporation. Distributions are tax free to the extent of a shareholder's basis and serve to reduce basis. Actual distributions are taxable only to the extent they exceed the shareholder's basis.)

---

[57] Code Sec. 1362(a).
[58] Code Sec. 1362(b).
[59] Code Sec. 1362(d)(2).
[60] Code Sec. 1362(d)(1).
[61] Code Sec. 1362(d)(3).
[62] Code Sec. 1375.
[63] Code Sec. 1366.

If a shareholder was not a shareholder for the entire year, the income is apportioned based on stock ownership and the number of days during the year the shareholder held the stock. Note that this income-splitting rule is absolute—there is no possibility of any "special allocations" of income or loss, as is the case of a partnership when the special allocations have substantial economic effect.

Example: An S corporation has three shareholders, A, B and C. A owns 25 percent, B owns 35 percent, and C owns 40 percent. Assuming these shareholders hold their stock for the entire tax year of the corporation and the corporation has $100,000 of income, A would report $25,000, B would report $35,000, and C would report $40,000.

Suppose, however, that C sold the stock to new shareholder D on May 1 of the current year and the corporation is a calendar year corporation. In this case, the $40,000 of income must be apportioned between C and D. C would report $13,150 ($40,000 × 120/365), and D would report $26,850 ($40,000 × 245/365).

¶ 247.1 *Built-In Gain*

There is an exception to the pass-through of income to an S corporation's shareholders. This exception taxes the "built-in gain" on corporate assets at the corporate level if the gain is recognized by the corporation within 10 years of the S election.[64] "Built-in gain" is essentially the amount by which the value of an asset exceeded its basis at the time the corporation became an S corporation. This tax applies only if the corporation was a regular C corporation before electing S status and only if the election was made after 1986. For corporations with a value of less than $5 million, the tax on built-in gain applies only if the S election was made after 1988 (partial relief is available for corporations worth between $5 million and $10 million if the S election was made before 1989). Any tax on built-in gains is passed on to S shareholders in pro rata fashion as a loss, as discussed below.

Under Code Sec. 1363(d), a corporation recognizes gain on a distribution of appreciated property to its shareholders. To the extent this appreciation represents built-in gain, the distribution of appreciated property by an S corporation to its shareholders may trigger the corporate level tax. Gain recognized by the corporation on a distribution of appreciated property to a shareholder, to the extent not taxed to the corporation, is passed through to the shareholders under the regular rule.

---

[64] Code Sec. 1374.

These rules can present a tax trap for unsuspecting S corporations that own appreciated real estate and for their shareholders. Individuals should become completely familiar with the S corporation provisions before choosing the S corporation as the owning entity for real estate or before converting a regular C corporation to S corporation status.

¶ 247.2 S Corporation Losses

Losses of an S corporation, just as income, are passed through to the shareholders. A loss is apportioned among the shareholders based on stock ownership and the number of days during the tax year they held the stock. For instance, in the example above on the apportionment of income, if the corporation had a $100,000 loss instead of income, the apportionment of the loss would be calculated in the same fashion.

In the case of a partnership, the basis of a partner's interest in the partnership limits the partner's deduction for losses sustained by the partnership. A similar rule applies to shareholders of an S corporation. The amount of losses and deductions taken into account by an S corporation shareholder cannot exceed the shareholder's adjusted basis for the stock plus the adjusted basis for any debt owed the shareholder by the corporation.[65]

While the rule is similar to the partnership rule, there is one critical difference that must be noted. Unlike a partner's basis for the partnership interest, a shareholder's basis in an S corporation does not include debt owed to outsiders. An S corporation shareholder's basis is equal to the cost of the stock, or adjusted basis of property contributed to the corporation to acquire the stock, plus the shareholder's share of corporate income, less distributions received from the corporation and losses previously passed through from the corporation and deducted by the shareholder. Also, an S corporation shareholder can deduct corporate losses to the extent of any debt owed to the shareholder by the corporation, but there is no increase in a shareholder's basis for corporate debt to outsiders, as there is for partners, when a partnership incurs a liability.

The basis rule for S corporations may have two significant effects on an S corporation used as the owning entity for real estate. First, of course, is that shareholders may not be able to fully utilize loss deductions if mortgaged real estate produces tax deductions in excess of income. Second, if real estate is refinanced, the distribution of the proceeds of the new financing to the shareholders may trigger a tax.

In a partnership, if real estate is refinanced, the mortgage debt increases the bases of the partners in the partnership. A distribution of

[65] Code Sec. 1366(d).

the refinancing proceeds is tax free to the partners to the extent of their bases in the partnership. In an S corporation, however, if real estate is refinanced, the mortgage debt to outsiders does not affect the bases of the shareholders in the S corporation. While the proceeds of the refinancing may be distributed tax free to the shareholders to the extent of their bases, their bases will not have been increased by the refinancing, and it is more likely that the distribution will be subject to tax.

¶ 251 OWNERSHIP IN TRUST

A trust is an entity that holds legal title to property for the benefit of another. The person who sets up or establishes a trust by transferring property to it is called the grantor of the trust. The property transferred by the grantor is managed by one or more trustees for the benefit of the beneficiaries of the trust. Legally, it is the trustees who hold the legal title to the trust property, while the beneficiaries hold what is termed beneficial title to the trust property.

As an owning entity for real estate operation or investment, the trust is likely to be used only when the beneficial owner is incapable of properly managing the property. It is a useful entity for making living or testamentary gifts to minors. Adults who do not have the time or experience to properly manage the trust property may also benefit from a trust, rather than being given the property outright. It is also a useful estate planning device when the grantor wants to preserve the property for more than one owner and more than one generation.

¶ 253 Tax Treatment of Trusts

The trust has something of a split personality when it comes to federal income tax treatment, and the following discussion of trust taxation is but a brief summary of the rules found in Code Secs. 641-683.

Generally, a trust is a taxable entity just like an individual taxpayer or corporation. The tax on trust income is higher than the tax on the same amount of income realized by an individual, however, because the income required to reach the higher tax brackets is less.

The higher tax on trusts would be a major discouragement to the use of trusts if it were not for the other aspect of trust taxation. A trust can be a conduit in a fashion similar to a partnership or an S corporation. A trust computes taxable income in much the same way an individual does, but a trust also may deduct amounts that are required to be distributed or that are distributed to trust beneficiaries under the terms of the trust. This deduction is limited to trust income. The beneficiaries include in their income and pay taxes on amounts deducted by the trust.

¶ 255 Depreciation

While the calculation of taxable income for a trust is similar to that made by an individual, there is a difference other than the distribution deduction that may be important for trusts owning real estate. The deduction for depreciation (and depletion as well) is allocated between the trust and its beneficiaries according to the terms of the trust or, if the trust is silent, according to the income of each. In other words, the trust instrument may spell out how depreciation is to be divided between the trust and its beneficiaries, but if no division is specified, then the division is made based on income. For instance, if the trust is silent on the apportionment of depreciation and 60 percent of trust income is distributed to beneficiaries, then 60 percent of any depreciation deduction is taken by the beneficiaries and the remaining 40 percent by the trust. (The tax deduction for depreciation is discussed at ¶ 903.)

¶ 257 Grantor Trusts

An individual who sets up a trust to achieve tax savings may be disappointed if that individual retains too much control over the trust property or if the income from the trust can be used for his or her benefit. Under the grantor trust rules, the grantor rather than the trust or beneficiary is taxed on trust income when the grantor attaches too many strings to the transfer of the property to the trust. Generally, a grantor is taxed on trust income in the following situations:

1. It is reasonable to expect that the grantor will get the trust property back (there is an exception for reversion in the case of the death of a minor income beneficiary who is a lineal descendent of the grantor).

2. The grantor can direct who will enjoy the trust property or the income of the trust after the trust is set up (this is subject to several exceptions for certain very limited powers).

3. The grantor can buy or sell trust property for less than adequate consideration.

4. The grantor can borrow from the trust without adequate interest or security.

5. The grantor can revoke the trust and obtain the trust property.

6. The income of the trust can be used for the benefit of the grantor or the spouse of the grantor.

¶ 257

¶ 261 CHOICE OF THE OWNING ENTITY

Making the choice of the owning entity for real estate requires a careful evaluation of the principal's personal and financial situation, as well as the nature and type of real estate involved. In many cases, there may be little choice involved, or no real practical choice. When only one principal is involved in the acquisition and ownership of the property, the choice is between individual ownership and corporate ownership. Corporate ownership, however, entails additional expense and added complexity. The extra cost and trouble may not be justified by the type or value of the real estate to be acquired. For instance, there usually is no reason to set up a corporation to own a personal residence. When a corporation is not justified by the facts, then there is no practical alternative to individual ownership.

The choice of the owning entity usually becomes more of a consideration when there is more than one principal involved in the acquisition and ownership of the property. Ownership as tenants in common may be acceptable for merely holding real estate, but if development or operation is contemplated, the principals usually will desire the more formal arrangement of a partnership or corporation. If a corporation is the choice, the question remains as to whether the corporation should elect to be treated as an S corporation.

The following paragraphs make some general observations as to factors that might be considered in choosing the owning entity for real estate by comparing and contrasting the corporation with the partnership and then the S corporation with the partnership. Following this discussion is a chart that compares, in summary form, many of the features of partnerships, C corporations, and S corporations (see ¶ 267).

¶ 263 Corporation or Partnership

The corporation boasts two possible advantages over a partnership that may make the corporation seem a likely choice as the owning entity for real estate. First, there is the liability protection afforded principals by the corporate veil. General partners are not protected by the partnership from liability arising out of the ownership or operation of real estate by the partnership. Second, shares of stock in a corporation are freely transferable, and transfers of stock do not affect the corporate entity. Partnership interests, on the other hand, generally are not readily transferable, and transfers of partnership interests may result in the termination of the partnership.

Unfortunately, these two possible advantages of corporate ownership over the use of a partnership may be more illusory than real. In a closely held corporation, true limited liability may be nonexistent from a practical standpoint. Banks and commercial lenders may require the personal guarantees of shareholders before lending to the corporation. Courts may "pierce the corporate veil" to provide relief to a party injured by the corporation. This is especially true if the corporation is undercapitalized or underinsured by the principals.

On the other hand, liability protection may be available in a partnership that equals or exceeds that available through a corporation. A limited partnership may protect limited partners from unlimited liability. (Although limited partnerships are discussed in greater detail in connection with securitized real estate in Part VI, limited partnerships may be set up by a small group of investors.) If the general partner in a limited partnership is a corporation, then the liability protection is essentially the same as with a corporation. Even in a general partnership, liability protection can be built in with insurance, nonrecourse financing and exculpatory provisions in mortgages.

The unlimited life and free transferability of stock in a closely held corporation also may be more theoretical than real. Shareholders often restrict stock transfers by shareholder agreement or restrictions incorporated in the stock. This is especially likely in an S corporation in order to prevent the transfer of stock to an ineligible shareholder. Partnership agreements may be drawn to allow continuation of the partnership following the death of a partner or other transfer of a partnership interest that would otherwise terminate the partnership.

What this all boils down to is that the choice between a corporation and a partnership may not really turn on the legal characteristics of the two entities. The extra expense of setting up and maintaining a corporation may be deciding in some cases. When expense is not a major factor, then the choice usually hinges on the tax treatment of the two entities.

Generally, organizing either a partnership or a corporation may be accomplished at no tax cost, so the initial tax burden will not be a deciding factor. Rather, it is in operation and liquidation that major tax differences occur which frequently tip the scale in favor of the partnership as the owning entity for real estate. Bear in mind, of course, that this is a general proposition that applies to "investment-type" real estate, that is, real estate that is owned to produce rents or held for appreciation rather than real estate that is owned to support a manufacturing or raw materials industry. In the latter case, it is the nature of the business that controls the choice of the form of business rather than the simple fact that the business owns real estate.

In any event, the separate existence of the corporation and its treatment as a separate taxpayer generally means that owning real

¶ 263

estate through a corporation increases the tax costs and eliminates the tax benefits to the principals involved. If the real estate is producing taxable income, the income may be locked in the corporation and removed only at the cost of a double tax. This would not be the case, however, if the principals were employed by the corporation and could justify salary and fringe benefits to themselves that would eliminate the corporation's taxable income. But this is not always possible, especially when the income of the corporation is derived from passive sources such as rents.

A corporation is also subject to the accumulated earnings and personal holding company penalty taxes which simply may exacerbate the double tax problem, especially for a real estate corporation. Partnerships have no similar tax problems.

Should real estate produce tax losses, which is often the case when the real estate is highly leveraged, those losses would be locked in the corporation if it were chosen as the owning entity. The losses could only be used to offset corporate income and would provide no tax benefit to the principals. This may be less of a factor now that the use of passive losses by individuals to offset various other classes of income has been severely limited, but it is nevertheless a factor to consider.

Finally, the potential for tax on the transfer or distribution of property (whether or not in liquidation of the entity) is now a major factor tilting the scales in favor of partnerships for real estate ventures. Generally, a partnership may distribute appreciated property to its partners without an immediate tax to either the partnership or its partners. Any potential tax is preserved through the basis mechanism until such time as the partner receiving the property disposes of the property in a taxable sale or exchange. Should the partner hold the property until death, the appreciation escapes tax entirely. Even if a partnership sells appreciated property and distributes the proceeds, there is but a single tax at the partner level on the gain.

Distributions of appreciated property by a corporation, on the other hand, generally produce immediate tax consequences to both the corporation and its shareholders. The corporation is subject to tax as if it had sold the property and the shareholder is taxed on the value of the property to the extent it is considered a dividend for tax purposes. Even a liquidating distribution, which is not subject to dividend treatment, produces similar results because the corporation is taxed on the appreciation of the property and the shareholders are taxed to the extent the distribution exceeds their bases in the corporation's stock. A sale and distribution of the proceeds produces the same result as a distribution of appreciated property directly to the shareholders.

¶ 263

What the rules on distributions mean for the real estate entity is that it may be very costly to get real estate assets or their value out of a corporation and into the hands of shareholders if and when this becomes desirable. Use of a partnership, on the other hand, means a lower tax cost down the road when real estate assets are distributed to the principals or sold for their benefit.

¶ 265   S Corporation or Partnership

The S corporation, with its special tax rules that are similar to a partnership, would seem to be a logical alternative to the partnership as the owning entity for real estate. The S corporation may offer the nontax advantages of a corporation combined with the tax advantages of a partnership. In some situations, this may, in fact, be the case. However, the dissimilarities between S corporation and partnership taxation are such that any hasty conclusion must be avoided.

Looking to the advantages of corporate operation found in the S corporation as compared to a partnership, the same general observations made in the comparison of regular C corporations to partnerships apply. Liability protection similar to that afforded by an S corporation can be built into a partnership with insurance, nonrecourse financing and exculpatory provisions. S corporation shareholders usually restrict stock transfers to protect the S election while partnership agreements can be drawn to allow continuation of the partnership following the death of a partner or other transfer of a partnership interest.

While the tax treatment of S corporations and partnerships is similar, it is not identical. Major differences in the two schemes of taxation do exist and, in many cases, will tip the choice of the owning entity for real estate to the partnership.

Leveraged real estate may produce tax losses that might be used to shelter other income of the owners, subject to the passive loss restrictions (passive loss rules are considered in some detail in Chapter 11). When leveraged real estate is owned by an S corporation, however, the loss ceiling imposed on shareholders may mean that they can derive no benefit from the losses produced by the leveraged property. S corporation shareholders do not get a basis step up for borrowings by the corporation to finance property, unlike partners who do get a basis step up to reflect borrowings by the partnership. With basis serving as the limiting factor on loss deductions in both partnerships and S corporations, the partnership has a clear tax advantage over the S corporation as a vehicle for owning and operating leveraged real estate.

Another potential drawback to the S corporation is the requirements that there be no more than 75 shareholders and only one class of stock. Partnerships are not limited to a certain number of partners and, perhaps more importantly in limited partnerships, various classes of partnership interests can be created. Also, the allocation of income, loss, deductions, and tax credits to shareholders in an S corporation must be made strictly according to stock ownership. The special allocations possible in a partnership, thereby permitting flexibility, are not available to an S corporation.

Finally, the S corporation, just as a regular corporation, presents some tax complications when appreciated property is distributed to shareholders. Unlike a partnership in which property distributions to partners generally produce no immediate tax, a property distribution to shareholders requires recognition of the gain on the property as if the corporation had sold the property. While this may not result in a tax at the corporate level because of the pass-through of the gain, the shareholders must report and pay taxes on their allocable shares of the recognized gain. Of course, if the gain recognized by the corporation is a built-in gain, the corporation as well as the shareholders will be subject to tax.

In sum, the S corporation, in some situations, may be a viable alternative to the partnership as the "entity of choice" for real estate investment and operation. The tax differences between the S corporation and partnership, however, are sufficiently broad as to require a very careful weighing of the factors involved. The potential tax disadvantages of an S corporation, although not as great as a C corporation, nevertheless may be enough to tip the scales in favor of partnership operation.

¶ 267 Comparison Chart of Business Entities

The following chart provides a concise comparison of many of the attributes of partnerships, S corporations, and C corporations. An LLC, depending on the status its members elect for tax purposes, will have characteristics of a partnership or corporation.

COMPARISON OF THE ATTRIBUTES OF PARTNERSHIPS, S CORPORATIONS, AND C CORPORATIONS

Attribute	Partnership	S Corporation	C Corporation
Entity Status	No state filing or tax elections required (state filing required for limited partnership)	State filing for incorporation; status must be elected for tax purposes	State filing for incorporation; status must be elected for tax purposes
Number of Owners	No limitations	No more than 75 shareholders	No limitations
Eligible Owners	No limitations	Must be qualified shareholders, generally individuals and certain trusts and estates	No limitations
Classes of Ownership Interests	General and limited partners; different classes of limited partners	Only one class of stock; differences in voting rights permitted	Multiple classes of stock permitted, including common and preferred, voting and nonvoting, etc.
Transfer of Ownership Interests	No, subject to partnership agreement	Yes, subject to shareholder agreement or stock restrictions	Yes, subject to shareholder agreement or stock restrictions
Tax Year	Same as principal partners unless business purpose for a different year	Calendar year unless business purpose for a different year	May choose any permitted fiscal year or calendar year
Passive Investment Income Effect	None	May cause termination of status	None
Termination of Entity Status for Tax Purposes	Transfer of 50% or more of partnership interests within 12 months; cessation of operations	Election by stockholders owning at least 50% of stock; failure to meet S requirements; excess passive investment income	Cessation of operations

Attribute	Partnership	S Corporation	C Corporation
Basis of Interests or Stock	Money plus basis of contributed property and services, increased by share of partnership liabilities	Money plus basis of other property contributed; value of contributed services included in income	Money plus basis of other property contributed; value of contributed services included in income
Adjustments to Basis	Increased by partnership taxable income and increases in partnership liabilities; decreased by distributions, depletion, losses and decreases in partnership liabilities	Increased by corporate income; decreased by distributions and corporate losses; no adjustment for corporate liabilities	Increased only for additional capital contributions; decreased only by return of capital distributions
Limited Liability	No for general partners; Yes for limited partners	Yes	Yes
"Double Tax"	No	No, subject to some limited exceptions	Yes
Deduction of Entity Losses	Limited to adjusted basis of partnership interest	Limited to adjusted basis of stock and basis of debt owned to shareholder by corporation	No pass-through of entity losses to shareholders
Special Allocations	Permitted, provided substantial economic effect	No; allocation strictly on a per-share/per-day basis	No

¶ 267

Attribute	Partnership	S Corporation	C Corporation
Distributions of Property	Gain not recognized	Gain recognized to extent value of property exceeds basis of property to corporation; built-in gain subject to corporate level tax	Gain recognized by corporation to extent value of property exceeds basis of property to corporation; value taxed to shareholder as dividend to extent of corporation earnings and profits; if distribution is liquidating distribution, gain recognized by shareholder to extent value of property exceeds shareholder's basis in stock

¶ 267

Chapter 3

Financing Real Estate

¶ 300 OVERVIEW OF CHAPTER

Financing the acquisition of real estate often involves third parties who are willing to lend money at interest based on the security afforded by the real estate. This financing is in addition to the equity financing in the form of money, property or services contributed to a partnership or corporation by its principals or the "down payment" made by an individual purchaser of real estate.

In most cases, the security for the real estate loan takes the form of a mortgage under which the borrower retains title to the property but gives the lender the right to take the property (foreclose) if the borrower fails to live up to the loan agreement. In some cases, however, financing real estate may involve the actual transfer of title to the "lender," who purchases the property but leases the property back to the "borrower" in a sale-leaseback transaction. Other leasing arrangements also may serve as financing devices.

Although seller financing is touched upon in this chapter, particularly in regard to the original issue discount and deferred payment sale rules of the tax code, installment sales and seller-financed transactions are explored further in Chapter 14. Also, interest on mortgages on taxpayers' personal residences is a topic covered in Chapter 17, along with other deductions for homeowners.

¶ 301 MORTGAGE FINANCING

As discussed at ¶ 101, the original cost basis of property includes the amount of any mortgage given to secure payment of any portion of the purchase price of the property. Similarly, the amount realized on the sale of property includes the amount of any mortgage that the seller is relieved of on the sale. If a mortgage is placed on previously owned property or an existing mortgage is refinanced, basis is not affected, nor does the owner realize taxable income from the proceeds of the loan. This rule applies even if the new mortgage exceeds the owner's adjusted basis in the property. Refinancing a previously owned property, therefore, is frequently a tax-free source of cash, but there is, of course, the obligation to repay the debt.

While mortgage financing is a popular way to finance real estate, it does entail certain costs for both the borrower and the lender, and these costs have tax consequences. Also, when a mortgage is satisfied at other than face amount, there may be tax consequences. These tax ramifications of mortgage financing are discussed in the following paragraphs. Gifts of mortgaged property are considered at ¶ 1615, and the sale of mortgaged property is discussed at ¶ 1303.

¶ 303   Mortgage Costs

Both the borrower (mortgagor) and the lender (mortgagee) are likely to incur various costs in connection with a mortgage loan. These costs may include legal fees, finders' or placement fees, brokers' commissions, appraisal costs, and the costs of surveys and title investigation.

¶ 303.1   *Borrower's Costs*

Fees, commissions, and other expenses paid by the borrower to obtain a mortgage or other loan on the property are not part of the cost of the property. Rather, they are more like capital expenditures that have a life that extends over the term of the loan. If business or income-producing property is involved, these costs may be amortized over the life of the loan and deducted accordingly.[1] Commissions paid to secure renewal of a loan also are subject to amortization.[2]

(For the treatment of the costs of obtaining a loan on a personal residence or other property that is held for personal rather than business or investment purposes, including the treatment of points, see ¶ 1703 and 1705.)

The term of the loan as specified in the loan agreement generally governs the period over which the borrower amortizes the costs, even if prepayment in full is allowed at any time. Amortization deductions for loan costs are taken on a straight-line basis. For instance, if a purchaser incurred $5,000 in costs in connection with a loan for the acquisition of business property and the term of the loan were 20 years, the purchaser would deduct $250 each year for 20 years. This would be the case regardless of whether the purchaser used the cash or accrual method of accounting.[3]

There are no rulings or case law actually on point governing the treatment of mortgage acquisition costs if the purchaser actually makes a partial prepayment on a loan for which the purchaser is amortizing costs. Presumably, if the prepayment merely shortens the

---

[1] Rev. Rul. 70-360, 1970-2 CB 103; *Detroit Consolidated Theatres, Inc.*, CA-6, 43-1 USTC ¶ 9222, 133 F.2d 200.

[2] *S. Spitzer*, 23 BTA 776, CCH Dec. 7038.

[3] *J.S. Lovejoy*, 18 BTA 1179, CCH Dec. 5830.

term remaining on the loan, the purchaser may refigure the amortization deductions to spread any unamortized costs out over the shorter period remaining on the loan.

If prepayment of the unpaid balance of a loan is made in full at any time, any unamortized costs of obtaining the loan are deductible at that time.[4] The same rule applies whenever the property is sold or disposed of before the costs are fully amortized. A taxpayer deducts the balance of unamortized loan costs when the liability for the loan and the property securing the loan are transferred.[5]

In the case of a corporation, any unamortized mortgage or loan costs are deductible in full in the year the corporation distributes assets to its shareholders in liquidation of the corporation.[6]

In the case of an individual, the balance of unamortized loan costs may be deducted on the income tax return for the year of the individual's death. Although the expenses incurred to obtain a loan are in the nature of capital expenditures that normally must be amortized over the term of the loan, the individual's death terminates the use of the loan proceeds, and the IRS has ruled that it is appropriate to deduct the balance of the unamortized loan costs on the deceased individual's final return.[7]

¶ 303.2 Lender's Costs

Generally, a lender who regularly engages in the business of making loans is entitled to deduct most costs associated with the making of the loans as ordinary and necessary business expenses under Code Sec. 162. The costs falling into this ordinary and necessary category would include most overhead costs. The IRS has ruled, however, that finders' fees and buying commissions paid by banks, building and loan associations, other classes of banks and financial institutions to brokers, title companies, and others for their introduction of an acceptable applicant for a mortgage loan are part of the acquisition cost of the loan, which must be capitalized and amortized over the term of the mortgage loan.[8] Capitalization and amortization also seems to be the rule for the occasional lender, that is, the lender who is not regularly engaged in the business of lending money and who, therefore, has no expenses falling into the ordinary and necessary category.

---

[4] *S&L Building Corp.*, 19 BTA 788, CCH Dec. 6019, Acq. X-1 CB 60, rev'd CA-2, 1932 CCH ¶ 9422, 60 F.2d 719, rev'd S. Ct. 3 USTC ¶ 1064, 288 U.S. 406.

[5] See *S&L Building Corp.* above; see also *O.C. Wacker*, 40 TCM 1009, CCH Dec. 37,166(M), T.C. Memo. 1980-324.

[6] *Longview Hilton Hotel Co.*, 9 TC 180, CCH Dec. 15,962, Acq. 1947-2 CB 3; *Anover Realty Corp.*, 33 TC 671, CCH Dec. 24,006.

[7] Rev. Rul. 86-67, 1986-1 CB 238.

[8] Rev. Rul. 57-400, 1957-2 CB 520.

¶ 305 Buy Downs and Similar Arrangements

In order to move homes out of inventory in times of high interest rates, builders may make it easier for purchasers to meet monthly mortgage payments by buying down or otherwise subsidizing the mortgage payments. For instance, the builder may work out an arrangement with a financial institution under which the institution will charge a lower rate of interest to purchasers of the builder's homes in exchange for up-front payments by the builder. Such an arrangement reduces a purchaser's debt service and makes it easier for a purchaser to buy a home, thus increasing the builder's sales. These payments by the builder should be considered an ordinary and necessary expense in order to sell homes, and, therefore, should be deductible by the builder. Alternatively, the payments might be considered a reduction of the sales price, which would have the same practical effect as the deduction.

In a Letter Ruling,[9] the IRS did rule that a builder who purchased loans from a financial institution which made below market-rate loans to purchasers of the builder's homes was entitled to deduct the excess of the purchase price paid for the loans over the fair market value of the loans. In this case, the builder was regularly engaged in the business of building and selling homes, and the premium paid by the builder for the loans was an expense incurred to permit the builder to sell his products. This ruling supports the idea that costs incurred by a builder to subsidize customers' mortgage payments, whatever the actual arrangement, are deductible ordinary and necessary business expenses.

¶ 307 Payoff of Mortgage

Just as the receipt of the proceeds of a mortgage produces no tax consequences, the repayment of the amount borrowed also has no tax consequences. Sometimes, lenders charge a premium, a "prepayment penalty," for the privilege of retiring a mortgage debt before the end of the loan term. In other cases, the lender may discount the mortgage debt for early payment. In either case, tax consequences flow from the satisfaction of a mortgage debt at other than its face amount.

¶ 307.1 *Prepayment Penalties*

A mortgagor who pays a penalty to the mortgagee for the privilege of prepaying a mortgage debt treats the prepayment penalty as additional interest.[10] When Rev. Rul. 57-198 was issued, of course, interest was deductible regardless of the nature of the underlying debt. Today, the interest deduction is subject to various limits based on the nature of the debt, although interest on property used in a trade or business is

---

[9] IRS Letter Ruling 8229120, April 23, 1982.   [10] Rev. Rul. 57-198, 1957-1 CB 94.

deductible in full. Presumably, a prepayment penalty treated as interest is subject to the same limitations.

In *12701 Shaker Blvd. Co.*,[11] a taxpayer attempted to amortize, as a mortgage cost, a prepayment penalty paid to one lender over the life of a new mortgage obtained from a different lender. Since the penalty was paid to extinguish an existing debt in a transaction that was independent of the new financing and was not part of the cost of the new financing, it had to be deducted in the year in which it was paid.

On the other hand, the purchaser of an apartment building could not deduct currently a subordination fee paid to refinance existing loans on the property purchased. The fee in this case was distinguished from the prepayment penalty in *12701 Shaker Blvd.* because the fee was not paid to extinguish an already existing debt, but was paid to obtain refinancing of the existing first and second mortgages.[12]

The mortgagee who receives a prepayment penalty treats the penalty as additional interest income. The prepayment penalty is an additional charge which the borrower pays for the privilege of using the mortgage money for a shorter period than originally agreed.[13] This is the rule regardless of whether the prepayment penalty is provided for in the loan agreement or is separately negotiated.[14]

¶ 307.2 Payment Discounts

The reduction of a purchase-money mortgage for a solvent debtor is treated as a reduction or adjustment in the purchase price, rather than as the discharge of a debt.[15] Accordingly, the debtor realizes no income, and the debtor's basis for the property is reduced to reflect the reduced purchase price. For the seller-lender, the debt reduction also is an adjustment to the sale price. This rule applies only to adjustments to purchase-money debts between original purchasers and sellers. It does not apply to purchase-money debts held or transferred to third parties or to mortgages held by other than the seller of the property, nor does it apply if the purchaser of the property has transferred the property to someone else.

Congress enacted the rule of Code Sec. 108(e)(5) to resolve the problem of whether an adjustment to a purchase-money obligation was an adjustment to the purchase price or income from the discharge of indebtedness. Congress has also enacted special statutory rules governing insolvent and bankrupt debtors and the discharge of qualified

---

[11] 36 TC 255, CCH Dec. 24,825, aff'd CA-6, 63-1 USTC ¶ 9194, 312 F.2d 749.
[12] IRS Letter Ruling 8614002, September 30, 1985.
[13] *General American Life Insurance Co.*, 25 TC 1265, CCH Dec. 21,631, Acq. 1956-2 CB 5.
[14] *S.R. Lewis*, 65 TC 625, CCH Dec. 33,563.
[15] Code Sec. 108(e)(5).

real property business indebtedness, and these are considered beginning at ¶ 1201 in Chapter 12, in which issues relating to troubled financings are discussed. Unfortunately, the enactment of Code Sec. 108(e)(5) did not resolve whether a discount applied to a mortgage debt is income or an adjustment to purchase price in other situations. For this, we must rely on a hodgepodge of case law that attempts to distinguish between price reductions and income from the discharge of indebtedness.

Generally, a taxpayer realizes income on the nongratuitous discharge of indebtedness to the extent the debt is cancelled or forgiven.[16] In Rev. Rul. 82-202,[17] the IRS ruled that an individual taxpayer realizes discharge of indebtedness income under Code Sec. 61(a)(12) on the discounted prepayment to a lender of all or a portion of mortgage debt. The amount of the discount is includible in income whether the mortgage note is recourse or nonrecourse. This would seem to be the rule whenever a mortgage debt is satisfied (other than in a gift situation) at less than face value and the fair market value of the property is more than the mortgage debt.[18] In Rev. Rul. 91-31,[19] the IRS amplified Rev. Rul. 82-202 so that it applies whether the fair market value of the property is greater or less than the principal balance of the mortgage.

There is, however, a line of cases that holds that when a buyer purchases property subject to a mortgage, or executes a mortgage as security for the unpaid portion of the purchase price or assumes an existing mortgage, and later satisfies the mortgage for less than the face amount of the mortgage but for more than the fair market value of the property at the time the mortgage is satisfied, the buyer does not recognize income. Rather, in such a case, the reduction in the mortgage debt is treated as an adjustment to the cost basis of the property.[20]

In *Hirsch,* a taxpayer purchased real estate for $10,000 cash and a $19,000 mortgage, which was reduced to $15,000. When the mortgage matured, the property was worth only $8,000, and the mortgagee accepted $8,000 in discharge of the debt. This was held to be an adjustment of the purchase price, and the solvent mortgagor realized no income from the discharge of the mortgage at a discount. In *Fifth Ave.-14th Street Corp.,*[21] however, the court expressed the opinion that the rule applied in *Hirsch* and a series of cases that followed it would be "limited to a case of a purchase money obligation where the vendor-mortgagee, in negotiations directly relating to the purchase price, agrees to a reduction; it has not been applied where the reduction

---

[16] Code Sec. 61(a)(12).
[17] 1982-2 CB 35.
[18] See *J.A. Michaels,* 87 TC 1412, CCH Dec. 43,555; *W. DiLaura,* 53 TCM 1077, CCH Dec. 43,973(M), T.C. Memo. 1987-291; *J.H. Sutphin,* Cls. Ct., 88-1 USTC ¶ 9269, 14 Cls. Ct. 545.

[19] 1991-1 CB 19.

[20] See, for example, *K. Hirsch,* CA-7, 40-2 USTC ¶ 9791, 115 F.2d 656.

[21] CA-2, 45-1 USTC ¶ 9115, 147 F.2d 453.

¶ 307.2

results from an arm's-length transaction relating solely to the debt itself, or from a purchase of the taxpayer's obligations at less than par in the market."

¶ 311 AT-RISK RULES

At one time, an investor could purchase an asset and take deductions for "tax losses" generated by the investment up to the full amount of the cost or other basis, even if the basis included borrowed amounts that the investor might never have to repay. With this as the rule, tax-shelter investments that were marketed primarily for their possible tax benefits proliferated. The main feature of many of these investments was the use of nonrecourse financing to provide investors with a high basis that could support large deductions, deductions that would exceed many times over any amount the investor might actually lose on the investment. (In a nonrecourse loan, the lender can look only to the asset financed by the loan for repayment, and the borrower is not personally liable for repayment of the borrowed amounts.)

Congress responded to the abuses in the use of nonrecourse financing by enacting "at-risk" rules in the Tax Reform Act of 1976. These original at-risk rules were limited in their application to four specific activities. A separate at-risk rule was enacted for partnerships, but real estate was not covered. Later, the rules were expanded to cover most activities, and the special partnership rule was dropped from the tax code; but again, real estate was exempted. In the Tax Reform Act of 1986, Congress finally extended the at-risk rules to real estate investments beginning in 1987, but limited the impact of the change by allowing nonrecourse financing from certain sources ("qualified nonrecourse financing") to be counted as amounts at risk.

Under the at-risk rules,[22] deductions from covered activities or investments are limited to the sum of the following amounts:

1. Money actually invested;
2. The adjusted basis of other property contributed to the activity;
3. Amounts borrowed for the activity for which the taxpayer is personally liable for repayment;
4. Amounts borrowed for the activity for which the taxpayer has pledged security property, other than property used in the activity, to the extent of the fair market value of the taxpayer's interest in the pledged property (but not if the pledged property has been financed with nonrecourse debt); and
5. Qualified nonrecourse financing for real estate.

[22] Code Sec. 465.

Note that tax basis generally is not affected by the at-risk rules other than for the purpose of determining any available investment credit. Tax basis is still determined under the rules discussed in Chapter 1, but losses (deductions) from an activity cannot exceed the amount considered at risk in the activity. For instance, depreciation (see Chapter 9) is still calculated on tax basis, which may include nonrecourse debt, but the owner of the property cannot deduct losses generated by the depreciation deductions in excess of the amount at risk.

¶ 313   Taxpayers and Activities Subject to the Rules

Taxpayers subject to the at-risk rules are:

1. Individuals;

2. Shareholders in S corporations; and

3. Corporations in which one-half of the stock (measured by value) is owned by five or fewer persons.[23]

There is a special exception for regular C corporations (but not S corporations) that are actively engaged in a trade or business other than a business involving master sound recordings, motion pictures, video tapes, or assets associated with literary, artistic, musical, or similar properties. This exception to the at-risk rules for regular corporations actively engaged in a trade or business, however, does not apply to personal holding companies and certain personal service corporations.[24] Also, regular corporations involved in equipment leasing are subject to the at-risk rules unless 50 percent or more of the corporation's gross receipts are from leasing or selling equipment.[25]

The at-risk rules generally apply to all activities including, since 1987, real estate. Each activity is treated separately under the rules, and a taxpayer cannot combine income from one activity and losses from another activity. There are, however, exceptions that permit the aggregation of income and losses from otherwise separate activities. Activities in connection with a trade or business are combined and treated together for purposes of applying the at-risk rules in the following situations:

1. If the person claiming the loss actively participates in the management of the business.[26]

---

[23] Code Sec. 465(a)(1).
[24] Code Sec. 465(c)(7).
[25] Code Sec. 465(c)(4).
[26] Code Sec. 465(c)(3)(B)(i).

2. If in a partnership or S corporation 65 percent or more of any losses go to partners or shareholders who actively participate in management.[27]

3. If a partnership or S corporation is engaged in equipment leasing, all leasing activities are treated together as a single activity.[28]

Generally, the aggregation rules in 1 and 3, above, apply to the activity of holding real property. Under these rules, if a taxpayer actively participates in the management of several partnerships, each engaged in a real estate business, the real estate activities of the various partnerships may be aggregated and treated as one activity as to that partner for purposes of the at-risk rules. Also, in the case of an affiliated group of corporations which is engaged principally in the real estate business, aggregation of the real estate activities is allowed if the component members of the group are actively engaged in the management of the real estate business (not including real estate financing other than between members of the affiliated group).[29]

¶ 315 Deduction Under the At-Risk Rules

In any tax year, there are two ways in which deductions generated by an activity subject to the at-risk rules may be allowed.[30] First, deductions from an activity may be taken to the extent of income received or accrued from the activity in that taxable year. Income, in this case, includes gain on a sale of assets whether that gain is long- or short-term. Simply put, there are no at-risk limitations on deductions from an activity to the extent that activity is also producing income. In other words, deductions generated by an activity may always be used to offset income generated by that activity.

In addition to deductions equal to income, deductions may be taken in excess of income from the activity to the extent the taxpayer is at risk.

Example: In 2002, the Taxpayer, who is on the calendar year, invested $50,000 in an activity subject to the at-risk rules by putting up $10,000 cash and obtaining nonrecourse financing for the balance. The Taxpayer's cost basis is $50,000, but the Taxpayer is at risk for only $10,000. At the end of 2002, the Taxpayer has a loss of $15,000 from the activity as a result of deductions generated by the activity.

---

[27] Code Sec. 465(c)(3)(B)(ii).
[28] Code Sec. 465(c)(2)(B)(i).
[29] See the Senate Finance Committee Report on the Tax Reform Act of 1986, P.L. 99-514.
[30] Prop. Reg. § 1.465-2(a).

¶ 315

The $15,000 loss reduces the Taxpayer's basis so that at the end of 2002 the Taxpayer's adjusted basis is $35,000. Of the $15,000 loss, however, the Taxpayer may deduct only $10,000 for 2002, the amount at risk. This deduction reduces the Taxpayer's amount at risk in the activity to zero. The balance of the loss, $5,000, is disallowed, but it may be carried over to be used against future income or if the Taxpayer otherwise increases the amount at risk in the activity.[31]

Assume that at the beginning of 2003, the Taxpayer sells the activity for the amount of the nonrecourse debt, or $40,000. Since the Taxpayer's adjusted basis is $35,000, the sale produces a $5,000 gain. Since this gain is income from the activity, the disallowed loss from 2002 that is carried over to 2003 may be taken as a deduction for 2003 to the extent of this income. Accordingly, the Taxpayer reports the $5,000 as income for 2003, but the Taxpayer also can deduct the $5,000 loss that was previously disallowed.

For additional examples of permitted deductions under the at-risk rules, see Prop. Reg. § 1.465-11.

¶ 315.1 Order of Deductions

When deductions from an activity exceed the amount at risk, the deductions are applied to the at-risk amounts and taken in the following order:[32]

1. Capital losses
2. All deductions that enter into the computation of Code Sec. 1231 gains and losses
3. Deductions that are not tax preferences under Code Sec. 57, to the extent not deducted under 1 or 2
4. All items of tax preference to the extent not deducted under 1 or 2

Deductions that are disallowed under the at-risk rules retain their identity according to this classification in succeeding years.

Example: The Taxpayer, who is on the calendar year, is engaged in an activity subject to the at-risk rules. At the end of 2002, the Taxpayer has $1,000 at risk in the activity. During 2003, the activity generates $3,000 of income and $7,500 in deductions. None of the deductions are capital losses or items subject to Code Sec. 1231, but $5,000 of the deductions are tax preferences. Assuming nothing else occurred in 2003 to affect the Taxpayer's amount

---

[31] Prop. Reg. § 1.465-2(b).

[32] Prop. Reg. § 1.465-38.

at risk, the Taxpayer will be allowed $4,000 of deductions, and $3,500 will be disallowed by the at-risk rules. The $4,000 of allowed deductions will consist of the entire $2,500 of deductions that are not tax preferences and $1,500 of the $5,000 of tax preferences. The disallowed deductions in the amount of $3,500 will be carried over and will retain their classification as tax preferences for purposes of applying them against future income from the activity or increases in the Taxpayer's amount at risk in the activity.

¶ 315.2 Recapture of Prior Deductions

Prior loss deductions that were allowed against amounts at risk in an activity must be recaptured and reported as income if an amount formerly at risk in the activity is converted to a nonrecourse liability or otherwise is no longer at risk.[33]

Example: The Taxpayer invested $100,000 in an activity in the form of $10,000 cash and $90,000 obtained through a recourse loan. The Taxpayer's original amount at risk in this activity, therefore, was $100,000. After taking $50,000 in loss deductions generated by this activity, the $90,000 recourse loan is converted to a nonrecourse loan. The Taxpayer now must report $40,000 of income, which represents a recapture of prior loss deductions to the extent the Taxpayer is no longer at risk.

¶ 317 Determining Amount at Risk

Amounts at risk in an activity include the amount of money invested, the adjusted basis of any property contributed to the activity, and borrowed amounts for which the borrower is personally liable for repayment or has pledged property, other than property in the activity, to secure payment. Amounts at risk in the case of a real estate activity also include qualified nonrecourse financing, which is separately discussed below. Amounts at risk do not include any amount protected against loss by nonrecourse financing (other than qualified nonrecourse financing for real estate), guarantees, stop-loss arrangements, or any other similar arrangement.[34]

The amount at risk in an activity for subsequent years is reduced by any allowable loss for the current year.[35]

---

[33] Code Sec. 465(e).

[34] Code Sec. 465(b)(4). See also Rev. Rul. 85-113, 1985-1 CB 184 (purported recourse note ruled nonrecourse because borrower could assign percentage of mine production in satisfaction of debt), and Rev. Rul. 80-72, 1980-1 CB 109 (option amounted to "other similar arrangement" to nonrecourse financing).

[35] Code Sec. 465(b)(5).

¶ 317.1 Borrowed Amounts

Borrowed money is not included in the amount at risk if the money is borrowed from a person who has an interest in the activity other than as a creditor or who is related to a person who has an interest in the activity other than as a creditor.[36] Related persons include brothers and sisters, spouses, ancestors, and lineal descendants; shareholders and 10 percent-owned corporations; partners and 10 percent-owned partnerships; beneficiaries and fiduciaries of a trust; and fiduciaries and grantors of a trust.

A special provision in Code Sec. 465(b)(2) prevents the use of circular arrangements to avoid the at-risk rules. For instance, if a taxpayer borrows money secured by livestock to buy real estate and borrows money secured by the real estate to pay for the livestock, none of the borrowed amounts would be considered at risk in either the livestock activity or the real estate activity.

Discounted Loans

In a case involving a recourse note that was not due for 10 years and for which the taxpayers were not liable for the stated interest on the note, the IRS asserted that the amount at risk should be discounted to reflect the time-value of money and that there was no personal liability for the interest. The Tax Court, however, ruled that the note did not have to be discounted to its value at the time of execution for purposes of determining the borrowed amount under the at-risk rules. The Court held that the tax code does not expressly or implicitly authorize a present value calculation in determining the borrowed amount.[37]

Guaranteed Loans

If a taxpayer guarantees repayment of an amount borrowed by another person (the primary obligor) for use in an activity, the guarantee does not increase the taxpayer's amount at risk.[38] If the taxpayer repays to the creditor the amount borrowed by the primary obligor, the taxpayer's amount at risk is increased when the taxpayer has no remaining legal rights against the primary obligor.

In *L.A. Bjerke*,[39] a limited partner was not entitled to deduct partnership losses based on debts that the partner guaranteed. The partnership debts that the partner guaranteed were not at risk because the partner could recover from the partnership as the primary obligor on the debt any guaranteed amounts that the partner might be compelled to pay.[40]

---

[36] Code Sec. 465(b)(3).
[37] *D.B. Follender*, 89 TC 943, CCH Dec. 44,305, Acq. 1989-1 CB 1.
[38] Prop. Reg. § 1.465-6(d).
[39] DC N.D., 87-2 USTC ¶ 9576, 677 F.Supp. 633.
[40] See also *E.H. Allen*, 55 TCM 641, CCH Dec. 44,718(M), T.C. Memo. 1988-166.

A limited partner was held to be at risk for the allocable share of the partnership's recourse indebtedness when the limited partner entered into legally enforceable contracts making the partner personally and ultimately liable for the share of the partnership's debt.[41] Since there was no primary obligor against whom the limited partner could recover amounts paid, the court concluded that the partner was not a mere guarantor of the share of the partnership's recourse debt but was ultimately liable for it.[42]

¶ 317.2 Avoidance of At-Risk Rules

Knowing that taxpayers would attempt to get around the at-risk rules whenever possible, the IRS has put forth some proposed regulations that are designed to block such attempts. These regulations are directed against arrangements that are outside of normal commercial practices or that are designed to convert recourse debt to nonrecourse debt.

Beyond Normal Commercial Practice

The proposed at-risk regulations state that if a taxpayer engages in conduct that is not within "normal commercial practice" or has the effect of avoiding the at-risk rules, the amount at risk may be adjusted to reflect more accurately the amount that is actually at risk.[43] For instance, if an event increases the amount at risk near the close of the taxable year and has the effect of increasing the amount of losses that can be deducted, and a corresponding event decreases the amount at risk after year-end, these amounts will be disregarded unless there is a valid business reason for the arrangement and the arrangement is not a device to avoid the at-risk rules.

The circumstances the IRS considers in deciding whether to adjust the amount at risk include:

1. The length of time between an increase and decrease in the amount at risk;
2. The nature of the activity and deviations from normal business practice in the conduct of the activity;
3. The use of those amounts that increased the amount at risk toward the close of the tax year;
4. Contractual arrangements between parties to the activity; and
5. The occurrence of unanticipated events which make a decrease in the amount at risk necessary.

---

[41] *T.S. Ockles*, 54 TCM 785, CCH Dec. 44,245(M), T.C. Memo. 1987-507.
[42] IRS Letter Ruling 8749009, August 21, 1987.
[43] Prop. Reg. § 1.465-4(a).

Recourse Liabilities Becoming Nonrecourse

If liabilities are recourse for a period of time and then later become nonrecourse, the amount of liabilities during the period they are recourse will be considered at risk only if the arrangement is primarily business motivated and consistent with the normal commercial practice of financing the activity for which the money is borrowed.[44]

In Rev. Rul. 82-225,[45] the IRS ruled that an investor was not at risk for a recourse note that could be converted into a nonrecourse note because the criteria for conversion did not require that the underlying property be of sufficient value to cover the amount of the note. Similarly, in *J. Porreca*,[46] a taxpayer that had a unilateral right to convert recourse notes to nonrecourse notes was not at risk because the right to convert was not tied to any substantial economic event.

A taxpayer was considered at risk, however, for a recourse note that was convertible to a nonrecourse note because substantial amounts were due and paid prior to the conversion of the note. The note could only be converted if payments were not in arrears. Also, the note provided no right to make up delinquencies, and payment was not contingent on the proceeds from the underlying activity. The at-risk amount, however, was limited to the extent of the payments made prior to conversion.[47]

¶ 317.3 Computation of At-Risk Amount

To determine the amount at risk in an activity for a particular tax year, one begins with the at-risk amount at the end of the previous year and adjusts that amount for events occurring during the current year. The following summarizes the events that increase or decrease the amount at risk in an activity.

Increase Amount At Risk for:

— Money contributed

— Income from activity in excess of deductions

— Property contributed, measured by its adjusted basis (even if property is encumbered, but only to the extent that the taxpayer is personally liable)

— Loans for which the taxpayer is personally liable

— Loans secured by property not in the activity, limited to the fair market value of the property (but a later contribution of the property to the activity will reduce at-risk amount)

— Loans that are qualified nonrecourse financing for real estate

---

[44] Prop. Reg. § 1.465-5.
[45] 1982-2 CB 100.
[46] 86 TC 821, CCH Dec. 43,022.
[47] *L. Lansburgh*, 53 TCM 454, CCH Dec. 43,803(M), T.C. Memo. 1987-164; 54 TCM 691, CCH Dec. 44,227(M), T.C. Memo. 1987-491.

Decrease Amount At Risk for:

— Money withdrawn

— Loss allowed

— Property withdrawn or distributed from the activity, measured by adjusted basis of the property in the taxpayer's hands less liabilities to which the property is subject and for which the taxpayer is not personally liable

The following example illustrating the application of the at-risk rules and the provisions of the proposed at-risk regulations is drawn from Prop. Reg. § 1.465-41.

Example: On January 1, 1990, A and B form an equal partnership called the AB partnership. A and B each contribute $5,000 to the partnership on January 1. On August 1, 1990, AB borrows $6,000 from a bank and A and B assume personal liability. On December 31, 1990, the bank loan is reduced to $4,500. There is no income or loss for 1990. A's at-risk amount is calculated as follows:

At risk January 1, 1990	$ 0
Plus: Contributions	5,000
Share of loan for which A has personal liability	3,000
	$8,000
Less: Share of loan reduction	750
At risk December 31, 1990	$7,250

On February 1, 1991, AB borrows $20,000 on a nonrecourse basis with the loan secured by equipment. On May 1, 1991, the bank loan is reduced to $4,000. On August 1, 1991, the nonrecourse loan is reduced to $19,000. On October 1, 1991, AB distributes $2,000 to each of its partners. On December 1, 1991, the bank loan is reduced to $2,500. On December 31, 1991, A and B are each allocated their $3,000 share of AB income for 1991. A's at-risk amount for 1991 is calculated as follows:

At risk January 1, 1991	$ 7,250
Plus: Income from activity	3,000
	$10,250
Less: Share in bank loan reductions	1,000
	$ 9,250
Less: Distribution	2,000
At risk December 31, 1991	$ 7,250

¶ 317.3

Note that since the loans were repaid with money in the activity, the repayment to the bank reduced the amount at risk, and the repayment on the nonrecourse debt did not increase the amount at risk.

On March 1, 1992, A and B each contribute $1,000 to the partnership. On September 1, 1992, A and B each contribute $1,500. AB reduces the bank loan to zero by paying $2,500. AB pays $500 on the nonrecourse loan. On December 31, 1992, A and B have $10,500 allocated to each of them as their shares of AB losses. A's at-risk amount for 1992 is calculated as follows:

At risk January 1, 1992	$7,250
Plus: Contributions	2,500
	$9,750
Less: Share of bank loan reduction	1,250
At risk December 31, 1992	$8,500

Since A's loss allocation for 1992 is $10,500, but the at-risk amount is $8,500, A's loss deduction is limited. A deducts $8,500 of the loss for 1992, and this reduces the at-risk amount as of December 31, 1992 to zero. The $2,000 loss that is not allowed is treated as a loss in 1993.

During 1993, A and B each contribute $1,000 to the AB partnership. On December 31, 1993, A and B are each allocated $500 of income. A's at-risk amount for 1993 is calculated as follows:

At risk January 1, 1993	$8,500
Less: Loss allowed for 1992	8,500
	$ 0
Plus: Contribution	1,000
At risk December 31, 1993	$1,000

Of the $2,000 loss not allowed in 1992, $500 is deductible due to 1993 income and $1,000 is deductible because A is at risk for 1993 to this extent. The remaining $500 of the loss is not deductible in 1993 but it is carried over and treated as a loss for the following year. A begins 1994 with an at-risk amount of zero.

¶ 319 Qualified Nonrecourse Financing

One reason real estate was exempted from the at-risk rules until 1987 was that it was generally thought that real estate investments were not subject to the abusive uses of nonrecourse financing to the same extent as other investments. Real estate has value that generally does not depreciate rapidly (in fact, it usually appreciates) and, therefore, investors have an incentive to protect their ownership of real estate even when financed on a nonrecourse basis. Abuse in real estate investments generally occurred when the nonrecourse financing was provided by the seller or promoter of the investment and the purchase price was set far above the actual fair market value of the property. With this in mind, when Congress extended the at-risk rules to real estate, it limited their application to truly abusive situations. Accordingly, qualified nonrecourse financing is treated as at risk under the rules.[48]

Qualified nonrecourse financing that is considered at risk must meet four requirements:

1. The borrowing must be for the activity of holding real property. Holding real property includes the holding of personal property and the provision of services that are incidental to the use of real property.

2. The borrowing must be from a qualified person or from any federal, state or local government or government instrumentality, or the loan must be guaranteed by federal, state or local government. Qualified persons include any person actively and regularly engaged in the business of lending money such as a bank, savings and loan, credit union, insurance company, or pension trust. Qualified persons do not include any person from which the taxpayer acquires the property or any person who receives a fee from the taxpayer's investment in the property or persons related to such persons. (Seller financing or promoter financing can never be qualified nonrecourse financing.)

3. No person may be personally liable for the financing, except as provided in regulations.

4. The borrowing may not be convertible debt.[49]

¶ 319.1 *Financing from Related Person*

Qualified nonrecourse financing may be obtained from a related person, but, if it is, the terms of the borrowing must be commercially reasonable and on substantially the same terms as loans involving unrelated persons.

According to the Conference Committee Report on the Tax Reform Act of 1986, the terms of nonrecourse financing are commercially reasonable if the financing is a written unconditional promise to pay on demand or on a specified date or dates a sum or sums certain in money,

---

[48] Code Sec. 465(b)(6).   [49] Prop. Reg. § 1.465-27.

and the interest rate is a reasonable market rate of interest, taking into account the maturity of the obligation.

Generally, an interest rate is not considered commercially reasonable if it is significantly below the market rate on comparable loans by qualified persons who are not related to the borrowers. Similarly, an interest rate that significantly exceeds the market rate on comparable loans by unrelated qualified persons is not considered commercially reasonable. Also, an interest rate that is contingent is not commercially reasonable, but floating rates keyed to a market index are permitted.

The terms of financing are not considered commercially reasonable if the term of the loan exceeds the useful life of the property. Also, if the right to foreclose or collect is limited, except to the extent provided under state law, the terms of the loan are not commercially reasonable. The intent of Congress, generally, is to limit qualified nonrecourse financing to financing that carries arm's-length terms.

¶ 319.2 Transfer of Property

A taxpayer who acquires property subject to a nonrecourse debt that constituted qualified nonrecourse financing in the hands of the original borrower also may treat the debt as qualified nonrecourse financing, provided all the requirements are met. The same rule applies to subsequent transfers of the property taken subject to the debt, and to the admission of new partners to a partnership and the sale or exchange of a partnership interest, so long as the debt constitutes qualified nonrecourse financing as to each transferee or new partner.

¶ 321 INTEREST

Interest is compensation for the use or forbearance of money. It is the cost paid by the owner of real estate for the use of another's money to finance the acquisition. In the case of the supplier of the money, it is the "rent" received while another makes use of the money.

At one time, it may have been possible to say simply that interest paid is deductible and interest received is income when the acquisition of real estate is financed through a mortgage or other lending arrangement. Such is not the case today. Massive changes in the tax code in recent years have created traps and pitfalls that must be carefully negotiated when structuring a loan transaction. While most of the complications focus on interest as a deductible expense, certain provisions affect both the borrower and the lender, either as to the amount or timing of interest income and expense, or both. These provisions include the rules on interest-free and below-market rate loans and the original issue discount and imputed interest rules for deferred payment sales.

¶ 323 Interest Income

Interest received by a mortgage lender is taxable income.[50] Interest income includes interest on a promissory note, a mortgage, and the interest portion of a condemnation award. Interest income also includes usurious interest, unless the usurious interest is automatically converted to principal payments under state law.[51] Prepayment penalties or premiums charged for the prepayment of a mortgage also are taxable as interest income to the recipient.[52]

Interest income, generally, is reported in the year it is received by a cash basis taxpayer and in the year it is earned by an accrual basis taxpayer.[53] An accrual basis taxpayer who receives an actual prepayment of interest, however, generally must report the interest income when received.[54] See, for example, *J.A. Mele*,[55] in which interest prepaid for five years on a promissory note was held accruable when received and could not be prorated over the five-year period; and *Bjornsen Investment Corp.*,[56] in which prepaid interest received by an accrual basis taxpayer in connection with a 20-year real estate contract was held taxable in full at time of receipt.

Mortgage discount points charged to the seller by a mortgagee and deducted from the proceeds of the mortgage loan before they are paid to the seller, however, are not included in the mortgagee's income for the year the mortgage is originated.[57] The discount is included in income ratably as payments are received from the buyer.[58]

Keep in mind that the general rule regarding the amount and timing of interest income may be affected by the original issue discount and imputed interest rules for deferred payment sales which are discussed below.

¶ 325 Interest Deduction

Code Sec. 163(a) states the general rule that a deduction is allowed for "all interest paid or accrued within the taxable year on indebtedness." Unfortunately, a plethora of other code provisions makes this general rule almost meaningless by limiting or denying completely deductions for interest relating to certain types of indebtedness. The provisions likely to apply to real estate financing include:

1. The deduction for interest on investment indebtedness is limited by Code Sec. 163(d) (see ¶ 325.2).

---

[50] Code Sec. 61.
[51] Reg. § 1.61-7.
[52] *General American Life Insurance Co.*, 25 TC 1265, CCH Dec. 21,631, Acq. 1956-2 CB 5.
[53] Code Sec. 451.
[54] Rev. Rul. 70-540, 1970-2 CB 101.
[55] 61 TC 358, CCH Dec. 32,260, Acq. 1975-1 CB 2.
[56] DC Iowa, 81-1 USTC ¶ 9258.
[57] Rev. Rul. 65-95, 1965-1 CB 208.
[58] IRS Letter Ruling 7820003, January 20, 1978.

2. Interest on personal debts is disallowed by Code Sec. 163(h), other than certain home mortgage debt (see ¶ 1703.3).

3. Interest incurred during the construction of real estate generally must be capitalized under Code Sec. 263A (see ¶ 127).

4. Interest that qualifies as carrying charges on certain real estate may be capitalized under Code Sec. 266 (see ¶ 135).

5. An accrual basis taxpayer may deduct interest paid to a related cash basis taxpayer only when actually paid.[59]

6. Prepaid interest generally must be capitalized and deducted ratably over the term of the loan under Code Sec. 461(g) (see ¶ 325.1).

7. Deductible interest may be limited under the at-risk rules of Code Sec. 465 (see ¶ 311).

8. Deductible interest may be limited under the passive loss limitations of Code Sec. 469 (see ¶ 1143.2).

To be deductible, generally, interest must be paid on the indebtedness of the taxpayer. In the case of interest paid by the legal or equitable owner on a mortgage on real property, the interest is deductible even if the owner is not directly liable on the bond or note secured by the mortgage.[60] Also, annual or periodic payments made under a redeemable ground rent are treated as interest payments under the tax code.[61] For instance, payments made under an agreement subject to the residential ground rent laws of Virginia are treated as interest.[62] Payments on nonredeemable ground rents, however, are not treated as interest, although the payments may be deductible if they qualify as a business or investment expense.

Subject to the special rules listed above, the general rule is that a cash basis taxpayer deducts interest when actually paid, and an accrual basis taxpayer deducts interest as it accrues ratably over the term or period of the debt.[63] For an accrual basis taxpayer, it is not material when actual payment occurs.[64] An accrual basis taxpayer, however, is placed on the cash method of accounting as to interest paid to a related cash basis person.[65] This rule prevents a related payor from taking advantage of an interest deduction before the interest is includible in the income of the recipient. The relationships covered by this rule are listed in Code Sec. 267(b) and include family members, controlled corporations, and various fiduciary relationships.

---

[59] Code Sec. 267.
[60] Reg. § 1.163-1(b).
[61] Code Sec. 163(c).
[62] Rev. Rul. 75-281, 1975-2 CB 65.
[63] Code Sec. 446; Reg. § 1.446-1(c).
[64] Rev. Rul. 68-643, 1968-2 CB 76.
[65] Code Sec. 267.

Cash basis taxpayers generally are allowed interest deductions only for interest actually paid in cash or its equivalent. Personal notes given to a creditor for interest due are not considered cash or its equivalent.[66] The IRS has announced that it will disallow any deduction claimed for interest paid on a loan if the payment is made with money obtained from the original creditor through a second loan, an advance, or any other arrangement that is similar to a loan.[67] A deduction is allowed, however, if the taxpayer borrows money from a third party and uses that money to pay interest which is owed to the original lender.

¶ 325.1 *Prepaid Interest*

An accrual basis taxpayer can deduct prepaid interest only in the period in which the use of money occurs and only to the extent of the interest cost of using the borrowed funds during that period. It is not material when actual payment occurs, and the existence of a fixed liability to make a prepayment of interest is not sufficient to justify a deduction.[68] Code Sec. 461(g) makes cash basis taxpayers subject to essentially the same rule.

Under Code Sec. 461(g), a cash basis taxpayer who pays interest that is properly allocable to a later tax year must charge that interest to a capital account and treat it as paid in the periods in which the interest represents a charge for the use or forbearance of borrowed money during each year. Interest on a "wraparound mortgage" is subject to this prepaid interest rule, although the IRS may recharacterize part or all of a borrower's "interest" payment on a wraparound mortgage as, in substance, an additional down payment of principal or as a nondeductible deposit of interest with a third party.[69]

Once prepaid interest is allocated over the term of the loan, then it becomes subject to the various other provisions that restrict or limit the deduction for interest.

Points are additional interest charges that are usually paid when a loan is closed and that generally are imposed by the lender in lieu of a higher interest rate. If points are paid as compensation for the use of borrowed money, and are therefore considered interest, rather than as payment for the lender's services, the points are prepaid interest and must be treated as paid over the term of the loan. Points paid in refinancing a mortgage are subject to this rule,[70] but an exception applies to points or prepaid interest to the extent the underlying debt is

---

[66] Rev. Rul. 70-647, 1970-2 CB 38.

[67] IRS News Release 83-93, July 6, 1983; see also *W.M. Roberts*, 53 TCM 787, CCH Dec. 43,900(M), T.C. Memo. 1987-235.

[68] Rev. Rul. 68-643, 1968-2 CB 76.

[69] Rev. Rul. 75-99, 1975-1 CB 197.

[70] Rev. Rul. 87-22, 1987-1 CB 146.

incurred for the purchase or improvement of the taxpayer's principal residence (see ¶ 1705).[71]

¶ 325.2 *Investment Interest*

For noncorporate taxpayers, the deduction of "investment interest" is limited by Code Sec. 163(d). Generally, a noncorporate taxpayer may deduct investment interest only to the extent of net investment income. Any investment interest disallowed as a deduction under this provision may be carried over and deducted against investment income realized in future years.

Investment interest includes interest on debt attributable to property that produces interest income, dividends, annuities, or royalties not derived in the ordinary course of a trade or business. Investment interest also includes interest on debt allocable to oil and gas activities that are not passive activities and that constitute a trade or business. Also, interest expense allocable to portfolio income under the passive loss rules (see ¶ 1143.1) and interest allocable to personal property used in a short sale is investment interest.

Investment interest does not include qualified residence interest (see ¶ 1703) or interest that is taken into account under the passive loss rules explained at ¶ 1103. Also, interest on debt allocable to rental real estate in which the taxpayer actively participates within the meaning of the passive loss rules is not considered investment interest.

Investment income is the income from property held for investment and includes capital gain derived from the sale of investment property. It includes interest income, dividends, annuities, and royalties not derived in the ordinary course of business, and income from activities that are trades or businesses in which the taxpayer does not materially participate but that are not passive activities under the passive loss rules.

Investment income must be reduced by investment expenses to determine the ceiling amount for the deduction of investment interest. Investment expenses are any expenses other than interest that are deductible in connection with the production of investment income. Deductible expenses are those allowed after the application of the two percent of adjusted gross income floor for the deduction of miscellaneous expenses by individual taxpayers. In computing the amount of investment expenses that exceed the two percent floor, non-investment expenses are disallowed before the disallowance of any investment expenses.

---

[71] Code Sec. 461(g)(2).

Investment income and expenses do not include any items taken into account under the passive loss rules.[72] (See Chapter 11 for a detailed discussion of the passive loss rules.)

Rental Real Estate

As noted above, interest on debt allocable to rental real estate in which the taxpayer actively participates within the meaning of the passive loss rules is not considered investment interest. Rental activities in which the taxpayer does not actively participate generally are considered passive activities under the passive loss rules. Therefore, income from such rental activities and interest on debt attributable to such activities would be covered by the passive loss rules and would not enter into the computation of the investment interest limitation.

Prior to 1987, interest on debt attributable to real property subject to a net lease was investment interest and income produced by net lease property was investment income. Now, of course, real property subject to a net lease produces income and loss subject to the passive loss rules, and not the investment interest limitation.

Vacant Land

Vacant land presents special problems in connection with the investment interest limitation. If land is acquired for investment, then interest on mortgages on that land would be investment interest deductible only to the extent of investment income.

Land, however, may be acquired for a number of reasons. A taxpayer may take the position that vacant land is acquired and held as part of a trade or business, that is, that the taxpayer is a dealer in property. In this case, interest attributable to debt on the land would not be subject to the investment interest limitation, but the sale of land would produce ordinary income, not capital gain.

Vacant land also may be acquired in order to construct rental real estate. If the rental real estate is a passive activity, then the interest on the land presumably would be governed by the passive loss rules rather than the investment interest limitation.

¶ 325.3 Tracing Debt Proceeds

The number of limitations and restrictions on the deduction of interest requires that some way be found to classify interest under the various categories—fully deductible interest relating to a trade or business, investment interest subject to the Code Sec. 163(d) limitation, passive activity interest subject to the Code Sec. 469 passive loss rules,

---

[72] Code Sec. 163(d)(4)(D).

and personal interest (other than qualified personal residence interest) disallowed under Code Sec. 163(h).

In general, the IRS has prescribed regulations[73] that call for interest expense on a debt to be allocated in the same manner as the debt to which the interest relates is allocated. Debt is allocated by tracing disbursements of debt proceeds to specific expenditures.[74] In other words, debt proceeds and related interest expense are allocated based entirely on the use of the proceeds. The allocation is not affected by the type of property (other than in the case of qualified residence interest) that is used to secure the debt.[75]

> **Example:** The Taxpayer pledges corporate stock held for investment to secure a loan and uses the proceeds to purchase an automobile for personal use. Interest expense accruing on the debt is personal interest even though the debt is secured by investment property. If the automobile were used in the Taxpayer's trade or business, the interest would be business interest.

The amount of interest expense that accrues during any period is determined by taking into account relevant loan provisions and any applicable Internal Revenue Code provision that affects the accrual of interest expense, such as the original issue discount and imputed interest rules.[76]

Loan Proceeds Not Paid to Borrower

If a lender disburses debt proceeds to a person other than the borrower for the sale or use of property, for services, or for any other purposes, the debt is treated as if the borrower used the debt proceeds for the property, services, or other purpose.[77] The same tracing rule applies if a taxpayer incurs or assumes a debt for the sale or use of property, for services, or for any other purpose, or takes property subject to a debt, and no debt proceeds are disbursed to the taxpayer.

Loan Proceeds Received in Cash

Generally, any debt proceeds a taxpayer (other than a corporation) receives in cash (including withdrawal of cash from an account) are treated as used to make personal expenditures.[78] The taxpayer, however, may treat any cash expenditure made within 15 days after receiving the cash as made from the debt proceeds and may treat the expenditure as made on the date the cash was received.[79]

---

[73] Temp. Reg. § 1.163-8T.
[74] Temp. Reg. § 1.163-8T(a)(3).
[75] Temp. Reg. § 1.163-8T(c)(1).
[76] Temp. Reg. § 1.163-8T(c)(2)(C).
[77] Temp. Reg. § 1.163-8T(c)(3).
[78] Temp. Reg. § 1.163-8T(c)(5)(ii).
[79] Temp. Reg. § 1.163-8T(c)(5)(i).

Example: The Taxpayer incurs a $1,000 debt on August 4 and receives the proceeds in cash. The Taxpayer deposits $1,500 cash in an account on August 15 and on August 27 writes a check on the account for an investment expenditure. The Taxpayer also engages in many other cash transactions throughout the month of August, and numerous deposits of borrowed and unborrowed amounts and expenditures occur through the account. Despite these other transactions, the Taxpayer may treat $1,000 of the deposit on August 15 as an expenditure made from the debt proceeds received on August 4. Also, the Taxpayer may treat the investment expenditure on August 27 as made from the $1,000 debt proceeds treated as deposited in the account.

Loan Proceeds Deposited in an Account

The deposit of debt proceeds in an account is an investment expenditure, and an amount held in an account (whether or not interest bearing) is considered property held for investment. The debt must be reallocated when the proceeds are withdrawn and used to make another expenditure.[80]

Example: The Taxpayer borrows $100,000 on January 1 and immediately uses the proceeds to open a noninterest-bearing checking account. No other deposits are made to the account and none of the loan is repaid during the year. On April 1, the Taxpayer uses $20,000 from the account to make a passive activity expenditure. On September 1, the Taxpayer uses an additional $40,000 for personal expenditures.

From January 1 through March 31, the entire $100,000 debt is allocated to an investment expenditure and the interest on the debt is investment interest. From April 1 through August 31, $20,000 of the debt is allocated to the passive activity, and $80,000 is allocated to the investment expenditure. Interest for this period is investment interest to the extent attributable to the $80,000 portion of the debt and interest subject to the passive loss rules to the extent attributable to the $20,000 portion of the debt. From September 1 through December 31, $40,000 of the debt is allocated to personal expenditures, $20,000 to the passive activity, and $40,000 to the investment expenditure. Interest on the debt is allocated accordingly.

When an account contains more than the proceeds of one loan and various deposits are made to the same account, an ordering rule is provided by Temp. Reg. § 1.163-8T(c)(4)(ii). Generally, debt proceeds deposited in an account are treated as expended before (1) any unbor-

---

[80] Temp. Reg. § 1.163-8T(c)(4)(i).

rowed amounts held in the account at the time the debt proceeds are deposited, and (2) any amounts (borrowed or unborrowed) that are deposited in the account after the debt proceeds are deposited.

Example: The Taxpayer opens a checking account on January 10 and deposits $500 of proceeds of debt A and $1,000 of unborrowed funds. The following summarizes the transactions through the account during the year:

January 10—$500 Debt A and $1,000 unborrowed funds deposited

January 11—$500 proceeds of Debt B deposited

February 17—$800 personal expenditure

February 26—$700 passive activity expenditure

June 21—$1,000 proceeds of Debt C deposited

November 24—$800 investment expenditure

December 20—$600 personal expenditure

The $800 personal expenditure is treated as made from the $500 proceeds of Debt A and $300 of the proceeds of Debt B. The $700 passive activity expenditure is treated as made from the remaining $200 proceeds of Debt B and $500 of unborrowed funds. The $800 investment expenditure is treated as made entirely from the proceeds of Debt C. The $600 personal expenditure is treated as made from the remaining $200 proceeds of Debt C and $400 of unborrowed funds. Debt is allocated to an investment expenditure for periods during which debt proceeds are held in the account.

Despite the general ordering rules, a taxpayer may treat any expenditure made from an account within 15 days after debt proceeds are deposited as made from the debt proceeds.[81]

Example: The Taxpayer incurs a $1,000 debt on June 5 and immediately deposits the proceeds in an account (Account A). On June 17, the Taxpayer transfers $2,000 from Account A to another account (Account B). On June 30, the Taxpayer writes a $1,500 check on Account B for an investment expenditure. In addition, numerous deposits of borrowed and unborrowed amounts and expenditures occur through both accounts throughout the month of June.

The Taxpayer may treat $1,000 of the deposit to Account B on June 17 as an expenditure from the debt proceeds deposited in Account A on June 5. Also, the Taxpayer may treat $1,000 of the investment expenditure on June 30 as made from the debt proceeds treated as deposited in Account B on June 17.

---

[81] Temp. Reg. § 1.163-8T(c)(4)(iii)(B).

¶ 325.3

If the proceeds of two or more debts are deposited in an account simultaneously, the proceeds are treated as deposited in the order in which the debts were incurred. If two or more debts are incurred simultaneously, the debts may be treated as incurred in any order the taxpayer selects.[82]

Debt Repayments

If debt is allocated to more than one expenditure when a portion of the debt is repaid, the debt is treated as repaid in the following order:

1. Amounts allocated to personal expenditures;
2. Amounts allocated to investment expenditures and passive activity expenditures other than rental real estate in which the taxpayer actively participates;
3. Amounts allocated to passive activity expenditures for rental real estate in which the taxpayer actively participates;
4. Amounts allocated to former passive activity expenditures; and
5. Amounts allocated to trade or business expenditures and to certain low-income housing projects.[83]

In the case of lines of credit or similar arrangements that permit borrowing periodically under a single loan agreement, all borrowings on which interest accrues at the same fixed or variable rate are treated as a single debt. Also, borrowings or portions of borrowings on which interest accrues at different fixed or variable rates are treated as different debts, and the debts are treated as repaid in the order in which the borrowings are treated as repaid under the loan agreement.[84]

Debt Refinancing

To the extent the proceeds of any debt (the replacement debt) are used to repay any portion of a debt, the replacement debt is allocated to the expenditures to which the repaid debt was allocated. The amount of the replacement debt allocated is equal to the amount of debt allocated to the expenditures which was repaid with the proceeds of the replacement debt. If the replacement debt exceeds the repaid debt, the balance of the replacement debt is allocated to expenditures under the other tracing rules.[85]

Reallocation of Debt

Debt allocated to an expenditure relating to an asset is reallocated to another expenditure on the earlier of:

---

[82] Temp. Reg. § 1.163-8T(c)(4)(v).
[83] Temp. Reg. § 1.163-8T(d)(1).
[84] Temp. Reg. § 1.163-8T(d)(3).
[85] Temp. Reg. § 1.163-8T(e)(1).

1. The date on which proceeds from a disposition of the asset are used for another expenditure, but not in excess of the proceeds from the disposition of the asset; or

2. The date on which the character of the first expenditure changes because of a change in the use of the asset, but not in excess of the fair market value of the asset on the date of change.[86]

If the proceeds from the disposition of an asset exceed the amount of debt reallocated because of the disposition, or two or more debts are reallocated because of the disposition of the asset, the proceeds of the disposition are treated as an account to which the rules discussed above for loan proceeds deposited to an account apply.[87]

Example: On January 1, the Taxpayer sells an asset for $25,000. Just prior to the sale, the amount of debt allocated to the asset was $15,000. The proceeds of the disposition are treated as an account consisting of $15,000 of debt proceeds and $10,000 of unborrowed funds. If the Taxpayer immediately makes a $10,000 personal expenditure from the proceeds and within 15 days deposits the remaining proceeds in a bank account, the Taxpayer may treat the entire $15,000 deposited in the bank account as proceeds of a debt.

¶ 327 Interest-Free and Below-Market Rate Loans

In most contexts, an interest-free or below-market interest rate loan is really more than a simple borrow and lend transaction. Generally speaking, these loans are made in settings that are removed from traditional commercial lending and involve borrowers and lenders that have some relationship beyond mere debtor and creditor. In an effort to recognize the true nature of these transactions, Code Sec. 7872 takes certain interest-free and below-market rate loans and recharacterizes them as arm's-length transactions.

In a loan transaction recharacterized under Code Sec. 7872, the lender is considered to have made a loan at a rate of interest fixed by statute and also made an additional payment to the borrower equal to the foregone interest. This additional payment may be considered a gift, dividend, contribution to capital, compensation, or some other payment, depending on the context of the loan. The borrower, in turn, is considered to have transferred back to the lender the amount of this foregone interest as an interest payment.

The amount of foregone interest is based on the "applicable federal rates" determined under the original issue discount rules.[88] These rates

---

[86] Temp. Reg. § 1.163-8T(j)(1).
[87] Temp. Reg. § 1.163-8T(j)(2).
[88] Code Sec. 1274(d).

are announced by the IRS each month. For term loans, the federal short-term rate is used for loans of three years or less, the federal mid-term rate for loans of more than three years but not more than nine years, and the federal long-term rate for loans with terms of more than nine years. For demand loans, the short-term rate is used. A special blended rate may be used when an interest-free or below-market rate loan remains outstanding for the entire calendar year.[89] Numerous examples illustrating the computation of foregone interest may be found in Prop. Reg. § 1.7872-13.

The rules of Code Sec. 7872 apply to interest-free and below-market loans made in the following contexts.[90]

1. Gifts—These are loans in which the foregone interest is in the nature of a gift and generally involve family members, although it is possible for there to be a gift loan between other than family members.

2. Compensation—These are loans made in connection with the performance of services between an employer and employee, an independent contractor and the person hiring the contractor, or a partner and partnership if the loan is for services by the partner other than in the capacity as a partner.[91]

3. Corporation-Shareholder—These are loans from a corporation to a shareholder of the corporation or from a shareholder to a corporation. Loans to shareholders who are also employees are considered shareholder loans if certain minimal stock ownership requirements are met.[92]

4. Tax Avoidance—These are loans in which one of the principal purposes for the interest arrangement is avoidance of federal tax by the borrower or lender or both.[93]

5. Tax Effect Loans—These are loans that have a significant effect on the tax liability of the lender or borrower as defined by IRS regulations. The IRS has not yet issued regulations under this provision.

Gift loans, compensation loans, and shareholder-corporation loans are considered in more detail below. Keep in mind that the rules of Code Sec. 7872 for interest-free and below-market rate loans generally do not apply to any loan given in consideration for the sale or exchange of property and covered by the original issue discount rules or paid on account of the sale or exchange of property and covered by the imputed

---

[89] Code Sec. 7872(f)(2).
[90] Code Sec. 7872(c).
[91] Prop. Reg. § 1.7872-4(c).
[92] Prop. Reg. § 1.7872-4(d).
[93] Prop. Reg. § 1.7872-4(e).

interest rules.[94] (The original issue discount rules and imputed interest rules governing deferred payment sales of property are separately considered later in this chapter.)

¶ 327.1 Gift Loans

An interest-free or below-market rate gift loan has both income and gift tax consequences. The same rules apply to the income tax treatment of both term loans and demand loans, but the gift tax treatment differs depending on whether a gift loan is a term loan or a demand loan.

Income Tax Treatment

In the case of a gift loan, the lender is treated as transferring to the borrower an amount equal to the interest foregone by the lender (the gift). The borrower, then, is treated as retransferring an equal amount back to the lender as interest. These transfers are considered to take place on the last day of the calendar year for loans outstanding for any period during the calendar year. Foregone interest is the difference between what would have been payable on the loan if interest accrued at the applicable federal rate and was paid on the last day of the calendar year and any interest actually payable on the loan allocable to the same period.

For the borrower, the amount of interest treated as transferred to the lender is subject to all the rules that govern the deductibility of interest. If the debt may be traced to a trade or business, the interest would be fully deductible. If the debt were traced to an investment, passive activity, or personal use, the interest deduction would be limited by the various provisions that apply to interest. For the lender, the interest received is, of course, gross income under Code Sec. 61.

The application of Code Sec. 7872 is limited in certain cases involving gift loans between individuals:

1. The rules do not apply to gift loans of $10,000 or less, as long as the loan is not used directly or indirectly to purchase or carry income producing assets.[95]
2. If gift loans between the parties do not exceed a total of $100,000 and one of the principal purposes of the loan arrangement is not the avoidance of federal income tax, then the interest treated as paid by the borrower is limited to the borrower's net investment income for the year (net investment income is the same as net investment income under the investment interest limitations discussed above). If the borrower's net investment income does not exceed $1,000, then it is

---

[94] Code Sec. 1274(c)(1); Code Sec. 483(c)(1); Prop. Reg. § 1.7872-2(a)(2)(ii).

[95] Code Sec. 7872(c)(2).

treated as zero. In other words, if the borrower has under $1,000 net investment income, there is no deemed transfer of interest between the parties on a gift loan of $100,000 or less.[96]

Gift Tax Treatment

The gift tax treatment of a demand gift loan follows the income tax treatment. The amount of foregone interest that the lender treats as a gift to the borrower is the amount determined using the short-term federal rate on the last day of the calendar year. This means that, in the case of a demand loan that remains outstanding, a new gift is made each year equal to the foregone interest for the year.

If the gift loan is a term loan, however, the lender is treated as having made a gift of the interest on the date the loan is made. The amount of the gift is equal to the difference between the amount loaned and the present value of all payments that the borrower is required to make under the terms of the loan. Rather than a potential for a gift each year the loan remains outstanding, as is the case with a demand loan, a term loan generates but a single gift at the time of the loan.

The following example illustrates the difference between the income tax treatment and the gift tax treatment of term and demand loans under Code Sec. 7872 and is taken from the Conference Committee Report on the Tax Reform Act of 1984.

Comprehensive Example: On January 1, the Father, a calendar year taxpayer, makes a $200,000 loan to the Son, also a calendar year taxpayer. The loan is repayable in two years, with five percent simple interest payable annually.

Assuming that the applicable federal rate is 12 percent compounded semiannually, the amount of the gift made by the Father is $24,760. This is the difference between the $200,000 transferred to the Son and the present value at 12 percent of the $10,000 interest payment due at the end of year one and the $10,000 interest payment and $200,000 principal payment due at the end of year two.

The amount treated as retransferred by the Son to the Father on the last day of each of the two calendar years is $14,720. This is the difference between interest computed at the applicable federal rate and the interest actually payable on the loan. This amount, in addition to the $10,000 interest called for by the loan agreement, is included in income by the Father and, subject to the rules that govern the interest deduction, is treated as interest paid by the Son.

---

[96] Code Sec. 7872(d)(1).

¶ 327.2 Compensation Loans

In the case of compensation-related interest-free or below-market rate loans, the treatment of the employer and employee or independent contractor depend on whether the loan is a demand loan or a term loan.

Demand Loans

When an employer makes an interest-free or below-market rate demand loan to an employee or independent contractor, the employer is considered to have paid compensation or wages equal to the amount of the foregone interest for any day that the loan is outstanding. The employee is considered to have received an equal amount of compensation income. The employee, in turn, is considered to retransfer an equal amount back to the employer as interest on the loan and the employer has interest income equal to the same amount.[97]

For the employer, an interest-free or below-market rate demand loan to an employee generally results in a wash as far as the tax consequences are concerned. The employer reports interest income from the loan, but is entitled to an equivalent deduction for the compensation deemed paid to the employee (provided the employee's compensation meets the usual "reasonable" requirement for deduction). For the employee, the interest foregone by the employer is compensation income, subject to FICA and FUTA taxes (but not income tax withholding). The equivalent amount deemed paid as interest back to the employer may or may not produce a tax deduction, depending on the use of the loan proceeds and the usual limits on the deduction of interest paid.

Term Loans

If a compensation-related loan is a term loan, the employee is treated as receiving compensation from the employer equal to the difference between the amount of the loan and the present value at the applicable federal rate of all payments that the employee is required to make under the terms of the loan. The employee must report this full amount of extra compensation as of the date the loan was received. The employee, however, is treated as making interest payments over the term of the loan.[98] In this case, even if the interest is deductible, the employee will not be able to fully offset the extra compensation received on the date of the term loan.

---

[97] Code Sec. 7872(a).

[98] Code Sec. 7872(b).

For the employer, the situation is reversed. The full amount of the foregone interest is deductible (assuming "reasonableness") when the loan is made, but additional interest income is reported over the term of the loan. Considering the harsh impact a term loan can have on the employee an employer is trying to benefit, the employer can structure a term loan to have it treated as a demand loan by making the benefits of the interest rate nontransferrable and conditioning them on the performance of substantial future services by the employee.[99]

De Minimis Exception

The rules of Code Sec. 7872 do not apply to compensation-related loans if the loans to an employee do not exceed $10,000 and do not have a principal purpose of tax avoidance.[100] In other words, an employee receiving an interest-free or below-market rate compensation loan of $10,000 or less reports no income and has no possible interest deduction as a result of the loan. Similarly, the employer is not considered to be paying additional compensation and reports no interest income (other than interest actually paid by the employee).

Employee Relocation Loans

Certain loans to employees are excepted from the interest-free and below-market rate loan rules of Code Sec. 7872 if they are to provide mortgage financing for an employee's new residence or bridge financing in connection with the transfer of the employee to a new principal place of work.[101]

¶ 327.3 Corporation-Shareholder Loans

Interest-free and below-market rate loans between corporations and their shareholders are subject to essentially the same rules as compensation-related loans. The same distinction exists between term and demand loans, and the same $10,000 de minimis exception applies. The difference, of course, is the nature of the deemed payments equal to the foregone interest.

In the case of a loan from a corporation to a shareholder, the amount equal to the foregone interest transferred to the shareholder represents a dividend, not deductible by the corporation but taxable to the shareholder. The interest transferred back to the corporation from the shareholder is income to the corporation and is treated as interest paid by the shareholder, subject to the usual limits on the interest deduction. Since the corporation may not deduct dividends paid, and the corporation is taxed on the interest deemed received from the

---

[99] Prop. Reg. § 1.7872-10(a)(5).
[100] Code Sec. 7872(c)(3).
[101] Temp. Reg. § 1.7872-5T(c).

shareholder, an interest-free or below-market rate loan to a shareholder may be quite costly to the corporation.

In the case of an interest-free or below-market rate loan from a shareholder to the corporation, the amount of foregone interest deemed transferred to the corporation is treated as a contribution to capital, which is not income to the corporation and not deductible by the shareholder. The amount of the contribution to capital, however, does increase the shareholder's basis for the interest in the corporation. The interest payment transferred back to the shareholder from the corporation is deductible by the corporation and income to the shareholder.

¶ 327.4 Reporting Requirements

A lender must attach a statement to the lender's income tax return for any taxable year in which the lender either has interest income or claims a deduction for an amount deemed transferred to a borrower under Code Sec. 7872. Similarly, a borrower must attach a statement to the borrower's return for any taxable year in which the borrower either has income from an imputed transfer or claims a deduction for interest under Code Sec. 7872.[102]

An individual who wants to take advantage of the provision that limits interest under Code Sec. 7872 to net investment income, in the case of gift loans totaling $100,000 or less, must notify the lender in a signed statement of the amount of the borrower's net investment income.[103]

¶ 331 ORIGINAL ISSUE DISCOUNT AND IMPUTED INTEREST ON DEFERRED PAYMENT SALES

In many cases, the sale of real estate does not involve outside third-party financing. Rather, the seller will provide financing and accept the buyer's debt in exchange for all or a part of the purchase price. Even when third-party financing is available, it may not be sufficient. In this case too, seller financing may be made available to the buyer to make up the difference. (Installment sales and seller-financed sales of real estate are considered in Chapter 14. Here we are concerned with the tax rules governing the financing of the transaction, rather than the sales transaction itself.)

On an installment or deferred payment sale of real estate, if the buyer and seller fail to provide adequate interest on the deferred payments, one of two Internal Revenue Code provisions may come into play to rewrite the parties' financing agreement for tax purposes. These

---

[102] The exact contents of these statements are detailed in Prop. Reg. § 1.7872-11(g).

[103] Prop. Reg. § 1.7872-11(g)(3).

provisions are the imputed interest rules of Code Sec. 483 and the original issue discount rules of Code Sec. 1274.

Before 1985, there was only one provision to deal with, the imputed interest rules of Code Sec. 483. In the Tax Reform Act of 1984, however, Congress expanded the original issue discount (OID) rules to cover many deferred payment sales of property. Previously, the OID rules were limited generally to publicly traded debt instruments and debt issued for publicly traded property.

The imputed interest rules were enacted in 1964 to close what was then perceived as a loophole in the tax law. At that time, an individual could convert what would be ordinary income into capital gain on the sale of a capital asset for installment or deferred payments. The strategy was simple. Instead of charging interest on the deferred payments, the seller would simply charge a higher price for the asset. The higher price, of course, was to compensate the seller for the interest the seller would otherwise receive. The buyer would pay no more than if the buyer paid a lower price plus interest, but the seller was able to report capital gain, which was subject to preferential tax treatment at that time, rather than ordinary interest income.

The imputed interest rules of Code Sec. 483 limited this strategy to convert ordinary income into capital gain by "imputing" interest in a contract for the sale of property unless a statutorily set minimum rate of interest was called for by the agreement. Since the fixed interest rate called for under the imputed interest rules did not always reflect current interest rates, Congress made the imputed interest rate under Code Sec. 483 conform to the OID rates when the OID rules were expanded in 1984 (how the rates are determined is discussed below for both the imputed interest rules and the OID rules).

While the imputed interest rules could block the conversion of ordinary income to capital gain as outlined above, Code Sec. 483 still left another loophole. If a cash basis seller sold an asset to an accrual basis buyer in an installment or deferred payment sale, a tax shelter of sorts could be constructed by manipulating the timing of the interest payments on the deferred amounts. The buyer could accrue and deduct the interest for the periods to which it related, even if the interest was not actually paid. The seller, however, would not have to report interest income until interest payments were actually received. In short, it was possible to generate an interest deduction for one taxpayer without a corresponding amount of interest income for another taxpayer. It is this second loophole, along with the conversion loophole, that the OID rules of Code Sec. 1274 are designed to close.

¶ 331

Unlike the imputed interest rules, the OID rules do more than merely convert "principal" into interest for tax purposes when insufficient interest is called for by the parties to a sale of property. The OID rules also require both the buyer and seller to account for any OID on an economic accrual basis by which OID is deemed to accrue at the applicable statutory rate with six-month compounding. Also, even if there is sufficient interest called for in a sale contract, the OID rules may require that the parties account for that interest for tax purposes under the OID accrual rule. (There is an exception that allows cash basis accounting in certain cases, and this is discussed in connection with the OID rules at ¶ 335.1.) In short, in addition to preventing the conversion of interest income into capital gain, the OID rules also match the buyer's interest deduction and the seller's interest income, regardless of their actual accounting methods and regardless of when interest payments are actually made.

Note: In 1986, the IRS issued proposed regulations that took up over 400 pages of typewritten copy and proposed additions or changes to the regulations under Code Secs. 163(e), 446, 482, 483, 1271, 1272, 1273, 1274, 1274A, and 1275. In 1992, the IRS withdrew most of those proposed regulations and issued new proposed regulations on the OID rules under Code Sec. 163(e) and Code Secs. 1271 through 1275, and proposed amendments to the Code Secs. 483, 1001, and 1012 regulations. The 1992 proposed regulations, with some changes, were adopted as final regulations on February 2, 1994.[104] Appropriate citations to the final regulations are made in the following discussion. The regulations also contain additional explanations and examples on how to determine imputed interest and original issue discount and how to accrue interest under the OID rules. The discussion here concentrates on the general concepts behind imputed interest and OID rather than any detailed mathematical computations. The reader who desires to delve into the mathematical intricacies is referred to the regulations.

¶ 333 Imputed Interest

The imputed interest rules of Code Sec. 483 apply to an installment or deferred payment sale only if the OID rules of Code Sec. 1274 discussed below do not apply.[105] The real estate sales transactions that are not subject to the OID rules and, therefore, that are subject to the imputed interest rules are:

1. Sales of farms by individuals or small businesses (as defined by Code Sec. 1244(c)(3)), if the sales price of the farm is $1,000,000 or less.[106]

---

[104] T.D. 8517, 59 F.R. 4799-4831.
[105] Code Sec. 483(d)(1).
[106] Code Sec. 1274(c)(3)(A).

2. Sales by individuals of their principal residences.[107]
3. Sales of property if the aggregate amount of debt payments and other consideration for the sale does not exceed $250,000.[108]
4. Sales of land between certain family members if the sales price does not exceed $500,000.[109]

¶ 333.1 *Unstated Interest*

Interest is imputed under Code Sec. 483 to a payment under a contract for the sale or exchange of property if the sales price is more than $3,000 [110] and if the following conditions are met:

1. The payment is due more than six months after the date of the sale or exchange;
2. Some or all of the payments called for by the contract are due more than one year after the sale or exchange; and
3. There is "unstated interest."[111]

There is unstated interest in a contract of sale to the extent the sum of the payments due under the contract exceed the present values of the payments plus the present values of any interest payments due under the contract.[112] Present values are calculated using a discount rate that is equal to the applicable federal rate (see ¶ 337). In the case of a sale-leaseback transaction in which the seller or related party leases a portion of the property after the sale, however, 110 percent of the applicable federal rate is used (sale-leasebacks as financing tools are discussed at ¶ 341).

Under this rule, a contract that specifies interest equal to the applicable federal rate cannot have unstated interest and cannot be subject to the imputed interest rules. To the extent that there is unstated interest, however, the unstated interest is imputed to the contract and treated as interest for all tax purposes. This also reduces the amount of principal. Accordingly, the imputation of interest under Code Sec. 483 not only produces interest income for the seller and a possible interest deduction for the buyer, it also reduces the amount realized by the seller from the sale and reduces the buyer's cost basis in the property.

¶ 333.2 *Land Sales Between Family Members*

In the case of a sale of land between family members for $500,000 or less, the discount rate used to determine if there is unstated interest

---

[107] Code Sec. 1274(c)(3)(B).
[108] Code Sec. 1274(c)(3)(C).
[109] Code Secs. 1274(c)(3)(F) and 483(e).
[110] Code Sec. 483(d)(2).
[111] Code Sec. 483(c).
[112] Code Sec. 483(b).

is set at a maximum of six percent compounded semiannually.[113] Of course, this also means that the related parties may use this rate if it is lower than the applicable federal rate and avoid the imputed interest rules.

While the statute speaks to the sales price in applying the $500,000 limitation, the proposed regulations look to the amount of the debt instrument. Reg. § 1.483-3(b)(2) provides that the special imputed interest rate applies to a debt instrument issued in a sale or exchange of land by an individual to a member of the individual's family if:

1. The individuals are the only parties to the debt instrument;
2. The debt instrument is not given in consideration for any property other than land (the exception does not apply to the sale of depreciable structures or improvements); and
3. The stated principal amount of the debt instrument, when added to the aggregate stated principal amount of any other debt instruments to which the exception applies and which were issued in prior qualified land sales between the individuals during the same calendar year, does not exceed $500,000.

If the property sold or exchanged does include property other than land, the maximum six percent rate applies only to the extent that the stated principal amount of the debt instrument issued in the sale or exchange is attributable to the land based on the relative fair market values of the land and the other property.[114]

Apparently, the regulations take the sensible position that sales for more than $500,000 can be fragmented so that the $500,000 limitation should be construed as applying to the debt. Presumably, the sales price may exceed $500,000, and even the amount of the sales price that is financed may exceed $500,000, but only $500,000 is eligible for the maximum six percent imputed interest rate.[115]

Family members eligible for the maximum six percent imputed interest rate on the sale of land are defined by Reg. § 1.483-3(b)(2)(i) to include only an individual's brother and sister (by the whole or half blood), spouse, parents, grandparents, children and grandchildren. Full effect is given to a legal adoption in determining these relationships.

¶ 335 Original Issue Discount

Generally, the OID rules of Code Sec. 1274 may apply to any sale or exchange of property that is not one of the exceptions listed at ¶ 333 as covered by the imputed interest rules. If the sale of property is one

---

[113] Code Sec. 483(e).
[114] Reg. § 1.483-3(b)(2)(iii)
[115] See the examples in Reg. § 1.483-4(b)(3).

that may be covered by the OID rules, the rules apply unless the contract of sale calls for interest at the applicable federal rate and the interest is payable currently at a constant rate over its term. If either inadequate interest is called for by the contract or adequate interest is not currently payable, the OID rules apply.[116]

If the interest rate called for by the contract is adequate but interest is not payable currently, the OID rules force the purchaser and seller to report the interest for tax purposes based on an economic accrual of interest with six-month compounding. If interest is less than the applicable federal rate, than an imputed principal amount is calculated by discounting all payments called for by the contract at the applicable federal rate. The difference between the stated principal amount and the imputed principal amount is original issue discount and is treated as interest for tax purposes. The parties account for the OID as if interest on the imputed principal amount were being compounded at six-month intervals.

> **Example:** In a sale subject to the OID rules, the Buyer and the Seller agree to a purchase price of $1,500,000 for commercial property. The Seller agrees to accept $500,000 in cash and the Buyer's note and purchase-money mortgage for $1,000,000. The mortgage calls for five percent interest payable annually with the full amount of principal due at the end of five years, or payments by the Buyer to the Seller of $50,000 each year for four years and a final payment after five years of $1,050,000. At the time of the sale, the applicable federal rate that applies to this transaction is eight percent.
>
> Since this deferred payment sale does not provide for adequate interest, an "imputed principal" amount and the original issue discount must be determined by discounting the payments required by the mortgage at eight percent compounded semiannually. Discounting the expected payments over the five-year term of the mortgage at eight percent gives a present value of $880,230, and this is the imputed principal amount. Subtracting the imputed principal from the stated principal ($1,000,000 − $880,230) yields original issue discount in the amount of $119,770.
>
> The original issue discount of $119,770 must be treated as interest for tax purposes by both the Buyer and the Seller, so the Seller reports the appropriate portion of the OID as additional interest income each year, and the Buyer may deduct an equal amount as interest, subject to the usual limitations on the deduction of interest. Also, the imputed principal amount is treated as

---

[116] Code Sec. 1274(c).

the principal amount of the debt for tax purposes. Accordingly, the Seller's gain or loss is determined based on his amount realized of $1,380,230 ($500,000 cash plus $880,230 mortgage debt), and the Buyer's cost basis for the property is also $1,380,230.[117]

¶ 335.1 *Cash Method Accounting*

Generally, for purposes of the OID rules, any original issue discount must be treated by the parties to the transaction on an economic accrual basis regardless of their actual tax accounting methods and regardless of when interest is actually paid. There is, however, an exception to the OID accrual rule which permits the parties to elect cash method accounting for OID that would otherwise be subject to Code Sec. 1274, if certain requirements are met.[118] Cash method accounting is available if:

1. The stated principal amount of the debt does not exceed $2,000,000;
2. The seller/lender does not use an accrual method of accounting for tax purposes;
3. The seller/lender is not a dealer in the property sold or exchanged; and
4. The election [119] to use the cash method is made jointly by both the buyer and seller.

If a debt instrument subject to a cash method election is transferred by the lender or assumed by a successor to the borrower, the election applies to the new party or parties. If a seller/lender's transferee is an accrual basis taxpayer, however, the cash method election does not apply and the transferee must use accrual accounting under the rules of Code Sec. 1272 to report any OID. [120]

¶ 335.2 *Assumptions and Modifications of Debt Instruments*

Neither the OID rules of Code Sec. 1274 nor the imputed interest rules of Code Sec. 483 apply on the assumption of an existing debt instrument unless the terms and conditions of the debt instrument are modified or the nature of the transaction is changed in connection with the assumption.[121]

Example: On the sale of property, the Seller provides a $3,000,000 purchase-money mortgage which calls for annual interest at 15 percent. Three years later, the property is resold and the new Buyer assumes the existing purchase-money mortgage, but the

---

[117] For many additional examples relating to OID calculations, including the calculation of the amount of OID that is reported for any year over the term of the loan, see the regulations under Code Sec. 1274.

[118] Code Sec. 1274A(c).
[119] Reg. § 1.1274A-1(c)(1).
[120] Reg. § 1.1274A-1(c)(2).
[121] Code Sec. 1274(c)(4).

Seller agrees to lower the interest rate on the mortgage to nine percent. Because the mortgage debt has been modified on the assumption, the modified debt is treated as a new debt provided by the Seller in consideration for the old debt.

If the lender and borrower, or successors to either, modify a debt instrument materially either in kind or in extent, the modified debt instrument is treated as a new debt given in consideration for the old, unmodified debt. The new debt instrument is eligible for the cash method election (¶ 335.1) if the other requirements are met. The new debt instrument is not eligible for the cash method election, however, if a principal purpose of the debt modification is to defer interest income or deductions through the election.[122]

¶ 337   Interest Rates Under the Imputed Interest and OID Rules

The interest rates, called federal rates, on which imputed interest or OID is determined are keyed to the interest rate on United States government obligations and the terms of the deferred payment sale.[123] The rates are adjusted each month based on the average market yield on outstanding government obligations and announced by the IRS. The rate for a particular sale or exchange is the rate in effect on the date of the transaction.

The applicable federal rate as announced by the IRS is determined by the term of the deferred payment obligation. If the term is three years or less, the applicable federal rate is the announced federal short-term rate. If the term is more than three years but not more than nine years, the applicable federal rate is the federal mid-term rate; and for terms in excess of nine years, the federal long-term rate is used.

Note that in the case of a sale-leaseback transaction involving seller financing, the applicable federal rates are 110 percent of the announced federal rates.[124]

To prevent taxpayers' planning of the sale or purchase of property from being adversely affected by monthly changes in the federal rates, a special rule permits the use of the federal rates announced for one month in the following two months as well.[125] The test rate generally is the lowest of the applicable federal rates in effect during either the three-month period that ends with the first month in which there is a binding written contract that contains the terms of the sale or exchange, or the three-month period that ends with the month in which the sale or exchange occurs.[126] For instance, a real estate sale that

---

[122] Reg. § 1.1274A-1(c)(3).
[123] Code Sec. 1274(d).
[124] Code Sec. 1274(e).
[125] Code Sec. 1274(d)(2).
[126] Reg. § 1.1274-4(a)(1).

closes in April may test for imputed interest or OID using the lowest federal rates announced for February, March, or April.

¶ 337.1 Maximum Interest Rate

If seller financing or other debt subject to the imputed interest or OID rules does not exceed $2,800,000, the maximum rate under the imputed interest or OID rules is nine percent.[127] This rate is merely a maximum. If the applicable federal rate announced by the IRS for the month of sale (or preceding two months) is lower, the lower rate may be used in place of the nine percent rate. The maximum nine percent rate generally does not apply to new tangible personal property.[128]

¶ 337.2 Installment Obligations

In the case of an installment obligation, the term of the instrument is the instrument's weighted average maturity as defined in Reg. § 1.1273-1(e)(3).[129]

¶ 337.3 Variable Interest Rate Obligations

Generally, for purposes of determining whether there is adequate interest, a variable rate debt keyed to an objective index (such as prime, federal rate, LIBOR, or average yield on treasuries) is treated as if the debt called for a fixed rate equal to the variable rate at the time the debt is tested for adequate interest.[130]

The general rule for variable rate obligations does not apply if, as a result of interest rate restrictions, such as an interest rate cap, the expected yield of the obligation taking the restrictions into account is significantly less than the expected yield of the obligation without regard to the restrictions. In this case, the interest payments on the obligation, other than any fixed interest payments, are treated as contingent payments.[131] An obligation is not subject to this rule if it contains reasonably symmetric interest rate caps and floors, or reasonably symmetric governors, that are fixed throughout the term of the obligation.

Example: A sells B property and as part of the consideration, B gives A a note for $1,000,000 payable in five years. Interest is payable monthly at a rate equal to one percentage point above the prime rate for the preceding month. If the applicable federal rate for this debt were 7.5 percent, and if, on the date this test rate is determined, the prime rate plus one percent equalled nine percent, the debt would have adequate interest.[132]

---

[127] Code Sec. 1274A(a).
[128] Code Sec. 1274A(b).
[129] Reg. § 1.1274-4(c)(1).
[130] Reg. § 1.1274-2(f)(1).
[131] Reg. § 1.1274-2(f)(1)(ii).
[132] For additional examples, see Prop. Reg. § 1.1274-3(d)(1)(v).

¶ 337.4 Contingent Interest

If a debt instrument provides for one or more contingent payments, the issue price of the debt instrument is the lesser of the instrument's noncontingent principal payments and the sum of the present values of the noncontingent payments determined under Reg. § 1.1274-2(c). If the debt instrument is issued in a potentially abusive situation, however, the issue price is the fair market value of the noncontingent payments.[133]

When an obligation containing contingent payments is subject to Code Sec. 1274, any noncontingent payments are treated as a separate debt instrument. The issue price of the overall debt instrument is determined as above (Reg. § 1.1274-2(g)).[134]

A contingent payment is treated as a payment of principal to the extent of the present value of the payment, determined by discounting the payment at the test rate from the date of the payment is made to the issue date. Any amount in excess of part of the payment treated as principal is interest.[135] The test rate is the rate that would be the test rate for the overall debt instrument if the term of the overall debt instrument began on the issue date and ended when the contingent payment is made. In the case of a contingent payment that consists of a payment of stated principal accompanied by a payment of stated interest at a rate that exceeds this test rate, however, the test rate is the stated interest rate.[136]

> *Example:* On January 1, 1997, A sells a newly constructed office building to B for a $1,000,000 in cash and a debt instrument that matures on December 31, 2001. The debt instrument provides for a payment at maturity of $5,000,000 and a contingent payment of interest on December 31 of each year equal to a fixed percentage of the gross rents B receives from the building in that year. On January 1, 1997, the short-term applicable federal rate is 5 percent, compounded annually, and the mid-term rate is 6 percent, compounded annually.
>
> The issue price of the debt instrument, determined under the rules of Reg. § 1.1274-2(g) is $3,736,291—the present value of the $5,000,000 noncontingent payment due on December 31, 2001, based on a discount rate equal to the mid-term applicable federal rate of 6 percent. (B's basis in the building is $4,736,291, the $1,000,000 cash plus the present value of the noncontingent payment.) The noncontingent payment is treated as a separate debt

---

[133] Reg. § 1.1274-2(g).
[134] Reg. § 1.1275-4(c)(3).
[135] Reg. § 1.1275-4(c)(4)(ii).
[136] Reg. § 1.1275-4(c)(4)(ii)(B).

instrument with an issue price of $3,736,291 and OID of $1,263,709.

If the contingent payment that is fixed and payable on December 31, 1997, is $200,000, the present value of that amount discounted at the short-term federal rate of 5 percent from the date the payment is made to the issue date, or $190,476, is principal, and the remainder of $9,524 is interest. (The amount treated as principal increases B's basis in the building.) The remaining contingent payments are accounted for in a similar fashion—discounted at 5 percent for the payments due at the end of 1998 and 1999, and discounted at 6 percent for the contingent payments due at the end of 2000 and 2001.[137]

¶ 337.5 Excessive Interest

The imputed interest and OID rules generally set the minimum interest rate that can be charged for tax purposes in a contract for the sale of property. But what about a maximum rate of interest? May a buyer and seller lower the purchase price and charge a higher rate of interest to provide a tax advantage for one of the parties? Corporations that issue certain "high yield" discount obligations may lose a portion of their interest deductions, but what of other taxpayers?

As discussed at ¶ 105.3, the IRS does have the power under Code Sec. 1274(b)(3) to limit the imputed principal amount of a debt instrument to the fair market value of the property acquired with the debt, and this power would seem to apply equally to a reduced purchase price to gain a tax advantage from interest deductions as to an inflated purchase price to gain depreciation or other tax advantages. Reg. § 1.1274-2(b)(3) specifically provides that in the case of a debt instrument issued in a potentially abusive situation, the issue price of the debt instrument is the fair market value of the property received in exchange for the debt instrument, reduced by the fair market value of any consideration other than the debt. An abusive situation includes a debt instrument with clearly excessive interest.[138] According to the regulations, interest on a debt instrument is clearly excessive, if the interest, in light of the terms of the debt instrument and the creditworthiness of the borrower, is clearly greater than the arm's length amount of interest that would have been charged in a cash lending transaction between the same two persons.[139]

---

[137] For additional examples, see Reg. § 1.1275-4(c)(7).

[138] Reg. § 1.1274-3(a)(2)(iv).
[139] Reg. § 1.1274-3(b)(3).

¶ 341 SALE-LEASEBACKS AND OTHER LEASE FINANCING

From a practical point of view, there may be very little difference between outright ownership of property and a long-term lease of the property, as far as the user of business property is concerned. In many cases, leasing transactions serve as a substitute for traditional financing. In a typical sale-leaseback, the owner of property sells the property to an investor and immediately leases the property back. A sale-leaseback can be arranged with any type of property, but it is real estate that is most often the subject of a sale and leaseback. The lease in a sale-leaseback is usually a net lease that assures the investor a return over and above the cost to him of financing the purchase of the property from the seller-lessee.

Apart from sale-leasebacks, a lease of property combined with an option to purchase by the lessee may be another way, in addition to a purchase-money mortgage, for the seller of property to provide financing for the prospective purchaser of property.

¶ 343 Straight Sale-Leaseback

In a straight forward sale-leaseback, the owner of property sells the property to an investor. The property may be newly constructed property or property that has been owned by the seller for some time. (In some deals, the seller may be a builder or developer who has constructed the property to the specifications of the future lessee. In these cases, the sale directly to the investor party eliminates the intermediate step of having the ultimate user of the property acquire title and then selling to the investor.) The investor may or may not obtain traditional mortgage financing from an outside third-party lender in order to finance the purchase. The investor then immediately leases the property back to the seller, usually on a long-term net lease. Under this arrangement, the seller-lessee is assured of the use of the property and is responsible for all property taxes, insurance, maintenance and upkeep expenses. The purchaser-lessor, through the net lease, is provided with a guaranteed return on his investment, and ownership of the property provides him with security for his investment.

In this form, the sale-leaseback is substituting for mortgage financing. Moreover, the amount of cash that is freed for the seller-lessee may be equal to the full value of the property, the equivalent of 100 percent financing.

> *Example:* A business owns a warehouse that is worth $500,000. The business would like to free up the cash that is tied up in the land and building for other uses, but wants to continue to use the warehouse in its business operations. One avenue open to this

business is to borrow against the property by obtaining a mortgage loan for 80 percent of the property's value, or $400,000. Instead of a mortgage loan, however, the business may want to explore a sale-leaseback that could free the entire $500,000 value of the building.

Assuming the mortgage loan could be obtained for a 25-year term at 10 percent, the business would be obligated to pay about $43,600 annually to amortize the loan over the 25 years. With a sale-leaseback, the business would sell the land and building to an investor for its full $500,000 value. Under the lease of the warehouse back from the investor, the lease might be for a 25-year term with annual payments of about $54,500, which is about the amount required to fully return the investor's $500,000 plus 10 percent interest over the 25-year term of the lease.

While the sale-leaseback as described above does free up the full value of the real estate assets, it does have significant drawbacks. First, at the end of the lease term, the investor and not the business owns the property, and the residual value, which may be significant, belongs to the purchaser-lessor. Second, the seller-lessee may want to continue using the property at the end of the lease term, but the property now belongs to the purchaser-lessor and the lease arrangement may have to be renegotiated. For these reasons, sale-leasebacks will contain various options for repurchase of the property or for the renewal of the lease on predetermined terms. These options, however, may complicate the tax treatment of the sale-leaseback.

¶ 343.1   Tax Benefits

Provided that the sale-leaseback is recognized as a sale and a lease for tax purposes, the seller-lessee deducts the full amount of its rental payments. If there is a gain or a loss on the sale portion of the transaction, the gain or loss is taxable under the usual rules. The purchaser-lessor has income from the rents received from the seller-lessee, but this income may be sheltered by the operating expenses and depreciation deductions available to the owner of real estate.

(Lease payments are considered at ¶ 401, sales of real property at ¶ 1301, real estate operating expenses at ¶ 721, and depreciation at ¶ 901.)

For the seller-lessee, the sale-leaseback may provide a tax benefit because the deduction for rental payments may be greater than depreciation and interest deductions from traditional financing. This is more likely to be the case if the property has already been fully depreciated or if the property is leased back for less than its useful life. The sale-leaseback also may provide benefits for the seller-lessee when the seller-lessee cannot utilize the tax benefits associated with the ownership of

¶ 343.1

depreciable property. The sale to an investor who can benefit from the tax advantages of ownership may permit the seller-lessee to lease at a favorable rate, in effect, splitting the tax benefits with the investor. Whether or not a sale-leaseback will actually provide a net benefit in a given situation may require extensive projections and computations. In many cases, the disadvantages of a sale-leaseback will outweigh the benefits.

Of course, to realize the tax benefits of a sale-leaseback, the transaction must be treated as a sale and leaseback for tax purposes, rather than as a mere financing device. The guidelines that have been applied are discussed at ¶ 345. If a sale-leaseback is not recognized as such for tax purposes, but is treated as a secured loan, the consequences are substantial. Since all calculations of the potential benefits of a sale-leaseback hinge on the tax treatment, it is essential that the parties to a proposed sale-leaseback be certain of the treatment of their transaction.

If a sale-leaseback is treated as a secured loan for tax purposes, the seller-lessee would be denied deductions for rent or lease payments. The seller-lessee's payments would be treated as payments on a loan—partly interest and partly the amortization of principal. Depreciation would be available to the seller-lessee who continues to be considered the owner of the property, but the rate and method of depreciation would be the same as before the purported sale of the property. The purchaser-lessor, instead of being in the position of the owner of property, would be in the position of a mortgagee. Depreciation deductions would not be available, nor would other deductions associated with the ownership of real property. To the extent payments received represent principal, however, the purchaser-lessor's income would be reduced.

¶ 343.2 *Like-Kind Exchange and the Sale-Leaseback*

Real estate held as an investment or used in a trade or business may be exchanged for other investment or business real estate without recognition of gain or loss. [140] Reg. § 1.1031(a)-1(c) provides that no gain or loss is recognized if a taxpayer exchanges "a leasehold of a fee with 30 years or more to run for real estate." This raises the danger that if the lease in a sale-leaseback is for 30 years or more, the sale-leaseback may be treated as a like-kind exchange of property, although it is not entirely clear that this provision governs when only one property is involved, that is, when a fee interest is exchanged for a

---

[140] Code Sec. 1031; like-kind exchanges are considered fully at ¶ 1311.

¶ 343.2

leasehold interest in the same property. There is a split of authority among the Circuit Courts of Appeals.

In *Century Electric Co.*,[141] the Eighth Circuit held that the sale of business property at a loss followed by a leaseback of the property for 95 years was a like-kind exchange which made the loss nondeductible. The court applied the regulation quoted above [142] and held it valid as applied to an exchange of a 30-year-or-longer leasehold for a fee interest, even though the rights exchanged are in the same property. On the other hand, the Second Circuit skirted the issue in *Jordan Marsh Co.*[143] In this case, a department store which sold the properties on which its store was operated for cash and simultaneously received a leaseback for 30 years and three days sustained a recognizable loss since, according to the court, there was in fact a sale for the full value of the properties conveyed, and not an exchange. The court found it unnecessary to pass on the validity of Reg. § 1.1031(a)-1(c) as applied to a leasehold of 30 years or more exchanged for a fee interest in the same property.[144] The key to sale-leaseback treatment rather than like-kind exchange treatment is that the sale must be for full fair market value and the rental must also be at fair rental value. Of course, if the term of the leaseback is less than 30 years, the problem cannot arise.

¶ 345 Recognition of a Sale-Leaseback for Tax Purposes

Determining whether a particular sale-leaseback will be recognized as such for tax purposes, or whether it will be treated as a mortgage financing arrangement is not an easy task. The Supreme Court has established some guidelines, and further guidance may be distilled from IRS pronouncements.

¶ 345.1 *Supreme Court Guidelines*

In *F. Lyon Co.*,[145] the Supreme Court held that the purchaser-lessor in a sale-leaseback was the owner of the building and that the arrangement was not merely a financing arrangement. The seller-lessee was a bank that could not itself finance the construction of a new building because of state and federal banking restrictions. The purchaser-lessor was a home furnishing company that agreed to take title to the building as it was being constructed and to lease it back to the bank with options to repurchase at various times. The purchaser-lessor obtained both a construction loan and permanent mortgage financing,

---

[141] CA-8, 51-2 USTC ¶ 9482, 192 F.2d 155, cert. denied, 342 U.S. 954, 72 S.Ct. 625.

[142] Reg. § 1.1031(a)-1(c).

[143] CA-2, 59-2 USTC ¶ 9641, 269 F.2d 453.

[144] The IRS will not follow the decision in *Jordan Marsh*. See Rev. Rul. 60-43, 1960-1 CB 687. For additional cases holding that the like-kind provisions do not apply to a genuine sale-leaseback transaction, see *Leslie Co.*, CA-3, 76-2 USTC ¶ 9553, 539 F.2d 943 and *Crowley, Milner & Co.*, CA-6, 82-2 USTC ¶ 9612, 689 F.2d 635.

[145] 78-1 USTC ¶ 9370, 435 U.S. 561, 98 S.Ct. 1291.

and made an initial investment of $500,000 in the building in order to diversify its operations.

The Court held that the sale-leaseback was genuine and pointed to the following factors:

1. A genuine multi-party transaction (financing was obtained from outside sources) with economic substance took place;
2. The sale-leaseback was compelled or encouraged by business or regulatory considerations and was not merely the result of tax avoidance considerations; and
3. The lessor retained significant and genuine attributes of the traditional lessor status.

Under these guidelines, if the purchaser-lessor supplied all of the funds for the purchase of the property, that is, did not obtain outside financing, and if the seller-lessee has a repurchase option that takes away any risk born by a lessor, the transaction would be treated as a financing arrangement, rather than as a sale and a leaseback.

¶ 345.2 *IRS Guidelines*

In a series of pronouncements, the IRS has established some guidelines of its own for determining whether there is a true lease or merely a financing arrangement. Although most of these pronouncements are directed to leveraged leasing of equipment, they may offer guidance by way of analogy in the case of the sale-leaseback of real estate. As distilled from Rev. Rul. 55-540,[146] Rev. Proc. 75-21,[147] Rev. Proc. 75-28,[148] Rev. Proc. 76-30,[149] and Rev. Proc. 79-48,[150] the IRS may characterize a lease transaction as a financed sale transaction if one of the following factors is present:

1. The lessee acquires equity through the lease payments;
2. The lessee acquires title to the property after the required number of lease payments have been made;
3. The lessee's total lease payments are due in a relatively short time, and the payments substantially cover the amount required to purchase the asset;
4. The lease payments substantially exceed the fair rental value of the property indicating that the transaction is financed over less than the life of the asset;
5. The property will be acquired by the lessee at the end of the lease term for a nominal sum;

---

[146] 1955-2 CB 39.
[147] 1975-1 CB 715.
[148] 1975-1 CB 752.
[149] 1976-2 CB 647.
[150] 1979-2 CB 529.

6. The lessee participates with the lessor in the acquisition of the asset by guaranteeing a loan or through similar agreements; or

7. The lessor has little or no at-risk investment in the property (in a leveraged equipment lease, the IRS looks for a minimum at-risk investment of 20 percent of the asset's cost).

¶ 347 Variations on the Sale-Leaseback

The straightforward sale-leaseback transaction may be modified in several respects to provide advantages to the parties and to accommodate various situations. The following discusses some of the more common variations.

¶ 347.1 Split Financing

Rather than a sale and leaseback of the entire real estate package, the real estate may be split into its components and only one component made the subject of the sale-leaseback. This is commonly done with a subordinated land lease. When a building is to be constructed, the land is sold to an investor and then leased back. Traditional mortgage financing is obtained by the seller-lessee of the land for the construction of the improvements. The lease is made subordinate to the mortgage. This arrangement provides financing for the land cost of a project which is not normally available through a traditional mortgage.

The tax treatment of these split financing sale-leasebacks hinges on the same factors as a regular sale-leaseback.

¶ 347.2 Related Party Sale-Leasebacks

Related party sale-leasebacks present problems in several respects. First, under Code Sec. 267, a loss on the sale of property to a related party is disallowed. A related party is defined to include family members, controlled corporations, and trustees. This, of course, would only be a consideration if the subject of the sale-leaseback had a value less than its basis.

Even more important, a sale-leaseback involving related parties does not fall squarely within the Supreme Court guidelines for a valid sale-leaseback, which are discussed at ¶ 345.1. There is also the danger that the sale and rental prices set by related parties will not be fair values.

Despite these problems, it is still possible to arrange a sale-leaseback between related parties, especially in light of Tax Court decisions upholding the validity of gift-leaseback transactions. A gift-leaseback is essentially the same as a sale-leaseback, except that the lessee gives the property to the lessor prior to the leaseback. In many cases, these transactions are between a property owner and a trust set up for the benefit of the owner's children. The validity of a sale-leaseback between related parties is more likely to be upheld if the arrangement conforms to the guidelines that have been applied to gift-leasebacks. The Tax Court would also support the transaction if the sale is for less than full value, since this arrangement may be split into a part-sale, part-gift and leaseback.

According to the Tax Court, a gift-leaseback transaction is valid if the following conditions are met:

1. The donor must not retain substantially the same control over the property after the gift-leaseback transaction;
2. The lease must be in writing and call for a reasonable rent;
3. The leaseback must have a bona fide business purpose (although the Fourth and Fifth Circuit Courts seem to look for a business reason for the gift as well); and
4. The donor must not retain any equity in the property and must not have the right to regain the property.[151]

¶ 347.3 *Equity Participation*

As noted above, one of the drawbacks in a sale-leaseback for the seller-lessee is that the property may have significant residual value at the end of the lease term. To overcome this, a sale-leaseback arrangement may give the seller-lessee an option to repurchase at the end of the lease term, although this may confuse the tax treatment of the transaction. Instead of an option to repurchase, the seller-lessee may be given a chance to share in any appreciation experienced by the property after the sale to the purchaser-lessee. This avoids the repurchase option, but may create other problems since, to the extent of the equity participation, the seller-lessee has not really parted with the property.

¶ 347.4 *Tax-Exempt Entity Leasing*

Tax-exempt organizations and government units gain no advantage from depreciation on property that they own or use. This makes these entities prime candidates for the role of seller-lessee in a sale-leaseback. Through a sale of property to an investor followed by a leaseback, tax-exempt entities may obtain indirectly, through reduced rentals, the benefits of depreciation. For the purchaser-lessor, however, a sale-leaseback with a tax-exempt entity means reduced benefits from depreciation. For real estate leased to a tax-exempt entity, the depreciation period is generally 40 years. (Depreciation is considered in Chapter 9.)

---

[151] See *C.J. Mathews*, 61 TC 12, CCH Dec. 32,161, rev'd CA-5, 75-2 USTC ¶ 9734, 520 F.2d 323, cert. denied 424 U.S. 967, 96 S.Ct. 1463, and *R.A. Serbousek*, 36 TCM 479, CCH Dec. 34,353(M), T.C. Memo. 1977-105.

¶ 349 Lease With Option as Conditional Sales Contract

In any lease with an option to purchase, there is the danger that the IRS may view the transaction as a sales contract and the lease as a mere financing device in which the parties are attempting to gain the tax advantages of a lease while giving the lessee the right to take title to the property. In any lease arrangement with a purchase option, the parties must keep the option price high enough and the rental payments low enough so that the transaction will be treated as a lease and the rents will be deductible.

The Tax Court seems to apply an economic reality or intent to purchase test. If the option is exercisable within a period which is clearly less than the useful life of the property, and the rental payments cover a substantial part of what would be the purchase price, the Tax Court is likely to hold that a sale and purchase are intended. This was the result when a taxpayer paid $300,000 for two years' rent on a farm and then exercised an option to buy for an additional $100,000.[152]

In *M&W Gear Co.*,[153] the Court denied a deduction for rents. Through the purported rental payments, the taxpayer acquired a substantial equity in land. Factors the Court considered were:

1. Evidence of an initial intent to purchase by the lessee;
2. Unreasonably high rent;
3. No provision for cancellation of the lease without cause;
4. The lessee was obligated to exercise the purchase option as a matter of economics, since the lessee had made costly improvements that could not be removed and that could be retained only if the option to purchase were exercised.

On the other hand, a 10-year lease with an option to purchase real estate was a lease and not a sale, and payments under the lease were held deductible in *Calcasieu Paper Co., Inc.*[154] The value of the property was not in excess of the option price, only payments made in the last two years of the lease were applied to the purchase price, the amount paid on exercise of the option was 40 percent of the total payments under the lease, the option could be exercised only after a period of six years, and the parties intended to make a lease.

WBSR, Inc.[155] involved the lease of the physical properties of a radio station for one year at a rent of $4,000 and an option to buy for $44,000 less any rent paid. The lessee exercised the option to purchase but was entitled to a deduction for the rent paid under the agreement.

---

[152] *M. Berry*, 11 TCM 301, CCH Dec. 18,882(M).
[153] CA-7, 71-2 USTC ¶ 9555, 446 F.2d 841.
[154] 12 TCM 74, CCH Dec. 19,445(M).
[155] 30 TC 747, CCH Dec. 23,061, Acq. 1958-2 CB 8.

The rent was not excessive in relation to the fair market value of the property. See also *Breece Veneer & Panel Co.,*[156] in which an agreement to pay rent of $100,000 in 60 monthly installments and an option to purchase for $50,000 was held a lease and the rent payments deductible because the lessee had no equity in the property until the option was exercised.

---

[156] CA-7, 56-1 USTC ¶ 9485, 232 F.2d 319.

Part II

Rental and Leasing Arrangements

Introduction to Part II

Acquiring ownership of property is not a prerequisite to obtaining the use of property. Rental and leasing arrangements are common. The desire or necessity by some individuals and businesses to use property without the burdens of ownership, and the desire of others to profit from filling this need, fuels a multi-billion-dollar market in investment real estate.

The tax consequences flowing from the more common payments between tenants and landlords are discussed in Chapter 4. The most common payment, of course, is cash rent. But rent can take many forms and guises. For the business tenant, rent is a deductible expense. For the landlord, rent is taxable income. The amount and timing of a tenant's tax deduction and a landlord's income is explored in some detail, including the special timing and reporting rules for certain deferred or stepped rental agreements. The discussion in this third edition reflects the IRS's adoption of final regulations that extend those special rules to decreasing, as well as increasing, rents.

While rent payments and deposits may be the most common payments that concern landlords and tenants, they are certainly not the only ones. Either party at both the inception and conclusion of a lease may incur substantial costs which are neither rents nor deposits. These costs, of course, have tax consequences. Careful advance planning, as discussed in Chapter 5, assures that all parties receive the most favorable tax treatment possible on the acquisition and the modification, cancellation, disposition, or other termination of a lease agreement.

Leasehold improvements and additions, the subject of Chapter 6, may be made by either the lessor or lessee, according to their agreement. How this responsibility is assigned determines the tax consequences, which can vary significantly depending on the exact arrangements made by the parties. This is one area in which the parties do have a great deal of power to shape the tax outcome by how they structure their lease agreement.

Chapter 4

Payments Between Landlord and Tenant

¶ 400 OVERVIEW OF CHAPTER

When a landlord and tenant enter into a lease agreement, the agreement may obligate the parties to make various payments. The most common of these payments, of course, are the periodic cash payments of rent. But rent can take many forms and guises. Other payments also may pass between landlord and tenant. For the landlord, the primary questions in any payment received from a tenant are whether the payment is income and, if so, when that income must be reported. For the tenant, the questions are whether a payment is deductible for tax purposes and, if so, when the deduction can be taken.

In this chapter, we examine the various forms of rent and their income tax consequences, beginning with an exploration of the concept of rent for tax purposes. The amount and timing of a tenant's tax deduction and a landlord's income are considered, as are the special timing and reporting rules for certain deferred or stepped rental agreements. In some cases, a purchase option written into a lease agreement may affect the characterization of payments between landlord and tenant, and this is also discussed in this chapter. The chapter concludes with a look at security deposits and similar payments.

While these topics cover most of the payments between landlord and tenant, there may be others that fall into the category of lease acquisition or disposition costs. These are considered in Chapter 5. Improvements and additions to leaseholds are the subjects of Chapter 6.

¶ 401 RENT

Rent is the payment by the user of property to the owner of property for its use and enjoyment. In general, gross income includes rentals received or accrued for the occupancy of real estate.[1] Rentals or other payments, required to be made as a condition to the continued use or possession, for purposes of the trade or business, of property to

---

[1] Code Sec. 61(a)(5); Reg. § 1.61-8(a).

which the taxpayer has not taken title or in which the taxpayer has no equity, are deductible as ordinary and necessary business expenses.[2]

The usual form of rent is periodic cash payments, but rent may also be paid in property or services. When rent is paid in this manner, the amount of rent is measured by the value of the property or services. Other arrangements also may govern the payment of rent. Rent may be set as a percentage of the lessee's sales, profits, or some other figure, rather than as a fixed amount. Rent may be paid indirectly, for example, through the payment of the lessor's expenses or debts by the lessee. The key is that if a payment is made as a condition to the use or occupancy of property, other than as a payment toward the purchase of the property, the payment, regardless of its form, is rent.

¶ 403 Percentage Rents

It is a common commercial practice to base rent or a portion of rent on a percentage of the lessee's sales, profits, or some other figure. Unless the parties to the lease are related (see ¶ 409), percentage lease agreements generally are respected for tax purposes and the percentage amounts are income to the lessor and deductible by the lessee. In upholding a lease which called for rent based on a percentage of gross sales, the Fifth Circuit Court of Appeals held that if a lease is fair and reasonable at the time it is executed, then deductions for rent paid during the term of the lease will be upheld regardless of the fact that the percentage of gross sales provision might produce low rental payments in poorer years and high rental payments in good years.[3]

¶ 405 Payment of Lessor's Expenses

Generally, if a lessee pays any of the lessor's expenses, the payments are considered additional rent.[4] Payment of the lessor's expenses by the lessee is a common practice in commercial leases, and these leases are commonly referred to as "net leases." Expenses of the lessor that may be paid by the lessee as additional rent include maintenance and repair expenses, insurance, utilities, real estate taxes, and interest on mortgage or other debt of the lessor. Some leases have even required the lessee to pay principal amortization, as well as interest, on mortgage debt secured by the leased property.

When a lessee pays a lessor's expenses, the lessor reports rental income, even if the expense is a deductible item for the lessor. For example, Reg. § 1.162-11(a) provides that "taxes paid by a tenant to or for a landlord for business property are additional rent and constitute a deductible item to the tenant and taxable income to the landlord, the

---

[2] Code Sec. 162(a)(3).
[3] *Brown Printing Co.*, CA-5, 58-2 USTC ¶ 9534, 255 F.2d 436.
[4] Reg. § 1.61-8(c).

amount of the tax being deductible by the latter." In fact, any ordinary and necessary business expense[5] paid by the lessee attributable to the property leased would be deductible by the lessor as a business expense. The tenant, however, is paying rent and the amount is deductible by the lessee only if the property is being used for business purposes. For example, if the tenant in a residential apartment pays the landlord's property tax on the apartment, the tax is additional rent. The landlord has additional rental income, but a corresponding tax deduction. The tenant, however, is paying rent, and not a property tax, and would not be entitled to a tax deduction for the amount of the property tax paid on behalf of the landlord.

If a lease requires the lessee to pay, as additional rent, the income tax of the lessor attributable to the rental income, the income tax paid by the lessee is additional rent which increases the income tax due. The additional tax increases the rent that, in turn, once again increases the tax due, and so on. This pyramiding that occurs when the lessee is required to pay the lessor's income tax under a net lease is why most net leases do not provide for the payment of the lessor's income tax. There is also the problem of determining the lessor's income tax attributable to the rental income. Most lessors do not want to disclose to their lessees the financial information necessary to determine the amount.

Annual payments made by the lessee following the assumption by the lessee of the lessor's mortgage indebtedness are income to the lessor when made.[6] The same rule applies even if the lessor is not personally liable on the mortgage.[7]

¶ 407 Property Transactions

In some situations, what appear to be transactions in, or sales or exchanges of, property may be treated as rental payments. In Rev. Rul. 73-276,[8] the IRS ruled that the payment of the rents collected by the purchaser after the sale, but which had accrued under a percentage rent agreement prior to the sale of a shopping center was rental income to the seller and not part of the purchase price.

A seller, who sold property for less than its fair value in exchange for the rent-free use of part of the property, received additional consideration for the property equal to the rental value of the property used. This rental value was then deductible by the seller as an advance rental.[9] (Treatment of advance rentals by lessors is considered at

---

[5] Code Sec. 162.
[6] *L.P. Wentz v. Gentsch*, DC Ohio, 40-2 USTC ¶ 9666.
[7] *E.S. Amey*, 22 TC 756, CCH Dec. 20,431.
[8] 1973-1 CB 210.
[9] *Steinway & Sons*, 46 TC 375, CCH Dec. 27,995, Acq. 1967-2 CB 3.

¶ 423.) Another advance rental situation involved the lessor of land who received a share of the proceeds of a leasehold mortgage in return for subordinating his fee interest in the land to the leasehold mortgage. The share of the proceeds received by the land lessor was advance rent.[10]

The sale of property to a lessee who improves the property and then resells the property back to the lessor may be a rental situation rather than two sales transactions. In *W.J. Haag*,[11] the sale of property to the lessee who improved the property and then resold the property to the lessor resulted in a loss to the lessee. This loss was held to be rent paid by the lessee to the lessor, deductible by the lessee and includible in the lessor's income.

¶ 409 Related Parties

The lease of property between related persons offers the potential for tax avoidance, and for this reason the IRS is more sensitive to rental agreements between family members or corporations and their shareholders. As a general rule, as long as a lease agreement is reasonable when entered into and one that would be arrived at in an arm's-length dealing between strangers, the IRS will not challenge the lease and the lessee's rent deductions.[12]

¶ 409.1 *Intra-Family Leases*

When business property is leased by a family member from another family member, there is the danger that the family may use the lease as a means of shifting income. If the lessee pays excessive rent, he will lose the deduction for rent above fair rental value (the amount of rent that would be charged in an arm's-length lease between strangers) since payment of the excess is not a "condition of the continued use or possession" of the property. In all likelihood, the excess rent will be treated as a gift to the lessor.

Determining the fair rental value of property leased to a family member, at times, may be difficult. If the property was previously leased to a stranger, the rent in that situation, most likely, would be considered the fair and reasonable rent that could be charged a family member. Rental figures for comparable properties, an appropriate capitalization rate applied to the value of the property, and professional appraisals also may be used to determine fair rental values.

---

[10] Rev. Rul. 75-226, 1975-1 CB 199.
[11] 40 TC 488, CCH Dec. 26,159, Acq. 1964-2 CB 7, aff'd, CA-8, 64-2 USTC ¶ 9634, 334 F.2d 351.

[12] *S. Imerman*, 7 TC 1030, CCH Dec. 15,429, Acq. 1947-1 CB 2; *H.G. Bender*, 6 TCM 421, CCH Dec. 15,762(M). See also *Brown Printing Co.* cited above.

¶ 409.2 Controlled Corporations

Leases of property between a controlled corporation and its shareholders can run in either direction, that is, the corporation may be either the tenant or landlord. When the corporation is the tenant, the shareholder, through the rental agreement, is able to draw money out of the corporation in a tax-deductible manner. When the shareholder is the tenant, the shareholder may obtain use of the corporate property while, in effect, paying rent to oneself. In either case, there is the temptation to use the lease as a tax avoidance device, and the IRS is sensitive to such arrangements.

If a corporation pays excessive rent to a shareholder, the excess rent is treated as the payment of a nondeductible dividend.[13] Similarly, a bargain rental of corporate property to a shareholder may be construed as payment of a constructive dividend equal to the bargain element.[14] The shareholder, however, would be entitled to deduct the bargain rent paid in this situation, provided the leased property was used in a trade or business of the shareholder.

As in an intra-family lease, as long as the rent, including percentage rent, in a lease between a controlled corporation and shareholder is fair when agreed to and would be accepted by parties dealing at arm's length, the IRS will accept the lease agreement.[15]

In some cases, it is possible for a shareholder to gain extra advantage by leasing unimproved property to a controlled corporation. If unimproved land, or property on which improvements can be made or added, is leased to the corporation, the corporation can make improvements. When the lease expires, the improvements become the property of the lessor-shareholder, and the shareholder may realize no taxable income because of the value added to the property by the corporation.[16] Although Code Sec. 109 does provide that the value of improvements made by the lessee is not gross income to the lessor on the termination of a lease, there is some danger that the IRS may find a constructive dividend if, following a lease to a controlled corporation, the property reverts to the shareholder-lessor long before the end of the improvement's useful life.[17]

Reallocation of Income

Lease agreements between shareholders and their controlled corporations also run the risk that the IRS may use its power to allocate

---

[13] *Limericks, Inc.,* 7 TC 1129, CCH Dec. 15,466, aff'd CA-5, 48-1 USTC ¶ 9146, 165 F.2d 483.
[14] Rev. Rul. 58-1, 1958-1 CB 173.
[15] *W.E. Davis & Sons, Inc.,* 41 TCM 1263, CCH Dec. 37,828(M), T.C. Memo. 1981-178; see also *Brown Printing Co.* cited above.
[16] Code Sec. 109.
[17] *Safway Steel Scaffolds Co. of Georgia,* CA-5, 79-1 USTC ¶ 9253, 590 F.2d 1360.

income among commonly controlled trades, businesses or organizations in order to properly reflect income.[18] Leasing property to a controlled corporation may be a trade or business, and the Tax Court has supported reallocation of income among shareholders and their corporations by the IRS.[19]

Reallocation of Rental Income and Deductions

Code Sec. 482 also applies to leases between two corporations that are owned by the same shareholders. If the rent charged one corporation by the other is either too high or too low, rental income and deductions may be reallocated between the corporations and cause the shareholders to receive constructive dividends from one corporation which are deemed to be capital contributions to the other corporation.[20]

¶ 409.3 Matching Lessee's Deduction to Lessor's Income

Were it not for Code Sec. 267, an accrual basis lessee could accrue and deduct rent owed to a related cash basis lessor before the lessor receives the rental income. Code Sec. 267(a)(2), however, requires the matching of deductions and income for expense and interest payments between certain related parties. Under this rule, a lessee is not allowed to deduct rent owed to a related taxpayer until the day that the corresponding income is includible in the lessor's income. In effect, an accrual basis lessee is placed on the cash basis as to rents owed to a related lessor.

The relationships that require the matching of deductions and income are the same as those for which losses on sales or exchanges are disallowed,[21] with one addition. Matching of expense deductions and income is required between a personal service corporation and any employee-owner of the corporation.[22] Matching is also required for any of the following relationships listed in Code Sec. 267(b):

1. Members of the same family, defined as including only brothers and sisters, spouse, ancestors, and lineal descendants;

2. A corporation and an individual who owns, directly or indirectly, more than 50 percent in value of the outstanding stock of the corporation;

---

[18] Code Sec. 482.

[19] *T.B. Fegan*, 71 TC 791, CCH Dec. 35,880, aff'd CA-10, 81-1 USTC ¶ 9436; *R.D. Cooper*, 64 TC 576, CCH Dec. 33,327; see also Rev. Rul. 88-38, 1988-1 CB 246.

[20] *Equitable Publishing Co.*, CA-3, 66-1 USTC ¶ 9609, 356 F.2d 514, cert. denied 385 U.S. 822, 87 S.Ct. 50.

[21] Code Sec. 267(b).

[22] Code Sec. 267(a)(2).

3. Two corporations that are members of the same controlled group (50 percent parent-subsidiary or brother-sister corporations);[23]
4. The grantor and fiduciary of a trust;
5. Fiduciaries of two different trusts if the same person is the grantor of both trusts;
6. The fiduciary and beneficiary of a trust;
7. A fiduciary and beneficiary of different trusts if the same person is the grantor of both trusts;
8. A trust fiduciary and a corporation if more than 50 percent in value of the outstanding stock of the corporation is owned, directly or indirectly, by or for the trust or the grantor of the trust;
9. A tax-exempt educational or charitable organization and a person who controls, directly or indirectly, the organization, or a member of the control person's family;
10. A corporation and a partnership if the same persons own more than 50 percent in value of the outstanding stock of the corporation, and more than 50 percent of the capital or profit interest in the partnership;
11. An S corporation and another S corporation if the same persons own more than 50 percent of the value of the outstanding stock of each corporation; and
12. An S corporation and a regular corporation if the same persons own more than 50 percent in value of the outstanding stock of each corporation.

¶ 411 TENANT'S RENT DEDUCTION

Rent, if it is paid for the use of business property, is deductible.[24] Rent that is considered a personal, living or family expense, however, is not deductible.[25] Therefore, rent on a personal residence, apartment, or vacation property generally is not deductible (personal residences are considered generally in Part V; mixed-use residences, part business/part personal, are specifically considered in Chapter 18).

If rent is paid in property other than money, the amount deductible is the fair market value of the property. If a tenant pays for rent by providing services for the landlord, the amount deductible is the amount of cash rental that was agreed to (provided, of course, that the cash rental was a reasonable fair rental). The tenant who pays rent by

---

[23] Code Secs. 267(f) and 1563(a).
[24] Code Sec. 162(a)(3).
[25] Code Sec. 262.

providing services, however, must include the value of the services in income. Presumably, the value of the services and the fair rental value are the same. In other words, the tenant has income from providing services and an equal offsetting deduction for rent.

Not everything denominated rent by the parties is deductible. Rent paid under a lease with an option to purchase may, in some cases, be treated as part payment of the purchase price (see ¶ 441). There may be no deduction for excessive rent paid to a related party as discussed above.

A lessee using the accrual method of accounting deducts rent for the year in which the rent accrues, regardless of when it is paid.

Example: The Taxpayer, who is an accrual-method, calendar-year taxpayer rents business property under a lease running from December 1, 2002, to November 30, 2003. Even if the Taxpayer makes no rent payments in 2002, the Taxpayer is still entitled to deduct the amount of rent attributable to December for the 2002 tax year. Similarly, if the Taxpayer pays three months' rent in December 2002, the deduction for 2002 is limited to one month's rent. The Taxpayer cannot deduct the other two months' rent in 2002, even though payment was made in 2002. The deduction for the two months' rent attributable to 2003 must be taken in 2003.

A lessee using the cash method of accounting cannot deduct rent until it is paid, regardless of the period to which it relates. Rent paid in advance, however, may not be currently deductible. Rather, the cash method lessee may have to take deductions for rent paid in advance over the periods to which the prepayment applies (see ¶ 413).

¶ 413 Advance Rents

The rationale for denying a cash method taxpayer a full deduction for advance payments of rent is that the payment is creating an asset, the interest in the leasehold. Reg. § 1.263(a)-2 provides that the cost of "acquisition, construction, or erection of buildings, machinery and equipment, furniture and fixtures, and similar property having a useful life substantially beyond the taxable year" is a capital expenditure. Also, in providing rules for the timing of deductions, Reg. § 1.461-1(a) provides that "under the cash receipts and disbursements method of accounting ... if an expenditure results in the creation of an asset having a useful life which extends substantially beyond the close of the taxable year, such an expenditure may not be deductible, or may be deductible only in part, for the taxable year in which made."

Accordingly, advance rentals are deductible on the cash basis only for the year to which they apply.[26] The same rule has been held to apply specifically to an accrual-method taxpayer.[27] See also Reg. § 1.162-11(a), which provides that "if a leasehold is acquired for business purposes for a specified sum, the purchaser may take as a deduction in his return an aliquot part of such sum each year, based on the number of years the lease has to run." (Note that an advance payment that applies to the entire lease term may be considered a lease acquisition cost. Lease acquisition costs are discussed further at ¶ 501.)

Despite the general rule for advance rents, some court decisions have allowed deductions for rent paid in advance when the prepaid rent applied in part to the current year and in part to the following year.[28] In *M.J. Zaninovich,* the Ninth Circuit applied Reg. § 1.461-1(a) to a 20-year lease that required the first year's rent, for the period December-November, to be paid in advance. The court allowed the deduction for the full year's rent when paid because, in the opinion of the court, one year was not "substantially beyond the close of the taxable year." The court also noted that the prepayment of 12 months' rent was a common business practice in the type of lease involved and that the prepayment did not distort income or permit the evasion of tax.

While *M.J. Zaninovich* provides precedent for taking a deduction for up to a year's rent when at least part of the payment applies to the current year, it does not support a deduction for prepayment of a year's rent in the year of payment when the lease term does not begin until the following year. In such a case, the deduction, most likely, would have to be deferred until the year the lease begins. For instance, the "one-year rule" of *M.J. Zaninovich* was not followed in *G.S. Sorrell, Jr.,*[29] in which rent-up fees paid in 1977 by a partnership to the general partner were not deductible in 1977 since the lease terms began in 1978. The payment was considered a capital expenditure, amortizable over the life of the leases, beginning no earlier than the year the leases began.

¶ 415 Graduated Rents

Rather than level rentals throughout the lease term, a lease may provide for graduated rentals that increase or decrease over time, beyond adjustments keyed to factors such as inflation or rises in taxes

---

[26] *N.B. Smith,* 51 TC 429, CCH Dec. 29,272; *Baton Coal Co.,* CA-3, 2 USTC ¶ 788, 51 F.2d 469, cert. denied 284 U.S. 674, 52 S.Ct. 129.
[27] *G.W. Keeling,* 30 TCM 954, CCH Dec. 30,968(M), T.C. Memo. 1971-224; *H.L. Wood,* 34 TCM 817, CCH Dec. 33,267(M), T.C. Memo. 1975-189.

[28] *M.J. Zaninovich,* CA-9, 80-1 USTC ¶ 9342, 616 F.2d 429; *H.H. Hoopengarner,* 80 TC 538, CCH Dec. 39,968, aff'd CA-9, 745 F.2d 66.

[29] 53 TCM 1362, CCH Dec. 44,054(M), T.C. Memo. 1987-351, rev'd on another issue CA-11, 89-2 USTC ¶ 9521, 882 F.2d 484.

or other expenses. Graduated rent arrangements are generally designed to accommodate special situations of the lessor or lessee.

¶ 415.1 Decrease in Rents

In the case of decreasing rents, there is the danger that the IRS may assert that the higher initial rents are advance rents that should be applied to later years of the lease. Advance rents do not have to be a single payment.

If advance rents are paid in installments over a period of years, the advance rents still must be deducted over the periods to which they relate. When a lease obligated the lessee to pay $10,000 annually during the first 25 years of a 99-year lease, with no payments required in the remaining years of the lease, only 1/99 of the aggregate rent was deductible in each year.[30] Said the court, "advance payments of rent, made in consideration of a lease for a longer period of time, have the character of capital investments whose benefits are spread throughout the life of the lease, and only an aliquot part of such expenditure is deductible in any tax year."

If there is some sound business reason for a lease with decreasing rents and the lease is a result of arm's-length bargaining, however, the lessee should take the higher deductions in the earlier years. See *Bellingham Cold Storage Co.*,[31] in which it was held that higher rents paid by the lessee on three leases in their earlier years were not advance rental payments allocable to the later years.

Renewal Options

Suppose that instead of decreasing rent over a fixed lease term, a lease fixes a level rent over the term of the lease, but also gives the lessee the option to renew at substantially reduced rental. Might the higher rents in the initial term be considered advance rentals applicable to the renewal term?

In Rev. Rul. 60-122,[32] the IRS ruled that a portion of the total payments in the first 36 months of a lease was advance rent applicable to a second 36-month renewal period that called for substantially reduced rents. While the lease involved equipment, the same rationale would seem applicable to real estate. Looking to whether the lessee would actually renew the lease, the IRS pointed to the nominal rent that had to be paid over the renewal period which made it "reasonable to assume . . . the lease will be renewed in accordance with the agree-

---

[30] *Main & McKinney Bldg. Co. of Houston, Texas*, CA-5, 40-2 USTC ¶ 9558, 113 F.2d 81, cert. denied 311 U.S. 688, 61 S.Ct. 66.

[31] 64 TC 51, CCH Dec. 33,145.
[32] 1960-1 CB 56.

ment." (See the discussion of the effect of renewal options on lease acquisition costs at ¶ 505.)

If factors other than low rent would influence the decision to renew beyond the initial term, it might be possible to show that it is not "reasonable to assume" that a lease will be renewed at a lower rent. In such a case, a lessee may be justified in taking the higher deductions during the initial term of the lease.[33]

Leases Involving More Than $250,000

Code Sec. 467(f) gives the IRS the power to prescribe regulations to make decreasing graduated rentals on leases involving more than $250,000 in rental payments subject to rules similar to those applicable to deferred or stepped rental agreements.

The IRS issued proposed regulations under Code Sec. 467 on June 3, 1996, that would apply to rental agreements that provide for decreasing, as well as increasing, rent, and to deferred or prepaid rent. The IRS adopted that rule as final in T.D. 8820 on April 30, 1999.

¶ 415.2 Increase in Rents

If a lease calls for graduated rents that increase over time, there is no question of advance rents. Generally, the deduction for rent would follow the usual rules, that is, a deduction would be allowed for the increasing rents as they were paid or accrued, depending on the lessee's method of accounting. However, if the graduated rents are on a lease involving more than $250,000, the rent payments would be subject to the special rules of Code Sec. 467 that apply to deferred or stepped rents. These rules are discussed at ¶ 431.

¶ 421 LANDLORD'S RENT INCOME

Gross income includes rents received or accrued for the occupancy of real estate.[34] A cash method lessor includes rents in income for the year in which they are received. An accrual-method lessor includes rents in income for the year in which they accrue or are received, whichever is earlier (see the discussion of advance rents at ¶ 423).

When a lease calls for percentage rents based on a percentage of the lessee's sales, a lessor using accrual accounting includes the rents in income for the period during which the sales are made, even if actual payment is not due until the following year. In *Heer-Andres Investment Co.*,[35] the Tax Court ruled that additional rent measured by the lessee's net sales, which the lessor was entitled to for its fiscal year

---

[33] *Gem, Inc.*, DC Miss, 61-1 USTC ¶ 9361, 192 F.Supp. 841.
[34] Code Sec. 61(a)(5); Reg. § 1.61-8(a).
[35] 17 TC 786, CCH Dec. 18,623, Nonacq. 1952-1 CB 5.

ending on January 31, accrued for the year ending on January 31, even though the additional rent was not payable until February. This ruling applies even if a portion of the additional rent might have to be returned to the lessee after the end of the taxable year.[36]

In some situations, improvements or additions made by a lessee to the lessor's property may be treated as rent income to the lessor (see ¶ 611).

¶ 423 Advance Rents

The regulations are quite clear as to the treatment by the lessor of advance rents: "Except as provided in section 467 and the regulations thereunder, gross income includes advance rentals, which must be included in income for the year of receipt regardless of the period covered or the method of accounting employed by the taxpayer."[37] (See ¶ 431 for a discussion of the Code Sec. 467 rules.)

If the Tax Code were symmetrical, of course, advance rents would be includible in income as earned rather than as received, just as payments of advance rents are deductible for the periods to which they relate rather than as paid. Unfortunately, the benefits of such symmetry are denied lessors. Despite the harshness of the rule and the possible bunching of income that it can create, the courts have been virtually unanimous in holding that rents received are income in the year of receipt, on a cash or accrual basis, even if no part of the advance payment is earned in the year of receipt.[38]

As long as the landlord has the unrestricted right to use advance rents, the rents must be included in income for the year received, even if the landlord may have to return some or all of the advance payment at some time in the future. For instance, the advance payment of the last year's rent under a 10-year lease was held to be income to an accrual basis lessor in the year received, even though the lessor was obligated to refund all or part of it if the premises were substantially destroyed prior to the expiration of the lease.[39]

¶ 425 Assignments and Loans

Sometimes, the parties to a lease may attempt to cast their transaction in some other form in order to avoid the immediate taxation of advance rents. An amount paid by the "purchaser" for the assignment of a lease was treated as an advance rental payment,

---

[36] *Rod Realty Co.*, 26 TCM 243, CCH Dec. 28,374(M), T.C. Memo. 1967-49.

[37] Reg. § 1.61-8(b).

[38] See, for example, *Hyde Park Realty, Inc.*, CA-2, 54-1 USTC ¶ 9305, 211 F.2d 462; *B.D. Lyon*, CA-9, 38-2 USTC ¶ 9356, 97 F.2d 70; *Kohler-Campbell Corp.*, CA-4, 62-1 USTC ¶ 9237, 298 F.2d 911; *J. & E. Enter-* *prises, Inc.*, 26 TCM 944, CCH Dec. 28,622(M), T.C. Memo. 1967-191.

[39] *New Capital Hotel, Inc.*, CA-6, 58-2 USTC ¶ 9912, 261 F.2d 437. See also Rev. Rul. 65-141, 1965-1 CB 210, in which the IRS ruled advance rents currently taxable even if paid to an escrow agent and even if the tenant may be entitled to a refund.

reportable by the "seller" as ordinary income in the year received, when the facts indicate the relationship between the parties to be that of lessor and lessee.[40] The value of a fee interest received on the execution of a lease, along with the right to annual rents, is an advance rental and taxable when received.[41]

W.B. Williams[42] involved an attempt to use a purported loan to avoid the inclusion of advance rents in the lessor's income when received. The lessee lent money to the lessor and the lessor was to repay the loan out of yearly payments received from the lessee for the use of land and timber. The court ruled that the "loan" was, in fact, prepaid rent. The lessor did not negotiate a loan separate from the lease, and the amount "loaned" was in direct relation to the annual rental payments. Of course, it should be possible for a lessor and lessee to work out a loan separate and apart from their lease agreement. The loan agreement should be embodied in a promissory note that contains a definite date for repayment. Also, the loan payments should not exactly match the rental payments called for in the lease agreement.

Not all payments received by a landlord, however, are immediately taxable. Advance payments that are in the nature of security deposits may escape current tax. See the discussion of deposits at ¶ 451.

¶ 431 DEFERRED OR STEPPED RENTAL AGREEMENTS

Deferred or stepped rental agreements offer the potential for tax savings when the lessor uses the cash method of accounting and the lessee uses the accrual method of accounting. Without some special statutory provision, the parties to a lease could agree to defer the payment of rent to the end of the lease. The amount of the payment, of course, would reflect the delay. In this fashion, the lessee could deduct rent as it accrued, but the landlord would not have to report income until the rent was actually paid. The Tax Reform Act of 1984 addressed this potential for tax avoidance with special rules for what are termed "Section 467 rental agreements."

Essentially, the rules of Code Sec. 467 are an extension of the original issue discount rules (discussed at ¶ 331) to leases that involve deferred or stepped rents. The essential thrust of the rules is to require the matching of rental income and deductions in Code Sec. 467 rental agreements and the inclusion of an interest factor on deferred rents in much the same fashion as the OID rules require the matching of income and deductions and the inclusion of an interest factor on deferred payment sales of property. Since April 30, 1999, similar rules apply to decreasing as well as increasing rentals.

---

[40] Rev. Rul. 57-537, 1957-2 CB 52.
[41] Rev. Rul. 66-209, 1966-2 CB 299.
[42] CA-5, 68-1 USTC ¶ 9394, 395 F.2d 508.

¶ 433 Section 467 Rental Agreements

A Section 467 rental agreement subject to Code Sec. 467 is any rental agreement for the use of tangible property under which:

1. There is at least one amount allocable to the use of property during a calendar year which is to be paid after the close of the following calendar year (a deferred rent), or

2. There are increases in the amount to be paid as rent under the agreement (stepped rents).

If the sum of the amounts to be paid under a rental agreement is $250,000 or less, Code Sec. 467 does not apply to the agreement, regardless of when the rent payments are made.[43]

In all Section 467 rental agreements that allocate rents (other than certain tax avoidance transactions discussed below), the lessor and lessee treat as rent for the current period the present value of rent to be paid after the close of the period that is allocable to the current period.[44] In addition, both the lessor and lessee take into account as interest an amount calculated by applying an interest rate equal to 110 percent of the applicable federal rate to the sum of rents taken into account in prior years but still unpaid as of the current year.[45] The applicable federal rates are the same as those under the imputed interest and original issue discount rules discussed in Chapter 3.

When Code Sec. 467 applies to rental payments, the lessor and lessee are both placed on the accrual method of accounting as to deferred or stepped rents, and both must recognize an interest element on the deferred rent. The rule eliminates any mismatching of income and deductions that would otherwise occur when there is a cash-basis lessor and an accrual-basis lessee.

While the terms of Code Sec. 467 are directed to deferred or stepped rents, the IRS was directed to issue regulations with comparable rules for agreements involving decreasing rents.[46] After 12 years, the IRS finally issued proposed regulations under Code Sec. 467 on June 3, 1996, and final regulations on April 30, 1999, that apply to rental agreements that provide increasing or decreasing rents, or deferred or prepaid rent. The regulations do not address the application of Code Sec. 467 to transactions known as "lease strips" or "stripping transactions," which are described in Notice 95-53 (1995-44 IRB 21). Regulations were issued under Code Sec. 7701(l) recharacterizing stripping transactions. The regulations also do not provide for an adjustment to Code Sec. 467 rent and interest if a Code Sec. 467 rental

---

[43] Code Sec. 467(d).
[44] Code Sec. 467(b)(1).
[45] Code Sec. 467(a)(2) and (e)(4).
[46] Code Sec. 467(f).

agreement is modified. However, if a modification is "substantial," it is treated as a new Code Sec. 467 rental agreement.

The regulations generally are effective after April 30, 1999, but the regulations that apply to tax avoidance transactions ("disqualified leasebacks and long-term agreements," see ¶ 435) apply to those transactions entered into after June 3, 1996.

As with the imputed interest and OID rules discussed in Chapter 3, the mathematics involved in the rent accrual and interest calculations for Code Sec. 467 rental agreements are best left to computers. The regulations do contain numerous examples.

¶ 435 Constant Rental Accrual in Tax Avoidance Transactions

If a Section 467 rental agreement does not allocate rents, the rent that accrues in a taxable year is determined on a level present-value basis. The amount is the amount that, if paid at the close of each lease period, would result in an aggregate present value equal to the present value of the aggregate payments required under the lease.[47] Present value is determined using 110 percent of the applicable federal rate. The same rule applies to tax avoidance transactions as defined in Code Sec. 467(b)(4).

A tax avoidance transaction is any Section 467 rental agreement that has as a principal purpose the avoidance of income tax and that involves either a:

1. Leaseback to any person who had an interest in the property at any time within two years before the leaseback (or a person related to such person), or

2. Long-term agreement, which is a lease for a term in excess of 75 percent of the statutory recovery period for the property.

The statutory recovery period for residential rental property and nonresidential real property is 19 years, and the period for 15-year and 20-year property (for purposes of computing depreciation under Code Sec. 168) is 15 years.[48] For most real property, therefore, a long-term lease agreement is one that is for a term of more than 14 years and three months.

Under regulations, the IRS, rather than the parties to the rental agreement, determine whether a rental agreement is a disqualified leaseback or long-term agreement.[49] The regulations also provide that if there is a significant difference in marginal tax rates of the lessor and the lessee, the rental agreement is closely scrutinized, and clear and

---

[47] Code Sec. 467(b)(2) and (e)(1).
[48] Code Sec. 467(e)(3).
[49] Reg. § 1.467-3(b).

convincing evidence is required to establish that tax avoidance is not as principal purpose for providing increasing or decreasing rent.[50]

¶ 435.1 Exemptions from Rental Agreement Rules

Certain agreements may be exempt from the Section 467 rental agreement rules under regulations issued by the IRS.[51] The IRS has issued regulations that incorporate the circumstances the IRS was directed to consider in drawing the exceptions.[52] These safe harbors include:

1. Changes in amounts paid determined by reference to price indices,
2. Rents based on a fixed percentage of lessee receipts or similar amounts,
3. Reasonable rent holidays, or
4. Changes in amounts paid to unrelated third parties (this would allow increases in rent keyed to increases in the lessor's operating costs without subjecting the lease to the Code Sec. 467 rules).

The final regulations also contain several safe harbors for various types of contingent payments that either are intended to compensate the lessor for costs unrelated to the lessor's continuing investment in the leased property or are so contingent that they should not be taken into account for purposes of Code Sec. 467 until the liability for the payment becomes fixed. Safe harbors are provided for payments required to be made by the lessee: in the event of damage, destruction, or loss of the leased property; for the failure of the property to maintain a specified residual value; for the failure of the property to be returned to the lessor at the end of the lease term in the condition specified in the agreement; or for the failure of the lessor to obtain the income tax benefits contemplated by the agreement. In addition, a provision requiring late payment charges is not taken into account in determining whether tax avoidance is present in a leaseback or long-term agreement. Limitations on the scope of these safe harbors are provided in order to ensure that the provisions are included in the agreement for a valid business purpose and that the provisions are not used to achieve tax avoidance.

The final regulations also added a safe harbor for certain variable interest rate provisions. Under that safe harbor, a rent adjustment provision is disregarded if it is based solely on the dollar amount of changes in the lessor's interest costs, and only if the lessor and the

---

[50] Reg. § 1.467-3(c).
[51] Code Sec. 467(b)(5).
[52] Reg. § 1.467-1(c)(2)(iii).

¶ 435.1

lender are not related and the indebtedness is evidenced by a variable rate debt instrument.

The regulations also contain a safe harbor that says that tax avoidance is not a principal purpose for providing increasing or decreasing rents, if the rents allocable to each calendar year of the lease do not vary from the average annual rents over the entire lease term by more than 10 percent (15 percent in the case of long-term leases of real estate).[53]

¶ 435.2   Recapture in Leasebacks and Long-Term Agreements

If the lessor under a Section 467 rental agreement that involves a leaseback or a long-term agreement which is not subject to the constant rental accrual rule sells the property, the lessor must recapture as ordinary income a portion of the gain realized on the sale.[54] The recapture provision prevents the conversion of ordinary income into capital gain that would occur when the seller receives consideration for the property that includes, in part, consideration for the higher rentals to be paid to the purchaser after the sale. The recapture amount is generally the prior understated inclusions, defined as the excess, if any, of:

1. The amount the lessor would have taken into account prior to the disposition of the property had the lessor been required to reflect income under the constant rental amount of a tax avoidance transaction, over

2. The actual amount taken into account under Code Sec. 467 by the lessor prior to the disposition.[55]

Recapture, however, is generally limited to the amount of gain realized on the property and may not be more than the excess of the amount realized (or fair market value in case of a disposition other than by sale, exchange or involuntary conversion) over the adjusted basis of the property, reduced by the amount of gain treated as ordinary income under any other income tax provision.[56]

¶ 441   LEASES WITH PURCHASE OPTIONS

A lease with an option to buy is a common business arrangement. The lessee secures the use of the property without an immediate commitment to purchase the property. The lessor, who is probably looking to sell, receives immediate cash from rent to carry the property until it is sold. The question for tax purposes in lease-option situations is whether the lessee is actually leasing the property or, in fact, is buying the property. Since the tax treatment of a purchase transaction

[53] Reg. § 1.467-3(c)(3).
[54] Code Sec. 467(c)(1).
[55] Code Sec. 467(c)(3).
[56] Code Sec. 467(c)(2)(B).

and a lease transaction is so different, it is important that the parties draft their agreement in order to obtain the desired results.

A deduction for rent under Code Sec. 162(a)(3) is available only if the taxpayer "has not taken or is not taking title" to the property or if the taxpayer "has no equity" in the property. If a purported lease is, in fact, a sale, the lessee may not deduct "rent" payments. Rather, these payments become part of the purchase price that must be capitalized and, in the case of business property, recovered through depreciation. Any payments received by the lessor that actually represent part of the purchase price for property might be treated as capital gain rather than ordinary income, and deductions for depreciation would be denied the lessor. As long as the tax rates on capital gain and ordinary income were the same, there was little meaning to this distinction as far as the lessor was concerned. However, on a purchase, the purported lessor realizes income only to the extent of gain on the property, while rent is taxable in full.

¶ 443 Lease as Sales Contract

In any lease with an option to purchase, there is the danger that the IRS may view the transaction as a sales contract and the lease as a mere financing device in which the parties are attempting to gain the tax advantages of a lease while giving the lessee an equity interest in the property. In any lease with a purchase option, the parties must keep the option price high enough and the rental payments low enough so that the transaction will be treated as a lease and the rents will be deductible. Rents that are unreasonably high when combined with an option price that is low indicate that the rent payments are, in fact, payments on the purchase price.

In *D.M. Haggard*,[57] a lease for land called for rent of $10,000 for 1948 and $12,000 for 1949. This was substantially higher than the rental value of the land. Along with the lease, the parties executed an option under which the lessor granted the lessee the right to purchase the land for $24,000 in 1950. The lessee paid the lessor $2,000 for this option. The lessor had previously negotiated for the sale of the land for $48,000. In this situation, the lessee was not allowed to deduct the "rent" payments because the lease and the option conferred an equity in the property to the lessee.[58]

In *W. Oesterreich*,[59] it was the nominal option price that tipped the scales in favor of a purchase rather than a lease transaction. The purported lease was for a term of 68 years, and, at the end of the lease,

---

[57] CA-9, 57-1 USTC ¶ 9230, 241 F.2d 288.
[58] See also *E.H. Beus*, 58-2 USTC ¶ 9945, CA-9, 261 F.2d 176.
[59] CA-9, 55-2 USTC ¶ 9733, 226 F.2d 798.

the lessee could acquire title to the property for a token consideration of $10. In this case, the payments under the "lease" were capital gains to the lessor and capital expenditures to the lessee because the "lease" was actually a contract of sale. Another factor in *W. Oesterreich* was that the lessee was required to make substantial improvements to the property and this investment could only be recovered by exercising the option to buy.[60]

¶ 445 Lease or Sale Distinguished

For a further discussion of how to distinguish between a lease and a sale, see the discussion relating to sale-leaseback transactions at ¶ 345 and the discussion of the treatment of a lease with an option as a conditional sales contract at ¶ 349. The IRS guidelines for distinguishing between a lease and a sale of equipment contained in Rev. Rul. 55-540, and discussed at ¶ 345.2, also may be helpful in distinguishing between a lease and a sale of real property.

¶ 451 DEPOSITS

The lessor of property may require the lessee to pay a deposit as security for faithful compliance with the terms of the lease. In a commercial transaction, the lessor may be free to use such deposits as the lessor sees fit and may not be required to pay the lessee interest on the deposit. In some states, however, the law requires that deposits be held in trust by lessors and that they be treated as the property of the lessee until such time as the lessor may apply the deposits to rent under the lease or until the lessee defaults on the lease.[61]

¶ 453 Lessee's Deduction

The lessee may not deduct a security deposit when paid if the deposit is to be returned. If the lessor may apply the security deposit against rent owed by the lessee, the proper time for the lessee's deduction is when the deposit is actually applied against the rent. If the lessee forfeits a deposit because of a breach of the lease, the lessee deducts the amount in the year of the breach.

Note that the question of whether a deposit is actually the payment of advance rent does not really arise as to the proper timing of the lessee's deduction. Since advance rents are deductible by the lessee only for the period to which they relate, the timing of the deduction is the same regardless of whether a payment is advance rent or a security deposit that may be applied against future rent. Such is not the case with regard to the timing of the lessor's income.

---

[60] See also *Wilshire Holding Corp.*, CA-9, 59-1 USTC ¶ 9123, 262 F.2d 51.

[61] See, for example, New York General Obligation Laws § 7-103.

¶ 455 Lessor's Income

A lessor includes in income advance rents when they are received regardless of the method of accounting and regardless of the periods which the advance rents apply, subject to the rent accrual and interest rules that apply to Code Sec. 467 rental agreements discussed at ¶ 431. A security deposit that must be returned to the lessee on the termination of a lease in the absence of a default is clearly not taxable to the lessor on receipt, even if the lessor has the unrestricted right to use the funds for his or her own purposes. On the other hand, if a deposit is to be applied to the rent for the last period under the lease, it may be treated as advance rent, even if it also serves as security, unless the deposit must be held in trust or in escrow on behalf of the lessee, either under the terms of the lease or under state law.

If the intention of the parties is that an amount equal to the rent for one period paid on execution of a lease is to stand as security for the lessee's performance and the lessor must account to the lessee for the amount of the deposit plus interest, the lessor does not report income in the year of receipt, even if the amount is to be applied to the last year's rent.[62]

If the lessor is not required to account to the lessee for the principal amount of the payment and interest, a security deposit is includible in income.[63] In *J. & E. Enterprises, Inc.*,[64] security deposits that the lessor had the option to refund after five years or to apply to rental payments due during the sixth year of a 10-year lease were held to be advance rental payments includible in the lessor's income in the year of receipt. The lessor had unrestricted use of the money.

See also the discussion of the difference between advance payments and security deposits contained in Rev. Rul. 72-519.[65] The IRS ruled that a deposit received by a supplier of fuel from service stations to protect its title to, and interest in, the fuel before its sale was a security deposit, but a deposit paid by a new customer to a water company was an advance payment for water. By analogy, a deposit to secure the lessor's interest in the lease by securing the tenant's performance would not be currently taxable

---

[62] *Clinton Hotel Realty Corp.*, CA-5, 42-2 USTC ¶ 9559, 128 F.2d 968; *R.L. Harcum*, DC Va, 58-2 USTC ¶ 9684, 164 F.Supp. 650; *J. Mantell*, 17 TC 1143, CCH Dec. 18,733, Acq. 1952-1 CB 3.

[63] *Astor Holding Co.*, CA-5, 43-1 USTC ¶ 9408, 135 F.2d 47.

[64] 26 TCM 944, CCH Dec. 28,622(M), T.C. Memo. 1967-191.

[65] 1972-2 CB 32.

Chapter 5

Lease Acquisition and Disposition

¶ 500 OVERVIEW OF CHAPTER

While rent payments and deposits may be the most common payments that concern lessors and lessees in business and commercial leases, they are certainly not the only ones. There may be substantial payments at both the inception and conclusion of a lease that are not rents, advance or otherwise, or security deposits. Both the lessor and the lessee may incur substantial costs merely to obtain the lease. Also, the modification, cancellation, disposition or other termination of a lease may entail significant payments. These payments may be made by the lessor, the lessee, or some third party acquiring the lease from the existing lessee. All of these costs and payments have tax consequences. Careful advance planning will assure that all parties receive the most favorable tax treatment possible.

¶ 501 LEASE ACQUISITION COSTS

Lease acquisition costs may be incurred by the lessor or lessee, or both. The lessee must amortize costs incurred to acquire a lease over the term of the lease.[1] For the lessor, a similar rule applies. Costs incurred by a lessor to secure a lease are capital expenditures that must be spread ratably over the term of the lease, regardless of its length, and regardless of whether the lessor uses the cash or accrual method of accounting.[2] The same rule applies to a lessee who incurs costs to obtain a sublessee.[3]

Example: A Corp. currently leases a building to B Corp. and the remaining term of the lease is five years. If C pays B Corp. $10,000 to assign the lease to C so that C can occupy the leased building, C would deduct $2,000 per year for each of the five years remaining on the lease to amortize the lease acquisition cost of $10,000.

Similarly, if A Corp. paid B Corp. $10,000 in order to vacate the lease so that it could lease the property to C for five years, A Corp. would deduct $2,000 per year for each of the five years of the term of the new lease.

---

[1] Reg. § 1.162-11(a).
[2] See, for example, *M.C. Young*, CA-9, 3 USTC ¶ 967 59 F.2d 691, cert. denied 287 U.S. 652, 53 S.Ct. 116; *E.A. Renwick*, CA-7, 37-1 USTC ¶ 9010, 87 F.2d 123;
P.W. Thielking, 53 TCM 746, CCH Dec. 43,891(M), T.C. Memo. 1987-227.
[3] *Bonwit Teller & Co.*, CA-2, 2 USTC ¶ 797, 53 F.2d 381, cert. denied 284 U.S. 690, 52 S.Ct. 266.

If B Corp. pays C $10,000 to sublease the building for the remaining five years on the lease, B Corp. would deduct $2,000 per year for each of the five years remaining on the lease.

As the example illustrates, the basic principle that lease acquisition costs must be amortized over the term of the lease is a simple one. Problems arise, however, in determining just what constitutes a lease acquisition cost and in fixing the exact term of the lease over which to amortize the costs when complicating factors such as renewal options are present.

¶ 503 Classification of Payments as Lease Acquisition Costs

Generally, any payment made to acquire a lease and any other payments related to the acquisition of the lease are lease acquisition costs. The classification of a payment as a lease acquisition cost may work for or against a taxpayer. If an item that might otherwise qualify as an ordinary business expense or other currently deductible item is classified as a lease acquisition cost, the taxpayer loses the benefit of a current deduction. On the other hand, if an otherwise nondepreciable and nonamortizable capital expenditure can be classified as a lease acquisition cost, the taxpayer benefits from deductions over the term of the lease.

¶ 503.1 Lessor's Costs

A lessor's normal expenses incurred to collect rents and manage property are ordinary and necessary business expenses that are currently deductible. The cost of acquiring a particular tenant, however, is a lease acquisition cost that must be amortized over the term of the lease. For instance, the entire amount of commission paid to a broker for obtaining a long-term lease is a lease acquisition cost.[4]

While some expenses, such as commissions for finding a tenant and attorney fees for services in connection with a particular lease, are readily seen as lease acquisition costs, other expenses may not be as obvious. Keep in mind that any payment that can be characterized as made to acquire a lease is amortizable over the life of the lease. In *G.S. Rush*,[5] a $2,500 expense for moving a house from one location on a lot to another, in order to lease the lot to an oil company, had to be amortized over the life of the lease. Similarly, the amount a lessor paid to a lessee in order to defray the cost of the lessee's move into the lessor's building had to be prorated over the lease term.[6]

Assume a lessor agrees to take over the leases between prospective tenants and other landlords in order to have the prospects move into

---

[4] Rev. Rul. 70-408, 1970-2 CB 68.
[5] DC Ala., 59-2 USTC ¶ 9752.
[6] *C.F. Bachman*, 21 BTA 36, CCH Dec. 6406.

the property. Is the rent paid by the lessor on the assigned leases a lease acquisition cost? It would seem to be similar to a lessor's payment of a lessee's expenses in order to induce the lessee to enter into a lease. In one case, however, the Second Circuit did not see it this way.[7] In this case, to obtain desirable tenants for its new office building, a taxpayer assumed the tenants' leases in other buildings and then attempted to rent these spaces for their remaining terms. The Tax Court denied a deduction to the taxpayer for the difference between what the taxpayer paid in rent and what was collected, characterizing this amount as a lease acquisition cost. On appeal, however, this decision was overturned. The Second Circuit Court characterized the payments on the old leases as part of the cost of operating the taxpayer's business, just as the income from subletting these spaces was part of the taxpayer's business income. The court pointed out that had the tenants remained in place and the owner of the old building granted a reduction in rent to keep them as tenants, the reduction would not be considered a capital investment to earn the reduced rent.

¶ 503.2 *Lessee's Costs*

In the case of lease acquisition costs incurred by a lessee, the lessee is in the same position as the lessor in that these costs do not produce a current deduction, but must be amortized over the life of the lease. A lessee's acquisition costs may include items such as brokers' commissions, attorneys' fees, or even the cost of an outright purchase of an existing leasehold. Acquisition costs also may include some not so obvious items.

In order to expand a business, a taxpayer wanted to obtain adjoining property that was leased by a merchandising company under a lease that had eight years to run. In order to induce the merchandising company to assign the lease on the adjoining property, the taxpayer purchased the stock and fixtures of the company. Following the assignment of the lease, the taxpayer sold the stock and fixtures at a loss and deducted the loss. According to the IRS, however, the loss was a cost of acquiring the lease and, as such, had to be spread over the remaining eight-year life of the lease.[8]

Sometimes, a lease will be acquired as part of a larger transaction, such as the purchase of a business or corporation. Normally, the cost of a business (other than the cost of depreciable physical or other wasting assets) is not deductible or amortizable. The same is true for stock in a corporation. In these situations, the purchaser may be able to gain a deduction if the purchaser can show that some specific amount is being

---

[7] *379 Madison Ave., Inc.*, CA-2, 1932 CCH ¶ 9397, 60 F.2d 68.

[8] Rev. Rul. 68-260, 1968-1 CB 86.

spent to acquire the lease. Advance planning and negotiation with the seller are required.

In *Washington Package Store, Inc.*,[9] the taxpayer purchased a liquor store that was operated from leased premises, but was denied an amortization deduction for any part of the purchase price because the taxpayer could not show that part of the consideration was paid to acquire the leasehold. Had the taxpayer separately negotiated to acquire the lease, in all likelihood, the cost would have been amortizable. In *N.W. Pugh Co., Inc.*,[10] the stock of a lessor corporation was acquired to obtain control of property leased to a corporation controlled by the taxpayer. The court held that no part of the cost of the stock could be allocated to the lease. Again, advance planning may have allowed the taxpayer to negotiate separately for an amortizable leasehold interest and a reduced price for the stock of the corporation.

A lessee also may assume some obligations of the lessor on entering a lease. As discussed at ¶ 405, the assumption of a lessor's obligation may be treated as advance rent. It also may be treated as a lease acquisition cost (see ¶ 503). From a practical standpoint, the classification of the assumption by the lessee of a lessor's obligation as either advance rent or a lease acquisition cost is not that important. In either case, the lessee does not get a current deduction, but must amortize the payment over the lease term. Some items that have been treated as lease acquisition costs when assumed by the lessee include delinquent taxes due on the leased property and mortgages on the leased property. Payments made to creditors of a previous lessee also may be lease acquisition costs when made to free the lease from claims.

¶ 503.3 *Unsuccessful Lease Attempt*

If the attempt to obtain a business lease is unsuccessful, the costs expended in the attempt generally are deductible when it is clear that the lease will not be acquired.[11] However, if the costs also are attributable to a later lease that is successful, the costs have to be amortized over the term of the successful lease. For example, attorney fees paid to negotiate a 20-year lease had to be deducted over the term of the lease.[12] The attorney had made several unsuccessful attempts to negotiate a lease with other prospects, but the attorney's work was not divisible. The successful negotiations were a continuation of the prior negotiations.

---

[9] 23 TCM 1805, CCH Dec. 27,041(M), T.C. Memo. 1964-294.
[10] CA DC, 1934 CCH ¶ 9227, 70 F.2d 776, cert. denied 293 U.S. 575, 55 S.Ct. 87.
[11] See, for example, *Levenson & Klein, Inc.*, 67 TC 694, CCH Dec. 34,221.
[12] *A.T. Galt*, 19 TC 892, CCH Dec. 19,491, aff'd and rev'd on other issues, CA-7, 54-2 USTC ¶ 9457, 216 F.2d 41.

¶ 505 Renewal Options

Once the amount of acquisition costs is determined, it is a simple matter to determine the annual amortization deduction when the lease has a fixed termination date. If the lease contains renewal options, however, the question arises as to whether acquisition costs should be amortized over the initial term of the lease only or over the initial term plus the periods of the renewal options.

Under Code Sec. 178, if a lease contains renewal options, lease acquisition costs are amortized over the initial term of the lease, ignoring any renewal periods, as long as at least 75 percent of the lease acquisition costs are attributable to the initial term. Lease acquisition costs must be amortized over the initial term plus any period for which the lease may be renewed or extended and any other period for which the parties reasonably expect the lease to be renewed, if more than 25 percent of the acquisition costs are attributable to the renewal periods.

Example: The Lessee pays $10,000 to acquire a lease with an initial term of 20 years. The lease also contains two options to renew for periods of five years each. Of the $10,000 lease acquisition cost, $8,000 was paid for the initial 20-year term. Since at least 75 percent of the cost is attributable to the initial 20-year term, the $10,000 lease acquisition cost is deductible over the initial term at a rate of $500 per year.

Had only $7,000 of the costs been paid for the initial 20-year term, the proper amortization period for the lease acquisition cost would include the renewal periods. In this event, the $10,000 lease acquisition cost would be deductible over 30 years at a rate of $333.33 per year.

While this rule is all well and good when the lease acquisition costs can be apportioned easily between initial term and renewal periods, in most situations, the proper apportionment is not readily apparent. There may be some latitude for the parties to negotiate what portion of lease acquisition costs is attributable to initial term and renewal periods, but Reg. § 1.178-1(b)(5) provides that the portion of lease acquisition costs attributable to the term of the lease, ignoring renewal periods or options, must be determined "on the basis of the facts and circumstances of each case." This would indicate that any allocation arrived at by the parties may not be given validity, especially if the person receiving the payments has no interest in how the allocation is made.

The regulations do provide an annuity method for apportioning lease acquisition costs between initial term and renewal periods when other evidence is lacking.[13] The annuity method looks at the present value (at an appropriate rate of interest) of annual savings of $1 over the initial term compared to the present value of annual savings of $1 over the initial term plus renewal periods. While the regulations under Code Sec. 178 were adopted before Code Sec. 178 was amended in 1986, they presumably have continuing application to lease acquisition costs under revised Code Sec. 178.

Example: The Lessee acquires a lease from a previous tenant at a cost of $100,000. At the time of acquisition, there are 20 years remaining on the initial lease term and the lease contains two renewal options of 10 years each. The lease calls for a uniform annual rental for the initial term and any renewal periods. If no other evidence of how much of the $100,000 of lease acquisition cost is attributable to the initial term, the Lessee may use the annuity method to apportion the cost. The annuity method calls for the use of a present value analysis based on a reasonable rate of interest. If the Lessee's cost of funds were 12 percent, this rate might be considered appropriate for the present value analysis.

The present value factor for the initial term of the lease, 20 years in this case, at 12 percent is 7.4694. The present value factor for 40 years, the initial term plus renewal periods, at 12 percent is 8.2438. The percentage of the $100,000 lease acquisition cost attributable to the initial term is: 7.4694/8.2438 = 90.6 percent. Since at least 75 percent of the acquisition cost is attributable to the initial term, the Lessee amortizes $100,000 over 20 years at a rate of $5,000 per year.

If the lease were such that the remaining initial term were 10 years with two renewal periods of 15 years each, however, the acquisition cost would have to be amortized over 40 years. The present value factor for 10 years at 12 percent is 5.6502, so the percentage of the lease acquisiti7on cost attributable to the initial 10-year term would be calculated under the annuity method as follows: 5.6502/8.2438 = 68.5 percent. Since less than 75 percent of the lease acquisition cost is attributable to the initial term in this case, the Lessee would have to amortize $100,000 over the 40 years of the initial term plus renewal periods at a rate of $2,500 per year.

¶ 507 Existing Improvements Costs

While lease acquisition costs must be amortized over the life of the lease, some costs incurred by a lessee to acquire a lease may not be lease acquisition costs. If a portion of the costs can be attributed to

---

[13] Reg. § 1.178-1(b)(5)(i).

improvements on the leased property with a life shorter than the remaining lease term, those costs may be recovered through depreciation deductions over the remaining life of the improvements.[14]

This rule was reflected in Reg. § 1.167(a)-4, which applied to both improvements purchased and constructed by a lessee prior to amendment of Code Sec. 168(i)(8) by the Tax Reform Act of 1986. While the cost of improvements constructed by a lessee on leased property now must be recovered over the life of the improvements, even if longer than the lease term, Code Sec. 168(i)(8) does not seem to affect the depreciation of assets purchased with a lease when the life of the improvements is less than the term of the lease.

Reg. § 1.167(a)-4 provides:

> . . . If the useful life of such improvements in the hands of the taxpayer is equal to or shorter than the remaining period of the lease, the allowance shall take the form of depreciation . . . If, on the other hand, the estimated useful life of such property in the hands of the taxpayer, determined without regard to the terms of the lease, would be longer than the remaining period of such lease, the allowances shall take the form of annual deductions from gross income in an amount equal to the unrecovered cost of such capital expenditures divided by the number of years remaining of the term of the lease.

In Rev. Rul. 61-217, a lessee constructed a commercial building on leased land. The lessee then assigned its interest in the improved property and lease to another party. The IRS ruled, in effect, that the assignee's payment to the original lessee to acquire the lease with the improved property was payment for two distinct assets. The portion of the payment attributable to the building was recoverable through depreciation over the useful life of the building. The part of the capital investment by the assignee that represented consideration for increased rental value, the lease acquisition cost, was recoverable only through amortization over the remaining period of the lease.

The Sixth Circuit Court adopted a similar approach in a later case.[15] In that case, the taxpayer acquired two 99-year leases with 64 and 68 years still to run. The leases covered both land and buildings, and the court held that the portion of the cost allocable to the buildings was depreciable over their estimated useful lives.

Now, of course, the concept of useful life has been replaced by statutory recovery periods. These periods are used in place of useful life for determining depreciation deductions (see ¶ 903.1). The key to tax

---

[14] Rev. Rul. 61-217, 1961-2 CB 49.

[15] *1220 Realty Co.*, CA-6, 63-2 USTC ¶ 9703, 322 F.2d 495.

savings on the acquisition of a lease is to allocate as much of the cost as is possible to improvements on the leased property that have a recovery period that is shorter than the remaining lease term.

Example: The Lessee acquires a lease with 50 years remaining to run by paying the current tenant $100,000. If all of the $100,000 is treated as a lease acquisition cost amortizable over the remaining term of the lease, the Lessee's deduction for these costs would be $2,000 for each of the 50 years.

Suppose, however, that the Lessee could show that $60,000 represented costs attributable to the acquisition of a commercial building located on the leased property. If this were the case, the Lessee would deduct $800 per year in each of 50 years as amortization of lease acquisition costs of $40,000. Also, the Lessee would deduct $1,538 in each of the first 39 years of the lease as depreciation of the cost attributable to acquiring the building.

Deductions in the early years of the lease could be further increased if the Lessee could show that some of the costs were attributable to property acquired under the lease with shorter recovery periods than the 39-year period for commercial buildings. (Recovery periods for various types of property are discussed at ¶ 903.1.)

¶ 511 LEASE CANCELLATION

For a wide variety of reasons, one party to a lease agreement may seek to cancel or terminate the agreement before the end of the lease term. Depending on the situation, the party seeking the cancellation may have to give some consideration to the other party in exchange for the cancellation.

If the lessee pays for the privilege of getting out of a business lease, the payment should be a deductible expense. For the lessor, of course, the payment from the lessee is income. On the other hand, if it is the lessor who pays the lessee for cancelling the lease agreement, the lessor is paying for the acquisition of property represented by the leasehold. A deduction for the payment may hinge on the reasons for the cancellation. For the lessee, the payment from the lessor is income. These concepts are explored more fully in the following paragraphs.

¶ 513 Payments By Lessee

A lessee's payments to a lessor to cancel a lease have tax consequences for both parties. If the lessee simply pays the lessor to cancel the lease and walks away from the property, the tax treatment is relatively straightforward. Complications may arise, however, if the lessee enters into a new lease agreement or if the lessee acquires a fee interest in the property.

¶ 513.1 *Lessee's Deduction*

An amount paid by a lessee to a lessor in consideration of the lessor's cancellation of a business lease is a deductible expense for years in which the payment is made or accrued depending on the lessee's accounting method. See Rev. Rul. 69-511,[16] in which the IRS ruled that a lump-sum payment by a lessee as damages for cancellation of a business lease that is equal to a certain amount for each month of the unexpired term is deductible.

The deduction for lease cancellation payments by an accrual basis lessee is taken when the lease is cancelled, even if the payments are spread out over a period of years. An accrual method lessee assumed the lessor's indebtedness of $45,100 in consideration of the cancellation of the lease. The lessee was required to deduct the amount in full in the year the lease was cancelled, even though the lessee would pay off the indebtedness assumed over an 11-year period.[17]

Not every payment by a lessee for the cancellation of a lease, however, gives rise to an immediate deduction. An amount paid by a lessee to obtain cancellation of a 20-year sublease on premises on which it owned a 99-year lease, in order to gain immediate possession, was amortizable over the remaining life of the 99-year lease.[18] Of course, in this situation, the payment made by the lessee is really in the nature of a payment made by a lessor to obtain possession of leased property (see ¶ 515).

What if the lessee pays to cancel a lease and then immediately enters into a new lease with the lessor? Are payments in this situation currently deductible? Generally, if a lease is cancelled on the acquisition of a new lease, any cost of the old lease, including the cost of its cancellation, becomes part of the cost of the new lease.[19] As a lease acquisition cost rather than a lease cancellation payment, the cost becomes deductible over the term of the new lease.

A lease agreement also may be cancelled by the lessee's acquisition of the fee interest in the leased property before the end of the lease term. The cost of acquiring the fee is a capital expenditure, not a currently deductible expense.[20] In *Millinery Building*, the taxpayer, as a lessee, constructed a building on leased property at a cost of $3 mil-

---

[16] 1969-2 CB 23.
[17] *C.L. Baumann & Co.*, 2 TCM 188, CCH Dec. 13,239(M).
[18] *Home Trust Co.*, CA-8, 3 USTC ¶ 1103, 65 F.2d 532.

[19] *Phil Gluckstern's, Inc.*, 15 TCM 41, CCH Dec. 21,521(M), T.C. Memo. 1956-9; *S. Peabody*, BTA Memo., CCH Dec. 8260-A, October 26, 1933.
[20] *Millinery Center Building Corp.*, S.Ct., 56-1 USTC ¶ 9391, 350 U.S. 456, 76 S.Ct. 493.

lion. Title to the building was to vest in the lessor at the end of the lease, or the lessor could require the lessee to raze it. At the end of the 21-year initial term of the lease, the lessee exercised its option to renew and shortly after that bought the premises for $2,100,000. The lessee, now the owner of the property, contended that the land was worth $660,000, and that it should be allowed to deduct the remainder as the cost of cancelling a lease under which it was paying excessive rent. The Supreme Court disallowed the claimed deduction and held the purchase price was the cost of acquiring the complete fee to the land and building. The purchase price had to be allocated to the land up to the land's value on the purchase date. Any amount paid over the value of the land had to be added to the lessee's remaining basis in the improvements.

¶ 513.2 *Lessor's Income*

"An amount received by a lessor from a lessee for cancelling a lease constitutes gross income for the year in which it is received, since it is essentially a substitute for rental payments." [21] This essentially reflects the position of the Supreme Court announced in *W.M. Hort*.[22] According to the Supreme Court, consideration received for cancellation of a lease of realty is essentially a substitute for rental payments and not a return of capital. The consideration is taxable in full, even if there is a difference between the present value of the unmatured rental payments and the fair rental value of the property for the unexpired period of the lease. Any reduction in value of the property because of the lease cancellation becomes a deductible loss only when fixed by a closed transaction.

If a lessee relieves the lessor of the obligation to return a security deposit, two Circuit Courts have held that the proper measure of income to the lessor is the discounted value of the retained security deposit.[23] The IRS, however, does not follow these cases.[24] According to the IRS, the entire amount of the released security deposit is includible in the lessor's gross income in the year of release, whether or not the lessor had the use of the security deposit, with or without an obligation to pay interest to the lessee for the use. It would seem that the position of the IRS is the stronger one in this situation, and it is quite likely that the courts today would not follow the earlier decisions measuring current income in terms of the present value of the future obligation to return a deposit.

---

[21] Reg. § 1.61-8(b).
[22] S.Ct., 41-1 USTC ¶ 9354, 313 U.S. 28, 61 S.Ct. 757.
[23] *Warren Service Corp.*, CA-2, 40-1 USTC ¶ 9333, 110 F.2d 723; and *Bradford Hotel Operating Co.*, CA-1, 57-2 USTC ¶ 9698, 244 F.2d 876.
[24] Rev. Rul. 68-19, 1968-1 CB 42.

Payments by the lessee to the lessor on cancellation of a lease may be for something other than the cancellation of the lease. If a lessor can show that all or part of the payments are not for cancelling the lease but are consideration for something else, the lessor may escape current taxation. For example, damages received from the lessee for the loss or destruction of leased property are a return of capital. As a return of capital, the damages are applied to reduce the lessor's basis for the property rather than included in current income.[25] If the damages exceed the lessor's basis, the excess is a capital gain.[26]

In *Sirbo Holdings, Inc.*,[27] however, a distinction was drawn between a lessee's payment for damages to the lessor's property and payments to the lessor in exchange for the lessor's relieving the lessee of an obligation to remove additions to the leased property added by the lessee and to restore the property to the condition it was in at the time the lease was executed. In this latter case, the payment was held to be ordinary income to the landlord since there was no "sale or exchange" to support capital gain treatment.

¶ 515 Payments By Lessor

Payments for the cancellation of a lease made by the lessor are treated as payments made for the acquisition of property rights. As such, the payments are capital expenditures under Code Sec. 263 and Reg. § 1.263(a)-2. For the lessee, the receipt of a lease cancellation payment from the lessor is income subject to the provisions of Code Sec. 1241.

¶ 515.1 *Lessor's Deduction*

Since lease cancellation payments made by the lessor are capital expenditures, the lessor is not entitled to a current deduction for these costs. Nevertheless, if the cancellation payments are made in connection with business property, the lessor is entitled to recover his costs. The question, then, is one of the proper period over which lease cancellation payments may be deducted.

As a general rule, an amount paid by a lessor to the lessee for the cancellation of the lease is for a capital asset, and the lessor may deduct the amount through amortization deductions over the unexpired term of the cancelled lease.[28]

Suppose, however, that the reason the lessor pays to cancel an existing lease is to regain the property in order to lease it to a new

---

[25] *Hamilton & Main, Inc.*, 25 TC 878, CCH Dec. 21,542.
[26] *Boston Fish Market*, 57 TC 884, CCH Dec. 31,321.
[27] CA-2, 75-1 USTC ¶ 9178, 509 F.2d 1220.
[28] Rev. Rul. 71-283, 1971-2 CB 168; *Peerless Weighing & Vending Machine Corp.*, 52 TC 850, CCH Dec. 29,713; *Handlery Hotels, Inc.*, CA-9, 82-1 USTC ¶ 9106, 663 F.2d 892.

tenant on more favorable terms. In this situation, the lease cancellation payment for the old lease also may be classified as a lease acquisition cost of the new lease. In fact, if the lessor makes the cancellation payment in order to enter a specific new lease, the lease cancellation payment is amortizable over the term of the new lease rather than the unexpired term of the old lease.[29]

In *Handlery Hotels, Inc.*, the court struggled with the question of when a lease cancellation payment should be treated as the cost of a new lease amortizable over the term of the new lease rather than over the unexpired term of the old lease. According to the court, the question is really one of clearly reflecting the lessor's income for the periods involved. In this case, the court decided that the payment involved was based on the value of the unexpired term of the old lease and, therefore, should be amortized over that period in order to clearly reflect the lessor's income over that period.

If a lessor pays an existing tenant to cancel an existing lease in order to execute a more favorable lease with a new tenant, the lessor may have a bunching of income problem if the lessor receives advance rent or bonus payments from the new tenant. The advance rent is reportable in full when received, as discussed at ¶ 423, but the lease cancellation payment is amortizable over either the term of the new lease or unexpired term of the old lease. In this case, the lessor may reduce taxes if a deal is struck to permit the new tenant to make a payment directly to the old tenant. As far as the old tenant is concerned, the tax treatment of the payment is the same whether it comes from the lessor or the new tenant. For the new tenant, advance rent paid to the lessor and a lease acquisition cost paid to the old tenant are both amortizable over the term of the lease, so the tax consequences for the new tenant are the same. The lessor, however, is better off, since advance rent is, in effect, immediately offset by what would otherwise be a lease cancellation payment.

If a lessor pays to cancel a lease in order to sell the property or in order to erect new buildings or improvements, the payments should be reflected in the basis of the property. In *Shirley Hill Coal Co.*,[30] it was held that an amount paid to a lessee for cancellation of a long-term lease of property which the lessor wished to sell enters into the computation of gain or loss on the sale. See also *American Spring & Wire Specialty Co.*,[31] in which it was held that a payment for accelerating the termination of a lease in order to obtain immediate possession of

---

[29] Wells Fargo Bank & Union Trust Co., Trustee, CA-9, 47-1 USTC ¶ 9359, 163 F.2d 521; *Montgomery Co.*, 54 TC 986, CCH Dec. 30,106, Acq. 1970-2 CB xx; *H. Latter*, 20 TCM 336, CCH Dec. 24,710(M), T.C. Memo. 1961-67.

[30] 6 BTA 935, CCH Dec. 2374.
[31] 20 TCM 116, CCH Dec. 24,646(M), T.C. Memo. 1961-26.

¶ 515.1

the property was part of the cost of the property and not deductible or amortizable over the remaining life of the lease.

When a taxpayer makes payments to acquire and cancel a lease and obtain early possession of the premises so that it can erect a new building for business use, the payments are part of the cost of the buildings and not of the land. The costs are recovered through depreciation over the useful life or recovery period of the new building and not over the shorter term of the cancelled lease.[32]

If a lessee makes lease cancellation payments to a sublessee, the lease cancellation payments are amortizable over the remaining term of the primary lease rather than the remaining term of the sublease.[33]

¶ 515.2 *Lessee's Income*

Amounts received by a lessee for cancellation of the lease are treated as amounts received "in exchange for such lease."[34] Note that Code Sec. 1241 does not have any bearing on the characterization of the amount received by the lessee other than to provide the requisite "exchange" necessary to support capital gain or loss or Code Sec. 1231 gain or loss. The actual character of the income is determined by the nature of the leasehold asset (see the discussion of the sale of a lease at ¶ 521). Also, Code Sec. 1241 does not prevent a transaction that does not qualify under that section from being treated as a sale.[35]

The cancellation of a lease covered by Code Sec. 1241 is the termination of all the contractual rights of a lessee in a particular premises, other than by the expiration of the lease in accordance with its terms. A payment made in good faith for a partial cancellation of a lease is treated as a cancellation payment under Code Sec. 1241, if the cancellation relates to a severable economic unit, such as a portion of the premises covered by the lease or a reduction in the unexpired term of the lease.[36] Payments made for other modifications of leases, however, are not treated as amounts received for cancellation under Code Sec. 1241.

In a case decided under the law before enactment of Code Sec. 1241, a lessee was accorded sale or exchange treatment for payments received from the lessor in exchange for the lessee's relinquishment of a covenant that barred the lessor from leasing other parts of the building

---

[32] *Third National Bank in Nashville*, CA-6, 72-1 USTC ¶ 9223, 454 F.2d 689. See also *J.W. Keiler, II*, CA-6, 68-1 USTC ¶ 9360, 395 F.2d 991; *Houston Chronicle Publishing Co.*, CA-5, 73-2 USTC ¶ 9537, 481 F.2d 1240, cert. denied, 414 U.S. 1129, 94 S.Ct. 867.

[33] *Steele-Wedeles Co.*, 30 BTA 841, CCH Dec. 8585; *Mid-State Products Co.*, 21 TC 696, CCH Dec. 20,157, Acq. 1955-2 CB 7.

[34] Code Sec. 1241.
[35] Reg. § 1.1241-1(a).
[36] Reg. § 1.1241-1(b).

to competitors of the lessee.[37] In Rev. Rul. 56-531,[38] the IRS did rule that amounts received by a lessee from his lessor in consideration of the lessee's relinquishment of a lease covenant restricting the use of the real estate by the lessor are the proceeds of a sale. Arguably, even under Code Sec. 1241, such a covenant may be a "severable economic unit."

If a lessee receives payments in connection with the cancellation of a lease that are not actually for the cancellation, those amounts are not treated under Code Sec. 1241. For instance, the lessor may return a security deposit with interest. The amount of the deposit is, of course, a return of the lessee's own funds (provided the deposit was treated as such and not as advance rent), and the interest is taxable as interest income. Returned advance rents that were previously deducted by the lessee are ordinary income.[39]

¶ 517 Unamortized Costs on Cancellation of Lease

As discussed at ¶ 503, lease acquisition costs are amortizable over the term of the lease. On the cancellation of a lease before its full term, either the lessor or lessee may have unamortized acquisition costs. Generally, a lessor's unamortized costs become fully deductible in the year of cancellation or termination.[40] A similar rule applies to the lessee, and a lessee may deduct unamortized lease acquisition costs in the year the lease is cancelled as a business expense.[41]

If the lessor cancels the lease in order to sell the property, however, unamortized costs are not deductible. Rather, they are added to the basis of the property and reduce the amount of gain or increase the amount of loss recognized.[42] Similarly, if the lessee purchases the property during the term of the lease, any unamortized lease acquisition cost becomes part of the basis of the property. The cost of the property then is the purchase price plus the remaining unamortized lease acquisition costs.[43]

Another situation in which the lessor does not enjoy an immediate deduction for remaining lease acquisition costs on the cancellation of a lease is when the lessor enters into a new lease for the same premises. In this case, the unamortized costs of acquiring the old lease are amortized over the term of the new lease.[44]

---

[37] *L.W. Ray*, CA-5, 54-1 USTC ¶ 9235, 210 F.2d 390, cert. denied, 348 U.S. 829, 75 S.Ct. 53.

[38] 1956-2 CB 983.

[39] *A.J. Gray*, CA-9, 81-1 USTC ¶ 9371, 642 F.2d 320. See also *Peerless Steel Equipment Co.*, 26 TCM 880, CCH Dec. 28,598(M), T.C. Memo. 1967-181.

[40] *Oliver Iron Mining Co.*, 13 TC 416, CCH Dec. 17,202, Acq. 1950-1 CB 4.

[41] *Guelph Hotel Corp.*, 7 BTA 1043, CCH Dec. 2693, Acq. VII-1 CB 13.

[42] *R.H. Post*, CA-2, 40-1 USTC ¶ 9187, 109 F.2d 135.

[43] *H. Boos*, 30 BTA 882, CCH Dec. 8593.

[44] *Pig & Whistle Co.*, 9 BTA 668, CCH Dec. 3198; *Phil Gluckstern's, Inc.*, 15 TCM 41, CCH Dec. 21,521(M), T.C. Memo. 1956-9.

Sometimes, a lease cancellation may be negotiated in one year, but the actual early termination of the lease will not take place until some time in the following year. In effect, the negotiation of early notice of cancellation shortens the remaining term of the lease. When this situation arises, any unrecovered lease acquisition costs, as of the time notice of cancellation is given, should be deducted ratably over the period from the beginning of the year in which notice is given until the termination of the lease.[45]

Example: The Lessee, who is a calendar year, accrual basis taxpayer, received notice on April 1, 2002, that its lease is being terminated. Lessee is given until May 31, 2003, to vacate the leased premises. The original term of the lease was not to expire until 2008. As of 2002, Lessee has $17,000 of lease acquisition costs remaining unamortized.

In this situation, Lessee's unamortized lease acquisition costs as of January 1, 2002, should be deducted ratably over the period from January 1, 2002, to May 31, 2003. This is a period of 17 months, so the Lessee should deduct 12/17 of the $17,000, or $12,000, for 2002, and 5/17 of the $17,000, or $5,000, for 2003.

Note that a rule similar to that for unamortized lease acquisition costs applies to unrecovered leasehold improvement costs when a lease is terminated. The unrecovered costs of improvements incurred by a lessee result in a loss in the year the lease is cancelled. See discussion at ¶ 615.2.

¶ 519 Modification of Lease

A lessee who receives a payment for modifying an existing lease agreement realizes income. The question is whether that income may qualify as capital gain as an amount received in a sale or exchange, either because Code Sec. 1241 applies, as discussed at ¶ 515.2, or because there is a sale of a lease by the lessee, as discussed at ¶ 521.

On the other hand, when a lessee pays for the modification of an existing lease, the lessee wants to maximize current deductions. Rev. Rul. 73-176 [46] illustrates the wrong way to do this. In the ruling, a lessee had entered into a 20-year lease for five floors of a building, but later found that it did not need that much space. The lessee negotiated a modification of the terms of the lease with a reduction in the amount of space leased. In addition to rent at the same rate per square foot as under the unmodified lease, the lessee agreed to pay a specific amount as "additional rent" over a period of 60 months. The IRS recharacterized this "rent" as a capital cost for the release from the future

---

[45] *Guelph Hotel Corp.*, 7 BTA 1043, CCH Dec. 2693, Acq. VII-1 CB 13.

[46] 1973-1 CB 146.

obligation to pay rent over the 20-year term of the lease. Accordingly, the deductions had to be spread out over the entire remaining term of the lease, rather than taken as paid over the five years.

Instead of a lease modification, the parties may have been able to increase the lessee's deductions by terminating the old lease and entering into an entirely new agreement. The lessor would not suffer because the lessor is taxed on receipt regardless of whether the extra amount is received as advance rent, a lease cancellation or modification payment, or as current rent.

¶ 521 SALE OF LEASE

Leasehold interests generally qualify as capital assets. Accordingly, if a lessee transfers all of the interest in the property to a third party, there is a sale of a capital asset. If leased land or buildings are used in a trade or business, the lease is a Section 1231 asset if the leasehold has been held for the required holding period.[47] The transaction is a sale even if the original lessee remains contingently liable to the lessor for the performance of the assignee under the lease. An exception does apply, however, if the holder of the leasehold is a dealer in leases. Dealer treatment converts an otherwise capital or Section 1231 asset into an ordinary income asset.[48]

Sale or exchange treatment is available on the sale of a leasehold by a lessee regardless of the source of the payments or who is actually acquiring the lease. Of course, payments may come from the lessor, in which case the payments, most likely, would qualify as capital gains from a sale under Code Sec. 1241, as discussed at ¶ 521, provided the payment is for the lessee's entire interest or a severable economic unit. The assignment or transfer of a lease to a third party also qualifies as sale,[49] as does the transfer of a lease to a sublessee.[50] Amounts received by a lessee from a sublessee for the lessee's release of its rights to the lessor, with whom the sublessee desired to negotiate a direct lease, were capital gains from the sale of the leasehold.[51]

The distinction between the sale of a lease and a sublease is less critical when capital gain is subject to the same rate of tax as ordinary income. Nevertheless, the distinction remains important because of the limits on the deduction of capital losses that prevent their deduction against ordinary income. The transfer by a lessee of less than the entire interest in the leased property, other than a severable economic unit,

---

[47] Rev. Rul. 72-85, 1972-1 CB 234.

[48] See Chapter 13 for a general discussion of the sale or exchange of real estate, and Chapter 10 for a discussion of dealer sales.

[49] *Metropolitan Building Co.*, TC 971, CCH Dec. 23,448, Acq. 1959-2 CB 6.

[50] *S.D. Miller*, 48 TC 649, CCH Dec. 28,565, Acq. 1968-1 CB 2.

[51] *Metropolitan Building Co.*, CA-9, 60-2 USTC ¶ 9686, 282 F.2d 592, rev'g and rem'g 31 TC 971, CCH Dec. 23,448, Acq. 1959-2 CB 6.

generally is treated as a sublease giving rise to ordinary income, rather than as a sale giving rise to capital gain.

In Rev. Rul. 57-537,[52] the IRS ruled that the amount paid by the purchaser for the assignment of a lease was an advance rental, reportable by the seller-lessee as ordinary income in the year received, if the seller-lessee reserved the exclusive right and option to purchase the land that was the subject of the lease. Also, a sublease has been found when an agreement among the lessor, lessee, and a third party provided for the lessee's continuing liability to the lessor, gave the lessee a right of reentry for breach of the agreement, and provided for the monthly payment of the "selling price" that resembled the payment of rent.[53]

---

[52] 1957-2 CB 52.

[53] *S. Voloudakis*, CA-9, 60-1 USTC ¶ 9192, 274 F.2d 209; see also *J.D. Price*, 17 TCM 660, CCH Dec. 23,079(M), T.C. Memo. 1958-124.

Chapter 6

Leasehold Improvements and Additions

¶ 600 OVERVIEW OF CHAPTER

Improvements and additions to leased property may be made by either the lessor or lessee, according to their agreement. Lease provisions often dictate what improvements are to be made and who is to make them and bear their cost. In this regard, the lessor and lessee should engage in some advance planning. How the responsibility is assigned will determine which party is entitled to depreciation deductions for the cost of improvements. The agreement between the parties may also determine whether improvements made by the lessee are to be treated as additional rent, deductible costs for the lessee and income to the lessor, or as a capital expenditure, for which the lessee may take depreciation deductions and which passes tax-free to the lessor at the expiration of the lease.

Another consideration when making improvements to leased property is whether any possible investment credit is available and who is entitled to claim the credit. The investment credit for rehabilitating older properties and historic structures may be quite significant. In some cases, the lessee may earn this credit, and in others, the lessor. When the credit is earned by the lessor, the lessor may pass this credit on to the lessee, or share the credit with the lessee, in certain situations. How the parties decide to handle the credit, as well the overall cost of improvements and additions, will turn on their relative tax positions. Leasehold improvements and additions are one area in which the parties have a great deal of power to shape the tax outcome through how they structure their lease agreement.

¶ 601 IMPROVEMENTS AND ADDITIONS BY LESSOR

The lessor who erects buildings or makes other improvements or additions to the property he leases generally is entitled to depreciation deductions for the cost of those improvements. The lessee who rents improved property is not entitled to depreciation deductions for the improvements when it is the lessor who has made the capital expenditures necessary to support the deductions. The lessor's depreciation deductions are taken over the usual recovery period for the property involved, regardless of the period of the lease.[1] Similarly, a lessor has no depreciable interest in improvements made by his lessee, even though the improvements become the property of the lessor.[2] (The computation of depreciation deductions for real estate and related improvements is the subject of Chapter 9.)

When the cost of improvements is borne by both the lessor and the lessee, both are entitled to depreciation deductions. The lessor is allowed depreciation on the amount contributed.[3] The cost of improvements borne by the lessee but treated as rent is considered to be a lessor's cost. (See the discussion of improvements as rent at ¶ 613.)

¶ 603 Restoration or Maintenance by Lessee

Leases usually contain provisions that impose some burden on the lessee to maintain the property. If the maintenance provision in a lease requires the tenant to return the property in its original condition on the expiration of the lease, there is some danger that the lessor will be denied deductions for depreciation. If the tenant must return property in its original condition, the lessor arguably cannot suffer a loss due to depreciation. A maintenance provision that will not jeopardize the lessor's depreciation deductions for improvements is one that excepts the lessee from any obligation to make good ordinary wear and tear or obsolescence. It is ordinary wear and tear and obsolescence that the depreciation deduction is designed to compensate.

The lessor has not been entitled to depreciation on property on which the lessee was bound to make good all depreciation by replacement and additions so as to return to the lessor at the expiration of the lease the value which the property had when the lease was made.[4] Similarly, depreciation deductions have been denied for furniture and fixtures when the lessee was required to replace them if they could not otherwise be kept in first-class condition.[5]

On the other hand, a requirement that the lessee keep the property in good repair and replace all or any part of the property whenever necessary does not prevent the lessor from taking depreciation deductions.[6] A similar result obtains if the lessee agrees to yield up the leased

---

[1] Reg. § 1.167(a)-4.
[2] *C.H. Reisinger*, CA-2, 44-2 USTC ¶ 9443, 144 F.2d 475.
[3] *P. Wilson*, 20 TCM 676, 20 TCM 676, CCH Dec. 24,833(M), T.C. Memo. 1961-135.
[4] *Georgia Ry. & Electric Co.*, CA-5, 35-2 USTC ¶ 9417, 77 F.2d 897, cert. denied 296 U.S. 601, 56 S.Ct. 117; *Terre Haute Electric Co., Inc.*, CA-7, 38-1 USTC ¶ 9228, 96 F.2d 383, cert. denied 292 U.S. 624, 54 S.Ct 629; *Watson Land Co.*, CA-9, 86-2 USTC ¶ 9679, 799 F.2d 571.

[5] *Royal St. Louis, Inc.*, CA-5, 78-2 USTC ¶ 9663, 578 F.2d 1017; see also *Hibernia National Bank* in New Orleans Tr. Div., CA-5, 84-2 USTC ¶ 9771, 740 F.2d 382, in which it was held that an amendment to the lease in *Royal St. Louis, Inc.* that incorporated a wear and tear exception did not entitle the lessor to depreciation because the lessor remained insulated from economic loss.
[6] *Alaska Realty Co.*, CA-6, 44-1 USTC ¶ 9256, 141 F.2d 675; *North Carolina Midland Ry. Co.*, Ct. Cls., 58-2 USTC ¶ 9701, 143 Ct. Cls. 30, 163 F. Supp. 610.

premises and all buildings and improvements thereon in first-class condition and repair.[7]

The critical distinction between the cases that have allowed depreciation and those that have disallowed depreciation seems to be one of value. If the lessor is guaranteed to get back the equivalent value of the property leased, there is no depreciation. On the other hand, if the lessor will get back the property in good repair and condition, but there is no guarantee as to value, the lessor is entitled to depreciation deductions that reflect a possible loss due to obsolescence and ordinary wear and tear. This is supported by Rev. Rul. 62-8.[8]

In Rev. Rul. 62-8, the IRS ruled that a lessor may, upon proper showing, be entitled to some allowance for depreciation, including obsolescence, of leased depreciable property, even though the lessee has agreed to so preserve, replace, renew, and maintain the property and all additions, amendments, and improvements to it that the property will be in at least as good a condition on the termination of the lease as at its beginning. The ruling distinguished G.C.M. 11933, which held that a lessor should not be entitled to depreciation when the lease provides that the property be maintained by the lessee and the same property or its equivalent in value be returned to the lessor on the termination of the lease.

While many of the cases dealing with the depreciation of leasehold improvements and additions predate enactment of the Accelerated Cost Recovery System (ACRS) and the Modified Accelerated Cost Recovery System (MACRS) of depreciation spelled out in Code Sec. 168, the principles generally should remain valid.[9]

The lessee, simply because required by the lease to keep buildings and improvements up to their present condition or to maintain and restore the property, is not entitled to depreciation deductions.[10] But the lessee is entitled to deductions for the cost of repairs and for the cost of restoration expenses on the termination of the lease.[11] The lessee also may deduct expenses during the term of the lease for replacements required under the lease to keep the property in good operating condition.[12]

¶ 605 Improvements to Benefit a Particular Lessee

Suppose the owner of property erects a building or other structure on the property in order to lease the property to a particular tenant.

---

[7] *Swoby Corp.*, 9 TC 887, CCH Dec. 16,123.
[8] 1962-1 CB 31.
[9] Code Sec. 168(a).
[10] *H.W. Weiss v. J. H. Wiener*, 1 USTC ¶ 393, 279 U.S. 333, 49 S.Ct. 337; *Ohio Cloverleaf Dairy Co.*, CA-6, 1929 CCH ¶ 9307, 34 F.2d 1022.
[11] G.C.M. 11933, XII-2 CB 52; O.D. 516, 2 CB 112.
[12] *Journal-Tribune Publishing Co.*, CA-8, 54-2 USTC ¶ 9630, 216 F.2d 138.

Further suppose that the improvement is only usable by that particular tenant and that when the tenant leaves the improvement will have no further value. In this situation, it would seem that deductions by the lessor for the cost of the improvement should be taken over the term of the lease, rather than the normal recovery period for the property, if the term of the lease is less than the recovery period. True, Reg. § 1.167(a)-4 says that depreciation for improvements to leased property by the lessor must be computed over the recovery period of the property, regardless of the lease term, but this seems to be based on the idea that the improvements will remain a benefit to the property and to the lessor at the expiration of a lease. This is not the case when the improvements benefit only a particular tenant and cannot be used by anyone else.

In *L.S. Ames*,[13] the court held that the useful life of a facility specifically constructed as a state social service center was the physical life of the facility rather than the term of the state's shorter lease. In this case, the specialized facilities would not have been suited for any use except a social service center, and the lessor took depreciation based on the term of the lease. In denying the more rapid depreciation, the court pointed to the lessor's failure to prove that he could reasonably foresee that the state would not exercise its option to renew the lease. Presumably, had the lessor been able to make such a showing, the cost of the improvements could have been depreciated over the shorter term of the lease.[14]

Even with the limited authority that existed before the Tax Reform Act of 1986 for writing off the cost of improvements made to benefit a particular lessee over the term of the lease rather than the recovery period for the improvement, the 1986 Act has probably foreclosed any such possibility for the future. Code Sec. 168(i)(8) provides that in "the case of any building erected (or improvements made) on leased property, if such building or improvement is property to which this section applies, the depreciation deduction shall be determined under the provisions of this section."

Although the lessor generally cannot write off improvements made for a particular lessee over a lease term that is shorter than the recovery period for the property while the lessee occupies the property, the Small Business Job Protection Act of 1996 did amend Code Sec. 168 to allow a possible write off at the end of the lease. Generally, a lessor of leased property that disposes of a leasehold improvement made for the lessee of the property may take the adjusted basis of the improvement

---

[13] CA-9, 80-2 USTC ¶ 9641, 626 F.2d 693.
[14] See also *L.C. Fieland*, 73 TC 743, CCH Dec. 36,749, in which there was no "practical certainty" that the improvements involved could not be used after the expiration of the lease.

into account for determining gain or loss if the improvement is irrevocably disposed of or abandoned by the lessee at the termination of the lease.

This does not mean that some tax planning cannot improve the position of the lessor who makes improvements to benefit a particular lessee. In the normal course of events, the lessor who makes such improvements will charge a higher rent in order to compensate for the cost of the improvements. Increased rental payments made in order to reimburse a lessor for improvements made on leased property are income to the lessor.[15]

Suppose, however, that the lessor agrees to accept a lower rent if the lessee agrees to repay the lessor for the cost of the improvements? Could what otherwise would be taxable rental income be converted to a tax-free reimbursement in this case? The answer appears to be yes, provided that the improvements are specially suited only to the particular tenant and "enhance by little or nothing the value of [the lessor's] real estate."[16]

When the lessor makes an improvement "for the account of the lessee," as in the *Beecham* case, the payments by the lessee to reimburse the lessor would be the lessee's cost of the improvements. The lessee would have to treat the improvements as if they were made directly by the lessee. (See the discussion of lessee-made improvements at ¶ 611.)

¶ 607 Purchase of Property with Lessee Improvements

A lessor who makes no investment in improvements to the property leased is not entitled to depreciation based on the cost or value of the improvements. Rather, it is the lessee who has made the investment and who is entitled to depreciation (see below). Suppose, however, that a lessor who has permitted a lessee to make improvements to the leased property sells that property subject to the lease. The seller had no investment in the improvements, but can the same be said of the purchaser? A portion of the purchase price may reflect the increased value of the property that flows from the improvements constructed by the lessee. In this situation, may the purchaser take depreciation deductions even though the predecessor could not? The answer is less than clear.

In Rev. Rul. 55-89,[17] the IRS ruled that a person who inherits property on which a lessee has constructed a building without cost to the lessor is not entitled to depreciation deductions for the building

---

[15] *D.G. Satterfield*, 34 TCM 872, CCH Dec. 33,287(M), T.C. Memo. 1975-203; see also Rev. Rul. 70-146, 1970-1 CB 18.

[16] *Beecham, Inc.*, DC Tenn., 73-2 USTC ¶ 9719.
[17] 1955-1 CB 284.

when the lease extends beyond the useful life (recovery period) of the building. The person who inherits the property acquires no depreciable interest in the building since possession of the building cannot be obtained until after the expiration of the lease. The application of this same rationale to a purchaser is supported by a decision of the First Circuit.[18]

While the First Circuit did hold that the purchaser had no depreciable interest in a building built by a lessee on the land subject to the lease because the seller of the lease had no interest in the building, the court indicated that it might not apply the same rationale to a situation in which the lease term is less than the useful life (recovery period) of the building. More importantly, the court indicated that it might support the idea that the purchaser of property on which a lessee has made improvements is entitled to some deduction for amortization of lease acquisition costs related to the acquisition of the lease.

Prior to the decision in *DeMatteo*, the Eighth Circuit had adopted a more pragmatic approach to the question of whether the purchaser of property from a lessor would be entitled to depreciation for lessee-constructed improvements.[19] The Eight Circuit saw no problem in allowing, in effect, two taxpayers (the lessee and the purchaser) to take deductions for the same property. The critical matter was whether the purchaser, as well as the lessee, had made some investment in a depreciable or wasting asset. Accordingly, the purchaser of leased land on which the lessee has constructed a building is entitled to depreciate or amortize the part of the cost that represents either the value of the building or a premium for the rent to be received. See also, *H.B. Pearson*,[20] in which it was held that it would be possible for the heir of a lessor to have a depreciable interest in a building erected by a lessee if the heir could show what part of the estate tax valuation was attributable to the building, as distinguished from the land.

The most recent of the confusing line of cases dealing with depreciation or amortization by a lessor's successor for lessee-constructed improvements is *Geneva Drive-In Theatre, Inc.*[21] In this case, part of the purchase price paid for the property clearly could be allocated to the improvements on the leased property constructed by the lessee. In this case, the court conceded that the purchaser was entitled to depreciation for this portion of the cost, but that the depreciation deductions could not begin until after the termination of the lease. Under this approach, the purchaser's interest in the lessee-constructed improve-

---

[18] *M. DeMatteo Construction Co.*, CA-1, 70-2 USTC ¶ 9684, 433 F.2d 1263.
[19] *World Publishing Co.*, CA-8, 62-1 USTC ¶ 9282, 299 F.2d 614.
[20] CA-5, 51-1 USTC ¶ 9236, 188 F.2d 72, 342 U.S. 861, 72 S.Ct. 88.
[21] CA-9, 80-2 USTC ¶ 9544, 622 F.2d 995.

ments is a reversionary one, and the purchaser does not actually own the improvements until they revert to the purchaser on termination of the lease.

In trying to draw some meaningful planning strategies out of the cases cited above, one is left with the feeling that the purchaser of property subject to a lease on which the lessee has constructed improvements is on shaky ground in claiming depreciation deductions for improvements on which the seller could not take depreciation. In such situations, the purchaser may be on firmer ground if some part of the cost is attributable to the acquisition of the lease rather than to the fee interest on the underlying property. The purchaser could negotiate for the purchase of two assets—the property without the improvements and the lease between the seller and the lessee. The latter cost, as a lease acquisition cost, would be subject to amortization deductions as discussed at ¶ 501. In this way, the whole matter of depreciation for the improvements may be avoided.

¶ 611 IMPROVEMENTS AND ADDITIONS BY LESSEE

A lessee who rents improved property has not made any investment in the improvements and is not entitled to depreciation deductions for the improvements. Since it is the owner of the property, the lessor, who has made the capital investment in the improvements, it is the lessor who is entitled to depreciation deductions (see ¶ 601). Obviously, the lessor renting improved property charges more rent than if the property were unimproved, and the lessee has a larger deduction for rent paid.

Under Code Sec. 110, which was added to the Code by the Taxpayer Relief Act of 1997, a lessee of retail space for a term of 15 years or less does not have to include in income construction or improvement allowances from the lessor for property that is nonresidential real estate that reverts to the lessor at the termination of the lease. The lessor must treat the amount excluded by the lessee as nonresidential real property.

If the lessee rents unimproved property and proceeds to make improvements to the property other than with payments or allowances from the lessor, it is an entirely different matter. In this situation, it is the lessee who is making the capital expenditures that will support a depreciation deduction. The lessor is not entitled to depreciation for improvements when the cost is borne by the lessee. The cost of improvements, however, may be treated as rent by the parties. If this is the case, then it is the lessor who is treated as making the improvements. The cost is deductible as rent by the lessee and the lessor includes the cost in income as rental income. The lessor, then, is entitled to the depreciation deductions for the improvements.

In any negotiation for the lease of property that will have to be improved, the parties should consider their tax and financial needs in deciding who should make the improvements and under what terms. Generally speaking, the process is one of trading off current and future income and deductions and current and future cash expenditures. When the lessee makes improvements, the lessor is accepting lower rents for the increase in value to the property that the lessor will realize at a later time. At the same time, the lessee will be paying less in rent, but will incur the up-front cost of the improvements. When the lessor makes improvements, the lessor charges more rent but incurs the up-front costs, while the lessee avoids the up-front improvement costs but pays more rent throughout the term of the lease.

¶ 613 Improvements as Rent

Whether the cost of improvements made by a lessee is treated as rent for tax purposes depends on the intent of the parties.[22] This intent may be found in either the terms of the lease or the circumstances surrounding the lease and the making of the improvements. Reg. § 1.61-8(c) provides, in part: "Whether or not improvements made by a lessee result in rental income to the lessor in a particular case depends upon the intention of the parties, which may be indicated either by the terms of the lease or by the surrounding circumstances."

If the lease describes a payment by the lessee as a rental payment, that description will generally control, even if the payment compensates the lessor for the cost of improvements. In *F.T.B. Martin*,[23] amounts described in the lease as rentals, which the lessor claimed were repayments to it of advances for remodeling the premises, were held to be rental income. The terms of the lease governed the characterization of the payments. See also *D.G. Satterfield,*[24] in which increased rental payments made to a lessor as reimbursement for improvements made on leased property were rental income to the lessor. On the other hand, if the payments really do represent repayment for improvements, the payments are not rental income to the lessor.[25]

When the cost of improvements made by a lessee may be credited against the rental obligation of the lessee, the cost of the improvements

---

[22] *M.E. Blatt Co.*, S.Ct., 38-2 USTC ¶ 9599, 305 U.S. 267.
[23] 11 BTA 850, CCH Dec. 3893.
[24] 34 TCM 872, CCH Dec. 33,287(M), T.C. Memo. 1975-203.
[25] *Beecham, Inc.*, DC Tenn., 73-2 USTC ¶ 9719; but see Rev. Rul. 70-146, 1970-1 CB 18, in which the entire amount, received by a lessor under a supplemental agreement by the lessee to pay an amount each month in addition to specified rent until the supplemental payments equaled one-half the cost of improvements made by the lessor, was ruled rental income.

is treated as rent.[26] Similarly, work performed by a tenant under an abatement agreement was additional rental income to the lessor since it was the intent of the parties to treat the improvements as a substitute for rent.[27] Also, when the lease permitted the tenant to make improvements and to reduce the amount of the stated rent by the cost of the improvements, the cost of the improvements was treated as rent and the tenant was treated as having made no investment in the improvements. The entire cost of the improvements was deductible by the tenant as rent.[28]

Generally, the cost of the improvements is the amount of rental income realized by the lessor and the amount of rent deemed paid by the lessee when improvements are treated as rent. In a ruling that preceded enactment of the 1954 Code, the IRS had accepted the idea that the lessor could include in income the value of the improvements discounted to reflect the fact that the lessor would not obtain the improvements until the end of the lease term.[29] It is not clear that the IRS would be willing to accept the same position today.[30]

When the cost of improvements is a direct offset against the rent stated in the lease agreement, the lessor's income is measured by the cost. This amount also becomes the lessor's basis for the improvements on which depreciation is calculated.[31] The lessee's rent deduction is based on the same amount that the lessor includes as rental income. Bear in mind, however, that different rules apply to the timing of the rental deduction and the inclusion in income of rent.

If the cost of improvements treated as rent is substantial, there is the likelihood that the cost represents advance rentals. The deduction for advance rentals by the lessee must be spread over the periods to which they relate (see ¶ 413), while the lessor includes advance rentals in income in full (see ¶ 423). Also, if the cost of an improvement treated as rent plus other rental payments called for by the lease exceed $250,000, income and deductions may have to be spread out under regulations under Code Sec. 467, dealing with deferred and stepped rental agreements (see ¶ 431).

¶ 615 Improvements as Capital Investment

A person who makes additions or improvements to his or her own business property may take depreciation deductions for the cost over the recovery period that applies to the particular addition or improvement involved. This same rule now applies to a lessee who makes

---

[26] *I. Brown*, CA-7, 55-1 USTC ¶ 9258, 220 F.2d 12.
[27] *B.E. McBride*, 53 TCM 158, CCH Dec. 43,713(M), T.C. Memo. 1987-94.
[28] *Your Health Club, Inc.*, 4 TC 385, CCH Dec. 14,250, Acq. 1945 CB 7.
[29] See I.T. 4009, 1950-1 CB 13.
[30] See, for example, Rev. Rul. 67-123, 1967-1 CB 383.
[31] See *I. Brown*, 22 TC 147, CCH Dec. 20,293, aff'd CA-7, 55-1 USTC ¶ 9258, 220 F.2d 12.

additions or improvements to business property that he or she leases, if the additions or improvements are not treated as rent.[32] It does not matter what the remaining term of the lease is at the time an improvement is made; depreciation is based on the full recovery period of the improvement. For improvements placed in service before 1987, their cost may be recovered over the normal recovery period or amortized over the remaining term of the lease if shorter than the appropriate recovery period (see ¶ 615.1). (See ¶ 903 for a discussion of how depreciation is calculated.)

As indicated at ¶ 611 and 613, whether lessee-made improvements are treated as a capital expenditure by the lessee or as additional rent depends on the intent of the parties.[33] The intent not to treat lessee-made improvements as additional rent may be found in the terms of the lease or in the circumstances of the situation. For example, if a lessee makes improvements that meet the special needs of the lessee and cannot be used by the lessor or other tenants, this would indicate that the improvements are not intended as rent.[34] In *G.H. Cunningham,* the principal stockholder of a corporation was held not to have received rental income from improvements made by the corporation to property it leased from the stockholder because neither party intended that the value of the improvements should be rent.

Another indication that improvements are not intended as rent is the actual rent charged for the property without the improvements. When controlled corporations erected buildings on land leased from the stockholder, it was held that the improvements were not in lieu of rent. The corporations were bona fide business corporations and if they had rented similar property on the open market from strangers, they could not have rented the property for any amount substantially less than the amount their actual occupancy cost them.[35]

¶ 615.1   *Pre-1987 Improvements*

For improvements made by a lessee and placed in service before 1987 (or after 1986 if they are subject to the pre-1987 depreciation rules under various transition rules), the lessee may amortize the cost of the improvements over the remaining term of the lease if that is less than the recovery period for the improvements. There are, however, some exceptions to this rule.

If a pre-1987 improvement may be removed by the lessee and used elsewhere, amortization over the lease term is not permitted. A lessee

---

[32] Code Sec. 168(i)(8).
[33] *M.E. Blatt Co.,* 38-2 USTC ¶ 9599, 305 U.S. 267; 59 S.Ct. 186; Reg. § 1.61-8(c).
[34] *G.H. Cunningham,* CA-9, 58-2 USTC ¶ 9771, 258 F.2d 231.
[35] *O.L. Bardes,* 37 TC 1134, CCH Dec. 25,416, Nonacq. 1964-1 CB (Part 1) 6.

was denied amortization deductions over a relatively short remaining lease term for the cost of fixtures, signs and wall cabinets. The lessee was unable to show that these assets could not be removed on termination of the lease and used elsewhere.[36] Also, a lessee who has a purchase option on the leased property may not amortize the cost of pre-1987 improvements over the lease term if it seems likely that the lessee will exercise the option, or if the lessee intends to exercise the option and it appears that the lessee will do so.[37]

Renewal Options

Generally, the lessee who made improvements to leased property and placed them in service before 1987 may amortize the cost over the remaining initial term of the lease and may ignore any renewal period or options, if the remaining initial term of the lease at the time the improvements were placed in service was at least 60 percent of the recovery period applicable to the improvements. If the remaining initial term was less than 60 percent of the recovery period, the renewal periods are counted as part of the lease term, unless the lessee can establish that it is more probable that the lease will not be renewed or extended than that the lease will be renewed or extended. Also, the amortization period must include renewal periods if the lease has been renewed or extended or the facts show with reasonable certainty that the lease will be renewed or extended.[38]

Purchase of Fee

If a lessee constructed a building or other improvement on leased property and placed that building or improvement in service before 1987, the lessee is entitled to amortize the cost over the lease term, if the lease term is less than the recovery period of the improvement. But what if the lessee now purchases the complete fee in the property? Obviously, a portion of the purchase price reflects the value of the lessor's right to the improvement at the end of the lease term as well as the value of the property without the lessee's improvement.

The excess of the purchase price of the fee over the value of the property without the lessee's improvement is not a deductible expense, and the lessee cannot amortize the portion of the purchase price allocable to the improvement over the remaining period of the extinguished lease.[39] According to the IRS, a lessee who purchases the fee must depreciate improvements made by the lessee before the purchase over their remaining recovery period as of the date the lessee acquires

---

[36] *Bell Electric Co.*, 45 TC 155, CCH Dec. 27,630, Acq. 1966-2 CB 4.
[37] *Dawson-Spatz Packing Co.*, CA-6, 61-1 USTC ¶ 9452, 289 F.2d 934; *S.J. Moss*, 38 TC 605, CCH Dec. 25,605.
[38] Former Code Sec. 178, as in effect before enactment of the Tax Reform Act of 1986, and the regulations under former Code Sec. 178.
[39] *Millinery Center Building Corp.*, S.Ct., 56-1 USTC ¶ 9391, 350 U.S. 456, 76 S.Ct. 493.

the fee.[40] See also *Wilshire Medical Properties, Inc.*,[41] in which it was held that a lessee who constructed a medical building on leased land and then purchased the lessor's interest in the property was entitled to show that some allocation of the purchase price between the land and the building should be made for the purposes of depreciation.

In Rev. Rul. 60-180, the IRS ruled that the purchase price paid by a lessee who had made improvements to leased land must be allocated to the land and the improvements in proportion to (1) the fair market value of the land as of the date of purchase and (2) the fair market value on the same date of the right to acquire at the end of the lease term the improvements made by the lessee. The amount of the purchase price allocated to the improvements is depreciable over their remaining recovery period as of the date of the purchase.

> *Example:* The Taxpayer entered into a 16-year lease for land in January 1986 and constructed a building on the land at a cost of $30,000. The building was completed in January 1987 and had a recovery period of 19 years. The Taxpayer is amortizing the cost of the building over the term of the lease at a rate of $2,000 per year ($30,000 cost divided by the 15 years remaining on the lease when the building was placed in service). On July 1, 1997, the Taxpayer purchases the premises from the lessor for $25,000. On that date, the fair market value of the land is $15,000 and the value of the lessor's right to acquire the building at the end of the lease term is $10,000. The Taxpayer's basis for depreciating the building over its remaining recovery period on July 1, 1997, is $19,000. This amount is the Taxpayer's unrecovered cost for the building of $9,000 ($30,000 less $21,000 in amortization for the period January 1987 through June 1997), plus $10,000 of the purchase price allocated to the building.

¶ 615.2 *Lease Termination*

If a lessee has made improvements to leased property, those improvements become the property of the lessor on the termination of the lease. At that time, we must be concerned with two questions:

1. What are the tax consequences to the lessee, who has been taking depreciation for the cost of the improvements?
2. What are the tax consequences, if any, to the lessor, who now comes into possession of the improvements?

Lessee's Loss Deduction

According to the Senate Finance Committee Report on the Tax Reform Act of 1986, a lessee who does not retain improvements that

---

[40] Rev. Rul. 60-180, 1960-1 CB 114.   [41] CA-9, 63-1 USTC ¶ 9334, 314 F.2d 333.

the lessee made to the leased property realizes gain or loss on termination of the lease measured by the adjusted basis of the improvements at that time. In other words, the termination of the lease is treated as if the lessee is selling the improvements and unless the lessee realizes some amount for the lease, the lessee suffers a tax loss equal to any unrecovered cost for the improvements when the lessee surrenders possession of the leased property. If the improvements were capital assets, the loss would be a capital loss. If the improvements were Code Sec. 1231 business property, the loss would be a Code Sec. 1231 loss. (See the discussion of sales and exchanges in Chapter 13.)

Lessor's Tax-Free Receipt

On the termination of a lease, the lessor recognizes no income because of the receipt of improvements that were made by the lessee to the leased property.[42] This income exclusion does not apply if the improvements represent the liquidation in kind of lease rentals. The exclusion applies only to the income realized by the lessor upon the termination of the lease and has no application to the cost of improvements made by the lessee that is treated as rent during the period of the lease. The exclusion has no application to income which may be realized by the lessor on the termination of the lease and which is not attributable to the value of the improvements made by the lessee, and it does not apply to income derived by the lessor after the termination of the lease as a result of the ownership of the improvements.[43]

In *Boston Fish Market Corp.*,[44] it was held that a payment to a lessor in settlement of a tenant's obligation under the lease agreement to restore the leasehold improvements to their original pre-lease condition was not excludable from income under Code Sec. 109 and was taxable to the lessor. Reg. § 1.109-1(b) contains the following example.

> **Example:** The A Corporation leased in 1945, for a period of 50 years, unimproved real property to the B Corporation under a lease providing that the B Corporation erect on the leased premises an office building costing $500,000, in addition to paying the A Corporation a lease rental of $10,000 per annum beginning on the date of completion of the improvements, the sum of $100,000 being placed in escrow for the payment of the rental. The building was completed on January 1, 1950. The lease provided that all improvements made by the lessee on the leased property would become the absolute property of the A Corporation on the termination of the lease by forfeiture or otherwise and that the lessor would become entitled on such termination to the remainder of the

---

[42] Code Sec. 109.
[43] Reg. § 1.109-1(a).
[44] 57 TC 884, CCH Dec. 31,321.

sum, if any, remaining in the escrow fund. The B Corporation forfeited its lease on January 1, 1955, when the improvements had a value of $100,000. Under the provisions of section 109, the $100,000 is excluded from gross income. The amount of $50,000, representing the remainder in the escrow fund, is forfeited to the A Corporation and is included in the gross income of that taxpayer.

A corresponding basis provision [45] prevents a lessor from increasing the basis for the property by the value of lessee improvements that are excluded from income under Code Sec. 109. What this means, of course, is that the lessor will be taxed on the improvements when the lessor disposes of them in a taxable transaction. The overall effect of Code Secs. 109 and 1019 is to defer the tax on the lessor for lessee improvements that are not treated as rent to a time when the lessor is in a position to pay the tax.

Example: The Lessor purchased land at a cost of $20,000 and leased this land for a number of years. The lessee constructed improvements on the land for its use. The cost of the improvements was borne solely by the lessee and was not treated as rent by the parties. On the termination of the lease, when the improvements had a fair market value of $75,000, these improvements became the property of the Lessor. At this time, the fair market value of the land was $40,000.

On the termination of the lease, the Lessor's basis for the property, land, and buildings is $20,000, the Lessor's basis for the land. If the Lessor immediately sells the property for its total fair market value of $115,000, the Lessor realizes a gain of $95,000, which represents the $20,000 gain on the land plus the value of the improvements received tax-free from the lessee on the termination of the lease. Code Sec. 109 does not prevent the recognition of this gain on the sale or other taxable disposition of the property.

¶ 621 INVESTMENT CREDIT

Prior to the Tax Reform Act of 1986, an investment credit was available for most tangible personal business property. This credit was 10 percent of the cost of qualifying property. For the most part, the credit was only of tangential interest to the owner of commercial or investment real estate since buildings and their structural components were not eligible for the credit. In addition to the regular 10 percent investment credit, however, an investment credit for the cost of rehabilitating certain buildings was introduced in 1978. While the 1986 Act repealed the regular investment credit, it retained the credit for qualified rehabilitation expenditures, but in modified form.

---

[45] Code Sec. 1019.

The current tax credit for rehabilitation expenditures is available for the cost of rehabilitating existing commercial buildings or residential and nonresidential historic structures. The tax credit is 10 percent of the cost of the qualified rehabilitation of a commercial building, but the building must have been first placed in service before 1936. The cost of rehabilitating a certified historic structure, regardless of its age, is eligible for a 20 percent tax credit. For qualified rehabilitations prior to 1987, commercial buildings 30 years old qualified for a 15 percent credit and buildings 40 years old qualified for a 20 percent credit. The pre-1987 credit for the rehabilitation of an historic structure was 25 percent of the cost of the rehabilitation.

The tax credit for rehabilitation expenditures is considered in detail at ¶ 821.

¶ 623 Qualified Rehabilitations by Lessee

The lessee of a building who makes qualified expenditures to rehabilitate the building can qualify for the 10 percent tax credit for older commercial buildings or the 20 percent tax credit for historic structures. To be eligible to take the credit, however, the expenditures must be capitalized by the lessee and not treated as rent by the parties. Also, there must be at least 39 years remaining on the term of the lease at the time the rehabilitation is completed (27½ years in the case of residential rental property).[46] The remaining term of the lease is determined without regard to any renewal periods.

The rules governing how a lessor may pass an investment credit to a lessee were preserved when the investment credit provisions were restructured in the Revenue Reconciliation Act of 1990.[47] This would indicate that a lessor who makes qualified rehabilitation expenditures may elect to pass the credit to the lessee under former Code Sec. 48(d) as in effect prior to 1991 (see ¶ 625.1). Presumably, the election to pass the credit through to the lessee would be available even if the remaining term of the lease is less than 39 years or other applicable recovery period for the property. A lessor who reimburses a lessee for the rehabilitation costs incurred by the lessee is treated as having made the qualified expenditures.

¶ 625 Qualified Rehabilitations by Lessor

A lessor who rehabilitates a building that is leased is eligible for the rehabilitation tax credit if the expenditures otherwise qualify.

Since the parties to the lease may arrange who is to actually claim the credit, by fixing who is to make the rehabilitation expenditures or by use of the election to pass the credit to the lessee (see ¶ 625.1), the

---

[46] Code Sec. 47(c)(2)(B)(vi).   [47] Code Sec. 50(d)(5).

lessor and lessee should carefully weigh who is in the best position to make full use of the credit. Various limits on the credit, which are discussed at ¶ 823.4, may limit the utility of the credit to certain taxpayers. By fixing who will claim the credit, and adjusting other lease terms accordingly, both lessor and lessee may gain from the credit.

¶ 625.1 Election to Pass Credit to Lessee

Generally, the lessee of property is not entitled to an investment credit for leased property when it is the lessor who makes the investment that qualifies for the credit. Under an exception to this rule, however, a lessee may claim the investment credit if the lessor of new investment credit property elects to pass the credit to the lessee.[48] In some cases, the election results in a split of the credit between the lessor and the lessee (see ¶ 625.2).

When the lessor elects to pass an investment credit to the lessee, the lessee calculates the credit on the basis of the fair market value of the property eligible for the credit.[49] If the lease is between component members of a controlled group of corporations, however, the credit is based on the lessor's basis in the property.[50] The election by a lessor to pass the credit to the lessee may be made on a property-by-property basis or under a general election. In either case, statements must be filed by the lessor with the lessee. Details on the procedure to pass the credit to the lessee may be found in Reg. § 1.48-4.

Lessee's Income

Generally, when a taxpayer makes qualified rehabilitation expenditures, the taxpayer must reduce the basis of the property for depreciation by the amount of the rehabilitation credit.[51] This basis reduction does not apply to the lessor, however, when the lessor elects to pass the credit through to the lessee.[52] Rather, when the lessor elects to pass the credit to the lessee, the lessee must include in gross income the amount of the credit ratably over the recovery period of the property.[53] A lessor who does not pass the credit to the lessee is subject to the basis reduction rule.

Subleases

A lessee who subleases property on which the lessor elected to pass on an investment credit may, in turn, elect to pass the credit on to the

---

[48] Former Code Sec. 48(d), as in effect prior to 1991; see Code Sec. 50(d)(5).

[49] Former Code Sec. 48(d)(1)(A), as in effect prior to 1991; see Code Sec. 50(d)(5).

[50] Former Code Sec. 48(d)(1)(B), as in effect prior to 1991; see Code Sec. 50(d)(5).

[51] Code Sec. 50(c).

[52] Former Code Sec. 48(d)(5)(A), as in effect prior to 1991; see Code Sec. 50(d)(5).

[53] Former Code Sec. 48(d)(5)(B), as in effect prior to 1991; see Code Sec. 50(d)(5).

sublessee. The lessee-sublessor, however, need not pass the credit on to the sublessee, but may retain it.[54]

When neither the lessor nor the lessee in a standard two-party lease can make immediate use of a rehabilitation investment tax credit, it may be possible to interpose a third party who can make use of the credit. This is essentially what happened in *Comdisco, Inc.*[55] A supplier corporation leased computer equipment directly to another corporation, but entered into a new lease for the property with a third party and assigned the former lease and elected to pass through the investment credit to the third party. The court ruled the transaction was a lease from the supplier to the third party and a sublease from the third party to the original lessee. The third party, as a lessee from the supplier, was entitled to the investment credit under the supplier's election to pass the credit to the lessee. It did not matter that the original lessee continued to make payments directly to the supplier because the third party was obligated to the primary lessor. While *Comdisco* involved the lease of equipment (which was eligible for the investment credit at the time), there would be no reason why the same principle could not apply to the lease of property that is being rehabilitated and is eligible for the investment credit for qualified rehabilitations.

¶ 625.2 *Credit Split on Short-Term Lease Property*

A lessor who elects to pass the investment credit to a lessee can transfer only part of the credit in the case of property leased under "certain short term leases."[56] A lease is subject to this special rule if the lease is of property that:

1. Is new investment credit property (qualified rehabilitations are always treated as new property);

2. Has a class life of more than 14 years under the ADR system;[57]

3. Is leased for a period of less than 80 percent of its class life; and

4. Is not leased subject to a net lease under which the lessor is guaranteed a specific return or is guaranteed against loss of income.[58]

---

[54] Rev. Rul. 71-243, 1971-1 CB 7.

[55] CA-7, 85-1 USTC ¶ 9245, 756 F.2d 569.

[56] Former Code Sec. 48(d)(2), as in effect prior to 1991; see Code Sec. 50(d)(5).

[57] See Rev. Proc. 87-56, 1987-2 CB 674, for a listing of the class lives for various assets.

[58] See former Code Sec. 57(c)(1)(B) as in effect before the enactment of the Tax Reform Act of 1986 for the definition of net lease for this purpose.

Since real estate is often leased under a net lease arrangement, there will be many occasions when an election to pass the credit to the lessee will result in a pass-through of the full credit, even if the lease term is relatively short. Unless the lessee remains in possession at least five years, however, all or part of the credit may be recaptured.[59] If the credit does have to be split between the lessor and the lessee when the lessor elects to pass the credit to the lessee, the credit is divided between the two parties in the same ratio that the lease term bears to the class life of the property.[60]

If the lessee of property subleases property that is subject to the short-term lease rules, the property is treated as being subject to a short-term lease in the hands of the sublessee. Property that is short-term lease property in the hands of the lessee is treated as such in the hand of the sublessee even if the property is leased to the sublessee under a net lease.[61] Of course, the credit must be split three ways if the sublessor elects to pass the credit to the sublessee after the primary lessor has elected to pass the credit to the sublessor.

---

[59] Code Sec. 50(a)(1).
[60] Reg. § 1.48-4(c)(3) and the examples in Reg. § 1.48-4(c)(4).
[61] Reg. § 1.48-4(e).

Part III

Real Estate Operation

Introduction to Part III

Chapter 7 looks at many of the common deductions associated with real estate operation. Also, the general rules relating to tax accounting are considered in this chapter, with special regard to the rules that are likely to affect the ownership and operation of real estate and those entities that may hold real estate for business or investment purposes.

Chapter 8 deals with additions and improvements to real estate in general and the special amortization and tax credit provisions available for particular types of improvements. This third edition reflects the additional deductions Congress enacted to assist economically depressed areas and New York City following the terrorist attacks of September 11, 2001. The more widely available deduction for depreciation is given special consideration in Chapter 9.

The development, subdivision, and sale of real estate in the ordinary course of business involves tax questions and problems that are unique when compared to those involved in the one-time sale of rental property or property used in a trade or business. These unique questions and problems are the subjects of Chapter 10.

While deductions generated by a specific property always can be used to reduce the taxable income from that property, there are limits on the use of deductions generated by real estate activities to reduce taxable income from other sources. Perhaps the most important limitations in this regard are the passive loss limitations discussed in Chapter 11. These limitations must be considered in any evaluation of the tax benefits that might be derived from the ownership and operation of real estate.

Finally, Part III concludes with an examination of one area of real estate operation that no one really wants to face—what happens when real estate just cannot support the debt incurred to finance its purchase, or support the debt incurred for other purposes and secured by the real estate. Troubled real estate financings, the topic of Chapter 12, may develop in the course of holding real estate for investment, for the production of rental income, or for use in a trade or business.

Chapter 7

Operating Expenses and Taxes

¶ 700 OVERVIEW OF CHAPTER

The income tax rates are applied to "taxable income," that is, to income after permitted deductions. The ownership and operation of real estate give rise to a host of deductions that often reduce substantially the amount of income from the real estate that is subject to tax. In this Chapter, many of the most common deductions associated with real estate operation are examined. Depreciation, a "non-cash" expenditure that is often one of the largest deductions associated with real estate operation, however, is singled out and treated separately in Chapter 9. Also, the deduction for interest is considered in Chapter 3 in connection with real estate financing. Deductions related to leasehold acquisition and disposition are considered in Chapter 5, and those related to leasehold improvements and additions in Chapter 6.

While deductions generated by a specific property always can be used to reduce the taxable income from that property, there are limits on the use of deductions generated by real estate activities to reduce taxable income from other sources. One such limitation is the at-risk rules discussed in Chapter 3. Another is the passive loss limitations discussed in Chapter 11. These limitations must be considered in any evaluation of the tax benefits that might be derived from the ownership and operation of real estate.

Taxable income must be determined using a consistent method of accounting to fix the taxable amount in a specific accounting period. The two most widely used accounting methods are cash and accrual, and the two most widely used accounting periods are the calendar and fiscal years. The general rules relating to tax accounting also are considered in this chapter, with special regard to the rules that are likely to affect the ownership and operation of real estate and those entities that may hold real estate for business or investment purposes.

¶ 701 TAX ACCOUNTING FOR REAL ESTATE

Most individuals are cash method, calendar year taxpayers. Individual ownership or co-ownership of real estate generally does not present an opportunity to make accounting changes. When real estate is acquired for business or investment purposes by a new entity and a

¶ 701

new taxpayer comes into existence, however, an opportunity exists to choose the accounting period and accounting method that will be most advantageous to the new entity and its owners. Of course, in many cases, the discretion to pick and choose among possible accounting periods and methods is not unfettered. The Internal Revenue Code contains a host of provisions designed to limit the tax advantages that might otherwise be gained through judicious tax accounting.

¶ 703 Accounting Period

Taxable income is computed on the basis of an annual accounting period called the tax or taxable year. This period generally may be either a fiscal year or the calendar year. The calendar year is the 12 months ending on December 31. A fiscal year is a 12-month period ending on the last day of any calendar month. Also, a fiscal year may be adopted that varies from 52 to 53 weeks and that always ends on the same day of the week and that always ends either on whatever date that day of the week last occurs in a calendar month or on whatever date that day of the week falls which is nearest to the last day of a calendar month.[1]

Since a new taxpayer may adopt either a fiscal year or the calendar year on the first return,[2] the formation of a new entity in connection with the acquisition and ownership of real estate offers the opportunity to select the most advantageous tax year. The ability to select any fiscal year as the tax year, however, is limited by special rules that apply to partnerships, S corporations, and personal service corporations and which are discussed at ¶ 703.1. When the choice of a tax year is not limited, the year may be selected to match income and deductions to limit tax liability, or to create a short initial year to minimize initial income taxes.

¶ 703.1 Required Tax Years for Partnerships, S Corporations, and Personal Service Corporations

Various provisions of the Internal Revenue Code generally require that partnerships,[3] S corporations,[4] and personal service corporations[5] conform their tax years to the tax years of their owners unless a business purpose can be shown for the use of some other year. S corporations and personal service corporations generally must use the calendar year.

The IRS has issued Rev. Proc. 2002-38,[6] which contains procedures for expeditious approval of requests by these entities to adopt, retain,

---

[1] Reg. § 1.441-2.
[2] Reg. § 1.441-1(c).
[3] Code Sec. 706(b).
[4] Code Sec. 1378(b).
[5] Code Sec. 441(i).
[6] 2002-22 IRB 1037.

or change their tax years. Rev. Proc. 2002-38 also contains a test for determining a natural business year that, if met, automatically establishes a business purpose for a particular fiscal year. Rev. Rul. 87-57 [7] contains examples of factors that are considered by the IRS in determining whether a business purpose exists for a specific tax year. Certain partnerships, S corporations, and personal service corporations may elect to use a tax year other than a required tax year,[8] as separately discussed at ¶ 703.2.

Partnerships

When a new partnership had the unrestricted right to choose a taxable year, partners often would take maximum advantage of this tax deferral opportunity. For example, if all partners were on the calendar year (which most likely would be the case when the partners were individuals), then choosing a fiscal year ending January 31 for the partnership would allow the partners to defer reporting partnership income for a period of 11 months. Partnership items from a partnership's tax year are reported by partners for their tax year that includes the last day of the partnership's tax year.

Now, however, Code Sec. 706(b) prevents this type of deferral by requiring a partnership to conform its tax year to that of the partners, unless the partnership can establish a business purpose for a different tax year. Under these tax year conformity rules, a partnership must use the same tax year as its majority partners, that is, the tax year used by the partners who have an aggregate interest in partnership profits and capital of more than 50 percent.[9] Since most individuals are calendar year taxpayers, this provision generally requires a partnership of individuals to use the calendar year.

If there is no combination of majority partners that have the same tax year, then the partnership's tax year must conform to the tax year of all the principal partners of the partnership, that is, all partners that have at least a five percent interest in partnership profits and capital.[10] If a partnership's tax year cannot be determined using majority partners or principal partners, then the tax year chosen must be the one that results in the least aggregate deferral of income to the partners.[11] Reg. § 1.706-1(b)(3)(iv) contains numerous examples of how to determine the tax year that results in the least aggregate deferral of income to the partners.

Once the partnership's tax year is fixed by the conformity rules (or by a business purpose), a partner cannot change tax years to achieve

---

[7] 1987-2 CB 117.
[8] Code Sec. 444.
[9] Code Sec. 706(b)(1)(B)(i).
[10] Code Sec. 706(b)(1)(B)(ii).
[11] Code Sec. 706(b)(1)(B)(iii); Reg. § 1.706-1(b)(3).

the deferral blocked by the conformity rules. A principal partner (five percent interest) cannot change to a tax year other than that of the partnership in which he or she is a principal partner unless a business purpose for the change is established.[12] The IRS, in effect, has extended this rule to all partners. Reg. § 1.706-1(b)(8)(ii) provides that no partner may change the taxable year without securing approval from the Commissioner of Internal Revenue.

A partnership may elect a tax year other than a required tax year under Code Sec. 444 as discussed at ¶ 703.2.

S Corporations

S corporations must use a tax year that is a "permitted year."[13] A permitted year is defined as a year ending on December 31 or any other accounting period for which the corporation is able to establish a business purpose.[14] Deferral of income to shareholders is not a business purpose that would justify a tax year other than the calendar year.

An S corporation may elect a tax year other than a required tax year under Code Sec. 444 as discussed at ¶ 703.2.

Personal Service Corporations

A personal service corporation must use the calendar year as its taxable year unless the corporation establishes a business purpose for having a different period for its taxable year.[15] Deferral of income to shareholders is not a business purpose that would justify a tax year other than the calendar year.

A corporation is a personal service corporation if:

1. The corporation is a C corporation;
2. The principal activity of the corporation is the performance of personal services in the fields of health, law, engineering, architecture, accounting, actuarial science, performing arts, or consulting;
3. The personal services are substantially performed by employee-owners (a person is an employee-owner if he is an employee of the corporation and owns any outstanding stock of the corporation); and
4. Employee-owners own more than 10 percent of the fair market value of the outstanding stock of the corporation.[16]

---

[12] Code Sec. 706(b)(2).
[13] Code Sec. 1378(a).
[14] Code Sec. 1378(b).
[15] Code Sec. 441(i)(1).
[16] Reg. § 1.441-3(c).

¶ 703.1

Reg. § 1.441-3 also contains an explanation of how to determine the "principal activity" of a corporation and how to determine whether personal services are "substantially performed" by employee-owners.

A personal service corporation may elect a tax year other than a required tax year under Code Sec. 444 as discussed at ¶ 703.2.

¶ 703.2 *Election to Use Other Than a Required Year*

Partnerships, S corporations, and personal service corporations that have a required tax year under the rules discussed above may elect, on Form 8716, to use a tax year other than their required year.[17] The election to use a tax year other than a required year, however, carries a cost—a "required payment" in the case of a partnership or S corporation, and minimum distributions to owner-employees in the case of a personal service corporation. The election is available to an entity if it meets the following three conditions:

1. The entity is not a member of a tiered structure (subject to a *de minimis* exception);

2. The entity did not previously have an election under Code Sec. 444 in effect; and

3. The elected tax year results in a deferral period of less than three months (or the deferral period of its current tax year if less than three months in the case of an entity that is changing its tax year).

For a partnership, S corporation, or personal service corporation that wants to adopt or change its taxable year by making the election under Code Sec. 444, the deferral period comprises the months that occur after the end of the taxable year desired under the election and before the close of the required tax year.[18] If an entity is using its required tax year as its tax year, the deferral period is deemed to be zero.[19] This latter precludes an entity that is already using its required tax year from changing to a different tax year, since an entity seeking to change its tax year cannot elect a tax year under Code Sec. 444 with a deferral period that is greater than the deferral period of its current tax year.

Example: The newly formed Partnership, in which all partners are calendar year individual taxpayers, desires to elect a tax year ending September 30. The Partnership's required tax year is the calendar year. The deferral period in this case is three months, the number of months between September 30 and December 31. The

---

[17] Code Sec. 444.
[18] Code Sec. 444(b)(4).
[19] Temp. Reg. § 1.444-1T(b)(4)(ii)(B).

new Partnership would be permitted to elect a fiscal year ending September 30 under Code Sec. 444.

On the other hand, suppose the Partnership were an existing partnership that had historically used the calendar year, its required year, and that the Partnership desired to change its tax year to the fiscal year ending September 30. In this case, the deferral period of its current tax year is zero and the deferral period of its desired tax year would be three months. The Partnership would not be permitted to elect the fiscal year ending September 30 under Code Sec. 444 because the deferral period for the new year would be greater than the deferral period of its existing tax year.

Election by Partnerships and S Corporations

A partnership or S corporation that makes the election to have a tax year other than the required tax year must make the payments required by Code Sec. 7519 for any tax year for which the election is in effect. The "required payment" is intended to represent the value of the tax deferral that the owners of the partnership or S corporation receive as a result of the election to use other than a required tax year. The payment is due by May 15 of the calendar year following the calendar year in which the elected tax year begins.[20] Required payments under Code Sec. 7519 are assessed and collected as if they were employment taxes and are paid with Form 720 or by FTD deposit. A worksheet included with the instructions for Form 1065 and Form 1120S is used to compute the required payment and must be included when the payment is made. A required payment is waived if it does not exceed $500. A partnership, S corporation, or its owners are not entitled to a deduction for any required payment under Code Sec. 7519.[21]

Election by Personal Service Corporations

A personal service corporation that elects a tax year other than the required tax year is subject to the deduction limits contained in Code Sec. 280H. These deduction limits are designed to eliminate the benefit that would otherwise result from the tax deferral. Code Sec. 280H limits the deductions that a personal service corporation using other than a required tax year may take for payments to employee-owners of the corporation unless certain minimum distributions are made to the employee-owners before the end of the calendar year. These minimum distributions must be made during the deferral period. See Temp. Reg. § 1.280H-1T for details on calculating the minimum distributions and

---

[20] Temp. Reg. § 1.7519-2T(a)(4)(ii).   [21] Temp. Reg. § 1.7519-2T(b).

any deduction limits imposed for failing to meet the minimum distribution requirements.

Termination of Election

The election to use a tax year other than the required tax year under Code Sec. 444 is terminated if:

1. The electing entity changes to its required tax year;
2. The electing entity liquidates;
3. A partnership or S corporation willfully fails to make the required payments or a personal service corporation willfully fails to comply with the minimum distribution requirements;
4. An entity becomes a member of a tiered structure (see discussion below);
5. An S corporation's S election is terminated (but a corporation that immediately becomes a personal service corporation following the termination of its status as an S corporation may continue the election); or
6. A personal service corporation ceases to be a personal service corporation (but a personal service corporation that ceases to be a personal service corporation but elects to be an S corporation may continue the election).

Once an election under Code Sec. 444 to use a tax year other than a required year is terminated under the above rules, the partnership, S corporation, or personal service corporation may not make another Code Sec. 444 election.[22]

Tiered Structures

An entity that is part of a tiered structure generally may not elect or continue a tax year other than a required year.[23] A partnership, S corporation, or personal service corporation is part of a tiered structure if the entity directly owns any portion of another partnership, S corporation, personal service corporation, or certain trusts. An entity is also a part of a tiered structure if any other partnership, S corporation, personal service corporation, or certain trusts directly own any portion of the entity.[24]

Certain ownership, however, may be disregarded under both "upstream" and "downstream" *de minimis* rules. Upstream, forbidden ownership in the entity seeking the Code Sec. 444 election is disregarded if it does not exceed five percent.[25] Downstream, forbidden

---

[22] Code Sec. 444(d)(2)(B); Temp. Reg. § 1.444-1T(a)(5).
[23] Code Sec. 444(d)(3).
[24] Temp. Reg. § 1.444-2T.
[25] Temp. Reg. § 1.444-2T(c)(3).

ownership by the entity seeking the Code Sec. 444 election is disregarded if the forbidden ownership contributes five percent or less of the entity's taxable income or two percent or less of the entity's gross income.[26]

¶ 705 Accounting Method

Taxpayers must compute taxable income using a method of accounting that clearly reflects income.[27] The two most commonly used methods of accounting are the cash receipts and disbursements method and the accrual method. Other methods may be allowed under other Internal Revenue Code sections, such as the installment method discussed at ¶ 1401, and hybrid methods may be authorized by regulations.[28] The general rules applicable to a specific accounting method may not always apply to specific items. Many income and expense items are subject to special rules that alter the timing or amount of reportable income or deduction from what would be the case under normal cash or accrual accounting rules. Examples of such items, include advance rents (see ¶ 415 and 423), prepaid and investment interest (see ¶ 325), original issue discount (see ¶ 335), and construction period expenses (see ¶ 127).

A taxpayer engaged in more than one trade or business may use a different method of accounting to compute taxable income for each trade or business.[29] This rule allows an individual to use the cash method for personal income and expenses and the accrual method for business income and expenses. It also allows an individual or other taxpayer to select a new method of accounting for a new business.[30]

¶ 705.1 *Cash Method*

Under the cash method of accounting, income is reported for the year in which it is actually or constructively received in the form of cash or its equivalent or other property or services.[31] Under the doctrine of constructive receipt, income must be reported under the cash method when the income is credited to the taxpayer's account, set apart for the taxpayer, or otherwise made available so that the taxpayer may draw upon it at any time. Deductions under the cash method generally are taken for the year in which the amounts are actually paid. The cash method is the method of accounting used by most individuals.

---

[26] Temp. Reg. § 1.444-2T(c)(2).
[27] Code Sec. 446.
[28] Code Sec. 446(c).
[29] Code Sec. 446(d).
[30] See, for example, *R.C. Hoffman,* 19 TCM 836, CCH Dec. 24,295(M), T.C. Memo. 1960-160, aff'd CA-3, 62-1 USTC ¶ 9218, 298 F.2d 784; *National Builders, Inc.,* 12 TC 852, CCH Dec. 16,985, Acq. 1949-2 CB 3; *Burgess Poultry Market, Inc.,* DC Tex, 64-2 USTC ¶ 9515.
[31] Reg. § 1.446-1(c).

A cash method taxpayer may control the timing of income, within the confines of the doctrine of constructive receipt, or deductions to the extent he has control over the timing of receipt of income or payment of expenses. Billing practices may hasten or defer collection of income, and accelerating or deferring payment of expenses may accelerate or defer tax deductions attributable to those expenses. There are, however, some limits on the taxpayers who are eligible to use the cash method of accounting, and these limitations are discussed below.

Limitations on Use of Cash Method

Under Code Sec. 448, certain taxpayers are not permitted to use the cash method of accounting, but must adopt and use the accrual method. These taxpayers are:

1. C corporations;
2. Partnerships that have at least one C corporation as a partner; and
3. Tax shelters.

Trusts that are subject to tax on unrelated trade or business income are treated as C corporations with respect to their unrelated business income.[32]

Tax shelters that are subject to the limitations on the use of the cash method of accounting are broadly defined to include:

1. Any enterprise, other than a C corporation, in which interests have been offered for sale in an offering that is subject to federal or state securities law registration;
2. A partnership or entity, other than a C corporation, if more than 35 percent of losses are allocable to limited partners or limited entrepreneurs; and
3. Any partnership or other entity, any investment plan or arrangement, or any other plan or arrangement, if the principal purpose is the avoidance of federal income tax.[33]

Exceptions to Limitations on Use of Cash Method

There are several exceptions to the limitations on the use of the cash method. Under these exceptions, small businesses, farmers and ranchers, and qualified personal service corporations may use the cash method of accounting, if otherwise qualified.

Except in the case of a tax shelter, a C corporation or partnership with a C corporation as a partner may use the cash method of

---

[32] Code Sec. 448(d)(6).   [33] Temp. Reg. § 1.448-1T(b).

accounting if the average annual gross receipts of the corporation or partnership do not exceed $5 million.[34]

Also, except in the case of a tax shelter, Code Sec. 448 does not apply to a farming business.[35] It should be noted, however, that certain farm corporations are required to use accrual accounting under the provisions of Code Sec. 447. Essentially, under Code Sec. 447, corporations engaged in farming are required to use accrual accounting unless the corporation is an S corporation or a corporation with less than $1 million in annual gross receipts ($25 million in the case of family farm corporations).[36]

Again, except in the case of a tax shelter, a qualified personal service corporation may use the cash method of accounting. A qualified personal service corporation is a corporation in which substantially all of the activities involve the performance of services in the fields of health, law, engineering, architecture, accounting, actuarial science, performing arts, or consulting. Also, for a corporation to be a qualified personal service corporation, substantially all of the stock of the corporation must be owned by employees who perform services for the corporation or former employees or their estates or heirs.[37]

¶ 705.2 Accrual Method

Under the accrual method of accounting, income is reported for the year in which it is earned, whether or not that income is actually or constructively received. Generally, it is the right to receive the income and not its actual receipt that controls.[38] Accrual of income may not be postponed because there is the possibility that some of the income may have to be returned or refunded.[39] Deductions or credits under the accrual method of accounting are taken in the year they are accrued or incurred, unless properly allowable in another year. As a general proposition, expenses incurred in and properly attributable to the process of earning income during an accounting period should be charged against that income, even if the expenses are not paid until a subsequent period.[40]

Economic Performance Requirement

In general, an accrual method taxpayer deducts expenses when (1) all events have occurred that determine the fact of the taxpayer's liability for the expense and (2) the taxpayer's liability can be determined with reasonable accuracy.[41] This "all events" test is not treated

---

[34] Code Sec. 448(b)(3) and (c).
[35] Code Sec. 448(b)(1) and (d)(1).
[36] Code Sec. 447(d).
[37] Code Sec. 448(d)(2); Temp. Reg. § 1.448-1T(e).
[38] *J.M. Enright Est.*, S.Ct., 41-1 USTC ¶ 9356, 312 U.S. 636, 61 S.Ct. 777.

[39] *A.M. Brown*, S.Ct., 4 USTC ¶ 1223, 291 U.S. 193, 54 S.Ct. 356.
[40] *P.C. Anderson*, S.Ct., 1 USTC ¶ 155, 269 U.S. 422, 46 S.Ct. 131.
[41] Code Sec. 461(h)(4); Reg. § 1.461-1(a)(2).

as satisfied with respect to a particular item unless and until economic performance with respect to that particular item has occurred.[42]

In the case of a liability that requires a payment for property or services provided to, or for the use of property by, an accrual method taxpayer, economic performance occurs when the property or services are provided or the property is used. In the case of a liability that requires a payment for property or services provided by an accrual method taxpayer, economic performance occurs and related expenses are deductible when the taxpayer actually provides the services or property.

> *Example:* In November of 2002, an accrual-method Taxpayer, using the calendar year as the accounting period, contracted with a third party to have the third party clean and paint the walls within a warehouse that the Taxpayer owns at a cost of $15,000. The work is not performed until sometime in 2003. Although the Taxpayer was contractually bound to pay the $15,000 as of November 2002, economic performance does not occur until 2003, and the Taxpayer may not accrue the expense deduction until 2003.

In order to avoid disrupting normal business and accounting practices, an exception to the economic performance rules applies in the case of certain recurring expense items. An expense deduction is allowed for an item, even if economic performance has not occurred, if:

1. The all events test, other than economic performance, is met;
2. Economic performance occurs within a reasonable time, but not more than 8½ months after the close of the year;
3. The item is recurring in nature and similar items are treated as incurred in the year in which the all events test is met without regard to economic performance; and
4. The recurring item is not material or the deduction for the year in which the all events test is met, without regard to economic performance, results in a better matching of income and expense.[43]

The recurring item exception to the economic performance requirement is not available to taxpayers that are considered tax shelters.[44]

Accrual of Real Property Taxes

Accrual method taxpayers may elect to accrue real property taxes over the period of time to which the property taxes relate.[45] A separate election may be made for the real property taxes attributable to each

---

[42] Code Sec. 461(h).
[43] Code Sec. 461(h)(3).
[44] Code Sec. 461(i).
[45] Code Sec. 461(c).

¶ 705.2

separate trade or business of the taxpayer.[46] If this election is not made, state and local property taxes are deemed to accrue (1) on the date that fixes when the tax becomes a lien on the property, (2) when personal liability for the tax arises, or (3) on any other basis appropriate to the specific situation.

Example: A calendar year Taxpayer using the accrual method owns real property for which the taxes become a lien on the property as of the first day of the property tax year, which runs from October 1 to September 30. Property taxes for the October 1, 1997, through September 30, 1998, period are $2,400. If the Taxpayer elects to ratably accrue the deduction for real property taxes, the Taxpayer deducts $600 of the $2,400 for the 1997 taxable year and $1,800 for the 1998 taxable year. In the absence of the election, the Taxpayer would accrue and deduct the entire $2,400 for the 1997 taxable year because the $2,400 becomes a lien against the property as of October 1, 1997.

¶ 705.3 *Long-Term Construction Contracts*

In the case of long-term contracts, that is, contracts that cannot be completed within one year, taxpayers generally must use the percentage-of-completion method of accounting.[47] Under the percentage-of-completion method, the taxpayer includes in income for the tax year the portion of the gross contract price that corresponds to the percentage of the entire contract that has been completed during the tax year.[48] Under the percentage-of-completion—capitalized-cost method of long-term contract accounting, which was available before July 11, 1989, and which remains available for contracts resulting from the acceptance of a bid made before July 11, 1989, the taxpayer takes 90 percent of the items with respect to the long-term contract into account under the percentage-of-completion method and 10 percent of the items under the completed-contract method or other normal method of accounting used by the taxpayer.[49]

These long-term contract rules of Code Sec. 460, which essentially require the use of the percentage-of-completion method of accounting for long-term contracts and block the use of the completed-contract method of accounting (under which income and expenses relating to a long-term contract are not taken into account until the contract is completed), do not apply to certain types of construction contracts.[50]

---

[46] Reg. § 1.461-1(c)(3).
[47] Code Sec. 460.
[48] Code Sec. 460(b).
[49] Former Code Sec. 460(a) as in effect prior to its amendment by Sec. 7621 of the Revenue Reconciliation Act of 1989, and Sec. 7621(d) of the 1989 Act.
[50] Code Sec. 460(e).

Small Construction Contracts

The long-term contract rules of Code Sec. 460 and the cost allocation rules for long-term contracts contained in Code Sec. 460(c) do not apply to "small construction contracts." A small construction contract is one that is expected to be completed within the two-year period beginning on the commencement date of the contract and that is performed by a taxpayer whose average annual gross receipts do not exceed $10 million.[51]

Home Construction Contracts

The long-term contract rules and cost allocation rules of Code Sec. 460 do not apply to "home construction contracts."[52] A home construction contract is a contract in which 80 percent or more of the estimated total contract costs are reasonably expected to be attributed to (1) the building, reconstruction or rehabilitation of dwelling units contained in buildings comprising four or fewer dwelling units, and (2) improvements to real property directly related to such dwelling units and located on the site of the dwelling units.[53]

Residential Construction Contracts

"Residential construction contracts" are contracts other than home construction contracts for which 80 percent or more of the total estimated costs under the contract are reasonably expected to be attributed to the building, construction, reconstruction, or rehabilitation of, or improvements to, real estate directly related to and located on the site of dwelling units.[54] Under a special rule for residential construction contracts, the percentage-of-completion—capitalized-cost method of accounting is applied with 70 percent of the contract items taken into account under the percentage-of-completion method and the remaining 30 percent of the items under the completed-contract or other normal method of accounting used by the taxpayer.[55]

¶ 707 Controlling the Timing of Income and Expense

The cash method taxpayer, because income is reported and deductions are taken as income is received or expenses paid, has a greater degree of control over the timing of income and expense than does the accrual method taxpayer. The accrual method taxpayer, because income and expense items must be reported in the year accrued or incurred, generally has less control over the timing of income and expense. Nevertheless, even the accrual method taxpayer has some strategies available to defer or accelerate income and expense items.

---

[51] Code Sec. 460(e)(1)(B).
[52] Code Sec. 460(e)(1)(A).
[53] Code Sec. 460(e)(6).
[54] Code Sec. 460(e)(6)(B).
[55] Code Sec. 460(e)(5).

In the usual case, regardless of the method of accounting employed by the taxpayer, a taxpayer will want to defer income and accelerate deductions to reduce current taxes. Through income deferral and expense acceleration, taxes are shifted to future years and, in the meantime, the taxpayer has the use of funds that would otherwise go to pay taxes. In some situations, however, accelerating income and deferring deductions may produce better overall tax results, for instance, when current income will be subject to lower tax rates than income reportable in the following year, either through application of the regular tax rates or the alternative minimum tax. For example, if income reportable this year would be subject to the alternative minimum tax, but income next year would be subject to the highest regular tax rates, accelerating income and deferring deductions could produce a tax advantage.

¶ 707.1   Deferring Income and Accelerating Deductions

As noted, the usual tax strategy is to seek to defer income and to accelerate deductions in order to shift tax liability to future years and gain the use of money that would otherwise go to the tax collector. The following is a checklist of some ideas for reducing current taxes through income deferral and expense acceleration.

1. A cash method taxpayer may delay billing and collection for property and services until after the end of the year.

2. An accrual method taxpayer may defer income by delaying the completion of services or the furnishing of property. For the accrual method taxpayer to achieve deferral, however, the taxpayer must actually hold back or delay completion of the work or delay shipment or transfer of the property. Merely delaying billing does not defer income once "all events" fixing the taxpayer's right to the income have occurred.

3. Profitable sales may be delayed, provided the delay is possible without undue risk of loss. Depending on the nature of the property, sales on consignment or approval may defer income realization while serving to fix price. In the case of real estate, simply setting a closing date after year end defers income from the sale.

4. When available, an installment sale may also defer income from the sale of property. An installment sale permits closing to take place in the current year while income is delayed until some future date. An installment sale also buys the taxpayer more time to assess the tax position. By electing out of installment reporting before a tax return is filed, the taxpayer can "reshift" income back into the year of sale.

¶ 707.1

Operating Expenses and Taxes

5. Cash method taxpayers may prepay real estate or state income taxes and accelerate deductions for these items.

6. Expenses can be accelerated by advance purchases of supplies, repairs and other deductible items. Legal and accounting fees for work in progress at year end may be paid. Cash method taxpayers must actually pay these items to garner a deduction, and accrual method taxpayers must be certain the expenses are incurred and accrued and economic performance has occurred.

7. Cash method taxpayers may pay bonuses before year end to accelerate the deduction. Accrual method taxpayers need not actually pay bonuses before year end but must be certain the necessary actions have been taken to fix liability for the bonuses before year-end, and the bonuses must actually be paid within 2½ months after the close of the year. Special rules apply to bonuses paid to related cash method taxpayers as discussed at ¶709 in connection with related party transactions.

8. Lease cancellation payments can accelerate deductions for rent on leased property that is no longer desirable or being used.

9. Charitable contributions are easily controlled for maximum advantage. Gifts of easements and appreciated real estate should be considered to effect a charitable deduction with no out-of-pocket cash cost.

10. Sales of property at a loss can be accelerated into the current year in order to use the loss deduction to offset other income.

11. Purchase of depreciable personal property before year end generates a deduction for the current year.

¶ 707.2 Accelerating Income and Deferring Deductions

When good tax planning calls for accelerating income into the current year and deferring deductions until the following year, the strategies available are essentially the opposite of those presented at ¶707.1. The following checklist highlights some of the more common strategies:

1. Accelerate billing and speed up shipments and delivery of goods and services.

2. Conclude profitable sales expeditiously so that closing takes place before year end.

3. Installment obligations or receivables may be sold to accelerate the receipt of income.

¶ 707.2

4. Installment obligations may be pledged to accelerate the realization of income.
5. Cash method taxpayers may delay the payment of deductible business expenses.
6. Purchase of supplies and repairs may be delayed.
7. Acquisition of depreciable personal property may be delayed until after year end.
8. Sales of property at a loss can be delayed or closing dates can be set after year end.

¶ 709 Related Party Transactions

Code Sec. 267 contains provisions that block the use of related parties to create tax losses through property sales and deductions for expenses and interest owed by an accrual method taxpayer to a related cash method taxpayer.

¶ 709.1 *Losses on Sales and Exchanges*

Generally, a taxpayer may make a sale or exchange of property in order to establish a loss and reduce income from other sources. If the sale of property that results in a loss is between related parties, however, no deduction is allowed for that loss.[56] This loss disallowance rule applies to sales between those related parties that are listed in Code Sec. 267(b) and set out at ¶ 709.3.

Were it not for Code Sec. 267(a), taxpayers could use related party sales to reduce current taxes even though, as a practical matter, no actual loss is realized. For example, if the sole owner of a corporation sells property at a loss to the corporation, the shareholder retains ownership and control over the property through the ownership and control over the corporation. Code Sec. 267 blocks the shareholder from taking a loss deduction for the sale of property in this case because, in effect, the shareholder still owns the property or otherwise has dominion and control over the property.

Following the sale of property at a loss between related parties, the transferee's basis in the property is determined under the normal rules, that is, the basis is its cost. The transferor realizes no benefit from the disallowed loss. However, if the original transferee of the property later sells or disposes of the property at a gain, the amount of gain realized by the transferee is reduced by the amount of the loss previously disallowed under Code Sec. 267.[57] The reduction of gain on a subsequent sale applies only to the original transferee and only to the property received from the related party or property received in exchange for that property in a tax-free exchange.

---

[56] Code Sec. 267(a)(1). [57] Code Sec. 267(d).

¶ 709.2 Deductions for Expenses and Interest

Code Sec. 267(a)(2) prevents the mismatching of expense and income that would otherwise occur when an accrual method taxpayer pays a deductible expense to a related cash method taxpayer. For example, an accrual method corporation could accrue salary owed to its sole shareholder. If the sole shareholder were a cash method taxpayer, the corporation could obtain a deduction even though the cash method shareholder would not be required to include the salary in income until such time as it is actually received. Under the current rule of Code Sec. 267(a)(2), however, an accrual method taxpayer may deduct expenses and interest owed to a related cash method taxpayer only when the related taxpayer is required to include the amount in his income. The rule applies to all deductible expenses and interest when the timing of the deduction depends on the taxpayer's method of accounting.

While the related persons covered by this matching of deductions and income rule are essentially the same as those covered by the loss disallowance rule, there are some additional related party rules for expenses and interest owed by partnerships and S corporations and their shareholders. Generally, the matching rules apply to amounts accrued by a partnership to its partners, by partners to their partnerships, by an S corporation to its shareholders, and by S corporation shareholders to their corporation.[58] Special constructive ownership rules apply to partnerships.[59]

¶ 709.3 Related Parties Defined

Related parties that are subject to the loss disallowance rule and income and expense matching rule of Code Sec. 267 include:

1. Members of a family, which includes only brothers, sisters, spouse, ancestors and lineal descendants;
2. An individual and a corporation if the individual owns 50 percent or more in value of the outstanding stock of the corporation;
3. Two corporations that are members of the same controlled group;[60]
4. A grantor and a fiduciary of any trust;
5. A fiduciary of a trust and a fiduciary of another trust, if the same person is the grantor of both trusts;
6. A fiduciary of a trust and a beneficiary of the trust;
7. A fiduciary of a trust and a beneficiary of another trust, if the same person is the grantor of both trusts;

---

[58] Code Sec. 267(e)(1).
[59] Code Sec. 267(e)(1)(C) and (e)(3).
[60] Code Sec. 267(f).

8. A fiduciary of a trust and a corporation, if more than 50 percent in value of the corporation is owned by or for the trust or by or for the grantor of the trust;

9. A person and a tax-exempt charitable or educational organization if the organization is controlled by that person or members of that person's family;

10. A corporation and a partnership, if the same persons own more than 50 percent in value of the outstanding stock of the corporation and more than 50 percent of the capital or profit interest in the partnership;

11. An S corporation and another S corporation if the same persons own more than 50 percent in value of the outstanding stock of each corporation;

12. An S corporation and a C corporation if the same persons own more than 50 percent in value of the outstanding stock of each corporation; and

13. An executor of an estate and a beneficiary of the estate, except for a sale or exchange to satisfy a pecuniary bequest.[61]

Code Sec. 267(c) contains a series of constructive ownership rules for determining stock ownership for purposes of Code Sec. 267. Also, Code Sec. 267(e) contains special related party rules for partnerships and S corporations.

¶711 START-UP EXPENSES

In order for "business expenses" to be deductible, there must be a trade or business. But what about the numerous expenses that arise before a business actually comes into existence? Without some special provision, these expenses would not be deductible. What's more, since most businesses have indefinite lifetimes, there could be no amortization of the cost of creating an asset (the business) over the life of the business. In short, a taxpayer who created a business could recover start-up and related costs only when the business was sold or otherwise ceased operation.

Fortunately, Code Sec. 195 provides the authority for recovering the cost of business start-ups sooner than the end of the business. The taxpayer who starts a business may treat the start-up and related expenditures as deferred expenses and deduct them ratably over a

---

[61] Code Sec. 267(b).

period of not less than 60 months, beginning with the month in which the business begins.[62] If the taxpayer disposes of the business before the end of the amortization period, the taxpayer may deduct any remaining start-up costs at that time, subject to the general provisions on deducting losses contained in Code Sec. 165.[63]

The election to deduct business start-up costs must be made on the tax return for the year in which business begins by attaching a statement that sets out the amount and description of the expenditures, the dates incurred, the month business began, and the number of months (at least 60) over which the costs will be amortized. It is important to claim the deduction as early as possible should there be any doubt about when the business actually begins. The right to deduct the costs could be lost if the IRS determines that business actually began in the year before that for which the election is made.

¶ 713 Amortization of Expenses

Generally, the expenditures eligible for amortization under Code Sec. 195 must be of the type that would be deductible if they were paid or incurred in connection with the expansion of an existing business in the same field.[64] In addition, the expenditures must fall within one of the three categories of expenses for which amortization is authorized. The expenditures must be paid or incurred in connection with (1) investigating the creation or acquisition of an active trade or business, (2) creating an active trade or business, or (3) an activity engaged in for profit and for the production of income before active business begins and in anticipation of the activity becoming an active trade or business.[65]

Expenses eligible for amortization under Code Sec. 195 do not include interest deductible under Code Sec. 163(a), taxes deductible under Code Sec. 164, and research and experimental expenses under Code Sec 174. Also, expenditures eligible for amortization do not include any amount for which a deduction would not be allowable to an existing trade or business. For example, securities registration expenses, underwriters' commissions, and other amounts paid in connection with the sale of stock, securities, or partnership interests are not amortizable under Code Sec. 195.

The amortization election also does not apply to amounts paid or incurred as part of the acquisition cost of a trade or business. Nor does it apply to amounts paid or incurred to acquire property for sale or for property that may be depreciated or amortized based on its useful life, including expenses relating to a lease and leasehold improvements.

---

[62] Code Sec. 195(b)(1).
[63] Code Sec. 195(b)(2).
[64] Code Sec. 195(c)(1)(B).
[65] Code Sec. 195(c)(1)(A).

Corporate or partnership organization expenditures that may be amortized under Code Sec. 248 or Code Sec. 709 are covered by those provisions and are not subject to the election under Code Sec. 195.

¶ 713.1 Investigatory Expenses

The first category of expenses eligible for amortization under Code Sec. 195 are those incurred in investigating the creation or acquisition of an active trade or business. These investigatory expenses are the costs incurred in reviewing a prospective business prior to reaching a final decision to acquire or enter that business. These costs include expenses incurred for the analysis or survey of potential markets, products, labor supply, transportation facilities, and similar expenses.

In the case of investigatory expenses incurred in connection with the acquisition of an existing business, the taxpayer must obtain an equity interest in, and actively participate in the management of, the trade or business. Amortization is not available for the costs incurred in investigating the acquisition of an investment interest represented by a bond or other debt instrument (even if convertible), preferred stock, or limited partnership interest. A taxpayer acquiring common stock is ordinarily acquiring an investment interest rather than a qualifying trade or business, and investigatory expenses relating to the acquisition of corporate stock generally may not be amortized under Code Sec. 195. However, if a stock acquisition is in substance the acquisition of a trade or business, the investigatory expenses are eligible for amortization even though one of the steps of the transaction involves the acquisition of stock—for example, the acquisition of a corporation that is then liquidated. Also, a corporation is considered to acquire the trade or business assets of an acquired corporation, rather than to make a portfolio investment in stock, if the acquired corporation becomes a member of an affiliated group which includes the corporation incurring the investigatory expenses and a consolidated income tax return is filed for the group.

A sole proprietor always is treated as having an operator equity interest in the trade or business. In the case of the acquisition of a general partnership interest, the taxpayer is treated as acquiring an active interest if the taxpayer actively participates in the management of the trade or business of the partnership.

¶ 713.2 Start-Up Expenses

The second category of expenses eligible for amortization under Code Sec. 195 are those incurred in actually creating an active trade or business. Start-up costs are those incurred after the decision is made to establish a particular business and before the time when the business begins. Start-up costs may be incurred by a taxpayer who is not engaged in any existing business, or by a taxpayer with an existing business who begins a new one that is unrelated, or only tangentially related, to the existing business.

Start-up costs include advertising, salaries and wages paid to employees who are being trained and their instructors, travel and other expenses incurred to line up prospective distributors, suppliers or customers, and salaries and fees paid for executives, consultants, and for similar professional services, including those for setting up books and records. In the case of an existing business, start-up expenses do not include ordinary and necessary business expenses paid or incurred in connection with an expansion of the business. These latter expenses are currently deductible and need not be amortized. Whether there is an expansion of an existing trade or business or a creation or acquisition of a new trade or business is, in the words of the Senate Finance Committee Report on P.L. 96-605, "based on the facts and circumstances of each case."

¶ 713.3 *Pre-Opening Expenses*

The final category of expenses eligible for amortization under Code Sec. 195 are those incurred in any activity engaged in for profit and for the production of income in anticipation of the activity becoming an active trade or business but before the day on which the active trade or business begins. This category of expenses, which represents an expansion of the definition of expenditures eligible for amortization, was added to the statute by the Tax Reform Act of 1984. The intent was to make pre-opening expenses, such as land rent during construction, amortizable under Code Sec. 195.

¶ 715 Trade or Business Requirement

To be eligible for amortization under Code Sec. 195, expenditures must relate to the investigation or creation of an active trade or business. Therefore, expenditures relating to an investment are not eligible. An activity for which related expenses are deductible only as itemized deductions for individuals under Code Sec. 212 is not treated as a trade or business. In addition, an activity is not treated as a trade or business activity solely because the property used in the activity may be eligible for capital gain or ordinary loss treatment under Code Sec. 1231.

In the case of rental activities, there must be significant furnishing of services incident to the rentals to constitute an active business rather than an investment. A rental activity is not considered an active business solely because deductions attributable to it are allowed in computing adjusted gross income. According to the Senate Finance Committee Report on P.L. 96-605, however, the operation of an apartment complex, an office building, or a shopping center would constitute an active trade or business.

¶ 721 REAL ESTATE OPERATING EXPENSES

Expenses of operating a real estate business or expenses associated with real estate used in a trade or business are deductible under Code Sec. 162, which allows a deduction for "all the ordinary and necessary expenses paid or incurred during the taxable year in carrying on any trade or business." Even if the holding of real estate does not rise to the level of a trade or business, an individual may deduct all the ordinary and necessary expenses paid "for the management, conservation, or maintenance of property held for the production of income." [66]

Under Code Sec. 212, it is not even necessary that the property be producing current income in order for a taxpayer to take deductions. Reg. § 1.212-1(b) provides that ordinary and necessary expenses of a building devoted to rental purposes are deductible "notwithstanding that there is actually no income therefrom in the taxable year, and regardless of the manner in which or the purpose for which the property in question was acquired." Further, if property is held for investment, expenses may be deductible under Code Sec. 212 even though the property is not currently productive and "there is no likelihood that the property will be sold at a profit or will otherwise be productive of income and even though the property is held merely to minimize a loss with respect thereto."

While the regulations seem to allow deductions for expenses related to the holding of raw land for investment, they apparently do not not allow deductions when there is some use of the property beyond a mere passive holding of the property unless there is a profit motive. A taxpayer was denied deductions for maintenance expenses of a house owned with a brother as tenants in common when the brother had the exclusive right to live there rent free. The expectation that the property would appreciate and eventually be sold at a profit was not sufficient to establish that it was held for the production of income.[67]

The proposition that rental property need not be producing current income in order for expenses to be deductible, however, has limits, although those limits may be hard to define. In *L. Hudson*,[68] a two-year vacancy in the other half of the taxpayer's duplex while the taxpayer was waiting for "desirable tenants" established that the property was no longer held for profit-making purposes. Longer periods of vacancy, however, may still not preclude deductions, given some special circumstances.[69]

---

[66] Code Sec. 212.
[67] *J. Hirschel*, 41 TCM 1298, CCH Dec. 37,842(M), T.C. Memo. 1981-189, aff'd, CA-2, February 25 1982.
[68] 41 TCM 1253, CCH Dec. 37,825(M), T.C. Memo. 1985-175.
[69] *G.C. Gorod*, 42 TCM 1569, CCH Dec. 38,388(M), T.C. Memo. 1981-632.

In *Gorod*, the taxpayer constructed a duplex apartment building and occupied the upper unit of the building. The Court held that the taxpayer held the lower unit of the building for the production of income, even though the lower unit was never rented over a period of about ten years. The lack of rental income was explained by the building's location in a high crime, rundown area. The taxpayer continued to advertise the lower unit, spent money keeping it in habitable condition, and did not use it for personal purposes. However, the Tax Court was unwilling to stretch its generosity when the same taxpayer appeared before the court four years later. By this time, the apartment had been vacant for 13 years, rent had never been collected, and the residence had become uninhabitable and had been boarded up. The court held that the taxpayer did not have a profit motive in keeping the vacant space.[70]

Once it is established that real estate is part of a trade or business or held for the production of income, the deduction of the routine operating expenses usually does not present a tax problem. Sometimes, though, it becomes difficult to separate the ordinary and necessary business expenses from expenditures that produce an extended benefit and that must be capitalized and recovered through depreciation, amortization, or, in some cases, on the sale or disposition of the property.

The following discussion focuses on the more common expense items which may be associated with the ownership and operation of business or investment real estate and the questions that relate to the timing and amount of the deductions for these items. Keep in mind that, in addition to the tax accounting rules discussed at ¶ 705, deductions attributable to real estate may be limited by the at-risk rules discussed at ¶ 311, and the passive loss rules discussed at ¶ 1103.

¶ 723 Repairs

The cost of repairing and maintaining real property used in a trade or business or held for the production of income is deductible as an ordinary and necessary business expense under Code Sec. 162 or an ordinary and necessary expense under Code Sec. 212. Reg. § 1.162-4 provides:

> The cost of incidental repairs which neither materially add to the value of the property nor appreciably prolong its life, but keep it in an ordinarily efficient operating condition, may be deducted as an

---

[70] *G. Gorod*, 49 TCM 526, CCH Dec. 41,827(M). T.C. Memo. 1985-33.

expense, provided the cost of acquisition or production or the gain or loss basis of the taxpayer's plant, equipment, or other property, as the case may be, is not increased by the amount of such expenditures. Repairs in the nature of replacements, to the extent that they arrest deterioration and appreciably prolong the useful life of the property, shall either be capitalized and depreciated . . . or charged against the depreciation reserve . . .

This regulation indicates the usual question that arises in taking a deduction for repairs, that is, whether the claimed deductible repair is actually a capital expenditure. An expenditure that goes beyond incidental repair for the purposes of keeping the property in ordinary efficient operating condition and materially adds to the value of the property or prolongs its life is not currently deductible. Rather, the cost of replacements, improvements or additions must be capitalized and recovered through depreciation or amortization. In the words of the Supreme Court in *Union Pacific R.R. Co.*:[71]

Theoretically, the expenses chargeable to earnings include the general expenses of keeping up the organization of the company, and all expenses incurred in operating the works and keeping them in good condition and repair; whilst expenses chargeable to capital include those which are incurred in the original construction of the works, and in subsequent enlargement and improvement thereof.

¶ 723.1 *Repair or Improvement*

A current deduction is not allowed for any amount paid out for new buildings or for permanent improvements or betterments made to increase the value of any property or estate, or for any amount expended in restoring property or in making good the exhaustion of property for which an allowance is or has been made in the form of a deduction for depreciation, amortization, or depletion.[72] These expenditures are those that add to the value, or substantially prolong the useful life, of property, or adapt property to a new or different use.[73]

While most repairs do add to the value of the property when measured against the value of the property just prior to the repair, this is not the test. The Tax Court explained the proper test for determining whether an expenditure should be treated as a capital expenditure, rather than a deductible repair, because of the value added to the property in *Oberman Mfg. Co.*[74] According to the Court, the proper test is whether "the expenditure materially enhances the value, use, life expectancy, strength, or capacity as compared with the status of the asset prior to the condition necessitating the expenditure."

---

[71] S.Ct. 99 U.S. 402.
[72] Code Sec. 263(a); Reg. § 1,263(a)-1(a).
[73] Reg. § 1.263-1(b).
[74] 47 TC 471, CCH Dec. 28,334.

Size of Expenditure

While large expenditures often fall into the capital expenditure category, it is not the size or amount of the expenditure that determines whether it is a deductible repair expense or a capital expenditure. Rather, it is the purpose for which the expenditure is made that controls. An expenditure that returns property to the state it was in prior to the condition necessitating the expenditure and that does not make the property more valuable, useful or long-lived, is a deductible repair, regardless of the amount. See, for example, *Plainfield-Union Water Co.*,[75] in which it was held that a substantial expenditure for cleaning and cement-lining tar-coated cast-iron piping was deductible since the useful life, strength, value, and capacity of the pipes were not increased by the cleaning and the lining.

Even when there is some incidental expansion or enlargement, a large expenditure nevertheless may be classified as a deductible repair. How far the courts may be willing to go in this area is illustrated by the Fifth Circuit Court of Appeals decision in *S.C. Evans*.[76]

A farmer had a large earthen dam that began to allow water to seep through. The farmer made several efforts to patch the dam, but was unable to stop the leakage. Finally, the farmer hired a contractor who drained the reservoir, excavated soil from the dam's front, and replaced the soil with clay in order to seal the dam. The cost to the farmer for the work was $50,000, and the repaired reservoir was one-fourth to one-half acre larger than prior to the repair. The Tax Court had characterized the $50,000 repair cost as a capital expenditure, but the Fifth Circuit disagreed. According to the Appeals Court:

> [The] taxpayer's sole purpose in undertaking the expense was to prevent the dam from leaking and thus to keep it in an ordinary operating condition over its probable useful life and for the use for which it was acquired. The work did not create a replacement for the dam, but merely restored the capability of retaining water which it had, so far as the record reflects, at the time taxpayer acquired it. If the work is considered repair, it did not in our view materially add to the value or materially prolong its ordinary life. Nothing of record establishes that the alleged enlargement constituted a material increase in value.

Forced Expenditures

Sometimes, property owners must make repairs, alterations, improvements, or other changes to their property in order to comply with

---

[75] 39 TC 333, CCH Dec. 25,740, Nonacq. 1964-2 CB 8.

[76] CA-5, 77-2 USTC ¶ 9596, 557 F.2d 1095.

some law or ordinance, or the requirements of some regulatory agency. Simply because an expenditure is forced on a property owner does not affect how that expenditure is classified, whether as a deductible repair or capital expenditure. If the required expenditures do not result in value added to the property or a longer useful life, they are deductible. On the other hand, if the required expenditures result in long-lived additions or improvements, the expenditure must be capitalized and recovered through depreciation or amortization.[77]

Under an order of the city building commissioner, the owner of rental property shored up the walls with steel rods, inserted new beams to support the roof, repaired portions of the roof, and underpinned the foundation of the building with cinder blocks. The expenses were held to be capital in nature, even though the expenditures were forced on the building owner by government authority.[78] A similar result was reached when the expenditures were forced on the taxpayer by a pending lawsuit. In *Mt. Morris Drive-In Theatre Co.*,[79] the taxpayer constructed an outdoor theater on sloping land. Later, the taxpayer had to spend over $8,000 to construct a drainage system extending onto adjacent land in compromise of a pending lawsuit by the adjoining landowner, who complained of concentrated drainage onto the land. The cost of the drainage system was a capital expenditure and not a deductible expense.

Classification of Expenditures

At one time or another, just about every expenditure imaginable made to repair or improve real property has been subject to challenge by the IRS over whether it should be classified as a currently deductible repair expense or a capital expenditure. Needless to say, it would be virtually impossible to catalog all the cases, but it may help to look at some expenditures by others and how they were treated.

The cost of painting, papering, whitewashing, decorating, etc., income-producing or business property is deductible.[80] But see the discussion at ¶ 723.2 on general renovations and remodeling. The cost of painting must be capitalized when it is done as part of or incidental to a general reconditioning or remodeling of the property.[81]

---

[77] *T.O. Campbell*, 32 TCM 451, CCH Dec. 31,953(M), T.C. Memo. 1973-101; *International Building Co.*, 21 BTA 617.

[78] *J.L. Boland*, 19 TCM 1030, CCH Dec. 24,370(M), T.C. Memo. 1960-199.

[79] 25 TC 272, CCH Dec. 21,338, aff'd per curiam 56-2 USTC ¶ 9994, 238 F.2d 85.

[80] *J.T. Rose v. Haverty Furniture Co.*, CA-5, 1927 CCH ¶ 7012, 15 F.2d 345; *M. Markovitz*, 11 TCM 823, CCH Dec. 19,138(M); *R.O. Watts*, 34 TCM 613, CCH Dec. 33,184(M), T.C. Memo. 1975-131.

[81] *J.M. Jones*, CA-5, 57-1 USTC ¶ 9517, 242 F.2d 616; *Bank of Houston*, 19 TCM 589, CCH Dec. 24,204(M), T.C. Memo. 1960-110.

Repairing rotting wood floors [82] and finishing a concrete floor in a storage room [83] are deductible repairs, but replacing a wood floor with a concrete floor is a capital expenditure.[84] Repairing a road without changing basic construction is a deductible repair expense,[85] but replacing a gravel driveway with a concrete driveway is a capital expenditure.[86] Sandblasting and pointing brick walls is a deductible repair,[87] but replacing a cracked old wall with a new wall is capital expenditure.[88] Replacing corrugated roofing that was blown away and replacing broken slate on slate roof are deductible repair expenses,[89] but replacing part of a foundry roof and supporting the roof are capital expenditures.[90]

¶ 723.2 Replacement, Renovation, and Reconditioning

Replacements that arrest deterioration and appreciably prolong the life of property are capital expenditures and are not currently deductible.[91] For example, the replacement of an old floor in a building with a new floor that permitted the use of heavy equipment made the building more valuable and was a capital expenditure and not a deductible repair.[92] Similarly, the replacement of a wooden factory door that had rotted because of termite damage with a new aluminum door and the construction of a new entrance had to be capitalized.[93] The cost of replacing a completely worn-out furnace and heating system is a capital expenditure when there is no repair of an existing system but a substantial replacement adding to the value of the property.[94]

Additions and improvements do not have to prolong useful life to be classified as capital expenditures, if the expenditures adapt the property to new or different uses, or make the property better suited to the business.[95] In *J.H. Rutter*,[96] expenditures made to add a lunch area, restrooms and loading and unloading ramps to clothing manufacturing

---

[82] *Farmers Creamery Corp. of Fredericksburg, Va.*, 14 TC 879, CCH Dec. 17,646, Acq. 1954-1 CB 4 in part and nonacq. 1954-1 CB 8 in part.

[83] *W.C. Hudlow, Jr.*, 30 TCM 894, CCH Dec. 30,959(M), T.C. Memo. 1971-218.

[84] *L.J. Best*, 13 TCM 948, CCH Dec. 20,601(M), T.C. Memo. 1954-170.

[85] *Almac's, Inc.*, 20 TCM 56, CCH Dec. 24,620(M), T.C. Memo. 1961-13.

[86] *A.R. Jones*, 25 TC 1100, CCH Dec. 21,590, Acq. 1958-2 CB 6, rev'd and rem'd on another issue, CA-5, 58-2 USTC ¶ 9832, 259 F.2d 300.

[87] *City National Bank*, 11 TCM 411, CCH Dec. 18,921(M), T.C. Memo. 1952.

[88] *Stewart Supply Co., Inc.*, 22 TCM 246, CCH Dec. 25,986(M), T.C. Memo. 1963-62, aff'd CA-2, 63-2 USTC ¶ 9824, 324 F.2d 233.

[89] *Knoxville Iron Co.*, 18 TCM 251, CCH Dec. 23,504(M), T.C. Memo. 1959-54.

[90] *Mountain State Steel Foundries, Inc.*, 18 TCM 306, CCH Dec. 23,522(M), T.C. Memo. 1959-59, rev'd on another issue, 60-2 USTC ¶ 9797, 284 F.2d 737.

[91] Reg. § 1.162-4.

[92] *Phillips & Easton Supply Co.*, 20 TC 455, CCH Dec. 19,691.

[93] *Alabama-Georgia Syrup Co.*, 36 TC 747, CCH Dec. 24,957, rev'd and rem'd on another issue sub nom. *L.B. Whitfield, Jr.*, 63-1 USTC ¶ 9124, 311 F.2d 640.

[94] *C.A. Boddie*, 20 TCM 350, CCH Dec. 24,717(M), T.C. Memo 1961-72.

[95] *Human Engineering Institute*, 37 TCM 619, CCH Dec. 35,100(M), T.C. Memo. 1978-145, aff'd CA-6, 80-2 USTC ¶ 9600, 629 F.2d 1160.

[96] 52 TCM 326, CCH Dec. 43,316(M), T.C. Memo. 1986-407, aff'd CA-5, 88-2 USTC ¶ 9500, 853 F.2d 1267.

plants were classed as capital expenditures. The purpose behind the expenditures was not merely to keep the property in efficient operating condition, but to add value to the plants and adapt them to different uses. Similarly, the cost of remodeling stores to adapt property to a different use is a capital expenditure.[97]

Courts generally hold that repairs that occur as part of an overall plan of renovation, modernization, alteration, or improvement must be capitalized. Items that would normally qualify as deductible repairs, such as painting, wallcovering, etc., are not deductible when they are incurred pursuant to an overall plan of capital improvements which substantially upgrade the condition of the property.[98] In *J.S. Moss*,[99] amounts spent on repairs as part of a renovation plan for a hotel were held not deductible by the Tax Court, but the decision was reversed by the Ninth Circuit Court of Appeals (see ¶ 803).

The propensity of courts to hold "repairs" made as part of overall renovations and reconditionings to be part of the capital expenditure, rather than separate deductible expenses, means that taxpayers should undertake to keep repairs separate from such general renovations. This usually requires that otherwise deductible repair procedures be undertaken at a different time from that at which the general renovations take place. If separating the time that repairs are done from the time of renovation is not possible, taxpayers should keep separate records for the cost of repairs, or even have the repairs done under separate contracts, in order to sustain the deduction for the repair costs.

In *B.W. Cohn*,[100] a taxpayer was allowed to deduct $50,000 as a repair expense out of $212,000 spent on improvements and repairs to a rundown farm purchased for $110,000. The district court held that the ordinary and necessary repairs to the farm buildings were deductible, even though they were made during an expansion and remodeling program.[101]

¶ 723.3 Removal of Architectural Barriers

A special deduction, of up to $15,000 per year, is allowed at the election of the taxpayer for the cost of removing architectural barriers to elderly and handicapped persons from business facilities.[102] Without

---

[97] *Bee Holding Co.*, 17 TCM 963, CCH Dec. 23,253(M), T.C. Memo. 1958-195.

[98] *First American National Bank of Nashville*, CA-6, 72-2 USTC ¶ 9694, 467 F.2d 1098; *Mountain Fuel Supply Co.*, CA-10, 71-2 USTC ¶ 9681; 449 F.2d 816, cert. denied 405 U.S. 989, 92 S.Ct. 1251; *Wolfsen Land & Cattle Co.*, 72 TC 1, CCH Dec. 35,975.

[99] 51 TCM 742, CCH Dec. 42,962(M), T.C. Memo. 1986-128, rev'd 87-2 USTC ¶ 9590, 831 F.2d 833.

[100] DC Tenn., 57-1 USTC ¶ 9457, aff'd CA-6, 58-2 USTC ¶ 9840, 259 F.2d 371.

[101] But see *A.L. Allen*, 15 TCM 464, CCH Dec. 21,680(M), T.C. Memo. 1956-88, in which it was held that expenditures which might have been deductible expenses for repairs were not allowed as deductions, even though they could be segregated, because they were part of a general plan of rehabilitation and betterment.

[102] Code Sec. 190.

this special statutory election, the costs of removing architectural barriers from business facilities normally would be capital expenditures that would be added to basis and recovered through depreciation. Costs in excess of $15,000 in any one year are treated as capital expenditures. Elderly persons are those aged 65 or older, and handicapped refers to blindness and deafness, as well as to difficulty in walking or using one's hands.

To qualify for the expense deduction, the removal of the barrier must bring the property into conformity with standards established by the Treasury on the advice of the U.S. Architectural and Transportation Barriers Compliance Board. These standards are contained in Reg. § 1.190-2. The procedure for electing to take advantage of the special deduction and the recordkeeping requirements are contained in Reg. § 1.190-3.

¶ 725 Materials and Supplies

The regulations provide some latitude in timing the deduction for materials and supplies, depending on the bookkeeping practices of individual taxpayers. Reg. § 1.162-3 provides:

> Taxpayers carrying materials and supplies on hand should include in expenses the charges for materials and supplies only in the amount that they are actually consumed and used in operation during the taxable year for which the return is made, provided that the costs of such materials and supplies have not been deducted in determining net income or loss or taxable income for any previous year. If a taxpayer carries incidental materials or supplies on hand for which no record of consumption is kept or of which physical inventories at the beginning and end of the year are not taken, it will be permissible for the taxpayer to include in his expenses and to deduct from gross income the total cost of such supplies and materials as were purchased during the taxable year for which the return is made, provided the taxable income is clearly reflected by this method.

In short, what the regulations say is that the cost of materials and supplies may be deducted as they are purchased, unless the taxpayer maintains inventory records for the materials and supplies, regardless of when the materials and supplies are actually used. In *Smith Leasing Co., Inc.*,[103] the Tax Court barred an IRS attempt to impose an inventory requirement on a taxpayer for supplies. The taxpayer kept no inventory of supplies and charged the cost of supplies purchased directly to expense. The taxpayer was entitled to deduct the cost of supplies purchased during the year and it was wrong for the IRS to set

---

[103] 43 TC 37, CCH Dec. 27,009, Acq. 1965-2 CB 6.

up a closing inventory of the supplies the taxpayer had on hand at the end of the year.

Of course, the deduction for supplies can be stretched too far, so that unusually large purchases during the year result in a distortion of income. When a corporation invested a large part of its earnings in supplies that would not be consumed until the following year, a deduction limited to those supplies consumed during the current year was held to more accurately reflect its net income than a deduction for supplies purchased.[104]

The ability to deduct the cost of materials and supplies as purchased puts a premium on classifying items, such as replacement parts, as materials and supplies. Here, too, there is quite a bit of latitude available to taxpayers. For example, the costs of replacement parts to be used in microwave towers, which did not increase the value of the towers, are deductible as supplies and materials.[105] In some cases, large purchases may be divided into long-lived assets and materials and supplies. In Rev. Rul. 73-357,[106] the IRS ruled that the cost properly allocable to tires and tubes on the purchase of used construction equipment is deductible as a business expense in the year of purchase if the average remaining useful life of the tires and tubes is less than one year. A careful review of all purchases with these cases and rulings in mind may boost current deductions.

¶ 727 Compensation

Ordinary and necessary business expenses include a reasonable allowance for salaries or other compensation for personal services actually rendered.[107] This sets up the test for deducting compensation payments: the payments must be reasonable and the payments must be in fact payments purely for services.[108]

Reasonable compensation is the amount that would ordinarily be paid for like services by like enterprises under like circumstances as of the date when the contract for services is made.[109] As a practical matter, the reasonable compensation question is likely to arise only in cases in which the business and the employee are related, such as when the employee is the sole or major stockholder of a corporate employer, or when the employee is a child, parent, or spouse of the employer. When an employee is not an owner or related to an owner, the arm's-length dealing involved means that the salary, almost by definition, is reasonable.

---

[104] *Spiegel, May, Stern Co.*, Ct. Cls., 2 USTC ¶ 474, 69 Ct. Cls. 110, 37 F.2d 988; see also *D. Baird & Son, Inc.*, 2 BTA 901, CCH Dec. 849.

[105] *F.K. Spain*, 37 TCM 1158, CCH Dec. 35,280(M), T.C. Memo. 1978-270.

[106] 1973-2 CB 40.

[107] Code Sec. 162(a)(1).

[108] Reg. § 1.162-7(a).

[109] Reg. § 1.162-7(b)(3).

Any amount paid in the form of compensation, but not in fact as the purchase price of services, is not deductible.[110] For instance, if salaries paid to shareholder-employees of a corporation are in excess of those paid for similar services and the excessive payments correspond or bear a close relationship to the stockholdings of the employees, it is likely that the excess payments represent a distribution of earnings. Also, an ostensible salary may be in part a payment for property. For example, partners may sell out to a corporation and agree to continue to work for the corporation. In this case, part of the salaries paid to the former partners may actually be payment for the transfer of the business.

How compensation is determined does not control its deductibility.[111] Compensation may be contingent, although contingent compensation is more open to challenge as unreasonable. Nevertheless, according to the regulation, "if contingent compensation is paid pursuant to a free bargain between the employer and the individual made before the services are rendered, not influenced by any consideration on the part of the employer other than of securing on fair and advantageous terms the services of the individual, it should be allowed as a deduction even though in the actual working out of the contract it may prove to be greater than the amount which would ordinarily be paid."

Methods of compensating employees, including salary, fringe benefits, retirement plans, vacations, bonuses, etc. are almost as numerous as employers. It is impossible for this work on real estate taxation to go into these areas in any depth, and the author leaves this area to others. The following discussion relating to compensation focuses on some areas that are most critical for the closely held real estate corporation or family real estate business.

¶ 727.1 Real Estate Corporation Officers

The Supreme Court has said that "extraordinary, unusual, and extravagant amounts paid by a corporation to its officers in the guise and form of compensation for their services, but having no substantial relation to the measure of services, and being utterly disproportioned to their value, are not in reality payment for services and cannot be regarded as 'ordinary and necessary expenses'. . . .".[112] Unfortunately, there is no set formula for determining the reasonableness of compensation, since reasonableness is a question of fact that is determined for each case. Many of the Tax Court's opinions on the reasonable compensation question begin with the following statement: "The question is one of fact. The finding [as to the amount which constitutes reasonable

---

[110] Reg. § 1.162-7(b)(1).
[111] Reg. § 1.162-7(b)(2).
[112] *Botany Worsted Mills*, S.Ct., 1 USTC ¶ 348, 287 U.S. 282, 49 S.Ct. 129.

compensation] which has been made is dispositive of the sole issue. It would serve no purpose to review the evidence or attempt to rationalize the conclusion reached."

Even though what constitutes reasonable compensation depends on the facts of each individual situation, it may be helpful to see what has been held to be reasonable in various situations. There are a number of cases that have dealt with reasonable compensation in the context of a real estate corporation.[113]

¶ 727.2   Family Members as Employees

The owner of a real estate business may achieve substantial tax savings by employing immediate family members in the business. The tax savings can be achieved without reducing the income to the total family unit.

Children

The owner of a real estate business may employ his or her children in the business. Each child can earn an amount equal to the standard deduction for the current year free of income tax, while the business deducts the amounts paid, provided they are reasonable compensation for the services actually rendered by the child. Even if the children earn more than the standard deduction, tax savings may be achieved since earned income is taxed in the child's tax bracket and not in the parent's tax bracket, as is the case with unearned income of a child under 14 years of age. The children, of course, are free to spend their earnings on personal items that would otherwise be purchased by the parents with their after-tax dollars. The personal exemptions for the children remain available to the parents, provided they continue to provide over half the support of the children, but the children are then not also entitled to the personal exemption.

It apparently does not matter how young a child is when the parent employs the child in the business, as long as the child can perform some useful service and effectively does perform the service. Even a seven-year-old child has been found able to perform valuable services for a parent's business so as to be entitled to reasonable

---

[113] *Bev Anderson Chevrolet, Inc.*, 26 TCM 338, CCH Dec. 28,403(M), T.C. Memo. 1967-64; *Langley Park Apartments, Sec. C., Inc.*, 44 TC 474, CCH Dec. 27,447, aff'd per curiam, CA-4, 66-1 USTC ¶ 9368, 359 F.2d 427; *B. Perlmutter*, 44 TC 382, CCH Dec. 27,434, aff'd, CA-10, 67-1 USTC ¶ 9246, 373 F.2d 45; *Marlo Coil Co.*, Ct. Cls., 697 CCH ¶ 7915; *S. & B. Realty Co.*, 54 TC 863, CCH Dec. 30,073, Acq. 1970-2 CB XXI; *Ettle Co., Inc.*, 30 TCM 351, CCH Dec. 30,751(M), T.C. Memo. 1971-86; *R.J. Nicoll Co.*, 59 TC 37, CCH Dec. 31,566, Acq. 1973-2 CB 3; *Roth Properties Co.*, 33 TCM 104, CCH Dec. 32,438(M), T.C. Memo. 1974-33, aff'd, CA-6, 75-1 USTC ¶ 9337, 511 F.2d 526; *P.E. Kummer Realty Co.*, 33 TCM 209 CCH Dec. 32,467(M), T.C. Memo. 1974-44, aff'd CA-8, 75-1 USTC ¶ 9262, 511 F.2d 313; *Chevy Chase Motor Co., Inc.*, 36 TCM 942, CCH Dec. 34,517(M), T.C. Memo. 1977-227; *Keller Street Development Co.*, 37 TCM 1451, CCH Dec. 35,383(M), T.C. Memo. 1978-350; *C.W. Clayton, Jr.*, 42 TCM 670, CCH Dec. 38,153(M), T.C. Memo. 1981-433.

compensation that is deductible by the business.[114] It does not matter that the child uses the pay received for part of his or her support.[115]

It is important that proper payroll records be keep for children who are employed by the business. Failure to keep the necessary records, and to withhold and pay any necessary payroll taxes, can result in the loss of the deduction.[116]

Spouses

Generally, there is not the same advantage to putting a spouse on the payroll as there is with putting a child on the payroll. If a joint return is filed, the tax is the same regardless of which spouse earns the income. In the case of an incorporated business, however, there may be some indirect tax advantages to putting a spouse on the payroll. If the owner-spouse's compensation has reached the limits of reasonableness, putting the spouse on the payroll allows more money to be drawn out of the corporation without a double tax. A spouse on the corporate payroll may also benefit from qualified retirement plan coverage and various fringe benefits that may be offered by the corporation. Another consideration is the Individual Retirement Account deduction that may be available to a spouse who has earned income.

Payroll Taxes

One disadvantage of employing family members in an incorporated real estate business is the added social security taxes and possible unemployment taxes that have to be paid by the family member and the corporation. While the corporation's share of social security and other payroll taxes is deductible, social security taxes paid by the family member are not deductible. This added tax burden should be taken into consideration when assessing the tax savings from employing family members in the business.

The added social security taxes may not be as much of a burden if the family member employed in the business is a parent or older family member who has not had sufficient earnings to qualify for full social security benefits. Added taxes, in this case, may be offset by future benefits. The opposite consideration is also important when employing older family members who are past the retirement age. That is, earnings may reduce the social security benefits for which the family member is currently eligible, at least until the family member is old enough to earn unlimited amounts without a reduction in benefits.

---

[114] *W.E. Eller,* 77 TC 934, CCH Dec. 38,391, Acq. 1984-2 CB 1.
[115] Rev. Rul. 73-393, 1973-2 CB 33.
[116] *A.R. Furmanski,* 33 TCM 225, CCH Dec. 32,472(M), T.C. Memo. 1974-47; *C. Tschupp,* 22 TCM 466, CCH Dec. 26,052(M), T.C. Memo. 1963-98.

The disadvantage of added payroll taxes when family members are employed by an incorporated business may not be present if the family members are employed by an unincorporated business. A child under 18 years of age who is employed in the business of a parent, or a spouse employed by a spouse, is exempt from social security and FUTA taxes. Income tax withholding generally is required, except in the case of a child who earns less than the standard deduction for the year.

A parent employed in a child's trade or business is subject to social security taxes, as well as income tax withholding. The parent is exempt from FUTA taxes. Just as in the case of an incorporated business, the added social security taxes paid by a parent employed in a child's business may be an advantage, if the added taxes purchase future benefits for the parent.

¶ 727.3 Independent Contractors and Employees

An employee's income is subject to income tax withholding by the employer. Also, an employee requires employer-paid FUTA and unemployment taxes, employer and employee FICA (social security) contributions, and, in many cases, coverage under workers' compensation statutes. On the other hand, an independent contractor is responsible for making his own income tax and FICA payments and is not covered by unemployment insurance or workers' compensation. Obviously, if a business can use independent contractors rather than employees, its tax and administrative burden can be greatly reduced.

Whether a business can characterize someone it employs to perform services for it as an independent contractor depends on whether the business controls both what the person performing the services does and how the work is performed. If the business does both, the individual is an employee. An independent contractor has discretion in how the work is performed.

As an aid to determining whether an individual is an employee under the common law rules, the IRS has identified 20 factors that indicate whether sufficient control is present to establish an employer-employee relationship. The IRS developed the factors based on an examination of cases and rulings considering whether an individual is an employee. The 20 factors are set out in Rev. Rul. 87-41.[117]

¶ 727.4 Licensed Real Estate Agents

Licensed real estate agents and direct salespersons may be exempt from income tax withholding, social security tax (FICA), and federal unemployment tax (FUTA). These individuals are treated as self-employed persons or independent contractors if the payments they

---

[117] 1987-1 CB 296.

receive are directly related to sales or other output and the services performed as a nonemployee are specified in a written contract. Direct sellers must be in the business of selling consumer products other than in a permanent retail place of business.

¶ 727.5 *Partners*

A partner in a partnership may be compensated for services rendered to the partnership. If the services rendered are within the normal scope of partnership duties, any compensation is treated as part of the partner's distributive share of partnership income, rather than as a deductible expense of the partnership.[118] When the partner renders the services as an outsider and not in his or her capacity as a member of the partnership, however, then the partnership is entitled to a deduction for the compensation paid to the partner as an outsider. Also, when the partner performs services as an outsider, then the partnership is treated as an unrelated entity for all purposes.[119]

In Rev. Rul. 81-301,[120] an advisor general partner, a corporate investment advisor, rendered services to the partnership which were substantially the same as the services it rendered as an independent contractor or agent to other persons. The IRS ruled that the 10 percent of daily gross income allocation paid to the advisor was not part of the advisor's distributive share of partnership income and was a payment that was subject to Code Sec. 707(a). As such, the payments were taxable to the advisor as compensation for services and were deductible by the partnership as a business expense.

Guaranteed Payments

Even when a partner is performing services in the capacity as a partner, payments to the partner for the services are deductible by the partnership if the payments can be classified as guaranteed payments under Code Sec. 707(c). Guaranteed payments are payments made by a partnership to a partner for services or capital, if the payments are determined without regard to the income of the partnership. Guaranteed payments are considered to be made to one who is not a partner, but only for the purpose of the partner's gross income under Code Sec. 61(a) and the partnership's expense deduction under Code Sec. 162(a).[121] Unlike payments under Code Sec. 707(a), which are treated as made to an outsider for all purposes, guaranteed payments under Code Sec. 707(c) are treated as made to an outsider only for the limited purpose of computing the partner's gross income and the partnership's deduction.

---

[118] *E.T. Pratt*, CA-5, 77-1 USTC ¶ 9347, 550 F.2d 1023.
[119] Code Sec. 707(a).
[120] 1981-2 CB 144.
[121] Reg. § 1.707-1(c).

While guaranteed payments must be "determined without regard to the income of the partnership," the IRS has ruled that guaranteed payments may include payments for services determined by reference to an item of gross income of the partnership and need not be a fixed amount.[122] In the ruling, general partners of a real estate limited partnership each received a fee of five percent of the gross rentals received by the partnership in exchange for management services provided to the partnership. The fees were ruled to be guaranteed payments under Code Sec. 707(c) because they were reasonable in amount and the method used to determine the compensation would have been used for an unrelated party.

The classification of payments for services rendered by a partner as payments to an outsider under Code Sec. 707(a) or guaranteed payments under Code Sec. 707(c) can have a significant impact on the taxable incomes of the partners, as illustrated in Reg. § 1.707-1(c), Example 3.

Example: Partner X in the XY partnership is to receive a payment of $10,000 for services, plus 30 percent of the taxable income or loss of the partnership. Partner Y receives 70 percent of the taxable income or loss. After deducting the payment of $10,000 made to Partner X as a guaranteed payment, the XY partnership has a loss of $9,000. Of this amount, $2,700 (30 percent of the loss) is Partner X's distributive share of the partnership loss. Partner X reports ordinary gross income in the amount of $10,000 and a loss from the partnership of $2,700. Partner Y's share of the loss is $6,300. If the $10,000 payment to Partner X did not qualify as a guaranteed payment or a deductible payment to an outsider under Code Sec. 707(a), the partnership would have taxable income of $1,000. Partner X would report only $300 of income, rather than $10,000 in gross income (which might be partially offset by Partner X's $2,700 share of the loss), and Partner Y's $6,300 loss would be converted into $700 of income.

Disguised Payments for Services

Sometimes, rather than seeking to classify payments to a partner as compensation, a partnership may want to disguise payments to a partner for services as a share of partnership income. This is likely to occur when the compensation would have to be capitalized and could not be taken as a deductible business expense. For example, payments to a partner that would be classified as organization or syndication fees, or payments relating to the construction of property (see ¶ 127), would have to be capitalized under the normal capitalization rules. If these

---

[122] Rev. Rul. 81-300, 1981-2 CB 143.

¶ 727.5

otherwise nondeductible compensation payments could be characterized as distributions of partnership income, the partners who are not receiving the payments would have the equivalent of a deduction (through a reduction in their shares of partnership income) for the payments made to the partner rendering the services.

Attempts to disguise payments for services that must be capitalized as distributions of partnership income, however, are thwarted by Code Sec. 707(a)(2)(A). If a partner performs services for a partnership and, in connection therewith, receives a related partnership allocation and distribution, the transaction is treated as a transaction between the partnership and an outsider if the transaction is more properly characterized as a payment to the partner acting in a non-partner capacity. In such a case, the amount paid to the partner is treated as a payment for services provided to the partnership and, when appropriate, the partnership is required to capitalize these amounts or otherwise treat the amounts in a manner consistent with the recharacterization. The partnership must treat the purported allocation to the partner performing the services as a payment to a non-partner in determining the partner's shares of taxable income or loss.

¶ 729 Commissions and Fees

Commissions and fees are deductible business expenses if they are incurred in connection with services for the business that produce only a short term benefit. For example, management fees that are paid to a real estate agent for collecting rents and managing rental property are deductible in the year paid or incurred.[123] If, however, the commissions or fees are paid for services that provide a long-lived benefit or a long-lived asset, the commissions or fees would have to be capitalized.[124] For example, a fee paid in connection with the negotiation of a long-term lease would have to be amortized over the term of the lease (see the discussion of lease acquisition costs at ¶ 501). Similarly, commitment fees or standby charges in connection with a bond sale agreement under which funds for construction are made available in stated amounts over a specified period must be amortized over the term of the loan.[125]

¶ 729.1 *Real Estate Commissions*

Generally speaking, commissions and fees paid in connection with the acquisition of real estate represent part of the acquisition cost of the property and are capital expenditures rather than currently deductible business expenses.[126] This rule would seem to be the same regardless of whether the purchaser is a real estate dealer or not.

---

[123] Reg. § 1.162-1(a).
[124] Reg. §§ 1.461-1(a) and 1.263(a)-2
[125] Rev. Rul. 81-160, 1981-1 CB 312.

[126] *R.V. Jacobson*, 47 TCM 499, CCH Dec. 40,640(M), T.C. Memo. 1983-719.

In the case of commissions paid on the sale of real estate, whether the sale is by a dealer or a non-dealer does make a difference in the treatment of the selling commissions. Real estate commissions paid by dealers in real estate for the sale of real estate are deductible as a business expense under Code Sec. 162 in the year in which paid or accrued.[127] Commissions on the sale of real estate by a non-dealer are not deductible as expenses, but they are an offset against the selling price and, accordingly, reduce the gain or increase the loss that is reportable on the sale.[128]

¶ 729.2 *Kickbacks*

Kickbacks, in the nature of fees or commissions, are deductible, if they fall in the category of an ordinary and necessary expense and are not illegal or do not frustrate sharply defined national or state policies proscribing particular types of conduct.[129]

A subcontractor at a large shopping mall construction site was allowed deductions for the lawful kickback payments it made to the supervisor of the primary contractor.[130] The subcontractor understood that it would not be allowed to continue the subcontract work and would not be timely paid if the kickbacks were not forthcoming. The court found an obvious logical relationship between the subcontractor's construction business and the kickback payments that it made to retain its construction contracts. Accordingly, the kickbacks were an ordinary cost of doing business, as well as a necessary one. Because deductions are allowable for such costs as long as the payments are within the bounds of federal and state law, they were deductible as current expenses and were not capital in nature.

In a later case, however, the Sixth Circuit distinguished its decision in *Raymond Bertolini Trucking Co.* on the question of ordinary and necessary and refused to allow a paving subcontractor to deduct kickback payments. The subcontractor obtained contracts for the construction of a mall by paying for services and materials used to construct the personal residence of the general contractor's vice president in charge of awarding the contracts. According to the court, the kickbacks in this case were neither ordinary nor necessary, since the subcontractor had obtained nearly all of its contracts, including 20 with the same general contractor, without paying kickbacks.[131]

---

[127] *C. Whitman,* CA-2, 1931 CCH ¶ 9393, 49 F.2d 1087.

[128] *E.A. Giffin,* 19 BTA 1243 CCH Dec. 6095; *A. Pickard,* 28 TCM 766, CCH Dec. 29,673(M), T.C. Memo. 1969-153; *C.F. Frick,* 47 TCM 564, CCH Dec. 40,656(M), T.C. Memo. 1983-733; I.T. 2340, VI-1 CB 43.

[129] *S.B. Heininger,* S.Ct., 44-1 USTC ¶ 9109, 320 U.S. 467, 64 S.Ct. 249.

[130] *Raymond Bertolini Trucking Co.,* CA-6, 84-2 USTC ¶ 9591, 736 F.2d 1120.

[131] *Car-Ron Asphalt Paving Co. Inc.,* CA-6, 85-1 USTC ¶ 9298, 758 F.2d 1132.

¶ 731 Insurance

Taxpayers may deduct insurance premiums against fire, storm, theft, accident, or other similar losses in the case of a business.[132] Insurance premiums paid on property under construction, however, must be capitalized as part of the cost of the property under the capitalization rules of Code Sec. 263A (see ¶ 127.1). But even before enactment of the uniform capitalization rules, insurance premiums to protect property under construction were not currently deductible. The Tax Court ruled that insurance premiums for fire and extended coverage on buildings during construction were capital expenditures and thus not currently deductible.[133] (similarly as to insurance premiums for public liability and workers' compensation insurance paid in connection with the construction of a new building when the taxpayer took on the responsibility of a general contractor).[134]

If insurance premiums on business property provide coverage extending beyond one year, a cash method taxpayer may have to spread the deduction out over the period to which the premiums relate. The IRS takes the position that the payment in advance of insurance premiums by a cash method taxpayer results in the creation of an asset, prepaid insurance, that is used up ratably over the period covered by the insurance contract. Only the pro rata portion of the insurance premium applicable to the taxable year is deductible.[135] But one-year premiums on fiscal year insurance are deductible in full in the calendar year in which paid by a taxpayer reporting on the calendar year.[136]

Life insurance premiums, even if business related, generally are not deductible if the payer is directly or indirectly a beneficiary under the policy. When a company that was selling homesites paid the premiums for life insurance on homesite purchasers, however, the IRS ruled that the life insurance premium payments were deductible as a business expense by the developer.[137]

The treatment of casualty losses is considered in Chapter 15.

¶ 733 Advertising

Advertising and similar expenses are deductible business expenses.[138] Advertising expenses to develop goodwill or to influence the public through intermediary organizations are also deductible. To be

---

[132] Reg. § 1.162-1(a).
[133] *H. Shainberg*, 33 TC 241, CCH Dec. 23,838, Acq. 1960-1 CB 5.
[134] Rev. Rul. 66-373, 1966-2 CB 103.
[135] Rev. Rul. 70-413, 1970-2 CB 103. See also *Boylston Market Assn.*, CA-1, 42-2 USTC ¶ 9820, 131 F.2d 966; *H.W. Guenther*, 34 TCM 834, CCH Dec. 33,272(M), T.C. Memo. 1975-194; *R.V. Jacobson*, 47 TCM 499, CCH Dec. 40,640(M), T.C. Memo. 1983-719.
[136] *Kauai Terminal, Ltd.*, 36 BTA 893, CCH Dec. 9810, Acq. 1939-2 CB 18; *I.L. Bell*, 13 TC 344, CCH Dec. 17,192, Acq. 1949-2 CB 1.
[137] Rev. Rul. 70-254, 1970-1 CB 31.
[138] Reg. § 1.162-1(a).

deductible, however, the expenses must be reasonable in amount and have a reasonable relationship to the business activities in which the taxpayer is engaged. For instance, a builder was not allowed a business deduction for advertising and promotional expenses incurred as a result of polo playing because the builder could not show a relationship between these expenses and a business purpose. [139] Expenses incurred by an automobile agency in sponsoring cars in auto races, however, were properly deductible as advertising expenses. [140]

¶ 735 Legal Expenses

Legal expenses paid or incurred as a result of a business transaction or paid to preserve an existing business are deductible under Code Sec. 162. On the other hand, expenditures incurred to defend or perfect title to property, or to recover property, or to develop or improve property are part of the cost of the property and are not deductible expenses.

Attorney fees paid to obtain a judicial determination of the title to land, or in successfully defending title to land, including suits to remove a cloud on the title, have been held to be additional costs of the land in numerous decisions. [141] Similarly, legal expenses in a suit to partition real property are nondeductible capital expenditures. [142] Expenses incurred in litigation to secure the right as a tenant to use and occupy a premises also have been held to be nondeductible costs of defending title to property. [143]

Legal expenses incurred in a condemnation proceeding are capital expenditures and are not deductible. [144] When the proceeding results in a condemnation and award, the expenses offset the award. [145]

Legal expenses incurred in connection with property held for the production of income or investment may not be deducted and must be capitalized, if they are incurred to defend or protect title, to acquire or dispose of the property, or to develop or improve the property. [146] Legal expenses incurred by a taxpayer in seeking a higher award in a state condemnation action against the taxpayer's property were not deductible as expenses paid or incurred for the production of income under

---

[139] *R.J. Sieber*, 38 TCM 48, CCH Dec. 35,816(M), T.C. Memo. 1979-15.

[140] *Lang Chevrolet Co.*, 26 TCM 1054, CCH Dec. 28,648(M), T.C. Memo. 1967-212.

[141] See for example, *Louisiana Land & Exploration Co.*, CA-5, 47-1 USTC ¶ 9266, 161 F.2d 842; *L.Q. Coupe*, 52 TC 394, CCH Dec. 29,610, Acq. 1970-2 CB xix; *Anderson-Tully Co.*, 48 TCM 415, CCH Dec. 41,314(M), T.C. Memo. 1984-338.

[142] *J.D. Cothran*, 33 TCM 547, CCH Dec. 32,568(M), T.C. Memo. 1974-109.

[143] *Bush Terminal Buildings Co.*, CA-2, 53-1 USTC ¶ 9392, 204 F.2d 575, cert. denied 346 U.S. 856, 74 S.Ct. 72.

[144] *Issac G. Johnson & Co.*, CA-2, 45-2 USTC ¶ 9338, 149 F.2d 851.

[145] *Casalina Corp.*, CA-4, 75-1 USTC ¶ 9311, 511 F.2d 1162; *J. Iske*, 39 TCM 1161, CCH Dec. 36,807(M), T.C. Memo. 1980-61, aff'd (unpublished opinion) November 18, 1980, cert. denied 451 U.S. 909, 101 S.Ct. 1978; Rev. Rul. 71-476, 1971-2 CB 308.

[146] Reg. § 1.212-1(k).

Code Sec. 212, but were capital expenditures.[147] Similarly, amounts paid by an individual for attorneys' fees in connection with the condemnation of property held for investment and the rezoning of the remainder of the tract were capital expenditures and were not deductible.[148] While rezoning costs normally are considered nondeductible capital expenditures, a loss deduction may be available if a rezoning effort fails. In *Chevy Chase Land Co.*,[149] the Tax Court allowed a deduction for an abandonment loss when the costs of a zoning effort were completely lost and worthless when the zoning change was denied.

On the other hand, if the expenses result in the collection of taxable income, for instance rent, then the expenses are deductible under Code Sec. 212. In *B.V. Sickle*,[150] the reasonable attorney's fees paid in an action to recover rent were held fully deductible under Code Sec. 212. The taxpayer was able to prove that the entire amount paid to the attorney under a contingency fee arrangement was paid for the action to recover rent and that the fee was reasonable. The cost of ejecting a trespasser so that income could be realized from property has also been held to be a currently deductible expense.[151]

¶ 737 Interest

The general rule is that a deduction is allowed for "all interest paid or accrued within the taxable year on indebtedness."[152] However, this rule is limited by many other provisions of the Internal Revenue Code. The interest deduction is considered in some detail at ¶ 321.

For a discussion of the requirement to capitalize construction period interest, see ¶ 127.2.

¶ 741 REAL ESTATE TAXES

Taxpayers may deduct state, local, and foreign real property taxes; state and local personal property taxes; and state, local, and foreign income taxes, regardless of whether those taxes are incurred in connection with a trade or business, property held for the production of income or investment, or purely personal activities.[153] Individuals generally take these deductions as itemized deductions. These taxes are not deductible for purposes of the individual alternative minimum tax, however, unless they are business related and deductible in computing adjusted gross income.[154] An individual who will be subject to the alternative minimum tax in a particular tax year should attempt to

---

[147] *S.E. Stickles*, DC NY, 70-1 USTC ¶ 9239; see also *S. Marcus*, 23 TCM 1240, CCH Dec. 26,908(M), T.C. Memo. 1964-206.

[148] *W.M. Soelling*, 70 TC 1052, CCH Dec. 35,429; see also, *J.D. Wallace*, 48 TCM 157, CCH Dec. 41,263(M), T.C. Memo. 1984-277.

[149] 72 TC 481, CCH Dec. 36,127.

[150] 52 TCM 982, CCH Dec. 43,480(M), T.C. Memo. 1986-538.

[151] *A. Bliss*, CA-5, 3 USTC ¶ 928, 57 F.2d 984.

[152] Code Sec. 163(a).

[153] Code Sec. 164(a).

[154] Code Sec. 56(b)(1)(A)(ii).

accelerate or defer the payment of deductible taxes so as not to lose the benefit of the tax deduction.

State, local, and foreign taxes, other than property and income taxes, are deductible if they are incurred in carrying on a trade or business or an activity for the production of income. In the case of these other state and local taxes, Code Sec. 164(a) requires that the taxes be treated as part of the cost of the property, or a reduction in the amount realized, if these taxes are imposed on the acquisition or disposition of property. Examples of these other taxes include mortgage recording taxes and state transfer taxes.

¶ 743 Real Property Taxes

Real property taxes deductible under Code Sec. 164(a) are taxes imposed on interests in real property that are levied for the general public welfare. Deductible real property taxes do not include taxes assessed against local benefits.[155] For example, a monthly charge based on usage made by a city for the use of its sewer system is not a tax and is not deductible as a tax.[156] Such a charge, however, may be deductible as a business expense or, if attributable to rental property, as an expense incurred in the production of income.[157] On the other hand, real estate tax increases imposed on all property owners within a municipality to pay off general revenue bonds that were sold to build and maintain a sewage disposal system are deductible as real property taxes.[158]

Annual assessments of a homeowners' association paid by its members for the purposes of promoting the recreation, health, safety, and welfare of residents and maintaining common areas are not deductible as real property taxes.[159] Also, annual fees earmarked for sanitation services that are imposed on all property in a county, based on the assessed value of the property, but which are subject to a maximum limit with additional fees for commercial and special services, are not deductible as real property taxes.[160]

Cash method taxpayers generally deduct taxes when they are paid. In this case, "paid" means paid to the proper taxing authority. A cash method mortgagor who makes monthly payments to the mortgagee that equal one-twelfth of the estimated annual real property taxes may deduct the taxes only in the year in which payment of the taxes is made by the mortgagee to the proper taxing authorities.[161]

---

[155] Reg. § 1.164-3(b).
[156] Rev. Rul. 75-346, 1975 CB-2 66.
[157] *M. Thornbrough*, 11 TCM 227, CCH Dec. 18,832(M).
[158] Rev. Rul. 74-52, 1974-2 CB 50.
[159] Rev. Rul. 76-495, 1976-2 CB 43.
[160] Rev. Rul. 77-29, 1977-1 CB 44.
[161] Rev. Rul. 78-103, 1978-1 CB 58. See also *F.L. Odom, Jr.*, 44 TCM 1132, CCH Dec. 39,344(M), T.C. Memo. 1982-531 (cash method taxpayer not credited with payment of taxes until paid out of escrow account to which taxpayer made deposits).

For a discussion on the accounting rule applicable to the accrual of real property taxes, see ¶ 705.2.

¶ 743.1 Deduction of Real Property Taxes

Generally, it is the owner of the property against which real property taxes are assessed that is entitled to the deduction. The owner, in this case, is not necessarily the owner of the legal title, and the equitable owner of property may be entitled to the tax deduction if the equitable owner actually pays the tax.

When taxpayers acquired a residence, legal title to the property was held by others as nominees, and the record title was never held by the taxpayers. The taxpayer's wife, however, made all of the payments on the purchase price of the residence and the mortgage payments. She claimed deductions for real estate taxes that she paid, but the deductions were disallowed by the IRS since she was not the record owner of the property. The Tax Court, however, held that the wife was the equitable owner of the residence and was entitled to deduct the real estate taxes paid, even though legal title was in the names of others.[162] Similarly, a taxpayer who took title to rental property in the names of his daughter and son-in-law for personal reasons could deduct the taxes he paid on the property when the record owners received no income from the property and paid no expenses on the property.[163]

A husband and wife may deduct on separate returns only the amount of property tax actually paid by each on property held as tenants by the entirety or as joint tenants.[164] Taxes paid by a husband on a home owned by his wife, however, are not deductible by the husband.[165]

¶ 743.2 Back Taxes Payments

Back taxes paid to redeem property to which the municipality had taken a tax collector's deed are deductible if, under local law, the taxpayer is personally liable for the arrearages until redemption or foreclosure of the right to redemption.[166] The same rule applies when the back tax payment is made directly to the person who acquired the property, subject to redemption, at a tax sale.[167]

For the apportionment of the real property tax deduction between buyer and seller on the purchase of real estate, see the discussion at ¶ 119.

---

[162] *G.B. Casey,* 24 TCM 1558, CCH Dec. 27,604(M), T.C. Memo. 1965-282.
[163] *A.J. Gilbert,* 11 TCM 457, CCH Dec. 18,958(M).
[164] *W.R. Tracy,* 25 BTA 1055, CCH Dec. 7510, Acq. X1-2 CB 10, rev'd on another issue, CA-6, 4 USTC ¶ 1269, 70 F.2d 93; Rev. Rul. 71-268, 1971-1 CB 58.
[165] *W.A. Colston,* CA DC, 3 USTC ¶ 947, 59 F.2d 867, cert. denied 287 U.S. 640, 53 S.Ct. 89; *W. Buff,* 58 TC 224, CCH Dec. 31,371.
[166] *J.R. Hopkins,* 15 TC 160, CCH Dec. 17,811, Acq. 1951-1 CB 2.
[167] *C.E. Baldwin,* 14 TCM 794, CCH Dec. 21,141(M), T.C. Memo. 1955-200.

¶ 745 Special Assessment and Local Benefit Taxes

Deductible real property taxes are those that are levied for the general public welfare by the proper taxing authorities at a like rate against all property in the territory over which the authorities have jurisdiction.[168] Taxes for local benefits or special assessments paid for local benefits such as streets, sidewalks, and other like improvements that are imposed because of and measured by some benefit that tends to increase the value of the property against which the assessment is levied are not deductible as taxes.[169] A tax is considered assessed against a local benefit when the property subject to the tax is limited to the property benefited. Special assessments are not deductible, even though an incidental benefit inures to the public welfare.[170] While the improvements envisioned by the statute are those that tend to increase the value of the property, there is no requirement that the improvements actually increase the value of the property assessed in every particular case.[171]

To the extent assessments against local benefits are made for maintenance or repair or to meet interest charges for the benefits, however, they are deductible.[172] It is up to the taxpayer to show the allocation of the assessments to the different purposes. If the allocation cannot be shown, none of the amount paid is deductible.[173] In Rev. Rul. 79-201,[174] the IRS ruled that the portion of a "front foot benefit charge" assessed against property benefited by the construction of a water system and added to the taxpayer's real property tax bill, which was properly allocated to interest and maintenance charges, was deductible as a tax under Code Sec. 164. However, the ruling went on to say that no part of a flat per unit charge or a two-part charge consisting of a metered charge and a uniform charge for maintenance and interest that a sewer or water authority imposed on all its customers was deductible.

The IRS has ruled that the following are taxes for local benefits and cannot be deducted under Code Sec. 164, except to the extent allocable to maintenance or interest charges:

1. Assessments paid by property owners to a city-created parking improvement district for the purpose of providing public parking facilities in or near the district.[175]

2. Assessments imposed by an irrigation district, a subdivision of a state, against farm property within the district for operation

---

[168] Reg. § 1.164-4(a).
[169] Code Sec. 164(c)(1).
[170] Reg. § 1.164-4(a).
[171] *Caldwell Milling Co.*, 3 BTA 1232, CCH Dec. 1379.
[172] Code Sec. 164(c)(1).
[173] Reg. § 1.164-4(b)(1).
[174] 1979-1 CB 97.
[175] Rev. Rul. 60-327, 1960-2 CB 65.

and maintenance, administration, water purchase costs, and repayment of the cost of a water distribution system.[176]

3. "Front foot benefit charges" assessed by the Washington Suburban Sanitary Commission against property in jurisdictions adjacent to the District of Columbia for water main and sewer improvements.[177]

4. Sewer, water, and solid waste disposal system taxes imposed on benefited lands only by municipal utility districts formed under state law to enhance the value and marketability of a certain tract of land.[178] But real estate tax increases imposed on all property owners within a municipality to pay off general revenue bonds sold to build a sewage disposal system and to provide for its maintenance are deductible as real estate taxes.[179]

¶ 747 Transfer Taxes

Prior to the Tax Reform Act of 1986,[180] state and local real estate transfer taxes were deductible if incurred in connection with a trade, business, or income-producing property.[181] These transfer taxes were not deductible if incurred by an individual in connection with the purchase of a personal residence.[182]

The following was added to Code Sec. 164(a) by the Tax Reform Act of 1986: ". . . any tax [other than real property, personal property, income and certain other taxes] which is paid or accrued by the taxpayer in connection with an acquisition or disposition of property shall be treated as part of the cost of the acquired property or, in the case of a disposition, as a reduction in the amount realized on the disposition." Accordingly, a taxpayer purchasing property and paying a state or local real estate transfer tax adds the transfer tax to the tax basis for the property. A taxpayer selling property and paying a state or local transfer tax reduces the amount realized on the sale by the amount of the tax, and this, in turn, reduces the gain or increases the loss that must be reported as a result of the sale.

For the capitalization of taxes in connection with the construction of property, see the discussion at ¶ 127.

---

[176] Rev. Rul. 67-337, 1967-2 CB 92.
[177] Rev. Rul. 75-455, 1975-2 CB 68.
[178] Rev. Rul. 76-45, 1976-1 CB 51. See also *G.A. Noble*, 70 TC 916, CCH Dec. 35,400, Nonacq. 1979-42 (taxpayer's one-time "tap fee" to hook up to city's sewer system is special assessment for improvement benefiting the taxpayer's business properties and is a nondeductible capital expenditure).
[179] Rev. Rul. 74-52, 1974-2 CB 50.
[180] P.L. 99-514.

[181] See Rev. Rul. 69-456, 1969-2 CB 30 (state and local transfer taxes paid by a corporation on the sale of a building used in the operation of its business); Rev. Rul. 71-590, 1971-2 CB 124 (Pennsylvania Realty Transfer Tax paid by a corporation on purchase of real estate).

[182] *L.C. Black*, 60 TC 108, CCH Dec. 31,942; *J.M. Gibbons*, 35 TCM 565, CCH Dec. 33,785(M), T.C. Memo. 1976-125.

¶ 749 **Impact Fees**

In some areas, developers must pay what are termed "impact fees" in order to develop land. These fees are designed to offset the increase in infrastructure cost that must be born by the community caused by the influx of new residents in connection with the development. In Florida, these fees must be paid for the approval and recordation of plats. The question arises whether these impact fees are deductible business expenses or capital expenditures.

Oriole Homes Corp. is a large residential home builder that deducted impact fees as an ordinary and necessary business expense. The IRS, however, asserted that the impact fees were nondeductible capital expenditures. A district court in Florida decided that impact fees must be capitalized as a development cost and recovered through an increase in the cost of goods sold as each house in a development is sold.[183] Citing that court decision, the IRS has ruled that impact fees incurred in connection with the construction of new buildings are capitalized costs allocable to the new buildings under Code Secs. 263 and 263A.[184]

---

[183] *Oriole Homes Corp. v. U.S.*, DC Fla., 89-2 USTC ¶ 9433.

[184] Rev. Rul. 2002-9, 2002-10 IRB 614.

Chapter 8

Property Additions and Improvements

¶ 800 OVERVIEW OF CHAPTER

When the owner of property makes additions or improvements to the property, generally the owner may not deduct the cost currently. Rather, the owner may add the cost to the tax basis of the property and recover the added cost through depreciation deductions, if available, or on the sale or other disposition of the property.

In some cases, however, the tax law provides for a faster recovery of the cost of certain additions or improvements to real property in order to encourage owners to take certain actions. An example of these special amortization provisions is the write-off for additions or improvements to industrial and other business property to control air and water pollution. Other incentives are provided for reforestation and soil and water conservation.

Another incentive that Congress often uses to promote socially desirable goals is a tax credit. Unlike a deduction, which reduces taxable income, a tax credit is a direct reduction in tax liability. Currently, there are two tax credits that may be used by owners of, and investors in, real estate. These tax credits are the investment credit for the rehabilitation of certain older commercial buildings and historic structures and the credit for the acquisition or improvement of low-income housing.

This chapter discusses additions and improvements to real estate in general and the special amortization and tax credit provisions that are available for particular types of improvements. The more widely available deduction for depreciation is given special consideration in Chapter 9.

¶ 801 IMPROVEMENTS TO REAL ESTATE AS CAPITAL EXPENDITURES

The Internal Revenue Code denies a deduction for any amount paid out for new buildings or for permanent improvements or betterments made to increase the value of any property or estate.[1] It also denies a deduction for any amount expended in restoring property or in

---
[1] Code Sec. 263(a)(1).

making good the exhaustion thereof for which an allowance is or has been made in the form of a deduction for depreciation, amortization, or depletion.[2]

In general, the nondeductible capital expenditures specified in Code Sec. 263 are those expenditures that add to the value, or substantially prolong the useful life, of property owned by the taxpayer, such as plants or equipment, or adapt property for a new or different use. Amounts paid or incurred for the incidental repairs and maintenance of property are not capital expenditures.[3] The distinction between repairs (currently deductible expenses, in the case of trade or business property or property held for the production of income) and improvements (nondeductible capital expenditures) is considered at ¶ 723.1 in connection with the discussion on deduction of repair expenses.

For the special considerations involved when landlords and tenants make improvements or additions to leased property, see ¶ 601 and 611.

¶ 803 Improvements to Land and Buildings

Capital expenditures include not only the cost of original construction but also subsequent improvements[4] and the cost of converting property to commercial use.[5] It is not necessary that expenditures which are made to convert property to business use or to make property suitable for use in business increase the actual value or assessed value of the property in order to be classified as capital expenditures.[6]

Nondeductible capital expenditures include the cost of improvements to land, as well as improvements to buildings. For example, amounts paid by the developer of a mobile home park to a public utility for underground electric and gas distribution systems are capital expenditures that are included in the developer's cost basis for the land.[7] Similarly, the costs of revetments and a berm built in connection with a lake landfill program and the cost of filling in the area are costs of improving and acquiring land.[8] The costs of land preparation were held to be nondeductible capital expenditures when the costs were incurred to increase the value of the farms for eventual resale and the activity was more than necessary annual maintenance.[9]

Expenditures to rehabilitate and restore an old office that had been uninhabitable when the taxpayer moved into it were capital expenditures and were not made for incidental repairs.[10] Similarly, taxpayers who purchased and renovated two apartment buildings were

---

[2] Code Sec. 263(a)(2).
[3] Reg. § 1.263(a)-1(b).
[4] *Simmons & Hammond Mfg. Co.*, 1 BTA 803, CCH Dec. 296.
[5] *I.T. Burden*, 1 TCM 610, CCH Dec. 12,991(M).
[6] *E. Dumble Co.*, 9 BTA 591, CCH Dec. 3188.
[7] Rev. Rul. 80-93, 1980-1 CB 50.
[8] Rev. Rul. 77-270, 1977-2 CB 79.
[9] *P.O. Huber*, 49 TCM 57, CCH Dec. 41,606(M), T.C. Memo. 1984-593.
[10] *K.A. Brown*, 39 TCM 397, CCH Dec. 36,406(M), T.C. Memo. 1979-434.

required to capitalize their expenditures.[11] The expenditures were not just for cosmetic changes but were made as part of a plan of rehabilitation for capital improvement. Even expenditures incurred after the apartments were occupied had to be capitalized because the taxpayers could not show that the plan of renovation ended with occupancy and they had not segregated their various expenses.

In *J.S. Moss*,[12] however, the Ninth Circuit allowed a current deduction for the costs of repairing a hotel and did not require capitalization of the costs merely because they were incurred as part of a plan to remodel the hotel with furniture and furnishings. The hotel remained in operation throughout the period of the remodeling and maintained its high rating throughout most of the period. The improvements merely served to maintain its status.

See also the discussion of the tax treatment of repair or improvement at ¶ 723.1.

¶ 805 Replacements of Building Components

The replacement of building components or other capital items generally is treated as a capital expenditure. For example, the replacement of attic beams and the installation of a support girder in a crawl space are capital expenditures.[13] Other examples of replacements as capital expenditures are:

Carpet, drapery, and refrigerator replacements in rental property [14]

Electrical system replacement in an office building [15]

Flooring (new) laid on top of old flooring, lumber and labor [16]

Furnace and water heater (new) in rental property [17]

Roof, doors, and carpeting (all new) for an office building [18]

Sewer replacement and reconnection of the lines [19]

Windows (new) [20]

Wooden floor replacement in an old building that was to be used for business purposes [21]

Wooden stairway replacement with steel stairway [22]

---

[11] *D.C. Ruttenberg*, 52 TCM 370, CCH Dec. 43,323(M), T.C. Memo. 1986-414.

[12] CA-9, 87-2 USTC ¶ 9590, 831 F.2d 833.

[13] *M. Mozayeny*, 53 TCM 566, CCH Dec. 43,835(M), T.C. Memo. 1987-188.

[14] *J.J. Otis*, 73 TC 671, CCH Dec. 36,716.

[15] *A.F. Harris*, 55 TCM 769, CCH Dec. 44,751(M), T.C. Memo. 1988-195.

[16] *Standard Fruit Product Co.*, 8 TCM 733, CCH Dec. 17,159(M).

[17] *B. Davis*, 37 TCM 42, CCH Dec. 34,914(M), T.C. Memo. 1978-12; *C.M. Hill, Jr.*, 45 TCM 821, CCH Dec. 39,930(M), T.C. Memo. 1983-112.

[18] *R.O. Watts*, 34 TCM 613, CCH Dec. 33,184(M), T.C. Memo. 1975-131.

[19] *Standard Fruit Product Co.*, 8 TCM 733, CCH Dec. 17,159(M).

[20] *B.T. Wright, Inc.*, 12 BTA 1149, CCH Dec. 4200, Nonacq. viii-1 CB 62.

[21] *La France Wine Co.*, 33 TCM 1130, CCH Dec. 32,786(M), T.C. Memo. 1974-254.

[22] *O.L. Thomas*, 21 TCM 708, CCH Dec. 25,526(M), T.C. Memo. 1981-128.

¶ 807 Abandonment of Improvement Plans

A loss incurred in a business or in a transaction entered into for profit and arising from the sudden termination of the usefulness of any nondepreciable property is allowed as a deduction under Code Sec. 165(a) for the taxable year in which the loss is actually sustained.[23]

For example, an architect's fees for a proposed building are a deductible loss for the taxable year in which the project is abandoned.[24] The same principle should apply to the abandonment of plans to improve or renovate an existing building. A current loss deduction should be available if it is clear that the plans have been completely abandoned and that the expense incurred has no further value to the taxpayer. In *R.B. Haspel*,[25] a loss deduction for the abandonment of an architect's plans was denied because the original plans were used or incorporated in part in later plans by a different architect.

In *Roux Laboratories, Inc.*,[26] an abandonment loss was allowed for the cost of plans drawn by an architectural firm for a building that was different from the one that the corporation eventually built. However, the corporation could not claim an abandonment loss for the cost of the materials handling consultant's report on which the original design was based because the report was of continued use to the corporation in making plans for its new building.

The cost of attempting to obtain a zoning change, if unsuccessful, also may be taken as an abandonment loss under Code Sec. 165.[27] But again, the project for which the zoning change is sought must be completely abandoned before there is a loss.[28]

When an improvement or replacement does not work out as intended, it does not mean that the cost of the improvement or replacement can be taken as an abandonment loss. For example, no loss was allowed for a marble floor that became defective and was covered with carpeting. The asset, which remained in the taxpayer's possession, was not completely abandoned but remained as a subfloor beneath the carpeting.[29] An abandonment loss has also been denied for one flooded apartment in an apartment complex that was converted to guestrooms and a clubhouse.[30]

---

[23] Reg. § 1.165-2(a).

[24] *Western Wheeled Scraper Co.*, 14 BTA 496, CCH Dec. 4547, Acq. and Nonacq. viii-1 CB 48, 61.

[25] 62 TC 59, CCH Dec. 32,549.

[26] DC Fla., 76-2 USTC ¶ 9751.

[27] *Chevy Chase Land Co. of Montgomery County, Md.*, 72 TC 481, CCH Dec. 36,127.

[28] *J.R. Clem*, 10 TCM 1248, CCH Dec. 18,718(M); *G. Weiss*, CA-8, 55-1 USTC ¶ 9365, 221 F.2d 152.

[29] *Wauwatosa Colony, Inc.*, 25 TCM 298, CCH Dec. 27,873(M), T.C. Memo. 1966-51.

[30] *E.V. Scott*, 38 TCM 115, CCH Dec. 35,839(M), T.C. Memo. 1979-29.

¶ 811 SPECIAL AMORTIZATION PROVISIONS

Some capital expenditures, as permitted by the Internal Revenue Code, may be amortized rather than added to basis and recovered through depreciation or on the sale or other disposition of the property. Amortization, in this case, is the ratable writeoff or deduction of the costs involved over some specified period. In the case of real property, the special amortization provisions that may apply are those for the cost of pollution control facilities and for certain reforestation expenses. Soil and water conservation expenditures, although technically not subject to special amortization since they are eligible for an immediate, although limited, deduction, are also covered in this section.

¶ 813 Pollution Control Facilities

Individuals and businesses may elect to amortize the cost of certified pollution control equipment over a period of 60 months.[31] The amortization deduction is available for treatment facilities that are used to abate or control water or air pollution in connection with any plant or other property.[32] In this regard, "plant or other property" includes any tangible property, whether or not the property is used in a trade or business or held for the production of income. For example, pollution control facilities or equipment installed in connection with paper mills, motor vehicles, or furnaces in an apartment house would all be eligible for the 60-month amortization.[33]

¶ 813.1 *Amortization Election Requirements*

A taxpayer who wants to elect the 60-month amortization for pollution control facilities generally must meet the following requirements contained in Code Sec. 169(d):

1. The pollution control facility must abate or control water or air pollution or contamination by removing, altering, disposing, storing or preventing the creation or emission of pollutants, contaminants, wastes, or heat.

2. The pollution control facility must be new tangible property. Buildings and their structural components generally do not qualify as pollution control facilities. However, if a building is used exclusively as a treatment facility, it does qualify.

3. The pollution control facility must be used in connection with a plant or other property that was in operation before January 1, 1976.

---

[31] Code Sec. 169(a).
[32] Reg. § 1.169-2(a)(2).
[33] Reg. § 1.169-2(a)(4).

4. The state certifying authority must certify that the pollution control facility is in conformity with the state program or requirements for pollution control.

5. The Environmental Protection Agency must certify the pollution control facility.[34]

6. The pollution control facility must not significantly increase the output or capacity, extend the useful life, or reduce the total operating costs of the plant or property to which it relates.

7. The pollution control facility must not alter the nature of the manufacturing or production process or facility.

The 60-month amortization period begins with the month following the month in which the pollution control facility is completed or acquired or with the first month of the next taxable year.[35] The procedure for filing the election is contained in Reg. § 1.169-4. An election to amortize pollution control costs may be discontinued or revoked at any time. Any unamortized pollution control facility cost that is unamortized when the election is discontinued is added to basis and recovered through normal depreciation rules.[36] A taxpayer may not renew the election to amortize pollution control facility costs once the original election has been terminated.

Corporations are subject to a 20 percent reduction in tax preferences under Code Sec. 291. Accordingly, only 80 percent of the cost of certified pollution control facilities may be amortized over 60 months by a corporation.[37] The 20 percent that is not eligible is recovered under the normal depreciation rules.

¶ 813.2 Limitation for Longer-Lived Facilities

The amortizable cost of pollution control facilities is limited in the case of facilities that have a useful life for depreciation purposes of more than 15 years.[38] This limitation, therefore, affects only pollution control facilities that come within the 20-year class of depreciable property or residential rental property (27.5-year depreciation period) or nonresidential real property (39-year depreciation period).

Under the limitation, only the portion of the pollution control facility cost that bears the same ratio to total cost as 15 years bears to the depreciable life of the facility is eligible for the 60-month amortization. The excess cost that is not amortizable over 60 months is added to

---

[34] The EPA issued regulations are at Reg. § 1.602-1—§ 1.602-10.
[35] Code Sec. 169(b).
[36] Code Sec. 169(c).
[37] Code Sec. 291(a)(5).
[38] Code Sec. 169(f)(2).

basis and recovered under the normal depreciation rules.[39] (Depreciation is the subject of Chapter 9.)

Example: A corporation constructs a building that is used exclusively as a treatment facility and qualifies as a certified pollution control facility. The cost of the treatment facility is $100,000 and it has a depreciable life of 39 years.

The amortizable basis of this pollution control facility is $38,462 ($100,000 × 15.0/39). This amount must be further reduced by 20 percent because the taxpayer is a corporation. This reduction is $7,692, leaving $30,770 to be amortized over 60 months at a rate of $512.83 per month. The $69,230 portion of the total cost of the pollution control facility that the corporation may not amortize over 60 months may be recovered under the normal depreciation rules over the 39-year depreciable life of the building.

¶ 815 Reforestation Expenses and Tax Credit

Under Code Sec. 194, a taxpayer may, over a period of 84 months, amortize up to $10,000 of reforestation expenses for qualified timber property incurred in a single tax year rather than adding the expenses to cost basis. The amortization period begins on the first day of the first month of the last half of the taxable year during which the taxpayer incurs the reforestation expenses.[40] If the taxpayer disposes of qualified timber property, the amortization deductions may be recaptured as ordinary income.[41]

Qualified timber property for which reforestation expenses may be amortized over 84 months is property located in the United States which will contain trees in significant commercial quantities and which the taxpayer holds for the growing and cutting of trees for sale or use in the commercial production of timber products.[42] The property may be a woodlot or other site, but must consist of at least one acre that is planted with tree seedlings in the manner normally used in forestation or reforestation.[43] Allowable reforestation expenses are limited to the direct costs incurred to plant or seed for forestation or reforestation purposes. Qualifying expenditures include site preparation, seed or seedlings, and labor and tool costs, including depreciation on equipment used in the planting or seeding.[44] Only costs that must be capitalized and are included in the adjusted basis of the property qualify as reforestation expenditures. Costs that are otherwise currently deductible do not qualify.[45]

---

[39] Code Sec. 169(g).
[40] Reg. § 1.194-1(b).
[41] Reg. § 1.194-1(c).
[42] Code Sec. 194(c)(1).
[43] Reg. § 1.194-3(a).
[44] Code Sec. 194(c)(3).
[45] Reg. § 1.194-3(c).

In the case of a partnership, the $10,000 limit applies at the partnership as well as the partner level.[46] Similar rules apply to S corporations.[47]

If a taxpayer is reimbursed under any governmental reforestation cost-sharing program, the expenditures do not qualify as reforestation expenses, unless the reimbursed amounts are included in the taxpayer's gross income.[48] The procedure for electing to amortize reforestation expenses is contained in Reg. § 1.194-4.

Although the regular investment credit was repealed for most types of property, a 10 percent tax credit remains available for reforestation expenses that are eligible for the special 84-month amortization.[49]

¶ 817 Soil and Water Conservation Expenditures

A taxpayer engaged in the business of farming may treat expenditures for soil and water conservation or to prevent erosion as current deductions rather than adding these costs to the basis of the land.[50] There is, however, an annual limit of 25 percent of the taxpayer's gross income from farming on the amount of soil and water conservation expenditures that the taxpayer can currently deduct.[51] Also, the expenditures that are eligible for this special treatment are limited to those that are consistent with a conservation plan approved by the Soil Conservation Service of the U.S. Department of Agriculture or, in the absence of a federally approved plan, a soil conservation plan of a comparable state agency.[52]

Soil and water conservation expenditures that are eligible for the special deduction include the cost of the treatment or moving of earth, such as leveling, grading, terracing, and contour furrowing, and the construction, control, and the protection of diversion channels, drainage ditches, earthen dams, watercourses, outlets, and ponds. The cost of eradicating brush and planting windbreaks is also eligible for the current deduction.[53]

The deduction for soil and water conservation expenditures, however, applies only to nondepreciable items. Taxpayers may not deduct expenditures for the purchase, construction, installation, or improvement of structures, appliances, or facilities subject to depreciation. The deduction is available for earthen items that are not subject to depreciation. For example, expenditures for structures such as tanks, reservoirs, pipes, conduits, canals, dams, wells, or pumps composed of

---

[46] Reg. § 1.194-2(b)(5)(ii).
[47] Reg. § 1.194-2(b)(6).
[48] Code Sec. 194(c)(3)(B).
[49] Code Sec. 46(b)(1).
[50] Code Sec. 175.
[51] Code Sec. 175(b).
[52] Code Sec. 175(c)(3).
[53] Code Sec. 175(c)(3).

masonry, concrete, tile, metal, or wood do not qualify, but expenditures for earthen terraces and dams that are nondepreciable do qualify.[54]

A taxpayer engaged in the business of farming may take a current deduction for the cost of fertilizer, lime, and similar items that are used to enrich, neutralize, or condition the land.[55] The current deduction is available for these items even though the effect on the land extends beyond one year and the cost would otherwise be treated as a capital expenditure.[56]

¶ 821 TAX CREDITS FOR BUILDING REHABILITATIONS

Before 1986, an investment tax credit was available for the purchase or construction of tangible personal property for use in a trade or business. The credit of up to 10 percent of the cost of qualifying property was not available for buildings or their structural components. In 1978, Congress expanded the investment credit to encourage the rehabilitation of existing commercial buildings and historic structures. When Congress repealed the regular investment credit in 1986, it largely left intact the credits for real estate rehabilitations. Today, a 10 percent credit is available for the rehabilitation of older commercial buildings, and a 20 percent credit is available for the rehabilitation of certified historic structures.[57]

The investment credit for rehabilitation expenditures is included with other credits that make up the general business credit of Code Sec. 38 for purposes of applying the ceiling on credits measured by tax liability. The other tax credits that are combined with the investment credit in the general business credit are the work opportunity credit, alcohol fuels credit, research credit, low-incoming housing credit, disabled access credit, enhanced oil recovery credit, renewable electricity production credit, empowerment zone employment credit, Indian employment credit, employer social security credit, and the orphan drug credit. The sum of these credits may be used to offset up to $25,000 in tax liability plus 75 percent of tax liability in excess of $25,000. Unused credits are subject to carryback and carryover rules.[58]

The rehabilitation credit is treated as a tax credit from real estate in which an investor actively participates, so that the limitation on passive losses does not apply, and an individual investor may use credit equivalents to shelter up to $25,000 of income per year from nonpassive sources. This $25,000 allowance is phased out for investors with adjusted gross incomes of $200,000 or more at a rate of 50 cents to the

---

[54] Reg. § 1.175-2(b).
[55] Code Sec. 180.
[56] See, for example, I.T. 3843, 1947-1 CB 12, holding that the cost of lime spread on farmland is a capital expenditure if the effectiveness of the lime extends substantially beyond the taxable year.
[57] Code Sec. 47(a).
[58] Code Sec. 39.

dollar in excess of $200,000. See Chapter 11 for a discussion of the passive loss limitations.

The tax credits for rehabilitating qualifying buildings are substantial inducements to renovate rather than relocate. Also, in appropriate cases, the purchase of older buildings or historic buildings, rather than new construction, may be more attractive because of the credits. These important tax incentives are discussed in the following materials.

¶ 823 Rehabilitation of Older Commercial Buildings

A tax credit of 10 percent of the qualified rehabilitation expenditures is available for buildings other than historic structures. A qualified rehabilitation is treated as an acquisition of new property, so that the used-property limitations that applied to the investment credit prior to 1991 do not apply to rehabilitation credits.[59] Should property that qualifies for the rehabilitation credit also qualify for energy credits, the energy credits may not be taken for the same expenditures.[60]

In order to qualify for the credit, the building that is being rehabilitated must have been originally placed in service before 1936.[61] In addition, the building must not be used for residential purposes other than on a transient basis.[62] This latter requirement excludes buildings such as apartment buildings from eligibility for the credit. Otherwise, all older buildings used for business or productive purposes qualify, including stores, warehouses, factories, hotels, and office buildings. The type of building is determined following the rehabilitation, so that an apartment building that was built before 1936 that is converted into an office building in a qualifying rehabilitation qualifies for the 10 percent tax credit.

In addition to the requirement that the building have been first placed in service before 1936, a building must meet the following three additional requirements in order for rehabilitation expenditures to qualify for the credit:

1. The building must be substantially rehabilitated;[63]

2. The building must have been placed in service before the beginning of the rehabilitation, but not necessarily by the taxpayer claiming the credit;[64] and

3. The building must retain in place 50 percent or more of its existing external walls as external walls, 75 percent of its

---

[59] Former Code Sec. 48(g)(4), as in effect prior to 1991.
[60] Code Sec. 48(a)(2)(C).
[61] Code Sec. 47(c)(1)(B).
[62] Code Sec. 50(b)(2).
[63] Code Sec. 47(c)(1)(A)(i).
[64] Code Sec. 47(c)(1)(A)(ii).

existing external walls as external or internal walls, and 75 percent of its existing internal structural framework.[65]

Requirements (1) and (3) are explored at ¶ 823.1 and 823.3.

Expenditures that qualify for the credit are capital expenditures for depreciable property that is nonresidential real property, residential rental property (but only in the case of historic structures), real property with a class life of more than 12.5 years, and an addition or improvement to these classes of property.[66] The expenditures must be made in connection with the rehabilitation of a qualified rehabilitated building that meets all of the requirements set out above.[67] Expenditures for work done to various facilities related to a building, such as sidewalks, parking lots, and landscaping, are not treated as made in connection with the rehabilitation of a qualified rehabilitated building.[68]

¶ 823.1 *Substantial Rehabilitation Test*

Rehabilitation expenditures do not qualify for the credit unless the building is "substantially rehabilitated." A building is substantially rehabilitated if the qualified rehabilitation expenditures for a 24-month period selected by the taxpayer and ending within the taxable year exceed the greater of (1) $5,000, and (2) the adjusted basis of the building and its structural components as of the first day of the 24-month period or of the holding period of the building, whichever is later.[69] Note that the adjusted basis used to determine whether a rehabilitation is substantial does not include the basis of land. Careful allocation of cost on the purchase of an older building and land may make it easier to obtain the rehabilitation credit at a later time.

The 24-month rehabilitation period may be extended to 60 months if the rehabilitation will be completed in phases. Architectural plans and specifications for the phased rehabilitation, however, must be completed before the rehabilitation begins for the 60-month period to apply.[70]

The substantial rehabilitation test is illustrated by the following example, adapted from Reg. § 1.48-12(b)(2)(x).

Example: The Taxpayer who is on the calendar year purchases a building for $140,000 on January 1, 2000. The Taxpayer incurs qualified rehabilitation expenditures of $48,000 ($4,000 per month) in 2000, $100,000 in 2001, and $20,000 ($2,000 per month) in the first ten months of 2002. The rehabilitation does not qualify as a phased rehabilitation because plans did not exist before work

---

[65] Code Sec. 47(c)(1)(A)(iii).
[66] Code Sec. 47(c)(2)(A)(i).
[67] Code Sec. 47(c)(2)(A)(ii).
[68] Reg. § 1.48-12(c)(5).
[69] Code Sec. 47(c)(1)(C)(i); Reg. § 1.48-12(b)(2).
[70] Code Sec. 47(c)(1)(C)(ii); Reg. § 1.48-12(b)(2)(v).

began. The Taxpayer places the building in service on October 31, 2002.

The Taxpayer may select any 24-month measuring period that ends in 2002 for purposes of meeting the substantial rehabilitation test. The Taxpayer selects the period that begins on February 1, 2000, and ends on January 31, 2002. The Taxpayer's basis in the building was $144,000 on February 1, 2000 ($140,000 plus $4,000 of rehabilitation expenditures incurred during January 2000). The amount of qualified rehabilitation expenditures incurred during the measuring period is $146,000 ($44,000 from February 1 to December 31, 2000, plus $100,000 in 2001, plus $2,000 in January 2002).

The building is treated as "substantially rehabilitated" for the Taxpayer's 2002 tax year because the $146,000 of expenditures incurred during the measuring period exceeded the taxpayer's adjusted basis of $144,000 at the beginning of the period. If the other requirements are met, the building is treated as a qualified rehabilitated building, and the Taxpayer has $168,000 of qualified rehabilitation expenditures ($146,000 incurred during the measuring period, $4,000 incurred before the beginning of the measuring period, and $18,000 incurred after the measuring period and during the year in which the measuring period ends).

The result would generally be the same if the property attributable to the rehabilitation expenditures were placed in service as the expenditures were incurred, but the Taxpayer would have $148,000 of qualified rehabilitation expenditures for 2001 and $20,000 for 2002.

¶ 823.2 *Expenditures Incurred by Predecessor*

If rehabilitation expenditures are incurred for a building by a person other than the taxpayer and the taxpayer subsequently acquires the building or a portion of the building to which some or all of the expenditures are allocable (for example, a condominium unit), the taxpayer acquiring the property is treated as having incurred the rehabilitation expenditures actually incurred by the transferor if:

1. The building or portion of the building acquired by the taxpayer was not used or placed in service after the rehabilitation expenditures were incurred and prior to the date of acquisition, and

2. No credit for the qualified rehabilitation expenditures is claimed by anyone other than the taxpayer acquiring the property.[71]

How this rule affects the substantial rehabilitation requirement is illustrated in the following example.

Example: The Seller owns a building with a basis of $10,000, and the Seller incurs $5,000 of rehabilitation expenditures. Before completing the rehabilitation project, the Seller sells the building to the Buyer for $30,000. The Buyer is treated as having incurred the $5,000 of rehabilitation expenditures actually incurred by the Seller. Because the Buyer's basis in the building is $30,000, which includes the property attributable to the Seller's rehabilitation expenditures, the Buyer's basis for purposes of the substantial rehabilitation test is reduced to $25,000 ($30,000 cost basis less the $5,000 rehabilitation expenditure treated as incurred by the Buyer). The Buyer, therefore, would be required to incur more than $20,000 of rehabilitation expenditures, in addition to the $5,000 incurred by the Seller and treated as having been incurred by the Buyer, during a measuring period selected by the Buyer in order to satisfy the substantial rehabilitation test.

¶ 823.3 The "Wall Test"

A building must meet the "wall test" in order to be considered a qualified rehabilitated building. This three-part test requires that 50 percent or more of the existing external walls be retained in place as external walls. Moreover, 75 percent of existing external walls must be retained as internal or external walls and 75 percent of the existing internal structural framework of the building must be retained in place.

The measurement of the walls is based on the total area of the walls, including both the supporting and nonsupporting elements. Therefore, a curtain, window, or door is counted in measuring the area of an external wall. An "external wall" is a wall that has one face exposed to the weather, earth, or an abutting wall of an adjacent building. A party wall, that is, a single wall shared with an adjacent building, also is considered an external wall, provided that the shared wall has no windows or doors in any portion of the wall that does not have one face exposed to the weather, earth, or an abutting wall.

External walls generally include only those walls that form part of the outline or perimeter of the building or that surround an uncovered courtyard. The walls of an uncovered internal shaft, such as a light well

---

[71] Reg. § 1.48-12(c)(3)(ii).

in the center of a building that is designed solely to bring light or air into the center of a building, which are completely surrounded by external walls and which enclose space not designed for use by people, are not considered external walls. Walls surrounding an outdoor space that is usable by people, however, such as a courtyard, are external walls.[72]

The "internal structural framework" includes all load-bearing internal walls and any other internal structural supports that are essential to the stability of the building. Internal supports include such things as columns, girders, beams, trusses, spandrels, and all other essential members.[73]

An external wall is retained in place even if it is covered with siding or is reinforced. Doors and windows may be replaced, enlarged, or eliminated. An existing curtain may be replaced, provided that the structural framework that supports the existing curtain is retained. The external wall may be disassembled and reassembled if the same supporting elements are used. For example, original bricks may be removed, cleaned and replaced to form the wall. An existing external wall is not retained in place, however, if the supporting elements of the wall are replaced by new supporting elements.[74]

Example: The Taxpayer rehabilitated a building that has two external walls measuring $75' \times 20'$ and two other external walls measuring $100' \times 20'$. The Taxpayer demolished one of the larger walls, including its supporting elements and constructs a new wall. Because one of the larger walls is more than 25 percent of the area of the building's external walls, the Taxpayer did not satisfy the requirement that 75 percent of external walls be retained and is not eligible for the rehabilitation credit.

Suppose, however, that the Taxpayer did not demolish the wall, but rather converted it into an internal wall by building a new external wall. In this case, the building would satisfy the external wall requirements and the building would qualify for the rehabilitation credit.

¶ 823.4 *Nonqualifying Expenditures*

Certain expenditures are specifically excluded from the definition of qualified rehabilitation expenditures by Code Sec. 47(c)(2)(B). These nonqualifying expenditures are:

1. Expenditures for which straight line depreciation is not used, other than tax-exempt bond financed property and tax-exempt

---

[72] Reg. § 1.48-12(b)(3)(ii).
[73] Reg. § 1.48-12(b)(3)(iii).
[74] Reg. § 1.48-12(b)(3)(iv).

Property Additions and Improvements

use property for which the alternative depreciation system must be used (depreciation is the subject of Chapter 9).

2. The cost of acquiring any building or an interest in any building.

3. Any expenditure attributable to the enlargement of an existing building. While rehabilitation includes renovation, restoration, or reconstruction, it does not include either enlargement or new construction. A building is enlarged if the total volume of the building is increased, but an increase in floor space that results from interior remodeling is not considered an enlargement.[75] If expenditures go to both enlargement and qualified rehabilitation, the expenditures must be apportioned between the original building and the enlargement.[76]

4. Any expenditure (with certain very limited exceptions) attributable to the rehabilitation of a certified historic structure or building in a registered historic district. These expenditures generally must qualify for the 20 percent credit discussed at ¶ 825.

5. Any expenditure by a lessee of a building if the remaining term of the lease is less than the depreciation period of the building when the rehabilitation is completed. See the discussion of investment credit considerations in connection with leasehold improvements and additions at ¶ 621.

6. Rehabilitation expenditures attributable to a building or portion of a building that is, or may reasonably be expected to be, tax-exempt use property. These expenditures, however, are considered in determining whether or not a building has been substantially rehabilitated.

¶ 823.5 Basis Reduction by Credit Amount

The basis of rehabilitated property must be reduced by the full amount of any rehabilitation credit.[77] This basis reduction, of course, reduces future depreciation deductions that may be taken for the property.

¶ 825 Rehabilitations of Certified Historic Structures

A taxpayer that rehabilitates an historic structure or building is entitled to a credit of 20 percent of the qualified rehabilitation expenditures.[78] This is a substantial tax incentive that has rather broad application. As long as the certification requirements are met, any type of building may qualify for the credit. Also, a certified historic struc-

---

[75] Reg. § 1.48-12(c)(10)(i).
[76] Reg. § 1.48-12(c)(10)(ii).
[77] Code Sec. 50(c).
[78] Code Sec. 47(a)(2).

ture does not have to be used for the same purpose after the rehabilitation as before the rehabilitation.

In general, the rehabilitation expenditures that qualify for the 20 percent credit are the same types of expenditures that qualify for the 10 percent credit for older commercial buildings. The rehabilitation of an historic building, in addition to the certification requirements discussed below, must qualify under the same rules that apply to the 10 percent credit, with the following three exceptions:

1. The building for which an historic rehabilitation credit is claimed does not have to have been originally placed in service before 1936. A building of any age qualifies, if it is a "certified historic structure."

2. The credit for the rehabilitation of historic structures is available even for residential property. An historic building may be used as an apartment building after the rehabilitation and still qualify for the credit.

3. The "wall test" for the rehabilitation of older commercial buildings does not apply. It is the opinion of Congress that the certifying procedure is sufficient to ensure that certified historic structures will be properly rehabilitated. The Senate Finance Committee, in repealing the wall test for historic structures, stated that it was expected that certification would be denied, however, when less than 75 percent of the external walls are retained.[79]

¶ 825.1 *Certification Requirements*

The rehabilitation of an historic building or structure must be a certified rehabilitation in order to be eligible for the 20 percent credit. A certified rehabilitation is the rehabilitation of a "certified historic structure" which the Secretary of the Interior has certified to the Treasury Secretary as consistent with the historic character of the property or the district in which the property is located.[80] Taxpayers must submit plans and specifications in order to obtain the certification, and the actual rehabilitation itself must be approved. At times, this certification process can be quite time-consuming.

A "certified historic structure" is a building and its structural components that is either (1) listed in the National Register of Historic Places or (2) located in a registered historic district and certified by the Secretary of the Interior as being of significance to the district.[81]

---

[79] See the Senate Finance Committee Report on the Tax Reform Act of 1986.

[80] Code Sec. 47(c)(2)(C).
[81] Code Sec. 47(c)(3)(A).

A registered historic district is any district that is (1) listed in the National Register of Historic Places, or (2) designated under a statute of a state or local government (if the statute is certified by the Secretary of the Interior as containing criteria that will substantially achieve the purpose of preserving and rehabilitating buildings of historic significance to the district) and is certified by the Secretary of the Interior as meeting substantially all of the requirements for the listing of districts in the National Register of Historic Places.[82]

¶ 825.2 Nonqualified Buildings Credit Allowance

The 10 percent credit for the rehabilitation of older commercial buildings generally is not available for certified historic structures or buildings in registered historic districts. The rehabilitation of these buildings generally must qualify for the 20 percent credit for historic rehabilitations. The 10 percent rehabilitation credit, however, is available for a building in a registered historic district if the building does not qualify for the 20 percent credit, but only if the following conditions are met:

1. The building must not be a certified historic structure.[83]

2. The Secretary of the Interior must certify to the Treasury Secretary that the building is not of historic significance to the district.[84]

3. If the required certification in 2 occurs after the rehabilitation of the building begins, the taxpayer must certify to the Treasury Secretary that he or she in good faith was not aware of the certification requirement at the beginning of the rehabilitation.[85]

¶ 827 Recapture of Rehabilitation Credits

The credits for the rehabilitation of older commercial buildings and historic structures are subject to recapture if a building for which a rehabilitation credit was taken is disposed of within five full years of the rehabilitation. Recapture also occurs if the Department of the Interior revokes or otherwise invalidates a certification after the property is placed in service or if a building, other than a historic structure, is moved from the place where it is rehabilitated after the property is placed in service. In addition, if all or a portion of a substantially rehabilitated building becomes tax-exempt use property for the first time within five years after the credit is claimed, the credit will be recaptured.[86]

---

[82] Code Sec. 47(c)(3)(B).
[83] Code Sec. 47(c)(2)(B)(iv)(I).
[84] Code Sec. 47(c)(2)(B)(iv)(II).
[85] Code Sec. 47(c)(2)(B)(iv)(III).
[86] Reg. § 1.48-12(f)(3).

To the extent a credit is recaptured, it increases the taxpayer's tax liability for the year in which the recapture event occurs. The credit is recaptured on a sliding scale as provided in Code Sec. 50(a)(1). If the recapture event occurs within one year of the rehabilitation, 100 percent of the credit is recaptured; if the recapture event occurs within two years of the rehabilitation, 80 percent of the credit is recaptured; if within three years, 60 percent; if within four years, 40 percent; and if within five years, 20 percent. There is no recapture potential after five full years.

Any credit that is recaptured, in addition to increasing tax liability, is added to the basis of the property because the basis was reduced by the full amount of the credit at the time the credit was claimed.

¶ 831 LOW-INCOME HOUSING CREDIT

Over the years, Congress has provided various tax incentives to encourage the development and maintenance of low-income rental housing. Those incentives have included special accelerated depreciation, five-year amortization of rehabilitation expenses, exemption from the capitalization requirement for construction period interest and taxes, and tax-exempt bond financing for multi-family rental properties. In the Tax Reform Act of 1986, Congress repealed many of the then existing tax incentives for low-income housing and enacted a tax credit that may be claimed by owners of residential property used for low-income housing.[87]

The credit is available for the cost of new construction, the cost of rehabilitation, or the cost of acquiring existing buildings by purchase and their rehabilitation. Generally, only the cost of buildings attributable to low-income units qualifies for the credit. Cost attributable to residential units other than low-income units and cost attributable to land are not eligible for the credit. The low-income housing credit is included in the general business credit and is subject to the tax liability limitation of Code Sec. 38 and the carryback and carryover rules of Code Sec. 39.

The low-income housing credit is taken annually, generally for a period of 10 years. New construction and rehabilitation expenditures for projects that were placed in service in 1987 were eligible for a credit equal to nine percent of the qualified cost each year for 10 years. The acquisition cost of existing projects and the cost of newly constructed projects receiving other federal subsidies placed in service in 1987 were eligible for a credit equal to four percent of the qualified cost each year for 10 years. For buildings placed in service after 1987, the credit

---

[87] Code Sec. 42.

percentages are adjusted figures. The exact percentages are redetermined each month in order to provide a total credit over the 10-year credit period equal to a present value of 70 percent of the qualified costs for new construction and rehabilitation. The credit rate is set to yield an amount with a present value equal to 30 percent of the cost if the construction or rehabilitation is financed with tax-exempt bonds or other federal subsidies. The lower credit is also available for the acquisition cost of low-income housing, whether or not construction or rehabilitation takes place.

The low-income housing credit is treated as a tax credit from real estate in which an investor actively participates, so that the limitation on passive losses does not apply. See Chapter 11 for a discussion of the passive loss limitations.

The low-income housing credit does not reduce the basis of a project for purposes of depreciation.

¶ 831.1 Overview of the Credit Process

The low-income housing credit program is jointly administered by the IRS and state tax credit allocation agencies. The following provides a brief overview of the process.

IRS Apportions Tax Credits

Code Sec. 42 directs the IRS to provide the tax credit allocating agencies of the states with information each year to compute the tax credits available to them for allocation. The allocation is limited annually to: (1) $1.75 ($1.50 for 2001) per state resident, (2) unused credits from the prior year, (3) credits initially allocated in previous years and returned in the current year, and (4) a portion of the unused tax credit returned to the IRS by other states. The state allocating agencies have up to two years to award the credits to housing projects; after that time, they must return any unused credits to the IRS for reassignment to other states. When the credits have been awarded, they are usually available to the owners/investors annually for a 10-year period as long as the project continues to meet the statutory and regulatory requirements.

Developers Apply to the Allocating Agencies

To apply for low-income housing tax credits, a developer must submit a detailed proposal to an allocating agency. The proposal must describe the housing project, indicate how much it will cost, and identify the sources and uses of the funds available to finance the project's development and operations. In describing the project, the developer must identify the total number of units and the number of units expected to qualify for tax credits. To qualify for consideration, a project must:

1. Be residential rental property;
2. Maintain at least 20 percent of the available units for households earning up to 50 percent of the area's median gross income adjusted for family size, or at least 40 percent of the units for households earning up to 60 percent of the area's median gross income adjusted for family size;
3. Restrict the rents (including the utility charges) for tenants in low-income units to 30 percent of either the 20/50 or 40/60 income limitations;
4. Maintain habitability standards; and
5. Operate under the program's rent and income restrictions for 15 years for projects placed in service before 1990 and for 30 or more years for later projects pursuant to extended use agreements.

State Agencies Award Tax Credits

The state allocating agencies are responsible for:

1. Awarding their tax credits to qualifying projects that meet their state's qualified allocation plans; and
2. Controlling the value of the tax credits awarded to projects.

When selecting developers' proposals for tax credit awards, an allocating agency must evaluate the proposed projects against a qualified allocation plan developed in accordance with the Internal Revenue Code's requirements. The qualified allocation plan must establish a procedure for ranking the projects on the basis of how well they meet the state's identified housing priorities and meet selection criteria that are appropriate to local conditions. In addition, the plan must give preference to projects that serve the lowest income tenants and serve qualifying tenants for the longest period of time.

In awarding tax credits to a project, a state allocating agency may provide no more credits than it deems necessary to ensure the project's financial feasibility throughout the 15-year tax credit compliance period. An allocating agency must consider any proceeds or receipts expected to be generated through tax benefits, the percentage of housing credit dollar amounts used for project costs other than the cost of intermediaries, and the reasonableness of developmental and operational costs. In general, the agency must compare the proposed project's developmental costs with the nontax credit financing, both private and governmental. The difference between the development costs and the nontax credit financing is the financing gap. Tax credits

¶ 831.1

are used to attract the equity investment needed to fill the gap, but are limited to a ceiling.

Under Code Sec. 42, the ceiling on tax credits limits the present value of the 10-year stream of tax benefits to: (1) 70 percent of the qualified basis for new construction or substantial rehabilitation of each qualified low-income building or (2) 30 percent of the qualified basis of acquired buildings that are substantially rehabilitated. To qualify as "substantial rehabilitation," the rehabilitation expenditures must equal at least 10 percent of the building's cost or at least $3,000 per low-income unit, whichever is greater.

For buildings placed in service in 1987, the credit was taken at annual rates of 9 percent (for the 70 percent value credit) and 4 percent (for the 30 percent value credit). Three types of credit are available for low-income buildings placed in service after 1987. The first type of credit is a 9 percent annual credit for the cost of a new building or qualifying rehabilitation costs, without a "federal subsidy." The second type of credit is a 4 percent annual credit for the cost of a new building or substantial rehabilitation built with a "federal subsidy." The third type of credit is a 4 percent annual credit for the cost of buying an existing building for which substantial rehabilitation expenditures are also incurred. Although the three types of credits are called 9 percent and 4 percent credits, the 9 percent and 4 percent figures are approximate. These figures are set each month by the IRS based upon fluctuating interest rates. A project can qualify for one of the three credits or a combination of the credits. For example, the same project can be eligible for the 4 percent credit, based on the cost of purchasing an existing building, and the 9 percent credit, based on the amount spent to substantially rehabilitate that building.

Low-income housing tax credit amounts are based on the cost of a building and the portion of the project that low-income households occupy. The cost of acquiring, rehabilitating, and constructing a building constitutes the building's eligible basis. The portion of the eligible basis attributable to low-income units is the building's qualified basis. In general, the qualified basis excludes the costs of land, obtaining permanent financing, rent reserves, syndication, and marketing. The applicable percentage (described in the previous paragraph) of the qualified basis may be claimed annually for 10 years as the low-income housing tax credit.

Low-income housing tax credit projects that use federal subsidies generally receive a smaller credit. If federally subsidized loans are used to finance substantial rehabilitation or new construction, either the eligible basis of the building must be reduced or the 4 percent credit must be used. Federally subsidized loans include below-market federal loans and tax-exempt financing. Projects funded by the Affordable Housing Program established under section 721 of the Financial Institutions Reform, Recovery, and Enforcement Act of 1989 (FIRREA), as well as Community Development Block Grants, are not treated as federally subsidized and, therefore, are eligible for the 9 percent credit. Below-market loans made after August 10, 1993, with Homes Investment Partnership Act Funds may also qualify for the 9 percent credit if 40 percent or more of the residential rental units in the building are occupied by individuals with income of 50 percent or less of the area median gross income.

State Agencies Monitor Compliance

A state agency cannot allocate low-income housing credits unless the state allocation plan contains a procedure that the agency (or an agent of, or private contractor hired by, the agency) will follow in monitoring compliance with the requirements of Code Sec. 42. The agency is required to notify the IRS of any noncompliance of which the agency becomes aware.

The requirement that a state agency monitor for compliance became effective on January 1, 1992, and applies to all buildings for which the low-income housing credit is, or has been, allowable at any time. Reg. § 1.42-5 provides the minimum standards for how a state agency must conduct its compliance monitoring activities. T.D. 8859 modified the regulations to reduce the inspection burden for new buildings and the changes were generally effective January 1, 2001.

The compliance monitoring regulations require the owner of a project, at a minimum, to certify annually to the state agency that for the preceding 12-month period the project was in compliance with Code Sec. 42 requirements. The certification covers a variety of requirements including that the owner has received an annual income certification from each low-income tenant and documentation supporting that certification, and that each building in the project was suitable for occupancy, taking into account local health, safety, and building codes. Reg. § 1.42-5(c)(1) lists the annual certification requirements.

The compliance monitoring regulations require agencies to report noncompliance or failure to certify, and whether the noncompliance or failure to certify was corrected, to the IRS on Form 8823, Low-Income Housing Credit Agencies Report of Noncompliance.

Incentive for Investors

Syndicators (usually investment partnerships) are a primary source of equity financing for tax credit projects. They recruit investors who are willing to become partners (generally, limited partners) in housing projects that, because of rent restrictions, are generally not expected to return rental profits to investors. Rather, the investors expect, for 10 years, to receive tax credits and other tax benefits, such as business loan deductions, that they can use to offset taxes. Those tax benefits (plus the possibility of cash proceeds from the sale of the project) represent the return on investment. The value of the tax benefits may vary from year to year, since the value of the tax credit depends on the number of habitable, rent-restricted units occupied by qualifying low-income households.

¶ 833 Qualification for the Credit

The low-income housing credit is available on a per unit basis for units located in qualified buildings within qualified low-income housing projects. A low-income unit is one that is rent restricted and occupied by individuals with incomes that are 50 percent or 60 percent of the area's median gross income, depending on the minimum set-aside (see ¶ 833.2) elected by the owner of the project. A unit that is used on a transient basis does not qualify as a low-income unit. Also, a unit in a building that has four units or fewer does not qualify if the owner or a person related to the owner occupies one of the units.[88]

¶ 833.1 *Qualified Low-Income Building*

A qualified low-income building is one that was part of a qualified low-income housing project for the 15 years beginning with the first tax year of the credit period.[89] After the end of the 15-year compliance period, the owner may elect to treat the building as not part of the project.[90]

¶ 833.2 *Qualified Low-Income Housing Project*

The low-income housing credit is available to the owner of a qualified low-income housing project. Residential rental property qualifies as a low-income housing project for purposes of the credit if it meets all of the following requirements.

Minimum Set-Aside

To be a qualified low-income housing project, 20 percent or more of the units in the project must be occupied by tenants whose incomes are 50 percent or less of the area median gross income, adjusted for family size (the 20-50 test), or at least 40 percent of the units must be occupied by tenants whose incomes are 60 percent or less of the area median gross income, adjusted for family size (the 40-60 test).[91] The owner of the project must elect the applicable test by the due date of

---

[88] Code Sec. 42(i)(3).
[89] Code Sec. 42(c)(2) and 42(i)(1).
[90] Code Sec. 42(g)(5).
[91] Code Sec. 42(g)(1).

the tax return. A building is treated as a qualified low-income building only if the project of which it is a part meets the minimum set-aside requirement by the close of the first year of the credit period for the building.[92] A special rule is provided for multi-building projects to allow several buildings to be tested together under the minimum set-aside requirement.[93]

Income limits under the minimum set-aside requirement may be adjusted for areas with unusually low family incomes or high housing costs relative to family incomes. The designation of an insignificant portion of the gross rent of a low-income housing unit for use toward the purchase of the unit by the tenant at the end of the 15-year credit compliance period does not affect a unit's eligibility for the credit. Amounts paid to the lessor toward the purchase of a unit, however, are considered part of the gross rent in determining whether the unit meets the requirement that it be rent restricted.[94]

Rent Restriction

The gross rent charged to a tenant in a low-income unit must not exceed 30 percent of the qualifying income level for the tenant's family size in order for a project to qualify for the credit.[95] Gross rent includes utilities, other than telephone, paid by the tenant. Gross rent does not include payments under Section 8 of the U.S. Housing Act or similar rental assistance payments. The gross rent paid by the tenant may exceed 30 percent of the income limit if required under the applicable federal housing program statute.[96]

State Credit Authority

Owners of qualified low-income projects may not claim a low-income housing credit without authorization by an appropriate state or local agency.[97] No credit authority is required, however, for projects financed by tax-exempt bonds subject to the private activity bond volume limitation of Code Sec. 146.

Generally, the owner of a project must obtain the allocation by the end of the calendar year in which a low-income building is placed in service.[98] A housing credit agency may authorize all or part of the credit to which the owner of a low-income project is otherwise entitled, and the owner may not claim a credit in excess of the credit dollar amount allocated to the project. State credit authority cannot increase the amount of the credit available to the owner of a low-income housing project above the amount calculated under the rules of Code Sec. 42. If

---

[92] Code Sec. 42(g)(3)(A).
[93] Code Sec. 42(g)(3)(B).
[94] Code Sec. 42(g)(6).
[95] Code Sec. 42(g)(2).
[96] Code Sec. 42(g)(2)(E).
[97] Code Sec. 42(h)(1).
[98] Code Sec. 42(h)(1)(B).

¶ 833.2

the owner of a project does not use the full credit authority, the authority is lost.

Certification

The owner of a low-income housing project must certify certain information to the IRS within 90 days after the end of the first tax year for which the low-income housing credit is claimed. Certification is made on Form 8609, Low-Income Housing Credit Allocation.

¶ 835 Calculation of the Low-Income Housing Credit

The owner of a qualified low-income housing project takes the low-income housing credit in each of 10 years, beginning with the year the property is placed in service or the following tax year.[99] The amount of the credit in each year is determined by multiplying the applicable credit rate for the type of project by the qualified basis allocable to low-income units in each qualified low-income building.[100]

¶ 835.1 *Applicable Credit Rates*

For newly constructed low-income units and rehabilitation expenditures that exceeded a specified minimum amount per unit (see ¶ 835.3) and were not federally subsidized, the credit rate for property placed in service in 1987 was nine percent. For projects placed in service after 1987, the credit rate is computed so that the present value of the 10 annual credit amounts as of the beginning of the credit period equals 70 percent of the qualified basis of the low-income units. The applicable credit rates after 1987 are published monthly by the IRS and apply for the month in which the building is placed in service.[101]

For subsidized construction or rehabilitation and the acquisition of existing housing, the credit rate was four percent for 1987. After 1987, the credit rate is computed so that the present value of the 10 annual credit amounts as of the beginning of the credit period equals 30 percent of the qualified basis of the low-income units.[102]

The owner of a low-income project may elect to determine the low-income housing credit rate applicable to a building in advance of the date the building is placed in service. The election must be made when a binding commitment for the amount of housing credit allocated to the building is received from the state credit agency or when tax-exempt bonds are issued for building financed with the bonds for which no state credit authorization is required.[103]

---

[99] Code Sec. 42(f)(1).
[100] Code Sec. 42(a).
[101] Code Sec. 42(b)(2)(A).
[102] Code Sec. 42(b)(2)(B).
[103] Code Sec. 42(b)(2)(A).

¶ 835.2 Qualified Basis for Determination of Credit

Qualified basis, the amount to which the low-income housing credit rate is applied to determine the credit amount, is the portion of eligible basis allocable to low-income housing units in a building. To determine the qualified basis portion of the eligible basis of a building, multiply the eligible basis by the lesser of the "unit fraction" and the "floor space fraction."[104] The unit fraction is the number of low-income units in the building divided by the total number of residential units in the building.[105] The floor space fraction is the total floor space of the low-income units in the building divided by the total floor space of all residential units in the building.[106]

The eligible basis of a new building is its adjusted basis.[107] The eligible basis of an existing building is the sum of (1) the portion of its adjusted basis attributable to its acquisition cost, and (2) capital expenditures incurred by the owner before the end of the first tax year in the credit period for depreciable property, improvements or additions.[108] Also, an existing building must meet the following requirements:

1. The building must be acquired by purchase;
2. There must be at least 10 years between the date of acquisition and the later of the date the building was last placed in service and the date of the most recent nonqualified substantial improvement of the building;
3. The building must not have been previously placed in service by the taxpayer or a related person as of the time previously placed in service; and
4. There must be a substantial rehabilitation, that is, rehabilitation expenditures during any 24-month period must equal the greater of $3,000 per low-income unit and 10 percent of the building's unadjusted basis.[109]

For purposes of requirement 2 above, a nonqualified substantial improvement is a capital improvement, subject to five-year amortization as a low-income housing rehabilitation cost under Code Sec. 167(k), if the capital costs of the improvements made within a two-year period are at least 25 percent of the adjusted basis of the building as of the beginning of the 24-month period.[110] Other special rules are provided for transfers in which the buyer has a carryover basis and for certain other transfers.[111]

---

[104] Code Sec. 42(c).
[105] Code Sec. 42(c)(1)(C).
[106] Code Sec. 42(c)(1)(D).
[107] Code Sec. 42(d)(1).
[108] Code Sec. 42(d)(2)(A).
[109] Code Sec. 42(d)(2)(B).
[110] Code Sec. 42(d)(2)(D)(i).
[111] Code Sec. 42(d)(2)(D)(ii).

If non-low-income units in a building are above the average quality standard of the low-income units in the building, the portion of the adjusted basis allocable to the above-average units is not included in the eligible basis.[112] An exception is provided that includes a portion of the basis allocable to above-average units in eligible basis when the disparity is not too great.[113] Under this exception, the cost per square foot of the disproportionate unit may not exceed 15 percent of the average cost per square foot of the low-income units. The cost of the entire disproportionate unit is excluded from eligible basis if this limit is exceeded.

A person who acquires an existing low-income building before the end of the prior owner's 10-year credit period generally cannot include the basis of the building in eligible basis. There is, however, an exception for the acquisition of an existing building before the end of the prior owner's 15-year compliance period for the building. In this case, the buyer steps into the shoes of the transferor and may take the credits to which the transferor would have been entitled had the transferor retained the property.[114] Under this exception, the three requirements that an existing building must meet to have eligible basis do not apply.

Special at-risk rules apply in determining qualifying basis for which a credit may be taken when the low-income housing is financed with nonrecourse financing.[115]

¶ 835.3 *Rehabilitation Expenditures*

Expenditures to rehabilitate low-income housing are treated as separate new buildings and are eligible for the higher credit rate, if certain conditions are met.[116] The separate new building treatment applies only if the qualified basis attributable to the rehabilitation expenditures during any 24-month period is at least $3,000 per low-income unit or 10 percent of the unadjusted basis of the building, whichever is greater.[117] The average expenditure per unit is determined at the end of the first tax year of the credit period for the expenditures.

Rehabilitation expenditures treated as a separate new building are considered placed in service at the end of the 24-month period used to compute average expenditures per unit. The requirements for an existing building to have an eligible basis do not apply when rehabilitation expenditures are treated as a new building. Rehabilitation expenditures eligible for treatment as a new building do not include:

1. Costs of acquiring property;

---

[112] Code Sec. 42(d)(3)(A).
[113] Code Sec. 42(d)(3)(B).
[114] Code Sec. 42(d)(7).
[115] Code Sec. 42(k).
[116] Code Sec. 42(e).
[117] Code Sec. 42(e)(3).

2. Expenditures for above-average quality units;
3. Expenditures that would not ordinarily be included in the adjusted basis of units for determining eligible basis; and
4. Cost of property that is not residential rental property.[118]

¶ 837 Compliance and Recapture Provisions

The owner of a qualified low-income housing project is required to repay a portion of the credits taken on the project if the project ceases to meet the qualification requirements at any time during the 15-year period that begins with the first credit year.[119] If there is a reduction in the qualified basis, but the project remains a qualified low-income housing project, the recapture is limited to the portion of the credit attributable to the reduction in qualified basis.

The following are the events that trigger recapture of the low-income housing credit:

1. The project fails to meet the minimum set-aside requirements (the 20-50 or 40-60 tests);
2. The gross rent charged tenants of the low-income units exceeds 30 percent of the qualifying income levels;
3. The project obtains financing from federal subsidies or the proceeds of tax-exempt bonds;
4. The owner disposes of the interest in the project; [120] and
5. There is a decrease in the qualifying basis of the project, even though the minimum set-aside requirement continues to be met.

The first four events listed above require recapture of the credit taken for the entire project. The fifth event listed requires recapture only for the units that go out of compliance. Insignificant changes in qualified basis because of changes in the floor space of low-income housing units do not trigger recapture.[121]

¶ 837.1 *Increases in Tenant Income*

A low-income unit does not lose its status as a low-income unit solely because of an increase in the tenant's income. Once a unit qualifies as a low-income unit, it continues to qualify until the tenant's income exceeds 140 percent of the qualifying income level applicable to low-income units. Even after a tenant's income exceeds 140 percent of the qualifying income level, the unit continues to qualify as a low-

---

[118] Code Sec. 42(e)(2)(B).
[119] Code Sec. 42(j).
[120] But recapture can be avoided if the owner furnishes a bond and it is expected that the building will continue to be operated as low-income housing for the remainder of the 15-year compliance period, see Code Sec. 42(j)(6).
[121] Code Sec. 42(j)(4)(F).

income unit as long as the owner continues to fill vacancies in comparable or smaller units with tenants who qualify as low-income tenants.

In the case of a "deep-rent skewing" set-aside, a unit is not disqualified as a low-income unit unless the tenant's income increases to more than 170 percent of the qualifying income level and a comparable unit in the project is rented to a tenant who does not qualify as a low-income individual. The owner may elect to have a qualified low-income housing project treated as a deep-rent skewed project if 15 percent or more of the low-income units in the project are occupied by tenants whose income is 40 percent or less of the area median gross income, gross rents are not more than 30 percent of the qualifying income level for the units, and the gross rent for each low-income unit does not exceed one-third of the average rent of units of comparable size that are not occupied by tenants who meet the applicable income limit.

¶ 837.2   *Large Partnerships*

A partnership with 35 or more partners (husband and wife count as one) is subject to recapture at the partnership level, unless the partnership elects not to have recapture apply at the partnership level.[122] Unless a partnership makes this election, no recapture event occurs because of a change in ownership unless more than 50 percent of the partnership interests (by value) change hands during a 12-month period. Should a partnership make the election not to have recapture apply at the partnership level, the disposition of a partnership interest by a partner will trigger recapture to the partner.

When recapture does occur at the partnership level, the increase in tax as a result of the recapture is allocated among the partners in the same manner as partnership taxable income.[123]

¶ 837.3   *Recapture Amount*

When a recapture event occurs, the owner of a qualified low-income housing project is required to pay additional tax for the year in which the recapture event occurs. This additional tax is equal to the "accelerated portion" of the credit allowable in earlier years.[124] In addition, interest is assessed from the dates the recaptured credit was claimed at the overpayment rate fixed by Code Sec. 6621.[125]

The "accelerated portion" of a credit is the aggregate of the credit taken over the aggregate of the credit that would have been allowed if the credit had been spread over 15 years rather than 10 years.[126] In the

---

[122] Code Sec. 42(j)(5).
[123] Code Sec. 42(j)(5)(A)(iv).
[124] Code Sec. 42(j)(2)(A).
[125] Code Sec. 42(j)(2)(B).
[126] Code Sec. 42(j)(3).

absence of previous recapture events, credits are recaptured in the following amounts:

Year of Recapture Event	Recapture Fraction
2 through 11	1/3
Year 12	4/15
Year 13	3/15
Year 14	2/15
Year 15	1/15

The credit for additions to the qualified basis after the first year of the credit period is computed at two-thirds the regular credit rate.[127] This means that there is no accelerated portion of the credit for additions, and there is no recapture when later reductions in qualifying basis occur except to the extent that reductions exceed the additions to qualified basis.

Example 1: Low-Income Housing Corporation built and placed in service a low-income housing project in 1999. The corporation claimed low-income housing credits beginning in 1999 based on the allocation of 30 percent of the basis of the project to units that met the 20-50 test (30 percent of the units were occupied by tenants earning 50 percent or less of the area median income). In 2002, vacancies in some of the low-income units are filled with tenants with nonqualifying income and, as a result, only 25 percent of the basis of the project is allocable to units with tenants whose income is 50 percent or less of the area median. The project, nevertheless, continues to meet the 20-50 test, so full recapture is not required. One-third of the credit claimed for the years 1999 through 2001 which is allocable to the five percent of basis that is no longer eligible for the credit, however, must be recaptured with interest.

In 2004, additional vacancies in the low-income units are filled with tenants with nonqualifying income and, as a result, only 15 percent of the basis of the project is now properly allocable to units whose tenants earn 50 percent or less of the area median income. The project no longer meets the 20-50 test of the minimum set-aside requirement, so full recapture is required. The recapture amount is one-third of the total of all credits taken for the years 1999 through 2003 which were allocable to the 25 percent of the basis of the project that represented units occupied by tenants with income of 50 percent or less of the area median up until 2004. The credits relating to the five percent of basis that were recaptured in 2002 are not taken into account again in 2004.

Example 2: Low-Income Housing Corporation built and placed in service a qualifying low-income housing project in 1999, and 25

---

[127] Code Sec. 42(f)(3).

percent of the basis of the project was allocable to units whose tenants had income of 50 percent or less of the area median. In 2001, additional low-income tenants rented units in the project, so that 35 percent of the basis of the project was allocable to low-income units. Low-Income began to take an additional credit for the additional 10 percent of qualified basis at two-thirds of the regular credit rate.

In 2003, vacancies in the low-income units were filled with tenants who were not low-income tenants and, as a result, only 30 percent of the basis of the project is properly allocable to units whose tenants have incomes of 50 percent or less of the area median. Although there is a decrease in the qualified basis of five percent, there is no recapture in 2003 because that five percent is allocable to additions to qualified basis after the first credit year.

Suppose, however, that qualified basis in 2003 falls to 20 percent of basis rather than 30 percent. In this case, one-third of the credit claimed for the years 1999 through 2002 attributable to five percent of the qualified basis would be recaptured. The first 10 percent of the reduction in qualified basis would be attributable to the additions to qualified basis which occurred after the first credit year and would not be subject to recapture.

If credits on a qualified low-income project could not be taken because of the limitations on the general business credit contained in Code Sec. 38, or because no tax was due against which the credit could be applied, no recapture is required.[128] An adjustment of carryovers, however, must be made.

¶ 837.4 *Casualty Losses*

Recapture does not apply to a reduction in qualified basis that occurs because of a casualty loss to the extent the loss is restored by reconstruction or replacement within a reasonable period established by the Treasury Secretary.[129]

¶ 841 RENEWAL COMMUNITIES AND NEW YORK LIBERTY ZONE

As part of a series of tax incentives to assist economically depressed areas and New York City following the terrorist attacks of September 11, 2001, Congress included additional deductions for the acquisition or revitalization of qualifying property.

---

[128] Code Sec. 42(j)(4)(B).

[129] Code Sec. 42(j)(4)(E).

¶ 843 Commercial Revitalization Deduction

A taxpayer can elect either to deduct one-half of commercial revitalization expenditures for the tax year a building is placed in service or amortize all the expenditures ratably over the 120-month period beginning with the month the building is placed in service.[130]

A commercial revitalization expenditure is the cost of a new building or the cost of substantially rehabilitating an existing building. The building must be used for commercial purposes and be located in a renewal community. In the case of the rehabilitation of an existing building, the cost of acquiring the building is a qualifying expenditure only to the extent that cost does not exceed 30 percent of the other rehabilitation expenditures.[131] The qualifying expenditures for any building cannot exceed $10 million.[132]

Each state is permitted to allocate up to $12 million of commercial revitalization expenditures to each renewal community located within the state for each calendar year after 2001 and before 2010. A state agency makes the allocations under a qualified allocation plan.[133]

No depreciation is allowed for amounts deducted under Code Sec. 1400I. Adjusted basis is reduced by the amount of the commercial revitalization deduction, and the deduction is treated as a depreciation deduction in applying the depreciation recapture rules. The commercial revitalization deduction is allowed in computing alternative minimum taxable income.[134]

The commercial revitalization deduction is treated in the same manner as the low-income housing credit in applying the passive loss rules of Code Sec. 469. Up to $25,000 of deductions (together with the other deductions and credits not subject to the passive loss limitation under Code Sec. 469(i)) are allowed to an individual taxpayer regardless of the taxpayer's adjusted gross income.

¶ 845 New York Liberty Zone

Code Sec. 1400L provides specific tax benefits for the area of New York City damaged by the terrorist attacks of September 11, 2001. The area is designated as the New York Liberty Zone and includes the area on or south of Canal Street, East Broadway (east of its intersection with Canal Street), or Grand Street (east of its intersection with East Broadway) in the Borough of Manhattan in the City of New York, New York.

---

[130] Code Sec. 1400I(a).
[131] Code Sec. 1400I(b).
[132] Code Sec. 1400I(c).
[133] Code Sec. 1400I(d).
[134] Code Sec. 1400I(f).

Among the benefits, Code Sec. 1400L(b) allows an additional first-year depreciation deduction of 30 percent of the adjusted basis of qualified New York Liberty Zone property. The additional first-year depreciation deduction is allowed for both regular tax and alternative minimum tax purposes for the tax year in which the property is placed in service. The basis of the property and the depreciation allowances in the year of purchase and later years are adjusted to reflect the additional first-year depreciation deduction.

Nonresidential real property and residential rental property is eligible for the additional first-year depreciation only to the extent it rehabilitates real property damaged, or replaces real property destroyed or condemned as a result of the terrorist attacks of September 11, 2001. Property is treated as replacing destroyed property if, as part of an integrated plan, the property replaces real property that is included in a continuous area that includes real property destroyed or condemned.

In addition, for property to qualify, the original use of the property in the New York Liberty Zone must begin with the taxpayer on or after September 11, 2001 (except for some leased property). Also, the taxpayer must purchase the property after September 10, 2001, and in the case of qualifying nonresidential real property and residential rental property, must place the property in service before January 1, 2010. Property does not qualify if a binding written contract for the acquisition of the property was in effect before September 11, 2001.

Chapter 9

Depreciation

¶ 900 OVERVIEW OF CHAPTER

Depreciation is a reasonable allowance for the exhaustion, wear and tear, and obsolescence of assets used to produce income. It is simply a deduction of a portion of the cost of an asset each year the asset is in use in recognition of the fact that income-producing assets gradually wear out or are used up. The deduction for depreciation is limited to property used in a trade or business or property held for the production of income.[1] Depreciation deductions are not available for the cost of property used purely for personal purposes, so depreciation would not be available on a personal residence, for example.

The manner of computing depreciation for tax purposes spelled out in the Internal Revenue Code is subject to constant change as Congress responds to political, economic, and revenue pressures. The system in use today was adopted in the Tax Reform Act of 1986 and generally applies to property placed in service after 1987. The Accelerated Cost Recovery System (ACRS) applies to property placed in service after 1980 and before 1987, but the ACRS system itself was modified several times during the six years between 1980 and 1987. Depreciation for property placed in service before 1981 is based on the "useful life" of the property, and straight-line and accelerated methods of calculating the deduction are permitted.

Depreciation is available only for tangible property and only for that part of the property which is subject to wear and tear, to decay or decline from natural causes, to exhaustion, and to obsolescence. Land is not depreciable, although certain improvements to land may be depreciable.[2] See the discussion of allocating costs on the purchase of real estate at ¶ 117.

Depreciation begins when property is placed in service, and the deduction is available to the owner of the property who has made a capital investment in the property and who has the benefits and burdens of ownership. The person entitled to depreciation deductions is not necessarily the owner of legal title to the property. See the discussion of ownership for tax purposes at ¶ 201.

---

[1] Code Sec. 167(a).
[2] Reg. § 1.167(a)-2.

While depreciation deductions are available for personalty, as well as realty, used in business or for the production of income, the discussion of depreciation in this chapter is essentially limited to the depreciation of real property. The cost of property that is not real property generally can be recovered over a much shorter period of time, and tax savings often result from a careful allocation of cost between realty and personalty on the purchase of a building.

¶ 901 MACRS DEPRECIATION SYSTEM

The depreciation deduction for property placed in service after 1986 is determined using the general depreciation system, also referred to as the Modified Accelerated Cost Recovery System (MACRS), unless the alternative depreciation system discussed at ¶ 911 applies. Depreciation rules for property placed in service before 1987 are taken up later in this chapter.

In some cases, property placed in service before 1991 may be depreciated under the ACRS system, which allowed recovery of the cost of real estate over 19 years, rather than the much longer period of current law. Generally, property constructed, reconstructed, or acquired under a written contract that was binding as of March 1, 1986, is depreciated under the pre-1987 rules, if it was placed in service before 1991. March 1, 1986, is also the critical date for other transitional rules that allow the shorter recovery period for self-constructed property, equipped buildings, and plant facilities that were placed in service before 1991.[3]

Under a transition rule contained in Sec. 1315(b)(2) of the Omnibus Budget Reconciliation Act of 1993, nonresidential real property placed in service before January 1, 1994, may be treated as 31.5-year property (rather than the 39-year property of current law) if the taxpayer or a qualified person entered into a binding written contract to purchase or construct the property before May 13, 1993, or construction began for those persons before that date. A qualified person is a person who transfers rights in a contract or property to the taxpayer before the property is placed in service.

Depreciation is calculated on the tax basis of the depreciable property. The determination of basis is taken up in considerable detail at ¶ 101-103. Other areas related to depreciation include the treatment of additions and improvements to leased property by lessor (see ¶ 601) and lessee (see ¶ 611), the distinction between repairs and improve-

---

[3] These transitional rules are explained in some detail in the Conference Committee Report on the Tax Reform Act of 1986 (P.L. 99-514).

ments (see ¶ 723.1), special amortization provisions (see ¶ 811), and recapture of "accelerated depreciation" on the sale of property (see ¶ 1307).

¶ 903 Computation of the Deduction

The depreciation deduction for property placed in service after 1986 is calculated by using the applicable depreciation method, the applicable recovery period, and the applicable convention.[4]

¶ 903.1 Recovery Periods

Under the general depreciation system, there are eleven classes of property, and these are assigned recovery periods of from three to 50 years.[5] In the case of real property, residential rental property has a recovery period of 27.5 years and nonresidential real property has a recovery period of 39 years. The recovery periods are based on full 12-month periods and are not based on taxable years.

A building or structure is residential rental property only if 80 percent or more of the gross rental income from the building or structure is rental income from dwelling units. If any portion of a building or structure is occupied by the taxpayer as a residence, the gross rental income from the building or structure includes the rental value of the portion occupied by the taxpayer.[6] Hotels, motels, inns, and similar establishments are excluded from the residential rental property class if more than one-half of the units are used on a transient basis.

Nonresidential real property is real property that is not residential rental property and that does not have a class life of less than 27.5 years. The class life of property is the class life that would be applicable to the property as of January 1, 1986, under Code Sec. 167(m). The class lives of property are set out in Rev. Proc. 87-56.[7]

¶ 903.2 Straight-Line Method

For residential rental and nonresidential real property, the applicable depreciation method is the straight-line method.[8] Salvage value is treated as zero.[9]

Under the straight-line method, the depreciation rate, in percentage terms, is determined by dividing one by the length of applicable recovery period remaining as of the beginning of the taxable year. The rate is applied to the unrecovered basis of the property, that is, the cost or other basis of the property adjusted for depreciation previously

---

[4] Code Sec. 168(a).
[5] Code Sec. 168(c) and (j).
[6] See Code Sec. 168(e)(2).
[7] 1987-2 CB 674.
[8] Code Sec. 168(b)(3).
[9] Code Sec. 168(b)(4).

allowed or allowable and for all other adjustments to basis. If the remaining recovery period as of the beginning of any tax year is less than one year, the depreciation rate for that year is 100 percent.

The computation of depreciation rates must reflect a reasonable and consistent rounding convention that, in the case of real property, is exact to at least one-thousandth of a percent. Under any rounding convention, no taxpayer may recover more than 100 percent of the recoverable basis of the property.[10]

¶ 903.3   *Mid-Month Convention*

A mid-month convention applies to all residential rental and non-residential real property.[11] The mid-month convention does not apply to any other classes of property.

Under the mid-month convention, property placed in service, disposed of, or retired during any month is treated as being placed in service, disposed of, or retired on the midpoint of the month. Therefore, regardless of when during the month a taxpayer places real property in service, the property is deemed to be placed in service on the midpoint of that month. Under the mid-month convention, depreciation is allowable for a fraction of a year for each property placed in service, disposed of, or retired during the year. The numerator of the fraction is equal to .5 plus the number of full months in the taxable year in which the property is in service. The denominator of the fraction is 12. Allowable depreciation for real property in a taxable year in which the mid-month convention applies is that fraction of the amount that would be allowable under the straight-line method for a full year. The remaining recovery period as of the beginning of the taxable year following a taxable year in which property is placed in service is equal to the property's applicable recovery period less the fraction of the first year for which depreciation is allowable.[12]

Example: On March 1, 2003, the Taxpayer who is on the calendar year places in service residential rental property. For 2003, the Taxpayer is entitled to 9.5/12 of the amount of depreciation that would be allowable under the straight-line method for a full year. As of January 1, 2004, the remaining recovery period for the property is 26 years and 8½ months (that is, 27 years and six months less the 9½ months for which depreciation was allowable in 2003).

---

[10] Rev. Proc. 87-57, 1987-2 CB 687.
[11] Code Sec. 168(d)(2).
[12] See Rev. Proc. 87-57, 1987-2 CB 687, as amplified and clarified by Rev. Proc. 89-15, 1989-1 CB 816.

Depreciation

First-Year Depreciation for Residential Rental Property

The following table lists the percentages of the basis of 27.5-year residential rental property that may be taken as depreciation for the first year based on the month in which the property is placed in service:

January	3.4848%
February	3.1818%
March	2.8788%
April	2.5758%
May	2.2727%
June	1.9697%
July	1.6667%
August	1.3636%
September	1.0606%
October	0.7576%
November	0.4545%
December	0.1515%

First-Year Depreciation for Nonresidential Property

The following table lists the percentages of the basis of 39-year nonresidential property that may be taken as depreciation for the first year based on the month in which the property is placed in service:

January	2.4572%
February	2.2435%
March	2.0299%
April	1.8162%
May	1.6025%
June	1.3888%
July	1.1752%
August	0.9615%
September	0.7478%
October	0.5341%
November	0.3205%
December	0.1068%

The calculation of depreciation under the general depreciation system (MACRS) is illustrated in the following example.

Comprehensive Example: In July 1997, the Taxpayer who is on the calendar year purchases land and a building with a single storefront and six residential apartments. Of the total $240,000 purchase price, $200,000 is allocated to the building, and $40,000

¶ 903.3

is allocated to the land (how such an allocation might be made is discussed at ¶ 117.1). The Taxpayer moves into one of the apartments and rents the others for $500 per month. The store rents for $700 per month.

Since the gross rental income from the apartments (including the apartment in which the owner lives) is more than 80 percent of the gross rental income from the building (6 × $500 = $3,000, which is more than 80 percent of $3,700), the building qualifies as residential rental real estate. If depreciation is allocated in proportion to rents, the Taxpayer's depreciation deduction for 1991 is $2,883. This figure is determined by computing a full year's depreciation ($200,000/27.5 = $7,273), dividing this full year figure by 12 to determine a full month's depreciation ($7,273/12 = $606), multiplying the full month's depreciation by 5.5 to reflect the number of months under the mid-month convention that the property is in service during 1997 ($606 × 5.5 = $3,333), and multiplying $3,333 by 32/37 ($3,200/$3,700) to limit depreciation to the portion of the building not used for personal purposes. (Note that the $3,333 figure could have been arrived at by multiplying $200,000 by 1.6667%, the percentage of basis for the first year when residential rental property is placed in service in July.)

Suppose, however, that the rental on the apartments was only $400 per month instead of $500. In this case, the building would not qualify as residential rental property because the gross rental from the apartments (6 × $400 = $2,400) is less than 80 percent of the gross rental income of the building ($2,400 + $700 = $3,100). As nonresidential real estate, depreciation must be based on a recovery period of 39 years. In this case, the Taxpayer's depreciation deduction for 1997 would be $2,045. This figure is determined by computing a full year's depreciation ($200,000/39 = $5,128), dividing this full year figure by 12 to determine a full month's depreciation ($5,128/12 = $427), multiplying the full month's depreciation by 5.5 to reflect the number of months under the mid-month convention that the property is in service during 1997 ($427 × 5.5 = $2,348), and multiplying $2,348 by 27/31 ($2,700/$3,100) to limit depreciation to the portion of the building not used for personal purposes. (Note that the $2,348 figure could have been arrived at by multiplying $200,000 by 1.1752%, the percentage of basis for the first year when nonresidential property is placed in service in July.)

¶ 903.3

¶ **903.4** *Use of Optional Tables*

The IRS has provided optional depreciation tables that may be used to compute the annual depreciation allowance for most types of property.[13] The optional depreciation tables specify schedules of annual depreciation rates that are applied to the *unadjusted* basis of property in each taxable year. If a taxpayer uses a table to compute the annual depreciation deduction for any item of property, the table must be used to compute the depreciation deductions for the entire recovery period.

---

[13] Rev. Proc. 87-57, 1987-2 CB 687.

OPTIONAL TABLE FOR 27.5-YEAR RESIDENTIAL RENTAL PROPERTY UNDER GENERAL DEPRECIATION SYSTEM

If the Recovery Year is:	And the Month in the First Recovery Year the Property is Placed in Service is:											
	1	2	3	4	5	6	7	8	9	10	11	12
	the Depreciation Rate is:											
1	3.485	3.182	2.879	2.576	2.273	1.970	1.667	1.364	1.061	0.758	0.455	0.152
2	3.636	3.636	3.636	3.636	3.636	3.636	3.636	3.636	3.636	3.636	3.636	3.636
3	3.636	3.636	3.636	3.636	3.636	3.636	3.636	3.636	3.636	3.636	3.636	3.636
4	3.636	3.636	3.636	3.636	3.636	3.636	3.636	3.636	3.636	3.636	3.636	3.636
5	3.636	3.636	3.636	3.636	3.636	3.636	3.636	3.636	3.636	3.636	3.636	3.636
6	3.636	3.636	3.636	3.636	3.636	3.636	3.636	3.636	3.636	3.636	3.636	3.636
7	3.636	3.636	3.636	3.636	3.636	3.636	3.636	3.636	3.636	3.636	3.636	3.636
8	3.636	3.636	3.636	3.636	3.636	3.636	3.636	3.636	3.636	3.636	3.636	3.636
9	3.636	3.636	3.636	3.636	3.636	3.636	3.636	3.636	3.636	3.636	3.636	3.636
10	3.637	3.637	3.637	3.637	3.637	3.637	3.637	3.637	3.637	3.637	3.637	3.637
11	3.636	3.636	3.636	3.636	3.636	3.636	3.636	3.636	3.636	3.636	3.636	3.636
12	3.637	3.637	3.637	3.637	3.637	3.637	3.637	3.637	3.637	3.637	3.637	3.637
13	3.636	3.636	3.636	3.636	3.636	3.636	3.636	3.636	3.636	3.636	3.636	3.636
14	3.637	3.637	3.637	3.637	3.637	3.637	3.637	3.637	3.637	3.637	3.637	3.637
15	3.636	3.636	3.636	3.636	3.636	3.636	3.636	3.636	3.636	3.636	3.636	3.636
16	3.637	3.637	3.637	3.637	3.637	3.637	3.637	3.637	3.637	3.637	3.637	3.637
17	3.636	3.636	3.636	3.636	3.636	3.636	3.636	3.636	3.636	3.636	3.636	3.636
18	3.637	3.637	3.637	3.637	3.637	3.637	3.637	3.637	3.637	3.637	3.637	3.637
19	3.636	3.636	3.636	3.636	3.636	3.636	3.636	3.636	3.636	3.636	3.636	3.636
20	3.637	3.637	3.637	3.637	3.637	3.637	3.637	3.637	3.637	3.637	3.637	3.637
21	3.636	3.636	3.636	3.636	3.636	3.636	3.636	3.636	3.636	3.636	3.636	3.636
22	3.637	3.637	3.637	3.637	3.637	3.637	3.637	3.637	3.637	3.637	3.637	3.637
23	3.636	3.636	3.636	3.636	3.636	3.636	3.636	3.636	3.636	3.636	3.636	3.636
24	3.637	3.637	3.637	3.637	3.637	3.637	3.637	3.637	3.637	3.637	3.637	3.637
25	3.636	3.636	3.636	3.636	3.636	3.636	3.636	3.636	3.636	3.636	3.636	3.636
26	3.637	3.637	3.637	3.637	3.637	3.637	3.637	3.637	3.637	3.637	3.637	3.637
27	3.636	3.636	3.636	3.636	3.636	3.636	3.636	3.636	3.636	3.636	3.636	3.636
28	1.970	2.273	2.576	2.879	3.182	3.485	3.636	3.637	3.636	3.637	3.636	3.637
29	0.000	0.000	0.000	0.000	0.000	0.000	0.152	0.455	0.758	1.061	1.364	1.667

¶ 903.4

Depreciation

OPTIONAL TABLE FOR 31.5-YEAR NONRESIDENTIAL REAL PROPERTY UNDER GENERAL DEPRECIATION SYSTEM

If the Recovery Year is:	And the Month in the First Recovery Year the Property is Placed in Service is:											
	1	2	3	4	5	6	7	8	9	10	11	12
	the Depreciation Rate is:											
1	3.042	2.778	2.513	2.249	1.984	1.720	1.455	1.190	0.926	0.661	0.397	0.132
2	3.175	3.175	3.175	3.175	3.175	3.175	3.175	3.175	3.175	3.175	3.175	3.175
3	3.175	3.175	3.175	3.175	3.175	3.175	3.175	3.175	3.175	3.175	3.175	3.175
4	3.175	3.175	3.175	3.175	3.175	3.175	3.175	3.175	3.175	3.175	3.175	3.175
5	3.175	3.175	3.175	3.175	3.175	3.175	3.175	3.175	3.175	3.175	3.175	3.175
6	3.175	3.175	3.175	3.175	3.175	3.175	3.175	3.175	3.175	3.175	3.175	3.175
7	3.175	3.175	3.175	3.175	3.175	3.175	3.175	3.175	3.175	3.175	3.175	3.175
8	3.175	3.174	3.174	3.174	3.174	3.175	3.175	3.175	3.174	3.175	3.175	3.175
9	3.174	3.175	3.175	3.175	3.175	3.175	3.175	3.175	3.175	3.175	3.175	3.175
10	3.175	3.174	3.174	3.174	3.174	3.174	3.174	3.175	3.174	3.174	3.174	3.174
11	3.174	3.175	3.175	3.175	3.175	3.175	3.175	3.174	3.175	3.175	3.175	3.175
12	3.175	3.174	3.174	3.174	3.174	3.174	3.174	3.175	3.174	3.174	3.174	3.174
13	3.174	3.175	3.175	3.175	3.175	3.175	3.175	3.174	3.175	3.175	3.175	3.175
14	3.175	3.174	3.174	3.174	3.174	3.174	3.174	3.175	3.174	3.174	3.174	3.174
15	3.174	3.175	3.175	3.175	3.175	3.175	3.175	3.174	3.175	3.175	3.175	3.175
16	3.175	3.174	3.174	3.174	3.174	3.174	3.174	3.175	3.174	3.174	3.174	3.174
17	3.174	3.175	3.175	3.175	3.175	3.175	3.175	3.174	3.175	3.175	3.175	3.175
18	3.175	3.174	3.174	3.174	3.174	3.174	3.174	3.175	3.174	3.174	3.174	3.174
19	3.174	3.175	3.175	3.175	3.175	3.175	3.175	3.174	3.175	3.175	3.175	3.175
20	3.175	3.174	3.174	3.174	3.174	3.174	3.174	3.175	3.174	3.174	3.174	3.174
21	3.174	3.175	3.175	3.175	3.175	3.175	3.175	3.174	3.175	3.175	3.175	3.175
22	3.175	3.174	3.174	3.174	3.174	3.174	3.174	3.175	3.174	3.174	3.174	3.174
23	3.174	3.175	3.175	3.175	3.175	3.175	3.175	3.174	3.175	3.175	3.175	3.175
24	3.175	3.174	3.174	3.174	3.174	3.174	3.174	3.175	3.174	3.174	3.174	3.174
25	3.174	3.175	3.175	3.175	3.175	3.175	3.175	3.174	3.175	3.175	3.175	3.175
26	3.175	3.174	3.174	3.174	3.174	3.174	3.174	3.175	3.174	3.174	3.174	3.174
27	3.174	3.175	3.174	3.175	3.174	3.175	3.175	3.174	3.174	3.174	3.174	3.175
28	3.175	3.174	3.175	3.174	3.175	3.174	3.175	3.174	3.175	3.174	3.175	3.174

¶ 903.4

OPTIONAL TABLE FOR 39-YEAR NONRESIDENTIAL REAL PROPERTY UNDER GENERAL DEPRECIATION SYSTEM

If the Recovery Year is:	And the Month in the First Recovery Year the Property is Placed in Service is:											
	1	2	3	4	5	6	7	8	9	10	11	12
					the Depreciation Rate is:							
1	2.461	2.247	2.033	1.819	1.605	1.391	1.777	0.963	0.749	0.535	0.321	0.107
2–39	2.564	2.564	2.564	2.564	2.564	2.564	2.564	2.564	2.564	2.564	2.564	2.564
40	0.107	0.321	0.535	0.749	0.963	1.177	1.391	1.605	1.819	2.033	2.247	2.461

¶ 903.4

¶ 905 Depreciation of Additions and Improvements

Additions and improvements to property are treated as separate property items for purposes of computing depreciation.[14] The recovery period for any addition or improvement to property begins the later of (1) the taxable year in which the addition or improvement is placed in service, or (2) the taxable year in which the property to which the addition or improvement relates is placed in service. The applicable recovery period, applicable convention, and applicable depreciation method for an addition or improvement to property are the same as those that would be applicable to the underlying property if the underlying property were placed in service at the same time as the addition or improvement.

Accordingly, an addition or improvement to residential rental real estate is depreciated over 27.5 years using the straight line method and the mid-month convention. An addition or improvement to nonresidential real estate is depreciated over 39 years using the straight line method and the mid-month convention.

In view of the long recovery period for additions and improvements, a premium is placed on classifying as much work on property as possible as currently deductible repairs rather than as depreciable improvements. See the discussion of repairs versus improvements at ¶ 723.

¶ 905.1 Land Improvements

Generally, those land improvements that do not permanently improve the land but improve it only for use with a specific building are depreciable. As the IRS has put it, land improvement costs are depreciable if they are directly associated with buildings rather than inextricably associated with the land.[15]

Land improvements are subject to depreciation over a recovery period of 15 years using the 150-percent declining balance method of depreciation and a half-year convention (unless more than 40 percent of the basis of depreciable property placed in service during the year is placed in service during the last quarter, in which case a mid-quarter convention applies).[16]

In Rev. Rul. 65-265, the IRS ruled that the cost of general grading of the land is part of the cost basis of the land and is nondepreciable. The cost of the digging and the removing of the soil that is necessary for the proper setting of the buildings and paving of the roadways,

---

[14] Code Sec. 168(i)(6).
[15] Rev. Rul. 65-265, 1965-2 CB 52.
[16] See Rev. Proc. 87-56, 1987-2 CB 674, Asset Class 00.3, which specifies that land improvements have a class life of 20 years and a recovery period under the general depreciation system of 15 years and a recovery period under the alternative depreciation system of 20 years.

however, is part of their cost and is depreciable. This ruling was further clarified by Rev. Rul. 68-193,[17] which allowed depreciation for certain grading costs for roads constructed to provide for movement of heavy materials between buildings in cases where the grading would be abandoned or replaced with the buildings with which it was directly associated.

Landscaping consisting of perennial shrubbery and ornamental trees adjacent to buildings was considered a depreciable land improvement when replacement of the buildings would require replacement of the landscaping. On the other hand, the cost of general landscaping of the grounds around the same buildings was considered a general land improvement cost and part of the basis of the nondepreciable land.[18]

Rev. Proc. 87-56 [19] contains the class lives and recovery periods for computing depreciation deductions for various assets. Under this Revenue Procedure, land improvements include depreciable improvements such as sidewalks, roads, canals, waterways, drainage facilities, docks, bridges, fences, landscaping, and shrubbery.

¶ 905.2 *Property Under Construction*

In regulations proposed on February 16, 1984, the IRS provided guidance on how to compute depreciation (cost recovery allowances) under ACRS for a building that is made available in stages.[20] Presumably the same principles apply to the calculation of depreciation under the general depreciation system (MACRS) using the applicable recovery period, depreciation method, and convention of current law.

Under Prop. Reg. § 1.168-2(e)(3), a building is considered placed in service only when a significant portion is made available for use in a finished condition—for example, when a certificate of occupancy is issued for the finished portion. If less than the entire building is made available, then the unadjusted basis that is taken into account for depreciation is the amount of the unadjusted basis of the building that is properly allocable to the portion made available. If another portion of the building is subsequently made available, then that amount of unadjusted basis that is properly allocable to the ensuing available portion is taken into account for depreciation when that portion becomes available. The taxpayer must use the same recovery period and method for all portions of the building.

The following example is based on Reg. § 1.168-2(e)(5), Examples (2) and (3).

---

[17] 1968-1 CB 79.
[18] Rev. Rul. 74-265, 1974-1 CB 56.
[19] 1987-2 CB 674.
[20] Prop. Reg. § 1.168-2(e)(3).

Comprehensive Example: The Taxpayer who is on the calendar year begins constructing a 10-story office building in 1982. All floors will have approximately the same amount of usable space. By 1983, the Taxpayer has paid $10 million for the building's shell, $4 million for work on the first three floors, and $5 million for work directly related to other floors. In March 1983, the Taxpayer receives a certificate of occupancy for the first three floors and begins offering those floors for rent to tenants. The building is considered placed in service in 1983, and no depreciation deductions are allowed for 1982.

The Taxpayer's depreciation deduction for 1983 is the properly allocated unadjusted basis times the applicable percentage (which for 1983 was 10 percent). The properly allocable unadjusted basis is $7 million, consisting of the amounts of unadjusted basis directly related to the portion of the building made available for use ($4 million) plus that amount of the unadjusted basis that is not directly related to any specific portion of the building ($10 million) properly allocable to the portion made available for use (that is, 3 floors/10 floors = 30% × $10 million = $3 million). No deduction is allowed for 1983 for the $5 million paid for work directly related to the top seven floors.

In January 1984, the Taxpayer receives a certificate of occupancy for the remaining seven floors and begins offering them for rent to tenants. The Taxpayer spent an additional $7 million to complete the building. In January 1984, the Taxpayer takes into account as basis for depreciation the $12 million not previously taken into account plus the $7 million of later expenditures. The Taxpayer begins depreciating the $19 million portion of the basis in January 1984.

¶ 911   ALTERNATIVE DEPRECIATION SYSTEM

Under the alternative depreciation system,[21] annual depreciation allowances are lower than allowances under the general depreciation system. The alternative depreciation system must be used by corporations to compute earnings and profits for the purpose of applying the rules relating to corporate distributions.[22] Also, the alternative depreciation system must be used in place of the general depreciation system in order to compute depreciation for purposes of the alternative minimum tax before 1999.[23] The alternative depreciation system also must be used for the following types of property (not all are real estate) to compute depreciation for regular tax purposes:

---

[21] Code Sec. 168(g).
[22] Code Sec. 312(k)(3).
[23] Code Sec. 56(a)(1)(A).

1. Tangible property that is used predominantly outside the United States during the taxable year;
2. Tax-exempt use property (discussed at ¶ 915.1);
3. Tax-exempt bond-financed property (discussed at ¶ 915.2);
4. Imported property covered by an Executive Order that finds that the country of origin is maintaining trade restrictions or engaging in discriminatory acts;
5. Plants and animals used in farming and placed in service during a taxable year in which the taxpayer elects not to have the uniform capitalization rules of Code Sec. 263A apply; [24] and
6. Property for which the taxpayer elects to have the alternative depreciation system apply (see ¶ 915).

¶ 913 Calculation of Alternative Depreciation

Alternative depreciation, as with general depreciation, is calculated using an applicable method, convention, and recovery period. The residential rental property and nonresidential real property classes are defined in the same manner for the alternative depreciation system as for the general depreciation system discussed above. Alternative depreciation for both classes of real property is calculated using the straight line method and the mid-month convention, but the recovery period for residential rental property and nonresidential real property is 40 years, rather than the 27.5 or 39 years under the general depreciation system.[25]

Under a special rule, the recovery period under the alternative depreciation system for any leased tax-exempt use property must be at least 125 percent of the lease term.[26] For example, if nonresidential real property is leased to a tax-exempt entity under a 99-year lease, the recovery period for the property is 123.75 years, rather than the 39 years that applies to nonresidential real property under the general depreciation system.

¶ 913.1 *Election of Alternative Depreciation*

A taxpayer may irrevocably elect to use the alternative depreciation system in lieu of the general depreciation system.[27] In the case of residential rental property and nonresidential real property, the election to use the alternative depreciation system may be made separately for each property. In the case of other classes of property, the election applies to all property within the class placed in service during the taxable year.

---

[24] Code Sec. 263A(d)(3) and (e)(2)(A).
[25] Code Sec. 168(g)(2).
[26] Code Sec. 168(g)(3)(A).
[27] Code Sec. 168(g)(7).

The election to have the alternative depreciation system apply must be made by the due date, including extensions, of the tax return for the first taxable year for which the election is being made. A statement identifying the election by reference to the Internal Revenue Code or Act section and identifying the property for which the election is being made must accompany the tax return.[28]

Since the alternative depreciation system provides lower annual depreciation deductions, most taxpayers will not want to elect to have the alternative depreciation system apply.

The calculation of depreciation under the alternative depreciation system is illustrated in the following example.

Comprehensive Example: In July, the Taxpayer who is on the calendar year purchases an office building for $250,000. Of the total purchase price, $200,000 is allocated to the building and $50,000 is allocated to the land (how such an allocation might be made is discussed in at ¶ 117.1). The building is nonresidential real property for depreciation purposes. If the Taxpayer uses the general depreciation system, the Taxpayer's depreciation deduction for the year is $2,348. This figure is determined by computing a full year's depreciation ($200,000/39 = $5,128), dividing this full year figure by 12 to determine a full month's depreciation ($5,128/12 = $427), and multiplying the full month's depreciation by 5.5 to reflect the number of months under the mid-month convention that the property is in service during the year ($427 × 5.5 = $2,348). (Note that the $2,348 figure could have been arrived at by multiplying $200,000 by 1.1752%, the percentage of basis from the optional table for the first year when nonresidential real property is placed in service in July.)

Suppose, however, that the Taxpayer elects to use the alternative depreciation system. In this case, depreciation must be based on a recovery period of 40 years, and the Taxpayer's depreciation deduction for the year would be $2,292. This figure is determined by computing a full year's depreciation ($200,000/40 = $5,000), dividing this full year figure by 12 to determine a full month's depreciation ($5,000/12 = $416.66), and multiplying the full month's depreciation by 5.5 to reflect the number of months under the mid-month convention that the property is in service during the year ($416.66 × 5.5 = $2,292). (Note that the $2,292 figure could have been arrived at by multiplying $200,000 by 1.1460, the percentage of basis from the optional table under the alternative depreciation system for the first year when nonresidential real property is placed in service in July. The optional table is set out at ¶ 913.2.)

---

[28] Temp. Reg. § 301.9100-7T.

¶ 913.2 *Use of Optional Tables*

The IRS has provided optional depreciation tables that may be used to compute the annual depreciation allowance under the alternative depreciation system for most types of property.[29] The optional depreciation tables specify schedules of annual depreciation rates that are applied to the *unadjusted* basis of property in each taxable year. If a taxpayer uses a table to compute the depreciation deduction for any item of property, the taxpayer generally must use the table to compute the depreciation deduction for the entire recovery period of the property. A taxpayer may not continue to use the table, however, if there are any adjustments to the basis of the property other than for depreciation or an addition or improvement that is subject to depreciation as a separate item of property.

OPTIONAL TABLE FOR RESIDENTIAL RENTAL AND NONRESIDENTIAL REAL PROPERTY UNDER ALTERNATIVE DEPRECIATION SYSTEM

If the Recovery Year is:	And the Month in the First Recovery Year the Property is Placed in Service is:					
	1	2	3	4	5	6
	the Depreciation Rate is:					
1	2.396	2.188	1.979	1.771	1.563	1.354
2 to 40	2.500	2.500	2.500	2.500	2.500	2.500
41	0.104	0.312	0.521	0.729	0.937	1.146

If the Recovery Year is:	And the Month in the First Recovery Year the Property is Placed in Service is:					
	7	8	9	10	11	12
	the Depreciation Rate is:					
1	1.146	0.938	0.729	0.521	0.313	0.104
2 to 40	2.500	2.500	2.500	2.500	2.500	2.500
41	1.354	1.562	1.771	1.979	2.187	2.396

---

[29] Rev. Proc. 87-57, 1987-2 CB 687.

¶ 915 Real Property Subject to Alternative Depreciation

The alternative depreciation system must be used for property used predominantly outside the United States,[30] tax-exempt use property,[31] and tax-exempt bond financed property.[32] Also, the alternative depreciation system must be used before 1999 to compute alternative minimum taxable income.[33] The predominant use of real property outside the United States is obvious. The other categories of property subject to alternative depreciation are discussed in the following paragraphs.

¶ 915.1 *Tax-Exempt Use Property*

Tax-exempt organizations and government units gain no benefit from depreciation or tax credits on property that they own or use. Through leasing from investors rather than buying and owning property, tax-exempt entities could obtain indirectly, through reduced rentals, the incentives intended for investments in property. The investors, because of the investment incentives of depreciation and tax credits, could offer the lower rentals.

Prior to the Tax Reform Act of 1984, the only limit on these mutually beneficial arrangements was a denial of the investment credit on property leased to or used by certain tax-exempt organizations and domestic government units. Sale-leasebacks involving almost every item of property that could be used by a tax-exempt organization or government unit, including the local town hall and city jail, were widespread and represented a severe drain on federal revenue. In 1984, Congress imposed a complicated series of restrictions on the tax advantages of leasing property to tax-exempt organizations and government units, including foreign governments. These restrictions included loss of the investment credit and accelerated depreciation, and longer recovery periods for property leased to or used by a tax-exempt entity. The required use of the alternative depreciation system for tax-exempt use property reflects a continuation of this policy.

Disqualified Lease Defined

In general, in the case of real property, tax-exempt use property is the portion of nonresidential real property leased to a tax-exempt entity in a disqualified lease.[34] A disqualified lease is any lease to a tax-exempt entity that falls into one of the following categories:

---

[30] Code Sec. 168(g)(1)(A).
[31] Code Sec. 168(g)(1)(B).
[32] Code Sec. 168(g)(1)(C).
[33] Code Sec. 56(a)(1)(A).
[34] Code Sec. 168(h)(1)(B).

1. All or part of the leased property is financed by a tax-exempt obligation, and the tax-exempt entity leasing the property, or a related entity, participates in the financing;
2. The lease includes a purchase or sale option at a fixed or determinable price which involves the tax-exempt entity, or there is the equivalent of such an option;
3. The lease term exceeds 20 years; or
4. The lease is made after a sale or other transfer of the property by, or lease of the property from, the tax-exempt entity or a related entity, and the property was used by the tax-exempt entity or a related entity before the sale or other transfer or lease.[35]

In the case of property leased to a partnership, whether the property is tax-exempt use property is determined at the partner level. Property leased to a partnership is treated as leased to the partners in proportion to their distributive share of partnership items. Similar rules apply to other pass-through entities.[36]

Exceptions from Definition

As is apparent from the definition of a disqualified lease, most commercial leases to tax-exempt entities will not be disqualified leases. Even when there is a disqualified lease, there are several exceptions that may prevent property leased to a tax-exempt entity from being subject to the alternative depreciation system.

Tax-exempt use property does not include any property if the portion of the property leased to tax-exempt entities in disqualified leases is 35 percent or less of the property.[37] The 35 percent is measured by the net rentable floor space in the property, computed without including any common areas. Tax-exempt use property does not include real estate that is leased to a tax-exempt entity for a period of less than three years.[38] Options to renew are included in the lease term, unless at fair market value at the date of renewal, and two or more successive leases that are part of the same transaction or series of transactions for the same or substantially similar property are treated as a single lease.[39]

Finally, tax-exempt use property does not include any portion of property predominantly used by the tax-exempt entity in an unrelated

---

[35] Code Sec. 168(h)(1)(B)(ii).
[36] Code Sec. 168(h)(5).
[37] Code Sec. 168(h)(1)(B)(iii).
[38] Code Sec. 168(h)(1)(C).
[39] Code Sec. 168(i)(3).

trade or business when the income from the trade or business is subject to tax under Code Sec. 511.[40]

Tax-Exempt Entities

Tax-exempt entities include: (1) The United States, any state or political subdivision, any possession of the United States, or agencies and instrumentalities of any of the foregoing; (2) An organization, other than a farmers' cooperative, that is exempt from income tax; and (3) A foreign person or entity, unless the property used by the foreign person or entity is subject to U.S. taxation.[41]

¶ 915.2   Tax-Exempt Bond Financed Property

Tax-exempt bond financed property subject to the alternative depreciation system is property placed in service after 1986 to the extent it is financed directly or indirectly by bonds on which the income is exempt from tax under Code Sec. 103(a).[42] The extent to which property is considered financed by the proceeds of tax-exempt bonds is determined based on the order in which property is placed in service.[43]

Tax-exempt bond financed property does not include qualified residential projects.[44] These are low-income housing projects that meet the minimum set-aside requirements that apply for the low-income housing credit (see ¶ 831). These are projects in which 20 percent or more of the units are occupied by tenants whose incomes are 50 percent or less of the area median gross income or in which 40 percent or more of the units are occupied by tenants whose incomes are 60 percent or less of the area median gross income.

¶ 915.3   Alternative Minimum Tax

The alternative depreciation system must be used for real estate to determine the depreciation deduction in computing alternative minimum taxable income before 1999 for purposes of the alternative minimum tax.[45] Since the basis of property for minimum tax purposes is adjusted under the alternative depreciation system, gain or loss on the sale of property may be different for regular tax and minimum tax purposes. For property placed in service after 1998, regular depreciation, not alternative depreciation, is used to compute alternative minimum taxable income.

For property placed in service before 1987, the excess of accelerated depreciation over straight-line depreciation for real estate is a tax

---

[40] Code Sec. 168(h)(1)(D).
[41] Code Sec. 168(h)(2).
[42] Code Sec. 168(g)(5)(A).
[43] Code Sec. 168(g)(5)(B).
[44] Code Sec. 168(g)(5)(C).
[45] Code Sec. 56(a)(1).

preference item subject to the minimum tax.[46] This rule continues to apply for purposes of the minimum tax in the case of property placed in service before 1987.

¶ 921 ACRS DEPRECIATION FOR PRE-1987 PROPERTY

For most property placed in service after 1980 and before 1987, the Economic Recovery Tax Act of 1981 allowed the cost of the property to be recovered under an accelerated schedule over much shorter periods than it was possible to recover this cost under the pre-1981 depreciation methods that were keyed to the property's useful life. While the Accelerated Cost Recovery System (ACRS) replaced the old depreciation system, the old system must continue to be used for property placed in service before 1981. Similarly, ACRS must continue to be used for most property placed in service after 1980 and before 1987, even though ACRS was replaced by the general depreciation system or Modified Accelerated Cost Recovery System for property placed in service after 1986.

¶ 923 Computation of Deduction

Under ACRS, as originally enacted, most real property was assigned a recovery period of 15 years. This recovery period applied to low-income housing and to all other real estate. The Tax Reform Act of 1984 extended the recovery period for real estate, other than low-income housing, from 15 to 18 years. Amendments in 1985 further extended the recovery period to 19 years.

The 18-year recovery period generally applies to property placed in service after March 15, 1984, and before May 9, 1985, although a separate schedule applies to 18-year property placed in service after June 22, 1984, to reflect the adoption of the mid-month convention. The 19-year recovery period generally applies to property placed in service after May 8, 1985 and before 1987.

Under the transition rules, the cost of property placed in service before 1987, however, may be recovered under the 15-year ACRS schedule if the taxpayer or qualified person entered into a binding contract to purchase or construct the property before March 16, 1984, or if construction of the property by or for the taxpayer or qualified person was begun before March 16, 1984. Similarly, the cost of property placed in service before 1987 may be recovered under the 18-year ACRS schedule if there was a binding contract to construct or acquire the property, or if construction was begun by or for the taxpayer after March 15, 1984, and before May 9, 1985. A qualified person is one who transfers his or her rights in the contract or the property to the

---

[46] Code Sec. 57(a)(7).

taxpayer, but only if the property was not placed in service before the transfer to the taxpayer.

The IRS has issued depreciation (or cost recovery) schedules based on an 18-year period and a 19-year period using the 175 percent declining balance method of depreciation and a mid-month convention for most real property, other than low-income housing, acquired after June 22, 1984. There are separate schedules for 18-year property acquired after March 15, 1984, and before June 23, 1984, which do not reflect the use of the mid-month convention. A similar schedule, but based on a 15-year recovery period applies to real property, other than low-income housing, acquired after 1980 but prior to March 16, 1984. The ACRS schedule for pre-1987 low-income housing is based on a 15-year period and 200 percent declining balance depreciation.

Computing the proper ACRS depreciation deduction is simply a matter of applying the percentage specified in the appropriate schedule to the unadjusted basis of the property. The ACRS schedules for real property are set out below.

Extended recovery periods and less accelerated depreciation were required for property outside the United States. Schedules are also provided for property falling in this category.

¶ 923.1 *Straight-Line Election*

Instead of using the percentages and recovery periods that reflect accelerated depreciation over the appropriate ACRS recovery period, a taxpayer could have elected straight-line depreciation over any one of three recovery periods. In the case of real estate, the straight-line election was available over the usual ACRS recovery period (*i.e.*, 15, 18, or 19 years) and over extended recovery periods of 35 or 45 years.

Since the straight-line election served to reduce depreciation deductions, at least in the initial years after the property was placed in service, the election was not often used. In the case of rehabilitated real estate, however, the tax credit for rehabilitation costs was available only if straight-line depreciation was used to recover costs. When the credit was a factor, the straight-line election was made.

¶ 923.2 *ACRS Schedules*

The ACRS schedules reproduced below are keyed to the year and to the month during the first year in which the property was placed in service. If ACRS property is sold before the end of the recovery period, the ACRS deduction for the year of disposition must be adjusted to reflect only the months during that year that the property was in service. Adjustments are also required in the case of short taxable years.

Accelerated Schedules

The following ACRS schedules apply when straight-line depreciation or optional longer recovery periods were not elected when the property was placed in service.

ACRS COST RECOVERY TABLES FOR REAL PROPERTY

Table 1*—15-Year Real Property (other than low-income housing)
(placed in service after December 31, 1980, and before March 16, 1984)
(15-Year 175% Declining Balance)
(Assuming No Mid-Month Convention)

Year	\multicolumn{12}{c}{Month Placed in Service}											
	1	2	3	4	5	6	7	8	9	10	11	12
1	12%	11%	10%	9%	8%	7%	6%	5%	4%	3%	2%	1%
2	10	10	11	11	11	11	11	11	11	11	11	12
3	9	9	9	9	10	10	10	10	10	10	10	10
4	8	8	8	8	8	8	9	9	9	9	9	9
5	7	7	7	7	7	7	8	8	8	8	8	8
6	6	6	6	6	7	7	7	7	7	7	7	7
7	6	6	6	6	6	6	6	6	6	6	6	6
8	6	6	6	6	6	6	5	6	6	6	6	6
9	6	6	6	6	5	6	5	5	5	6	6	6
10	5	6	5	6	5	5	5	5	5	5	6	5
11	5	5	5	5	5	5	5	5	5	5	5	5
12	5	5	5	5	5	5	5	5	5	5	5	5
13	5	5	5	5	5	5	5	5	5	5	5	5
14	5	5	5	5	5	5	5	5	5	5	5	5
15	5	5	5	5	5	5	5	5	5	5	5	5
16	—	—	1	1	2	2	3	3	4	4	4	5

* Notice 81-16, 1981-2 CB 545 (same as T.D. News Rel. 9-10-81).

Table 2*—18-Year Real Property
(placed in service after March 15, 1984 and before June 23, 1984)
(18-Year 175% Declining Balance)
(Assuming No Mid-Month Convention)

Year	\multicolumn{11}{c}{Month Placed in Service}										
	1	2	3	4	5	6	7	8	9	10-11	12
1	10%	9%	8%	7%	6%	6%	5%	4%	3%	2%	1%
2	9	9	9	9	9	9	9	9	9	10	10
3	8	8	8	8	8	8	8	8	9	9	9
4	7	7	7	7	7	7	8	8	8	8	8
5	6	7	7	7	7	7	7	7	7	7	7
6	6	6	6	6	6	6	6	6	6	6	6
7	5	5	5	5	6	6	6	6	6	6	6
8-12	5	5	5	5	5	5	5	5	5	5	5
13	4	4	4	5	5	4	4	5	4	4	4
14-18	4	4	4	4	4	4	4	4	4	4	4
19	—	—	1	1	1	2	2	2	3	3	4

* Notice 84-16, 1984-2 CB 475 (same as T.D. News Rel. R-2890, 10-22-84).

¶ 923.2

Table 3*—18-Year Real Property
(placed in service after June 22, 1984 and before May 9, 1985)
(18-Year 175% Declining Balance)
(Assuming Mid-Month Convention)

Year	\multicolumn{12}{c}{Month Placed in Service}											
	1	2	3	4	5	6	7	8	9	10	11	12
1	9%	9%	8%	7%	6%	5%	4%	4%	3%	2%	1%	0.4%
2	9	9	9	9	9	9	9	9	9	10	10	10
3	8	8	8	8	8	8	8	8	9	9	9	9
4	7	7	7	7	7	8	8	8	8	8	8	8
5	7	7	7	7	7	7	7	7	7	7	7	7
6	6	6	6	6	6	6	6	6	6	6	6	6
7	5	5	5	5	6	6	6	6	6	6	6	6
8-12	5	5	5	5	5	5	5	5	5	5	5	5
13	4	4	4	5	4	4	5	4	4	4	5	5
14-17	4	4	4	4	4	4	4	4	4	4	4	4
18	4	3	4	4	4	4	4	4	4	4	4	4
19	—	1	1	1	2	2	2	3	3	3	3	3.6

*Notice 84-16, 1984-2 CB 475 (same as T.D. News Rel. R-2890, 10-22-84).

Table 4*—19-Year Real Property
(placed in service after May 8, 1985, and before 1987)
(19-Year 175% Declining Balance)
(Assuming Mid-Month Convention)

Year	\multicolumn{12}{c}{Month Placed in Service}											
	1	2	3	4	5	6	7	8	9	10	11	12
1	8.8%	8.1%	7.3%	6.5%	5.8%	5.0%	4.2%	3.5%	2.7%	1.9%	1.1%	.4%
2	8.4	8.5	8.5	8.6	8.7	8.8	8.8	8.9	9.0	9.0	9.1	9.2
3	7.6	7.7	7.7	7.8	7.9	7.9	8.0	8.1	8.1	8.2	8.3	8.3
4	6.9	7.0	7.0	7.1	7.1	7.2	7.3	7.3	7.4	7.4	7.5	7.6
5	6.3	6.3	6.4	6.4	6.5	6.5	6.6	6.6	6.7	6.8	6.8	6.9
6	5.7	5.7	5.8	5.9	5.9	5.9	6.0	6.0	6.1	6.1	6.2	6.2
7	5.2	5.2	5.3	5.3	5.3	5.4	5.4	5.5	5.5	5.6	5.6	5.6
8	4.7	4.7	4.8	4.8	4.8	4.9	4.9	5.0	5.0	5.1	5.1	5.1
9	4.2	4.3	4.3	4.4	4.4	4.5	4.5	4.5	4.5	4.6	4.6	4.7
10-19	4.2	4.2	4.2	4.2	4.2	4.2	4.2	4.2	4.2	4.2	4.2	4.2
20	0.2	0.5	0.9	1.2	1.6	1.9	2.3	2.6	3.0	3.3	3.7	4.0

* Rev. Proc. 86-14, 1986-1 CB 542, modifying and superseding Rev. Proc. 86-6, 1986-1 CB 503.

¶ 923.2

Table 5*—15-Year Low-Income Housing
(placed in service after December 31, 1980, and before May 9, 1985)
(15-Year 200% Declining Balance)
(Assuming No Mid-Month Convention)

Year	\multicolumn{12}{c}{Month Placed in Service}
	1	2	3	4	5	6	7	8	9	10	11	12
1	13%	12%	11%	10%	9%	8%	7%	6%	4%	3%	2%	1%
2	12	12	12	12	12	12	12	13	13	13	13	13
3	10	10	10	10	11	11	11	11	11	11	11	11
4	9	9	9	9	9	9	9	9	10	10	10	10
5	8	8	8	8	8	8	8	8	8	8	8	9
6	7	7	7	7	7	7	7	7	7	7	7	7
7	6	6	6	6	6	6	6	6	6	6	6	6
8	5	5	5	5	5	5	5	5	5	5	6	6
9	5	5	5	5	5	5	5	5	5	5	5	5
10	5	5	5	5	5	5	5	5	5	5	5	5
11	4	5	5	5	5	5	5	5	5	5	5	5
12	4	4	4	5	4	5	5	5	5	5	5	5
13	4	4	4	4	4	4	5	4	5	5	5	5
14	4	4	4	4	4	4	4	4	4	5	4	4
15	4	4	4	4	4	4	4	4	4	4	4	4
16	—	—	1	1	2	2	2	3	3	3	4	4

* Notice 81-16, 1981-2 CB 545 (same as T.D. News Rel. 9-10-81).

Table 6*—15-Year Low-Income Housing
(placed in service after May 8, 1985, and before 1987)
(15-Year 200% Declining Balance)
(Assuming No Mid-Month Convention)

Year	\multicolumn{12}{c}{Month Placed in Service}
	1	2	3	4	5	6	7	8	9	10	11	12
1	13.3%	12.2%	11.1%	10.0%	8.9%	7.8%	6.6%	5.6%	4.4%	3.3%	2.2%	1.1%
2	11.6	11.7	11.9	12.0	12.1	12.3	12.5	12.6	12.7	12.9	13.0	13.2
3	10.0	10.1	10.2	10.4	10.5	10.7	10.8	10.9	11.1	11.2	11.3	11.4
4	8.7	8.8	8.9	9.0	9.1	9.2	9.3	9.5	9.6	9.7	9.8	9.9
5	7.5	7.6	7.7	7.8	7.9	8.0	8.1	8.2	8.3	8.4	8.5	8.6
6	6.5	6.6	6.7	6.8	6.9	6.9	7.0	7.1	7.2	7.3	7.4	7.4
7	5.7	5.7	5.8	5.9	5.9	6.0	6.1	6.1	6.2	6.3	6.4	6.5
8	4.9	5.0	5.0	5.1	5.2	5.2	5.3	5.3	5.4	5.5	5.5	5.6
9	4.6	4.6	4.6	4.6	4.6	4.6	4.6	4.6	4.6	4.7	4.8	4.8
10	4.6	4.6	4.6	4.6	4.6	4.6	4.6	4.6	4.6	4.6	4.6	4.6
11	4.6	4.6	4.6	4.6	4.6	4.6	4.6	4.6	4.6	4.6	4.6	4.6
12	4.5	4.6	4.6	4.6	4.6	4.6	4.6	4.6	4.6	4.6	4.6	4.6
13	4.5	4.5	4.6	4.5	4.6	4.6	4.6	4.6	4.6	4.5	4.6	4.6
14	4.5	4.5	4.5	4.5	4.5	4.5	4.6	4.6	4.5	4.5	4.5	4.5
15	4.5	4.5	4.5	4.5	4.5	4.5	4.5	4.5	4.5	4.5	4.5	4.5
16	0.0	0.4	0.7	1.1	1.5	1.9	2.3	2.6	3.0	3.4	3.7	4.1

* Rev. Proc. 86-14, 1986-1 CB 542, modifying and superseding Rev. Proc. 86-6, 1986-1 CB 503.

¶ 923.2

Table 7 *—Low-Income Housing Used Predominantly Outside the United States
(placed in service after December 31, 1980 and before May 9, 1985)
15-Year Real Property Used Predominantly Outside the United States
(placed in service after December 31, 1980 and before March 16, 1984)
18-Year Real Property Used Predominantly Outside the United States
(placed in service after March 15, 1984 and before June 23, 1984)
(35-Year 150% Declining Balance)
(Assuming No Mid-Month Convention)

Year	Month Placed in Service				
	1	2-3	4-6	7-8	9-12
1	4%	4%	3%	2%	1%
2-5	4	4	4	4	4
6	3	3	3	4	4
7-24	3	3	3	3	3
25	3	2	3	2	3
26-35	2	2	2	2	2
36		1	1	2	2

* Prop. Reg. § 1.168-2(g)(2)(ii); Notice 84-16, I.R.B. 1984-52, 64 (same as T.D. News Rel. R-2890, 10-22-84).

Table 8 *—18-Year Real Property Used Predominantly Outside the United States
(placed in service after June 22, 1984 and before May 9, 1985)
(35-Year 150% Declining Balance)
(Assuming Mid-Month Convention)

Year	Month Placed in Service						
	1	2	3	4-5	6-8	9-11	12
1	4%	4%	3%	3%	2%	1%	0.2%
2-5	4	4	4	4	4	4	4.0
6	3	3	3	3	4	4	4.0
7	3	3	3	3	3	3	3.8
8-24	3	3	3	3	3	3	3.0
25	3	2	3	2	2	3	3.0
26-35	2	2	2	2	2	2	2.0
36		1	1	2	2	2	2.0

* Notice 84-16, I.R.B. 1984-52, 64 (same as T.D. News Rel. R-2890, 10-22-84).

Depreciation

Table 9 *—19-Year Real Property Used Predominantly Outside the United States
(placed in service after May 8, 1985, and before 1987)
(35-Year 150% Declining Balance)
(Assuming Mid-Month Convention)

Year	\multicolumn{12}{c}{Month Placed in Service}
	1	2	3	4	5	6	7	8	9	10	11	12
1	4.1	3.7	3.4	3.0	2.7	2.3	2.0	1.6	1.3	0.9	0.5	0.2
2	4.1	4.1	4.1	4.2	4.2	4.2	4.2	4.2	4.2	4.3	4.3	4.3
3	3.9	4.0	4.0	4.0	4.0	4.0	4.0	4.0	4.1	4.1	4.1	4.1
4	3.8	3.8	3.8	3.8	3.8	3.8	3.9	3.9	3.9	3.9	3.9	3.9
5	3.6	3.6	3.6	3.6	3.7	3.7	3.7	3.7	3.7	3.8	3.7	3.7
6	3.5	3.5	3.5	3.5	3.5	3.5	3.5	3.5	3.5	3.6	3.6	3.6
7	3.3	3.3	3.3	3.3	3.3	3.4	3.4	3.4	3.4	3.4	3.4	3.4
8	3.2	3.2	3.2	3.2	3.2	3.2	3.2	3.2	3.3	3.3	3.3	3.3
9	3.0	3.0	3.0	3.1	3.1	3.1	3.1	3.1	3.1	3.1	3.1	3.1
10	2.9	2.9	2.9	2.9	2.9	2.9	3.0	3.0	3.0	3.0	3.0	3.0
11	2.8	2.8	2.8	2.8	2.8	2.8	2.8	2.8	2.9	2.9	2.9	2.9
12	2.6	2.7	2.7	2.7	2.7	2.7	2.7	2.7	2.7	2.7	2.8	2.8
13-29	2.6	2.6	2.6	2.6	2.6	2.6	2.6	2.6	2.6	2.6	2.6	2.6
30-35	2.5	2.5	2.5	2.5	2.5	2.5	2.5	2.5	2.5	2.5	2.5	2.5
36	0.0	0.2	0.5	0.7	0.9	1.2	1.3	1.7	1.7	1.8	2.2	2.5

* Rev. Proc. 86-14, 1986-1 CB 542, modifying and superseding Rev. Proc. 86-6, 1986-1 CB 503.

Table 10 *—Low-Income Housing Used Predominantly Outside the United States
(placed in service after May 8, 1985, and before 1987)
(35-Year 150% Declining Balance)
(Assuming No Mid-Month Convention)

Year	\multicolumn{12}{c}{Month Placed in Service}
	1	2	3	4	5	6	7	8	9	10	11	12
1	4.2	3.9	3.6	3.2	2.8	2.5	2.1	1.8	1.4	1.1	0.7	0.4
2	4.1	4.1	4.1	4.2	4.2	4.2	4.2	4.2	4.2	4.2	4.3	4.3
3	3.9	3.9	4.0	4.0	4.0	4.0	4.0	4.0	4.0	4.1	4.1	4.1
4	3.8	3.8	3.8	3.8	3.8	3.8	3.8	3.8	3.9	3.9	3.9	3.9
5	3.6	3.6	3.6	3.6	3.7	3.7	3.7	3.7	3.7	3.7	3.7	3.7
6	3.4	3.5	3.5	3.5	3.5	3.5	3.5	3.5	3.5	3.6	3.6	3.6
7	3.3	3.3	3.3	3.3	3.3	3.4	3.4	3.4	3.4	3.4	3.4	3.4
8	3.2	3.2	3.2	3.2	3.2	3.2	3.2	3.2	3.3	3.3	3.3	3.3
9	3.0	3.0	3.0	3.1	3.1	3.1	3.1	3.1	3.1	3.1	3.1	3.1
10	2.9	2.9	2.9	2.9	2.9	2.9	3.0	3.0	3.0	3.0	3.0	3.0
11	2.8	2.8	2.8	2.8	2.8	2.8	2.8	2.8	2.8	2.8	2.9	2.9
12	2.6	2.7	2.7	2.7	2.7	2.7	2.7	2.7	2.7	2.7	2.7	2.8
13-28	2.6	2.6	2.6	2.6	2.6	2.6	2.6	2.6	2.6	2.6	2.6	2.6
29	2.6	2.5	2.5	2.5	2.6	2.6	2.6	2.6	2.6	2.6	2.6	2.6
30-35	2.5	2.5	2.5	2.5	2.5	2.5	2.5	2.5	2.5	2.5	2.5	2.5
36	0.0	0.2	0.4	0.6	0.8	1.0	1.3	1.6	1.8	1.9	2.1	2.3

* Rev. Proc. 86-14, 1986-1 CB 542, modifying and superseding Rev. Proc. 86-6, 1986-1 CB 503.

¶ 923.2

Optional Straight-Line Schedules

The following depreciation schedules apply when straight-line depreciation or optional longer recovery periods were elected when the property was placed in service.

Table 11 *—15-Year Real Property (placed in service after December 31, 1980 and before March 16, 1984)
Low-Income Housing (placed in service after December 31, 1980 and before March 16, 1984)
(Straight Line Method Over a 15-Year Period)
(Assuming No Mid-Month Convention)

Year	\multicolumn{7}{c}{Month Placed in Service}
	1	2-3	4	5-6	7-8	9-10	11-12
1	7%	6%	5%	4%	3%	2%	1%
2-10	7	7	7	7	7	7	7
11-15	6	6	6	6	6	6	6
16		1	2	3	4	5	6

* Prop. Reg. § 1.168-2(c)(4)(ii)(A).

→ *Caution: Table 12, below, does not reflect changes made to Code Sec. 168(b)(3)(A) by P.L. 99-514 that specify a 15-year recovery period for low-income housing.* ←

Table 12 *—18-Year Real Property (placed in service after March 15, 1984 and before June 23, 1984)
Low-Income Housing (placed in service after March 15, 1984 and before May 9, 1985)
(Straight Line Method Over an 18-Year Period)
(Assuming No Mid-Month Convention)

Year	\multicolumn{6}{c}{Month Placed in Service}
	1	2-3	4-5	6-7	8-9	10-11	12
1	6%	5%	4%	3%	2%	1%	0.5%
2-10	6	6	6	6	6	6	6
11	5	5	5	5	5	5	5.5
12-18	5	5	5	5	5	5	5
19		1	2	3	4	5	5

* Notice 84-16, I.R.B. 1984-52, 64 (same as T.D. News Rel. R-2890, 10-22-84).

Table 13 *—18-Year Real Property (other than low-income housing) (placed in service after June 22, 1984 and before May 9, 1985)
(Straight Line Method Over an 18-Year Period)
(Assuming Mid-Month Convention)

Year	\multicolumn{6}{c}{Month Placed in Service}
	1-2	3-4	5-7	8-9	10-11	12
1	5%	4%	3%	2%	1%	0.2%
2-10	6	6	6	6	6	6
11	5	5	5	5	5	5.8
12-18	5	5	5	5	5	5
19	1	2	3	4	5	5

* Notice 84-16, I.R.B. 1984-52, 64 (same as T.D. News Rel. R-2890, 10-22-84).

¶ 923.2

Depreciation

Table 14 * —19-Year Real Property (other than low-income housing)
(placed in service after May 8, 1985, and before 1987)
(Straight Line Method Over a 19-Year Period)
(Assuming Mid-Month Convention)

Year	\multicolumn{12}{c}{Month Placed in Service}
	1	2	3	4	5	6	7	8	9	10	11	12
1	5.0	4.6	4.2	3.7	3.3	2.9	2.4	2.0	1.5	1.1	0.7	0.2
2-13	5.3	5.3	5.3	5.3	5.3	5.3	5.3	5.3	5.3	5.3	5.3	5.3
14-19	5.2	5.2	5.2	5.2	5.2	5.2	5.2	5.2	5.2	5.2	5.2	5.2
20	0.2	.6	1.0	1.5	1.9	2.3	2.8	3.2	3.7	4.1	4.5	5.0

* Announcement 86-5, I.R.B. 1986-3, 43; Rev. Proc. 86-14, 1986-1 CB 542, modifying and superseding Rev. Proc. 86-6, 1986-1 CB 503.

→ *Caution: Table 15, below, does not reflect changes made to Code Sec. 168(b)(3)(A) by P.L. 99-514 that specify a 15-year recovery period.* ←

Table 15 * —Low-Income Housing (placed in service after May 8, 1985)
(Straight Line Method Over a 19-Year Period)
(Assuming No Mid-Month Convention)

Year	\multicolumn{12}{c}{Month Placed in Service}
	1	2	3	4	5	6	7	8	9	10	11	12
1	5.3	4.8	4.4	3.9	3.5	3.1	2.6	2.2	1.8	1.3	0.9	0.4
2-12	5.3	5.3	5.3	5.3	5.3	5.3	5.3	5.3	5.3	5.3	5.3	5.3
13	5.2	5.3	5.3	5.3	5.3	5.3	5.3	5.3	5.3	5.3	5.3	5.3
14-19	5.2	5.2	5.2	5.2	5.2	5.2	5.2	5.2	5.2	5.2	5.2	5.2
20	0.0	0.4	0.8	1.3	1.7	2.1	2.6	3.0	3.4	3.9	4.3	4.8

* Rev. Proc. 86-14, 1986-1 CB 542, modifying and superseding Rev. Proc. 86-6, 1986-1 CB 503.

Table 16 * —Low-Income Housing (placed in service after December 31, 1980 and before May 9, 1985)
15-Year Real Property (placed in service after December 31, 1980 and before March 16, 1984)
18-Year Real Property (placed in service after March 15, 1984 and before June 23, 1984)

(Straight Line Method Over a 35-Year Period)
(Assuming No Mid-Month Convention)

Year	\multicolumn{3}{c}{Month Placed in Service}
	1-2	3-6	7-12
1	3%	2%	1%
2-30	3	3	3
31-35	2	2	2
36	—	1	2

* Prop. Reg. § 1.168-2(c)(4)(ii)(B); Notice 84-16, I.R.B. 1984-52, 64 (same as T.D. News Rel. R-2890, 10-22-84).

Note: Table 16 may also be used for the above described property that is used predominantly outside the United States for which a straight line election is made under the full month convention over a 35-year recovery period.

¶ 923.2

Table 17*—18-Year Real Property (placed in service after June 22, 1984, and before May 9, 1985)
(Straight Line Method Over a 35-Year Period)
(Assuming Mid-Month Convention)

Year	Month Placed in Service				
	1-2	3-6	7-10	11	12
1	3%	2%	1%	0.4%	0.1%
2-30	3	3	3	3	3
31	2	2	2	2.6	2.9
32-35	2	2	2	2	2
36		1	2	2	2

* Notice 84-16, 1984-2 CB 475 (same as T.D. News Rel. R-2890, 10-22-84).

Note: Table 17 may also be used for the above described property that is used predominantly outside the United States for which a straight line election is made under the mid-month convention over a 35-year recovery period.

Table 18*—19-Year Real Property (placed in service after May 8, 1985, and before 1987)
(Straight Line Method Over a 35-Year Period)
(Assuming Mid-Month Convention)

Year	Month Placed in Service											
	1	2	3	4	5	6	7	8	9	10	11	12
1	2.7	2.5	2.3	2.0	1.8	1.5	1.3	1.1	0.8	0.6	0.4	0.1
2-20	2.9	2.9	2.9	2.9	2.9	2.9	2.9	2.9	2.9	2.9	2.9	2.9
21-35	2.8	2.8	2.8	2.8	2.8	2.8	2.8	2.8	2.8	2.8	2.8	2.8
36	0.2	0.4	0.6	0.9	1.1	1.4	1.6	1.8	2.1	2.3	2.5	2.8

* Rev. Proc. 86-14, 1986-1 CB 542, modifying and superseding Rev. Proc. 86-6, 1986-1 CB 503.

Note: Table 18 may also be used for the above-described property that is used predominantly outside the United States for which a straight line election is made under the mid-month convention over a 35-year recovery period.

Table 19*—Low-Income Housing (placed in service after May 8, 1985, and before 1987)
(Straight Line Method Over a 35-Year Period)
(Assuming No Mid-Month Convention)

Year	Month Placed in Service											
	1	2	3	4	5	6	7	8	9	10	11	12
1	2.9	2.6	2.4	2.1	1.9	1.7	1.4	1.2	1.0	0.7	0.5	0.2
2-20	2.9	2.9	2.9	2.9	2.9	2.9	2.9	2.9	2.9	2.9	2.9	2.9
21-35	2.8	2.8	2.8	2.8	2.8	2.8	2.8	2.8	2.8	2.8	2.8	2.8
36	0.0	0.3	0.5	0.8	1.0	1.2	1.5	1.7	1.9	2.2	2.4	2.7

* Rev. Proc. 86-14, 1986-1 CB 542, modifying and superseding Rev. Proc. 86-6, 1986-1 CB 503.

Note: Table 19 may also be used for the above described property that is used predominantly outside the United States for which a straight line election is made under the full month convention over a 35-year recovery period.

¶ 923.2

Depreciation

Table 20*—Low-Income Housing (placed in service after December 31, 1980)
15-Year Real Property (placed in service after December 31, 1980, and before March 16, 1984)
18-Year Real Property (placed in service after March 15, 1984, and before June 23, 1984)
(Straight Line Method Over a 45-Year Period)
(Assuming No Mid-Month Convention)

Year	\multicolumn{12}{c}{Month Placed in Service}
	1	2	3	4	5	6	7	8	9	10	11	12
1	2.3%	2.0%	1.9%	1.7%	1.5%	1.3%	1.2%	0.9%	0.7%	0.6%	0.4%	0.2%
2-10	2.3	2.3	2.3	2.3	2.3	2.3	2.3	2.3	2.3	2.3	2.3	2.3
11-45	2.2	2.2	2.2	2.2	2.2	2.2	2.2	2.2	2.2	2.2	2.2	2.2
46		0.3	0.4	0.6	0.8	1.0	1.1	1.4	1.6	1.7	1.9	2.1

* Prop. Reg. § 1.168-2(c)(4)(ii)(C); Notice 84-16, 1984-2 CB 475 (same as T.D. News Rel. R-2890 10-22-84). Low-income housing rates in the above proposed regulation are the same as in Rev. Proc. 86-14, 1986-1 CB 542, modifying and superseding Rev. Proc. 86-6, 1986-1 CB 503.

Note: Table 20 may also be used for the above described property that is used predominantly outside the United States for which a straight line election is made under the full month convention over a 45-year recovery period.

Table 21*—**18-Year Real Property** (placed in service after June 22, 1984 and before May 9, 1985)
(Straight Line Method Over a 45-Year Period)
(Assuming Mid-Month Convention)

Year	\multicolumn{12}{c}{Month Placed in Service}
	1	2	3	4	5	6	7	8	9	10	11	12
1	2.1%	1.9%	1.8%	1.6%	1.4%	1.2%	1.0%	0.8%	0.6%	0.5%	0.3%	0.1%
2-11	2.3	2.3	2.3	2.3	2.3	2.3	2.3	2.3	2.3	2.3	2.3	2.3
12-45	2.2	2.2	2.2	2.2	2.2	2.2	2.2	2.2	2.2	2.2	2.2	2.2
46	0.1	0.3	0.4	0.6	0.8	1.0	1.2	1.4	1.6	1.7	1.9	2.1

* Notice 84-16, 1984-2 CB 475.

Note: Table 21 may also be used for the above described property that is used predominantly outside the United States for which a straight line election is made under the mid-month convention over a 45-year recovery period.

Table 22*—**19-Year Real Property** (placed in service after May 8, 1985, and before 1987)
(Straight Line Method Over a 45-Year Period)
(Assuming Mid-Month Convention)

Year	\multicolumn{12}{c}{Month Placed in Service}
	1	2	3	4	5	6	7	8	9	10	11	12
1	2.1%	1.9%	1.8%	1.6%	1.4%	1.2%	1.0%	0.8%	0.6%	0.5%	0.3%	0.1%
2-11	2.3	2.3	2.3	2.3	2.3	2.3	2.3	2.3	2.3	2.3	2.3	2.3
12-45	2.2	2.2	2.2	2.2	2.2	2.2	2.2	2.2	2.2	2.2	2.2	2.2
46	0.1	0.3	0.4	0.6	0.8	1.0	1.2	1.4	1.6	1.7	1.9	2.1

* Rev. Proc. 86-14, 1986-1 CB 542, modifying and superseding Rev. Proc. 86-6, 1986-1 CB 503.

Note: Table 22 may also be used for the above described property that is used predominantly outside the United States for which a straight line election is made under the mid-month convention over a 45-year recovery period.

¶ 923.2

¶ 925 Additions and Improvements

In the case of improvements and additions to pre-1987 ACRS property, different rules apply to additions and improvements that are merely components of the original property and additions and improvements that qualify as substantial improvements. In general, the deduction for any component of a building added to the building before 1987 must be computed in the same way as the deduction for the building itself.[47] This general rule, however, was modified by transition rules to reflect the changing recovery periods for real property between 1981 and 1987.

The ACRS recovery period for real property placed in service after 1980 and before March 16, 1984, is 15 years. This recovery period was changed to 18 years for most real property other than low-income housing placed in service after March 15, 1984, and before May 9, 1985. The first component added after March 15, 1984, and before May 9, 1985, must be treated as a separate building and depreciated using the 18-year cost recovery schedules, if the building was placed in service before March 16, 1984. The deduction for any subsequent components added to the building before May 9, 1985, must be calculated in the same way as the deduction for the first component added after March 15, 1984, and before May 9, 1985.

The ACRS recovery period for most real property placed in service after May 8, 1985, and before January 1, 1987, was extended to 19 years. Rules similar to those for the transition from a 15-year recovery period to an 18-year recovery period apply to the transition from an 18-year recovery period to a 19-year recovery period. The first component added after May 8, 1985, and before January 1, 1987, must be treated as a separate building and depreciated using the 19-year cost recovery schedules, if the building was placed in service before May 9, 1985. The deduction for any subsequent components added to the building before 1987 must be calculated in the same way as the deduction for the first component added after May 8, 1985, and before 1987.

¶ 925.1 *Substantial Improvements as Separate Property*

An exception to the general rule that cost recovery deductions for pre-1987 additions and improvements to a building are computed in the same way as the deduction for the building (or, when the transition rules apply, the first component added after March 15, 1984, or May 9, 1985) applies to "substantial improvements" made three or more years after the building was placed in service. Under this rule, a substantial

---

[47] Former Code Sec. 168(f)(1) of the Internal Revenue Code of 1954.

improvement is treated as a separate property for purposes of computing the ACRS deduction. As separate property, the various elections and options under the ACRS system were available for a substantial improvement.

¶ 925.2 Qualification as Substantial Improvement

To qualify as a substantial improvement, the capital expenditures for improvements to the building during a 24-month period had to be at least 25 percent of the adjusted basis of the building as of the first day of the 24-month period. Adjusted basis for this purpose was calculated by ignoring any prior depreciation or cost recovery deductions.

¶ 931 DEPRECIATION OF PRE-1981 PROPERTY

Taxpayers that placed depreciable property in service before 1981 were generally free to use any reasonable method of computing depreciation, as long as the method chosen was used consistently throughout the life of the property. Depreciation deductions were spread over the useful life of the property. Useful life was based on how long the property could reasonably be expected to be used for the purpose in which it was employed. In many cases, the useful life of real property could be as long as 40 years or more.

While the consistent application of any reasonable method of depreciation was permitted for pre-1981 property, the Internal Revenue Code of 1954 specifically authorized three methods:

1. Straight-line method
2. Declining-balance method
3. Sum-of-the-years digits method

Also, in the case of real property, the use of accelerated methods of depreciation was limited.

¶ 933 Calculation of Deduction for Real Property

Accelerated depreciation is a depreciation method other than the straight-line method. For real property placed in service before 1981, accelerated depreciation is limited. Property that was new commercial property when placed in service cannot be depreciated faster than the 150 percent declining-balance method permits, and used commercial property cannot be depreciated faster than the straight-line method permits.

Residential property placed in service before 1981 is subject to more liberal restrictions on the use of accelerated depreciation methods. Property that was new residential property when placed in service may be depreciated using the double (200%) declining-balance method or the sum-of-the-years digits method. Used residential property may be depreciated using the 125 percent declining-balance method.

¶ 933.1 Depreciation Methods

Straight-line depreciation is simply the amount calculated by dividing the basis of property (less salvage value and prior depreciation) by the number of years remaining in the useful life of the property. The cost of any improvements are simply added to basis for purposes of computing depreciation. Property or improvements acquired, sold, or disposed of during a year are allowed a proportionate part of a full year's deduction.

The *declining-balance method* of depreciation provides greater depreciation deductions during the early years of a property's useful life and progressively smaller deductions in later years (hence the term "accelerated depreciation"). Under the declining-balance method, the deduction is calculated by applying a percentage of the straight-line rate to the property's adjusted basis. For instance, a building with a 50-year useful life would have a straight-line rate of 2% (100%/50 years). The double declining-balance (200 percent) rate for this building would be 4% (200% × 2%); the 150 percent declining-balance rate would be 3%; and the 125 percent declining-balance rate would be 2.5%. Property held for only part of the year is entitled to only a proportionate part of a full year's deduction.

The *sum-of-the-years digits method* of depreciation is also an accelerated method. Under this method, a fraction of the property's original basis (less salvage value) is deducted each year. The fraction for any year is set by adding the years of the property's useful life to determine the denominator and using the number of years left in the property's useful life for the numerator. For instance, if real property had a useful life of 40 years, the denominator of the fraction would be calculated by adding the digits 1 through 40 (1 + 2 + 3 + 4, etc.) to arrive at 820. The fraction to determine the deduction for this property for its first year (when there are 40 years in its useful life) would be 40/820; the fraction for the second year would be 39/820; for the third year, 38/820; etc. Property in service for only part of a year is entitled to only a proportionate part of a full year's deduction.

¶ 933.2 Change of Depreciation Methods

A change in depreciation methods for property placed in service before 1981 is considered a change in accounting method that generally requires IRS consent. A change from a declining-balance method to the straight-line method, however, may be made without prior IRS consent.[48] It is often beneficial to switch to the straight-line method when the depreciation deductions from the declining-balance method are about to fall below the deductions that would be available if the remaining basis of the property were depreciated using the straight-line method.

¶ 935 Anti-Churning Rules

When the ACRS system was adopted for assets placed in service after 1980, Congress moved to block attempts by taxpayers to get the more generous deductions under ACRS for property that they had already placed in service. The anti-churning rules, as they were called, prevented taxpayers from transferring property to related parties to gain the larger ACRS deductions. The same rules were adopted when the MACRS system was adopted for post-1987 property. However, these anti-churning rules do not apply to real property because the depreciation deductions for real property under the general depreciation system (MACRS) are much less generous than those that were available under ACRS.

¶ 935.1 *Real Property Rules*

The anti-churning rules exclude certain property from the definition of recovery property under ACRS. In the case of real property, recovery property entitled to ACRS does not include any property that was:

1. Owned by the taxpayer or a related person at any time during 1980;
2. Leased to a person, or related person, who owned the property at any time during 1980; and
3. Acquired in a tax-free exchange or acquisition under Code Secs. 1031, 1033, 1038, or 1039 to the extent of the basis of the property given up in the transaction.[49]

¶ 935.2 *Related Party Transfers*

The relationships that bring property within the ambit of the anti-churning rules are:

1. Family, which includes brothers, sisters, spouse, ancestors, and lineal descendants;
2. Fiduciary, which includes a trust, its grantor, trustee, and beneficiary;

---

[48] Rev. Rul. 74-324, 1974-2 CB 66.

[49] Former Code Sec. 168(e)(4) of the 1954 Internal Revenue Code and Code Sec. 168(f)(5) of the 1986 Internal Revenue Code.

3. Corporation and shareholder owning at least 10 percent of the corporation;
4. Partnership and partner owning at least 10 percent of the partnership; and
5. Corporations under 50 percent common control.

¶ 935.3 *Tax-Free Transfers*

Restrictions are imposed on tax-free transfers of recovery property under ACRS. Transfers covered by this transferee rule include:

1. Liquidation of a subsidiary;
2. Transfer to a controlled corporation;
3. Tax-free reorganization;
4. Bankruptcy or receivership;
5. Contribution to a partnership; or
6. Distribution from a partnership.

In these transactions, the transferee must continue to use the transferor's depreciation recovery period and method in computing the ACRS deduction for the portion of the transferee's basis that does not exceed the transferor's adjusted basis. The transferee must, as a result, compute depreciation on the carried-over adjusted basis as if the transfer had not occurred. The transferee may, however, depreciate the excess basis as if it were newly acquired property.

Chapter 10

Development, Subdivision, and Sales in the Ordinary Course of Business

¶ 1000 OVERVIEW OF CHAPTER

The development, subdivision, and sale of real estate in the ordinary course of business involves tax questions and problems that are unique when compared to those involved in the one-time sale of either rental property or property used in a trade or business.

The cost or basis of the property must be apportioned among the parcels that are sold in order to determine income as the parcels are sold. Also, there are the development costs that must be included in the basis of the property and allocated among the parcels. In many cases, a developer will sell lots before all development costs have been incurred. In this case, the developer may estimate future development costs and allocate a share to the lots already sold in order to reduce the taxable income that the developer must report. (How basis is determined generally is considered at ¶ 103.)

Apart from the amount of income that must be reported as subdivided property is sold, there is the question of the character of that income. The sale of property held for investment generally produces capital gain or loss, while property that is sold in the ordinary course of business produces ordinary income or loss. The distinction usually turns on whether the seller is considered a "dealer" in real property. Dealer sales generally produce the ordinary income or loss result. Of course, the distinction between capital gain and ordinary income is less important when the two types of income are subject to the same or nearly the same tax rates, but Congress is constantly changing the treatment of capital gain. Even when the two types of income are subject to the same tax rates, the distinction remains important because of the rules limiting deduction of capital losses. Capital losses can always offset capital gain, but the deduction of capital losses against ordinary income is severely limited.

At times, an investor may hold property that cannot be sold unless the property is subdivided. The subdivision and sale of separate parcels may create dealer status. There is, however, a statutory provision that

¶ 1000

allows an investor to realize capital gain when the investor must subdivide holdings for sale.

¶ 1001 DEVELOPMENT COSTS

In the early stages of development, a developer incurs costs and realizes no income as the property is readied for sale. During this time, some of the costs may qualify as ordinary and necessary business expenses which are currently deductible. Many costs, however, are expenditures that have to be capitalized as part of the cost of the property under the capitalization rules discussed at ¶ 127 or under those that apply to additions and improvements discussed at ¶ 801. Development costs are also capital expenditures. These capitalized costs can be recouped only as sales are made. The total cost of the property, including development costs, must be apportioned among units or parcels that are sold separately to determine the amount of income or loss on each unit or parcel.

¶ 1003 Equitable Apportionment Rule

Under the regulations, when part of a larger property is sold, the cost or other basis of the entire property must be equitably apportioned among the several parts, and the gain realized or loss sustained on the part of the entire property sold is the difference between the selling price and the cost or other basis allocated to the part sold.[1] The sale of each part is treated as a separate transaction and the gain or loss is computed separately on each part. The seller cannot defer reporting gain or loss until the entire property has been sold.

Even if the taxpayer did not contemplate subdivision at the time the real estate was purchased but intended to sell it as a whole, the subsequent sale of part of the property in separate tracts creates a series of separate transactions for purposes of accounting for gain or loss.[2]

The rule of equitable apportionment applies to condominiums. A taxpayer who purchases a rental apartment building, converts that building into condominiums, and then sells the units individually cannot use the cost recovery method of accounting for the income from the sales and thus defer reporting income until the taxpayer recovers the entire basis.[3] The equitable apportionment rule also applies to the subdivision and sale of cemetery lots.[4]

---

[1] Reg. § 1.61-6(a).

[2] *F. Skinner*, 20 BTA 491, CCH Dec. 6241, Acq. x-1 CB 60.

[3] Rev. Rul. 79-276, 1979-2 CB 200.

[4] *Cedar Park Cemetery Assn., Inc.*, CA-7, 50-2 USTC ¶ 9376, 183 F.2d 553, cert. denied 292 U.S. 639, 54 S.Ct. 773.

Development costs expended or to be expended are added to basis that is apportioned.[5] These costs include such items as the cost of water and sewer facilities, even though the facilities are transferred to a public service company without consideration.[6] Other costs added to basis include the cost of surveying boundaries and expenditures for platting, grading and cindering streets, and installing sidewalks.[7] The addition of development costs to the basis of subdivided real estate is considered further at ¶ 1005.

¶ 1003.1 Manner of Apportionment of Basis

The cost or other basis of property must be "equitably apportioned" among the parts that are sold separately. Equitable apportionment is not ratable apportionment. The apportionment of basis must reflect differences in the relative values of the parcels being sold, if such differences exist. Of course, when there is no difference in value, apportionment may be done on a pro rata basis. For instance, in *J.D. Byram*,[8] the Court of Appeals upheld an IRS determination to allocate the basis of a parcel of land that had been subdivided into two tracts on a pro rata basis. The taxpayer was unable to show that the value per acre of Tract One was greater than that of Tract Two on the date of purchase.

In many cases, however, there will be a difference in relative values because of size, location, or other factors, and the apportionment of basis must reflect this difference. There is an opportunity for tax planning in this. If more basis can be allocated to the earlier sales, income can be deferred until later sales. For example, in a housing subdivision, some lots may be located on a lake. These lots, most likely, will have a higher value than interior lots. If the lakefront lots are sold first, a greater portion of the total basis will be available to offset the selling price of these lots.[9]

In smaller subdivisions, apportioning basis may be a relatively simple matter, as illustrated in Reg. § 1.61-6(a), Example (2).

> **Example:** The Taxpayer purchases for $25,000 property consisting of a used car lot and an adjoining gas station. At the time of purchase, the fair market value of the gas station is $15,000 and the fair market value of the used car lot is $10,000. Five years later, the Taxpayer sells the gas station for $20,000 at a time when $2,000 has been properly allowed as depreciation. The Taxpayer's

---

[5] *Colony, Inc.*, 26 TC 30, CCH Dec. 21,665, Acq. 1958-1 CB 4, aff'd CA-6, 57-1 USTC ¶ 9636, 244 F.2d 75.

[6] *G.W. Offutt*, CA-4, 64-2 USTC ¶ 9757, 336 F.2d 483.

[7] *Frishkorn Real Estate Co.*, 15 BTA 463, CCH Dec. 6588.

[8] CA-5, 77-2 USTC ¶ 9541, 555 F.2d 1234.

[9] See *Biscayne Bay Islands, Co.*, 23 BTA 731, CCH Dec. 7030, Acq. XI-1 CB 2, in which the total cost of a group of lots was partly allocated to interior lots as well as to waterfront lots, but on a ratio of one to three, and not on a ratable proportion.

gain on the sale is $7,000 since $7,000 is the amount by which the selling price of the gas station ($20,000) exceeds the portion of the cost equitably allocable to the gas station at the time of purchase reduced by the depreciation ($15,000 − $2,000 = $13,000).

In larger projects and subdivisions, however, the apportionment of basis, which includes both on- and off-site development costs can become rather involved. The trick for the developer is to choose a method of equitable apportionment that results in the greatest possible portion of basis being allocated to the earlier sales in order to boost cash flow during those early critical stages of a development, but without having the method struck down by the IRS.

¶ 1003.2   Methods of Apportionment of Basis

As a general proposition, the Tax Court has required that the allocation of basis be made at the time of purchase rather than at the time of sale.[10] Under this principle, the equitable apportionment may be based on an appraisal of the relative value of the different lots or other parcels before actual sales are made.

Example: The Developer purchases a tract of land for $500,000 and subdivides this tract into 25 lots. The expected selling price of the lots ranges from $25,000 to $75,000 per lot, depending on size, location, etc. The total appraised price at which the Developer expects to sell the lots is $1,100,000. During the first year of sales, 10 lots are sold for a total of $450,000. These sales represent lots that were originally appraised at $462,500. The Developer spent $50,000 in improving the 10 lots that are sold and estimates further development costs for these lots at an additional $50,000.

Since the initial appraisal would seem to be a method of equitably apportioning basis in this case, the Developer could assign about 42 percent (462,500/1,100,000) of the original cost basis to the 10 lots sold, or $210,227.25. Adding the $100,000 in development costs for these lots to the $210,227.25 cost basis, gives the Developer a total basis for the 10 lots sold of $310,227.25. Subtracting this basis from the actual sales price of the 10 lots results in a gain of $139,772.75 ($450,000 − $310.227.25).

Use of the gross profit from sales has been approved in some cases, even though this method ignores the principle that the allocation should be made at the time the property is acquired. For instance, in *R.W. Ewing*,[11] the gross receipts from the lots sold were divided by the sum of the receipts and the tentative selling price of the unsold land.

---

[10] *W.A. Ayling*, 32 TC 704, CCH Dec. 23,647, Acq. 1959-2 CB 3.

[11] 17 TCM 626, CCH Dec. 23,042(M), T.C. Memo. 1958-115.

This fraction was multiplied by the total cost of the land, and the resulting figure was allocated to the lots sold.

In still other cases, the selling price has been used as the basis for equitable apportionment. The Tax Court has held that an IRS allocation of the cost based on selling price was reasonable when nothing had occurred from the date of purchase until the time of sale to alter the relative values.[12] The taxpayer had sought an allocation to two separate frontages in one parcel of 90 percent and 10 percent, but the IRS allocation based on selling price was 65 percent and 35 percent.

Apportionment of cost to each lot sold on the basis of assessed valuation by the local property tax assessor has been approved in the absence of a better method.[13]

Considering the wide variety of methods available to equitably apportion the cost of property, it would seem that almost any method chosen should be acceptable, provided it fairly matches costs with revenues. A method that distorts the income realized by the developer when lots or other units are sold, however, would not be acceptable.

¶ 1005 Inclusion of Development Costs in Basis

The basis of subdivided lots generally includes a pro rata portion of the cost of developing the parcel and making it suitable for subdivision. A developer may add to the cost of the lots the cost of land set aside for streets[14] or the release of frontage for a road.[15]

The IRS has also ruled that a pro rata portion of the cost of water lines should be added to the basis of each lot in a subdivision.[16] The developer agreed to build water lines and convey them to a water utility company because the developer needed water service for the subdivision; but once the developer conveyed the water lines to the water company, the developer retained no rights to them.

Deposits required to have public utilities extended to subdivided real estate are added to the basis of the subdivided lots.[17] The cost of a sewage disposal system operated by a corporation was includible in the basis of lots sold by a real estate developer, even though he owned the corporation and therefore the plant.[18] The same result was reached when water and sewer facilities were conveyed to a utility company wholly owned by an individual who owned 40 percent of the stock in the development company.[19]

---

[12] *R.M. Clayton*, 15 TCM 105, CCH Dec. 21,537(M), T.C. Memo. 1956-21, aff'd CA-6, 245 F.2d 238, 57-1 USTC ¶ 9447.

[13] *J.S. Cullinan*, 5 BTA 996, CCH Dec. 2041, Acq. vii-1 CB 8.

[14] *Laguna Land & Water Co.*, CA-9, 41-1 USTC ¶ 9302, 118 F.2d 112.

[15] Rev. Rul. 57-488, 1957-2 CB 157.

[16] Rev. Rul. 81-83, 1981-1 CB 434.

[17] *T.M. Divine, Jr.*, DC Tenn., 62-2 USTC ¶ 9632.

[18] *M.A. Collins Est.*, 31 TC 238, CCH Dec. 23,228, Acq. 1959-2 CB 4.

[19] *G.W. Offutt*, CA-4, 64-2 USTC ¶ 9757, 336 F.2d 483.

In Rev. Rul. 60-3,[20] the basis of each lot was held to include a pro rata portion of the payment for installing water lines in a subdivision, even though the developer might receive a repayment of all or part of the payment. See also, *A. Gersten*,[21] in which it was held that allocable portions of the cost of extending water lines paid by the subdivider were properly added to the cost of the properties sold, even though all or part of the cost would be recovered over a 10-year period out of collections from the subdivision.

The value of lots donated to a recreation center increased the basis of the remaining lots when membership in the center would be open to purchasers of lots in the subdivision.[22] In *Country Club Estates, Inc.*,[23] the taxpayer, a corporation formed to develop a tract of land as a residential subdivision, donated a part of the land to a country club. Since the donation was intended as an inducement for people to buy nearby lots, the cost of the land donated was part of the cost basis of the lots sold. The IRS extended this position and ruled that the basis of subdivided lots includes a pro rata portion of the payments made for construction of a golf course, dam, lake, and related recreational facilities, as well as the cost of land donated to the nonprofit country club.[24]

¶ 1005.1 Development Improvements as Separate Interest

While the cost of improvements such as streets, water, and sewage utilities and recreational facilities that benefit a real estate development as a whole may be added to the basis of the property sold, these same costs generally may not be added to basis when the developer retains ownership and control of the improvements and is able to commercially exploit them or operate them as a business separate from the subdivision.

In *Colony, Inc.*,[25] a developer applied the cost of a water supply system to the cost of lots sold. Water meters were installed, and the developer was paid for the water purchased by the consumers. In this situation, the Tax Court held that the cost of the system constructed by the developer was not a development expense that could be added to the developer's basis in the subdivision lots because the developer retained ownership of the system and did not part with the property for the benefit of the subdivided lots. A similar result was reached in *R.J. Sabinske*,[26] in which it was held that subdividers could not add the

---

[20] 1960-1 CB 284.

[21] 28 TC 756, CCH Dec. 22,466, Acq. 1958-1 CB 4, aff'd CA-9, 59-1 USTC ¶ 9303, 267 F. 2d 195.

[22] *Sevier Terrace Realty Co.*, 21 TCM 1289, CCH Dec. 25,707(M), T.C. Memo. 1962-242, aff'd CA-6, 64-1 USTC ¶ 9268, 327 F.2d 999.

[23] 22 TC 1283, CCH Dec. 20,575, Acq. 1955-1 CB 4.

[24] Rev. Rul. 68-478, 1968-2 CB 330.

[25] 26 TC 30, CCH Dec. 21,665, Acq. 1958-1 CB 4, aff'd CA-6, 244 F.2d 75, 57-1 USTC ¶ 9636.

[26] DC Tex., 62-1 USTC ¶ 9210.

aliquot portion of the costs of water systems to the basis of each lot sold because the operation of the water systems was a separate business.

In *M.J. Noell*,[27] the taxpayer was not permitted to add the basis in an adjoining airport runway and taxiways to the basis in subdivided residential lots. The taxpayer retained sufficiently complete control and ownership over the landing facilities for ancillary but independent commercial exploitation. Accordingly, the facilities represented a separate asset and their cost was not properly allocable to the cost of the lots.

Even when the improvements are not commercially exploited on a separate basis, their cost may not be added to the basis of subdivided lots when they benefit some other enterprise of the developer and not just the subdivided lots. For instance, the cost of water systems that were constructed to benefit the developer's substantial recreational facilities and not merely to make lots more salable could not be included in computing the basis of subdivided lots.[28]

¶ 1005.2 *Estimated Future Costs*

Generally, when subdivided lots are sold prior to completion of the development work, the subdivider, in determining the gain or loss from the sale of the lots, may add to the actual cost or other basis of the property sold the estimated costs of future improvements to the property.[29] In order to add to the actual cost or other basis of the property sold the estimated costs of future improvements, the following conditions must be met:

1. The subdivider must be contractually obligated to make the future improvements;
2. The costs of the future improvements must not be recoverable through depreciation by the subdivider;
3. The subdivider must sign a consent fixing the period of limitation on the assessment of income tax to expire one year after the expiration of the estimated period within which the subdivider expects to make the improvements, or one year after the expiration of a five-year period, whichever is shorter, calculated from the date of the tax return to which the consent relates; and
4. The subdivider must furnish the data and information required by section 4.02 of Rev. Proc. 75-25 in order to establish the correctness of the estimated costs.

---

[27] 66 TC 718, CCH Dec. 33,927, Acq. 1977-2 CB 2.
[28] *Bryce's Mountain Resort, Inc.*, 50 TCM 164, CCH Dec. 42,164(M), T.C. Memo. 1985-293.

[29] Rev. Proc. 75-25, 1975-1 CB 720.

A subdivider who does not comply with the provisions of Rev. Proc. 75-25 may not add estimated costs of future improvements to the cost or other basis of the property sold for the purpose of determining gain or loss resulting from the sale of the property. Once a subdivider obtains approval to add estimated costs of future improvements to basis, the subdivider must file follow-up statements along with each tax return.[30] If a subdivider of real estate who has added estimated future costs to basis determines that the estimate was understated or overstated, the subdivider must make an adjustment to the costs in and for the year the correct determination was made, not for the prior taxable year when the estimate was made.[31]

¶ 1011 DEALER STATUS

Property held primarily for sale to customers in the ordinary course of business is not a capital asset. In real estate, property held for sale is commonly called "dealer property," although a dealer in real property may still hold property for investment. The gain or loss on the sale of dealer property is ordinary income or loss, rather than a capital gain or loss. Also, real property held primarily for sale to customers in the ordinary course of business is not eligible for installment reporting, while the sale of real property used in a trade or business or held for investment may be reported on the installment method (see ¶ 1405).

The question of whether a particular piece of property is dealer property, that is, held primarily for sale, has been the source of a great deal of litigation. The reason for this is that the question of whether land or improved realty is held primarily for sale to customers in the ordinary course of a taxpayer's trade or business or for investment is one of fact, and is determined on a case-by-case, property-by-property basis.[32]

¶ 1013 Characterization of Dealer Property

The Supreme Court has interpreted the word "primarily" to mean "principally" or "of first importance."[33] According to the Court in *Malat*, the purpose of the "primarily" requirement is to distinguish between ordinary profits arising in the everyday operation of a business and the realization of appreciation in the value of an asset accrued over a substantial period of time. While *Malat* involved a dual purpose on the part of the taxpayer, investment or sale, other cases have held that the same principles are equally applicable when property is acquired with the single purpose of selling it sometime in the future.[34]

---

[30] Rev. Proc. 75-25, 1975-1 CB 720, Section 5.
[31] Rev. Proc. 78-25, 1978-1 CB 270.
[32] *E.L. Freeland*, CA-9, 68-1 USTC ¶ 9278, 393 F.2d 573, cert. denied 393 U.S. 845, 89 S.Ct. 132.
[33] *W. Malat v. Riddell*, S.Ct., 66-1 USTC ¶ 9317, 393 U.S. 569, 86 S.Ct. 1030.
[34] See, for example, *W.A. Scheuber*, CA-7, 67-1 USTC ¶ 9219, 371 F.2d 996.

As a general matter, there does not seem to be any one single factor or combination of factors that controls the characterization of property as dealer property. For example, in *W.K. Dean Est.*,[35] a corporation treated certain parcels of real estate on its books and in every corporate audit report as current assets held primarily for sale to customers in the ordinary course of business. This practice was found not conclusive as to the status of the real estate because the purpose for holding real estate is subject to change based on a change in circumstances.

Dealer status does not automatically attach to a parcel of property merely because a substantial part of the owner's business is devoted to the business of selling real estate. Gain from the sale of an apartment house by a real estate broker was capital gain when the property was not held primarily for sale in the course of business.[36] See also *J.S. Murray*,[37] in which a real estate dealer was found to be an investor as to some properties sold and to be entitled to treat the proceeds from the sale of these properties as capital gain. As to other pieces of property, the dealer was found to be in the business of selling real estate, and sales proceeds were ordinary income.

¶ 1013.1 Tests Applied for Classification of Property

To aid in deciding whether property is held primarily for sale to customers in the ordinary course of business, the courts have developed several tests. Among these, one of the most frequently applied concerns the purpose or reason for the taxpayer's acquisition and disposition of the property. Real estate is not dealer property if the sales purpose is substantial but not dominant.[38]

The Tax Court applied the purpose test of the Eighth Circuit's *Municipal Bond* decision in the following fashion. If the rental of a piece of realty is merely incidental to its eventual sale, such as might be the case when the property is in a bad rental area, the principal purpose for which the property is held is sale. On the other hand, if the property is held for a long period of time, if no effort is made to sell it, and if the property is a good income producer, the principal purpose for holding the property is investment. In cases where sales are made reluctantly, such as when condemnation proceedings are threatened or actually commenced, the principal purpose for holding property is investment.

---

[35] 34 TCM 631, CCH Dec. 33,192(M), T.C. Memo. 1975-137.

[36] *P.A. Miller*, 20 BTA 230, CCH Dec. 6170, Acq. X-1 CB 44.

[37] CA-4, 67-1 USTC ¶ 9181, 370 F.2d 568, cert. denied 389 U.S. 834, 88 S.Ct. 38.

[38] *Municipal Bond Corp.*, CA-8, 65-1 USTC ¶ 9247, 341 F.2d 683.

In *C.T. Au*,[39] the court held that a taxpayer did not hold property primarily for sale to customers in the ordinary course of business. The court noted that the taxpayer's stated purpose for acquiring the property was either the construction of a shopping center or its sale for a profit. In addition, the facts that the taxpayer was not a real estate dealer and that his entire income was derived from sources other than transactions in real estate suggested that the property was not held for sale. On the other hand, gain on the sale of six parcels of unimproved land from a larger tract of land was taxable as ordinary income (dealer property) because the taxpayer was engaged in the business of selling real estate, the taxpayer had held the property for the purpose of selling it and had sold numerous other parcels of land from the property over a period of many years, and the profits realized from the sale were contemplated in the ordinary operation of the taxpayer's business.[40]

In addition to the purpose test, other tests applied by the courts in deciding whether property is dealer property are:

1. The continuity of sales or sales-related activity over a period of time;
2. The number and frequency of sales;
3. The extent of sales activities such as developing or improving the property, soliciting customers, and advertising;
4. The volume of sales in relation to the taxpayer's other sources of income;
5. The desire to liquidate land acquired unexpectedly, such as by inheritance;
6. Reluctance on the part of the taxpayer to sell the property; and
7. The amount of the gain obtained on the sale.

Frequent sales and continuity of sales effort are often enough to tip the scales in favor of classifying property as dealer property, even in the absence of many other factors indicating dealer property.[41] In *B.B. Margolis*,[42] an individual engaged in buying and selling real estate on a broad basis was found to have held residential lots for sale in the ordinary course of business, even though they were acquired with the intent of holding them for a substantial period before sale. In the same case, however, commercial lots were found to have been held as an investment because they were acquired with the intent of converting the lots into income-producing properties.

---

[39] Cls. Ct., 84-1 USTC ¶ 9256, 4 Cls. Ct. 441.
[40] *Suburban Realty Co.*, CA-5, 80-1 USTC ¶ 9351, 615 F.2d 171, cert. denied 449 U.S. 920, 101 S.Ct. 318.
[41] *D.B. Goodman*, Ct. Cls., 68-1 USTC ¶ 9171, 390 F.2d 915, cert. denied 393 U.S. 824, 89 S.Ct. 87.
[42] CA-9, 64-2 USTC ¶ 9755, 337 F.2d 1001.

¶ 1013.1

If sales are infrequent, result from unsolicited offers, or are required by a change in circumstances, property is more likely to be treated as investment property than as dealer property.[43]

While normally adverse, an acquisition with the primary intent to resell may not result in the property's classification as dealer property if the taxpayer is not in the business of selling real estate.[44] Merely because the owner realizes at the outset that the property may be sold in the future does not mean that the property was acquired for sale.[45] In *Biedenharn*, the Court of Appeals found that a realty company derived ordinary income, not capital gain, from the sale of certain subdivided lots. The property was originally acquired for investment but was transformed into ordinary business property as a result of the substantiality and frequency of the company's sales over an extended period of time, the improvements it made, its solicitation and advertising efforts, and brokers' activities.

¶ 1013.2 *Subdivided Realty as Dealer Property*

Often an investor or other taxpayer acquires unimproved real estate with the intention of holding it for investment purposes or for use in a trade or business other than a real estate business but then subdivides and sells the property in lots or parcels. Although the property was not dealer property when it was acquired, the later sales of the lots or parcels closely resemble the sale of property in the ordinary course of business. Code Sec. 1237 provides a precise set of circumstances under which subdivided realty will not be treated as dealer property solely because of the subdivision. This statutory "safe harbor" is discussed at ¶ 1021. When Code Sec. 1237 does not apply, however, the taxpayer is faced with a conflicting collection of cases and rulings as to whether the mere fact that property is subdivided for sale creates dealer status.

The IRS has ruled that when sizable improvements are made to facilitate the sale of lots, the property becomes dealer property.[46] When one portion of a tract is subdivided and the remaining part is not, however, the taxpayer is not in the business of selling real estate as to the unsubdivided part.[47]

---

[43] *W.E. Starke*, CA-9, 63-1 USTC ¶ 9199, 312 F.2d 608. See also *South Texas Properties Co.*, 16 TC 1003, CCH Dec. 18,267, Acq. 1951-2 CB 4 (infrequent and unusual sales of unimproved property by a corporation organized to own and rent properties resulted in capital gain); *H.C. Martin*, DC Ga., 54-1 USTC ¶ 9157, 119 F.Supp. 468 (sales by a partnership engaged in the management and ownership of real estate were sales of capital assets where the property was sold only when it became unprofitable, the partnership wished to improve its holdings, or an unsolicited offer was too good to refuse).

[44] *G.W. Mitchell*, 47 TC 120, CCH Dec. 28,177, Nonacq. 1970-2 CB xxii.

[45] *Biedenharn Realty Co.*, CA-5, 76-1 USTC ¶ 9194, 526 F.2d 409, cert. denied 429 U.S. 819, 97 S.Ct. 64.

[46] Rev. Rul. 59-91, 1959-1 CB 15.

[47] Rev. Rul. 57-565, 1957-2 CB 546. See also *O. Patrick*, 60-1 USTC ¶ 9334, CA-7, 275 F.2d 437 (lots were held to be for sale in the ordinary course of

In *R. Herndon*,[48] the sale of subdivided farm property used by a real estate dealer as his summer home and for farming after his wife's illness was the liquidation of a capital asset and not a sale to customers in the ordinary course of his real estate business. Similarly, dealer status did not arise on the sales by a trust to liquidate lands acquired by gift.[49] On the other hand, taxpayers' desire to liquidate their investment in repossessed lots and lands acquired on tax sales did not prevent the sales from being classified as sales in the ordinary course of business.[50]

Land acquired by an attorney as a fee was held to be for sale in the ordinary course of business after he engaged a real estate company to develop, subdivide, and sell the land.[51] But an attorney who subdivided land and sold several lots over a period of years was found not to have made the sales in the ordinary course of business.[52]

When a taxpayer abandoned farming because of a lack of farm labor and sold lots, it was held that such sales were not dealer sales.[53] The same result was reached when a doctor bought a 160-acre farm with the intention of going into the dairy business but sold subdivided lots after deciding to liquidate the farmland holdings because of a serious illness.[54]

On the other hand, the sales of lots from farm land that was held by the taxpayer for 27 years, during which he neither bought nor sold any other property, were treated as made in the ordinary course of business.[55] See also *J.W. Kelley*,[56] in which it was held that subdivision and sales activities, including substantial improvements, in connection with ranch land after the taxpayer's ranching business failed were sufficient to make the taxpayer a real estate dealer.

¶ 1015   Tax Effects of Classification as a Dealer

When property is classified as dealer property, that is, property held primarily for sale in the ordinary course of business, there are two important tax effects. First, dealer property produces ordinary income or loss, not capital gain or loss. Second, the sale of dealer property, with a limited exception, may not be reported on the installment basis.

(Footnote Continued)

business where taxpayer originally acquired land for investment but later subdivided and built houses).

[48] 27 TCM 662, CCH Dec. 29,028(M), T.C. Memo. 1968-135.

[49] *A. Moore*, 30 TC 1306, CCH Dec. 23,188, Acq. 1959-1 CB 4.

[50] *W. Critzer Est.*, 13 TCM 1087, CCH Dec. 20,691(M), T.C. Memo. 1954-211; *W.J. Lewis, Jr.*, 13 TCM 1161, CCH Dec. 20,724(M), T.C. Memo. 1954-232.

[51] *W.N. Foster*, 2 TCM 595, CCH Dec. 13,425(M).

[52] *W.T. Minor, Jr.*, 18 TCM 14, CCH Dec. 23,404(M), T.C. Memo. 1959-4.

[53] *R.L. Harcum*, DC Va., 58-2 USTC ¶ 9684, 164 F.Supp. 650.

[54] *T. Berberovich v. Menninger*, DC Mich., 57-1 USTC ¶ 9390, 147 F.Supp. 890.

[55] *M.A. Nieman Est.*, 17 TCM 105, CCH Dec. 22,851(M), T.C. Memo. 1958-24.

[56] CA-9, 60-2 USTC ¶ 9635, 281 F.2d 527.

(Installment reporting for sales of real estate is considered in detail at ¶ 1401).

The increased capital gain preference enacted as part of the Taxpayer Relief Act of 1997, has increased the stakes in having gain property classified as nondealer property and loss property classified as dealer property.

¶ 1015.1 Dealer Installment Sales

In general, gain on any disposition of real property held for sale to customers in the ordinary course of business may not be reported under the installment method.[57] Certain exceptions, however, are provided, and installment reporting is permitted for sales to individuals in the ordinary course of business of:

1. Timeshare rights to use or timeshare ownership interests in residential real property for not more than six weeks, or rights to use specified campgrounds for recreational purposes; and
2. Residential lots, but only if the taxpayer (or any related person) is not to make improvements to the lots.[58]

Installment reporting is also available for sales of any property used or produced in the trade or business of farming.[59]

¶ 1015.2 Dealer Sales of Timeshares and Residential Lots

In the case of sales of timeshares and residential lots, installment reporting by a dealer is permitted only if the dealer elects to pay interest on the tax deferred by the use of the installment method.[60] This interest is added to the dealer's income tax. The amount of interest is based on the tax for the year attributable to installment payments received during the year and is calculated from the date of sale to the date the payments are received. The interest rate that is applied is the applicable federal rate, compounded semiannually, in effect at the time of the sale under the original issue discount rules (how this rate is set is explained at ¶ 331). No interest is assessed in the case of installment payments received in the year of sale. Any interest paid under this rule is treated as interest in determining the dealer's interest deduction.

¶ 1021 SUBDIVISION BY INVESTOR

Real estate that is held primarily for sale to customers in the ordinary course of business produces ordinary income on its sale. As discussed at ¶ 1013.2, this tax treatment may result when a larger parcel is subdivided and sold as separate lots or smaller parcels. There

---

[57] Code Sec. 453(b).
[58] Code Sec. 453(l)(2)(B).
[59] Code Sec. 453(l)(2)(A).
[60] Code Sec. 453(l)(3).

is, however, a special rule that assures an individual or taxpayer other than a C corporation capital gain treatment when a large tract is subdivided and sold.[61] This special rule is merely a safe harbor, and it does not determine whether or not real property is held primarily for sale in the ordinary course of business if its requirements are not met. Code Sec. 1237 does not apply to the conversion of rental units in an apartment building into condominiums and the sale of condominiums to the general public.[62]

When its conditions are met, Code Sec. 1237 provides that if there is no other substantial evidence that a taxpayer holds real estate primarily for sale to customers in the ordinary course of business, the taxpayer is not considered a real estate dealer holding it primarily for sale merely because the taxpayer has subdivided the tract into lots or parcels and engaged in advertising, promotion, selling activities, or the use of sales agents in connection with the sale of lots in the subdivision. The subdivision and selling activities are disregarded in determining the purpose for which a taxpayer held real property sold from a subdivision whenever these activities constitute the only substantial evidence that the taxpayer ever held the property primarily for sale to customers in the ordinary course of business.[63]

When other substantial evidence shows that the taxpayer held real property for sale to customers in the ordinary course of business, however, the taxpayer's activities in connection with the subdivision and sale of the property sold are taken into account in determining the purpose for which the taxpayer held both the subdivided property and any other real property. For example, other evidence may consist of the taxpayer's selling activities in connection with other property in prior years during which the taxpayer was engaged in subdividing or selling activities in connection with the subdivided tract, the taxpayer's intention in prior years (or at the time the subdivided property was acquired) to hold the tract primarily for sale, subdivision of other tracts in the same year, holding other real property for sale in the same year, or construction of a permanent real estate office which could be used in selling other real property. On the other hand, if the only evidence of the taxpayer's purpose in holding real property consisted of not more than one of the following, that would not be considered substantial other evidence:

1. Holding a real estate dealer's license;
2. Selling other real property that was clearly investment property;

---

[61] Code Sec. 1237.
[62] Rev. Rul. 80-216, 1980-2 CB 239.
[63] Reg. § 1.1237-1(a)(2).

¶ 1021

3. Acting as a salesman for a real estate dealer, but without any financial interest in the business; or
4. Mere ownership of other vacant real property without engaging in any selling activity whatsoever in connection with it.

If more than one of the above exists, the circumstances may or may not constitute substantial evidence that the taxpayer held real property for sale in the ordinary course of business, depending on the particular facts in each case.[64]

If a taxpayer meets the requirements of Code Sec. 1237, the gain on the sale of lots from a subdivision will be treated as capital gain except for up to five percent of the selling price, which is treated as ordinary income after five lots in the same tract have been sold.

¶ 1023 Qualification for Special Tax Treatment

Generally, any lot or parcel that is part of a tract of real property that is not owned by a C corporation (S corporations are eligible) is not treated as held primarily for sale to customers in the ordinary course of business at the time of sale merely because the owner subdivides the tract for sale or because of any activity incident to the subdivision, if the following requirements are met:

1. The tract or any part of the tract has not been held previously by the owner for sale in the ordinary course of business and, in the year of sale, the owner does not hold any other property for sale in the ordinary course of business (this automatically disqualifies real estate dealers);
2. No substantial improvements have been made by the owner while the property was held and no substantial improvements will be made under a contract of sale between the owner and the buyer; and
3. The property, except in the case of property acquired by inheritance, has been held by the owner for at least five years.[65]

If a taxpayer fails to meet the requirements of Code Sec. 1237, it does not necessarily imply that the taxpayer held property primarily for sale. Also, even if the requirements are met, Code Sec. 1237 does not apply if the property sold would not have been considered real property held primarily for sale in the ordinary course of business. Code Sec. 1237 has no application to losses realized on the sale of realty from subdivided property.[66]

---

[64] Reg. § 1.1237-1(a)(3).
[65] Code Sec. 1237(a).
[66] Reg. § 1.1237-1(a)(4). See also *R.E. Gordy*, 36 TC 855, CCH Dec. 24,982, Acq. 1964-1 CB (Part 14).

¶ 1023.1 Holding Period Rules

A taxpayer is considered as holding property that the taxpayer owns individually, jointly, or as a member of a partnership.[67] To apply Code Sec. 1237, the taxpayer must either have inherited the lot sold or have held it for five years. Generally, the holding period rules contained in Code Sec. 1223 apply to determine the period for which the taxpayer has held the property.

Example: An individual held a tract of land for three years under circumstances that would otherwise qualify for capital gain treatment under Code Sec. 1237. The individual made a gift of the tract to the Taxpayer at a time when the fair market value of the tract exceeded the donor's basis for the tract. The Taxpayer held the tract for two more years under similar circumstances. The Taxpayer then sold four lots from the tract. The Taxpayer is entitled to the benefits of Code Sec. 1237 since the lots were held for five years [68] and all other requirements of Code Sec. 1237 are met.

Although an individual is not considered to hold property that is held by family members, a taxpayer is considered to have made improvements made by family members while the tract was held by the taxpayer.[69]

Example: The Father held a tract of land for three years during which time he made substantial improvements that substantially enhanced the value of every lot on the tract. He then made a gift of the tract to his Son, who made no further improvements on the tract, but held it for three years and then sold several lots. The Son is not entitled to the benefits of Code Sec. 1237 because, under Code Sec. 1237(a)(2), the Son is deemed to have made the substantial improvements made by the Father, and under Code Sec. 1223(2) the Son is treated as having held the property for the period it was held by the Father. Accordingly, the disqualifying improvements are deemed to have been made by the Son while the tract was held by him. (Disqualifying improvements are discussed at ¶ 1023.2.)

¶ 1023.2 Improvements to Land Tracts

Sales of subdivided lots do not qualify under Code Sec. 1237 if the lots were substantially enhanced in value as a result of substantial improvements made anywhere on the tract by the taxpayer, or by anyone else pursuant to the contract of sale between the taxpayer and the buyer.[70] An improvement is considered to be made by the taxpayer

---

[67] Reg. § 1.1237-1(b)(3).
[68] See Code Sec. 1223(2) which provides for the tacking of holding period in the case of a gift.
[69] Reg. § 1.1237-1(c)(2)(i)(a).
[70] Code Sec. 1237(a)(2); Reg. § 1.1237-1(c)(3).

if, while the tract is held by the taxpayer, the improvement is made by a family member, by a corporation controlled by the taxpayer, an S corporation that includes the taxpayer as a shareholder, or by a partnership in which the taxpayer is a partner. Also, if an improvement is made by a lessee and the improvement is treated as rental income to the taxpayer, the improvement is deemed made by the taxpayer. If an improvement is made by the federal government, or a state or local government or political subdivision, and the improvement increases the taxpayer's basis (as in the case of a special assessment for a local benefit), the improvement is considered made by the taxpayer.[71]

Whether improvements substantially increase the value of a lot depends on the circumstances in each case. If improvements increase the value of a lot by 10 percent or less, the increase is not considered substantial, but if the value of the lot is increased by more than 10 percent, then all relevant factors are considered to determine whether the increase is substantial.[72] Improvements may increase the value of some lots in a tract without equally affecting other lots in the same tract. Only lots whose value is substantially increased are ineligible under Code Sec. 1237.[73] The improvement that enhances the value of the lots must itself be substantial to disqualify the lots under Code Sec. 1237. Among the improvements considered substantial are shopping centers, or other commercial or residential buildings, and the installation of hard surface roads or utilities such as sewers, water, gas, or electric lines. On the other hand, a temporary structure used as a field office, surveying, filling, draining, leveling and clearing operations, and the construction of minimum all-weather access roads, including gravel roads where required by the climate, are not substantial improvements.[74]

¶ 1023.3 *Necessary Improvements to Property After 10 Years*

After 10 years, certain necessary improvements, such as water, sewer, roads, etc., may be made to the property without disqualifying the property under Code Sec. 1237. The owner, however, must elect not to add the cost of the improvements to the tax basis in the land. Also, the owner must show that the property could not be marketed at the prevailing local price for similar building sites without the improvements.[75]

> ***Example:*** The Taxpayer, an individual, purchased land 15 years ago for $100 per acre and has just been offered $500 per acre for a tract of the land without roads, water, or sewer facilities. An adjacent tract has been subdivided and improved with water

---

[71] Code Sec. 1237(a)(2); Reg. § 1.1237-1(c)(2).
[72] Reg. § 1.1237-1(c)(3)(ii).
[73] Reg. § 1.1237-1(c)(3)(iii).
[74] Reg. § 1.1237-1(c)(4).
[75] Code Sec. 1237(b)(3); Reg. § 1.1237-1(c)(5).

facilities and roads, and has sold for $4,000 per acre. The estimated cost of roads and water facilities on the tract under consideration is $2,500 per acre. The prevailing local price for similar building sites in the vicinity is $1,500 per acre ($4,000 − $2,500). If the Taxpayer installs roads and water at a cost of $2,500 per acre, the tract would sell for about $4,000 per acre rather than the $500 that has been offered.

In this case, the Taxpayer can add the roads and water facilities and still qualify under Code Sec. 1237. However, if the tract is sold for $4,000 per acre, the Taxpayer's gain would be $3,900 ($4,000 − $100 tax basis). The Taxpayer cannot add the cost of the roads and water facilities to the tax basis and still qualify under Code Sec. 1237. If the Taxpayer does add the cost of the improvements to the basis, the property may be treated as property held for sale in the ordinary course of business (dealer property), and this would result in ordinary income in the amount of $1,400 per acre ($4,000 − $2,600 tax basis).

If the Taxpayer could sell the unimproved tract for $1,500 per acre without the improvements, rather than $500, any improvements would not be considered necessary improvements because the Taxpayer could obtain the prevailing local price without any improvement.

As can be seen from the example, qualifying under Code Sec. 1237 when substantial necessary improvements are made after 10 years is not necessarily an advantage. The inability to offset sale proceeds by the cost of the improvements, in fact, can create a substantial tax disadvantage when the tax preference for capital gain is not enough to offset the increased taxable gain.

¶ 1025 Calculation of the Amount and Character of Gain

When a subdivision qualifies under Code Sec. 1237, gain realized on the sale of lots is all capital gain until the year in which the sixth lot is sold. For the year in which the sixth lot is sold and all subsequent years, five percent of the selling price of the lots is treated as gain from the sale of property held primarily for sale to customers in the ordinary course of business, that is, ordinary income.[76]

¶ 1025.1 *Five-Percent Rule*

Under this rule, a subdivider who sells or exchanges only five lots or less in the first taxable year of the subdivision sales realizes all capital gain. If the subdivider sells or exchanges more than five lots or parcels in the first taxable year, then the amount by which five percent

---

[76] Code Sec. 1237(b)(1).

Development, Subdivision, and Sales

of the selling price of each lot exceeds the expenses incurred in its sale is ordinary income to the extent it represents gain.[77] In computing the number of lots or parcels sold, two or more contiguous lots sold to a single buyer in a single sale is counted as only one parcel.[78]

Note that an exchange is counted as a sale or exchange for determining if five lots or parcels have been sold, even if gain or loss is not recognized on the exchange. The "selling price" in the case of an exchange is the fair market value of property received plus any money received in exchange for the lot.[79]

Application of the five percent rule is illustrated in the following example taken from Reg. § 1.1237-1(e)(2).

Comprehensive Example: The selling price of the sixth lot of a tract is $10,000. The basis of the lot is $5,000, and the expenses of sale are $750. The sale is subject to Code Sec. 1237. On the sale, the subdivider realizes a gain of $4,250. The entire amount of this gain is capital gain, computed as follows:

Selling price		$10,000
Basis		5,000
Excess over basis		5,000
5% of selling price	$500	
Expenses of sale	750	
Ordinary income		0
Excess over basis		5,000
5% of selling price	500	
Excess expenses over 5% of selling price	250	750
Amount of gain from sale of property not held for sale in ordinary course of business		$ 4,250

Suppose, however, that the expenses of sale of the sixth lot were $300 rather than $750. In this case, the subdivider realizes a gain of $4,700 on the sale, and of this amount, $200 is ordinary income and $4,500 is gain from the sale of property not held for sale in the ordinary course of business, computed as follows:

Selling price		$10,000
Basis		5,000
Excess over basis		5,000
5% of selling price	$500	
Expenses of sale	300	
Ordinary income		200

---

[77] Reg. § 1.1237-1(e)(2)(ii).
[78] Reg. § 1.1237-1(e)(2)(i).
[79] Reg. § 1.1237-1(e)(2)(iii).

¶ 1025.1

Excess over basis		5,000
5% of selling price	500	
Excess expenses over 5% of selling price	0	500
Amount of gain from sale of property not held for sale in ordinary course of business		$ 4,500

¶ 1025.2 Five-Year Rule

If a subdivider does not sell or exchange any lots from the tract for a period of five years after the sale or exchange of at least one lot in the tract, then the remainder of the tract is treated as a new tract when counting the number of lots sold from the same tract under Code Sec. 1237(b)(1). The pieces in the new tract need not be contiguous, and the five-year period is measured between the dates of the sales or exchanges.[80] In other words, if five years elapse after the last sale of a lot, any new sales after the end of the five-year period are treated as if they are being made from a tract that is newly subdivided.

A "tract" is either a single piece of real property or two or more pieces of real property if they were contiguous at any time while held by the taxpayer, or would have been contiguous but for the interposition of a road, street, railroad, stream, or similar property. Properties are contiguous if their boundaries meet at one or more points. The single piece or contiguous properties need not have been conveyed by a single deed. The taxpayer may have assembled them over a period of time and may hold them separately, jointly, or as a partner, or in any combination of these forms of ownership.[81]

A subdivider selling lots in separate tracts applies the "sixth-lot rule" and the "five-year rule" to each tract independently of the sales or exchanges of lots from the other tract.

---

[80] Reg. § 1.1237-1(g)(2). [81] Reg. § 1.1237-1(g)(1).

Chapter 11

Passive Activity Loss Rules

¶ 1100 OVERVIEW OF CHAPTER

Before the Tax Reform Act of 1986, there were no general limitations placed on the ability of a taxpayer to use tax deductions from a particular activity to offset income from other activities. Also, most tax credits could be used to offset tax attributable to income from any of a taxpayer's activities. Without such limitations, taxpayers with substantial sources of income frequently invested in tax shelters that offered the opportunity to reduce or avoid tax liability by making available deductions and credits, often exceeding real economic costs, in advance of the income from the tax shelters.

In the wisdom of Congress, the passive activity loss rules[1] were adopted to limit sheltering activities. The passive activity loss rules, however, went beyond limiting traditional tax sheltering activities by limiting deductions for actual out-of-pocket expenses as well as deductions for noncash items such as depreciation and accrued but unpaid expenses. As they stand today, the passive activity loss rules may prevent the current recognition of real cash losses, as well as paper losses.

In concept, the passive activity loss rules are simple. Generally, under the rules, losses from "passive activities" can be used only to offset income from passive activities. Similarly, a tax credit generated by a passive activity can be used only to offset a tax liability attributable to a passive activity. Any loss or credit that cannot be used by a taxpayer because of the rules may be carried over to future years and applied to passive income (or tax liability attributable to passive income in the case of credits) in subsequent years. A loss attributable to a passive activity that remains unused at the time the taxpayer disposes of that activity may be deducted at that time.

While the concept of the passive activity loss rules may be simple to state, there is certainly no simplicity in their application, nor in the several hundred pages of Internal Revenue Code and Income Tax Regulations (with more to come) that attempt to explain the rules. Moreover, tracking losses and making sure disallowed losses are tied to

---
[1] Code Sec. 469.

the right activity to figure the proper deduction when a taxpayer disposes of a passive activity creates a recordkeeper's nightmare. In any event, taxpayers must deal with these rules. The material in this chapter tries to explain the important aspects of the passive loss rules as they might apply to the owner of real property, whether the real property is held for investment, as rental property, or for use in a trade or business.

¶ 1103 GENERAL PROVISIONS

In order to apply the passive activity loss rules, it is necessary to know what taxpayers are subject to the rules, the activities that are covered by the rules, and the concept of "material participation" that applies to most activities other than rental activities. It is generally the material participation by the taxpayer in an activity that separates a passive activity from a nonpassive activity.

Whenever the passive activity loss rules apply to an activity of a taxpayer, the taxpayer may lose the current benefit of any tax deductions and tax credits to which the taxpayer is entitled under other provisions of the Internal Revenue Code. These rules must be kept in mind whenever a taxpayer attempts to determine the value of a tax deduction or credit.

¶ 1105 Taxpayers Subject to the Rules

The passive activity loss rules apply to the following taxpayers:

1. Noncorporate taxpayers, including individuals, trusts (except to the extent governed by the grantor trust rules), and estates;
2. Closely held regular C corporations; and
3. Personal service corporations.[2]

The rules apply at the taxpayer level. Therefore, income, deductions, and credits from passthrough entities (partnerships and S corporations) are subject to the passive activity loss rules at the individual partner or shareholder level.

¶ 1105.1 *Closely Held C Corporations*

A closely held C corporation is subject to the passive activity loss rules, but a less stringent version applies if the corporation is not also a personal service corporation. A regular C corporation is closely held if, at any time during the last half of the tax year, more than 50 percent in value of the corporation's stock is owned by five or fewer individuals.[3]

---

[2] Code Sec. 469(a)(2).

[3] Code Sec. 469(j)(1).

Under a limited exception to the passive loss rules, a closely held C corporation, other than a personal service corporation, may use passive activity losses and credits to offset income from business operations, but not from portfolio income. Portfolio income is generally income from dividends, interest, annuities, and royalties, and is not considered passive income under the passive loss rules.[4]

The limited exception may be important for corporations that can take advantage of investments to produce passive losses for offsetting operating income. Closely held corporations, in the past, often served as tax shelters for their shareholders. Now, however, the top tax rate for corporations exceeds the top rate for individuals. Also, to get money out of a corporation now usually requires payment of a double tax, once at the corporate level and again at the shareholder level, and this further reduces the tax shelter potential of a closely held corporation. In this climate, many closely held corporations may find that passive activity investments are viable parking places for corporate funds that are not needed as working capital.

¶ 1105.2 *Personal Service Corporations*

Personal service corporations are subject to the passive activity loss rules. A corporation may be subject to the rules as both a closely held corporation and a personal service corporation. If this is the case, the limited exception to the rules that permits passive losses to offset operating income does not apply. A personal service corporation is a corporation that meets the following requirements:

1. It is a regular C corporation and not an S corporation;
2. The principal activity of the corporation is the performance of personal services;
3. The personal services are substantially performed by employee-owners; and
4. Employee-owners, in the aggregate, own more than 10 percent of the stock of the corporation.[5]

A person is an employee-owner of a personal service corporation if the person is an employee of the corporation and owns any of the outstanding stock of the corporation. Ownership of stock is determined under the constructive ownership rules of Code Sec. 318. Personal services include only services performed in the fields of health, law, engineering, architecture, accounting, actuarial science, performing arts, and consulting. Personal services are substantially performed by employee-owners if the corporation's compensation cost for personal

---

[4] Code Sec. 469(e)(1).   [5] Code Sec. 469(j)(2).

services performed by employee-owners is more than 20 percent of the corporation's total compensation cost for personal services.[6]

¶ 1107 Activities Subject to the Rules

Passive activities, that is, those subject to the passive activity loss rules, in most cases depend for their classification on the relationship of the taxpayer to the activities. It is quite possible for an activity conducted through a partnership to be a passive activity for some of the partners and an active or nonpassive activity for other partners. Under the general rule, an activity is passive if it involves a trade or business in which the taxpayer does not materially participate.[7]

Rental activities are subject to a special rule and are automatically classified as passive activities,[8] but there are two exceptions for rental real estate activities that may permit deductions generated by rental real estate to offset nonpassive activity income. First, a limited exception is provided in Code Sec. 469(i) for real estate activities in which a taxpayer actively participates, as discussed at ¶ 1131. Second, as discussed at ¶ 1133, the rental activities rule does not apply to any rental real estate activity of a taxpayer in the real property business as defined in Code Sec. 469(c)(7).

¶ 1107.1 Limited Partnership Interests

A limited partner, generally, does not take part in the management of the partnership and cannot actively participate in the limited partnership activity. Therefore, the ownership of a limited partnership interest is generally treated as a passive activity.[9] There are, however, four exceptions to the general rule provided by the regulations:

1. If the limited partner participates in the limited partnership activity for more than 500 hours during the year, the activity is not a passive activity;

2. If the limited partner materially participated in the activity for any five tax years, whether or not consecutive, during the 10 tax years immediately preceding the current tax year, the activity is not a passive activity;

3. If the activity of the partnership is a personal service activity and the limited partner materially participated in the activity for any three tax years, whether or not consecutive, preceding the current tax year, the activity is not a passive activity; and

---

[6] Temp. Reg. § 1.469-1T(g)(2) and Reg. § 1.441-3(c).
[7] Code Sec. 469(c)(1).
[8] Code Sec. 469(c)(2).
[9] Temp. Reg. § 1.469-5T(e)(1).

4. If the limited partner is also a general partner, the partner is not treated as a limited partner and the limited partnership rule does not apply.[10]

A special version of the passive activity loss rules applies to publicly traded partnerships and is discussed at ¶ 1151.

¶ 1107.2   Oil and Gas Property Working Interests

A working interest in an oil and gas property is not a passive activity if the taxpayer holds the interest directly or through an entity that does not limit the taxpayer's liability.[11] It does not matter whether or not the taxpayer materially participates. A working interest is a working or operating mineral interest in any tract or parcel of land within the meaning of Reg. § 1.612-4(a).[12]

The working interest exception to the passive activity rules does not apply to a working interest held through an entity that limits the taxpayer's liability. Holding an interest through the following forms of ownership will be considered an interest in an entity that limits the taxpayer's liability:

1. A limited partnership interest in a partnership in which the taxpayer is not a general partner;
2. Stock in a corporation; or
3. An interest in any entity other than a limited partnership or corporation that, under state law, limits the potential liability of the holder of an interest for all obligations of the entity to a determinable fixed amount, such as the amount of the holder's capital contributions.[13]

Protection against loss through an indemnification agreement, a stop-loss agreement, insurance, or any similar arrangement is not considered in determining whether a taxpayer holds a working interest through an entity that limits the taxpayer's liability.[14]

¶ 1109   Material Participation

In many cases, material participation in an activity determines whether or not the activity is subject to the passive activity loss rules. Material participation, however, is not relevant in many rental activities (see ¶ 1121) or when the activity involves a working interest in oil and gas property as discussed at ¶ 1107.2. A limited partner may or may not be affected by the material participation standard, as discussed at ¶ 1107.1. Generally, a trade or business in which a taxpayer

---

[10] Temp. Reg. § 1.469-5T(e)(2).
[11] Code Sec. 469(c)(3)(A).
[12] Reg. § 1.469-1(e)(4)(iv).
[13] Temp. Reg. § 1.469-1T(e)(4)(v)(A).
[14] Temp. Reg. § 1.469-1T(e)(4)(v)(B).

materially participates is not an activity subject to the passive loss rules.[15]

¶ 1109.1 *Material Participation by an Individual*

The regulations provide seven tests for determining material participation.[16] Material participation is established if the individual satisfies any one of the following tests:

1. The individual participates in the activity for more than 500 hours during the tax year.

2. The individual's participation in the activity for the tax year constitutes substantially all of the participation in the activity of all individuals, including individuals, such as employees, who are not owners (this test covers activities that do not require 500 hours to operate).

3. The individual participates in the activity for more than 100 hours during the tax year and the individual's participation in the activity is not less than the participation of any other individual, including individuals who are not owners (this test covers activities that do not require more than 500 hours by any one individual to operate).

4. The activity is a significant participation activity (the individual participates in the activity for more than 100 hours during the tax year but fails to satisfy any other test for material participation) and the individual's aggregate participation in all significant participation activities during the tax year exceeds 500 hours (this test treats individuals who participate in multiple activities equally with those who devote the same amount of time to one activity).

5. The individual materially participated in the activity for any five tax years, whether or not consecutive, during the 10 tax years immediately preceding the current tax year (this test recognizes that material participation over a long period of time usually represents more than a mere passive investment).

6. The activity involves the performance of personal services in the fields of health, law, engineering, architecture, accounting, actuarial science, performing arts, consulting, or any other trade or business in which capital is not a material income-producing factor, and the individual materially participated in the activity for any three tax years, whether or not consecutive, preceding the current tax year (this test recognizes that a personal service business in which the taxpayer materially

---

[15] Code Sec. 469(c)(1).   [16] Temp. Reg. § 1.469-5T(a).

participates over a period of time is likely to be the taxpayer's livelihood rather than a mere investment).

7. Based on all of the facts and circumstances, the individual participates in the activity on a regular, continuous, and substantial basis during the tax year. Under this test, an individual's management services are not considered if a paid manager participates in the activity or if someone else performs management services that exceed (based on hours) those performed by the individual.[17] Also, the test does not apply if an individual participates in an activity for less than 100 hours during the tax year.[18]

Generally, any work done by an individual in connection with an activity in which the individual owns an interest is considered participation in the activity. It does not matter in what capacity the individual does the work.[19] However, work done in connection with an activity is not counted as participation if the work is not the type that is customarily done by an owner and one of the principal purposes for doing the work is to avoid disallowance of a loss or credit under the passive activity loss rules.[20]

Work done in the capacity of an investor in an activity is not counted as participation in the activity. This type of work includes studying and reviewing financial statements or reports on operations of the activity, preparing or compiling summaries or analyses of the finances or operations of the activity for the individual's own use, and monitoring the finances or operations of the activity in a nonmanagerial capacity.[21]

The participation of an individual's spouse is combined with that of the individual in determining material participation by the individual. It does not matter whether the participating spouse owns an interest in the activity or whether the spouses file a joint return.[22]

¶ 1109.2 *Material Participation by a Corporation*

A closely held C corporation or personal service corporation materially participates in an activity if and only if:

1. One or more individuals, each of whom materially participates in the activity for the year, directly or indirectly hold in the aggregate more than 50 percent in value of the outstanding stock of the corporation, or

---

[17] Temp. Reg. § 1.469-5T(b)(2)(ii).
[18] Temp. Reg. § 1.469-5T(b)(2)(iii).
[19] Reg. § 1.469-5(f)(1).
[20] Temp. Reg. § 1.469-5T(f)(2)(i).
[21] Temp. Reg. § 1.469-5T(f)(2)(ii).
[22] Temp. Reg. § 1.469-5T(f)(3).

2. In the case of a closely held corporation, the corporation is considered an active business as defined for purposes of the at-risk rules in Code Sec. 465(c)(7)(C).[23]

In order to apply the significant participation test for determining material participation by a corporation in an activity, an activity is treated as a significant participation activity only if the corporation is not treated as materially participating in the activity for the tax year, and one or more individuals, each of whom significantly participates in the activity, directly or indirectly hold in the aggregate more than 50 percent in value of the outstanding stock of the corporation.[24] An individual is treated as materially participating or significantly participating in an activity for purposes of determining a corporation's material participation if the individual meets one of the seven tests set out above for individual material participation. In applying these tests, however, the following factors apply:

1. All activities of the corporation must be treated as activities in which the individual holds an interest to determine whether the individual participates in an activity of the corporation; and

2. The individual's participation in all activities other than activities of the corporation must be disregarded to determine whether the individual's participation in an activity of the corporation is material participation under the test for significant participation in multiple activities.[25]

¶ 1111 IDENTIFICATION OF SEPARATE ACTIVITIES

To apply the passive activity loss rules, taxpayers must determine just what constitutes an activity. The material participation standard is applied to each "activity." If several undertakings of the taxpayer are one activity, then the taxpayer must establish material participation only for the activity as a whole to avoid the passive loss rules. On the other hand, if several undertakings are separate activities, then the taxpayer must establish material participation for each separate activity. Also, knowing what constitutes an activity is important in determining whether a taxpayer has disposed of his entire interest or only a portion of an activity.

The IRS has issued regulations that define an activity for purposes of the passive activity loss rules.[26] The following discussion is based on those regulations and summarizes their application.

---

[23] Temp. Reg. § 1.469-1T(g)(3)(i).
[24] Temp. Reg. § 1.469-1T(g)(3)(ii).
[25] Temp. Reg. § 1.469-1T(g)(3)(iii).
[26] Reg. § 1.469-4.

¶ 1113 General Rule

One or more trade or business activities or rental activities may be treated as a single activity if the activities are an appropriate economic unit for the measurement of gain or loss under the passive activity loss rules.[27] Trade or business activities are activities, other than rental activities or activities that are treated under Reg. § 1.469-1T(e)(3)(vi)(B) (see ¶ 1123) as incidental to holding property for investment, that:

1. Involve the conduct of a trade or business;
2. Are conducted in anticipation of the beginning of a trade or business; or
3. Involve research or experimental expenditures that are deductible under Code Sec. 174 (or would be deductible if the taxpayer adopted the current expense method for R&E costs).[28]

An activity is a rental activity if tangible property held in connection with the activity is used by, or held for use by, customers, and the gross income from the activity represents amounts paid or to be paid primarily for the use of property.[29]

A taxpayer may use any reasonable method of applying relevant facts and circumstances in grouping activities. The IRS gives the factors listed below the greatest weight in determining whether activities are an appropriate economic unit for the measurement of gain or loss under the passive activity loss rules:

1. Similarities and differences in types of trades or businesses;
2. The extent of common control;
3. The extent of common ownership;
4. Geographical location; and
5. Interdependencies between or among the activities (for example, the extent to which the activities purchase or sell goods between or among themselves, involve products or services that are normally provided together, have the same customers, have the same employees, or are accounted for with a single set of books and records).[30]

Example: Taxpayer has a significant ownership interest in a bakery and a movie theater at a shopping mall in Baltimore and in a bakery and a movie theater in Philadelphia. After taking into account all the relevant circumstances, there may be more than

---

[27] Reg. § 1.469-4(c)(1).
[28] Reg. § 1.469-4(b)(1).
[29] Reg. § 1.469-4(b)(2).
[30] Reg. § 1.469-4(c)(2).

one reasonable method for grouping Taxpayer's activities. For instance, depending on the circumstances, the following groupings may or may not be allowed: a single activity; a movie theater activity and a bakery activity; a Baltimore activity and a Philadelphia activity; or four separate activities. Also, once Taxpayer groups the activities into appropriate economic units, Taxpayer generally must continue to use that grouping in later tax years unless a material change in circumstances makes it clearly inappropriate.

¶ 1115 Limitations on Grouping

The grouping of activities for the passive activity loss rules is subject to several limitations.

A rental activity may not be grouped with a trade or business activity unless the activities being grouped together are an appropriate economic unit (see ¶ 1113) and:

1. The rental activity is insubstantial in relation to the trade or business;

2. The trade or business is insubstantial in relation to the rental activity; or

3. Each owner of the trade or business has the same proportionate ownership interest in the rental activity, in which case the portion of the rental activity that involves the rental of items of property for use in the trade or business may be grouped with the trade or business.[31]

Example 1: Attorney is a sole practitioner in his hometown. Attorney also owns residential real estate in the town that he rents to third parties. Attorney's law practice is a trade or business and the residential real estate is a rental activity and is insubstantial in relation to Attorney's law practice. Under the circumstances, the law practice and the residential real estate are not an appropriate economic unit and Attorney may not treat the law practice and real estate as a single activity.

Example 2: Husband and Wife are married and file a joint return. Husband is the sole shareholder of an S corporation that runs a grocery store business. Wife is the sole shareholder of an S corporation that owns and rents out a building. Part of the building is rented to Husband's grocery store. The grocery store rental and the grocery store business are not insubstantial in relation to each other.

---

[31] Reg. § 1.469-4(d)(1).

Because they file a joint return, Husband and Wife are considered one taxpayer for the passive activity loss rules. The sole owner of the trade or business activity (the married couple) is also the sole owner of the rental activity. Each owner of the trade or business activity has the same proportionate ownership interest in the rental activity and the grocery store rental and the grocery store business may be grouped together into a single trade or business activity, if the grouping is otherwise appropriate (see ¶ 1113).

An activity that involves the rental of real property and an activity that involves the rental of personal property (other than personal property provided in connection with the real property or real property provided in connection with the personal property) may not be treated as a single activity.[32]

A taxpayer who owns an interest as a limited partner or limited entrepreneur in an activity described in Code Sec. 465(c)(1), which deals with the at-risk rules (see ¶ 311), may not group that activity with any other activity. A taxpayer who owns an interest as a limited partner or a limited entrepreneur in a Code Sec. 465(c)(1) activity may group that activity with another activity in the same type of business if the grouping is otherwise appropriate as discussed at ¶ 1113.[33]

Example: Individual owns and operates a farm. Individual is also a member of a limited liability company (LLC) that conducts a cattle-feeding business, but does not actively participate in the management of the LLC. Individual is also a limited partner in an oil and gas production limited partnership.

Because Individual does not actively participate in the management of the LLC, Individual is a limited entrepreneur in the LLC's activity. The cattle-feeding business is described in Code Sec. 465(c)(1)(B) and may not be grouped with any other activity that does not involve farming. Further, Individual's farm may not be grouped with the cattle-feeding activity unless the grouping is an appropriate economic unit for the measurement of gain or loss.

Because Individual is a limited partner and the partnership's oil and gas activity is described in Code Sec. 465(c)(1)(D), Individual may not group the partnership's oil and gas activity with any other activity that does not involve oil and gas. The partnership's activity may not be grouped with Individual's farm or with LLC's cattle-feeding business.

A C corporation subject to the passive activity loss rules, an S corporation, or a partnership (a Sec. 469 entity) must group its activi-

---

[32] Reg. § 1.469-4(d)(2).   [33] Reg. § 1.469-4(d)(3).

¶ 1115

ties under the grouping rules. Once the Sec. 469 entity groups its activities, a shareholder or partner may group those activities with each other, with activities conducted directly by the shareholder or partner, and with activities conducted through other Sec. 469 entities under the grouping rules. A shareholder or partner may not treat activities grouped together by a Sec. 469 entity as separate activities.[34]

¶ 1117 Regrouping

Once a taxpayer has grouped activities for the passive activity loss rules, the taxpayer generally may not regroup those activities in later tax years. Taxpayers must comply with disclosure requirements that the IRS may prescribe for both their original groupings and the addition and disposition of specific activities within those chosen groupings in later tax years. If a taxpayer determines that the original grouping clearly was inappropriate or if a material change in circumstances occurs that makes the original grouping clearly inappropriate, however, the taxpayer must regroup the activities and must comply with disclosure requirements that the IRS may prescribe.[35]

The IRS may regroup a taxpayer's activities if any of the activities resulting from the grouping is not an appropriate economic unit and a principal purpose of the taxpayer's grouping, or failure to regroup, is to circumvent the underlying purposes of the passive activity loss rules.[36]

For the tax year in which there is a disposition of substantially all of an activity, a taxpayer may treat the part disposed of as a separate activity, but only if the taxpayer can establish with reasonable certainty: (1) the amount of deductions and credits allocable to that part of the activity for the tax year under Reg. § 1.469-1(f)(4), and (2) the amount of gross income and of any other deductions and credits allocable to that part of the activity for the tax year.[37]

¶ 1121 LIMITS ON RENTAL ACTIVITIES

A rental activity generally is classified as a passive activity regardless of the taxpayer's level of participation in the activity.[38] This sometimes, but not always, makes classification of an activity as a rental activity disadvantageous for a person who participates in the activity. There are, however, occasions when classification of an activity as a rental activity producing passive income may be advantageous: for instance, when a taxpayer has passive losses that may be used to offset the income. In these situations, taxpayers would be inclined to rearrange their business or investment holdings in an effort to produce passive income. So, in addition to the rules defining rental activities as

---

[34] Reg. § 1.469-4(d)(5).
[35] Reg. § 1.469-4(e).
[36] Reg. § 1.469-4(f).
[37] Reg. § 1.469-4(g).
[38] Code Sec. 469(c)(2).

passive activities, there are rules that block such a classification in certain situations and require that the income produced be treated as income that is not from a passive activity.

In the case of real estate, there are special rules that create two exceptions to the general rule that all rental activities are passive activities. First, a limited exception is provided in Code Sec. 469(i) for real estate activities in which a taxpayer actively participates, as discussed at ¶ 1131. Second, as discussed at ¶ 1133, the rental activities rule does not apply to any rental real estate activity of a taxpayer in the real property business as defined in Code Sec. 469(c)(7). In other situations, even if a taxpayer can show that a particular activity is not a rental activity, the taxpayer still must show material participation, as discussed at ¶ 1109.1, to avoid the passive activity loss rules.

¶ 1123 Rental Activity Defined

An activity is considered a rental activity if tangible property held in connection with the activity is used by, or held for use by, customers, and the gross income from the activity represents amounts paid or to be paid primarily for the use of property.[39] If any one of the following six tests is met, the activity will not be considered to be a rental activity:

1. The average period of customer use of the rental property is seven days or less. This test excludes short-term use of hotel and motel rooms from the passive loss rules.

2. The average period of customer use is 30 days or less and significant personal services are provided by or on behalf of the owner. Whether services are significant is based on factors such as their frequency, their value relative to the amount charged for the use of the property, and the type and amount of labor required. Services are not significant if they (a) are necessary to permit lawful use of the property, (b) are for construction, improvements or repairs that extend the life of the property substantially beyond the average period customers use the property, or (c) are similar to those commonly provided in connection with long-term rentals of high-grade commercial or residential real property, such as cleaning of common areas, routine repairs, trash collection, elevator service, and entrance or perimeter security.[40]

3. Extraordinary personal services are provided by or on behalf of the owner, even if the average period of customer use is greater than 30 days. Services are extraordinary only if they

---

[39] Temp. Reg. § 1.469-1T(e)(3).   [40] Temp. Reg. § 1.469-1T(e)(3)(iv).

are performed by individuals and the use of the property by customers is incidental to the services. For example, boarding facilities at a hospital are incidental to the personal services of the hospital staff, or boarding facilities at a school are incidental to the services of the teaching staff.[41]

4. The rental of the property is treated as incidental to a nonrental activity. This test applies to rentals of property that are incidental to the holding of property for investment, the use of property in a trade or business activity, or the holding of property for sale to customers in the ordinary course of business. (See further discussion at ¶ 1123.1.)

5. The property is customarily made available during defined hours of business for the nonexclusive use of customers. This test excludes the operation of facilities such as golf courses that are used by customers.

6. Property is provided to a partnership, S corporation, or joint venture in which the taxpayer holds an interest, if the property is provided in the taxpayer's capacity as owner rather than rented to the entity. (See further discussion at ¶ 1123.2.)

The following example illustrates the application of the significant services and extraordinary services tests (see tests 2 and 3 above).

Example: The Taxpayer is engaged in an activity of owning and operating a residential apartment hotel. For the taxable year, the average period of customer use for apartments exceeds seven days but does not exceed 30 days. In addition to cleaning public entrances, exits, stairways, and lobbies, and collecting and removing trash, the Taxpayer provides a daily maid and linen service at no additional charge. All of the services, other than the maid and linen services, are similar to those commonly provided in connection with long-term rentals of high-grade residential real property. The value of the maid and linen services, measured by the cost to the Taxpayer of employees performing these services, is less than 10 percent of the amount charged to tenants for occupancy of apartments. Under these facts, the Taxpayer provides neither significant personal services (test 2) nor extraordinary personal services (test 3) in connection with making the apartments available for use by customers. Accordingly, the activity is a rental activity.

Additional examples may be found in the regulations at Temp. Reg § 1.469-1T(e)(3)(viii).

---

[41] Temp. Reg. § 1.469-1T(e)(3)(v).

¶ 1123.1 Rentals Incidental to Nonrental Activities

The rental of property that is incidental to a nonrental activity is not considered a rental activity. This exception applies to rentals of property that are incidental to holding property for investment, the use of property in a trade or business activity, or holding property for sale to customers in the ordinary course of business.[42]

The rental of property is incidental to the activity of holding the property for investment only if:

1. The principal purpose for holding the property is to realize gain from the appreciation of the property; and
2. The gross rental income from the property for the taxable year is less than two percent of the unadjusted basis of the property or the fair market value of the property, whichever is less.

The rental of property is incidental to a trade or business activity only if:

1. The taxpayer owns an interest in the trade or business during the taxable year;
2. The property was predominantly used in the trade or business during the taxable year or during at least two of the five tax years immediately preceding the current year; and
3. The gross rental income from the property for the taxable year is less than two percent of the unadjusted basis of the property or the fair market value of the property, whichever is less.

Lodging provided to an employee or an employee's spouse or dependents for the convenience of the employer (within the meaning of Code Sec. 119) is incidental to the activity of the taxpayer in which the employee performs services.[43]

Example 1: The Taxpayer owns 1,000 acres of unimproved land with a fair market value of $350,000 and an unadjusted basis of $210,000. The Taxpayer holds the land for the principal purpose of realizing gain from appreciation. In order to defray the cost of carrying the land, the Taxpayer leases the land to a rancher for grazing cattle. The rancher pays $4,000 per year as rent. The gross rental income from the land is less than two percent of the lesser of the fair market value and the unadjusted basis of the land (2% × $210,000 = $4,200). The rental of the land is not a rental activity because the rental is incidental to holding the property for investment.

---

[42] Temp. Reg. § 1.469-1T(e)(3)(vi).   [43] Reg. § 1.469-1(e)(3)(vi)(D).

Example 2: In 2002, the Taxpayer acquires vacant land for the purpose of constructing a shopping mall. Before beginning construction, the Taxpayer leases the land under a one-year lease to an automobile dealer who uses the land to park cars held in inventory. The Taxpayer begins construction in 2003.

The Taxpayer acquired the land for the principal purpose of constructing the shopping mall, not for the principal purpose of realizing gain from the appreciation of the property. The rental of the property in 2002 is not incidental to holding the property for investment. Also, since the land has not been used in any trade or business of the Taxpayer, the rental of the property in 2002 is not treated as incidental to a trade or business activity. Since the rental of the property in 2002 is not incidental to a nonrental activity of the Taxpayer, the rental of the land in 2002 is a rental activity.

A special rule relating to the treatment of income from the rental of nondepreciable property is discussed at ¶ 1129.

¶ 1123.2   Property Provided to a Partnership, Joint Venture, or S Corporation

Providing property to a partnership, joint venture, or S corporation conducting an activity other than a rental activity in which the taxpayer holds an interest is not a rental activity if the property is provided in the taxpayer's capacity as owner rather than rented to the entity.[44] For instance, if a partner contributes the use of property to a partnership, none of the partner's distributive share of partnership income is income from a rental activity unless the partnership is engaged in a rental activity. In addition, a partner's gross income attributable to a guaranteed payment is not income from a rental activity under any circumstances.[45] The determination of whether property used in an activity is provided by the taxpayer in the capacity as owner of an interest in a partnership, S corporation, or joint venture is made on the basis of all of the facts and circumstances.

Example: The Taxpayer makes farmland available to a tenant farmer under an arrangement designated a "crop-share lease." Under the arrangement, the tenant is required to use his best efforts to farm the land and produce marketable crops. The Taxpayer is obligated to pay 50 percent of the costs incurred in the activity, regardless of whether crops are successfully produced or marketed, and is entitled to 50 percent of the crops produced or 50 percent of the proceeds from marketing the crops. The Taxpayer is

---

[44] Reg. § 1.469-1(e)(3)(vii).   [45] Temp. Reg. § 1.469-2T(e)(2).

providing the farmland for use in a farming activity conducted by a joint venture in the capacity as an owner of an interest in the joint venture. The Taxpayer is not engaged in a rental activity, regardless of whether the Taxpayer performs any services in the farming activity.

¶ 1125 Self-Rented Property

An amount of the taxpayer's gross rental activity income for the taxable year from an item of property equal to the net rental activity income for the year from the property is treated as not from a passive activity if the property is rented for use in a trade or business activity in which the taxpayer materially participates and the property is not rented incident to development as discussed below.[46] This rule is aimed primarily at situations in which a taxpayer conducts a trade or business that must make use of property, typically real estate, that may be owned or leased. For instance, an individual may run a retail operation as a corporation, but own the store from which the operation is conducted in the individual's name. If the rental of the store to the corporate business produced passive income, the taxpayer would be able to offset that income with passive losses. At the same time, the rent deduction for the corporation would reduce its regular taxable operating income. Reg. § 1.469-2(f)(6) prevents this by, in effect, converting the otherwise passive income from the rental into nonpassive income so that the taxpayer cannot shelter this rental income with passive losses from other activities.

¶ 1127 Rental Incident to Development

Generally, a rental activity is a passive activity and gain from the sale or disposition of property used in a passive activity is treated as passive activity income.[47] A taxpayer that materially or significantly participates in the development of property that is rented during the year of its sale, however, may have nonpassive income in the year of the sale.[48] Net rental activity income from the rental or sale of property used in a rental activity for the taxable year is not treated as passive income if the following three conditions are met:

1. The taxpayer recognizes gain from the sale, exchange, or other disposition of the property for the taxable year;
2. The use of the property in a rental activity began less than 24 months before the date of disposition of the property;[49] and
3. The taxpayer materially participated or significantly participated (as defined at ¶ 1109 above) for any taxable year in an

---

[46] Reg. § 1.469-2(f)(6).
[47] Temp. Reg. § 1.469-2T(c)(2).
[48] Reg. § 1.469-2(f)(5).
[49] Rental begins when substantially all of the property is first held out for rent and is in a state or readiness for rental; Reg. § 1.469-2(f)(5)(ii).

activity that involved the performance of services for the purpose of enhancing the value of the property.

Services that enhance the value of property include, but are not limited to, construction, renovation, and lease-up as long as the taxpayer acquires an interest in the property before a substantial portion of the property is leased.[50]

Example: The Taxpayer, a calendar-year individual, is a partner in Partners, a calendar-year partnership which develops commercial real estate. In 2000, Partners acquires undeveloped land and arranges for the financing and construction of an office building on the land. Construction is completed in February 2002, and substantially all of the building is held out for rent and is in a state of readiness for rental beginning on March 1, 2002.

Partners holds the building for rent for the remainder of 2002 and all of 2003, and sells the building on January 15, 2004, under a contract that was signed on January 15, 2003. Partners did not hold out the office building or any other building for sale to customers in the ordinary course of business. The Taxpayer's share of Partners' taxable losses from the rental of the building is $50,000 for 2002 and $30,000 for 2003. All of the Taxpayer's losses from the rental building are disallowed passive activity losses. The Taxpayer's share of the gain recognized by Partners on the sale of the building is $150,000. The Taxpayer has no other income or deductions from the activity of renting the building.

In 2000, 2001, and 2002, the real estate development activity that the Taxpayer holds through Partners involves the performance of services for the purpose of enhancing the value of the building. The date on which the use of the building in the rental activity began was less than 12 months before the date on which a binding contract for the sale was executed. If the Taxpayer materially participated in the real estate development activity in 2000, 2001, or 2002, regardless of whether the Taxpayer materially participated in the activity in more than one of those years, an amount of the Taxpayer's gross rental activity income for 2004 from the building equal to the Taxpayer's net rental activity income for 2004 from the building ($150,000 − $80,000 of previously disallowed losses = $70,000) is gross income that is not from a passive activity.

---

[50] Reg. § 1.469-2(f)(5)(iii).

¶ 1129 Rental of Nondepreciable Property

Income from the rental of nondepreciable property is not treated as passive activity income but as portfolio income. Property is nondepreciable if less than 30 percent of its unadjusted basis is subject to depreciation. Unadjusted basis is adjusted basis determined without regard to any adjustments under Code Sec. 1016 that decrease basis.[51] This rule primarily affects ground rents and other rentals of undeveloped land.

Example: The Taxpayer is a limited partner in a partnership. The partnership acquires vacant land for $300,000, constructs improvements on the land at a cost of $100,000, and leases the land and improvements to a tenant. The partnership then sells the land and improvements for $600,000, thereby realizing a gain on the disposition. The unadjusted basis of the improvements ($100,000) equals 25 percent of the unadjusted basis of all property ($400,000) used in the rental activity. Therefore, an amount of the Taxpayer's gross income from the activity equal to the net passive income from the activity, which is computed by taking into account the gain from the disposition including gain allocable to the improvements, is treated as not from a passive activity.

¶ 1131 Active Participation in Rental Real Estate

A limited exception to the passive activity loss rules is available to an individual taxpayer for rental real estate in which the individual "actively participates." [52] The active participation standard requires much less participation on the part of the taxpayer than the material participation standard that generally applies under the passive loss rules. The taxpayer, however, must participate in the making of management decisions or arrange for others to provide services such as repairs in a significant and bona fide sense. The active participation requirement does not apply, however, to rehabilitation and low-income housing tax credits.[53]

An individual is not considered to actively participate, regardless of the actual level of participation, if the individual and spouse together own less than 10 percent of the value of all interests in the activity (Code Sec. 469(i)(6)). Also, the active participation requirement precludes investing as a limited partner in order to realize tax deductions in excess of income from passive activities. The exception does permit deductions from real estate against nonpassive income for individual owners and investors who participate in the rental activity

---

[51] Temp. Reg. § 1.469-2T(f)(3).
[52] Code Sec. 469(i).
[53] Code Sec. 469(i)(6)(B).

through a general partnership or S corporation, provided they meet the 10 percent ownership requirement.

¶ 1131.1 *$25,000 Limit*

Under the exception to the passive activity loss rules for rental real estate in which an individual actively participates, up to $25,000 of losses and credits, in a deduction equivalent sense, may be used to offset nonpassive income.[54] The $25,000 amount is applied by first netting income and loss from all real estate activities in which the taxpayer actively participates. If there is a net loss from these activities, net passive income, if any, from other activities is then applied against the net loss in determining the amount eligible for the $25,000 deduction.

¶ 1131.2 *Filing Status*

The exception is generally available to single individuals and married taxpayers who file joint returns. Married individuals who file separate returns are not eligible for the exception, unless they lived apart at all times during the tax year. Married individuals living apart and filing separate returns each may qualify for up to $12,500 in deductions.[55]

¶ 1131.3 *Phase-Out of Deduction*

The maximum $25,000 deduction under the exception to the passive activity loss rules for rental real estate is reduced for higher income individuals. The $25,000 amount is reduced by 50 cents for each dollar of adjusted gross income in excess of $100,000. Individuals with incomes in excess of $150,000, therefore, cannot benefit from the exception to the passive activity loss rules for active participation in rental real estate.[56] The dollar amounts for the phase-out, as with the $25,000 limit itself, are cut in half for married individuals living apart who file separate returns.

In the case of a rehabilitation credit determined under Code Sec. 47, the phase-out starts at $200,000 rather than $100,000. Further, there is no phase-out for a passive activity loss attributable to the commercial revitalization deduction under Code Sec. 1400I or the low-income housing credit under Code Sec. 42. Ordering rules to reflect those exceptions and separate phase-out are contained in Code. Sec. 469(i)(3)(E).

For purposes of computing the reduction in the $25,000 limit for individuals with adjusted gross income in excess of $100,000, adjusted

---

[54] Code Sec. 469(i)(2).
[55] Code Sec. 469(i)(5).
[56] Code Sec. 469(i)(3).

gross income is computed without regard to any passive activity loss, taxable social security or railroad retirement benefits, or deductions made for contributions to an individual retirement account.[57]

¶ 1133 Real Property Business Exception

Rental real estate activities of qualifying taxpayers, generally those in a real property business, are not subject to the rule that treats all rental activities as passive.[58] As a result, a real estate activity of a qualifying taxpayer is not passive if the taxpayer materially participates in the activity. Further, each of a qualifying taxpayer's interests in rental real estate is treated as a separate activity unless the taxpayer elects to treat all interests in real estate as a single activity.[59]

To qualify for the real property business exception to the rule that treats all rental activities as passive, a taxpayer must perform:

1. More than one-half of the personal services performed in trades or businesses during the tax year in real property trades or businesses in which the taxpayer materially participates; and

2. More than 750 hours of services during the tax year in real property trades or businesses in which the taxpayer materially participates.[60]

In the case of a joint return, the requirements are satisfied if and only if either spouse separately satisfies the requirements. For a closely held C corporation, the requirements are met if more than 50 percent of the gross receipts of the corporation are derived from real property trades or businesses in which the corporation materially participates.[61] Personal services performed as an employee do not count, unless the employee is a 5-percent owner.

A real property trade or business is any real property development, redevelopment, construction, reconstruction, acquisition, conversion, rental, operation, management, leasing, or brokerage trade or business.[62]

For any tax year in which a qualifying taxpayer materially participates in a rental real estate activity, that activity is treated as a former passive activity if disallowed deductions or credits are allocated to the activity.[63]

---

[57] Code Sec. 469(i)(3)(D).
[58] Code Sec. 469(c)(7).
[59] Code Sec. 469(c)(7)(A)(ii).
[60] Code Sec. 469(c)(7)(B).
[61] Code Sec. 469(c)(7)(D).
[62] Code Sec. 469(c)(7)(C).
[63] Reg. § 1.469-9(e)(2).

¶ 1133.1 *Grouping Rental Real Estate Activities*

A taxpayer who qualifies for the real estate business exception to the passive activity loss rules may not group a rental real estate activity with any other activity. For instance, if a qualifying taxpayer develops real property, constructs buildings, and owns an interest in rental real estate, the taxpayer's interest in rental real estate may not be grouped with the taxpayer's development activity or construction activity. This means that only the participation of the taxpayer as to the rental real estate may be used to determine if the taxpayer materially participates in the rental real estate activity.[64]

A qualifying taxpayer may participate in a rental real estate activity through participation in the management of rental real estate, even if this management activity is conducted through a separate entity. In determining whether the taxpayer materially participates in the rental real estate activity, however, work the taxpayer performs in the management activity is taken into account only to the extent it is performed in managing the taxpayer's own rental real estate interest.[65]

Example: Taxpayer owns interests in three rental buildings, X, Y, and Z. In 2002, Taxpayer has $30,000 of disallowed passive losses allocable to building X, and $10,000 allocable to building Y. In 2003, Taxpayer has $5,000 of net income from building X, $5,000 of net losses from building Y, and $10,000 of net income from building Z. In 2003, Taxpayer is a qualifying taxpayer for the real property business exception. Each building is treated separately unless Taxpayer elects to treat them as a single rental real estate activity. If the buildings are treated as separate activities, material participation is determined separately for each building. If Taxpayer elects to treat the buildings as a single activity, all participation relating to the buildings is aggregated to determine whether Taxpayer materially participates in the combined activity.

Assume Taxpayer elects to treat the buildings as a single activity in 2003 and works full-time managing the buildings so that he materially participates in the combined activity. The combined activity is not a passive activity in 2003, and the disallowed passive losses from 2002 of $40,000 are allocated to the combined activity. Taxpayer's net income from the rental real estate activity for 2003 is $10,000, and this net income is nonpassive income. Because the three buildings are treated as one activity and this activity is a former passive activity, however, Taxpayer may offset the $10,000 of net income from the buildings with an

---

[64] Reg. § 1.469-9(e)(3)(i).   [65] Reg. § 1.469-9(e)(3)(ii).

equal amount of disallowed passive losses allocable to the buildings, regardless of which building produced the income or losses. Taxpayer has $30,000 of disallowed passive losses remaining from the buildings after 2003.

¶ 1133.3 *Limited Partnership Interests*

If a taxpayer elects to treat all interests in rental real estate as a single rental activity, and at least one interest is held as a limited partnership interest, the combined rental real estate activity is treated as a limited partnership interest in order to determine material participation.[66] What this means is that the taxpayer will not be treated as materially participating in the combined rental real estate activity unless the taxpayer materially participates in the activity under the tests for determining material participation by a limited partner and set out at ¶ 1107.1.

If a taxpayer elects to treat all interests in rental real estate as a single rental activity, and the taxpayer's share of gross rental income from all of the taxpayer's limited partnership interests in rental real estate is less than 10 percent of the taxpayer's share of gross rental income from all interests in rental real estate, the taxpayer may determine material participation under any of the tests that apply to rental real estate activities.[67]

¶ 1133.5 *Coordination with Active Participation Exception*

Passive losses and credits from rental real estate activities are allowed to a limited extent when the taxpayer actively participates in the activity (see ¶ 1131). The amount of losses or credits that are allowed under that exception is determined after the exception for a rental real estate business is applied. Losses allowed by the rental real estate business exception, however, are not taken into account to determine adjusted gross income for the phase-out of the limited $25,000 exception for active participation (see ¶ 1131.3).[68]

Example: Taxpayer owns two rental buildings, X and Y. In 2003, Taxpayer qualifies for the rental real estate business exception to the passive activity loss rules, but does not elect to treat the two buildings as a single activity. Taxpayer materially participates in building X that has $100,000 of disallowed losses from prior years and produces $20,000 of losses in 2003. Taxpayer does not materially participate in building Y that produces $40,000 of income in 2003. Taxpayer also has $50,000 of nonpassive income from other sources in 2003.

---

[66] Reg. § 1.469-9(f)(1).
[67] Reg. § 1.469-9(f)(2).
[68] Reg. § 1.469-9(j).

For 2003, Taxpayer may use the $20,000 of losses produced by building X to offset part of the $50,000 of nonpassive income. This leaves Taxpayer with $30,000 of nonpassive income. Also, Taxpayer may offset the $40,000 of passive income from building Y with $40,000 of the prior years' $100,000 of disallowed passive losses from building X. Because Taxpayer still has $60,000 of passive losses remaining from building X and meets the requirements for the exception for active participation in rental real estate, Taxpayer may offset up to $25,000 of nonpassive income (the limit under the active participation exception) with passive losses from building X. The final result leaves Taxpayer with $5,000 of nonpassive income and disallowed passive losses from building X of $35,000 in 2003.

¶ 1141 TAX TREATMENT OF PASSIVE LOSSES AND CREDITS

If the passive activity loss rules apply to one or more activities, the taxpayer faces the hurdle of computing the deductible loss, if any, and the extent to which any tax credit generated by a passive activity may be used to offset tax liability. Generally, losses from passive activities can be used only to offset income from passive activities and a tax credit generated by a passive activity can be used only to offset tax liability attributable to a passive activity.

¶ 1143 Computation of Deductible Loss

A passive activity loss is not deductible.[69] A passive activity loss, in the case of a taxpayer other than a closely held corporation, is the amount by which the passive activity deductions exceed the passive activity gross income for the taxable year.[70] In order to compute the passive activity loss, then, it is necessary to first compute passive activity gross income and passive activity deductions. Since a closely held corporation may use passive losses to offset operating income, a modified computation, as discussed below, is required.

¶ 1143.1 *Passive Activity Gross Income*

Passive activity gross income for a taxable year includes an item of gross income only if the income is from a passive activity.[71]

Portfolio Income

Passive activity income does not include portfolio income.[72] Portfolio income is all gross income, other than income derived in the ordinary course of business, that is derived from the following sources:

---

[69] Code Sec. 469(a)(1)(A).
[70] Temp. Reg. § 1.469-2T(b)(1).
[71] Temp. Reg. § 1.469-2T(c)(1).
[72] Temp. Reg. § 1.469-2T(c)(3)(i).

1. Interest, annuities, royalties, dividends on C corporation stock, and income from a real estate investment trust, regulated investment company, real estate mortgage investment conduit, common trust fund, controlled foreign corporation, qualified electing fund (described in Code Sec. 1295(a)), or cooperative;
2. Dividends on S corporation stock that exceed the corporation's accumulated adjustment account but not earnings and profits;
3. Gain or loss attributable to the disposition of any property that produces income of the types described in 1, and
4. Gain or loss on the disposition of property held for investment.

If income falls into any of the classifications above but is derived in the ordinary course of a trade or business, it is not considered portfolio income. Gross income derived in the ordinary course of a trade or business includes only the following:

1. Interest income on loans and investments made in the ordinary course of a trade or business. For example, interest on mortgage loans received by a mortgage company would not be portfolio income.
2. Interest on accounts receivable arising from the performance of services or the sale of property in the ordinary course of a trade or business of performing the services or selling the property, but only if credit is customarily offered to customers of the business.
3. Income from investments made in the ordinary course of a trade or business of furnishing insurance or annuity contracts or reinsuring risks underwritten by insurance companies.
4. Income or gain derived in the ordinary course of an activity of trading or dealing in any property if the activity constitutes a trade or business. A dealer's income or gain is not business income, and is therefore portfolio income, however, if the income or gain is from property that the dealer held for investment at any time before the income or gain is recognized.
5. Royalties derived by the taxpayer in the ordinary course of a trade or business of licensing intangible property, but only if the taxpayer created the property or performed substantial services or incurred substantial costs to develop or market the property.[73]

---

[73] Temp. Reg. § 1.469-2T(c)(3)(iii)(B).

¶ 1143.1

6. Amounts included in the gross income of a patron of a cooperative for any payment or allocation to the patron based on patronage occurring with respect to a trade or business of the patron.

7. Other income identified by the IRS as income from a trade or business.

See Temp. Reg. § 1.469-2T(c)(3)(ii).

Example 1: A partnership operates a rental apartment building for low-income tenants. Under local law, the partnership is required to maintain a reserve fund to pay for the maintenance and repair of the building. The partnership invests the reserve fund in short-term interest-bearing deposits. The interest the partnership receives from investing this reserve fund is not derived in the ordinary course of a trade or business under the rules set out above. Therefore, the partnership's interest income from the deposits is portfolio income.

Example 2: An individual engaged in the trade or business of farming sells farmland in an installment sale. The individual is not engaged in the trade or business of selling farmland. In this situation, the individual's interest income from the installment sale is portfolio income since it is not derived in the ordinary course of a trade or business.

Gain on Sale or Disposition

Generally, gain recognized on the sale, exchange, or other disposition of an interest in property used in an activity or of an interest in an activity held through a partnership or S corporation is treated as passive activity gross income for the tax year or years in which it is recognized if the activity is a passive activity for the tax year of disposition.[74] Any material portion of property that was used in any activity at a time when the remainder of the property was not used in the activity is treated as a separate interest in property and the amount realized from the disposition and the adjusted basis of the property must be allocated among the separate interests in a reasonable manner.[75]

Example 1: The Taxpayer sold a 10-floor office building that the Taxpayer had owned for three years. For the entire time the building was held, the Taxpayer used seven floors of the building in a trade or business activity and three floors in a rental activity. The fair market value per square foot is substantially the same

---

[74] Temp. Reg. § 1.469-2T(c)(2)(i)(A).   [75] Temp. Reg. § 1.469-2T(c)(2)(i)(C).

¶ 1143.1

throughout the building, and the Taxpayer did not maintain a separate adjusted basis for any part of the building.

The seven floors used in the trade or business activity and the three floors used in the rental activity are treated as separate interests in property. The amount realized and the adjusted basis of the building must be allocated between the separate interests in a reasonable manner. Accordingly, an allocation based on the square footage of the parts of the building used in each activity would be reasonable.

If an interest in property is used in more than one activity during the 12 months before its disposition, the amount realized and the adjusted basis of the interest must be allocated among the activities in a manner that reasonably reflects the use of the interest in property during that 12-month period. An allocation of the amount realized and the adjusted basis solely to the activity in which an interest in property is predominantly used during the 12-month period reasonably reflects the use of the interest in property, if the fair market value of the interest does not exceed $10,000 or 10 percent of the sum of the fair market value of the interest and the fair market value of all other property used in the activity immediately before the disposition, whichever is less.[76]

Example 2: Assume the same facts as in Example 1, except that two of the seven floors used in the trade or business activity were used in the rental activity until five months before the sale. The five floors used exclusively in the trade or business activity and the two floors used first in the rental activity and then in the trade or business activity are treated as separate interests in property.

For the amount realized and the adjusted basis of the building, the Taxpayer allocates 30 percent to the three floors used exclusively in the rental activity, 50 percent to the five floors used exclusively in the trade or business activity, and 20 percent to the two floors used first in the rental activity and then in the trade or business activity. The amount realized and the adjusted basis allocated to the two floors that were used in both activities during the 12 months before the sale must also be allocated between the activities. Under these facts, an allocation of 7/12 to the rental activity and 5/12 to the trade or business activity would reasonably reflect the use of the two floors during the 12-month period.

If an interest in property used in an activity is substantially appreciated at the time of its disposition, any gain from the disposition is treated as not from a passive activity, unless the interest was used in

---

[76] Temp. Reg. § 1.469-2T(c)(2)(ii)

a passive activity for either 20 percent of the time the taxpayer held the interest or the entire 24 months before the disposition.[77] An interest in property is substantially appreciated if the fair market value of the interest exceeds 120 percent of the adjusted basis of the interest.[78]

> *Example 3:* The Taxpayer acquired a building on January 1, 1993, and uses the building in a trade or business activity in which the Taxpayer materially participates until March 31, 2004. On April 1, 2004, the Taxpayer leases the building. On December 31, 2005, the Taxpayer sells the building when the interest is substantially appreciated. Assuming the Taxpayer's lease of the building is a rental activity, the building is used in a passive activity for 21 months (April 1, 2004, through December 31, 2005). The building was not used in a passive activity for the entire 24 months before its sale. In addition, the 21-month period during which the building was used in a passive activity is less than 20 percent of the Taxpayer's holding period of 13 years for the building. Therefore, the gain from the sale is not treated as passive activity income.

Special rules apply to dealer property (held primarily for sale to customers in the ordinary course of business) used in a nondealer activity. Holding an interest in property in a dealing activity (the marketing of the property) is treated as the use of the interest in a nondealing activity if the marketing of the property is incidental to the nondealing use. When these rules apply, the interests in property are treated as used in the last nondealing activity in which they were used prior to their disposition. The marketing of the property is treated as incidental to the nondealing use if the interest in the property was used in nondealing activities for more than 80 percent of the taxpayer's holding period in the property and the taxpayer did not acquire and hold the interest for the principal purpose of selling it to customers in the ordinary course of a trade or business.[79]

A taxpayer is rebuttably presumed to have a dealing purpose unless the interest in property was used in nondealing activities for more than 24 months or 20 percent of the property's recovery period, whichever is less. The same presumption applies if the interest in property was offered for sale to customers during more than 25 percent of the period in which the interest was held in nondealing activities.[80]

Personal Service Income

Passive activity gross income does not include compensation paid to or on behalf of an individual for personal services performed or to be

---

[77] Reg. § 1.469-2(c)(2)(iii)(A).
[78] Reg. § 1.469-2(c)(2)(iii)(C).
[79] Reg. § 1.469-2(c)(2)(v).
[80] Reg. § 1.469-2T(c)(2)(v)(A)*(1)(ii)*.

performed by the individual at any time. Compensation for personal services includes only:

1. Earned income, including payments by a partnership to a partner that represent compensation for services by the partner;
2. Amounts includible in income as property transferred for services under Code Sec. 83;
3. Distributions from qualified retirement plans;
4. Payments under deferred compensation arrangements other than qualified plans;
5. Social security benefits included in gross income; and
6. Other income that the IRS designates as income derived from personal services.

A partner's distributive share of partnership income or a shareholder's pro rata share of income from an S corporation, however, cannot be treated as compensation for personal services.[81]

Change of Accounting Method

If a change in accounting method results in an increase in income from an activity as a result of the adjustments required by Code Sec. 481, a ratable portion of the amount taken into account for a tax year as a result of the adjustment is treated as gross income from the activity for the tax year. This income is passive activity gross income only if the activity is a passive activity for the year of the change in accounting method.[82]

Other Income Items

Passive activity gross income does not include the following items:

1. Gross income from intangible property, such as a patent, copyright, or literary, musical, or artistic composition, if the individual's personal efforts significantly contributed to the creation of the property;
2. Gross income from a qualified low-income housing project, as defined in Sec. 502 of the Tax Reform Act of 1986, for any taxable year in the relief period;
3. Gross income from a refund of any state, local, or foreign income, war profits, or excess profits tax;
4. Gross income from a covenant not to compete; and
5. Gross income that is treated as not from a passive activity under the Code Sec. 469 regulations.

---

[81] Temp. Reg. § 1.469-2T(c)(4).   [82] Temp. Reg. § 1.469-2T(c)(5).

¶ 1143.2 Passive Activity Deductions

Passive activity deductions are the deductions that may be taken against passive activity gross income in order to compute passive activity income or loss. Generally, a deduction is a passive activity deduction for a tax year only if the deduction arises in connection with the conduct of a passive activity for the tax year or is a carryover deduction from a prior year.[83]

Exceptions

Passive activity deductions do not include the following:

1. A deduction for an expense item, other than interest, that is clearly and directly allocable to portfolio income;
2. A deduction for dividends received by a corporation if the dividends are not included in passive activity gross income;
3. Interest expense, but only if it is allocated to a passive activity expenditure and is not a qualified residence interest or capitalized under a capitalization provision;
4. A deduction for a loss from the disposition of property that produces portfolio income;
5. A deduction that is allowed on the disposition of a passive activity;
6. A deduction for any state, local, or foreign income, war profits, or excess profits tax;
7. A miscellaneous itemized deduction that is subject to the two-percent floor;
8. A charitable contribution deduction;
9. Net operating loss, depletion allowance, or capital loss that is carried over to the tax year;
10. An item of loss or deduction that would have been allowed for a tax year before 1987, had it not been subject to the at-risk rules;
11. A casualty or theft loss deduction if losses that are similar in cause and severity do not recur regularly in the activity; and
12. A deduction or loss allocable to business or rental use of a dwelling when deduction or loss is limited to the income from the business or rental use under Code Sec. 280A(c)(5).[84]

---

[83] Temp. Reg. § 1.469-2T(d)(1).
[84] Temp. Reg. § 1.469-2T(d)(2) and Reg. § 1.469-2(d)(2).

An expense is clearly and directly allocable to portfolio income only if the expense is incurred as a result of, or incident to, an activity in which the portfolio income is derived or in connection with property from which the portfolio income is derived. For example, general and administrative expenses and compensation paid to officers attributable to the performance of services that do not directly benefit or are not incurred because of a particular activity or particular property are not clearly and directly allocable to portfolio income.[85]

Loss on Sale or Disposition

Generally, loss recognized on the sale, exchange, or other disposition of an interest in property used in an activity or of an interest in an activity held through a partnership or S corporation, and any deduction allowed because of the abandonment or worthlessness of the interest, is treated as a deduction from a passive activity if the activity is a passive activity for the tax year of disposition.[86]

Generally, the rules discussed above in connection with the discussion of when gain on a sale or disposition is treated as passive activity gross income apply to deductions. This includes all the allocation rules for separate interests and the use of property in more than one activity during the 12 months before the sale or disposition.

Change of Accounting Method

If a change in accounting method results in a decrease in income from an activity as a result of the adjustments required by Code Sec. 481, a ratable portion of the amount taken into account for a tax year as a result of the adjustment is treated as a deduction from the activity for the tax year. This deduction is a passive activity deduction only if the activity is a passive activity for the year of the change in accounting method.[87]

¶ 1143.3 *Partners and S Corporation Shareholders*

Partners and S corporation shareholders determine the character of items from these passthrough entities as passive activity income and deductions, when participation is relevant, based on their participation in the activities generating the income or deduction items. Participation is determined for the tax year of the passthrough entity and not the partner or shareholder.[88]

Example: The Taxpayer is a calendar-year taxpayer and a partner in a partnership that has a tax year ending January 31. During the partnership year ending January 31, 2003, the partnership engages in only one trade or business activity and the Taxpayer

---

[85] Temp. Reg. § 1.469-2T(d)(4).
[86] Temp. Reg. § 1.469-2T(d)(5).
[87] Temp. Reg. § 1.469-2T(d)(7).
[88] Temp. Reg. § 1.469-2T(e)(1).

does not materially participate in this activity during the partnership's tax year. On the Taxpayer's return for the calendar year 2003, the Taxpayer's share of the partnership's gross income and deductions from the activity are passive activity gross income and passive activity deductions. This would be the case even if the Taxpayer materially participated in the activity from February 1, 2003, through December 31, 2003.

Payments to Partners

Partners may receive payments that are not distributions of the partners' shares of income. These payments are subject to special rules.[89]

Any income or deductions attributable to a transaction between a partner and a partnership that is treated as occurring between the partnership and an outsider is characterized under the passive activity loss rules in a manner that is consistent with the treatment of the transaction under Code Sec. 707(a).[90]

In the case of a guaranteed payment made to a partner for services or capital under Code Sec. 707(c), the payment is characterized as a payment for services or as the payment of interest and not as a distributive share of partnership income.[91]

Any gain or loss taken into account by a retiring partner or a deceased partner's successor in interest as a result of a payment under Code Sec. 736(b) for the deceased or retiring partner's interest in the partnership is treated as passive activity gross income or a passive activity deduction only to the extent that the gain or loss would have been passive income or a passive deduction of the retiring or deceased partner if it had been recognized at the time the liquidation of the partner's interest began.[92] Payments made to a retiring partner or a deceased partner's successor in interest under Code Sec. 736(a) for unrealized receivables and goodwill are passive activity income only in the same percentage as the percentage that the retiring or deceased partner would have recognized as passive activity income if the unrealized receivables and goodwill had been sold at the time that the liquidation of the partner's interest began.[93]

Sale or Exchange of Interest in Entity

If a partner or S corporation shareholder disposes of an interest in the passthrough entity, a ratable portion of any gain or loss from the disposition is treated as gain or loss from the disposition of an interest

---

[89] Temp. Reg. § 1.469-2T(e)(2).
[90] Temp. Reg. § 1.469-2T(e)(2)(i).
[91] Reg. § 1.469-2(e)(2)(ii).
[92] Reg. § 1.469-2(e)(2)(iii)(A).
[93] Reg. § 1.469-2(e)(2)(iii)(B).

in each trade or business, rental, or investment activity in which the passthrough entity owns an interest on the applicable valuation date.[94]

The applicable valuation date is the beginning of the taxable year of the partnership or S corporation, or the date on which the disposition occurs, depending on which date is selected by the passthrough entity. However, the applicable valuation date is the date immediately preceding the date of disposition if any of the following occur between the beginning of the entity's tax year and the date of disposition of the interest by the partner or shareholder:

1. The passthrough entity disposes of more than 10 percent of its interest, measured by value as of the beginning of the taxable year, in any activity;
2. More than 10 percent of the property, by value as of the beginning of the taxable year, used in any activity of the passthrough entity is disposed of; or
3. The holder of the interest contributes substantially appreciated property or substantially depreciated property to the entity, and the total fair market value of appreciated property or adjusted basis of depreciated property exceeds 10 percent of the total fair market value of the holder's interest in the passthrough entity as of the beginning of the taxable year.[95]

Examples of the application of these rules may be found in Temp. Reg. § 1.469-2T(e)(3)(vii).

¶ 1145 Closely Held Corporation's Passive Activity Loss

The manner of computing a closely held corporation's passive activity loss is slightly different because closely held corporations may use deductions generated by passive activities to offset certain operating income as well as income from passive activities. A closely held corporation's passive activity loss for the taxable year is the amount by which the corporation's passive activity deductions for the taxable year exceed the sum of the corporation's passive activity gross income and its net active income for the taxable year.[96] Passive activity gross income and passive activity deductions are determined in the same fashion as discussed above for other taxpayers subject to the passive activity loss rules.

A corporation's net active income is the corporation's taxable income computed without regard to the following items:

1. Passive activity gross income;
2. Passive activity deductions;

---

[94] Temp. Reg. § 1.469-2T(e)(3)(ii)(A).
[95] Temp. Reg. § 1.469-2T(e)(3)(ii)(D)(*1*).
[96] Temp. Reg. § 1.469-1T(g)(4)(i).

3. Portfolio income;
4. Income from working interests in oil and gas properties which is not subject to the passive activity loss rules;
5. Income and deductions from a trade or business activity of trading personal property, but only if the corporation did not materially participate in the activity;
6. Deductions attributable to portfolio income; and
7. Interest expense that is allocable to a portfolio expenditure.[97]

The following examples illustrate the computation of a closely held corporation's passive activity loss.

Comprehensive Example 1: Closely Held Corporation (CHC) is engaged in two activities for 2002. One is a trade or business activity in which CHC materially participates for 2002, and the other is a rental activity. CHC also holds portfolio investments. CHC's gross income and deductions for 2002 are:

Gross Income:	
Rents	$ 60,000
Business income	100,000
Portfolio income	35,000
Total	$195,000

Deductions:	
Rental deductions	$100,000
Business deductions	80,000
Interest expense allocable to portfolio expenditures	10,000
Deductions allocable to portfolio income	5,000
Total	$195,000

CHC's net active income for 2002 is $20,000, computed as follows:

Gross income		$195,000
Amounts not included in net active income:		
Rents	$ 60,000	
Portfolio income	35,000	
	$ 95,000	95,000
Gross active income		$100,000
Deductions		$195,000
Amounts not included in net active income:		
Rental deductions	$100,000	
Interest expense for portfolio income	10,000	
Other deductions for portfolio income	5,000	
	$115,000	115,000
Deductions from active income		$ 80,000

---

[97] Temp. Reg. § 1.469-1T(g)(4)(ii).

Gross active income	$100,000
Deductions from active income	80,000
Net active income	$ 20,000

CHC's passive activity loss for 2002 is $20,000, the amount by which the passive activity deductions ($100,000) exceed the sum of the passive activity gross income ($60,000) and the net active income ($20,000). The $20,000 of deductions from CHC's rental activity that are disallowed for 2002 are treated as deductions from the rental activity for 2003 (see the discussion of disallowed losses below). If computed without regard to the net active income, CHC's passive activity loss would be $40,000 ($100,000 of rental deductions minus $60,000 of rental income). The effect of including active income in the computation of passive activity loss is to reduce CHC's passive activity loss for the year by the amount of CHC's net active income for the year.

Under these facts, CHC's taxable income for 2002 is $20,000, computed as follows:

Gross income		$195,000
Deductions:		
Total deductions	$195,000	
Passive activity loss	20,000	
Allowable deductions	$175,000	175,000
Taxable income		$ 20,000

Comprehensive Example 2: Assume the same facts as in Comprehensive Example 1, except that in 2003, CHC has a loss from the trade or business activity, and a net operating loss (NOL) of $15,000 that is carried back to 2002. Since NOL carrybacks are taken into account in computing net active income, CHC's net active income for 2002 must be recomputed as follows:

Net active income before NOL carryback	$20,000
Less: NOL carryback	15,000
Net active income	$ 5,000

Under these facts, CHC's disallowed passive activity loss for 2002 is $35,000, the amount by which the passive activity deductions for the taxable year ($100,000) exceed the sum of the passive activity gross income for the taxable year ($60,000) plus the net active income for the taxable year ($5,000).

The $35,000 of deductions for CHC's rental activity that are disallowed for 2002 are treated as deductions from the rental

¶ 1145

activity for 2003. CHC's taxable income for 2002 is $20,000, computed as follows:

Gross income		$195,000
Deductions:		
Total deductions	$210,000	
Passive activity loss	35,000	
Allowable deductions	$175,000	175,000
Taxable income		$ 20,000

Taking the NOL carryback into account in computing net active income for 2002 does not affect CHC's taxable income for 2002, but increases the deductions from CHC's rental activity for 2003 and decreases CHC's NOL carryover to years other than 2002.

¶ 1147 Disallowed Losses

Generally, losses from passive activities can be used only to offset income from passive activities. Any loss that cannot be used by a taxpayer because of the passive activity loss rules may be carried over to future years and applied to passive income in subsequent years.[98] A loss that remains unused as of the time the taxpayer disposes of the passive activity that generated the loss may be deducted at that time.[99] These rules require that disallowed passive activity losses be allocated among activities.

¶ 1147.1 Allocation of Disallowed Loss

If any portion of a taxpayer's passive activity loss is disallowed for the taxable year, a ratable portion of the loss, if any, from each passive activity of the taxpayer is disallowed. The ratable portion of a loss from an activity is computed by multiplying the passive activity loss that is disallowed for the taxable year by the fraction that is obtained by dividing:

1. The loss from the activity for the taxable year; by
2. The sum of the losses for the taxable year from all activities having losses for the year.[100]

The allocation may be computed using the worksheets that accompany the instructions to Form 8582, Passive Activity Loss Limitations.

Example: An individual holds interests in three passive activities, A, B, and C. For the taxable year, activity A produces $7,000 of gross income and $16,000 in deductions, activity B produces gross

---

[98] Code Sec. 469(b).
[99] Code Sec. 469(g).
[100] Temp. Reg. § 1.469-1T(f)(2)(i)(A).

income of $4,000 and deductions of $20,000, and activity C produces gross income of $12,000 and deductions of $8,000.

The individual's passive activity loss for the taxable year in the amount of $21,000 ($23,000 total income less $44,000 total deductions) is disallowed. Therefore, a ratable portion of the losses from activities A and B is disallowed. The disallowed portion for each activity is calculated by multiplying the passive loss by a fraction which has the net loss from the activity as its numerator and total net losses from all loss activities as its denominator. In this case, the results are as follows:

For A: $21,000 × $9,000/$25,000 = $7,560.

For B: $21,000 × $16,000/$25,000 = $13,440.

A special allocation rule applies to significant participation activities when passive activity gross income from these activities exceeds the passive activity deductions attributable to these activities. In this case, the significant participation activities are treated as a single activity that does not have a loss for the taxable year.[101] This rule allows all significant participation activities to be treated as one activity only for purposes of allocating the loss among activities and allows a taxpayer to avoid piecemeal allocation to significant participation activities when the net result of all significant participation activities is passive income rather than loss.

Example: An individual holds interests in four passive activities, A, B, C, and D. Activity A produces gross income of $15,000 and deductions of $5,000, or net income of $10,000. Activity B produces gross income of $5,000 and deductions of $10,000, or a net loss of $5,000. Activity C produces $10,000 of gross income and deductions of $20,000, or a net loss of $10,000. Activity D produces $10,000 of gross income, and $8,000 of deductions, or net income of $2,000. The total result of all of the individual's passive activities is gross income of $40,000, deductions of $43,000, and a net loss of $3,000.

Activities A and B are significant participation activities. The gross income from these activities for the taxable year ($20,000) exceeds the passive activity deductions from these activities for the taxable year ($15,000) by $5,000. Solely for applying the allocation rule, activities A and B are treated as a single activity that does not have a loss for the taxable year. The individual's passive activity loss for the taxable year is $8,000 ($43,000 of passive activity deductions minus $35,000 of passive activity gross income). The result of treating activities A and B as a single activity

---

[101] Temp. Reg. § 1.469-1T(f)(2)(i)(C).

¶ 1147.1

that does not have a loss for the year is that none of the $8,000 passive activity loss is allocated to activity B, even though the individual incurred a loss in that activity.

¶ 1147.2   Allocation Within Loss Activities

Once a taxpayer allocates the passive activity loss among all the passive activities that produced a loss, the taxpayer must then allocate the ratable portion applied to each loss among the deductions from the activity that produced the loss. A ratable portion of each passive activity deduction, other than an excluded deduction, from the activity is disallowed. The ratable portion of a passive activity deduction is the amount of the disallowed portion of the loss from the activity multiplied by the fraction obtained by dividing:

1. The amount of the deduction; by
2. The sum of all passive activity deductions, other than excluded deductions, from the activity.[102]

An excluded deduction is any passive activity deduction that is taken into account in computing the taxpayer's net income from an item of property in which an amount of the gross income from the item of property is treated as not being from a passive activity.[103]

¶ 1147.3   Carryover of Disallowed Deductions

If any deductions are disallowed for a taxable year under the passive activity loss rules, the disallowed deductions must be allocated among the taxpayer's activities for the succeeding taxable year in a manner that reasonably reflects the extent to which each activity continues the business and rental operations that constituted the loss activity. Also, the disallowed deductions allocated to an activity are treated as deductions from the activity for the succeeding year.[104]

> **Example:** The Taxpayer owns interests in a convenience store and an apartment building that are treated as interests in two separate passive activities. A $5,000 loss from the convenience store and a $3,000 loss from the apartment building are disallowed for 2002.
>
> The $5,000 loss from the convenience store is allocated among the passive activity deductions from that activity for 2002, and the $3,000 loss from the apartment building is treated similarly. In 2003, the business and rental operations that constituted the convenience store activity are continued in a single activity, and the business and rental operations that constituted the apartment building activity are similarly continued in a separate activity.

---

[102] Temp. Reg. § 1.469-1T(f)(2)(ii).
[103] Temp. Reg. § 1.469-1T(f)(2)(ii)(B).
[104] Reg. § 1.469-1(f)(4)(i).

Passive Activity Loss Rules

The disallowed deductions from the convenience store for 2002 must be allocated to the Taxpayer's convenience store activity in 2003. Similarly, the disallowed deductions from the apartment building for 2002 must be allocated to the Taxpayer's apartment building activity in 2003. The disallowed deductions allocated to the convenience store in 2003 are treated as deductions from that activity for 2003, and the disallowed deductions allocated to the apartment building for 2003 are treated as deductions from that activity for 2003.

If a taxpayer continues part or all of the business and rental operations that constitute a loss activity through a C corporation or similar entity, the taxpayer's interest in the entity is treated for purposes of the carryover of disallowed deductions as an interest in a passive activity that continues the business and rental operations. An entity is similar to a C corporation if the owners of interests in the entity derive only portfolio income from the ownership interests.[105]

Example: The Taxpayer owns stock in an S corporation for the taxable year 2002. After 2002, the S corporation is a C corporation. For 2002, the Taxpayer's pro rata share of the corporation's loss from a rental activity is $5,000, and the entire loss is disallowed under the passive activity loss rules.

The Taxpayer's $5,000 loss from the rental activity is allocated among the deductions from that activity for 2002. In 2003, the business and rental operations that constituted the rental activity are continued through the C corporation, and the Taxpayer's interest in the C corporation is treated as a passive activity that continues the rental operations. The Taxpayer must allocate the disallowed deductions from the rental activity for 2002 to the C corporation activity in 2003 and treat them as deductions from the C corporation activity for 2003.

The Taxpayer's treatment of the interest in the C corporation as an interest in a passive activity that continues the operations of the rental activity does not change the character of the dividend income from the C corporation. The Taxpayer's dividend income is portfolio income and is not included in passive activity gross income. The Taxpayer's loss from the C corporation activity for 2003 is $5,000.

¶ 1147.4 Disposition of a Passive Activity

If a taxpayer disposes of the entire interest in a passive activity or former passive activity in a taxable transaction, any passive activity

---

[105] Temp. Reg. § 1.469-1T(f)(4)(ii)(A).

loss on that activity that has been carried over from prior years, as well as any loss for the current year, becomes deductible as a nonpassive activity loss to the extent it exceeds passive income from other activities for the year. If the taxpayer realizes income or gain from the passive activity in the year of its disposition, the suspended losses from prior years must be used first to offset this gain. Any loss in excess of this gain is then used to offset passive income for the year from other activities. Only then may the taxpayer use the loss to offset nonpassive income or gain.[106] This rule does not apply, however, if the taxpayer and transferee of the passive activity are related. In this case, the suspended loss remains suspended until the passive activity is acquired by another person who is not related to the taxpayer.[107]

Transfer at Death

A similar rule applies to the transfer of a passive activity on the death of a taxpayer. In this case, however, a suspended loss may be deducted from the deceased taxpayer's other income for the year of death only to the extent the loss exceeds any increase in the basis of the interest in the passive activity that occurs as a result of the transfer (the step-up in basis).[108]

Installment Sale

If the taxpayer disposes of the entire interest in a passive activity through an installment sale, the suspended loss may not be deducted in full in the year of sale. Rather, the taxpayer deducts the loss as the income from the sale is reported, that is, the taxpayer deducts the loss in the same ratio as the income from the installment sale is reported.[109]

Income realized after 1986 as a result of an installment sale that occurred before 1987 is passive income if the activity from which the sale arose would have been a passive activity in the year of sale had the passive activity loss rules applied.[110]

¶ 1149 Passive Activity Credits

Tax credits generated by passive activities (passive activity credits) generally may not be used to offset income tax liability attributable to nonpassive activities. A taxpayer's passive activity credit for a taxable year is the amount by which the sum of all tax credits that are subject to the passive activity loss rules for the year exceeds the taxpayer's regular tax liability allocable to all passive activities for the

---

[106] Code Sec. 469(g)(1)(A).
[107] Code Sec. 469(g)(1)(B).
[108] Code Sec. 469(g)(2).
[109] Code Sec. 469(g)(3).
[110] Technical and Miscellaneous Revenue Act of 1988, Sec. 1005(a)(10).

year.[111] The tax credits that are subject to the passive activity loss rules are:

1. Investment credit under Code Sec. 46, made up of the rehabilitation credit, the energy credit, and the reforestation credit
2. Work opportunity credit
3. Alcohol fuels credit
4. Research credit
5. Low-income housing credit
6. Enhanced oil recovery credit
7. Disabled access credit
8. Renewable electricity production credit
9. Empowerment zone employment credit
10. Indian employment credit
11. Employer Social Security credit
12. Orphan drug credit
13. New markets tax credit
14. Small employer pension plan start-up cost credit
15. Employer-provided child care credit
16. Puerto Rico economic activity credit
17. Clinical testing of drugs credit
18. Electric vehicle credit
19. Nonconventional fuel credit [112]

A taxpayer's regular tax liability allocable to all passive activities, against which credits from passive activities may be used, is the excess of the taxpayer's regular tax liability over the amount of tax that the taxpayer would pay if taxable income were reduced by passive activity gross income in excess of passive activity deductions.[113]

The application of the rule limiting the use of credits is illustrated by the following example. In any calculation involving the determination of tax liability, the tax rates in effect for the 2002 tax year have been used.

Comprehensive Example: A single individual acquires an interest in a partnership that rehabilitates a building and places it in service in a trade or business activity in which the individual does not materially participate. For the year in which the building is

---

[111] Code Sec. 469(d)(2).
[112] Code Sec. 469(d)(2).
[113] Temp. Reg. § 1.469-3T(d).

placed in service, the individual has the following items of gross income, deductions, and credits:

Gross Income:
Nonpassive income	$110,000	
Passive activity income	20,000	$ 130,000

Deductions:
Nonpassive deductions	$ 23,950	
From passive activities	18,000	41,950
Taxable income		$ 88,050

Credits:
Rehabilitation credit from passive activity	$ 8,000

The amount by which the individual's passive activity gross income exceeds the passive activity deductions (the individual's net passive income) is $2,000. The individual's regular tax liability allocable to passive activities is determined as follows:

Taxable income	$88,050	
Regular tax liability		$20,730
Taxable income less net passive income	86,050	
Tax liability on income of $86,050		20,130
Regular tax liability allocable to passive activities		$ 600

The individual's passive activity credit is the amount by which credits from passive activities for the year ($8,000) exceed regular tax liability allocable to passive activities ($600). Therefore, the individual's passive activity credit that is suspended and carried over to future years is $7,400.

Suppose, however, that the individual had an additional $100,000 in deductions from a trade or business in which the individual materially participated. This would produce a taxable loss for the individual in the amount of $11,950, rather than taxable income of $88,050.

In this case, since regular tax liability cannot exceed the tax imposed, the individual's regular tax liability allocable to passive activities is zero. Although the net operating loss is reduced by net passive income and regular tax liability for other taxable years may increase as a result of the reduction, the increase does not change regular tax liability allocable to passive activities for the current year. Therefore, the individual's passive activity credit that is suspended is the full $8,000 credit attributable to passive activities.

¶ 1149

¶ 1149.1 Closely Held Corporation

A closely held corporation that is subject to the passive activity loss rules may use losses from passive activities to offset operating income as well as passive income. Similarly, these corporations may use tax credits generated by a passive activity to offset tax liability attributable to operating income as well as passive income. Under Temp. Reg. § 1.469-1T(g)(5), a closely held corporation's passive activity credit for the taxable year (the amount of the credit that is suspended) is reduced by the corporation's net active income tax liability for the year.

A corporation's net active income tax liability is the amount by which:

1. The corporation's regular tax liability for the taxable year, determined by reducing the corporation's taxable income by an amount equal to the excess, if any, of the corporation's passive activity gross income over the corporation's passive activity deductions; exceeds

2. The sum of (a) the corporation's regular tax liability determined by reducing the corporation's taxable income by an amount equal to the excess, if any, of the sum of the corporation's net active income (as defined above in connection with the discussion of a corporation's passive activity loss) and passive activity gross income over the corporation's passive activity deductions, plus (b) the corporation's credits, other than credits from passive activities, that are allowable for the taxable year.[114]

Special rules apply in the case of affiliated groups filing consolidated returns.[115]

¶ 1149.2 Carryover of Suspended Credit

If a taxpayer's passive activity credit is disallowed for the taxable year under the passive activity loss rules, a ratable portion of each credit from each passive activity is disallowed.[116] A taxpayer need not account separately for any credit unless the credit may, if separately taken into account, result in an income tax liability for any year other than that which would result were the credit not taken into account separately. Credits that must be accounted for separately include, but are not limited to:

---

[114] Temp. Reg. § 1.469-1T(g)(5)(ii).
[115] Temp. Reg. § 1.469-1T(h).
[116] Temp. Reg. § 1.469-1T(f)(3)(i).

1. Credits, other than the low-income housing and rehabilitation credits, from a rental real estate activity in which the taxpayer actively participates;
2. Credits, other than low-income housing and rehabilitation credits, from a rental real estate activity in which the taxpayer does not actively participate; and
3. Low-income housing and rehabilitation credits from a rental real estate activity.[117]

If any credits from an activity are disallowed under the passive activity loss rules, the disallowed credits are allocated among the taxpayer's activities for the succeeding year in a manner that reasonably reflects the extent to which each activity continues the business and rental operations that constituted the loss activity, and the disallowed credits allocated to an activity are treated as credits from the activity for the succeeding taxable year.[118] This is the same rule that applies to disallowed deductions from passive activities, as discussed above.

While credits that are disallowed under the passive loss rules are suspended and carried over to succeeding years, just as disallowed losses are suspended and carried over to succeeding years, there is no provision that allows a taxpayer to take suspended credits when the taxpayer sells or otherwise disposes of the entire interest in a passive activity that gave rise to the suspended credit. Once a suspended credit becomes allowable under the passive loss rules, because of the tax liability attributable to passive income or under the limited exception for real estate activities in which the taxpayer actively participates, the credits are then aggregated with credits from nonpassive activities in order to apply the various other limitations on tax credits, such as the tax-liability limitation and the limitation on the use of credits to reduce alternative minimum tax.

¶ 1151 PUBLICLY TRADED PARTNERSHIPS

In response to the growing use of publicly traded partnerships to combine the organizational and operational advantages of a corporation with the tax advantages of a partnership, Congress enacted Code Sec. 7704, which treats certain publicly traded partnerships as corporations for federal income tax purposes. A publicly traded partnership is defined by Code Sec. 469(k) as a partnership in which interests are traded on an established securities market or are readily tradable on a secondary market, or the substantial equivalent of a secondary market.

---

[117] Temp. Reg. § 1.469-1T(f)(3)(iii).   [118] Reg. § 1.469-1(f)(4)(i).

While many publicly traded partnerships are now treated as corporations under this rule, those publicly traded partnerships that are not, such as real estate partnerships, are subject to a special passive activity loss rule. This rule, generally, isolates losses from publicly traded partnerships and bars their use to offset other passive income. Publicly traded partnerships treated as corporations and public limited partnerships in general are considered further in Chapter 21. The following discussion focuses on the special passive activity loss rule that applies to publicly traded partnerships that are not treated as corporations.

¶ 1153 Partnerships Subject to the Rule

The treatment of publicly traded partnerships as corporations is subject to some very important exceptions, primarily for partnerships engaged in real estate and natural resource (such as oil and gas) operations.[119] A publicly traded partnership is not treated as a corporation, and the special passive activity loss rule for publicly traded partnerships applies, if 90 percent or more of the partnership's gross income is qualifying income. Qualifying income includes the following:

1. Interest, but this category does not include amounts contingent on profits or interest earned in the course of a financial or insurance business;
2. Dividends;
3. Rents from real property, including real property rents based on a fixed percentage of receipts or a fixed percentage of gross sales, but not amounts contingent on profits;
4. Gain from the disposition of real property (gross income is not reduced by the inventory costs of property taken into account in determining gain from the sales in the case of real property sold to customers in the ordinary course of business);
5. Income and gains from natural resource activities (natural resources include fertilizer, geothermal energy, and timber, as well as oil and gas and products of oil and gas);
6. Any gain from the disposition of a capital asset or asset held for the production of income that falls within the first five categories; and
7. Income and gains from commodities (other than those held for sale to customers in the ordinary course of business), futures, options, or forward contracts on commodities (including foreign currency transactions of a commodity pool), but only if the principal activity of the partnership is the buying and selling of the commodities, futures, options, or forward con-

---

[119] Code Sec. 7704(c).

tracts (this category of qualifying income excludes typical commodity pools from treatment as corporations).[120]

¶ 1157 Partnerships Subject to Grandfather Rule

In addition to the exception to treating publicly traded partnerships as corporations based on qualifying income, there is another exception for partnerships that were in existence on December 17, 1987. These publicly traded partnerships are not treated as corporations until after December 31, 1997. After 1997, a publicly traded partnership that was in existence on December 17, 1987, and to which the grandfather rule applied through 1997, may elect to continue to be subject to the grandfather rule at a tax cost of 3.5 percent of its gross income.[121] Publicly traded partnerships not treated as corporations under the grandfather rule are subject to the special passive activity loss rule.

¶ 1159 Application of the Special Passive Activity Loss Rule

Generally, as discussed above, an interest in a limited partnership as a limited partner is considered a passive activity. Publicly traded partnerships that are not treated as corporations because they have qualifying income or are subject to the 10-year grandfather rule for partnerships in existence on December 17, 1987, however, are subject to a special passive activity loss rule.[122] The thrust of the rule is to block the use of income or loss generated by a publicly traded partnership to offset passive income or loss from other passive activities, as well as income and loss from other sources.

Each partner in a publicly traded partnership treats a loss, if any, from the partnership as separate from income and loss from any other publicly traded partnership and also as separate from income or loss from other passive activities. Net income from a publicly traded partnership is treated as portfolio income under the passive activity loss rules. A net loss attributable to an interest in a publicly traded partnership may not be deducted against the partner's other income but must be suspended and carried forward. These net losses can be applied against net income from the partnership in future years. When a partner disposes of the entire interest in a publicly traded partnership, any remaining suspended losses may be deducted against other income at that time.[123]

There is an exception that allows a partner to use his or her share of low-income housing credits and rehabilitation credits from a publicly traded partnership against tax liability attributable to nonpartnership

---

[120] Code Sec. 7704(c).
[121] Code Sec. 7704(g).
[122] Code Sec. 469(k).
[123] Code Sec. 469(k)(3).

income to the extent of the unused $25,000 deduction-equivalent allowance. The credits are allowable under the partner's $25,000 allowance to the extent that the partner has not fully utilized the allowance for losses and credits otherwise allowed under the regular passive activity loss rules.[124]

The application of the passive activity loss rule to publicly traded partnerships that are not treated as corporations is illustrated by the following example.

> ***Comprehensive Example:*** The Taxpayer owns limited partnership interests in two limited partnerships, A and B, but owns no interest in any other passive activity. Limited partnership A is a publicly traded limited partnership but is not subject to being treated as a corporation because 90 percent of its gross income is from real estate activities. Limited partnership B is not a publicly traded partnership.
>
> For the current tax year, partnership A produced a net loss passed through to the Taxpayer in the amount of $1,000. Partnership B produced net income passed through to the Taxpayer in the amount of $1,500. The income from B was not portfolio income to the partnership. Neither partnership produced income or loss for the Taxpayer in any prior tax year. The Taxpayer cannot use the $1,000 loss from partnership A to offset the $1,500 of income from partnership B. The Taxpayer must report the $1,500 of passive activity income from partnership B, which is not a publicly traded partnership. The Taxpayer's loss from publicly traded partnership A is suspended, and the Taxpayer may carry this amount forward to offset income that may eventually be realized from partnership A. If the loss is still unused when the Taxpayer disposes of the entire interest in partnership A, the Taxpayer may take a deduction for the unused loss at that time.
>
> Suppose, however, the situation were reversed. Assume that partnership A, the publicly traded partnership, produces net income for the Taxpayer in the amount of $1,500 and that partnership B, the partnership that is not publicly traded, produces a net loss for the Taxpayer in the amount of $1,000. In this situation, the Taxpayer cannot use the loss from partnership B to offset the $1,500 of income from partnership A. The $1,500 of income realized by the Taxpayer from partnership A is treated as portfolio income under the passive activity loss rules. The $1,000 loss from partnership B, however, is a passive loss under the passive activity loss rules. If the Taxpayer realized income from other passive

---

[124] Code Sec. 469(k)(1).

activities, this loss could be used to offset that passive income. In the absence of income from passive sources, the $1,000 loss is suspended and carried over to future years under the regular passive activity loss rules, and the Taxpayer may deduct this loss against income realized in the future from any passive activity, not just partnership B.

If neither limited partnership A nor limited partnership B were a publicly traded partnership, the Taxpayer could deduct the $1,000 loss realized from one partnership against the $1,500 in income realized from the other partnership under the usual passive activity loss rules. The net result for the Taxpayer in this case would be taxable income from the partnerships in the amount of $500.

Chapter 12

Troubled Financings

¶ 1200 OVERVIEW OF CHAPTER

While owners of real estate may be reluctant to admit it, there are times when real estate cannot support the debt incurred to finance its purchase or support the debts incurred for other purposes and secured by the real estate. Troubled real estate financings may develop in the course of holding real estate for investment, for the production of rental income, or for use in a trade or business. As the mortgagor tries to meet payments, the mortgagor may seek ways to get out from under the burden that the real estate now represents. The mortgagee who sees late payments and, finally, a default in payments may take steps to realize as much as possible on the value represented by the real estate.

The first course of action for the mortgagee, assuming the mortgagor wants to continue ownership of the property, may be an attempt at some compromise or settlement of the debt at a discount. This is most likely if a decline in value, through no fault of the mortgagor, means that the real estate is no longer worth as much as the debt secured by the real estate and cannot generate the cash flow necessary to meet the payment obligations. Settlement of a mortgage debt at a discount has tax consequences for both the mortgagor and the mortgagee.

When the mortgagor wants out, or the mortgagee is unwilling to compromise or wait for payments, foreclosure looms. From the mortgagor's point of view, a foreclosure is essentially a sale on which he or she may realize gain or loss, even though the sale may not be voluntary. For the mortgagee, a foreclosure may have more complicated consequences, depending on whether the foreclosure results in a sale to a third party or whether the mortgagee is forced to bid because of the lack of acceptable bids from third parties.

To avoid foreclosure, a mortgagor may convey the property to a creditor. Again, there are tax consequences to both debtor and creditor. In the rare case when real estate has declined in value so much that neither the mortgagor nor the mortgagee wants the property, the mortgagor may simply walk away from the property and abandon it. When this occurs, there is a question of whether the abandonment generates a deductible loss for tax purposes.

¶ 1200

Finally, special considerations arise when the troubled financing is seller financing in the form of a purchase-money mortgage. Is a reduction in the debt merely a reduction in the selling price, or does it produce a deductible loss? And what if the seller reacquires the property through foreclosure or conveyance from the purchaser? Here, too, there are special tax considerations that come into play.

¶ 1201 SETTLEMENT OF DEBT AT DISCOUNT

In the normal course of events, when a debtor satisfies the debt at its face amount, there are no tax consequences for either the debtor or the creditor. There is no economic benefit to either party in addition to the original bargain that gave rise to the debt. The same cannot be said, however, when a mortgage debt is satisfied at less than face value. In this case, the borrower may be receiving an economic benefit, and the lender may be suffering an economic detriment. Generally, the tax law recognizes this and taxes the benefit realized by the borrower and allows the lender a deduction for the economic loss.

¶ 1203 Tax Treatment of Debtor

While the tax law does tax the debtor on the benefit received from the discharge of a debt at a discount, the timing of that tax is another matter. The actual treatment of the debtor who satisfies the debt at a discount hinges on the status of the debtor at the time. The solvent debtor, who presumably would have no problem meeting a current tax payment for the benefit of the discharged debt, generally is subject to an immediate tax on income from the discharge of indebtedness.[1] Insolvent and bankrupt debtors, however, may escape an immediate tax under the rules of Code Sec. 108 (see ¶ 1203.2). There also is a special rule that allows income from the discharge of "qualified real property business indebtedness" to escape current tax (see ¶ 1203.3). Special rules in Code Sec. 108(g) apply to the discharge of qualified farm indebtedness.

¶ 1203.1 Solvent Debtor

At one time, solvent debtors were able to defer the tax on income from the discharge of indebtedness. This rule was repealed in the Tax Reform Act of 1986 on the theory that a solvent debtor had the capacity to pay the tax currently and there was no reason to permit a deferral. Of course, the reduction of a mortgage debt does not produce any immediate cash flow with which to fund the tax payment and, if the value of the property has declined, may never produce a cash amount corresponding to the "benefit" of the debt reduction. Nevertheless, in the case of a solvent debtor, other than in the case of qualified

---

[1] Code Sec. 61(a)(12).

real property business indebtedness and qualified farm indebtedness, gross income includes income from the discharge of indebtedness.[2]

The term "income from discharge of indebtedness" is broad and seems to encompass any debt reduction. The IRS has ruled that an individual taxpayer realizes income from the discharge of indebtedness under Code Sec. 61(a)(12) on the discounted prepayment to a lender of all or a portion of mortgage indebtedness. Further, according to the IRS, the amount of the discount is includible whether the mortgage note is recourse or nonrecourse.[3]

Debt Forgiveness as Gift

One exception to this rule would be when the forgiveness or reduction of the debt is really a gift from the creditor to the debtor. Whether the reduction or cancellation of the debt is voluntary or involuntary does not matter. Simply because a debt is reduced or cancelled on a voluntary basis does not establish a gift. Rather, a gift depends on donative intent. As the Supreme Court has put it, "the transfer of something for the best price available" does not amount to a gift.[4] In *W. DiLaura*,[5] the discharge of a mortgage for an amount less than the principal balance due was taxable as income to the mortgagor because the mortgagee did not act with disinterested generosity but was motivated by the sound economic reason of ridding itself of a low-interest mortgage.[6]

For the treatment of a reduction in a purchase-money mortgage as a reduction in the selling price in the case of seller financing, see ¶ 1203.5.

Acquisition of Debt by Related Parties

Forgiveness of the debt by the creditor is not the only way in which a debtor can be relieved of the obligation to repay the debt. The Internal Revenue Code recognizes this in Code Sec. 108(e), which provides some general rules for the discharge of indebtedness, including discharges outside of bankruptcy or insolvency. Under Code Sec. 108(e)(4), an outstanding debt acquired from an unrelated creditor by a person related to the debtor is treated as if the debtor had acquired the debt. To the extent provided in Reg. § 1.108-2(f), this gives rise to income from the discharge of indebtedness. Parties related to the debtor that trigger this rule are:

---

[2] Code Secs. 61(a)(12) and 108(a)(1).
[3] Rev. Rul. 82-202, 1982-2 CB 35.
[4] *American Dental Co.*, S.Ct., 43-1 USTC ¶ 9318, 318 U.S. 322, 63 S.Ct. 577.
[5] 53 TCM 1077, CCH Dec. 43,973(M), T.C. Memo. 1987-291.
[6] See also *M.H. Juister, Jr.*, 53 TCM 1079, CCH Dec. 43,974(M), T.C. Memo. 1987-292; *J.H. Sutphin*, Cls. Ct., 88-1 USTC ¶ 9269, 14 Cls. Ct. 545.

¶ 1203.1

1. Members of a controlled group of corporations of which the debtor is also a member;
2. Trade or business under common control;
3. Partner in a partnership controlled by the debtor of a controlled partnership, as defined in Code Sec. 707(b)(1); and
4. Family members, that is, an individual's spouse, children, grandchildren, parents, and a spouse of the individual's children or grandchildren.

¶ 1203.2 Insolvent or Bankrupt Debtor

Prior to the Bankruptcy Tax Act of 1980, there were exceptions to the general rule that gross income includes income from the discharge of indebtedness. Under a judicially developed insolvency exception, no income arose from discharge of indebtedness if the debtor were insolvent both before and after the transaction.[7] If the transaction left the debtor with assets whose value exceeded the remaining liabilities, however, income was realized, but only to the extent of the excess.[8] The old Bankruptcy Act (repealed in 1979 by P.L. 95-598) provided that no income was recognized on cancellation of indebtedness in an insolvency reorganization under Chapter X. The debtor corporation would reduce the basis of its assets by the amount of the indebtedness discharged. Similar rules applied to arrangements under Chapter XI, real property arrangements under Chapter XII, and wage earner plans under Chapter XIII of the old Bankruptcy Act.

When the old Bankruptcy Act was repealed, the tax provisions contained in that Act also were repealed. This led to the passage of the Bankruptcy Tax Act of 1980, which provided tax rules in Code Sec. 108 that apply to debt discharge in the case of bankrupt or insolvent debtors. The 1980 Act also made related changes to existing law applicable to solvent debtors outside of bankruptcy and codified them in Code Sec. 108. Now, there is no insolvency exception, other than that in Code Sec. 108, from the general rule that gross income includes income from the discharge of indebtedness.[9]

Insolvent Debtor

An insolvent debtor who has a debt discharged or cancelled outside of bankruptcy does not recognize income from the discharge of indebtedness.[10] The exclusion, however, is limited to the amount of the debtor's insolvency.[11] The amount of the debtor's insolvency is measured by the excess of the debtor's liabilities over the assets immedi-

---

[7] *Dallas Transfer & Terminal Warehouse Co.*, CA-5, 4 USTC ¶ 1270, 70 F.2d 95; Reg. § 1.61-12(b)(1).
[8] *Lakeland Grocery Co.*, 36 BTA 289, CCH Dec. 9707.
[9] Code Sec. 108(e)(1).
[10] Code Sec. 108(a)(1)(B).
[11] Code Sec. 108(a)(3).

ately before the discharge.[12] The excluded amount of an insolvent debtor's income from the discharge of indebtedness is used to reduce tax attributes, as discussed below. The amount of the debt that is not excluded from income because it exceeds the debtor's insolvency is subject to the rules discussed at ¶ 1203.1 that apply to the discharge of a solvent debtor.

Bankrupt Debtor

If the discharge of debt occurs in a bankruptcy proceeding, the debtor excludes the amount of the discharged debt from income[13] and reduces tax attributes by the amount of the debt discharged.[14] To benefit from this exclusion, the debtor must be under the jurisdiction of the court in a bankruptcy case,[15] and the discharge of indebtedness must be granted by the court or carried out under a plan approved by the court.[16]

Reduction of Tax Attributes

Income from the discharge of indebtedness that is excluded from the income of an insolvent or bankrupt debtor under Code Sec. 108(a) is not forgiven, but merely deferred through the mechanism of reductions in the taxpayer's "tax attributes."[17] The excluded amount reduces the following tax attributes in the order shown:

1. Any net operating loss for the taxable year of the discharge, and any net operating loss carryover to that year;
2. Carryovers of the general business credit;
3. The minimum tax credit as of the beginning of the tax year following the year of discharge;
4. Any net capital loss for the taxable year of the discharge, and any capital loss carryover to that year;
5. The basis of depreciable and nondepreciable property;
6. Any passive activity loss or credit carryover from the year of the discharge; and
7. Foreign tax credit carryovers.[18]

Tax attributes, other than credit carryovers, are reduced one dollar for each dollar of discharged debt that is excluded from income.[19] The reduction in credit carryovers is 33 1/3 cents for each dollar of excluded discharged debt.[20] The required reductions are made in the order of tax years in which the items would be used, without regard to the exclusion

---

[12] Code Sec. 108(d)(3).
[13] Code Sec. 108(a)(1)(A).
[14] Code Sec. 108(b)(1).
[15] Title 11 of the United States Code.
[16] Code Sec. 108(d)(2).
[17] Code Sec. 108(b)(1).
[18] See Code Sec. 108(b)(2).
[19] Code Sec. 108(b)(3)(A).
[20] Code Sec. 108(b)(3)(B).

¶ 1203.2

from income of the debt discharged or to the limitations on the use of credits. The excluded amount of discharged debt first reduces the current year's loss and then reduces the loss carryovers in the order in which they arose, and the credit carryovers are reduced in the order in which they would be used against taxable income.[21]

Election to Reduce Basis

An insolvent or bankrupt debtor may take advantage of a special election to reduce the basis of the depreciable property first, rather than apply the excluded discharged debt to reduce tax attributes in the order listed above. The debtor applies the reduction in basis to the property held at the beginning of the taxable year following the year in which the discharge occurs.[22] In an election within an election, this basis reduction may include real property that is dealer property, that is, real property held for sale in the ordinary course of business.[23] If the amount of discharged debt that is excluded from income exceeds the aggregate adjusted basis of depreciable or dealer real property, the excess is then applied to reduce tax attributes in the order specified above.

Proposed Reg. § 1.1017-1 provides ordering rules for reducing the basis of property in the context of both the reduction of tax attributes and the election to first reduce basis before reduction of other tax attributes.

The election to reduce the basis of depreciable and dealer property gives a debtor flexibility to account for a debt discharge amount in a way that is most favorable to the debtor's tax situation. For example, a bankrupt or insolvent debtor who wishes to retain net operating losses and other carryovers is able to elect to reduce the basis of depreciable assets and real property held for sale in the ordinary course of business. On the other hand, a debtor with an expiring net operating loss that would otherwise be "wasted" is able to apply the excluded amount of the discharged debt first against the net operating loss.

To insure that income from the discharge of indebtedness that is excluded under Code Sec. 108 eventually does result in ordinary income and cannot be converted into capital gain, Code Sec. 1017(d) provides that any gain on a subsequent disposition of the reduced-basis property is subject to recapture as ordinary income.

¶ 1203.3   Qualified Real Property Business Debt

A taxpayer other than a C corporation can elect to exclude from income the discharge of qualified real property business debt.[24] A

---

[21] Code Sec. 108(b)(4).
[22] Code Sec. 1017(a).
[23] Code Sec. 1017(b)(3)(E).
[24] Code Sec. 108(a)(1)(D).

taxpayer who makes this election must reduce the basis of depreciable real property by the excluded amount.[25]

Qualified real property business debt is debt, other than qualified farm debt, that was:

1. Incurred or assumed in connection with real property used in a trade or business;
2. Secured by the real property; and
3. Incurred or assumed before January 1, 1993, or incurred or assumed to acquire, construct, or substantially improve the real property.

The taxpayer must elect to apply the rules to the property. Qualified real property business debt includes refinancing of debt described in 3 above, but only to the extent it does not exceed the debt being refinanced.[26]

A taxpayer cannot exclude more than either:

1. The excess of outstanding principal of the debt before the discharge over the fair market value before the discharge of the business real property reduced by the outstanding amount of any other qualified real property business debt secured by the property before the discharge, or
2. The total adjusted bases of depreciable real property held immediately before the discharge. (The bases are determined after any basis reduction due to a discharge in bankruptcy, insolvency, or of qualified farm debt.)[27]

¶ 1203.5 *Purchase-Money Mortgage Reduction*

When the seller of real estate provides financing to the purchaser in the form of a purchase-money mortgage, two relationships are created. There is, of course, the buyer-seller relationship. Buyers and sellers may negotiate over the purchase price and increase or decrease that price based on a number of factors, including their relative bargaining powers. There is also a debtor-creditor relationship created. This dual relationship can create a question when, after the sale is complete and the financing is arranged, the parties agree to reduce the amount of the debt. Is the reduction one that flows from the debtor-creditor relationship so that the reduction produces discharge of indebtedness income for the buyer-debtor? Or does the reduction flow from the buyer-seller relationship, so that the reduction is nothing more than a reduction in the purchase price paid by the buyer-debtor?

---

[25] Code Sec. 108(c)(1).
[26] Code Sec. 108(c)(3).
[27] Code Sec. 108(c)(2) and Reg. § 1.108-6.

Congress enacted Code Sec. 108(e)(5) to eliminate disagreements between the IRS and debtors as to whether, in a particular case to which the provision applies, the debt reduction should be treated as income from the discharge of indebtedness or a true price adjustment. If the seller of specific property reduces the debt of the purchaser which arose out of the purchase, and the reduction to the purchaser does not occur in a bankruptcy case or when the purchaser is insolvent, then the reduction to the purchaser of the purchase-money mortgage is treated as a purchase price adjustment on the property. This rule applies only if the amount of the reduction otherwise would be treated as income from the discharge of indebtedness.[28]

The treatment of a reduction in the amount of a purchase-money mortgage as a price adjustment only applies when it occurs between the original buyer and original seller of the property. If the debt is transferred by a seller to a third party, even a party related to the seller, or if the property is transferred by the buyer to a third party, even a party related to the buyer, Code Sec. 108(e)(5) does not apply to determine whether a reduction in the amount of a purchase-money mortgage should be treated as income from the discharge of indebtedness or a true price adjustment. Also, Code Sec. 108(e)(5) does not apply if the debt is reduced because of factors that do not involve direct agreements between the buyer and seller, such as the running of the statute of limitations on the enforcement of the obligation.

¶ 1205 Tax Treatment of Creditor

In the typical case, the mortgagee lends the mortgagor the face amount of the debt. The amount of the loan becomes the mortgagee's basis for the loan. As the mortgagor pays off the loan, the mortgagee is merely recovering the basis and there are no tax consequences. However, if the mortgagee receives less than the face amount of the debt or the basis, then the mortgagee obviously realizes a loss. This loss may be deductible simply as a loss under Code Sec. 165, or as a bad debt under Code Sec. 166.

If the mortgage is a purchase-money mortgage provided by the seller of property to the buyer, the rule that treats a reduction in the amount of the mortgage as a reduction in the purchase price (discussed at ¶ 1203.5 in connection with the tax treatment of the debtor) applies equally to the creditor. Therefore, if the conditions of Code Sec. 108(e)(5) are met, the creditor must treat a reduction of a purchase-money mortgage as a reduction of the selling price rather than as a loss or bad debt.

---

[28] Code Sec. 108(e)(5)(C).

¶ 1205.1 *Loss on Discount*

Generally, a loss that is not compensated for by insurance or otherwise is deductible in full for the year in which it is sustained.[29] In the case of individuals, losses are deductible under Code Sec. 165 only if they are incurred in a trade or business or in a transaction entered into for profit.[30] Since a loss on a mortgage loan will be from a transaction entered into for profit, if not actually a trade or business, most taxpayers would benefit from being able to deduct the reduction in a mortgage loan as a loss under Code Sec. 165, rather than a bad debt under Code Sec. 166. Only "business bad debts" are deductible in full. Other bad debts are treated as capital losses (see ¶ 1205.2).

The distinction between a loss under Code Sec. 165 and a bad debt deduction under Code Sec. 166 for a mortgagee evidently turns on the reason for the reduction in the amount of debt and the financial status of the debtor. If a mortgagee agrees to settle a debt at a discount because the mortgagor is unable to pay, or refuses to pay because the property has declined in value, the situation obviously involves a bad debt. But what if the mortgagor is able and willing to pay, but only according to the terms of the mortgage loan? How can there be a "bad debt" in this situation?

The obvious answer to these questions is that there really is no bad debt. The mortgagee may want to eliminate a loan that carries a low interest rate and be willing to accept less than the basis and take the loss in order to obtain cash that can be put to better use. The mortgagee also simply may need the cash and cannot wait for the mortgagor to make the agreed payments. When the mortgagee offers and accepts less than the remaining balance on the mortgage in these situations, the loss should be deductible under Code Sec. 165. The deduction would be the difference between the amount received and the remaining basis for the mortgage.

While there is limited authority for this viewpoint, it is not without some support. In Letter Ruling 8547001, June 26, 1985, the IRS permitted a cash method domestic federal savings and loan association to deduct a loan discount that was used to encourage an early payoff of a low-interest mortgage as an ordinary loss in the year that the mortgage was repaid.[31] Loss due to compromise of debt is not deductible as a bad debt if the debtor is solvent.[32]

---

[29] Code Sec. 165(a).
[30] Code Sec. 165(c).
[31] See also I.T. 4018, 1950-2 CB 20; but also see Rev. Rul. 69-43, 1969-1 CB 310.
[32] *G.C. Peterson Co.*, 1 BTA 690, CCH Dec. 259, Acq. iv-1 CB 3; *Raffold Process Corp.*, 3 TCM 1050, CCH Dec. 14,170(M), aff'd CA-1, 153 F.2d 168, 52-1 USTC ¶ 9359.

A mortgagee must not assume that discounting a mortgage and assigning the mortgage to a third party will produce the same tax result as discounting the mortgage on behalf of the mortgagor. While the economic results are essentially the same, that is, the mortgagee receives less than the remaining basis in the mortgage note, the assignment of the mortgage to a third party is a sale or exchange of the mortgage rather than the compromise of a debt. If the mortgage debt is a capital asset in the hands of the mortgagee, the assignment means that the loss is subject to the limits on the deduction of capital losses. For instance, in *Yates Holding Corp.*,[33] the taxpayer's assignment of a mortgage to a partnership formed by certain members of the mortgagor was held to be the sale of a capital asset and not a compromise of debt because the transaction took place between the taxpayer and the partnership, rather than between the taxpayer and the mortgagor. In this case, the taxpayer was allowed only a capital loss on the transaction.

¶ 1205.2 Bad Debt Deduction

A mortgagee who is unable to collect on a mortgage note is entitled to a bad debt deduction under Code Sec. 166. The deduction is taken in the year the debt becomes worthless.[34] If the mortgagee can show that the debt is recoverable only in part, a deduction may be allowed for the part that cannot be collected.[35] The deduction for a corporate mortgagee is always an ordinary deduction that is deductible in full against ordinary income. The deduction for a noncorporate taxpayer, however, hinges on whether the debt is considered a business bad debt or a nonbusiness bad debt. Business bad debts are deductible in full, but nonbusiness bad debts are treated as capital losses subject to the limits on the deduction of capital losses.[36]

The sale of mortgaged property in a foreclosure for less than the amount of the mortgage debt may establish the amount of the worthless debt (see discussion at ¶ 1211 in connection with foreclosure). Otherwise, in determining whether a debt is worthless in whole or only in part, the IRS considers "all pertinent evidence, including the value of the collateral, if any, securing the debt and the financial condition of the debtor."[37]

Going to the expense and trouble of reducing a debt to judgment and showing that it is uncollectible is not always necessary. Reg. § 1.166-2(b) provides that if the surrounding circumstances indicate that a debt is worthless and uncollectible and that legal action to

---

[33] 39 TCM 303, CCH Dec. 36,373(M), T.C. Memo. 1979-416.
[34] Code Sec. 166(a)(1).
[35] Code Sec. 166(a)(2).
[36] Code Sec. 166(d).
[37] Reg. § 1.166-2(a).

enforce payment would in all probability not result in the satisfaction of execution on a judgment, this is sufficient to establish the bad debt deduction. However, a taxpayer who makes what he or she considers a bona fide loan cannot refrain from pressing for collection of the full amount from a solvent debtor simply because the taxpayer is faced with the necessity of litigation and then deduct the difference between what the debtor is willing to pay and the face amount of the loan as a "loss." [38]

Bankruptcy, generally, is proof of worthlessness of at least a part of an unsecured and unpreferred debt.[39] In bankruptcy cases, a debt may become worthless before settlement in some instances, while in others, it may become worthless only when a settlement in bankruptcy is reached. This may make it difficult to decide when a bad debt deduction should be taken. In the usual situation, a mortgagor does not fall into financial straits overnight, but gradually slips into financial difficulty. This makes establishing the worthlessness of a debt at a particular time extremely difficult.

A mere refusal of a debtor to pay its debt does not warrant the debt's deduction as a bad debt,[40] nor does the refusal to pay combined with the creditor's belief that collection might be barred by the statute of limitations;[41] but the creditor is not required to be an "incorrigible optimist."[42] Generally, there must be some identifiable events that form a basis for abandoning hope of recovery.[43] An attorney's unsuccessful attempts to collect on accounts turned over to the attorney for collection was held to be sufficient proof of the worthlessness of the debts.[44]

¶ 1205.3 *Nonbusiness Bad Debts*

Unlike "business bad debts," nonbusiness bad debts are not deductible in full, but are subject to the limitations on the deduction of capital losses. Moreover, no deduction is allowed for the partial worthlessness of a nonbusiness bad debt.[45] This places a premium on classifying a bad debt as a business bad debt. A business bad debt is a debt (1) that is created or acquired in connection with a taxpayer's trade or business, or (2) whose worthlessness results in a loss which is incurred in the taxpayer's trade or business. Any other debt is a nonbusiness debt.[46]

---

[38] *N. D'Alonzo*, 10 TCM 817, CCH Dec. 18,509(M).
[39] Reg. § 1.166-2(c).
[40] *P.C. Hughes*, 10 TCM 204, CCH Dec. 18,180(M).
[41] *C.C. Cooke*, 10 TCM 881, CCH Dec. 18,556(M), aff'd and rev'd CA-10, 203 F.2d 258.
[42] *Home Agency Co.*, 25 TCM 272, CCH Dec. 27,868(M), T.C. Memo. 1966-48.

[43] *W. Ockrant*, 25 TCM 333, CCH Dec. 27,885(M), T.C. Memo. 1966-60.
[44] *J.M. Clarkston*, 17 TCM 446, CCH Dec. 22,986(M), T.C. Memo. 1958-91.
[45] Code Sec. 166(d).
[46] Code Sec. 166(d)(2).

The use to which the borrowed funds are put by the debtor is of no consequence in determining whether a debt is a business or nonbusiness debt. The character of the debt is determined by the relation which the loss resulting from the debt's becoming worthless bears to the trade or business of the taxpayer. If that relation is a proximate one in the conduct of the trade or business in which the taxpayer is engaged at the time the debt becomes worthless, the debt is a business debt and not a nonbusiness debt.[47] The settlement of a mortgage at a discount resulted in a business bad debt when the mortgage was held for sale in the ordinary course of the taxpayer's real estate business.[48] An individual with extensive investments in real estate and stocks and bonds, however, was not entitled to a business bad debt since his activities consisted solely of keeping records of investments and collecting dividends and interest.[49]

¶ 1211 FORECLOSURE

When a mortgagor fails to make payments on a mortgage note and a settlement or compromise cannot be reached, the mortgagee is likely to take steps to secure payment of the debt through a foreclosure and sale of the property. In the case of a deed of trust, as opposed to a mortgage, the trustee sells the property under the powers contained in the deed of trust. In the usual case, a foreclosure sale is simply the sale of the property securing the mortgage debt to a third party. The sale proceeds are then turned over to the mortgagee in full or partial satisfaction of the debt, and neither the mortgagee nor mortgagor has any further interest in the property, unless the mortgagor retains a right of redemption under local law.

For the mortgagor, the foreclosure is simply a sale for tax purposes on which gain or loss is realized. The mortgagee who receives payment in full as a result of the foreclosure merely receives back the basis in the mortgage debt, and there are no further tax consequences. If the foreclosure results in less than full satisfaction of the debt, however, the mortgagee may have a bad debt or loss deduction. A bad debt deduction may be available to the mortgagee, even if it is the mortgagee who purchases the property in the foreclosure.

¶ 1213 Tax Treatment of the Debtor

A foreclosure is a "sale" for tax purposes.[50] It is immaterial whether the taxpayer is personally liable on the mortgage.[51] See also

---

[47] Reg. § 1.166-5(b).
[48] *Theodore Gutman Est.*, 18 TC 112, CCH Dec. 18,923, Acq. 1952-2 CB 2; *R.E. Keller*, 29 TCM 369, CCH Dec. 30,043(M), T.C. Memo. 1970-79.
[49] *E. Higgins*, S.Ct., 41-1 USTC ¶ 9233, 312 U.S. 312, 61 S.Ct. 475.

[50] *G. Hammel*, S.Ct., 41-1 USTC ¶ 9169, 311 U.S. 504, 61, S.Ct. 368.
[51] *E.F.C. McLaughlin*, 43 BTA 528, CCH Dec. 11,642; *J.G. Abramson*, CA-2, 42-1 USTC ¶ 9200, 124 F.2d 416.

Rev. Rul. 78-164,[52] in which the IRS ruled that a voluntary conveyance of real property to a mortgagee by a mortgagor who was not personally liable on the mortgage was a sale. Nor does the "involuntary" nature of a foreclosure make the foreclosure an involuntary conversion that would allow postponement of tax under Code Sec. 1033.[53]

Since the foreclosure is a sale of the property, the mortgagor realizes gain or loss on the sale as measured by the difference between the adjusted basis for the property and the amount realized on the foreclosure sale.[54]

¶ 1213.1   Calculation of Gain or Loss

When a foreclosure sale produces proceeds that, after the expenses of sale, exceed the amount of the mortgage, the net proceeds are the amount realized by the mortgagor. This is fairly easy to see, since the proceeds are applied first to the unpaid mortgage, and any excess then is paid to the mortgagor.

Example 1: The Mortgagor purchased real property for $50,000, paying $5,000 in cash and financing the balance with a $45,000 mortgage. After amortizing $1,000 of the outstanding mortgage debt, the Mortgagor experiences financial difficulty and stops making payments on the debt. The mortgagee forecloses and the real property is sold for $49,000 after sale expenses. Up to the time of the foreclosure, the Mortgagor had taken $3,000 in depreciation deductions on the property, so that the adjusted basis at the time of the foreclosure was $47,000.

In this case, the $49,000 sale proceeds are applied first to the $44,000 of outstanding mortgage debt. The balance of $5,000 belongs to the Mortgagor and is paid to the Mortgagor. The Mortgagor realizes a gain of $2,000 on this sale, measured by the difference between the adjusted basis and the net proceeds of the sale ($49,000 − $47,000 = $2,000).

A foreclosure can also produce a loss for the mortgagor, even if the net proceeds of the foreclosure exceed the outstanding balance of the mortgage debt.

Example 2: Assume the same facts as in Example 1, except that the net proceeds from the foreclosure sale are $45,000, rather than $49,000.

---

[52] 1978-1 CB 264.
[53] *Cooperative Publishing Co.,* CA-9, 40-2 USTC ¶ 9823, 115 F.2d 1017; *J.A. Woolf,* 42 TCM 63, CCH Dec. 37,970(M), T.C. Memo. 1981-286.
[54] Code Sec. 1001(a).

In this case, the $45,000 sale proceeds are applied first to the $44,000 of outstanding mortgage debt. The balance of $1,000 belongs to the Mortgagor and is paid to the Mortgagor. The Mortgagor realizes a loss of $2,000 on this sale, measured by the difference between the adjusted basis and the net proceeds of the sale ($45,000 − $47,000 = ($2,000)).

A situation that is less easy to see arises when the proceeds of the foreclosure sale are not sufficient to pay off the outstanding mortgage debt. In this situation, is the amount realized by the mortgagor limited to the proceeds of the sale? The answer to this is "no," based on the principle established in *B.B. Crane* [55] and discussed at ¶ 105.

While this result is clearly called for when the mortgagor is not personally liable for the mortgage debt, there may be some question as to whether this rule should apply when the mortgagor remains liable for the deficiency. In any event, the case law seems to support the proposition that the amount realized includes the entire mortgage, not just the net proceeds of the foreclosure sale. The theory seems to be that any deficiency payment made at a later time is merely part of the mortgagor's cost that had been fully accounted for in the basis at the time of the foreclosure. This result applies regardless of whether the mortgagor realizes a gain or loss on the foreclosure and sale for less than the outstanding mortgage debt.

When a taxpayer acquired mortgaged property in a tax-free exchange and subsequently the mortgagee foreclosed and bought the property for a nominal sum, the foreclosure was held a "disposition," and the amount realized was the amount of the mortgage. Treating the amount of the mortgage as the amount realized resulted in a gain to the taxpayer measured by the difference between the mortgage and the taxpayer's adjusted basis.[56] In Rev. Rul. 73-36,[57] a foreclosure resulted in a loss. The mortgage foreclosure was ruled a sale of real estate in consideration of the cancellation of the mortgage debt, and the taxpayer sustained a loss equal to the excess of the adjusted basis of the property over the amount of the cancelled mortgage.[58]

Example: The Mortgagor purchased real property for $50,000, paying $5,000 in cash and financing the balance with a $45,000 mortgage. After amortizing $1,000 of the outstanding mortgage debt, the Mortgagor experiences financial difficulty and stops making payments on the debt. The mortgagee forecloses and the real property is sold for $43,000 after sale expenses. The Mortgagor remains liable for the $1,000 deficiency between the outstanding

---

[55] 47-1 USTC ¶ 9217, 333 U.S. 1, 67 S.Ct. 1047.
[56] *Woodsam Associates, Inc.*, CA-2, 52-2 USTC ¶ 9396, 198 F.2d 357.
[57] 1973-1 CB 372.
[58] See also *E. Harris*, 34 TCM 597, CCH Dec. 33,173(M), T.C. Memo. 1975-125.

¶ 1213.1

mortgage balance of $44,000 and the $43,000 sale proceeds. Up to the time of the foreclosure, the Mortgagor had taken $3,000 in depreciation deductions on the property, so that the adjusted basis at the time of the foreclosure was $47,000.

In this case, the $43,000 sale proceeds are insufficient to pay in full the $44,000 of outstanding mortgage debt. The balance of $1,000 is eventually paid to the mortgagee by the Mortgagor. The Mortgagor realizes a loss of $3,000 on this sale, measured by the difference between the adjusted basis and the amount of the outstanding mortgage debt ($44,000 − $47,000 = ($3,000)). When the Mortgagor eventually pays the $1,000 deficiency, there are no further tax consequences and no loss to the Mortgagor because that portion of the debt, as well as the portion paid with the foreclosure proceeds, was reflected in the adjusted basis for purposes of computing the gain or loss on the foreclosure sale.

Suppose, however, that the Mortgagor had taken $8,000 in depreciation deductions prior to the foreclosure so that the adjusted basis at the time of the foreclosure is $42,000. In this case, the Mortgagor realizes a gain of $2,000 on this sale, measured by the difference between the adjusted basis and the outstanding mortgage balance ($44,000 − $42,000 = $2,000). Again, when the Mortgagor eventually pays the $1,000 deficiency, there are no further tax consequences and no loss to the Mortgagor because that portion of the debt, as well as the portion paid with the foreclosure proceeds, was reflected in the adjusted basis for purposes of computing the gain or loss on the foreclosure sale.

Sometimes, the holder of a second or subordinate mortgage on real estate will make payments to the holder of the first mortgage in order to protect the interest when the mortgagor defaults. When this occurs, the mortgagor becomes indebted to the second mortgagee for the amount of the payments in addition to the amount of the second mortgage. The payments made by the holder of the second mortgage are added to the amount of the second mortgage to determine the amount of cancelled mortgage debt on a foreclosure of the second mortgage.[59]

Generally, the mortgagor reports the gain or loss from the foreclosure sale in the year in which the foreclosure occurs. The definitive event fixing the amount of gain or loss is the foreclosure sale, not the foreclosure decree that orders and precedes the sale.[60] When the mortgagor retains a right of redemption under local law, however, the gain

---

[59] *E. Harris*, 34 TCM 597, CCH Dec. 33,173(M), T.C. Memo. 1975-125.

[60] *G. Hammel*, S.Ct., 41-1 USTC ¶ 9169, 311 U.S. 504, 61 S.Ct. 368.

¶ 1213.1

or loss is not reportable until that right expires.[61] If the mortgagor releases the right to redeem prior to the expiration of the redemption period, however, the mortgagor reports gain or loss on release of the redemption right.[62] Essentially, a mortgagor in a jurisdiction that grants a right of redemption may choose the year in which to report the gain or loss. If the mortgagor wants to delay, the mortgagor merely allows the redemption period to run its course. To accelerate the gain or loss, the mortgagor merely releases the redemption right early.

¶ 1213.2 Character of Gain or Loss

Since a foreclosure is a sale for tax purposes, the character of the gain or loss realized by the mortgagor on a foreclosure depends on the nature of the property. If the foreclosed property is a capital asset, the gain or loss resulting from the foreclosure is a capital gain or loss.[63] A taxpayer realized a capital loss when real estate that had been purchased in a joint venture was sold at a foreclosure sale because the joint venture did not hold the real estate primarily for sale to customers in the ordinary course of business.[64]

The gain or loss on foreclosed property may also be an ordinary gain or loss [65] or a Section 1231 gain or loss.[66] In Rev. Rul. 67-188, the IRS ruled that if a general partner is engaged in the real estate business individually as a dealer, and the partnership operates a hotel, the general partner's share of the partnership loss resulting from the foreclosure of a mortgage on the hotel property is a Section 1231 loss. The individual business activities of the partner were not taken into account in determining the nature of the partner's share of partnership gains or losses.

For more on the treatment of the sale of real estate other than in the ordinary course of business, see ¶ 1301. For a discussion of the sale of real property in the ordinary course of business, see Chapter 10.

¶ 1215 Treatment of the Creditor

A foreclosure may result in the sale of the mortgaged property to a third party or to the mortgagee. When the sale is to a third party, the tax consequences are fairly straightforward since the mortgagee has no further interest in the property and merely receives whatever proceeds are available to fully or partially satisfy the mortgage debt. If no third party comes forward with a reasonable bid in the foreclosure, however,

---

[61] *J.C. Hawkins*, CA-5, 37-2 USTC ¶ 9412, 91 F.2d 354; *G.J. Kolowich*, 1 TCM 416, CCH Dec. 12,936-C.
[62] *Atmore Realty Co.*, BTA Memo., CCH Dec. 12,517-A; *S.A. Hill, Admr.*, 40 BTA 376, CCH Dec. 10,796, Nonacq. 1939-2 CB 53.
[63] *G. Hammel*, S.Ct., 41-1 USTC ¶ 9169, 311 U.S. 504, 61 S.Ct. 368; *Electro-Chemical Engraving Co.*,
Inc., S.Ct., 41-1 USTC ¶ 9170, 311 U.S. 513, 61 S.Ct. 372.
[64] *K.R. Terry*, 48 TCM 906, CCH Dec. 41,431(M), T.C. Memo. 1984-442.
[65] *H. Rothschild v. H.A. Berliner*, DC Cal., 50-2 USTC ¶ 9521.
[66] Rev. Rul. 67-188, 1967-1 CB 216.

the property may be purchased by the mortgagee in order to protect the mortgagee's interest. When this occurs, the mortgagee is placed in the role of both creditor and purchaser. As a creditor, the mortgagee may have a bad debt loss, and, as a purchaser, the mortgagee may realize a gain or loss. Whatever the final results of the foreclosure, however, the mortgagee can be sure that expenses will be incurred in protecting the property before the foreclosure, for the foreclosure itself, and, if the mortgagee acquires the property, for charges that have accumulated against the property.

¶ 1215.1 *Foreclosure Expenses*

The costs of the foreclosure itself borne by the mortgagee, such as legal fees and court costs, reduce the proceeds of the foreclosure.[67] These expenses, therefore, may increase the mortgagee's loss from the foreclosure or decrease any gain the mortgagee might realize if the mortgagee reacquires the property as a result of the foreclosure.

Taxes and water rates against property that are paid by the mortgagee prior to acquiring title on foreclosure increase the amount of mortgage debt and, as a result, are recognized in determining gain or loss from the foreclosure.[68] The same rule would apply to any other charges against the property that the mortgagee pays prior to the foreclosure proceedings.

On the other hand, if the mortgagee acquires the property in the foreclosure and pays charges against the property at the time of foreclosure or afterwards, these charges are part of the mortgagee's basis for the acquired property. In *Schieffelin*, the taxpayer purchased other mortgaged property at the foreclosure sale, with taxes and water rates outstanding against the property. The court ruled that payment of these charges in the year after the foreclosure was an additional capital investment in the property and did not enter into the calculation of gain or loss on the foreclosure. See also *M.S. Rogers*,[69] in which taxes paid by the mortgagee as a condition precedent to the acquisition of title by foreclosure increased the basis for depreciation of the buildings on the foreclosed realty. If the mortgagee does not acquire the property, these charges would presumably be added to the mortgage debt and increase the mortgagee's basis for the debt in the same fashion as charges incurred prior to the foreclosure.

¶ 1215.2 *Purchase by Third Party*

If the proceeds of the foreclosure sale are less than the amount of the debt, and the portion of the mortgage debt that remains unsatisfied

---

[67] GCM 19573, 1938-1 CB 214.
[68] *L.S. Schieffelin Est.*, 44 BTA 137, CCH Dec. 11,752, Acq. 1941-1 CB 9.
[69] DC Conn., 46-2 USTC ¶ 9361, 69 F.Supp. 8.

after the sale is wholly or partially uncollectible, the mortgagee is entitled to a bad debt deduction for the taxable year in which it becomes wholly worthless or is charged off as partially worthless.[70] The mortgagee may also include accrued and unpaid interest on the mortgage as part of the bad debt deduction, but only if the mortgagee previously reported the accrued interest as income.[71] Generally, if the mortgagee obtains a deficiency judgment for the amount of the mortgage debt that is not covered by the proceeds of the foreclosure sale, a bad debt deduction cannot be taken until the judgment becomes uncollectible.

For the treatment of a bad debt as a business bad debt or a nonbusiness bad debt, and the determination of when a debt becomes worthless, see the discussion of the bad debt deduction at ¶ 1205.2.

>*Example:* The Mortgagor defaults when a balance of $52,000 is owed on the mortgage obtained to finance the purchase of a parcel of real estate. In order to protect the interest before foreclosure, the Mortgagee pays real estate taxes on the parcel in the amount of $2,500. The real estate taxes paid by the Mortgagee are considered an additional loan and increase the Mortgagee's basis for the debt to $54,500 ($52,000 + $2,500).
>
>In the foreclosure sale, the parcel is sold for $49,000. The expenses of the foreclosure, including legal fees and court costs, are $3,600. These expenses reduce the proceeds of the foreclosure sale to $45,400 ($49,000 − $3,600). The Mortgagee's bad debt deduction therefore is $9,100. This is the Mortgagee's basis in the debt of $54,500, less the net proceeds of the foreclosure of $45,400 ($54,500 − $45,400 = $9,100).

¶ 1215.3 *Purchase by Mortgagee*

Just as with a purchase by a third party, if the proceeds, or in this case the amount bid by the mortgagee, are less than the amount of the debt, and the portion of the mortgage debt that remains unsatisfied after the sale is wholly or partially uncollectible, the mortgagee is entitled to a bad debt deduction for the taxable year in which the debt becomes wholly worthless or is charged off as partially worthless. Thus, the mortgagee realizes a bad debt loss measured by the difference between the bid price and the amount of the outstanding mortgage debt whenever the bid price is less than the outstanding debt.[72]

A mortgagee who bids for and acquires the property in a foreclosure sale, however, wears a second hat in addition to that of a creditor. The mortgagee is also a purchaser of the property and, in this role, may

---

[70] Reg. § 1.166-6(a)(1).
[71] Reg. § 1.166-6(a)(2).
[72] Reg. § 1.166-6(a)(1).

realize a gain or loss on the transaction, in addition to any possible bad debt loss. This gain or loss is measured by the difference between the amount of the obligations of the debtor that are applied to the purchase or bid price of the property and the fair market value of the property.[73] The fair market value of the property is presumed to be the amount for which it is bid in by the mortgagee, in the absence of clear and convincing proof to the contrary.[74]

The effect of these rules is that the mortgagee realizes no gain or loss, apart from any bad debt loss, if the bid price is equal to the fair market value of the property. If the bid price is less than the fair market value of the property, however, any bad debt loss is offset by the gain realized, so that the actual economic gain or loss realized by the mortgagee is reflected in his taxable income or loss. Similarly, if the bid price is more than the fair market value of the property, the additional economic loss is added to the bad debt loss. While this might give a mortgagee an incentive to bid low if the gain would be treated as a capital gain, the IRS has ruled that if a taxpayer receives an ordinary deduction on foreclosure, any offsetting gain is taxable as ordinary income.[75] The ruling involved a real estate investment trust that engaged primarily in short-term financing activities. The trust had made a construction loan on which it later foreclosed and bid in the property for less than its fair market value. Since the trust's basis in the mortgage note exceeded the property's value, and the balance due on the note was wholly uncollectible, the trust sustained an ordinary bad debt loss. The gain realized by the trust as a result of the bid on the property at less than fair market value was ruled to be ordinary income.

As to the presumption in Reg. § 1.166-6(b)(2) that the bid price is equal to the fair market value of the property, the Tax Court has defined the workings of the presumption in the following manner. The fair market value is presumed to be the bid price absent clear and convincing proof to the contrary. Upon proof of the bid price, the mortgagee comes within the presumption and meets the burden of proof as to the fair market value of the property. The presumption applies even when the value of the property is greater than the bid price and the presumption is not limited to cases in which the alleged fair market value is lower than the bid price. The IRS cannot disregard the presumption without producing evidence to indicate that the bid price is not representative of the fair market value.[76] The IRS, however, may use evidence to prove that the fair market value is different

---

[73] Reg. § 1.166-6(b)(1).
[74] Reg. § 1.166-6(b)(2).
[75] Rev. Rul. 80-56, 1980-1 CB 154.
[76] *Community Bank*, 62 TC 503, CCH Dec. 32,679, Acq. 1975-1 CB 1.

than the bid price, even if state law provides that a successful bid price at a foreclosure proceeding determines the fair market value of real property.[77] The IRS may use an expert witness to rebut the presumption and establish a fair market value other than the bid price.[78]

> **Example:** The Mortgagor owes a balance of $53,000 on a parcel of real estate when the Mortgagee acquires the property in a foreclosure by bidding in $50,000. The remaining amount of the debt is uncollectible. The Mortgagee's bad debt deduction is $3,000 ($53,000 basis of debt − $50,000 bid = $3,000 bad debt loss). If the fair market value of the property is $50,000, or if there is no clear and convincing evidence that the fair market value is anything other than the bid price, the Mortgagee would realize no further gain or loss as a result of the purchase of the property in the foreclosure.
>
> Suppose, however, that the fair market value of the property is $45,000. In this case, in addition to the bad debt loss, the Mortgagee would realize an additional loss of $5,000 ($50,000 obligations of debtor applied to bid price − $45,000 fair market value = $5,000 loss on purchase). This loss may be a capital loss if the debt is a capital asset in the hands of the Mortgagee.
>
> If the fair market value of the property is $55,000, however, the Mortgagee would realize a gain on the purchase of $5,000 ($55,000 fair market value − $50,000 obligations of debtor applied to bid price = $5,000 gain on purchase). The gain may be capital gain if the debt is a capital asset. However, as noted above, the IRS applies tax benefit principles to treat gain offsetting a deduction from ordinary income as ordinary income (Rev. Rul. 80-56, 1980-1 CB 154). Therefore, if the $3,000 bad debt loss produces an ordinary loss deduction for the Mortgagee, $3,000 of the $5,000 gain on the purchase transaction would be ordinary income, even if the debt qualified as a capital asset in the hands of the Mortgagee.

In Rev. Rul. 72-238,[79] the IRS ruled that gain realized in a foreclosure proceeding by a bank that purchases mortgaged property at a bid price less than the fair market value of the property is ordinary income. The loan is not a capital asset in the hands of a bank originating the loan.

As a general rule, a mortgagee will want to bid as low as possible in order to produce the greatest bad debt deduction on a foreclosure. The

---

[77] *Community Bank,* 79 TC 789, CCH Dec. 39,481, Aff'd CA-9, 87-2 USTC ¶ 9379.
[78] See, for example, *C.J. Heath,* 30 TCM 545, CCH Dec. 30,812(M), T.C. Memo. 1959-80.
[79] 1972-1 CB 65.

lower bounds, taking into account the bid necessary to acquire the property, should be such as to come within the presumption that the bid price is equal to fair market value, that is, not so low as to invite a challenge. The mortgagee can support the position taken with appraisals or other evidence showing that the bid price is equal to fair market value. While a bid that is lower than fair market value would produce an even larger bad debt loss, the additional loss would be offset by the gain realized on the purchase transaction.

The mortgagee's basis for property bid in at a foreclosure sale is the fair market value of the property.[80] The fair market value of the property, rather than the bid price, is used to fix the mortgagee's basis because any difference between the bid price and the fair market value of the property is reflected in the mortgagee's income at the time of the foreclosure. If the mortgagee pays charges against the property at the time of foreclosure or afterwards, these charges are added to the mortgagee's basis for the acquired property (see further discussion of expenses of foreclosure, at ¶ 1215.1).

For the special rules that apply when the seller reacquires property subject to a purchase-money mortgage, see the discussion at ¶ 1231.

¶ 1221 CONVEYANCE AND ABANDONMENT OF MORTGAGE

The settlement of the mortgage debt at a discount or foreclosure are not the only options open to the parties when a mortgage loan is in trouble. A mortgagee may be willing to accept the conveyance of the mortgaged property in full satisfaction of the mortgage debt. This course may appeal to the mortgagee who wants to avoid the time-consuming and costly process of foreclosure. It is also likely to appeal to a mortgagee who foresees an unnecessary loss on a foreclosure sale because of market or other conditions that may improve with time.

A mortgagor who is unable to meet mortgage obligations on the property may be willing to simply "walk away" from the property. Whether such an abandonment produces tax results that differ from foreclosure or conveyance to the mortgagee is a question that has troubled the courts for years. Earlier cases indicate that when there is an abandonment there is no sale or exchange necessary to support capital loss treatment and, therefore, abandonment automatically produces an ordinary loss. More recent cases, however, do not accept this notion.

¶ 1223 Conveyance to Mortgagee

A mortgagee may be willing to accept the mortgaged property in full satisfaction of the mortgage debt in some cases when the mortgagor

---

[80] Reg. § 1.166-6(c).

is no longer able to make the required payments. The conveyance of the mortgaged property to the mortgagee has tax consequences for both parties to the mortgage loan.

¶ 1223.1 Tax Treatment of Mortgagor

The transfer of the mortgaged property by the mortgagor to the mortgagee in satisfaction of the mortgage debt is treated as a sale of the mortgaged property. The outstanding mortgage debt is the amount realized from the sale, and if this is less than the mortgagor's basis for the property, the mortgagor realizes a loss.[81] However, regulations issued under Code Sec. 1001 may require the mortgagor to recognize income from the discharge of indebtedness in the case of a recourse mortgage which exceeds the fair market value of the property. If the mortgage debt is greater than the mortgagor's basis for the property, the mortgagor realizes a gain, regardless of whether the mortgagor is personally liable on the debt.[82]

The general rule is that the amount realized from a sale or other disposition of property includes the amount of liabilities from which the transferor is discharged as a result of the sale or disposition.[83] However, the amount realized on a sale or other disposition of property that secures a recourse liability does not include amounts that are or would be, if realized and recognized, income from the discharge of indebtedness.[84] This rule applies only if the amount of debt were included in the basis of the property.[85]

Example: The Mortgagor transfers to the mortgagee property with a fair market value of $60,000, and the mortgagee discharges a $75,000 mortgage for which the Mortgagor was personally liable. The amount of the mortgage was included in the Mortgagor's basis for the property. The amount realized by the Mortgagor on the transfer of the property is its fair market value of $60,000. In addition, the Mortgagor has income from the discharge of indebtedness of $15,000 ($75,000 − $60,000 = $15,000).

Under the regulations, a disposition of property includes a transfer of the property in satisfaction of liabilities to which it is subject.[86] The sale or other disposition of property that secures a recourse liability discharges the transferor from liability if another person agrees to pay the liability, regardless of whether the transferor is in fact released from liability.[87] The sale or other disposition of property that secures a nonrecourse liability discharges the transferor from liability.[88]

---

[81] *A.A. Kaufman,* CA-9, 41-1 USTC ¶ 9468, 119 F.2d 901.
[82] *Lutz & Schramm Co.,* 1 TC 682, CCH Dec. 13,014, Nonacq. 1943 CB 35.
[83] Reg. § 1.1001-2(a)(1).
[84] Reg. § 1.1001-2(a)(2).
[85] Reg. § 1.1001-2(a)(3).
[86] Reg. § 1.1001-2(a)(4)(iii).
[87] Reg. § 1.1001-2(a)(4)(ii).
[88] Reg. § 1.1001-2(a)(4)(i).

¶ 1223.2 Tax Treatment of Mortgagee

The mortgagee realizes a loss when the mortgaged property is accepted in satisfaction of the mortgage debt if the value of the property is less than the mortgagee's basis for the debt. This loss is deductible as a bad debt since there is no sale or exchange of the mortgage notes.[89] See also *National Bank of Commerce of San Antonio*,[90] in which the court ruled that a bank had a deductible bad debt loss, not a capital loss, equal to the difference between the amount of its loans to an estate and the value of property conveyed to it by the debtor in settlement of the loans—the transaction was not a sale.

If the value of the mortgaged property exceeds the mortgagee's basis for the debt, the mortgagee realizes a gain. If there is accrued but unreported interest on the debt, or if the excess represents discount, to this extent the gain is ordinary income. Interest income cannot arise, however, if the value of the property does not exceed the principal of the mortgage loan.

Special rules apply when a mortgagee reacquires property that was sold subject to a purchase-money mortgage. These rules are discussed at ¶ 1231.

Mortgaged property may be conveyed to the mortgagee in full satisfaction of the mortgage debt under court order in foreclosure. The tax consequences to the mortgagee of such an involuntary conveyance are the same as those discussed at ¶ 1223.1 that apply in the case of a voluntary transfer by the mortgagor. If the fair market value of the property exceeds the mortgagee's basis for the debt, the mortgagee realizes gain. If the basis of the debt is greater than the fair market value of the property, the mortgagee realizes a bad debt loss. If the mortgagor retains a right of redemption, however, the deduction for the bad debt loss may be delayed until the right expires or is released or abandoned.

¶ 1225 Abandonment by Mortgagor

The abandonment of property by the mortgagor leaves the mortgagor in essentially the same economic position the mortgagor would be in had the property been conveyed to the mortgagee or had the mortgagee foreclosed. Nevertheless, early case law looked upon abandonment as producing a different tax result, at least if the mortgagor were not personally liable on the debt. If a taxpayer did not assume the mortgage on property at the time of purchase, notice to the mortgagee of abandonment of all rights in the property resulted in an ordinary loss.[91]

---

[89] *H.P. Bingham*, CA-2, 39-2 USTC ¶ 9636, 105 F.2d 971; *A.B. Spreckles*, CA-9, 41-2 USTC ¶ 9546, 120 F.2d 517.

[90] CA-5, 40-2 USTC ¶ 9550, 112 F.2d 946.

[91] *W.W. Hoffman*, CA-2, 41-1 USTC ¶ 9280, 117 F.2d 987. See also *T. Stokes*, CA-3, 41-2 USTC ¶ 9770,

The theory behind these decisions was that there was no sale or exchange when the property was abandoned, and, therefore, without a sale or exchange, gain or loss would not be a capital gain or loss.

If the mortgagor was personally liable on the mortgage debt, however, the early cases did recognize that a sale or exchange took place, with the discharge of the debt treated as property received by the mortgagor.[92] Also, the early cases found a sale or exchange rather than an abandonment whenever any consideration at all flowed to the mortgagor. For instance, a capital loss resulted after a mortgagor decided to abandon property and then directed a conveyance of the title for nominal consideration, which he never received.[93] In *H.C. Aberle*,[94] there was a sale resulting in a capital loss when the owner of property subject to a mortgage on which he was not personally liable conveyed the property to the mortgagee in consideration for the mortgagee's agreement to pay real property taxes which were the personal liability of the owner.

More recently, however, the Tax Court has found that a sale or exchange can occur when property is abandoned and that a capital loss, rather than an ordinary loss, is the result for the mortgagor (assuming, of course, that the property is a capital asset in the hands of the mortgagor). This more recent line of decisions is based on the Tax Court's decision in *E.L. Freeland*,[95] in which the Court ruled that a transaction in which the purchaser of real property reconveyed the property to the mortgagee without consideration, when the fair market value of the property was less than the unpaid mortgage principal, was the sale of a capital asset, and thus the loss was capital rather than ordinary.

While *E.L. Freeland* did not deal directly with abandonment, the same principle was soon extended to the abandonment of property by a mortgagor who was not personally liable on the mortgage debt. When a partnership that held real property subject to nonrecourse mortgages in excess of the fair market value of the property abandoned the property, the Tax Court held that the losses from the abandonment were capital losses, not ordinary losses.[96] The Tax Court specifically followed its decision in *E.L. Freeland* and ruled that to the extent *W.W. Hoffman* held to the contrary, it was no longer controlling. Other decisions soon followed.

(Footnote Continued)

124 F.2d 335; *Realty Operators, Inc.*, 40 BTA 1051, CCH Dec. 19,914, Nonacq. 1940-1 CB 8.

[92] See, for example, *P. Green*, CA-3, 42-1 USTC ¶ 9277, 126 F.2d 70.

[93] *A. Blum*, CA-2, 43-1 USTC ¶ 9283, 133 F.2d 447.

[94] CA-3, 41-2 USTC ¶ 9558, 121 F.2d 726.

[95] 74 TC 970, CCH Dec. 37,127.

[96] *M.L. Middleton*, 77 TC 310, CCH Dec. 38,124, aff'd per curiam CA-11, 693 F.2d 124, 82-2 USTC ¶ 9713.

In *L.J. Arkin*,[97] the taxpayer's abandonment of the interest in a land trust was ruled a sale or exchange of a capital asset, and the loss deductible as a capital loss rather than an ordinary loss. The taxpayer's interest was admittedly a capital asset, and the relinquishment of the bundle of rights constituting the interest in the land trust in return for being relieved of the obligation to bear a proportionate share of the costs of the mortgage payment, trustee's fees, insurance costs, taxes, and tort or contract liability constituted a sale or exchange, regardless of whether a technical abandonment also occurred under state law.

A taxpayer, a member of a joint venture that held unimproved property subject to a nonrecourse mortgage in excess of the property's fair market value, sustained a long-term capital loss from the sale or exchange of a capital asset at the time the joint venture abandoned the property. The Tax Court's characterization of the loss from the abandonment of unimproved real estate as a long-term capital loss, rather than an ordinary loss, was affirmed on appeal.[98] According to the appellate court, the abandonment of unimproved real estate held subject to a nonrecourse mortgage exceeding its fair market value constituted a "sale or exchange" because the taxpayer received the benefit of being relieved of the obligation to pay the debt and taxes and assessments against the property.[99]

What the recent decisions have done is to bring the tax treatment of abandonment into conformity with the treatment of foreclosure and voluntary conveyance as a means of dealing with troubled real estate financings. Considering the economic equivalence of these transactions from the mortgagor's point of view, the uniform treatment seems justified.

¶ 1231 REPOSSESSION OF SELLER-FINANCED PROPERTY

When the seller of real property provides financing to the purchaser through a purchase-money mortgage, a foreclosure puts the mortgagee (seller) in the position of reacquiring property that he previously owned. This situation differs from third-party financing, and the tax law recognizes this difference. Generally, under Code Sec. 1038, the mortgagee recognizes neither gain nor loss on the reacquisition of seller-financed property, except to the extent of payments received in excess of gain reported on the original sale.

In the case of an all-cash sale, or when there is third-party financing, Code Sec. 1038 does not apply. If the seller of property

---

[97] 76 TC 1048, CCH Dec. 38,017.
[98] *J.W. Yarbo*, CA-5, 84-2 USTC ¶ 9691, aff'g 45 TCM 170, CCH Dec. 39,513(M), T.C. Memo. 1982-675.
[99] See also *F.L. LaPort*, CA-7, 82-1 USTC ¶ 9230, 671 F.2d 1028, aff'g 40 TCM 1134, CCH Dec. 37,202(M), T.C. Memo. 1980-355.

receives the entire purchase price and then accepts a reconveyance of the property and returns the buyer's funds in the same taxable year, no gain is recognized by the seller on the sale. If the reconveyance occurs after the taxable year of the sale, the seller reports the sale in the tax year of the sale and acquires a new basis in the property when it is reconveyed equal to the amount paid for the reconveyance.[100]

¶ 1233 Nonrecognition of Gain or Loss

The general rule of Code Sec. 1038 is that if the sale of real property gives rise to indebtedness to the seller which is secured by the real property that is sold, and the seller of the property reacquires the property in full or partial satisfaction of the indebtedness, then the seller recognizes neither gain nor loss as a result of the reacquisition.[101] The property need not be reacquired from the purchaser, but may be reacquired from the purchaser's transferee or assignee, as long as the indebtedness that is partially or completely satisfied in the reacquisition arose in the original sale and was secured by the property.[102]

The mortgagee reacquiring the property must have been the seller of the property for the nonrecognition provisions to apply. When a taxpayer acquired real property on the foreclosure of a mortgage, but had obtained the mortgage for a note that had been acquired as part payment for the sale of stock, Code Sec. 1038 did not apply to the gain attributable to the acquisition of the real property through the foreclosure. Code Sec. 1038 applies only when the reacquired property was previously sold by the mortgagee.[103] Similarly, the IRS has ruled that the nonrecognition provisions do not apply to a former shareholder who has received an installment obligation in a corporation's liquidation when that shareholder, on the buyer's default, receives the real property used to secure the debt. In this case, the liquidated corporation, not the former shareholder, is the seller of the property.[104]

The nonrecognition provision applies regardless of whether the seller realized a gain or loss on the sale of the property. Also, it does not matter what method of accounting the seller used to report gain or loss from the sale or whether at the time of reacquisition the property has appreciated or depreciated since the original sale.[105] The nonrecognition provision even applies on the repossession of improved property in satisfaction of an obligation resulting from the sale of the same property prior to the improvements.[106] The only gain that must be recognized is that from payments received that exceed previously reported gain, as discussed below.

---

[100] Rev. Rul. 80-58, 1980-1 CB 181.
[101] Code Sec. 1038(a).
[102] Reg. § 1.1038-1(a)(4).
[103] *E.R. Held,* DC Ala., 75-2 USTC ¶ 9678.
[104] Rev. Rul. 86-120, 1986-2 CB 145.
[105] Reg. § 1.1038-1(a)(1).
[106] *R.R. Connners,* 88 TC 541, CCH Dec. 43,750.

Title does not have to pass to the purchaser in order for there to be a sale, so that the nonrecognition provision applies on a repossession in a contract-type sale. If the purchaser has a contractual right to retain possession of the property as long as the obligations under the contract are performed and to obtain title on the completion of the contract, a sale has taken place for purposes of Code Sec. 1038. A sale may have occurred even if the purchaser does not have the right to possession until the purchaser partially or fully satisfies the terms of the contract.[107]

Code Sec. 1038 applies only when the seller reacquires the property in partial or full satisfaction of the indebtedness to the seller that arose from the sale of the real property and that was secured by the property. It is not necessary, however, that the purchaser default or that default be imminent. As long as the seller is reacquiring the property only in exchange for the discharge of the purchaser's obligation to the seller, and does not pay any additional consideration, the nonrecognition provision applies.[108] If additional consideration is paid by the seller on the reacquisition, the reacquisition and additional consideration must be provided for in the original sale contract or the purchaser must be in default or default must be imminent. For example, if the purchaser is in arrears on the payment of interest or principal or has in any other way defaulted on the contract for the purchase of the property, or if the facts indicate that the purchaser is unable to perform the obligations satisfactorily under the contract, and the seller reacquires the property from the purchaser for consideration in addition to discharging the purchaser's indebtedness to the seller which arose from the sale and was secured by the property, Code Sec. 1038 applies to the reacquisition.

¶ 1233.1 *Prior Bad Debt Deductions*

A bad debt deduction is not allowed on the reacquisition of property under Code Sec. 1038.[109] If the seller-mortgagee previously took a bad debt deduction for the partial or complete worthlessness of the debt secured by the property, the seller must report an equal amount of income on the reacquisition of the property under Code Sec. 1038. Income inclusion is not required, however, to the extent the seller-mortgagee did not receive a tax benefit from the prior bad debt deduction.[110]

¶ 1233.2 *Holding Period of Reacquired Property*

Since the reacquisition of seller-financed property is essentially a nullification of the original sale of the property, the holding period of the property after its reacquisition includes the period the seller held

---

[107] Reg. § 1.1038-1(a)(2).
[108] Reg. § 1.1038-1(a)(3).
[109] Code Sec. 1038(a).
[110] Reg. § 1.1038-1(f)(2).

the property prior to its original sale. The holding period does not include the period of time beginning with the date following the date on which the property is originally sold and ending with the date on which the seller reacquires the property.[111]

¶ 1233.3 Basis of Reacquired Property

In order to preserve any gain or loss that goes unrecognized under Code Sec. 1038 on the disposition of the mortgage, the seller-mortgagee's basis for the reacquired property is a substituted basis, *i.e.*, the property generally takes the basis the seller-mortgagee had in the mortgage debt prior to the reacquisition of the property securing that debt.[112] This basis is adjusted for any gain recognized, as discussed below, and for any extra consideration paid by the seller in reacquiring the property. Specifically, Reg. § 1.1038-1(g)(1) provides that the basis of any real property acquired in a reacquisition to which Code Sec. 1038 applies is the sum of the following amounts:

1. The adjusted basis of all indebtedness of the purchaser to the seller which is secured by the property at the time of reacquisition;
2. The amount of gain that results because payments received by the seller exceed the amount of gain previously reported; and
3. The amount of money and the fair market value of other property paid by the seller in connection with the reacquisition of the real property.

The calculation of basis is illustrated in the examples below dealing with the recognition of gain.

¶ 1235 Recognition of Gain

Although the general rule provides that gain or loss is not recognized when seller-financed real property is reacquired by the seller, an exception applies when the seller has received money or other property from the purchaser in excess of gain reported on the sale of the property for periods prior to the reacquisition.[113] This may occur if the seller is reporting the original sale on the installment basis or if the seller elected out of installment reporting.

In either case, the gain reported under Code Sec. 1038 is limited to the potential gain on the original sale (selling price less adjusted basis), reduced by the sum of: (1) the amount of gain reported by the seller prior to the reacquisition, and (2) the expenses and other costs incurred by the seller in the reacquisition. In determining the potential gain from the original sale, the gross sales price is reduced by the selling

---

[111] Reg. § 1.1038-1(g)(3).
[112] Code Sec. 1038(c).
[113] Code Sec. 1038(b)(1).

commissions, legal fees, and other expenses incident to the sale of the property which are properly taken into account in determining gain or loss on the sale.[114]

To determine the amount of gain reported as income prior to the reacquisition, the seller includes gain resulting from payments received in the taxable year in which the reacquisition occurs, if the payments are received prior to the reacquisition.[115]

> **Example:** The Seller, a calendar year taxpayer, sells property with an adjusted basis of $15,000 to the Purchaser for $50,000. The sale takes place in 2002, and the Seller elects to report the gain from the sale under the installment method. During 2002 and 2003, the Seller receives a total of $20,000 on the contract. On May 15, 2004, the Seller receives $5,000 on the contract. After this payment, the Purchaser defaults and the Seller reacquires the property on October 1, 2004. The gain the Seller reported as income prior to the reacquisition includes gain attributable to the payment received in 2004, as well as the payments received in 2002 and 2003. Under the installment method, of the $25,000 in payments received prior to the reacquisition, 70 percent ($35,000 gain/$50,000 contract price), or $17,500, would have been reported as gain. The Seller would report the remaining $7,500 in payments received prior to the reacquisition as gain under Code Sec. 1038. (Installment sales are considered in Chapter 14.)

In determining the amount of payments and other property received prior to the reacquisition, the seller includes payments made by the purchaser for the purchaser's benefit, as well as payments made and other property transferred directly to the purchaser. If the purchaser makes payments on a mortgage or other indebtedness to which the property was subject at the time of the sale, or on which the seller was personally liable at the time of the sale, the seller includes these amounts as payments received prior to the reacquisition. If after the sale the purchaser borrows money and uses the property as security for the loan, however, payments by the purchaser in satisfaction of this indebtedness are not considered amounts received by the seller from the sale of the property, even though the seller does benefit indirectly when the purchaser makes these payments.[116]

Payments received by the seller also include payments made by the purchaser at the time of the reacquisition which are attributable to the original sale of the property.[117] For instance, if the purchaser makes a payment in partial or complete satisfaction of the original purchase-

---

[114] Code Sec. 1038(b)(2).
[115] Reg. § 1.1038-1(b)(1)(ii).
[116] Reg. § 1.1038-1(b)(2)(i).
[117] Reg. § 1.1038-1(b)(2)(ii).

money mortgage when the seller reacquires the property, the seller treats the payment as received prior to the reacquisition with respect to the original sale. Interest, stated or unstated, is excluded from the computation of gain on the sale of the property and is not considered money or other property received with respect to the sale.[118]

¶ 1235.1 Reacquisition Following Installment Sale

The seller who makes an installment sale of property and later repossesses the property is subject to Code Sec. 1038. The determination of the amount of gain that the seller must report on the reacquisition of the property, as well as the basis for the reacquired property, is illustrated by the following example.

Example: The Seller purchased real property for $80,000 and later sold that property to the Purchaser for $100,000. At the time of the sale to the Purchaser, there was no existing mortgage on the property. Under the contract of sale from the Seller to the Purchaser, the Purchaser paid $10,000 down and executed a note for the balance of $90,000, with interest at the current market rate. The principal, together with accrued interest, was to be paid in nine annual installments. The Seller elected to report the gain from the sale on the installment method. After the second $10,000 annual payment, the Purchaser defaults and the Seller accepts a voluntary reconveyance of the property in complete satisfaction of the purchase-money debt. The Seller incurs $5,000 in expenses in connection with the reacquisition of the property. At the time of the reacquisition, the property is worth $110,000.

The gain the Seller reports as a result of the reacquisition of the property is $9,000, determined as follows:

Gain before limitation:		
Money received prior to reacquisition................		$ 30,000
Less gain previously reported as income ($30,000 × $20,000/$100,000)		6,000
Gain before limitation.............................		$ 24,000
Limitation on reportable gain:		
Sales price		$100,000
Less:		
Basis at time of sale	$80,000	
Gain reported prior to reacquisition	6,000	
Expense of reacquisition.....................	5,000	91,000
Limitation on amount of gain.......................		$ 9,000

The basis of the reacquired property at the time of reacquisition by the Seller is $70,000, determined as follows:

---

[118] Reg. § 1.1038-1(b)(2)(iii).

Troubled Financings

Adjusted basis of indebtedness ($70,000 − ($70,000 × $20,000/$100,000))	$ 56,000
Gain from reacquisition	9,000
Expense of reacquisition	5,000
Basis of reacquired property	$ 70,000

¶ 1235.2   Reacquisition Following Election Out of Installment Reporting

If the seller does not report the gain from the original sale on the installment method, the taxable gain on the reacquisition of the property depends on whether the seller valued the purchaser's obligation at face value or less than face value.

Example: The Seller purchased real property for $80,000 and later sold that property to the Purchaser for $100,000. At the time of the sale to the Purchaser, there was no existing mortgage on the property. Under the contract of sale from the Seller to the Purchaser, the Purchaser paid $10,000 down and executed a note for the balance of $90,000, with interest. The principal, together with accrued interest, was to be paid in nine annual installments. At the time of sale, the Purchaser's note had a fair market value of $90,000. The Seller elected not to report the gain from the sale on the installment method, but to treat the transaction as a deferred-payment sale. After the third $10,000 annual payment, the Purchaser defaults and the Seller forecloses. Under the foreclosure sale, the Seller bids in the property at $70,000 (its fair market value at the time), cancels the Purchaser's outstanding obligation of $60,000, and pays $10,000 to purchaser. The Seller incurs no additional expenses in connection with the reacquisition of the property.

The gain the Seller reports as a result of the reacquisition of the property is zero, determined as follows:

Gain before limitation:		
Money received prior to reacquisition		$40,000
Less gain previously reported as income (($10,000 + $90,000) − $80,000)		20,000
Gain before limitation		$20,000
Limitation on reportable gain:		
Sales price		$100,000
Less:		
Basis at time of sale	$80,000	
Gain reported prior to reacquisition	20,000	
Expense of reacquisition	10,000	110,000
Limitation on amount of gain (not less than zero)		$ 0

¶ 1235.2

The basis of the reacquired property at the time of reacquisition by the Seller is $70,000, determined as follows:

Adjusted basis of indebtedness (face value at time of reacquisition)	$60,000
Gain from reacquisition	0
Expense of reacquisition	10,000
Basis of reacquired property	$70,000

Suppose that the Purchaser's note at the time of sale was valued at $75,000, instead of $90,000, by the Seller. In this case, the gain the Seller would report as a result of the reacquisition of the property would be $5,000, determined as follows:

Gain before limitation:		
Money received prior to reacquisition		$ 40,000
Less:		
Gain previously reported as income (($10,000 + $75,000) − $80,000)		5,000
Gain before limitation		$ 35,000
Limitation on reportable gain:		
Sales price		$100,000
Less:		
Basis at time of sale	$80,000	
Gain reported prior to reacquisition	5,000	
Expense of reacquisition	10,000	95,000
Limitation on amount of gain		$ 5,000

The basis of the reacquired property at the time of reacquisition by the Seller in this case would be $60,000, determined as follows:

Adjusted basis of indebtedness	$45,000
Gain from reacquisition	5,000
Expense of reacquisition	10,000
Basis of reacquired property	$60,000

¶ 1235.3   *Third-Party Mortgages*

In the examples above, it was assumed that the only indebtedness on the property reacquired by the seller was the original purchase-money mortgage. This may not always be the case. For example, the purchaser may obtain a first mortgage from a bank and a second mortgage from the seller. When the seller reacquires the property and assumes a debt to a third party secured by the property, or takes the property subject to an indebtedness that is not owed by the purchaser to the seller, the seller treats the amount of the outstanding third-party debt as money paid him by the seller in connection with the reacquisition of the property.[119] In effect, regardless of whether the seller assumes a third-party mortgage or takes the property subject to the third-party mortgage, the existence of such a mortgage reduces the amount of gain the seller reports as a result of the reacquisition and increases the seller's basis for the reacquired property.

¶ 1235.4 *Character of Gain*

Logically, it would seem reasonable to characterize gain realized on the reacquisition of property under Code Sec. 1038 in the same fashion as the gain realized from the original sale; that is, if the original sale produced capital gain, gain on repossession also would be capital gain. This simple and logical approach is denied by the regulations, which provide a rather complicated rule for determining the character of gain realized on the reacquisition of seller-financed real property.

Under Reg. § 1.1038-1(d), the character of the gain resulting from the reacquisition depends on whether the gain on the original sale was reported on the installment method, or, if not, on whether title to the real property was transferred to the purchaser and whether the reconveyance of the property to the seller was voluntary.

If the gain on the original sale of the reacquired property was reported on the installment method, the character of the reacquisition gain is determined under Reg. § 1.453-9. This means that if the property were a capital asset, the reacquisition gain would be a capital gain. Similarly, a Section 1231 asset would produce a Section 1231 gain on reacquisition.

If the original sale was not on the installment method but was a deferred-payment sale, the reacquisition gain is ordinary income if title to the real property was transferred to the purchaser and the seller accepts a voluntary reconveyance of the property. If the purchaser was a corporation, however, and the obligations of the corporation satisfied on the reacquisition are securities, reacquisition gain is capital gain.

---

[119] Reg.   § 1.1038-1(c)(4)(ii).

Part IV

Disposition of Real Estate

Introduction to Part IV

Part IV examines the disposition of real estate through various taxable and nontaxable transactions. Chapter 13 focuses on sales and exchanges of real estate, both taxable and nontaxable. Generally, the sale or exchange of real estate is treated in much the same fashion as the sale or exchange of other assets, and the basic rules for computing taxable gain or loss apply equally to both sales and exchanges. The tax on the gain from an exchange of property, however, may be deferred if certain requirements are met. This third edition also includes a discussion of the reduced or zero tax rates for the sale of qualifying property in designated depressed areas.

Although a seller generally must report recognized gain from the sale of real estate in the year of the sale, an important exception to this rule applies when the seller does not receive the full purchase price in the year of sale. This is most likely to occur when the seller provides financing to the buyer in the form of a purchase money mortgage. Seller financed sales and installment reporting are the subject of Chapter 14. Also included in this Chapter is a discussion of the tax consequences of a disposition or pledge of installment obligations received by the seller of real estate.

The tax consequences of the involuntary disposition of real estate are explored in Chapter 15. Casualties and condemnations may produce either a gain or loss, much like a sale. Timely reinvestment of the proceeds of an involuntary conversion can avoid a current tax on a gain. Finally, the income tax consequences of a gratuitous transfer of real estate, whether as a gift to charity or family members, is the subject of Chapter 16.

Chapter 13

Sales and Exchanges

¶ 1300 OVERVIEW OF CHAPTER

In this chapter, the basic rules for determining the amount of gain or loss on the sale or exchange of real estate are considered. For the most part, the sale or exchange of real estate is treated in the same fashion as the sale or exchange of other assets. While there may be a gain or loss on the transfer of an asset not all transfers produce immediate tax consequences. Generally, the first requirement for a taxable transaction is that there be a sale or exchange. A sale is the transfer of property for money or a promise to pay money, such as a mortgage or note. An exchange is the transfer of property for other property or services.

The basic rules for computing taxable gain or loss apply equally to both sales and exchanges, but not all exchanges that produce a gain are immediately taxable. The tax on the gain produced by the exchange of like-kind property may be deferred, if certain requirements of the Internal Revenue Code are met.

While the basic rules for sales and exchanges are covered in this chapter, special situations involving the sale, exchange or transfer of real estate are considered in other chapters. The distinction between a lease and a sale is explained in Chapter 3. The sale of real estate in the ordinary course of business by real estate dealers, as well as the subdivision and sale of real estate, is the subject of Chapter 10. The rules governing the transfer of real estate in satisfaction of a debt or in bankruptcy are covered in Chapter 12. The special rules governing installment sales are the subject of Chapter 14, while the loss or transfer of real estate assets as the result of casualty or condemnation is considered in Chapter 15.

The gain on the sale of a personal residence, subject to limitations, may not be subject to tax. The special rules relating to the sale of a personal residence are the subject of Chapter 20.

¶ 1301 SALE OF REAL ESTATE

In order to determine the proper tax treatment for the sale of real estate, the amount of gain or loss, of course, must be computed. But knowing the amount of gain or loss is only a beginning. The character of that gain or loss, that is, ordinary or capital, must be determined from the character of the property in the hands of the seller prior to the sale. In some cases, the character of any gain or loss may depend on the length of time the seller held the property. Also, various "recapture" provisions may convert an otherwise capital gain into ordinary income.

¶ 1303 Computation of Gain or Loss

Computing the gain or loss on an item or parcel of real estate requires two figures—the "adjusted basis" for the property sold and the "amount realized" from the sale. Gain is simply the excess of the amount realized from the sale over the adjusted basis of the property. Similarly, loss is the excess of the adjusted basis for the property over the amount realized.[1]

¶ 1303.1 *Adjusted Basis*

A taxpayer's adjusted basis for real estate is the property's original basis to the taxpayer as affected by events occurring while the taxpayer held the property.[2] As more fully explained at ¶ 103, the original basis for real estate is determined by the manner in which the taxpayer acquired the property. The most common adjustments to the original basis in the case of real estate are increases for capital improvements or additions and decreases for depreciation, amortization, and casualty losses.

The following chart summarizes the method of determining basis for property acquired through various transactions. The adjustments to basis are discussed throughout this volume in connection with the specific activities or events that give rise to the adjustments.

BASIS OF PROPERTY ACQUISITIONS

Acquisition	Basis
Arm's-length purchase	Cost
Bargain purchase	Cost, unless saving is gift, compensation, dividend, or other
Bequest	Before 2010, fair market value at date of decedent's death, but value assigned at settlement in the case of property acquired in lieu of specific amount of bequest
Cash purchase	Cost
Cash purchase plus mortgage assumed or given	Full purchase price including the amount of the mortgage

[1] Code Sec. 1001(a).

[2] Code Sec. 1011; Reg. § 1.1011-1.

Acquisition	Basis
Cash purchase plus redeemable ground rent assumed or property taken subject to ground rent	Full purchase price including amount of redeemable ground rent
Corporate property acquired for stock by controlled corporation	Transferor's basis for property
Corporate property acquired for stock in taxable transaction	Fair market value of stock at time of exchange
Corporate property contributed by nonstockholders	Zero
Corporate property acquired as paid-in surplus	Transferor's basis
Dividend	Fair market value
Divorce or separation agreement	Same as gift
Gift	Donor's basis plus gift tax, but basis for loss limited to lesser of donor's basis or fair market value at time of gift
Lessor's acquisition of lessee's improvements	Zero, if excluded from income
Mortgaged property or property subject to redeemable ground rent	Basis includes mortgage or ground rent
Partnership property received as contribution for interest	Partner's adjusted basis for property contributed
Partnership property received in distribution from partnership	Partnership's adjusted basis, limited to partner's basis for his interest
Partnership property received in liquidation of partnership	Adjusted basis of partnership interest less cash received
Purchase for more than fair market value	Cost, but may be limited to fair market value if excess is a gift
Repossessed real property reacquired in satisfaction of purchaser's debt secured by the property	Adjusted basis of debt plus gain from the reacquisition and reacquisition costs
Residence	Cost minus gain not recognized
Transfer in trust	Grantor's basis, plus gain or minus loss recognized by grantor on transfer

¶ 1303.2 Amount Realized

The amount realized on the sale of real estate is the total of all money received plus the fair market value of all property or services received.[3]

---

[3] Code Sec. 1001(b).

Mortgages and Other Liabilities

The amount realized by the seller of property includes any liabilities that are assumed by the buyer and any liabilities to which the property sold is subject.[4] Therefore, the seller of real estate must include the face amount of any mortgage on the property in the "amount realized" for the purpose of determining the gain or loss. This rule applies regardless of whether the seller is personally liable on the mortgage or whether the buyer actually assumes the mortgage or merely purchases the property subject to the mortgage.

See *B.B. Crane*[5] and the discussion of mortgage and basis at ¶ 105.

Selling Expenses

Generally, the amount realized on a sale is the selling price of the property reduced by any selling expenses. Except for property sold by dealers (see ¶ 1013), fees and commissions paid by the seller to brokers or others are offset against the selling price to determine the amount realized from the sale and are not taken as separate deductions.[6]

State and local taxes, such as state stamp taxes, mortgage recording taxes, and other transfer taxes, paid by the seller in connection with the sale of real estate also are treated as reductions in the amount realized.[7] State, local, and foreign income taxes imposed on the seller, however, are deductible from income and are not treated as reductions in the selling price or amount realized.[8] According to the IRS, the Vermont land gains tax is not an income tax and is, therefore, an offset to the selling price and cannot be taken as a separate deduction from income.[9]

Example: The Taxpayer bought an apartment building for $350,000. As owner of the building, the Taxpayer made improvements that cost $100,000 and claimed depreciation deductions in the amount of $50,000. The Taxpayer sold the building for $500,000 in cash, plus property with a fair market value of $100,000. The Buyer assumed the current real estate taxes of $15,000 (a liability of the Taxpayer) and a mortgage of $85,000. The selling expenses of the Taxpayer in connection with the sale of this property are $20,000. The gain on the property is computed as follows:

---

[4] Reg. § 1.1001-2.

[5] S.Ct., 47-1 USTC ¶ 9217, 331 U.S. 1, 67 S.Ct. 1047.

[6] Reg. § 1.263(a)-2(e); see also the discussion of expenses at ¶ 729.

[7] Code Sec. 164(a).

[8] Code Sec. 164(a)(3).

[9] Rev. Rul. 80-121, 1980-1 CB 43.

Amount Realized:		
Cash	$500,000	
Property received	100,000	
Taxes assumed by buyer	15,000	
Mortgage assumed by buyer	85,000	
	$700,000	
Less: Selling expenses	20,000	
Amount Realized		$680,000
Adjusted Basis:		
Cost	$350,000	
Improvements	100,000	
	$450,000	
Less: Depreciation	50,000	
Adjusted Basis		400,000
Gain Realized		$280,000

Sale on Contract for Deed

A cash basis taxpayer who sells property on contract without receiving a note or similar obligation of the purchaser may not be taxable until the receipts exceed the adjusted basis for the property.[10] By contrast, a seller on the accrual basis is taxable on the amount owed under a contract for sale as soon as the purchaser becomes unconditionally obligated to pay for the property. This obligation may arise on transfer of title or possession, whichever occurs earlier. Therefore, an accrual basis seller who sells property under a contract for deed realizes gain on the execution of the contract under which the buyer takes possession.[11] For both cash and accrual taxpayers, loss on a sale is deductible in the year of sale, regardless of when the consideration is to be paid under the contract.

The IRS has taken the position, however, that contracts must be valued, and only in rare circumstances will a contract be one that cannot be valued for purposes of "closing" a transaction for tax purposes.[12] Later cases lean to this view and support the idea that even a cash basis taxpayer must report the gain from a sale contract when the contract is executed. In *Warren Jones Co.*,[13] the fair market value of a real estate sales contract was treated as an amount realized in the year of sale by a cash basis seller even though payments were to be received over a 15-year period and even though the contract could not have been sold without a discount of the sales price.[14]

---

[10] See, for example, *N.J. Ennis*, 17 TC 465 CCH Dec. 18,543; *C. Hurlburt Est.*, 25 TC 1286, CCH Dec. 21,637, Nonacq. 1956-2 CB 10,; *R.W. Ewing*, 17 TCM 626, CCH Dec. 23,042(M), T.C. Memo. 1958-115.

[11] *North Texas Lumber Co.*, S.Ct., 2 USTC ¶ 484, 281 US 11, 50 S. Ct. 184.

[12] Rev. Rul. 58-402, 1958-2 CB 15.

[13] CA-9, 75-2 USTC ¶ 9732, 524 F.2d 788.

[14] See also *D.J. Corley*, 51 TCM 280, CCH Dec. 42,818(M), T.C. Memo. 1986-17; *J.M. Smith*, CA-9, 424 F.2d 219, 70-1 USTC ¶ 9327; *W.A. Ehlers v. R.P. Vinal*, CA-8, 67-2 USTC ¶ 9612, 382 F.2d 58.

¶ 1303.2

Sale of Easement

Granting or selling an easement usually is not a taxable sale of property. Rather, the amount received for the easement is subtracted from the basis of the property. If only a part of the entire tract of property is permanently affected by the easement, only the basis of that part is reduced by the amount received, unless it is impossible or impractical to separately determine the basis of the part of the property on which the easement is granted.

If the amount received for an easement is more than the basis of the property to which the easement relates, the excess is a taxable gain. In this case, the granting of the easement is reported as if it were a sale of property.

¶ 1303.3 Disallowed Losses

A loss on the sale or exchange of property is not deductible if the transaction is between certain specified related parties.[15] The relationships that trigger the loss disallowance rule are listed in Code Sec. 267(b) and include the following:

1. Members of the same immediate family, including brothers and sisters, half-brothers and half-sisters, spouse, ancestors, and lineal descendants;[16]
2. An individual and a corporation, if the individual owns, directly or indirectly, more than 50 percent in value of the outstanding stock of the corporation;
3. Two corporations that are members of the same controlled group as defined in Code Sec. 1563(a), except that "more than 50 percent" is substituted for "at least 80 percent" in the definition[17] (controlled group does not include a DISC for this purpose);[18]
4. A trust fiduciary and a corporation, if the trust or the grantor of the trust owns, directly or indirectly, more than 50 percent in value of the outstanding stock of the corporation;
5. A grantor and fiduciary, and the fiduciary and beneficiary, of any trust;
6. A fiduciary and beneficiary of two different trusts, if the same person is the grantor of both trusts;
7. A tax-exempt educational or charitable organization and a person who, directly or indirectly, controls the organization, or a member of that person's family;

---

[15] Code Sec. 267(a).
[16] Code Sec. 267(c)(4).
[17] Code Sec. 267(f)(1).
[18] Code Sec. 267(f)(3).

8. Fiduciaries of two different trusts, if the same person is the grantor of both trusts;
9. A corporation and a partnership if the same persons own more than 50 percent in value of the outstanding stock of the corporation and more than 50 percent of the capital interest or the profits interest in the partnership;
10. Two S corporations if the same persons own more than 50 percent in value of the outstanding stock of each corporation;
11. Two corporations, one of which is an S corporation, if the same persons own more than 50 percent in value of the outstanding stock of each corporation; and
12. An executor and beneficiary of an estate, except in the case of a sale or exchange in satisfaction of a pecuniary bequest.

If a sale or exchange is between any of the related parties listed above and involves the sale of a number of parcels of real estate, the gain or loss must be computed separately for each parcel. The gain on each parcel is taxable, but the loss on any parcel is not deductible. Also, gains from the sales of any of the parcels may not be reduced by losses on the sales of any of the other parcels.[19]

Controlled Group Loss Deferral

Losses on transactions between members of the same controlled group are deferred rather than denied. The losses are deferred until the property is transferred outside and the loss recognized under consolidated return principles or until such other time as may be prescribed in regulations.[20]

Constructive Ownership Rules

In determining whether an individual directly or indirectly owns any of the outstanding stock of a corporation in applying the loss disallowance rules, the following rules of constructive ownership apply:[21]

1. Stock owned directly or indirectly by or for a corporation, partnership, estate, or trust is considered to be owned proportionately by or for its shareholders, partners, or beneficiaries.
2. An individual is considered to own the stock owned directly or indirectly by or for the family (brothers and sisters, half-brothers and half-sisters, spouse, ancestors, and lineal descendants).

---

[19] Reg. § 1.267(d)-1(b).
[20] Code Sec. 267(f)(2).
[21] Code Sec. 267(c).

3. An individual who owns (other than by constructive ownership from a family member) any stock in a corporation is considered to own the stock owned directly or indirectly by or for a partner.

4. For purposes of applying the first three rules, stock constructively owned by a person under rule 1 is treated as actually owned by that person, but stock constructively owned by an individual under rule 2 or 3 is not treated as owned by the individual for again applying either rule 2 or 3 to make another person the constructive owner of the stock.

Tax Treatment of Disallowed Losses

If a taxpayer sells or exchanges at a gain property received from a related party, the taxpayer recognizes the gain only to the extent that it is more than the loss previously disallowed to the transferor-related party.[22] This rule applies only to the original transferee.

Example: A sells a parcel of real estate to his brother B for $76,000. The adjusted basis of the real estate in A's hands was $100,000. Under Code Sec. 267, A's loss of $24,000 is not deductible. Later, B sells the property to an unrelated person for $105,000. B's gain is $29,000 ($105,000 amount realized − $76,000 adjusted cost basis), but B's reportable gain is only $5,000. This is the excess of B's gain of $29,000 over the amount of the loss that was previously disallowed to A of $24,000.

Suppose, however, that B sells the property to an unrelated person for $69,000 rather than $105,000. In this case, B's reportable loss is $7,000 ($76,000 adjusted basis − $69,000 loss realized). B cannot deduct the loss of $24,000 that was previously disallowed to A.

¶ 1303.4   Sale Between Spouses and Former Spouses

Whenever property is transferred from one spouse to another, or from one spouse to a former spouse incident to a divorce, the transfer is a tax-free event and no gain or loss is realized by the transferor spouse.[23] The transferee spouse's basis for the property is the adjusted basis the property had in the hands of the transferor spouse.[24] The transfer of property from a spouse to a former spouse is considered incident to a divorce if the transfer takes place within one year after the date on which the marriage ends or is related to the cessation of the marriage.

---

[22] Code Sec. 267(d).
[23] Code Sec. 1041(a).
[24] Code Sec. 1041(b).

¶ 1305 Character of Gain or Loss

Once the amount of any recognizable gain or loss for tax purposes is determined following the sale or exchange of real estate, it still is necessary to fix the character of that gain or loss as either capital or ordinary. In some cases, especially for property used in a trade or business, the character of the gain or loss may be either capital or noncapital, depending on the taxpayer's particular circumstances.

¶ 1305.1 *Capital Gains and Losses*

Generally all property is classified as one of three types by the Internal Revenue Code:

1. Capital asset, which produces capital gain or loss on its sale or exchange;
2. Noncapital asset, which produces ordinary income or loss on its sale or exchange; or
3. Section 1231 asset used in a trade or business, which may produce capital or ordinary gain or loss, depending upon whether sales and exchanges of all such assets produce a net gain or loss for the year.

For the most part, all personal and investment assets are capital assets. In fact, the Internal Revenue Code, in defining capital assets, takes a negative approach by listing those assets that are *not* capital assets rather than attempting to list those assets that are capital assets. According to Code Sec. 1221(a), a capital asset is any property except:

1. Property held mainly for sale to customers or property that will actually become part of merchandise or property that is for sale to customers (these assets are essentially "inventory" assets);
2. Depreciable property used in a trade or business;
3. Real property used in a trade or business;
4. Accounts or notes receivable acquired in the ordinary course of business, for services rendered as an employee, or from the sale of inventory assets;
5. Copyright, literary, musical, or artistic composition, letter or memorandum or similar property created by the holder or, in the case of a letter or memorandum or similar property, held by the person for whom the asset in question was produced (these assets remain noncapital assets in the hands of a transferee who acquires them from the creator or the one for whom produced, if they have the same basis as in the hands of the transferor);

¶ 1305.1

6. U.S. government publications received for free or for less than the normal sales price;

7. Commodities derivative financial instruments held by a commodities derivatives dealer;

8. Hedging transactions that are clearly identified as such before the close of the day on which acquired, originated, or entered into; and

9. Supplies of a type regularly used or consumed by the taxpayer in the ordinary course of a trade or business.

Investment property is a capital asset, and a gain or loss on its sale is a capital gain or loss. Rental property, however, is treated as business property. Real property used in a trade or business is subject to the special capital gain/ordinary loss treatment of Code Sec. 1231 discussed at ¶ 1305.2. Note that while real property used for personal purposes, such as a personal residence or vacation home, is a capital asset and gain from its sale is a capital gain, losses from sales and exchanges of such property are not deductible unless they result from a casualty. Of course, if real estate is held for sale in the ordinary course of business, it is not a capital or Section 1231 asset but is "dealer" property. Dealer property and sales of real property in the ordinary course of business are discussed at ¶ 1013.

Gain on Related Party Sales

Capital gain treatment is denied, and any gain recognized is ordinary income, for the sale or exchange of property, including leaseholds, if the property is depreciable property in the hands of the buyer and if the buyer and seller are related.[25] Related parties that bring this rule into play are:

1. A person and an entity controlled by that person[26] (what constitutes a controlled entity is discussed below);

2. A taxpayer and any trust in which the taxpayer (or spouse) is a beneficiary, unless the beneficiary's interest in the trust is a remote contingent interest, that is, the value of the interest computed actuarially is five percent or less of the value of the trust property;[27]

3. An employer and any person related to the employer under rules 1 and 2, above;[28]

---

[25] Code Sec. 1239(a).
[26] Code Sec. 1239(b)(1).
[27] Code Sec. 1239(b)(2).
[28] Code Sec. 1239(d)(1).

¶ 1305.1

Sales and Exchanges

4. A welfare benefit fund (as defined in Code Sec. 419(e)) that is controlled directly or indirectly by persons related to the employer under rules 1 and 2, above;[29] and

5. An executor and beneficiary of an estate, except in the case of a sale or exchange in satisfaction of a pecuniary bequest.[30]

A "controlled entity" is defined by Code Sec. 1239(c)(1) and includes:

1. A corporation in which more than 50 percent of the value of all outstanding stock, or a partnership in which more than 50 percent of the capital interest or profit interest, is owned directly or indirectly by or for one person;

2. A corporation and a partnership, if the same persons own more than 50 percent in value of the outstanding stock of the corporation and more than 50 percent of the capital interest or profits interest in the partnership;

3. Two corporations that are members of the same controlled group;

4. Two S corporations if the same persons own more than 50 percent in value of the outstanding stock of each corporation; and

5. Two corporations, one of which is an S corporation, if the same persons own more than 50 percent in value of the outstanding stock of each corporation.

Control is based on constructive, as well as actual, ownership.[31] In figuring stock ownership for purposes of determining control:

1. Stock owned directly or indirectly by or for a corporation, partnership, estate, or trust is treated as owned proportionately by or for its shareholders, partners, or beneficiaries;

2. An individual is treated as owning stock that is directly or indirectly by or for the individual's family, including only brothers and sisters, half-brothers and half-sisters, spouse, ancestors, and lineal descendants; and

3. Stock that is constructively owned by a person under rule 1 is treated as actually owned by that person for applying rules 1 and 2, but stock that is constructively owned by an individual under rule 2 is not treated as owned by that individual for again applying rule 2 to make another person the constructive owner of that stock.

---

[29] Code Sec. 1239(d)(2).
[30] Code Sec. 1239(b)(3).
[31] Code Sec. 1239(c)(2).

¶ 1305.1

Tax Treatment of Individual Capital Gains and Losses

The tax treatment of capital gains and losses differs depending on whether the taxpayer is an individual or corporate taxpayer. In either case, however, short-term gains and losses must be separated from long-term gains and losses. The long-term holding period is more than one year (see ¶ 1305.3). For assets held more than one year, the maximum tax rate for most capital gains realized after May 6, 1997, is 20 percent. Effective in 2001, the 20 percent rate dropped to 18 percent for assets acquired after 2000 and held more than five years. Taxpayers were able to elect to treat assets held on January 1, 2001, as if they had been sold for their fair market value in order to reset the acquisition date and qualify future appreciation for the lower rate. (Note that installment payments received after May 6, 1997, are subject to the lower rate even if the sale took place before May 7, 1997.)

In the case of an individual, short-term capital gains and losses realized during the year are combined to compute a net short-term capital gain or loss. Similarly, long-term capital gains and losses realized during the year are combined to compute a net long-term capital gain or loss. If net long-term gain exceeds net short-term loss, the net gain is eligible for the lower tax rates on net capital gain. If the individual realizes a net loss, the loss is deductible, subject to the limitation discussed immediately below.

An individual with a net capital loss for a year may deduct that loss against ordinary income only to the extent of $3,000 or the net capital loss, whichever is less. In the case of married taxpayers filing separate returns, the limit is $1,500 rather than $3,000.[32] Note that an individual must deduct a net capital loss up to the $3,000 limit, even if the individual has no ordinary income to offset the loss.

The limitation on the deduction of a net capital loss is mitigated by the carryover provision found in Code Sec. 1212. An individual with a net capital loss in excess of the deduction limit may carry over the excess to later years until it is completely used up. The unused loss is carried over as a short-term or long-term loss, as the case may be.[33]

> **Example:** A married couple sold property in 2002. The sale resulted in a capital loss of $7,000, and the couple had no other capital transactions in 2002. On their joint return, the couple deducts $3,000, the lower of $3,000 or $7,000. The unused part of the loss, $4,000 ($7,000 − $3,000) is carried over to 2003. If this couple had no taxable income in 2002, the carryover to 2003 would still be $4,000. The allowable $3,000 deduction is considered used,

---

[32] Code Sec. 1211(b).   [33] Code Sec. 1212(b).

even if they had no income against which the deduction could be used to produce a tax benefit.

If the couple had incurred a $2,500 loss rather than a $7,000 loss in 2002, their deduction for 2002 would have been $2,500 and they would have no carryover to 2003.

In computing a capital loss carryover, short-term losses are deducted before long-term losses.

Tax Treatment of Corporate Capital Gains and Losses

Generally, a corporation's net capital gain is taxed at the same rates as other corporate income, unless the corporate tax rate exceeds 35 percent. If the corporate tax rate exceeds 35 percent, a corporation's net capital gain is taxed at 35 percent.[34] A corporation's net capital gain is "the excess of the net long-term capital gain for the taxable year over the net short-term capital loss for such year".[35]

A corporation's capital losses, unlike an individual's, may be deducted only to the extent of capital gains. A corporation cannot use capital losses to offset ordinary income.[36] An unused capital loss may be carried back three years and carried forward five years and used to offset capital gains in those years until used up. The unused loss generally must be carried to the earliest year in which it can be used. Any capital loss carryback or capital loss carryforward is treated as a short-term loss in the year(s) to which it is carried.[37]

¶ 1305.2 Property Used in a Trade or Business: Section 1231 Assets

Real property used in a trade or business and depreciable business property are given special capital gain/ordinary loss treatment in Code Sec. 1231. The split treatment came about as a result of pressure from business, which was not happy with the exclusion of most business property from the definition of capital assets when these assets were sold at a gain, but did not want to give up the benefit of ordinary loss treatment when these assets were sold at a loss. Generally, all gains and losses for the year on Section 1231 assets are combined. If the net result is a loss, then all Section 1231 gains and losses are treated as ordinary gains and losses. If the net result is a gain, then all Section 1231 gains and losses are treated as capital gains and losses.

Keep in mind that Code Sec. 1231 only serves to characterize the nature of gain or loss as capital or ordinary. The section has no other function.

---

[34] Code Sec. 1201(a).
[35] Code Sec. 1222(11).
[36] Code Sec. 1211(a).
[37] Code Sec. 1212(a).

When gain is treated as a capital gain under Code Sec. 1231, other Internal Revenue Code provisions may convert that gain into ordinary income. The depreciation recapture provisions (Code Secs. 1245 and 1250, discussed at ¶ 1307.1 and ¶ 1307.2) take precedence over Code Sec. 1231. Also, prior Section 1231 losses are subject to recapture when Section 1231 gains are realized in later years.

Section 1231 Assets

Code Sec. 1231 requires combining gains and losses on all Section 1231 assets, not just real property used in a trade or business. Code Sec. 1231(b) requires taxpayers to take the following assets into account:

1. Depreciable personal property used in a trade or business and held for more than one year.
2. Real property used in a trade or business and held for more than one year.
3. Property held for the production of rents or royalties and held more than one year.
4. Leaseholds used in a trade or business and held more than one year.
5. Timber, coal, and iron ore to which Code Sec. 631 applies.
6. Cattle and horses held for draft, breeding, dairy, or sporting purposes and held for two years or more from the acquisition date.
7. Livestock, other than cattle, horses, and poultry, held for draft, breeding, dairy, or sporting purposes and held for more than one year.
8. Unharvested crops on land used in farming, if the crop and land are sold, exchanged, or involuntarily converted at the same time and to the same person, and if the land has been held more than one year.[38]
9. Compulsory conversions (*i.e.,* condemnations, eminent domain, etc.) and involuntary conversions through casualty or theft of business property, property held for the production of rents and royalties, and investment property, but only if total compulsory and involuntary conversion gains exceed total compulsory and involuntary conversion losses.[39]

Inventory and property held for sale to customers in the ordinary course of business, "dealer" property, is excluded from Code Sec. 1231. Apartments, office buildings, and other income-producing real estate generally qualify as Section 1231 assets. A leasehold of land with

---

[38] Code Sec. 1231(b)(4).   [39] Code Sec. 1231(a)(4)(C).

improvements used in the taxpayer's trade or business also qualifies as a Section 1231 asset, provided the taxpayer is not a "dealer" in leases.[40]

Growing crops sold with a lease on the land, even though to the same person in the same transaction, are not considered Section 1231 assets. Reg. § 1.1231-1(f) says a leasehold or estate for years is not "land" for Code Sec. 1231 purposes.[41] Also, a sale, exchange, or involuntary conversion of an unharvested crop with land is not included in Code Sec. 1231 if the taxpayer keeps any right or option to reacquire the land, directly or indirectly, other than a right customarily incident to a mortgage or other security interest.[42]

Tax Treatment of Section 1231 Gains and Losses

In order to apply Code Sec. 1231, combine all gains and losses from the sales and dispositions of all Section 1231 property for the tax year. If the Section 1231 gains exceed the Section 1231 losses, there is a net Section 1231 gain and all the Section 1231 gains and losses are treated as long-term capital gains or long-term capital losses, as the case may be.[43] On the other hand, an excess of Section 1231 losses over Section 1231 gains results in a net Section 1231 loss. If the Section 1231 losses equal or exceed the Section 1231 gains, then each item is treated as an ordinary gain or loss.[44]

Example: An individual taxpayer sells two Section 1231 assets during 2002. Asset #1 has an adjusted basis of $100,000 and is sold for $120,000. Asset #2 has an adjusted basis of $60,000 and is sold for $20,000. Since the net result is a $20,000 loss ($20,000 gain on Asset #1 and $40,000 loss on Asset #2), the $20,000 gain on Asset #1 is ordinary income and the $40,000 loss on Asset #2 is a fully deductible ordinary loss which, when combined, result in a fully deductible $20,000 loss.

Suppose, however, that the individual sells Asset #1 for $140,000 and Asset #2 for $40,000, instead of the selling prices assumed above. In this case, the individual realizes a net gain of $20,000 ($40,000 gain on Asset #1 and a $20,000 loss on Asset #2). If the individual did not realize a net loss on Section 1231 property in 1997 through 2001, the $40,000 gain on Asset #1 would be a capital gain and the $20,000 loss on Asset #2 would be a capital loss which, when combined, result in a $20,000 net capital gain.

Generally speaking, it is better to have ordinary losses rather than capital losses, and capital gain rather than ordinary income. Therefore,

---

[40] Rev. Rul. 72-85, 1972-1 CB 234.
[41] *Bidart Bros.*, CA-9, 59-1 USTC ¶ 9193, 262 F.2d 607, cert. denied 359 U.S. 1003, 79 S.Ct. 1141.
[42] *J.F. Nutt Est.*, CA-9, 71-2 USTC ¶ 9607, 447 F.2d 1109.
[43] Code Sec. 1231(a)(1).
[44] Code Sec. 1231(a)(2).

the usual strategy for tax savings under Code Sec. 1231 is to segregate gains and losses into different tax years. Keep in mind, however, that the Section 1231 recapture rule can convert current capital gains into ordinary income.

Recapture of Prior Section 1231 Losses

The relatively straightforward rule for Section 1231 assets and the opportunities for tax planning through segregating sales at a gain and loss sales into different tax years were complicated by a recapture rule introduced by the Tax Reform Act of 1984. Generally, a net Section 1231 gain is no longer automatically treated as capital gain. It is necessary to "look back" to the preceding five years to see if sales of Section 1231 property in any of those years produced a net loss deducted from ordinary income. If there was a net loss in any of those years, a net gain in the current year must be treated as ordinary income to the extent any prior net losses exist which have not been used already to convert otherwise capital gain into ordinary income on the sale or other disposition of Section 1231 property.[45]

Example: The calendar-year Corporation had a net Section 1231 loss of $12,000 in 2000. The Corporation had no net Section 1231 losses in 1998, 1999, or 2001. The Corporation had a net Section 1231 gain of $7,750 in 1996 and has a net Section 1231 gain of $6,900 in 1997. In computing its taxable income for 1996, the Corporation treated its net Section 1231 gain of $7,750 as ordinary income by recapturing $7,750 of its $12,000 net Section 1231 loss from 1994. Then in 1997, the Corporation applies the remaining net Section 1231 loss of $4,250 ($12,000 − $7,750) against its net Section 1231 gain of $6,900. The Corporation reports $4,250 as ordinary income and also reports $2,650 ($6,900 − $4,250) as long-term capital gain.

Despite the Section 1231 recapture rule, planning the sale or disposition of Section 1231 property remains a matter of timing. Section 1231 gains are recaptured as ordinary income only if they *follow* Section 1231 losses. If several Section 1231 assets are to be sold within a relatively short period of time, dividing the sales between two tax years will still produce the capital gain/ordinary loss advantage if the sales at a gain are made in the year *before* the loss sales.

¶ 1305.3   Holding Period

The holding period for an asset is the length of time a taxpayer owns the asset before disposing of it. If a capital asset is held for one year or less, the gain or loss from its disposition is short term. If the

---

[45] Code Sec. 1231(c).

capital asset is held longer than one year, the gain or loss on its disposition is long term.[46] Also, application of Code Sec. 1231 to the sale or disposition of business property depends on the holding period for the property. Generally, property must be held for "more than one year" for Code Sec. 1231 to apply.

The holding period for property generally begins on the day following the day the property is acquired and includes the day the property is disposed of or sold.[47] For example, if a taxpayer purchases an asset on July 19, 2002, the taxpayer begins counting the holding period on July 20, 2002. If the taxpayer sells the property on July 19, 2003, the holding period is not more than one year, but if the taxpayer sells on July 20, 2003, the holding period is more than one year.

While the passing of title generally indicates when a sale has taken place and when a new owner's holding period begins, a taxpayer's holding period may begin before title passes. The holding period of property that is the subject of an unconditional contract of sale begins on the day following that on which title passes, or on the day following that on which delivery of possession is made and the burdens and benefits of ownership are assumed by the purchaser, whichever occurs first.[48] However, taking delivery of possession of real property under an option agreement is not enough to start the holding period. The holding period cannot start until there is an actual contract of sale. The holding period of the seller cannot end before that time.[49]

In *Edwards Industries, Inc.*,[50] the holding period of real estate began when the purchase price was paid under an escrow agreement. This was the time when the parties intended the burdens and benefits of ownership to shift to the purchaser. The period during which the purchaser held an option on the property was not included in the holding period.

When land is acquired and a building or other improvement is constructed upon it, there may be more than one holding period. The holding period of a newly constructed building does not begin with the date of acquisition of the land.[51] The IRS has ruled that the holding period of an office building which was constructed for use in the taxpayer's business and which was sold shortly after completion to an unrelated party began progressively as the building was being constructed. The portion of the building actually completed more than one

---

[46] Code Sec. 1222.
[47] Rev. Rul. 66-7, 1966-1 CB 188; *H.M. Hooper*, 26 BTA 758, CCH Dec. 7689.
[48] Rev. Rul. 54-607, 1954-2 CB 177.
[49] *V. Hoven*, 56 TC 50, CCH Dec. 30,721, Acq. 1971-2 CB 3.
[50] 33 TCM 569, CCH Dec. 32,581(M), T.C. Memo. 1974-120.
[51] *M.A. Paul*, CA-3, 53-2 USTC ¶ 9527, 206 F.2d 763.

year before the date of sale is considered held for more than one year for purposes of Code Sec. 1231.[52]

When property is acquired other than by purchase, the holding period does not necessarily begin on the date the property is acquired. Under Code Sec. 1223, the holding period of newly acquired property may include the holding period of other property which is "tacked on" to the holding period of the newly acquired property.

The most usual situation in which an additional period is tacked on to the holding period of property is following a nontaxable exchange. If a taxpayer acquired an asset in exchange for another asset and the basis for the new asset is figured, in whole or in part, by the taxpayer's basis in the old property, the holding period of the new property includes the holding period of the old property.[53]

The holding period of property acquired by gift includes the donor's holding period if basis is determined using the donor's basis.[54] Property acquired from a decedent automatically has a long-term holding period.[55]

¶ 1307 Depreciation Recapture

The good, or positive, side of depreciation is presented in Chapter 9. Depreciation, as a "noncash" expense, can shelter from taxation the income generated by real estate. Of course, as depreciation deductions are taken on property, the adjusted basis of that property is reduced. This reduction in basis for depreciation means that the shelter will be reversed and that any depreciation deductions in excess of actual economic depreciation (or loss in value) will be taxed as gain on the sale or other taxable disposition of the property.

Although depreciation in excess of any real decline in value would eventually be recovered by the government because of the basis mechanism, one problem remains. Depreciation could convert ordinary income into capital gain, that is, the deductions for depreciation would offset ordinary taxable income, but any later gain on the sale of the property resulting from the prior depreciation deductions would be taxed only as capital gain under the characterization rule of Code Sec. 1231. This is where the recapture rules of Code Secs. 1245 and 1250 come into play. It is this conversion of ordinary income into capital gain that the recapture rules are designed to prevent.

While the principle of depreciation recapture is easy enough to state, the application of the recapture mechanism is complicated by two sets of rules that apply to two different types of property, that is,

---

[52] Rev. Rul. 75-524, 1975-2 CB 342.
[53] Reg. § 1.1223-1(a).
[54] Reg. § 1.1223-1(b).
[55] Code Sec. 1223(11); Reg. § 1.1223-1(j).

Section 1245 property and Section 1250 property. Generally, the dividing line between Section 1245 and Section 1250 property is that between "personalty" (Code Sec. 1245) and "realty" (Code Sec. 1250), but the line is not completely clear cut. Further complication is added because different recapture rules may apply to the same property for depreciation taken over different periods of time.

¶ 1307.1 Section 1245 Property Recapture

Under Code Sec. 1245, all prior depreciation and amortization deductions, plus any basis reduction as a result of an investment credit taken on the property, are recaptured as ordinary income to the extent of any gain realized on the disposition of the property. The Internal Revenue Code achieves this result by requiring that gain be treated as ordinary income on the sale, exchange, or involuntary conversion of Section 1245 property, including a sale and leaseback transaction, to the extent of the lesser of:

1. The recomputed basis of the property minus the adjusted basis of the property, or
2. The amount realized from the sale minus the adjusted basis of the property.[56]

The recomputed basis of Section 1245 property is the adjusted basis of the property plus all adjustments reflected in that adjusted basis because of deductions allowed *or allowable* for depreciation or amortization.[57] Depreciation includes the amount allowed or allowable based on useful life for depreciable property and the regular or alternate ACRS deductions for recovery property. Amortization includes any first-year expense deduction under Code Sec. 179 and deductions for clean-fuel vehicles, the removal of barriers for the handicapped and elderly, child-care facilities, on-the-job training facilities, pollution control facilities, reforestation expenditures, and certain expenditures for historic structures.

Property subject to Code Sec. 1245 recapture includes any property that is or has been subject to an allowance for depreciation and that is:

1. Personal property, both tangible and intangible.[58]
2. Tangible depreciable property, except a building or its structural components, that is or has been an integral part of manufacturing, production, or extraction, or an integral part of the furnishing of transportation, communication, electrical energy, gas, water, or sewage disposal services. Also included

---

[56] Code Sec. 1245(a)(1).
[57] Code Sec. 1245(a)(2).
[58] Code Sec. 1245(a)(3)(A); Reg. § 1.1245-3(b).

are research facilities or storage facilities used in connection with any of these activities.[59]

3. Single-purpose agricultural or horticultural structures.[60]

4. Storage facilities used in connection with the distribution of petroleum or any primary product of petroleum.[61]

5. Real property, not included in 2, 3, or 4, above, to the extent its adjusted basis has been reduced by certain amortization deductions, including those for certified pollution control facilities, on-the-job training and child-care facilities, removal of architectural barriers to the handicapped and elderly, clean-fuel vehicle refueling property, and reforestation expenditures, or by a first-year expense deduction under Code Sec. 179.[62]

6. Railroad grading or tunnel bore.[63]

¶ 1307.2 Section 1250 Property Recapture

Section 1250 property generally includes all buildings and other improvements to land that are not Section 1245 property and that were placed in service before 1981. For property placed in service after 1980, Section 1250 property includes:

1. Residential real property;

2. Real property located outside the United States;

3. Any real property depreciated on a straight-line basis; and

4. Low-income housing.[64]

Note that, since most real property placed in service after 1986 must be depreciated using the straight-line method, it generally will be Section 1250 property. Also, since only "excess" depreciation generally is subject to recapture in the case of Section 1250 property, as discussed below, there will be no recapture on real property that was placed in service after 1986.

Reduced Capital Gain Preference

Although there is no recapture for straight-line depreciation on real estate under Code Sec. 1250, gain from the sale of depreciable property by a noncorporate taxpayer may not be eligible for the most favorable capital gain tax rates. Gain on real property held for more than one year and not recaptured under Code Sec. 1250 is subject to a 25 percent maximum capital gain tax rate, rather than the maximum rate of 20

---

[59] Code Sec. 1245(a)(3)(B); Reg. § 1.1245-3(c).
[60] Code Sec. 1245(a)(3)(D).
[61] Code Sec. 1245(a)(3)(E).
[62] Code Sec. 1245(a)(3)(C).
[63] Reg. § 1.1245-3.
[64] Code Sec. 1250(c).

percent that applies to most other assets.[65] (See the discussion under "Tax Treatment of Individual Capital Gains and Losses" at ¶ 1305.1.)

Gain Subject to Recapture

The amount of gain that is subject to recapture on the sale or disposition of Section 1250 property is determined as follows:

1. Determine the excess of the amount realized over the adjusted basis of the property in a sale, exchange, or involuntary conversion or the excess of fair market value over adjusted basis in the case of any other disposition,

2. Determine any "excess" depreciation for periods after 1975, and

3. Multiply the lesser of 1 or 2 by the applicable percentage for the particular type of property involved.[66] (The applicable percentage for various types of properties is discussed below.)

4. Determine the "excess" depreciation for periods after 1969 but before 1976,

5. Multiply the lesser of the remaining gain (1 less 2 or 4) by the applicable percentage for the particular type of property involved.[67]

6. Add the results from 3 and 5 to figure the gain subject to recapture as ordinary income, in the case of taxpayers other than corporations. In the case of corporations, an additional amount is subject to recapture, as discussed below.

"Excess" depreciation is the amount by which depreciation deductions exceed the amount of the deductions that would be available if depreciation were figured under the straight-line method for the same period.[68] If property is held less than 12 months, however, all depreciation is treated as excess depreciation. Also, any reduction in basis for investment credit is treated as a deduction for depreciation. Generally, recapture can arise if Section 1250 property has been depreciated under the regular ACRS method, the declining-balance method, the sum-of-the-years-digits method, the units-of-production method, or any other method of rapid or accelerated depreciation. The 60-month write-off for the rehabilitation of low-income housing before 1987 also may produce excess depreciation subject to recapture.

The amount of excess depreciation that is subject to recapture (the "applicable percentage") depends on the type of property that is disposed of in the sale, exchange, or other transaction.

---

[65] Code Sec. 1(h)(1)(D).
[66] Code Sec. 1250(a)(1)(A).
[67] Code Sec. 1250(a)(2)(A).
[68] Code Sec. 1250(b)(1).

Nonresidential Real Property

For real property that is neither residential real property nor low-income housing, the applicable percentage of excess depreciation that is subject to recapture is 100 percent for periods after 1969.[69] There is no recapture of depreciation for excess depreciation attributable to periods before 1970.

Residential Real Property

For residential real property, other than low-income housing, the applicable percentage of excess depreciation that is subject to recapture is 100 percent for periods after 1975.[70] For periods after 1969 and before 1976, the applicable percentage of excess depreciation that is subject to recapture is 100 percent minus one percent for each full month the property was held in excess of 100 months. There is no recapture of depreciation for periods before 1970. Because of the one percent per month reduction in excess depreciation for periods before 1976, anyone now holding property held before 1976 will not be subject to depreciation recapture, although noncorporate taxpayers will be subject to the 25 percent maximum capital gain tax rate rather than the 20 percent maximum rate generally applicable to capital gains other than real property gains.

For periods after 1975, 85 percent of the gross income from the property must be from dwelling units in order for the property to be considered residential property. For periods before 1976, only 80 percent of the gross income had to be from dwelling units to be considered residential property.

> **Example:** The Taxpayer, an individual, acquired an apartment house that qualified as residential rental property on January 1, 1975, and sold the apartment house on January 4, 1997. The Taxpayer realized $50,000 over the adjusted basis on the sale of the property. Excess depreciation on the property totaled $20,000, of which $18,000 was attributable to the period the Taxpayer held the property after 1975, and $2,000 was attributable to the period the Taxpayer held the property before 1976.
>
> The applicable percentage of excess depreciation subject to recapture as ordinary income for the period after 1975 is 100 percent, and for the period before 1975, the applicable percentage is zero. The applicable percentage for the period before 1975 is determined by reducing an applicable percentage of 100 percent by one percent for each month the Taxpayer held the property over 100 months. In this case, the Taxpayer held the property well

---

[69] Code Sec. 1250(a)(1)(B)(v) and (a)(2)(B)(v).   [70] Code Sec. 1250(a)(1)(B)(v).

¶ 1307.2

over 200 months, so the reduction in the applicable percentage is 100 percent (100 percent − 100 percent = zero percent recapture).

The Taxpayer's gain that is treated as ordinary income because of the Section 1250 recapture rule is then computed as follows:

1. Excess of amount realized over adjusted basis $50,000
2. Excess depreciation after 1975 .... $18,000

Since gain exceeds post-1975 excess depreciation, it is necessary to take into account pre-1976 depreciation.

3. Lesser of 1 or 2 times 100% $18,000
4. Pre-1976 excess depreciation .... $ 2,000
5. Lesser of 4, or the excess of 1 over 2, times 0% 0

Gain recaptured as ordinary income $18,000

The Taxpayer's remaining gain of $32,000 is subject to characterization as ordinary income or capital gain under the rules of Code Sec. 1231, as discussed at ¶ 1305.2, because the rental property qualifies as a Section 1231 asset. If it is capital gain, the $32,000 is subject to a maximum capital gain tax rate of 25 percent.

Low-Income Housing

Low-income housing includes the following types of property:

1. Federally assisted housing projects, if the mortgage is insured under Sections 221(d)(3) or 236 of the National Housing Act, or housing financed or assisted by a direct loan or tax abatement under similar provisions of state or local laws; [71]
2. Low-income rental housing for which a depreciation deduction for rehabilitation expenditures is allowed; [72]
3. Low-income rental housing held for occupancy by families or individuals who are eligible to receive subsidies under Section 8 of the United States Housing Act of 1937, or under the provisions of state or local laws that authorize similar subsidies for low-income families; [73] and
4. Housing financed or assisted by direct loan or insured under Title V of the Housing Act of 1949.[74]

The applicable percentage of excess depreciation subject to recapture for periods after 1975 for low-income housing is 100 percent minus

---

[71] Code Sec. 1250(a)(1)(B)(i) and (a)(2)(B)(ii).
[72] Code Sec. 1250(a)(1)(B)(iii) and (a)(1)(B)(iv).
[73] Code Sec. 1250(a)(1)(B)(ii).
[74] Code Sec. 1250(a)(1)(B)(iv).

one percent for each full month the property was held in excess of 100 months.[75] For low-income housing described in categories 2, 3, and 4, above, the applicable percentage for periods after 1969 and before 1976 is 100 percent minus one percent for each full month the property is held over 100 months. For low-income housing in category 4 above, however, the applicable percentage is 100 percent minus one percent for each full month the property was held over 20 full months.[76] There is no recapture for periods before 1970.

Summary of Section 1250 Recapture

The following charts summarize the recapture rules for real property for the periods 1970-1975, 1975-1980, and post-1980, based on the type of property involved and the holding period for the property.

DEPRECIATION AFTER 1969 AND BEFORE 1976

Type of Property	Holding Period	Recapture
Nonresidential	Not more than 12 months	All depreciation is subject to recapture.
	More than 12 months	All excess depreciation; that is, all depreciation in excess of what would have been allowed under the straight-line method.
Residential other than low-income housing	Not more than 12 months	All depreciation is subject to recapture.
	More than 12 months but not more than 100 months	All excess depreciation; that is, all depreciation in excess of what would have been allowed under the straight-line method.
	More than 100 months but not more than 200 months	All excess depreciation less 1% per month for each full month property held over 100 months.
	More than 200 months (16 2/3 years)	No recapture.

---

[75] Code Sec. 1250(a)(1)(B).

[76] Code Sec. 1250(a)(2)(B).

¶ 1307.2

Sales and Exchanges

DEPRECIATION AFTER 1969 AND BEFORE 1976

Type of Property	Holding Period	Recapture
Low-income housing with federally insured mortgage or direct loan or tax abatement	Not more than 12 months	All depreciation is subject to recapture.
	More than 12 months but not more than 20 months	All excess depreciation; that is, all depreciation in excess of what would have been allowed under the straight-line method.
	More than 20 months but not more than 120 months	All excess depreciation less 1% per month for each full month property held over 20 months.
	Over 120 months	No recapture.
Other low-income housing	Not more than 12 months	All depreciation is subject to recapture.
	More than 12 months but not more than 100 months	All excess depreciation; that is, all depreciation in excess of what would have been allowed under the straight-line method.
	More than 100 months but not more than 200 months	All excess depreciation less 1% per month for each full month property held over 100 months.
	More than 200 months	No recapture.

DEPRECIATION AFTER 1975 AND BEFORE 1981

Type of Property	Holding Period	Recapture
Nonresidential and residential other than low-income housing	Not more than 12 months	All depreciation is subject to recapture.
	More than 12 months	All excess depreciation; that is, all depreciation in excess of what would have been allowed under the straight-line method.

¶ 1307.2

DEPRECIATION AFTER 1975 AND BEFORE 1981

Type of Property	Holding Period	Recapture
Low-income housing	Not more than 12 months	All depreciation is subject to recapture.
	More than 12 months but not more than 100 months	All excess depreciation; that is, all depreciation in excess of what would have been allowed under the straight-line method.
	More than 100 months but not more than 200 months	All excess depreciation less 1% per month for each full month property held over 100 months.
	More than 200 months	No recapture.

DEPRECIATION AFTER 1980

Type of Property	Holding Period	Recapture
Nonresidential depreciated under the accelerated schedules (Section 1245 property)		All depreciation is subject to recapture.
Residential other than low-income housing	Not more than 12 months	All depreciation is subject to recapture.
	More than 12 months	All excess depreciation; that is, all depreciation in excess of what would have been allowed under the straight-line method.
Low-income rental housing	Not more than 12 months	All depreciation is subject to recapture.
	More than 12 months but not more than 100 months	All excess depreciation; that is, all depreciation in excess of what would have been allowed under the straight-line method.
	More than 100 months but not more than 200 months	All excess depreciation less 1% per month for each full month property held over 100 months.
	More than 200 months	No recapture.

¶ 1307.2

DEPRECIATION AFTER 1980

Type of Property	Holding Period	Recapture
Property located outside the United States	Not more than 12 months	All depreciation is subject to recapture.
	More than 12 months	All excess depreciation; that is, all depreciation in excess of what would have been allowed under the straight-line method.
All real property depreciated on a straight-line basis	Not more than 12 months	All depreciation is subject to recapture.
	More than 12 months	No recapture.

Substantial Improvements

Substantial improvements to Section 1250 property may be treated separately for purposes of determining recapture.[77] To be considered a separate element, the cost of improvements added to the capital account for the property during a 36-month period ending on the last day of a taxable year must exceed the greatest of:

1. 25 percent of the adjusted basis of the property;
2. 10 percent of the original basis of the property, plus the cost of any improvements made prior to the current improvements, less the cost of retired components; or
3. $5,000.

Improvements in any one year are not counted under the rule if they are (a) $2,000 or less, or (b) one percent or less of the basis in 2, above, whichever is greater.

The amount of depreciation subject to recapture when substantial improvements are treated as separate properties is the sum of the recapture amounts applicable to each separate element of the property.

Additional Recapture for Corporations

If a corporation disposes of property subject to Section 1250 recapture, an extra amount must be recaptured as ordinary income in addition to the recapture called for by the Section 1250 rules. Generally, the corporation determines Section 1250 recapture in the normal fashion. To this amount, the corporation adds 20 percent of the differ-

---

[77] Code Sec. 1250(f).

ence between the normal Section 1250 recapture amount and the amount that the corporation would have had to recapture had the Section 1250 property been Section 1245 property.[78]

> *Example:* Several years ago, a corporation purchased real property for use in its trade or business. The corporation claimed depreciation deductions on this property in the amount of $50,000 and recently sold this property for $60,000 in excess of its adjusted basis. If the corporation had used straight-line depreciation, its depreciation deductions would have been $32,000 instead of $50,000.
>
> Under Code Sec. 1250, the normal recapture amount for this property is the amount of excess depreciation, or $18,000 ($50,000 − $32,000). To this amount, the corporation must add 20 percent of the difference between the Section 1250 recapture and the amount that would have been recaptured if the property were Section 1245 property. Under Code Sec. 1245, all depreciation to the extent of gain is recaptured, in this case $50,000. The difference between $50,000 and the Section 1250 recapture amount of $18,000 is $32,000. The corporation must add 20 percent of $32,000, or $6,400, to its normal Section 1250 recapture. Total depreciation subject to recapture, therefore, is $24,400 ($18,000 + $6,400).

Rehabilitated Buildings

If certain requirements are met as discussed in Chapter 8, the cost of rehabilitating older commercial buildings and historic structures is eligible for a tax credit. Generally, straight-line depreciation applies to the rehabilitation costs (even for property placed in service before 1987), and the amount of the credit reduces the basis for depreciation. In most cases, straight-line depreciation for real property eliminates future recapture under Code Sec. 1250. This, however, is not the case if the rehabilitation tax credit was taken for the property.

The reduction in adjusted basis as a result of the rehabilitation tax credit is treated as a deduction for depreciation for purposes of the depreciation recapture provisions.[79] Furthermore, in the case of Section 1250 property, recapture applies to deductions in excess of those that would have been allowed under the straight-line method on the basis of the property unreduced by the rehabilitation tax credit.[80] In other words, the tax credit for rehabilitation expenses produces excess depreciation subject to recapture under Code Sec. 1250. Note that if a building is held less than five years following a rehabilitation eligible

---

[78] Code Sec. 291(a)(1).
[79] Code Sec. 50(c)(4)(A).
[80] Code Sec. 50(c)(4)(B).

¶ 1307.2

for a tax credit, some or all of the tax credit is recaptured (see discussion at ¶ 827). This credit recapture would increase the basis of the building and also reduce the amount of the basis reduction treated as depreciation for Section 1250 recapture purposes.

¶ 1309 Alternative Minimum Tax

The alternative minimum tax imposed by Code Sec. 55 is designed to assure that everyone with income pays at least some tax. Although it is not directed particularly at the owners of real estate, the workings of the alternative minimum tax frequently bring real estate owners within its grasp. The alternative minimum tax applies to individuals and corporations, but there are some differences in the required adjustments and preferences for corporations as compared to other taxpayers. The following discussion is not meant to be a complete exposition of all the intricacies involved in the calculation of the alternative minimum tax. It is meant to bring the possible effects of this tax on the ownership, operation, and sale of real estate to the attention of those taxpayers who might be affected by the tax. Also, while the following discussion generally applies to all taxpayers, some of the preferences and adjustments that apply only to corporations are not considered.

¶ 1309.1 *Basic Computation*

Essentially, all taxpayers must compute their tax liability for the regular tax and the alternative minimum tax. Once this is done, a taxpayer simply pays the higher of the two, although technically it is the difference between the tentative minimum tax and the regular tax that is added to the regular tax if the alternative minimum tax figure is the higher of the two.[81] Taxpayers must consider any possible alternative minimum tax in making estimated tax payments since estimated tax payments are required against the alternative minimum tax as well as the regular income tax.

In order to compute the alternative minimum tax, a taxpayer begins with taxable income, computed in the usual fashion, makes certain adjustments, and then adds tax preferences. This new figure is known as the alternative minimum taxable income.[82] For corporate taxpayers, a tax rate of 20 percent is applied to alternative minimum taxable income in excess of a $40,000 exemption.[83] For other taxpayers, the rate is 26 percent of the first $175,000 ($87,500 in the case of married individuals filing separately) of alternative minimum taxable income in excess of the exemption amount, plus 28 percent of any additional alternative minimum taxable income. In the case of

---

[81] Code Sec. 55(a).
[82] Code Sec. 55(b)(2).
[83] Code Sec. 55(d)(2).

noncorporate taxpayers, the exemption is based on filing status as follows: [84]

Married taxpayers filing a joint return	$45,000 ($49,000 for 2001–2004)
Single or head-of-household filers	$33,750 ($35,750 for 2001–2004)
Married taxpayers filing separate returns	$22,500 ($24,500 for 2001–2004)
Estates and trusts	$22,500

For noncorporate taxpayers, the exemption amounts are phased out or reduced as alternative minimum taxable income rises above a certain level. The exemption is reduced by 25 percent of alternative minimum taxable income in excess of the following amounts, based on filing status: [85]

Married taxpayers filing a joint return	$150,000
Single or head-of-household filers	$112,500
Married taxpayers filing separate returns and for estates and trusts	$ 75,000

Generally, nonrefundable tax credits cannot be used to reduce the alternative minimum tax, with the exception of a modified foreign tax credit.[86] Tax credits that are not used because of the alternative minimum tax generally can be carried over and used against the regular tax in later years under the tax credit carryover rules.

To prevent capital gain from aggravating alternative minimum tax problems, Code Sec. 55(b)(3) applies the same preferential rates that apply for regular tax purposes to capital gains realized by noncorporate taxpayers for alternative minimum tax purposes (see ¶ 1305.1).

¶ 1309.2 Small Business Exception

A small business corporation is exempt from the alternative minimum tax if the corporation had average annual gross receipts of $7.5 million or less for all three-tax-year periods before the current year. For the first three-year period, the amount is $5 million.[87]

---

[84] Code Sec. 55(d)(1).
[85] Code Sec. 55(d)(3).
[86] Code Secs. 55(c), 59(a).
[87] Code Sec. 55(e).

Qualifying corporations with unused minimum tax credits after 1997 that would otherwise be available to offset regular tax in excess of tentative minimum tax, may use the credit to offset 75 percent of regular tax.[88]

¶ 1309.3 Adjustments to Taxable Income

Part of the process of going from regular taxable income to alternative minimum taxable income involves making adjustments to the way certain deductions and other items are treated for alternative minimum tax purposes as opposed to the regular tax. To compute alternative minimum taxable income, the following items are treated in the manner indicated.

Depreciation

Depreciation on property placed in service after 1986 and before 1999 must be redetermined using the alternative depreciation system (see Chapter 9) for alternative minimum tax purposes.[89] Generally, the alternative depreciation system provides for smaller deductions through longer depreciation periods and, in the case of personal property, a less accelerated method of calculating deductions. For property placed in service after 1998, the adjustment is still required, but it is computed using regular tax depreciation lives. For property placed in service before 1987, accelerated depreciation (excess of depreciation over the straight-line amount) is a tax preference that is added to alternative minimum taxable income.[90]

Another aspect of depreciation and the alternative minimum tax is that the alternative depreciation system also must be used to calculate the adjusted basis of property for minimum tax purposes.[91] This means that on the sale or exchange of property, the property may have a different adjusted basis for minimum tax purposes than for regular tax purposes and, accordingly, the amount of gain for minimum tax purposes may be different than for regular tax purposes.

Mining Exploration and Development Costs

The deduction for mining exploration and development costs must be redetermined for minimum tax purposes based on the capitalization of these costs and 10-year amortization.[92]

Long-Term Contracts

Income from long-term contracts must be redetermined for minimum tax purposes using the percentage-of-completion method of ac-

---

[88] Code Sec. 55(e)(5).
[89] Code Sec. 56(a)(1).
[90] Code Sec. 57(a)(6).
[91] Code Sec. 56(a)(6).
[92] Code Sec. 56(a)(2).

counting if the completed-contract method of accounting is used for regular tax purposes.[93]

Net Operating Loss

Any net operating loss deduction must be redetermined using the rules contained in Code Sec. 56(d) to determine the alternative tax net operating loss deduction.[94] The net operating loss cannot offset more than 90 percent of alternative minimum taxable income.

Pollution Control Facilities

Deductions for pollution control facilities placed in service after 1986 must be calculated using the alternative depreciation system for minimum tax purposes.[95] This makes pollution control facilities subject to the same depreciation rules as other property in computing the alternative minimum tax. For property placed in service after 1998, the deduction is determined under Code Sec. 168 using the straight-line method.

Miscellaneous Itemized Deductions

Deductions for miscellaneous itemized expenses (except as noted below) or for state and local taxes are not allowed in computing alternative minimum taxable income.[96] Medical expenses are deductible for alternative minimum tax purposes only to the extent they exceed 10 percent of the taxpayer's adjusted gross income.[97] The deduction for interest is generally allowed to the same extent as for regular tax purposes, but there is a special limitation put on the deduction of interest on a refinanced home mortgage. In this latter case, the interest deduction for alternative minimum tax purposes is limited to the amount of the debt prior to the refinancing.[98]

Circulation Expenditures

Circulation expenditures of periodicals must be amortized over three years for alternative minimum tax purposes.[99]

Research and Experimental Expenditures

R&D expenses must be amortized over 10 years for alternative minimum tax purposes, unless the taxpayer materially participates in the R&D activity.[100]

---

[93] Code Sec. 56(a)(3).
[94] Code Sec. 56(a)(4).
[95] Code Sec. 56(a)(5).
[96] Code Sec. 56(b)(1)(A).
[97] Code Sec. 56(b)(1)(B).
[98] Code Sec. 56(b)(1)(C) and (e).
[99] Code Sec. 56(b)(2)(A)(i).
[100] Code Sec. 56(b)(2)(A)(ii).

Sales and Exchanges

Passive Farm Losses

Losses from farming activities in which the taxpayer does not materially participate are generally not allowed in computing alternative minimum taxable income.[101]

Passive Activity Losses

Generally, the passive activity loss rules (see Chapter 11) apply in determining alternative minimum taxable income as well as regular taxable income. The various adjustments for the alternative minimum tax apply.[102] Any deduction that is a tax preference under the minimum tax is not taken into account under the passive loss rules.[103]

¶ 1309.4 Tax Preferences

After a taxpayer makes the adjustments listed above to regular taxable income, tax preferences are added to arrive at alternative minimum taxable income. Tax preferences for noncorporate taxpayers include the following items:

Depletion

Percentage depletion in excess of the basis of the property at the end of the year is a tax preference.[104]

Intangible Drilling Costs

The tax preference for intangible drilling costs is the amount by which the deduction for such costs on successful wells exceeds the amount that could be deducted if the costs were amortized over 10 years, but only to the extent that this amount exceeds 65 percent of the taxpayer's net income from oil, gas, and geothermal wells for the year.[105]

Tax-Exempt Interest

The interest on certain private activity bonds issued after August 7, 1986, which continues to be exempt from regular tax, is a tax preference for minimum tax purposes.[106] Private activity bonds are bonds issued by government for nonessential functions.

Small Business Stock Gain

Forty-two percent of gain from the sale of small business stock that is excluded from income under Code Sec. 1202 is a tax preference.[107]

---

[101] Code Sec. 58(a).
[102] Code Sec. 58(b)(1).
[103] Code Sec. 58(b)(2).
[104] Code Sec. 57(a)(1).
[105] Code Sec. 57(a)(2).
[106] Code Sec. 57(a)(5).
[107] Code Sec. 55(a)(7).

Accelerated Depreciation

The excess of accelerated depreciation, including the amortization of certified pollution control facilities, over the straight-line amount for property placed in service before 1987 is a tax preference.[108]

¶ 1309.5 Optional 10-Year Writeoff

Taxpayers may elect to amortize certain costs in order to avoid adjustments or preferences for alternative minimum tax purposes.[109] Generally, if the following are amortized over 10 years, they are not considered in computing alternative minimum taxable income:

1. Research and experimental expenditures;
2. Intangible drilling costs;
3. Mine exploration expenses; and
4. Mine development expenses.

Circulation expenditures that are amortized over three years do not enter into the alternative minimum taxable income calculation.[110] Also, the adjustment for depreciation on property placed in service after 1986 is avoided if the alternative depreciation system is used for regular tax purposes.

¶ 1309.6 Alternative Minimum Tax Credit

In order to prevent the double taxation of certain amounts that may show up in alternative minimum taxable income in one year and in regular taxable income in another year, the alternative minimum tax paid may be used as a tax credit against regular tax, but not alternative minimum tax, in future years.[111] The credit is allowed to the extent that alternative minimum tax results from "deferral" preferences and adjustments. Only alternative minimum tax that results from "exclusion" preferences and adjustments may not be used to offset future regular tax in excess of alternative minimum tax. The exclusion preferences and adjustments include:

1. Individual itemized deductions;
2. Depletion;
3. Tax-exempt interest; and
4. Exclusion for gain on small business stocks.[112]

¶ 1311 TAX-FREE EXCHANGE OF PROPERTY

Under the general rules of Code Secs. 1001 and 1002, an exchange of one parcel of real estate for another parcel of real estate is taxable to

---

[108] Code Sec. 57(a)(6).
[109] Code Sec. 59(e).
[110] Code Sec. 59(e)(1).
[111] Code Sec. 53.
[112] Code Sec. 53(d).

the same extent as a cash sale. The fair market value of the property received in the exchange is the "amount realized," and the difference between this figure and the adjusted basis of the property given up is the amount of gain or loss realized.

The Internal Revenue Code, however, recognizes that when a taxpayer gives up property in exchange for similar property, the taxpayer has not effectively "realized" a profit on the transaction. Rather, the exchange of similar properties actually represents a continued investment on the part of the taxpayer, and it is inappropriate to impose a tax at this point. Practical considerations also may have played a part in Congress's decision to exempt various exchange transactions from current taxation. From an administrative standpoint, it may be difficult to value property that is exchanged solely or primarily for similar property. Even more importantly, in a pure exchange of one property for another, no cash is generated with which to pay a tax. Accordingly, Code Sec. 1031(a)(1) provides that:

> No gain or loss shall be recognized on the exchange of property held for productive use in a trade or business or for investment if such property is exchanged solely for property of like kind which is to be held either for productive use in a trade or business or for investment.

The tax consequences from any potential gain or loss on property, however, are not completely avoided. The nonrecognition rule is coupled with a basis rule in Code Sec. 1031(d) that preserves any unrecognized gain or loss in the adjusted basis of the replacement property. A future taxable disposition of the replacement property ultimately results in the recognition of this previously unrecognized gain or loss.

The nonrecognition rule of Code Sec. 1031, as noted, applies to losses as well as to gains. Moreover, the nonrecognition provisions are not elective. If the requirements are met, Code Sec. 1031 applies. In cases where there is a potential loss on real estate, it may be better to sell the property, recognize the loss, and use the proceeds to purchase replacement property.

¶ 1313 Like-Kind Exchange Requirements

In order for an exchange of properties to qualify as a tax-free like-kind exchange under Code Sec. 1031, six basic requirements or conditions must be satisfied:

1. The property received and the property given up in the exchange must be business or investment property.

¶ 1313

Business property may be exchanged for investment property or investment property for business property.[113] The use of either the property given up or the property received for personal purposes takes the transaction out of the like-kind exchange provisions and results in current taxation. For instance, the exchange of business or investment property for property that will be used as a personal residence does not qualify as a tax-free exchange.[114]

2. The property must not be property held for sale.

Neither the property received nor the property given up in the exchange may be property that is sold to customers.[115] Real estate that dealers hold for sale to customers does not qualify for like-kind exchange treatment.[116] A corporation engaged in the business of real estate development and sale was not entitled to nonrecognition of gain on the exchange of an orange grove for grazing land when the grazing land was held primarily for sale rather than for investment.[117]

3. There must be an exchange of like property.

An exchange occurs when there is a reciprocal transfer of property, as distinguished from a transfer of property for money consideration only.[118] The transfer of money along with qualifying property, however, does not completely disqualify the exchange. Money received in addition to like-kind property results in the recognition of gain, but only to the extent of the money received.[119] (See the discussion of partially tax-free exchanges at ¶ 1315.) Also, a transaction that appears to be an "exchange" may, in fact, be a sale. For instance, a company transferred its old plant to a contractor, who accepted the property to apply to the construction cost of a new building for the company. The contractor did not own the land on which the building was constructed, nor did the contractor own the building he was constructing. In this situation, the contractor was not exchanging property that he owned, and the transaction was a sale with the old plant serving as part of the consideration.[120]

4. The property must be tangible property.

This requirement is not a problem in the case of real estate, which is tangible property. Code Sec. 1031(a)(2) specifically excludes the following from the like-kind exchange provision: (a) stocks, bonds, and notes, (b) other securities and evidences of indebtedness or interest,

---

[113] Reg. § 1.1031(a)-1(a).
[114] *D.H. Click*, 78 TC 225, CCH Dec. 38,790.
[115] Code Sec. 1031(a)(2)(A).
[116] *California Delta Farms, Inc.*, 6 BTA 1301, CCH Dec. 2455, Acq. VII-1 CB 5.
[117] *Land Dynamics*, 37 TCM 1119, CCH Dec. 35,263(M), T.C. Memo. 1978-259.
[118] Reg. § 1.1002-1(d).
[119] Code Sec. 1031(b).
[120] *Bloomington Coca-Cola Bottling Co.*, CA-7, 51-1 USTC ¶ 9320, 189 F.2d 14.

(c) interests in a partnership, (d) certificates of trust and beneficial interest, and (e) choses in action.

5. The property to be exchanged must be identified within 45 days.

Property to be received in a like-kind exchange must be identified on or before the day which is 45 days after the date on which the taxpayer transfers the property given up in the exchange.[121] This identification requirement may be met by designating the property in the contract between the parties. The requirement is also met if the contract specifies a limited number of properties that may be transferred and the particular property to be transferred is determined by contingencies beyond the control of both parties. For instance, if A transferred real estate in exchange for a promise by B to transfer Property #1 to A if zoning changes were approved and Property #2 if they were not, the exchange would qualify for like-kind treatment, provided the other requirements were met.

6. There must be a completed transaction.

Property to be received in a tax-free like-kind exchange must be received on or before the earlier of (a) the 180th day after the date on which the taxpayer transfers the property given up, and (b) the due date, including extensions, for the taxpayer's return for the tax year in which the transfer of the property given up occurs.[122]

¶ 1313.1 *Like-Kind Real Estate Defined*

The tax-free exchange provision of Code Sec. 1031 applies only to exchanges of properties that are of a "like kind." Like kind refers to the nature or character of the property, not to its grade or quality. That real estate involved in an exchange is improved or unimproved is not material because that relates only to the grade or quality of the property, to its kind or class.[123]

Whether property is new or used does not affect a like-kind exchange. The distinction between new and used property is one of grade or quality, not one of kind. City real estate may be exchanged tax-free for a farm or ranch. A leasehold with 30 years or more to run may be exchanged for a fee interest in real estate.[124]

The Tax Court has listed several factors to consider in determining whether property is of a like kind:

1. Respective interests in the physical properties;
2. Nature of title conveyed;

---

[121] Code Sec. 1031(a)(3)(A).
[122] Code Sec. 1031(a)(3)(B).
[123] Reg. § 1.1031(a)-1(b).
[124] Reg. § 1.1031(a)-1(c).

3. Rights of the parties;
4. Duration of the interests; and
5. Any other factor bearing on the nature or character of the properties as distinguished from their grade or quality.

Applying these factors and pointing out that "like kind" does not mean "identical," the Court held that taxpayers who exchanged fee interests in unimproved real estate for the fee interest in improved property were entitled to like-kind exchange treatment, even though the property they received was subject to a long-term lease.[125]

Mineral rights are interests in real property, and the transfer of an undivided interest in oil, gas and other minerals for an undivided interest in a city lot is a nontaxable exchange.[126] The IRS has ruled that an exchange of a producing oil lease extending until exhaustion of the deposit for a fee interest in an improved ranch is a like-kind exchange.[127] Similarly, if water rights are considered real property rights under state law, the exchange of water rights for a fee interest in land may qualify as a like-kind exchange.[128]

The exchange of leaseholds may qualify for like-kind exchange treatment.[129] However, the transfer of a lot for the execution of a leasehold interest in the lot and in other properties was not a like-kind exchange on the part of the transferee-lessor, although it was for the transferor-lessee. The lot received by the transferee-lessor was an advance rental.[130]

An exchange of one remainder interest in real property for a remainder interest in another parcel of real property qualifies as a like-kind exchange.[131] The exchange of a life estate in real property owned by a son for a remainder interest in real property owned by his 70-year-old father, however, was ruled not to be a like-kind exchange.[132]

In a private letter ruling,[133] the IRS has approved like-kind treatment for an investor-shareholder's exchange of stock in a cooperative for a condominium interest. Although stock is explicitly excluded from the like-kind exchange rules under Code Sec. 1031(a)(2)(B), the IRS noted that the investor-shareholder in a cooperative was in a unique position that called for different treatment than the normal shareholder in a corporation. In the ruling, the IRS pointed to the regulation (Reg. § 1.1031(a)-1(c)) that treats a leasehold interest with 30 years or more to run as an interest in real estate (the lease on the cooperative had 92

---

[125] *C.E. Koch*, 71 TC 54, CCH Dec. 34,062, Acq. 1980-2 CB 1.
[126] *W. Fleming v. Campfield*, CA-5, 53-2 USTC ¶ 9469, 205 F.2d 549.
[127] Rev. Rul. 68-331, 1969-2 CB 352.
[128] Rev. Rul. 55-749, 1955-2 CB 295.
[129] Rev. Rul. 76-301, 1976-2 CB 241.
[130] Rev. Rul. 66-209, 1966-2 CB 299.
[131] Rev. Rul. 78-4, 1978-1 CB 256.
[132] Rev. Rul. 72-601, 1972-2 CB 467.
[133] IRS Letter Ruling, December 10, 1987.

¶ 1313.1

years to run). Also, the investor-shareholder's interest was characterized as real estate under the laws of California, where the cooperative was located.

Under prior law, the exchange of real estate could qualify for like-kind treatment even if one parcel was located in a foreign country.[134] For exchanges after July 10, 1989, however, real property located in the United States and real property located outside the United States are not properties of a like kind.[135]

The exchanging taxpayer must hold both the property transferred and the property received for business or investment use in order for the nonrecognition provision to apply. Accordingly, the IRS has ruled that when an individual exchanged land and buildings used in a business for land and an office building and immediately thereafter, in a prearranged plan, transferred the land and office building to a newly created corporation, there was no like-kind exchange.[136] Similarly, the IRS has also ruled that an individual's prearranged transfer of a shopping center, received from the liquidation of the individual's wholly owned corporation and immediately exchanged for like-kind property held by an unrelated party, did qualify for nonrecognition of gain or loss under Code Sec. 1031.[137]

The Tax Court and the Ninth Circuit Court of Appeals, however, have disagreed with Rev. Rul. 77-337. These courts have held that an exchange of real property which was acquired as a corporate liquidating distribution for three parcels of realty qualified for nonrecognition of gain as a like-kind exchange of property "held for investment," even though the exchange was contemplated before the liquidating distribution occurred. The realty received as a liquidating distribution did not have to be held, even briefly, with the intention of keeping it indefinitely in order to qualify as being "held for investment." The requirement that the property be held for investment was satisfied because the property was not acquired with the intention of liquidating it or using it for personal pursuits.[138]

Related Parties

If a taxpayer exchanges property with a related party (as defined in Code Sec. 267, relating to disallowed losses as discussed at ¶ 1303.3) and the taxpayer would otherwise be eligible for nonrecognition treatment under Code Sec. 1031, the exchange does not qualify for nonrecognition if either the related party disposes of the property received or the taxpayer disposes of the like-kind property within two years of the

---

[134] Rev. Rul. 68-363, 1968-2 CB 336.
[135] Code Sec. 1031(h).
[136] Rev. Rul. 75-292, 1975-2 CB 333.
[137] Rev. Rul. 77-337, 1977-2 CB 305.
[138] *J.R. Bolker*, CA-9, 85-1 USTC ¶ 9400, 760 F.2d 1039, aff'g 81 TC 782, CCH Dec. 40,558.

¶ 1313.1

exchange.[139] This related party rule generally applies to exchanges after July 10, 1989. Any gain or loss not recognized by the taxpayer as of the date of the original exchange is recognized as of the date of the subsequent disposition, subject to the disallowed loss rules of Code Sec. 267. Adjustments to the basis of the properties involved in the exchange also are made as of the date of the subsequent disposition.

A disposition of the property exchanged by related parties does not invalidate the nonrecognition treatment of the original exchange if the subsequent disposition is due to the death of either party or the involuntary conversion of the property, provided that the original exchange occurred before the threat or imminence of the conversion.[140] A disposition also does not invalidate the nonrecognition treatment of the original exchange if it is established that neither the exchange nor the subsequent disposition had as one of its principal purposes the avoidance of Federal income tax.[141] According to the Senate Committee Report on the Revenue Reconciliation Act of 1989, it is intended that the non-tax avoidance exception generally will apply to the following:

1. Transactions involving an exchange of undivided interests in different properties that results in each taxpayer's holding the entire interest in a single property or a larger undivided interest in any of the properties;

2. Dispositions of property in nonrecognition transactions; and

3. Transactions that do not involve the shifting of basis between properties.

A disposition includes indirect dispositions of the property, such as by means of the disposition of the stock of a corporation or interests in a partnership that owns the property.

Nonrecognition of gain or loss under Code Sec. 1031 is not available for any exchange which is part of a transaction or series of transactions structured to avoid the purpose of the related party rules.[142] For example, if a taxpayer, under a prearranged plan, transfers property to an unrelated party who then exchanges the property with a party related to the taxpayer within two years of the previous transfer in a transaction otherwise qualifying under Code Sec. 1031, the related party will not be entitled to nonrecognition treatment under Code Sec. 1031.

---

[139] Code Sec. 1031(f)(1).
[140] Code Sec. 1031(f)(2).
[141] Code Sec. 1031(f)(2)(C).
[142] Code Sec. 1031(f)(4).

¶ 1313.1

Delayed Exchanges

The requirement that property to be exchanged be identified within 45 days and that the exchange be completed within 180 days were added to the like-kind exchange requirements in 1984. Prior to that, delayed or nonsimultaneous exchanges were possible, although they did risk challenge from the IRS. In *T.J. Starker*,[143] however, the court held that an exchange qualified for like-kind treatment, even though the property to be exchanged could be designated by the transferor for up to five years after the transaction and even though the transferor could have ultimately received cash rather than like-kind property if suitable property could not be found to complete the exchange. It was in response to *Starker* that Congress enacted the 45-day identification requirement and 180-day completed transaction requirement for like-kind exchanges.

Of course, nonsimultaneous exchanges remain possible within the confines of the identification and completed transaction time limits. Generally, the contract between a seller who wants like-kind treatment and a purchaser will provide that the purchaser is to deliver the purchase price to the owner of the property that is desired by the seller and that the owner of that property will convey it to the seller (a form of a multi-party exchange, see ¶ 1317). If suitable property cannot be found within the time limits, the purchase price is delivered to the seller and the transaction becomes a taxable sale. The contract to pay cash if suitable exchange property cannot be located within the necessary time limits does not destroy a tax-free exchange if suitable property is found.

Suppose, however, that the prospective parties to a like-kind exchange need more time than that provided by the identification and completed transaction requirements. Is it possible to have the equivalent of an exchange that exceeds the time limits yet still qualifies as a tax-free exchange?

The IRS has ruled on the tax consequences of an option to purchase real property that permitted the option price to be paid in either cash or other real property. When the option was ultimately exercised by the purchaser by acquiring property equal in value to the option price and transferring that property to the seller, the seller was given tax-free like-kind exchange treatment on the exercise of the option by the purchaser.[144] Only the cash originally received for the option was taxable.

---

[143] CA-9, 79-2 USTC ¶ 9541, 602 F.2d 1341.   [144] Rev. Rul. 84-121, 1984-2 CB 168.

¶ 1313.1

While a simple option does permit a delayed like-kind exchange, what if the purchaser wants immediate possession of the property? In this case, it may be possible for the seller, who wants to achieve a like-kind exchange, to lease the property to the purchaser in connection with the purchase option. Under this strategy, the purchaser receives immediate use of the property to be given up by the seller in the exchange but does not have to find suitable replacement property until it is time to exercise the option. The danger in this strategy is that the IRS may insist that when the purchaser takes possession under the lease a "transfer" has occurred that triggers the running of the 45-day and 180-day requirements for a like-kind exchange. Retention of ownership by the seller and a contract that does not actually bind the purchaser to purchase the property until the option is exercised may minimize the danger of such an IRS attack.

Build-to-Suit Exchange

The owner/seller of property may find a purchaser who is willing to construct new facilities for the seller so that the seller can take advantage of the like-kind exchange provision. The IRS has approved such a build-to-suit arrangement in Rev. Rul. 75-291.[145]

In the ruling, the purchaser wanted to acquire the seller's land and factory, but the seller wanted a tax-free exchange. The parties agreed for the purchaser to buy land and construct a new factory to the seller's specifications. The contract allowed the purchaser to cancel if the cost of buying the replacement land and constructing the new factory exceeded a specified amount. The purchaser ultimately bought land, constructed the factory, and exchanged properties with the seller. The IRS ruled that the transaction qualified as a like-kind exchange for the seller under Code Sec. 1031, even though the property received in the exchange was acquired by the purchaser solely to complete the exchange. The IRS emphasized that the purchaser had to act on the purchaser's own behalf, and not as agent for the seller, in buying the land and constructing the new factory. The purchaser was not eligible for like-kind exchange treatment, however, because the land and factory exchanged were not held for business or investment purposes. In most cases, this would not matter to a prospective purchaser.

¶ 1313.2 Basis Rule

In order to preserve the potential gain or loss when property is exchanged in a like-kind exchange under Code Sec. 1031, the basis of the property acquired in the exchange is the same as the adjusted basis of the property transferred at the time of the exchange.[146] This basis is

---

[145] 1975-2 CB 332.

[146] Code Sec. 1031(d).

known as a "substituted basis." A cash payment or the value of other consideration given in connection with a tax-free like-kind exchange is added to the substituted basis of the acquired property.[147]

> *Example:* The Taxpayer exchanges land and a building worth $100,000, but with an adjusted basis of $60,000, for land worth $100,000. The exchange qualifies for like-kind treatment. The Taxpayer's basis for the land received is $60,000 and the potential gain of $40,000 on the land and building given up is preserved.
>
> If the land received by the Taxpayer was worth $110,000, the Taxpayer may have completed the exchange by paying $10,000 cash in addition to the land and building given up in the exchange. In this case, the Taxpayer's basis for the land received would be $70,000 ($60,000 adjusted basis of the property given up + $10,000 cash paid).

Generally, if a taxpayer receives money or nonqualifying property in an otherwise tax-free like-kind exchange, the taxpayer is taxed on any gain up to the amount of money or other property received (see partially tax-free exchanges, at ¶ 1315). In this case, the basis of the acquired property is the adjusted basis of the property given up, decreased by the amount of money or value of other property received and increased by the amount of gain recognized on the exchange.[148] Application of this rule is illustrated at ¶ 1315.3 in connection with the discussion of partially tax-free exchanges.

¶ 1313.3 Basis Allocation Among Multiple Properties

If more than one property is received in a like-kind exchange, the adjusted basis of the property given up must be allocated among the properties received according to their fair market values on the date of the exchange.[149] When multiple properties are received, appraisals of the fair market values of the properties should be obtained to facilitate this allocation. Allocation of basis also is required when land and a building are acquired in the exchange, since the land and building are two separate properties (see allocation of costs at ¶ 117).

> *Example:* A corporation exchanges land and buildings with a total adjusted basis of $110,000 ($100,000 is the basis of the land and $10,000 is the basis of the buildings) for two lots, A and B. Each of the lots received has a building on it. The fair market values of these properties received by the corporation are:

---

[147] Reg. § 1.1031(d)-1(a).
[148] Code Sec. 1031(d); Reg. § 1.1031(d)-1(b).
[149] Rev. Rul. 68-36, 1968-1 CB 357.

Lot A:
Land .... $ 20,000
Building   80,000

   Total $100,000

Lot B:
Land .... $ 30,000
Building 120,000

   Total $150,000

The basis of the property given up is allocated to the land and building for each lot received in proportion to its fair market values. Accordingly, 2/5 ($100,000/$250,000) of the $110,000 adjusted basis of the property given up is allocated to property A, and 3/5 ($150,000/$250,000) is allocated to property B:

Property A: 2/5 × $110,000 = $44,000.

Property B: 3/5 × $110,000 = $66,000.

The basis allocated to property A and property B must then be allocated between the land and building. Since the building on lot A represents 4/5 of the total value of A ($80,000/$100,000) and the land represents 1/5 of the total value of A ($20,000/$100,000), 4/5 of the basis allocated to A is allocated to the building and 1/5 to the land:

Building A: 4/5 × $44,000 = $35,200.

Land A: 1/5 × $44,000 = $8,800.

A similar allocation is made between the land ($30,000/$150,000 = 1/5) and building ($120,000/$150,000 = 4/5) located on lot B based on their relative fair market values:

Building B: 4/5 × $66,000 = $52,800.

Land B: 1/5 × $66,000 = $13,200.

The basis to the corporation for the two acquired properties is, therefore, $44,000 for lot A (with $8,800 allocated to the land and $35,200 allocated to the building) and $66,000 for lot B (with $13,200 allocated to the land and $52,800 allocated to the building).

¶ 1315 Partially Tax-Free Exchanges

It is the rare exchange of properties that does not require some payment or other consideration to equalize the values of the properties. An exchange of real estate is only partially tax free for the party who receives money or other property, often called "boot," in addition to the like-kind property. The tax-free status of an exchange is not affected by the giving of boot, only by its receipt. [150] While the receipt of boot will trigger the recognition of gain, the receipt of boot does not permit the recognition of any loss realized on the exchange. [151]

¶ 1315.1 Other Property or Money

The receipt of money or other unlike property, in addition to property that may be received tax free in a like-kind exchange, is taxable to the party receiving it if the recipient realizes a gain on the exchange. The recipient of the boot pays a tax on gain, but only to the extent of the money and fair market value of the other property received. [152]

> *Example:* The Taxpayer, who is not a dealer in real estate, exchanges real property held for investment, which was acquired several years before and which has a basis of $50,000, for other real estate to be used in a trade or business and $20,000 in cash. The value of the real estate received is $60,000. The Taxpayer's amount realized is $80,000 ($20,000 cash plus $60,000 like-kind property). The Taxpayer's gain from the transaction is, therefore, $30,000 ($80,000 amount realized less $50,000 basis), but the gain is recognized only to the extent of the cash received of $20,000. [153]

The disposition of property in a like-kind exchange transaction is subject to the depreciation recapture provisions as discussed at ¶ 1307. However, income results from the recapture of depreciation on a like-kind exchange only to the extent gain is otherwise recognized [154] or if the amount of recapture on the property exchanged exceeds the value of the depreciable property received. [155]

Gain recognized in a like-kind exchange may be reported on the installment method if the transaction otherwise qualifies as an installment sale. [156]

¶ 1315.2 Mortgages and Other Liabilities

The assumption of liabilities by the other party to the exchange, or the other party's acquisition of property subject to a liability, is treated as money received by the taxpayer on the exchange. [157] It does not matter whether the taxpayer is personally liable for the debt or whether the other party actually assumes the debt. [158] An individual who made a like-kind exchange of investment real property for other investment real property, cash, and the transferee's assumption of a

---

[150] Reg. § 1.1031(a)-1(c).
[151] Code Sec. 1031(c).
[152] Code Sec. 1031(b); Reg. § 1.1031(b)-1(a).
[153] Reg. § 1.1031(b)-1(b).
[154] Code Sec. 1250(d)(4)(A)(i).
[155] Code Sec. 1250(d)(4)(C).
[156] Rev. Rul. 65-155, 1965-1 CB 356. See the discussion of installment reporting at ¶ 1405.
[157] Code Sec. 1031(d); Reg. § 1031(b)-1(c).
[158] *G.P. Allen,* 10 TC 413, CCH Dec. 16,288.

liability on the transferred property was required to recognize gain to the extent of the cash received and the liability assumed. [159]

Example 1: Individual B owns an apartment house which has an adjusted basis in B's hands of $500,000, but which is subject to a mortgage of $150,000. B transfers the apartment house to individual C in exchange for $50,000 in cash and another apartment house with a fair market value on the date of the transfer of $600,000. The transfer to C is subject to the $150,000 mortgage. B realizes a gain of $300,000 on the exchange, computed as follows:

Value of property received	$600,000
Cash	50,000
Liabilities transferred	150,000
Amount realized	$800,000
Less: Basis of property transferred	500,000
Gain realized	$300,000

Under Code Sec. 1031(b), B's recognized gain is limited to $200,000 of the $300,000 total gain. This is the amount of boot received by taxpayer, consisting of the $50,000 cash and the $150,000 of mortgage debt to which the transferred property was subject.

When a taxpayer exchanges mortgaged property for other mortgaged property and each party to the exchange assumes the mortgage of the other, a balancing of the liabilities takes place. [160] Only the net reduction of the taxpayer's mortgage debt, if any, is treated as money received. According to the regulations:

Where, on an exchange described in section 1031(b), each party to the exchange either assumes a liability of the other party or acquires property subject to a liability, then, in determining the amount of "other property or money" for purposes of section 1031(b), consideration given in the form of an assumption of liabilities (or a receipt of property subject to a liability) shall be offset against consideration received in the form of an assumption of liabilities (or a transfer subject to a liability).[161]

Example 2: D, an individual, owns an apartment house with an adjusted basis in D's hands of $100,000. The fair market value of this apartment house is $220,000, but it is subject to a mortgage of $80,000. D transfers the apartment house to E, also an individual, in exchange for $40,000 in cash and another apartment house. The apartment house owned by E before the exchange has an adjusted

---

[159] *D.W. Westall,* 56 TCM 66, CCH Dec. 45,040(M), T.C. Memo. 1988-421.
[160] Rev. Rul. 59-229, 1959-2 CB 180.
[161] Reg. § 1.1031(b)-1(c).

¶ 1315.2

basis in E's hands of $175,000 and a fair market value of $250,000, but it is subject to a mortgage of $150,000. As part of the exchange, each apartment house is transferred subject to the mortgage on it.

D realizes a gain of $120,000 on the exchange, computed as follows:

Value of property received	$250,000
Cash	40,000
Liabilities transferred	80,000
Amount realized	$370,000
Less: Basis of property transferred	100,000
	$270,000
Less: Liabilities received	150,000
Gain realized	$120,000

For purposes of Code Sec. 1031(b), the amount of "other property or money" received by D is $40,000. Consideration received by D in the form of a transfer subject to a liability of $80,000 is offset by consideration given in the form of a receipt of property subject to a $150,000 liability. Accordingly, only the consideration received in the form cash, $40,000, is treated as boot, and D recognizes only $40,000 of the $120,000 gain.

As for the other side of the exchange, E realizes a gain of $75,000 on the exchange, computed as follows:

Value of property received	$220,000
Liabilities transferred	150,000
Amount realized	$370,000
Less: Basis of property transferred	175,000
	$195,000
Less: Cash paid	40,000
	$155,000
Less: Liabilities received	80,000
Gain realized	$ 75,000

For purposes of Code Sec. 1031(b), the amount of "other property or money" received by E is $30,000. Consideration received by E in the form of a transfer subject to a liability of $150,000 is offset by consideration given in the form of a receipt of property subject to an $80,000 liability and by the $40,000 cash paid by E. Although consideration received in the form of cash or other property is not offset by consideration given in the form of an assumption of liabilities or a receipt of property subject to a liability, consideration given in the form of cash or other property

¶ 1315.2

is offset against consideration received in the form of an assumption of liabilities or a transfer of property subject to a liability. Accordingly, E recognizes only $30,000 of the total gain of $75,000.

¶ 1315.3 Basis in Partially Tax-Free Exchanges

The application of the substituted basis rule to a like-kind exchange is complicated by adjustments when the exchange is only partially tax free, or if a loss is recognized because unlike property is transferred in the exchange along with the like-kind property.

When boot is received in a like-kind exchange, the basis of the like-kind property acquired is the basis of the property transferred, decreased by the amount of money received and increased by the amount of gain recognized on the exchange.[162] The basis of the "other" or unlike property received in an otherwise tax-free exchange is its fair market value on the date of the exchange.[163]

Example 1: The Taxpayer trades an apartment building worth $230,000 for another apartment building worth $190,000 and $15,000 in cash and stock with a fair market value of $25,000. The Taxpayer's adjusted basis at the time of the exchange for the building being given up is $150,000. The Taxpayer realizes a gain on the exchange of $80,000, but only $40,000 (the amount of boot received) is recognized. The Taxpayer's basis for the property received in the exchange is computed as follows:

Basis of property given up	$150,000
Less: Money received	15,000
	$135,000
Plus: Gain recognized	40,000
	$175,000
Less: Basis of stock (fair market value)	25,000
Basis of property received	$150,000

If a loss is recognized on a partially tax-free exchange because the taxpayer transfers unlike property to the other party to the exchange, the recognized loss decreases the basis of the property received in the exchange. The amount received for the other property given up is considered to be its fair market value on the date of the exchange.[164]

Example 2: The Taxpayer exchanges a building with an adjusted basis of $150,000 and equipment worth $20,000 (but with a basis of $30,000) for land worth $170,000. The Taxpayer's $10,000 loss is recognized because the loss is on "unlike" property. The Tax-

---

[162] Code Sec. 1031(d); Reg. § 1.1031(d)-1(b).
[163] Reg. § 1.1031(d)-1(c).
[164] Reg. § 1.1031(d)-1(e).

payer's basis for the land received is $170,000, that is, the basis of the properties transferred ($150,000 building + $30,000 equipment = $180,000) − the $10,000 loss recognized.

The amount of any liabilities of the taxpayer assumed by the other party to the exchange, or of any liabilities to which the property exchanged by the taxpayer is subject, is treated as money received by the taxpayer on the exchange. The amount of the liability, therefore, decreases the basis of the property acquired by the taxpayer.[165] The following examples illustrate these rules and are continuations of the examples set out above illustrating the effect of mortgages on the amount of gain recognized.

Example 3: Individual B owns an apartment house which has an adjusted basis in B's hands of $500,000, but which is subject to a mortgage of $150,000. B transfers the apartment house to individual C in exchange for $50,000 in cash and another apartment house with a fair market value on the date of the transfer of $600,000. The transfer to C is subject to the $150,000 mortgage. B realizes a gain of $300,000 on the exchange, but the recognized gain is limited to $200,000. The basis of the apartment house acquired by B is $500,000, computed as follows:

Basis of property transferred	$500,000
Less: Cash received	50,000
	$450,000
Less: Liabilities transferred	150,000
	$300,000
Plus: Gain recognized	200,000
Basis of property acquired	$500,000

If both the property given up and the property received in a like-kind exchange are subject to liabilities, a balancing or netting of the liabilities is permitted. If the mortgage or liability on the property received is at least as much as the liability on the property transferred, there is no "money" received for purposes of determining the basis of the property received.[166]

Example 4: D, an individual, owns an apartment house with an adjusted basis in the individual's hands of $100,000. The fair market value of this apartment house is $220,000, but it is subject to a mortgage of $80,000. D transfers the apartment house to E, also an individual, in exchange for $40,000 in cash and another apartment house. The apartment house owned by E before the

---

[165] Code Sec. 1031(d); Reg. § 1.1031(d)-2.
[166] Rev. Rul. 59-229, 1959-2 CB 180; Reg. § 1.1031(d)-2.

exchange has an adjusted basis in E's hands of $175,000, a fair market value of $250,000, but it is subject to a mortgage of $150,000. As part of the exchange, each apartment house is transferred subject to the mortgage on it.

D realizes a gain of $120,000 on the exchange, but recognizes only $40,000 of the gain. The basis of the apartment house acquired by D is $170,000, computed as follows:

Basis of property transferred	$100,000
Liabilities received	150,000
	$250,000
Less: Money received	40,000
	$210,000
Less: Liabilities transferred	80,000
	$130,000
Plus: Gain recognized	40,000
Basis of property acquired	$170,000

As for the other side of the exchange, E realizes a gain of $75,000 on the exchange, but recognizes only $30,000 of the gain. The basis of the apartment house acquired by E is $175,000, computed as follows:

Basis of property transferred	$175,000
Money paid	40,000
Liabilities received	80,000
	$295,000
Less: Liabilities transferred	150,000
	$145,000
Plus: Gain recognized	30,000
Basis of property acquired	$175,000

¶ 1315.4 Commissions and Other Expenses

Money paid in connection with a like-kind exchange for commissions, legal fees, and similar expenses is offset against money received in computing realized and recognized gain, and is added in determining the basis of property received.[167] The following examples taken from Rev. Rul. 72-456 illustrate the effect of commissions on realized gain and basis of property received in connection with like-kind exchanges.

Example 1: The Taxpayer exchanged investment real estate with an adjusted basis of $120,000 for investment real estate with a fair market value of $200,000 and $100,000 in cash. The Taxpayer

---

[167] Rev. Rul 72-456, 1972-2 CB 468.

paid commissions and fees of $20,000 in connection with the exchange.

Received:	
Land—F.M.V.	$200,000
Cash	100,000
	$300,000
Less: Commissions and fees	20,000
Amount realized	$280,000
Given up:	
Land—basis	120,000
Realized gain (loss)	$160,000
Recognized gain (lesser of realized gain or net cash received)	$ 80,000
Basis:	
Land given up—basis	$120,000
Less: Cash received	100,000
Plus: Recognized gain	80,000
Plus: Commissions and fees	20,000
Basis of land received	$120,000

Example 2: The Taxpayer exchanged investment real estate with an adjusted basis of $295,000 for investment real estate with a fair market value of $200,000 and $100,000 in cash. The Taxpayer paid commissions and fees of $20,000 in connection with the exchange.

Received:	
Land—F.M.V.	$200,000
Cash	100,000
	$300,000
Less: Commissions and fees	20,000
Amount realized	$280,000
Given up:	
Land—basis	295,000
Realized gain (loss)	($15,000)
Recognized gain (lesser of realized gain or net cash received)	$–0–
Basis:	
Land given up—basis	$295,000
Less: Cash received	100,000
Plus: Recognized gain	–0–
Plus: Commissions and fees	20,000
Basis of land received	$215,000

¶ 1315.4

Example 3: The Taxpayer exchanged investment real estate with an adjusted basis of $100,000 for investment real estate with a fair market value of $200,000. The Taxpayer paid commissions and fees of $20,000 in connection with the exchange.

Received:	
Land—F.M.V.	$200,000
Cash	–0–
	$200,000
Less: Commissions and fees	20,000
Amount realized	$180,000
Given up:	
Land—basis	100,000
Realized gain (loss)	$ 80,000
Recognized gain (lesser of realized gain or net cash received)	$ –0–
Basis:	
Land given up—basis	$100,000
Less: Cash received	–0–
Plus: Recognized gain	–0–
Plus: Commissions and fees	20,000
Basis of land received	$120,000

¶ 1317 Multi-Party Exchanges

The tax-free, like-kind exchange provisions also apply to property exchanges that involve three-party and four-party transactions. Any part of these multi-party exchanges may qualify as a like-kind exchange if it generally meets the requirements discussed above for such an exchange. Also, if the like-kind exchange includes money or unlike property, in addition to like-kind property, gain realized is taxed to the extent of the money and fair market value of the unlike property.[168]

¶ 1317.1 *Three-Way Exchange*

A problem frequently faced by the owner of business or investment property who would like to exchange it in a tax-free exchange is that the other party does not want the owner's property or wants only cash for the property. Another problem arises when the owner of property has a potential purchaser for the property, but wants to acquire property that the potential purchaser does not own. In these situations, it may be possible to work out a three-way exchange.

Example: Individual A owns land held for investment and wishes to exchange it for improved business property owned by B. B does

---

[168] See, for example, Rev. Rul. 57-244, 1957-1 CB 247, which involved a triangular exchange among three lot owners.

not want A's land but is willing to sell the business property. If A can find a buyer for the land, an exchange can be worked out. This third party may be a buyer who actually wants A's land, or an intermediary or broker who will arrange an exchange on behalf of A and ultimately resell A's land. The third party purchases B's business property and acquires title. The third party then exchanges the business property for A's land. In this case, A has a tax-free, like-kind exchange. Neither B nor the third party, however, qualify for like-kind exchange treatment. B does not qualify because the property was sold, and the third party does not qualify because the business property was never held by the third party for use in a trade or business or for investment.

While there are many possible variations of the three-party exchange, the taxpayer who directs the other party to purchase like-kind property in a three-way exchange generally must show that there was no intent to sell the property that was transferred in the exchange. The agreement must show an intent to make an exchange rather than a sale for cash.[169] A provision for alternative sale possibilities or the receipt of cash if the exchange is not completed, or the existence of a sales contract, however, does not destroy an otherwise tax-free exchange if the parties exhibited an intent to exchange properties and if the exchange actually occurs. For instance, when a taxpayer who was holding business property originally entered into an agreement to sell the property for cash but arranged to exchange the property with his purchaser for like-kind property before the sales contract was implemented, the exchange qualified as a like-kind exchange.[170]

Generally, the property transfers in a three-way exchange must be part of an integrated plan, although contractual interdependence between the taxpayer's transfer and the receipt of properties is not necessary for tax-free treatment.[171] The taxpayer may undertake to locate the exchange property and negotiate with the third party for its acquisition by the purchaser.[172]

¶ 1317.2 Four-Way Exchange

If a taxpayer wants to make a tax-free exchange and the prospective purchaser does not want to take title to the taxpayer's property, they may be able to work out a four-way exchange. Generally, a four-way exchange involves a taxpayer who wants the exchange property, a

---

[169] *J. Alderson*, CA-9, 63-2 USTC ¶ 9499, 317 F.2d 790.

[170] *L.Q. Coupe*, 52 TC 394, CCH Dec. 29,610, Acq. 1970-2 CB xix. See also, *Coastal Terminals, Inc.*, CA-4, 63-2 USTC ¶ 9623, 320 F.2d 333; *F.B. Biggs*, CA-5, 81-1 USTC ¶ 9114, 632 F.2d 1171.

[171] *A.E. Brauer*, 74 TC 1134, CCH Dec. 37,200.

[172] *J. Alderson*, CA-9, 63-2 USTC ¶ 9499, 317 F.2d 790. See also *Coastal Terminals, Inc.*, CA-4, 63-2 USTC ¶ 9623, 320 F.2d 333; *L.A. Woodbury*, 49 TC 180, CCH Dec. 28,696, Acq. 1969-2 CB xxv.

prospective purchaser of the taxpayer's property, a prospective seller of the property that the taxpayer wants to receive in the exchange, and a fourth party. The fourth party receives the taxpayer's property and sells that property to the prospective purchaser. The fourth party then purchases the prospective seller's property and transfers that property to the taxpayer, who wants like-kind exchange treatment. The fourth party ends up holding no property other than whatever compensation for facilitating the transaction was agreed to among the parties.

The fourth party to a four-way exchange may be an agent of one of the parties. In one case upholding like-kind exchange treatment, the fourth party was the prospective purchaser's agent,[173] and in another case, the fourth party was the taxpayer's bank, which the taxpayer controlled as majority shareholder.[174] The IRS's argument that the purchaser must have title to the exchange property as a prerequisite for a tax-free like-kind exchange has been rejected by the Fifth Circuit Court of Appeals.[175]

¶ 1321 REPORTING REQUIREMENTS

Code Sec. 6045(e)(1) provides that the "real estate reporting person" must file a return and statement in the case of a "real estate transaction." This provision was added to the Internal Revenue Code by the Tax Reform Act of 1986 in order to prevent sellers of real estate from avoiding tax on gain by not reporting the transaction on their tax returns. Reporting is not required on the sale of a personal residence for $250,000 ($500,000 in the case of married taxpayers) or less, if the residence is a principal residence and the gain is not subject to tax under Code Sec. 121.[176] (See ¶ 2007.) The IRS has issued regulations that spell out the details of the reporting requirement.[177]

¶ 1323 Transactions Subject to Reporting

Sales or exchanges of real estate for money, indebtedness, property other than money, or services are subject to the information reporting requirements.[178] Real estate subject to reporting includes land, including air space; any inherently permanent structure, including residential, commercial, or industrial buildings; any condominium unit, including appurtenant fixtures and common elements; or any stock in a cooperative housing corporation.[179]

A gift or a financing or refinancing that is not related to the acquisition of real estate is not subject to reporting.[180] Involuntary conversions also are not subject to reporting, but other tax-free sales or exchanges are subject to the reporting requirements.[181]

---

[173] *L.Q. Coupe*, 52 TC 394, CCH Dec. 29,610, Acq. 1970-2 CB xix.
[174] *H. Rutland*, 36 TCM 40, CCH Dec. 34,215(M), T.C. Memo. 1977-8.
[175] *F.B. Biggs*, CA-5, 81-1 USTC ¶ 9114, 632 F.2d 1171.
[176] Code Sec. 6045(e)(5).
[177] Reg. § 1.6045-4.
[178] Reg. § 1.6045-4(b)(1).
[179] Reg. § 1.6045-4(b)(2).
[180] Reg. § 1.6045-4(c).
[181] Reg. § 1.6045-4(b)(1).

¶ 1323.1 Reporting Person

The person who is required to report real estate transactions under Code Sec. 6045(e) is generally the person responsible for closing the transaction.[182] If no person is responsible for closing the transaction,[183] the person who must report is the first-listed of the following who participates in the transaction as:

1. Mortgage lender;

2. Seller's broker;

3. Buyer's broker; or

4. Transferee of the property.[184]

To avoid any uncertainty as to who is responsible for reporting a real estate transaction, a designation agreement may be used. The agreement must be in writing and must be between the designated person and the person who would otherwise be treated as the real estate broker.[185] The person designated by the agreement must be an eligible person. Eligible persons are:

1. Persons responsible for closing the transaction described above;

2. Transferee's attorney, the transferor's attorney, or the title or escrow company, regardless of whether responsible for the closing; or

3. Mortgage lender.[186]

¶ 1323.2 Multiple Transferors

If more than one person is transferring an interest in the same one-to-four-family real estate, the reporting person must make a separate information return for each transferor. A husband and wife who hold the real estate as tenants in common, joint tenants, tenants by the entirety, or community property, however, are treated as a single transferor.[187] If there are multiple transferors, the reporting person must request the transferors to provide an allocation of the gross proceeds among themselves at or prior to the closing.[188] The request or the response does not have to be in writing.

---

[182] Reg. § 1.6045-4(e)(1).
[183] Reg. § 1.6045-4(e)(3).
[184] Reg. § 1.6045-4(e)(4).
[185] Reg. § 1.6045-4(e)(5)(i).
[186] Reg. § 1.6045-4(e)(5)(ii).
[187] Reg. § 1.6045-4(f).
[188] Reg. § 1.6045-4(i)(5).

¶ 1325 Information Return and Statement

The real estate broker in a real estate transaction subject to the reporting requirements must file an information return with the IRS [189] and furnish the transferor with a statement.[190]

¶ 1325.1 Form and Content of Return

Unless filing is done on magnetic media,[191] the information is filed using Form 1099. The form must contain the following information: [192]

1. The name, address, and taxpayer identification number of the transferor. The transferor is required by law to furnish the reporting person with his or her TIN.[193]

2. A general description of the real estate transferred. This includes the complete address of the property and a legal description if the address would not be sufficient to identify the property.[194]

3. The date of closing, which is the date described as the Settlement Date if a Uniform Settlement Statement is used, or the earlier of the date on which the title is transferred and the date on which the burdens and benefits of ownership shift to the transferee.[195]

4. The gross proceeds, which are generally the total cash received or to be received by the transferor. Gross proceeds do not include the value of any property other than cash transferred as part of the transaction. Liabilities transferred with the property as assumed by the transferee are included in the gross proceeds.[196]

5. If the transferor received or will receive property other than cash and consideration treated as cash in computing gross proceeds, or services, as part of the consideration for the transaction, an indication that such property or services were or will be received.

6. The real estate reporting person's name, address, and TIN.

7. Any other information required by Form 1099 or its instructions.

¶ 1325.2 Statement for Transferor

The reporting person who is required to file the information return must furnish a written statement to the transferor, whose TIN must be

---

[189] Code Sec. 6045(a).
[190] Code Sec. 6045(b).
[191] Reg. § 1.6045-4(k).
[192] Reg. § 1.6045-4(h)(1).
[193] Reg. § 1.6045-4(l).
[194] Reg. § 1.6045-4(h)(2)(i).
[195] Reg. § 1.6045-4(h)(2)(ii).
[196] Reg. § 1.6045-4(i).

shown on the information return. The written statement must contain the legend on the recipient copy of Form 1099 or the following:

> This is important tax information and is being furnished to the Internal Revenue Service. If you are required to file a return, a negligence penalty or other sanction will be imposed on you if this item is required to be reported and the IRS determines that it has not been reported.[197]

The requirement that the reporting person furnish the transferor with a statement may be satisfied by giving the transferor a recipient copy of a completed Form 1099. In the case of a real estate transaction for which a Uniform Settlement Statement is used, the requirement is also satisfied by giving the transferor a copy of a completed statement in compliance with Reg. § 1.6045-4(m) and by designating on the Uniform Settlement Statement the items of information required on Form 1099. The statement may be given to the transferor in person, either at or after the closing, or mailed to the transferor at the transferor's last known address.

The statement for the transferor must be given to the transferor on or after the date of closing and before February 1 of the following calendar year.[198]

¶ 1327 Penalties

A responsible person who fails to file the necessary information return or furnish the transferor with the required statement may be subject to one or more of the following penalties:

1. Failure to file an information return (Code Sec. 6721);
2. Failure to furnish a statement to the transferor (Code Sec. 6722);
3. Failure to include correct information (Code Sec. 6723); and
4. Willful failure to supply information (Code Sec. 7203).

¶ 1331 REDUCED TAXES ON DEPRESSED AREA PROPERTY

To encourage investment in various depressed areas, Congress has enacted a series of incentives. Among those incentives are reduced or zero tax rates when qualifying property within one of the designated areas is sold.

¶ 1333 Rollover of Empowerment Zone Investment

A taxpayer can elect to roll over capital gain from the sale or exchange of any qualified empowerment zone asset purchased after December 21, 2000, and held for more than one year if the taxpayer

---

[197] Reg. § 1.6045-4(m)(1). [198] Reg. § 1.6045-4(m)(2).

uses the proceeds to purchase other qualifying empowerment zone assets in the same zone.[199] The taxpayer must purchase the replacement property within 60 days of the sale of the asset.[200]

A qualified empowerment zone asset is an asset that would be a qualified community asset under Code Sec. 1400F (see ¶ 1335), if the empowerment zone were a renewal community and the asset is acquired after December 21, 2000.[201] Assets in the D.C. Enterprise Zone (see ¶ 1337) are not eligible for the tax-free rollover treatment.[202]

The holding period of the replacement asset includes the holding period of the original asset, except that the replacement asset must actually be held for more than one year to qualify for another tax-free rollover.[203] The basis of the replacement asset is reduced by the gain not recognized on the rollover. However, if the replacement asset is qualified small business stock (as defined in Code Sec. 1202), the exclusion in that section does not apply to gain accrued on the original zone asset.[204]

¶ 1335 Renewal Community Capital Gain

A zero percent capital gain tax rate applies to gain from the sale of a qualified community asset acquired after December 31, 2001, and before January 1, 2010, and held for more than five years.[205] A qualified community asset includes:

1. original-issue stock in a renewal community business purchased for cash;
2. a partnership interest in a renewal community business acquired for cash; and
3. tangible property originally used in a renewal community business by the taxpayer and that is purchased or substantially improved after December 31, 2001.

¶ 1337 D.C. Zone Capital Gain

Economically depressed census tracts in the District of Columbia are designated as the D.C. Enterprise Zone. Businesses and individual residents in the zone are eligible for special tax incentives. Under Code Sec. 1400B, a zero percent capital gain tax rate applies to capital gains from the sale of qualified District of Columbia zone assets held for more than five years. Qualified D.C. zone assets include D.C. zone business stock, D.C. zone partnership interests, and D.C. zone business property.

---

[199] Code Sec. 1397B.
[200] Code Sec. 1397B(a).
[201] Code Sec. 1397B(b)(1).
[202] Code Sec. 1397B(b)(1)(B).
[203] Code Sec. 1397B(b)(5).
[204] Code Sec. 1397B(b)(4).
[205] Code Sec. 1400F.

Qualified capital gain eligible for the zero percent rate does not include any gain attributable to periods before January 1, 1998, or after December 31, 2008. It also doesn't include any gain that would be treated as ordinary income because of recapture under Code Sec. 1245 or under Code Sec. 1250 if Code Sec. 1250 applied to all depreciation rather than the additional depreciation. Further, qualified capital gain doesn't include any gain that's attributable to real property, or an intangible asset, that is not an integral part of a D.C. zone business. Finally, qualified capital gain doesn't include any gain attributable to a transaction with a related person.

In general, D.C. zone business stock is stock in a U.S. corporation originally issued after December 31, 1997, if (1) the stock is acquired by the taxpayer before January 1, 2004, at its original issue solely for cash; (2) at the time the stock was issued, the corporation was a D.C. zone business; and (3) during substantially all of the taxpayer's holding period for the stock, the corporation qualified as a D.C. zone business.

A D.C. zone partnership interest is a capital or profits interest in a U.S. partnership originally issued after December 31, 1997, if (1) the interest is acquired by the taxpayer before January 1, 2004, from the partnership solely for cash; (2) at the time the interest was acquired, the partnership was a D.C. zone business; and (3) during substantially all of the taxpayer's holding period for the interest, the partnership qualified as a D.C. zone business.

In general, D.C. zone business property is tangible property if (1) the property was acquired by the taxpayer by purchase after December 31, 1997, and before January 1, 2004; (2) the original use of the property in the D.C. zone begins with the taxpayer; and (3) during substantially all of the taxpayer's holding period for the property, substantially all of the use of the property was in a D.C. zone business of the taxpayer. A special rule applies for buildings that are substantially improved. A D.C. zone business is any enterprise zone business (as defined in Code Sec. 1397C), subject to some modifications.

Chapter 14

Seller-Financed Sales

¶ 1400 OVERVIEW OF CHAPTER

Chapter 13 examined the basic tax rules that affect the sale or exchange of real estate, including the manner of computing gain or loss and the character of the gain or loss. A taxpayer generally must report any recognized gain from the sale or exchange of real estate for the tax year in which the sale or exchange occurs, which is generally when title passes or the burdens and benefits of ownership shift from the seller to the buyer. An exception to this rule applies, however, when the seller does not receive the full purchase price in the year of sale.

The acquisition of real property usually is financed by a mortgage loan from a third-party lender (see Chapter 3). In this case, the general rule of reporting recognized gain in full in the year of sale generally does not impose an undue burden on the seller since the seller receives the full purchase price immediately, even though the buyer makes payments over a period of time to the holder of the mortgage. However, the seller of real estate may be willing to assist in the financing when adequate financing cannot be obtained from a third-party lender or if the seller's financing of the sale will provide the seller with tax or financial advantages. When the seller finances the sale, the seller typically takes back a purchase-money mortgage from the buyer to secure the future payment of the full purchase price. If the seller-financed sale qualifies as an installment sale under Code Sec. 453, then the seller may report gain from the sale as payments actually are received.

¶ 1401 INSTALLMENT SALES

When the seller finances the sale of real property, the seller's receipt of the buyer's note would require the seller to report the entire gain in the year of sale if there were no Internal Revenue Code provision for installment reporting. Absent installment reporting, the seller could face the undesirable prospect of paying tax on gain the seller has not actually received and, possibly, might never receive.

The installment method permits the seller to report the gain in excess of any amount of depreciation recapture as payments from the buyer actually are received. When installment reporting is available, it can be an important tax and financial planning tool for both the seller and the buyer. The seller is able to pay the tax from the sale proceeds and may retain a larger portion of the buyer's down payment for reinvestment or other purposes. Tax savings to the seller also may result if the gain from the sale would place the seller in a higher tax bracket for the year of sale. Gain spread out over more than one year may result in a lower total tax on the gain.

Of course, an installment sale is not right in every situation. In some cases, the seller may have losses from other sources that would wholly or partially offset the gain on the sale. In such cases, it may be advisable for the seller to elect out of installment reporting. An election out also may be warranted if tax rates will increase or the seller's tax bracket will be higher in future years when the installment payments are received. The tax on each payment received in future years is at the rate in effect in the year of receipt.

If depreciation recapture is significant, the seller may not be inclined to make an installment sale and may insist on full payment up front, either through a cash sale or third-party financing. Recapture income, as discussed at ¶ 1405.1, is currently taxable whether payments are received or not. At a minimum, the seller may want to consider recapture in setting the down payment or other payments to be received in the year of sale. The seller may want to insist that these initial payments be at least sufficient to cover the projected tax liability from recapture.

In general, the regular tax rules that apply in the case of loans from third-party lenders, as discussed at ¶ 1301, also apply to determine the effect of a purchase-money mortgage given by the seller on basis, income, and the amount realized on the sale of the property. Also, as a general proposition, the treatment of interest, discount, and costs associated with a purchase-money mortgage given by the seller is the same as third-party loans, as discussed at ¶ 301. The ability of sellers and buyers to manipulate tax consequences by varying interest and discount terms in seller-financed transactions, however, is limited by the imputed interest and the original issue discount rules. These rules are discussed at ¶ 331.

¶ 1403 Sales that Qualify as Installment Sales

An installment sale is simply the disposition of property when at least one payment is to be received by the seller after the close of the taxable year in which the disposition occurs.[1] Generally speaking, if the seller finances the buyer's purchase of the property, the transaction

---

[1] Code Sec. 453(b)(1).

probably is an installment sale for tax purposes. The buyer's obligation to make future payments may be in the form of a deed of trust, a note, a land contract, a mortgage, or some other evidence of the buyer's indebtedness to the seller. Installment reporting is permitted, regardless of the amount of payments received in the year of sale, as long as at least one payment is to be received in a subsequent taxable year. Also, installment reporting is permitted even if the entire purchase price is to be received in a lump sum in a taxable year subsequent to the year of sale.[2] The installment sales provisions also permit installment reporting when the sales price is contingent.[3] This may facilitate some transactions and is discussed further below. These provisions allow the parties to control the amount and timing of payments to suit their individual financial and tax positions.

The installment sales provisions do not apply when the sale of property results in a loss. Losses are always reported in full for the year of sale. Also, installment reporting is not permitted if the sale is between certain related persons, as discussed further at ¶ 1407.[4]

¶ 1403.1 *Dealer Sales*

In the Omnibus Budget Reconciliation Act of 1987, Congress repealed the installment method of reporting income for dealers in property.[5] The apparent rationale, other than a need to raise revenue, was that dealers do not need the benefits of installment reporting since they generally are able to finance their receivables and frequently do. Thus payment of tax for the year of sale by a dealer does not create the cash flow problem that occurs in the case of non-dealers.

In general, gain on any disposition of personal property by a person who regularly sells or disposes of property on the installment plan, and gain on the sale or disposition of real property held for sale to customers in the ordinary course of business, subject to some limited exceptions, may not be reported under the installment method.[6] The ban on the use of the installment method does not affect the treatment of installment obligations that arose out of dispositions before March 1, 1986.

Despite the general disallowance of installment reporting for dealer sales, installment reporting remains available for sales or disposi-

---

[2] Reg. § 15A.453-1(b).

[3] Code Sec. 453(f)(8)(B).

[4] Code Sec. 453(g).

[5] Code Sec. 453(b)(2).

[6] Code Sec. 453(l)(1). For a discussion of who is a dealer and what constitutes "dealer property," see ¶ 1013.

tions of any property used or produced in the trade or business of farming.[7] Also, installment reporting is permitted for sales to individuals in the ordinary course of business of:

1. Time-share rights to use, or time-share ownership interests in, residential real property for not more than six weeks, or rights to use specified campgrounds for recreational purposes, and

2. Residential lots, but only if the taxpayer (or any related person) is not to make any improvements to the lots.[8]

In the case of sales of timeshares and residential lots, installment reporting by dealers is permitted only if the dealer elects to pay interest on the tax deferred by the use of the installment method.[9] This interest is added to the dealer's income tax.[10] The amount of interest is based on the tax for the year attributable to installment payments received during the year and is calculated from the date of sale to the date the payments are received.[11] The interest rate that is applied is the applicable federal rate, compounded semiannually, in effect at the time of the sale under the original issue discount rules.[12] No interest is assessed in the case of installment payments received in the year of sale.[13] Any interest paid under this rule is treated as interest in determining the dealer's interest deduction.[14]

¶ 1403.2   *Escrow Arrangements*

In some cases, a sales agreement may require the buyer to establish an escrow account, out of which the installment payments are to be made. Generally, if there is no restriction on the seller's right to receive payments from the escrow account, other than the passage of time, the sale will not qualify for installment reporting. In this situation, the IRS views the buyer's obligation as paid in full when the purchase price is deposited into the escrow account. With the escrow account, the seller is no longer relying on the buyer for the rest of the payments, but on the escrow arrangement.[15]

Substitution of an escrow agreement as security following an installment sale also ends the seller's right to report the transaction on the installment basis. The IRS has ruled that an agreement to sell real property did not qualify for installment reporting when the installment

---

[7] Code Sec. 453(l)(2)(A).
[8] Code Sec. 453(l)(2)(B).
[9] Code Sec. 453(l)(3).
[10] Code Sec. 453(l)(3)(A).
[11] Code Sec. 453(l)(3)(B)(i).
[12] Code Sec. 453(l)(3)(B)(i)(III). For an explanation of how this rate is set, see the discussion of the original issue discount rules at ¶ 331.
[13] Code Sec. 453(l)(3)(B)(iii).
[14] Code Sec. 453(l)(3)(C).

[15] Rev. Rul. 73-451, 1973-2 CB 158. See also, *E. Pozzi*, 49 TC 119, CCH Dec. 30,842; *J.E. Oden*, 56 TC 569, CCH Dec. 28,681. But see *E. Grannemann*, DC Mo., 87-1 USTC ¶ 9287, 649 F.Supp. 949, in which the district court held that sellers were entitled to choose not to accept the buyer's offer to pay the full purchase price in cash and could insist on installment payments using an escrow arrangement solely to reduce the tax consequences of the sale.

obligations were secured by a deed of trust and the sales agreement was changed in the year of sale by a later agreement that required the seller to cancel the deed of trust in exchange for the buyer's deposit of the balance of the purchase price to an irrevocable escrow account. Under the new agreement, the buyer continued to be liable for the note payments, but the annual payments were made by the escrow agent from the escrow account.[16]

A similar result occurs when the escrow arrangement is established in a year after the sale. For instance, a sale of realty ceased to qualify for installment reporting when the purchaser made an escrow deposit in exchange for the release of the seller's security interest and the payment schedule was the only restriction on the seller's right to receive the total sales proceeds.[17]

On the other hand, if an escrow arrangement imposes a substantial restriction on the seller's right to receive the sale proceeds, the sale may be reported on the installment method, provided the sale otherwise qualifies for installment reporting. In order for an escrow arrangement to impose a substantial restriction, it must serve a bona fide purpose of the buyer, that is, a real and definite restriction placed on the seller or a specific economic benefit conferred on the buyer. For instance, an escrow agreement that secures the seller's agreement not to compete with the buyer following the sale, as well as securing the buyer's payments, would impose a definite restriction on the seller and would not defeat installment reporting. In *R.J. Murray*,[18] more than 75 percent of the purchase price was placed in escrow as security for the seller's agreement not to compete, and the escrow agent was to release one-fifth of the escrow funds each year provided the seller had not entered a competing business. In this situation, the receipt of the purchase price by the escrow agent was not constructive receipt by the seller and the sale could be reported on the installment method.

¶ 1403.3 *Election out of Installment Reporting*

Under current law, use of the installment method is automatic for any sale that qualifies as an installment sale.[19] The seller, however, may elect not to have the installment sale rules apply.[20] A seller who makes this election must recognize gain on the sale in accordance with the seller's regular method of accounting, which, in the case of a cash method taxpayer, means that the seller must report the entire gain from the sale for the year of the sale even though the seller will not be paid all of the selling price until later.

---

[16] Rev. Rul. 77-294, 1977-2 CB 173.
[17] Rev. Rul. 79-91, 1979-1 CB 179.
[18] 28 BTA 624, CCH Dec. 8151, Acq. XII-2 CB 10.
[19] Code Sec. 453(a).
[20] Code Sec. 453(d)(1).

In determining the amount realized on the sale, the seller must include the buyer's notes or obligations to make the future payments at their fair market value. In making the fair market value determination, any provision of contract or local law restricting the transferability of the installment obligations is disregarded.[21] Notes, mortgages, land contracts, and even an oral promise enforceable under local law are examples of obligations that must be included in the seller's amount realized at their fair market value when the seller elects not to report on the installment method.

Example: The Taxpayer, a cash method, calendar year taxpayer, sold a parcel of land to the Buyer for $50,000, payable $10,000 down with the balance over a period of 10 years at $4,000 per year plus 12 percent interest. The Buyer gave the Taxpayer a note for $40,000, and the note had a fair market value of $30,000. The Taxpayer's basis for the land at the time of the sale was $25,000, and the Taxpayer paid a commission of $3,000 in connection with the sale. The Taxpayer elects out of installment reporting. The Taxpayer's recognized gain for the year of sale is $12,000, computed as follows:

Cash		$10,000
Market value of note		30,000
Amount realized		$40,000
Less:		
Basis of property	$25,000	
Commission	3,000	28,000
Gain realized and recognized in the year of sale		$12,000

Provided the land was a capital asset in the Taxpayer's hands, the $12,000 gain would be a capital gain. However, since the Taxpayer included only the fair market value of the note (75 percent of its face value in this case) in the amount realized in the year of sale, the Taxpayer must report 25 percent of each payment of principal received in later years as ordinary income. Of course, the Taxpayer must also report the interest on the note as ordinary interest income.

Determination of Fair Market Value

The regulations provide guidelines for determining the fair market value of the buyer's obligations when the seller elects out of installment reporting. If the amount payable under the buyer's obligation is fixed, the fair market value of the obligation to a cash method seller can never be less than the fair market value of the property sold (minus any other consideration received by the seller on the sale). An accrual

---

[21] Reg. § 15A.453-1(d)(2)(i).

¶ 1403.3

method seller treats as an amount realized in the year of sale the total amount payable under the installment obligation.[22] Under no circumstances does the IRS allow an installment sale for a fixed amount obligation to be treated as an "open" transaction in which the seller reports income only as payments are received.

The fair market value of a contingent payment obligation may be determined from, and in no event will be considered less than, the fair market value of the property sold (less the amount of any other consideration received in the sale). A cash method taxpayer must include the fair market value of the contingent payment obligation in the amount realized for the year of sale. An accrual method taxpayer reports the amount realized from a contingent obligation in the year of sale in accordance with the accrual method of accounting, but in no event can the amount realized be less than the fair market value of the contingent payment obligation.[23]

Unlike a sale involving fixed payment obligations, the IRS has left the door open for reporting installment sales involving contingent payment obligations as open transactions when the seller elects out of installment reporting. Reg. § 15A.453-1(d)(2)(iii) provides:

> Only in those rare and extraordinary cases involving sales for a contingent payment obligation in which the fair market value of the obligation cannot reasonably be ascertained will the taxpayer be entitled to assert that the transaction is "open." Any such transaction will be carefully scrutinized to determine whether a sale in fact has taken place.

Making the Election

A seller makes the election not to report a qualifying installment sale under the installment method by reporting the entire gain on a timely filed tax return for the year of sale.[24] Late elections are generally not permitted, unless the IRS concludes that the taxpayer had good cause for failing to make a timely election. A recharacterization of a transaction as a sale in a taxable year subsequent to the taxable year in which the transaction occurred does not justify a late election.[25] For example, a transaction initially reported as a lease that is later determined to be an installment sale would not be good cause that would permit a late election out of installment reporting. A valid election out of installment reporting can be revoked only with the consent of the IRS.[26]

---

[22] Reg. § 1.15A.453-1(d)(2)(ii)(A).
[23] Reg. § 15A.453-1(d)(2)(iii).
[24] Reg. § 15A.453-1(d)(3)(i).
[25] Reg. § 15A.453-1(d)(3)(ii).
[26] Reg. § 15A.453-1(d)(4).

¶ 1405 Reporting Installment Income

If a sale qualifies as an installment sale, the taxpayer must report the sale on the installment method unless, as discussed above, the taxpayer elects out of installment reporting.[27] Generally, each installment payment consists of three parts: the return of the seller's basis in the property sold, the gain on the sale, and interest. A sale that results in a loss cannot be reported under the installment method, and the loss, if it is otherwise deductible, must be taken for the year of the sale.

¶ 1405.1 *General Rules*

Each year that a seller receives payments following an installment sale, the seller must report as income the portion of the payments that represents gain from the sale and must also report the interest portion of each payment as interest income (see the discussion of unstated interest, below). As with any sale, the seller does not report as income the portion of the amount realized that represents a return of the seller's basis in the property.

Under the installment method, gain is reported ratably as each installment payment is received. The amount of each payment treated as income is determined by multiplying the payment received by a fraction known as the "gross profit ratio." The gross profit ratio is simply the ratio of the gross profit realized (or to be realized) to the total contract price.[28] To convert this ratio or fraction into numbers, it is necessary to deal with several definitions.

"Gross profit," the numerator of the fraction, is the selling price of the property less its adjusted basis. Commissions and selling expenses are added to basis in order to determine the gross profit.[29] If any gain from the sale may be postponed or excluded from income (*e.g.*, gain on the sale of a personal residence by a taxpayer over 55 years of age), this gain is subtracted from the gross profit. The selling price that is included in the gross profit is the gross selling price without reduction to reflect any existing mortgage or other encumbrance on the property, regardless of whether the obligation is assumed or taken subject to by the buyer, and without reduction for selling expenses. Also, interest, whether stated or unstated, or original issue discount is not part of the selling price.[30]

The "total contract price," the denominator of the gross profit ratio, is the selling price reduced by any debt assumed or taken subject to by the buyer which does not exceed the seller's basis in the property adjusted for commissions and other selling expenses.[31] If the amount of

---

[27] Code Sec. 453(a); Reg. § 15A.453-1(a).
[28] Code Sec. 453(c); Reg. § 15A.453-1(b)(2)(i).
[29] Reg. § 15A.453-1(b)(2)(v).
[30] Reg. § 15A.453-1(b)(2)(ii).
[31] Reg. § 15A.453-1(b)(2)(iii).

any mortgage or other debt assumed or taken subject to by the buyer exceeds the seller's basis for the property, the excess does not reduce the selling price in determining the contract price.

The following worksheet outlines the basic method of determining the seller's gross profit ratio following an installment sale:

1. Selling Price .... _____
2. Minus the sum of:
    Basis of property sold   .... _____
    Selling expenses   .... _____ _____
3. Gross Profit (Line 1 minus Line 2) .... _____
4. Contract Price .... _____
5. Gross Profit Ratio (Line 3 divided by Line 4) .... _____

> *Example:* A, a calendar year taxpayer, sells Blackacre, an unencumbered capital asset in A's hand, to B for $100,000 on the following terms: $10,000 down and the remainder payable in equal annual installments over the next nine years, together with adequate stated interest. A's basis in Blackacre, exclusive of selling expenses, is $38,000. Selling expenses paid by A are $2,000.
>
> The gross profit is $60,000 ($100,000 selling price − $40,000 basis inclusive of selling expenses). The gross profit ratio is 3/5 (gross profit of $60,000 divided by $100,000 contract price). Therefore, $6,000 (3/5 of $10,000) of each $10,000 payment is gain from the sale and $4,000 ($10,000 − $6,000) is recovery of basis. A also must report the interest received each year as ordinary interest income.

Depreciation Recapture

When property sold on the installment basis is subject to depreciation recapture (see discussion at ¶1307), the recapture must be reported in full for the year of the sale. This provision was added to the Internal Revenue Code by the Tax Reform Act of 1984, which provided that "... any recapture income shall be recognized in the year of the disposition and any gain in excess of the recapture income shall be taken into account under the installment method."[32] Current regulations do not specify how the gain in excess of recapture should be calculated for installment reporting purposes. Presumably, the recapture income reported in the year of sale reduces the gross profit in the gross profit ratio. This can be accomplished by simply adding the recapture amount to the adjusted basis of the property for purposes of determining gross profit for installment reporting purposes.

> *Example:* Assume the same facts as in the example above, except that the sale of Blackacre is subject to depreciation recapture in

---

[32] Code Sec. 453(i).

the amount of $20,000. A must report the $20,000 recapture income for the year of sale, even though A receives only $10,000 on the purchase price in that year. A then reports the gain in excess of recapture on the installment basis. The gross profit is $40,000 ($100,000 selling price — $60,000 basis inclusive of selling expenses and depreciation recapture). The gross profit ratio is 2/5 (gross profit of $40,000 divided by $100,000 contract price). Therefore, $4,000 (2/5 of $10,000) of each $10,000 payment is gain from the sale and $6,000 ($10,000 — $4,000) is recovery of basis and previously reported recapture income.

Reduced Selling Price

If the parties to an installment sale later agree to reduce the selling price, the gross profit on the sale changes. The seller must then refigure the gross profit ratio for the remaining payments. The seller cannot go back and refigure the gain reported in earlier years.

Example: In 2001, A sold land with a basis (inclusive of selling expenses) of $40,000 for $100,000. A received $20,000 as a down payment and the buyer's note for $80,000. Payments of $20,000 each plus adequate stated interest are due on each July 1 beginning in 2002. A's gross profit was $60,000 and his gross profit ratio was 3/5 ($60,000 divided by $100,000). On each of the payments received in 2001 and 2002, A reported a gross profit of $12,000 (3/5 of $20,000).

In 2003, A and the buyer agree to reduce the selling price of the property to $85,000 and the payments in 2003, 2004, and 2005 to $15,000. A's adjusted gross profit on the sale is now $45,000, and the total amount of profit remaining to be reported is $21,000 ($45,000 gross profit — $24,000 profit already reported in 2001 and 2002). The remaining profit to be received by A of $21,000 is divided by the remaining selling price to be received by A of $45,000 ($85,000 adjusted selling price — $40,000 of selling price received in 2001 and 2002), to determine the new gross profit ratio of 7/15. A reports a gross profit of $7,000 (7/15 of $15,000) on each of the $15,000 payments due in 2003, 2004, and 2005.

¶ 1405.2 Payments

The seller of property under the installment method applies the gross profit ratio to "payments" received, including any down payment and each later payment of principal.[33] While the term "payment" usually denotes a cash payment, the term has much broader meaning when applied to installment reporting for federal income tax purposes.

---

[33] Code Sec. 453(c).

Payments include amounts actually or constructively received.[34] For example, if the buyer assumes and pays expenses of the seller in connection with the sale, it is considered a payment to the seller. The expenses also are included in both the selling price and the contract price when computing the gross profit ratio.

Receipt of the purchaser's evidence of indebtedness, such as the buyer's note, generally does not constitute a payment.[35] Even if the buyer's evidence of indebtedness comes with a third-party guarantee, it is not a payment. Receipt of an evidence of indebtedness that is secured directly or indirectly by cash or a cash equivalent, such as a bank certificate of deposit or treasury note, however, is treated by the regulations as the receipt of a payment.[36] Debt secured by a standby letter of credit, that is, a nonnegotiable, nontransferable letter of credit issued by a bank or other financial institution, is not treated as a payment. A letter of credit is not a standby letter of credit if it may be drawn upon in the absence of default in payment of the underlying debt.[37]

Mortgages and Other Debts Assumed

If the buyer assumes a mortgage on the property or otherwise takes the property subject to a mortgage, it is generally not treated as a payment. Also, other indebtedness not secured by the property but incurred or assumed by the buyer incident to the buyer's acquisition, holding, or operation in the ordinary course of business of the property generally is not treated as a payment for installment sale purposes.[38] These rules apply to qualifying indebtedness so long as the debt assumed or taken subject to by the buyer does not exceed the seller's basis in the property.

> **Example:** C sells Whiteacre to D for a selling price of $160,000. Whiteacre is encumbered by a longstanding mortgage in the amount of $60,000. D assumes the $60,000 mortgage and pays the remaining $100,000 in ten equal annual installments together with adequate stated interest. C's basis in Whiteacre is $90,000 and there are no selling expenses in connection with this sale.
>
> The contract price is $100,000, the $160,000 selling price reduced by the mortgage of $60,000. Gross profit is $70,000 ($160,000 selling price less C's basis of $90,000). C's gross profit ratio is $7/10$ (gross profit of $70,000 divided by contract price of $100,000). Therefore, C must report $7,000 ($7/10$ of $10,000) of

---

[34] Reg. § 15A.453-1(b)(3)(i).
[35] Code Sec. 453(f)(3).
[36] Reg. § 15A.453-1(b)(3)(i).
[37] Reg. § 15A.453-1(b)(3)(iii).
[38] Reg. § 15A.453-1(b)(2)(iv).

¶ 1405.2

each $10,000 annual payment as gain from the sale and $3,000 as return of basis.

If the buyer assumes a mortgage or other qualifying debt and the debt exceeds the seller's basis for the property, the portion of the debt assumed in excess of basis is treated as a payment.[39] Also, if the debt assumed or taken subject to by the buyer exceeds the seller's basis, the seller recovers the entire basis in the year of sale and the seller's gross profit ratio will always be 1/1.

Example: Assume the same facts as in the example above, except that C's basis in Whiteacre is $40,000 rather than $90,000.

In this case, C is treated as receiving a payment of $20,000, the amount by which the mortgage assumed by D ($60,000) exceeds C's basis in the property ($40,000). Since C has fully recovered basis in the year of sale, the gross profit ratio is one (gross profit of $120,000 divided by contract price of $120,000), and C must report 100 percent of the $20,000 payment from the assumption of the mortgage in excess of basis and each $10,000 annual payment as gain from the sale of Whiteacre.

If the buyer assumes any type of debt other than qualifying indebtedness in connection with the sale, the full amount of the debt is treated as a payment in the year of sale. Qualifying indebtedness does not include an obligation of the seller incurred incident to the disposition of the property, such as legal fees relating to the sale, or an obligation unrelated to the acquisition, holding, or operation of the property, such as the seller's medical bills or a personal loan.

In an attempt to frustrate last minute borrowing on the property by the seller just prior to a sale in order to pull cash out without having a taxable payment, the regulations provide the following: "Any obligation created subsequent to the taxpayer's acquisition of the property and incurred or assumed by the taxpayer or placed as an encumbrance on the property in contemplation of disposition of the property is not qualifying indebtedness if the arrangement results in accelerating recovery of the taxpayer's basis in the installment sale." [40] While this rule leaves open the question of when a debt is incurred "in contemplation of the disposition of the property," it is unlikely that the IRS could successfully challenge a mortgage placed on property before any offer is made to buy or sell the property.

Wraparound mortgages have presented a special problem when it comes to determining the amount of payments received by the seller in connection with an installment sale. A wraparound mortgage is an

---

[39] Reg. § 15A.453-1(b)(3)(i). [40] Reg. § 15A.453-1(b)(2)(iv).

¶ 1405.2

agreement in which the buyer issues to the seller an installment obligation in an amount that equals or exceeds the seller's outstanding mortgage or other debt on the property (the wrapped debt), but the existing mortgage or other debt is neither paid off nor assumed by the buyer. In the usual case, the seller uses payments received from the buyer on the wraparound mortgage to make payments on the wrapped debt.

Under the regulations, use of a wraparound mortgage is treated as a sale in which the buyer takes the property subject to the seller's outstanding mortgage.[41] This is the case, according to the regulations, even though the seller remains liable for the wrapped debt and the buyer does not assume the seller's debt, and even though title to the property does not actually change hands. If the wrapped debt exceeds the seller's basis, then, under the regulations, the portion of the wrapped debt in excess of the seller's basis is a payment. The Tax Court, however, has held that the treatment of wraparound mortgages under the regulations is invalid.[42] According to the Tax Court, the buyer should not be treated as taking the property subject to or having assumed the existing mortgage when there is an installment sale of property with a wraparound mortgage, and the seller should not have to reduce the total contract price by the amount of the wrapped debt.

The IRS has acquiesced to the decision of the Tax Court[43] but has not withdrawn or modified the regulations dealing with wraparound mortgages.

If the buyer of the property in an installment sale is the holder of an existing mortgage on the property or other qualifying indebtedness, the seller's debt is not assumed on the sale but is cancelled.[44] In this case, the seller is treated as receiving a payment equal to the outstanding amount of the cancelled debt.

Demand and Readily Tradable Obligations

If the seller can immediately convert an obligation received into cash, there is really no reason to postpone tax through installment reporting. After all, installment reporting is designed to avoid the difficulties or "cash crunch" that might occur when a tax liability arises from a transaction that does not generate the funds with which to pay the tax. Accordingly, the installment sale provisions provide that those obligations which the holder can convert to cash at will must be treated as payments rather than as installment obligations subject to installment reporting.

---

[41] Reg. § 15A.453-1(b)(3)(ii).
[42] *Professional Equities, Inc.*, 89 TC 165, CCH Dec. 44,064, Acq. 1988-2 CB 1.
[43] 1988-2 CB 1.
[44] Reg. § 15A.453-1(b)(3)(i).

A bond or other evidence of indebtedness issued by any person and payable on demand is a payment in the year received under the installment sale rules.[45] Also, an obligation issued by a corporation or a government or political subdivision is a payment under the installment sale rules and not an installment obligation payable in future years if the obligation is issued:

1. With interest coupons attached (whether or not the obligation is readily tradable in an established securities market);
2. In registered form (other than an obligation issued in registered form which the taxpayer establishes will not be readily tradable in an established securities market); or
3. In any other form designed to render the obligation readily tradable in an established securities market.[46]

An obligation is considered to be in registered form if it is registered as to principal, interest, or both and if its transfer must be effected by the surrender of the old instrument and either reissuance by the corporation of the old instrument to the new holder or the issuance by the corporation of a new instrument to the new holder.[47] The definition of the terms "designed to be readily tradable in an established securities market," "readily tradable in an established securities market," "readily tradable," and "established securities market" may be found in Reg. § 15A.453-1(e)(4).

The seller reports a payment in the form of a demand or readily tradable obligation under his normal accounting method. If the seller is a cash method taxpayer, the amount realized on the payment in the form of a demand or readily tradable obligation is the fair market value of the obligation. If the seller uses the accrual method of accounting, the amount realized on receipt of a demand obligation is the face amount of the obligation, and the amount realized on receipt of a readily tradable obligation is the stated redemption price at maturity less any original issue discount or, if there is no original issue discount, the stated redemption price at maturity appropriately discounted to reflect total unstated interest, if any.[48]

Example: Several individuals owning equal interests in a tract of land with a fair market value of $1 million sell the land to C Corporation. The $1 million sales price is paid with bonds issued by C to the individuals. The bonds are not in registered form and do not have interest coupons attached. The bonds are payable in 120 equal installments, each due on the first day of each month over

---

[45] Code Sec. 453(f)(4)(A).
[46] Code Sec. 453(f)(4)(B) and (f)(5).
[47] Reg. § 15A.453-1(e)(1)(i).
[48] Reg. § 15A.453-1(e)(2). Original issue discount and unstated interest are considered at ¶ 331.

the next ten years. The bonds are negotiable and may be assigned by the holder to any other person, but the bonds are not quoted by any brokers or dealers who deal in corporate bonds and there are no comparable obligations of C which are so quoted.

In this case, the bonds are not treated as readily tradable in an established securities market. Also, under these particular facts, the bonds will not be considered to be in a form designed to render them readily tradable in an established securities market. The receipt of the bonds by the sellers of the land is not treated as payment under the sale provisions, even though the bonds are freely assignable.[49]

¶ 1405.3 Sale of Multiple Assets

When a taxpayer sells two or more assets in a single installment sale to one buyer and there is more than one type or class of asset, the taxpayer must apportion the selling price and payments among the assets sold.[50] Generally, an arm's-length allocation of the selling price and of the payments received in the year of sale made by the parties to the sale is acceptable to the IRS. In the absence of a specific arm's-length allocation, the seller must allocate selling price and payments among the assets sold according to their respective net fair market values.[51] The net fair market value of any asset is its fair market value reduced by any debt on the asset that the buyer assumes or takes the asset subject to.

If the selling price, the down payment, or both are separately stated for different assets in the sale of a going business, there must be an allocation of the selling price and the payments received in the year of sale to the following:

1. Inventory assets which the seller may not report on the installment method;
2. Assets sold at a loss which the seller must report in full in the year of sale;
3. Depreciable assets sold at a gain, part or all of which the seller must report in the year of sale because of depreciation recapture;
4. Real property sold at a gain which the seller may report on the installment method; and
5. Personal property sold at a gain which the seller may report on the installment method.[52]

---

[49] Reg. § 15A.453-1(e)(4)(v), Example (1).
[50] Rev. Rul. 55-79, 1955-1 CB 370.
[51] Rev. Rul. 55-79; see also *J.A. Johnson*, 49 TC 324, CCH Dec. 28,802.
[52] Rev. Rul. 68-13, 1968-1 CB 195.

Since some gains reported on the installment method may be ordinary income and others capital gain, the seller may have to make separate computations to report the gain properly for each asset.

> **Example:** The Taxpayer sells a business in an arm's-length transaction for $350,000 and receives $100,000 as a down payment in the year of sale. The Seller receives no other payments in the year of sale. The price of the inventory included in the sale is 40 percent of the total selling price, or $140,000. The balance of the selling price of $210,000 is for noninventory property.
>
> In the absence of bona fide arm's-length allocation of the down payment, it must be ratably allocated to the inventory and noninventory property. Forty percent of the down payment ($40,000) is allocable to inventory property and 60 percent ($60,000) is allocable to noninventory property. The Seller may report gain from the sale of the noninventory property, other than depreciation recapture, on the installment method. The Seller must report any gain on the inventory property in full for the year of sale.

A taxpayer who sells separate and unrelated assets of the same type under a single contract may report the sale as a single transaction for installment sale purposes. If the taxpayer has a loss on one or more of the assets, however, the taxpayer may not report the sales at a loss on the installment method but must report the loss sales separately. The taxpayer may report only the assets sold at a gain together on the installment method.[53]

> **Example:** The Taxpayer sold three separate and unrelated parcels of real property, A, B, and C, under a single contract. The total selling price for all three properties of $260,000 consisted of a cash down payment of $40,000, the buyer's assumption of a $60,000 mortgage on parcel B, and an installment obligation of $160,000 payable in eight annual installments with adequate stated interest. The sales contract did not allocate the selling price or the down payment among the individual parcels. The fair market value of parcels A and B was $120,000 each. The fair market value of parcel C was $20,000. The Taxpayer's basis for each parcel was $30,000, so the net gain was $170,000 ($260,000 amount realized − $90,000 basis). The Taxpayer decides to report the gain on the installment method and not to elect out of installment reporting.
>
> Since the basis of parcel C was more than its fair market value, parcel C was sold at a loss and must be treated separately. The Taxpayer must allocate the total selling price and the amounts received in the year of sale between parcel C and the other two

---

[53] Rev. Rul. 76-110, 1976-1 CB 126.

¶ 1405.3

parcels. The total selling price of $260,000 is allocated as $240,000 for parcels A and B together and $20,000 for parcel C. The cash payment of $40,000 received in the year of sale and the buyer's note are allocated on the basis of the proportionate net fair market value of the properties. The net fair market value is the fair market value minus any debt assumed or which the property is taken subject to. The allocation is:

	A and B	C
Net fair market value:		
Fair market value	$240,000	$20,000
Less: Mortgage assumed	60,000	0
Net fair market value	$180,000	$20,000
Proportionate net FMV:		
Percentage of total	90%	10%
Payments in year of sale:		
$40,000 × 90%	$ 36,000	
$40,000 × 10%		$ 4,000
Excess of mortgage assumed over basis—parcel B	30,000	
Allocation of payments in year of sale	$ 66,000	$ 4,000

The Taxpayer may not report the sale of parcel C on the installment method because the sale results in a loss. The Taxpayer reports this loss of $10,000 ($20,000 selling price − $30,000 basis) in full for the year of sale, unless the Taxpayer held parcel C for personal purposes.

The buyer's installment obligation of $160,000 is allocated to the properties sold according to their proportionate net fair market values. Ninety percent of each payment received is from parcels A and B, and 10 percent of each payment is a return of basis from parcel C. If the Taxpayer receives any payments on the buyer's installment obligation in the year of sale, the Taxpayer includes them with the other payments received in the year of sale.

¶ 1405.4   Like-Kind Exchanges

Gain on property that is exchanged for "like-kind" property may be deferred under Code Sec. 1031, as discussed at ¶ 1313. Essentially, gain attributable to the receipt of the like-kind property is deferred, but gain attributable to money or other property received as part of the exchange is currently taxed. If, in addition to like-kind property, a taxpayer receives an obligation of the buyer that may be reported on the installment method, the following rules apply:

1. The contract price does not include the fair market value of the like-kind property the taxpayer receives in the trade.[54]
2. The gross profit is reduced by any gain on the exchange that can be postponed.[55]
3. Like-kind property received in the trade is not considered a payment on the installment obligation.[56]

Accordingly, in reporting the gain on the exchange under the installment method when an installment obligation is received in addition to the like-kind property, the gross profit is the amount of gain that will be recognized on the exchange if the installment obligation is satisfied in full at its face amount. Also, the total contract price does not include the value of the like-kind property, but consists solely of the sum of the money and fair market value of other property received plus the face amount of the installment obligation.

The basis of the like-kind property received is determined as if the obligation were satisfied at its face amount.[57] Thus, the taxpayer's basis in the property given up in the exchange is first allocated to the like-kind property received, but not in excess of the property's fair market value, and any remaining basis is used to determine the gross profit ratio.

Example: The Taxpayer exchanges property with a basis of $400,000 for like-kind property worth $200,000. The Taxpayer also receives an installment note for $800,000. The note is payable $100,000 (plus interest) one year after the exchange and $700,000 (plus interest) two years after the exchange.

The Taxpayer's gross profit is $600,000 ($1,000,000 selling price — $400,000 basis). The contract price is $800,000 ($1,000,000 — $200,000 fair market value of property received). The gross profit ratio is 3/4 or 75 percent ($600,000 divided by $800,000). The Taxpayer reports no gain in the year of the exchange because the like-kind property received is not treated as a payment. The Taxpayer reports $75,000 gain when the $100,000 installment (75% × $100,000) is received and $525,000 gain when the $700,000 installment (75% × $700,000) is received. The Taxpayer's basis for the like-kind property received in the exchange is $200,000.

¶ 1405.5 Contingent Sales

A contingent sale is one in which the total selling price cannot be determined by the end of the tax year in which the sale occurs.

---

[54] Code Sec. 453(f)(6)(A).
[55] Code Sec. 453(f)(6)(B).
[56] Code Sec. 453(f)(6)(C).
[57] Rev. Rul. 65-155, 1965-1 CB 356.

Generally, contingent sales must be reported on the installment basis, unless the seller elects out of installment reporting.[58] In directing the IRS to issue rules for reporting contingent payment sales on the installment method, Congress wanted to reduce the justification for treating transactions as "open" transactions. In an open transaction, the taxpayer may first recover basis before reporting any gain, and thus defer taxes. The cost-recovery method of reporting open transactions was sanctioned by the Supreme Court in 1931.[59]

With a contingent payment sale, since the selling price cannot be determined by the end of the year, the contract price and the gross profit ratio cannot be determined using the same rules that apply to an installment sale that has a fixed selling price. The regulations provide rules for allocating the seller's basis to payments received and to be received so that contingent sales may be reported on the installment basis. The rules distinguish contingent payment sales for which a maximum selling price can be determined, sales for which a maximum selling price cannot be determined but the time over which payments will be received can be determined, and sales for which neither a maximum selling price nor a definite payment term can be determined.

Stated Maximum Selling Price

A contingent payment sale has a stated maximum selling price if the seller can determine the maximum proceeds from the sale by the end of the year in which the sale occurs. The seller must determine the stated maximum selling price by assuming that all of the contingencies contemplated by the agreement are met or otherwise resolved in a way that maximizes the selling price and accelerates the payments to the earliest date or dates permitted by the agreement. The seller treats the stated maximum selling price as the selling price for installment reporting purposes unless and until that maximum amount is reduced. If the maximum amount is reduced, the seller recomputes the gross profit ratio for payments received in or after the year in which the event requiring the reduction occurs.[60]

> *Example:* C owns Blackacre, which is encumbered by a long-standing mortgage of $100,000. C sells Blackacre to D under the following payment arrangement: $100,000 in cash on closing; nine equal annual payments of $100,000 beginning in the year after the sale; and nine annual payments equal to five percent of the gross annual rental receipts from Blackacre generated during the preceding calendar year. The agreement also calls for adequate stated interest on the deferred payments and limits the maximum

---

[58] Code Sec. 453(j)(2); Reg. § 15A.453-1(c)(1).
[59] *D. Burnet v. E.A. Logan,* S.Ct., 2 USTC ¶ 736, 283 US 404, 51 S.Ct. 550.
[60] Reg. § 15A.453-1(c)(2)(i).

amount payable to C, exclusive of interest, to $2,100,000. Also, D assumes the existing mortgage on Blackacre. C's basis in Blackacre plus the selling expenses total $300,000.

The selling price is $2,100,000 and the contract price is $2,000,000 (selling price of $2,100,000 less the $100,000 existing mortgage assumed by the buyer). The gross profit ratio is 9/10 (gross profit of $1,800,000 divided by the $2,000,000 contract price). C reports $90,000 of the $100,000 payment received in the year of sale as gain attributable to the sale of Blackacre, and $10,000 is recovery of basis.[61]

Fixed Period

If a stated maximum selling price cannot be determined, but the maximum period over which the seller may receive payments under the contingent sale price agreement is fixed, the seller recovers the basis, including selling expenses, in equal annual increments over the fixed period. If payments in any year are less than the portion of basis allocated to that year, unrecovered basis allocated to that year is carried over to the following year. No loss is allowed until the final payment year, unless future payment obligations under the agreement have become worthless.[62]

The following examples from Reg. § 15A.453-1(c)(3)(ii) illustrate the rules for recovery of basis in a contingent payment sale in which stated maximum selling price cannot be determined but the period over which payments are to be received under the agreement is fixed.

Example 1: A sells Blackacre to B for 10 percent of Blackacre's gross yield for each of the next five years. A's basis in Blackacre is $5 million. Since the sales price is indefinite and the maximum selling price is not ascertainable from the terms of the contract, basis is recovered ratably over the period during which payment may be received under the contract. Thus, assuming A receives the payments, exclusive of interest, listed in the following table, A will report the following:

Year	Payment	Basis Recovered	Gain Attributable to the Sale
1	$1,300,000	$1,000,000	$ 300,000
2	$1,500,000	$1,000,000	$ 500,000
3	$1,400,000	$1,000,000	$ 400,000
4	$1,800,000	$1,000,000	$ 800,000
5	$2,100,000	$1,000,000	$1,100,000

Example 2: The facts are the same as in Example 1, except that the payment in Year 1 is only $900,000. Since the installment

---

[61] Reg. § 15A.453-1(c)(2)(i)(B), Example (2). [62] Reg. § 15A.453-1(c)(3)(i).

payment is less than the amount of basis allocated to that year, the unrecovered basis, $100,000, is carried forward to Year 2.

Year	Payment	Basis Recovered	Gain Attributable to the Sale
1	$ 900,000	$ 900,000	$ -0-
2	$1,500,000	$1,100,000	$ 400,000
3	$1,400,000	$1,000,000	$ 400,000
4	$1,800,000	$1,000,000	$ 800,000
5	$2,100,000	$1,000,000	$1,100,000

Fifteen-Year Basis Recovery

If a contingent price sale agreement neither specifies a maximum selling price nor limits payments to a fixed period, the seller recovers basis in equal amounts over a 15-year period, provided the agreement is, in fact, a sale. The regulations point out that when terms are so indefinite, "a question arises [as to] whether a sale realistically has occurred or whether, in economic effect, payments received under the agreement are in the nature of rent or royalty income." The regulations go on to warn that the IRS will closely scrutinize arrangements of this sort.[63]

Income Forecast Method

The IRS recognizes that there are cases in which the failure to take account of the nature or productivity of the property sold in a contingent payment sale may result in a distortion of the taxpayer's income over time because payments will be greater in earlier years and decline over time. Such cases involve property qualifying for depreciation under the income forecast method, such as movies, mineral rights when the selling price is based on production, a sale under which the amount payable is based on a declining percentage of the buyer's revenues, and similar sales. In these cases, the seller may recover basis using an income forecast method of basis recovery.[64]

¶ 1405.6 Unstated Interest

Generally, the parties to an installment sale provide that each deferred payment on the sale will include interest or that there will be an interest payment in addition to the principal payment. Interest that is provided for by the parties is "stated interest." If an installment sale with some or all of the payments due more than one year after the date of sale does not provide for interest, a part of each payment due more than six months after the date of sale is treated as interest. The amount treated as interest is "unstated interest" or "imputed interest." When stated interest is under the rate specified by the Internal Revenue

---

[63] Reg. § 15A.453-1(c)(4).   [64] Reg. § 15A.453-1(c)(6).

Code, the unstated interest is the difference between the specified rate of interest and the stated interest. Imputed interest on deferred payment sales is considered in some detail at ¶ 333.

In an installment sale, imputed interest affects the selling price and the contract price. It also affects the amount of gain on the sale, whether the seller reports on the installment method or elects out. For installment reporting, both the selling price and the contract price must be reduced by any imputed interest. If the seller elects out of installment reporting, imputed interest reduces the selling price before the seller computes gain or loss. For the rules on determining whether unstated interest exists and for imputing interest when a contract calls for less than the required amount of interest, see ¶ 333.1.

¶ 1407 Sales to Related Party

Two special rules apply to installment sales between related persons. First, installment reporting is not permitted in the case of sales of depreciable property between specified related persons.[65] Second, in the case of installment sales to family members and other related persons, a resale by the related person may trigger recognition of gain to the original installment seller.[66] The first rule prevents a sale to a related person to obtain the benefits of a stepped-up basis for depreciation without a concurrent reporting of income by the related seller. The second rule prevents the use of a related person to obtain the economic benefit of the full sales price while deferring the recognition of gain attributable to that sales price. While both rules apply to what are termed "related persons," the definition of "related persons" is not the same for both rules.

¶ 1407.1 Sales of Depreciable Property

A taxpayer who sells depreciable property (depreciable by the buyer) to certain related persons may not report the sale using the installment method.[67] Rather, the seller treats all payments to be received as received in the year of sale.[68] Payments to be received include the total amount of all payments that are not contingent and the fair market value of any payment that is contingent as to amount. If the fair market value of contingent payments is not reasonably ascertainable, the seller recovers basis ratably and the buyer may not increase the basis of any property acquired in the sale by any amount before the seller includes the amount in income.[69]

---

[65] Code Sec. 453(g).
[66] Code Sec. 453(e).
[67] Code Sec. 453(g)(1)(A).
[68] Code Sec. 453(g)(1)(B)(i).
[69] Code Sec. 453(g)(1)(B)(ii).

Related Persons

The following are "related persons" for purposes of the rule denying installment reporting in the case of sales of depreciable property to related persons.[70]

1. The seller and a controlled entity. A controlled entity is a partnership in which the seller owns, directly or indirectly, more than 50 percent of interest in its capital or profits, or a corporation in which the seller owns, directly or indirectly, more than 50 percent of the value of the outstanding stock.

2. The seller and any trust in which the seller or the seller's spouse is a beneficiary unless the interest is a remote contingent interest. A beneficiary's contingent interest in a trust is remote if, under the maximum exercise of discretion by the trustee for the beneficiary, the value of the interest is five percent or less of the value of the trust property.

3. An executor and beneficiary of an estate, except for sales and exchanges to satisfy a pecuniary bequest.

4. Two corporations that are members of the same controlled group.

5. Two S corporations if the same persons own more than 50 percent in value of the outstanding stock of each corporation.

6. An S corporation and a corporation that is not an S corporation if the same persons own more than 50 percent in value of the outstanding stock of each corporation.

7. A corporation and a partnership if the same persons own more than 50 percent in value of the outstanding stock of the corporation and more than 50 percent of the capital interest or profit interest in the partnership.

8. Two or more partnerships if the same persons own, directly or indirectly, more than 50 percent of the capital interest or profit interest in each partnership.

Constructive Ownership

Rules of constructive ownership are applied to determine indirect ownership interests:[71]

---

[70] The definition of "related person" for this rule is borrowed from Code Sec. 1239(b).

[71] The constructive ownership rules are borrowed from Code Sec. 267(c), other than paragraph (3). See Code Sec. 1239(c)(2).

¶ 1407.1

1. Stock owned by or for a corporation, partnership, estate, or trust is constructively owned proportionately by or for its shareholders, partners, or beneficiaries, and
2. An individual constructively owns the stock owned by or for the individual's spouse, brothers and sisters (whether by whole or half blood), lineal descendants, and ancestors.

In applying the constructive ownership rules, an individual's constructive ownership of stock under 1 is considered to be actual ownership of that stock and the individual's ownership may be attributed to a member of that individual's family. An individual's constructive ownership under 2, however, is not considered to be actual ownership and the individual's ownership may not be attributed to another member of the individual's family.

Exception to Reporting Rule

A sale of depreciable property to a related person may be reported on the installment method if the seller can show, to the satisfaction of the IRS, that avoidance of federal income taxes was not one of the principal purposes of the sale.[72] Installment reporting may also be allowed if the seller will derive no significant tax deferral benefits from the sale.

¶ 1407.2   Resale by Related Purchaser

Generally, if a taxpayer makes an installment sale of property (a "first disposition") to a related person, as defined below, who resells the property (a "second disposition") within two years of the first disposition, and before all payments are made under the first disposition, a special rule may come into play. Under this rule, part or all of the amount the related person realizes as a result of the second disposition is treated by the taxpayer as if it had been received from the first disposition at the time of the second disposition.[73]

A second disposition generally is a disposition of the property by the related person and includes a sale, exchange, gift, or cancellation of the installment note. If the second disposition is not a sale or exchange, the amount realized is equal to the fair market value of the property disposed of at the time of the second disposition. A transfer of the property after the death of the person making the first disposition or the related person's death, whichever is earlier, and any later transfer is not a second disposition.[74] Also, an involuntary conversion is not a second disposition if the taxpayer made the first disposition before any

---

[72] Code Sec. 453(g)(2).
[73] Code Sec. 453(e)(1).
[74] Code Sec. 453(e)(6)(C).

knowledge of the possibility that the property would be subject to an involuntary conversion.[75]

Related Person

The following are "related persons" for purposes of applying the rule that taxes the installment seller of property to a related person on a second disposition by the related person.[76]

1. Members of the seller's family, defined to include a spouse, brother, sister, half-brother, half-sister, or any ancestor or lineal descendant.
2. Partnership in which the seller is a partner.
3. Estate in which the seller is a beneficiary.
4. Trust in which the seller is a beneficiary or of which the seller is treated as an owner.
5. Corporation (other than an S corporation) in which the seller owns 50 percent or more in value of the stock.
6. S corporation in which the seller is a shareholder.
7. Corporation and an individual who owns directly or indirectly more than 50 percent of the value of the outstanding stock of that corporation.
8. Two corporations that are members of the same controlled group.
9. Fiduciary of a trust and a corporation, if more than 50 percent of the value of the outstanding stock is owned directly or indirectly by or for the trust or by or for the grantor of the trust.
10. Grantor and fiduciary of any trust, and the fiduciary and beneficiary of any trust.
11. Fiduciaries of two different trusts, and the fiduciaries and beneficiaries of two different trusts, if the same person is the grantor of both trusts.
12. Certain educational and charitable organizations and any person (in the case of an individual, including the members of the individual's family) who directly or indirectly controls the organization.
13. Two S corporations if the same persons own more than 50 percent in value of the outstanding stock of each corporation.

---

[75] Code Sec. 453(e)(6)(B).
[76] See Code Sec. 453(f)(1), which borrows the definition of "related person" from Code Secs. 318(a) and 267(b).

¶ 1407.2

14. S corporation and a corporation that is not an S corporation if the same persons own more than 50 percent in value of the outstanding stock of each corporation.
15. A corporation and a partnership if the same persons own more than 50 percent in value of the outstanding stock of the corporation and more than 50 percent of the capital interest, or profits interest, in the partnership.
16. An executor and beneficiary of an estate, except for sales and exchanges to satisfy a pecuniary bequest.

The constructive ownership rules discussed at ¶ 1407.1 in connection with an installment sale of depreciable property to a related person also apply in the case of the related party resale rule.

Limit on Amount Treated as Received

There is a limit on the amount the installment seller is treated as receiving in a tax year as a result of a second disposition by a related person.[77] To compute this limit:

1. Take the lesser of (a) the total amount realized from any second disposition of the property that occurred before the close of the tax year, or (b) the total contract price for the first disposition.
2. Add (a) the total of all payments received by the end of the tax year from the first disposition to (b) the total of all amounts treated as received in earlier tax years as a result of a second disposition.
3. The limit is (1) minus (2). If less than zero, the installment seller does not treat any amount realized from the second disposition by a related person as if it were received from the first disposition.

The total amount realized from a second disposition is reduced by any amount attributable to improvements made by the related person while the related person held the property.[78]

Two-Year Cutoff

Except for marketable securities, the rules that apply to second dispositions by related persons apply only if the second disposition occurs within two years of the first disposition.[79] This two-year period is extended for any property by any period in which the related person's risk of loss is substantially reduced by:

---

[77] Code Sec. 453(e)(3).
[78] See the Senate Finance Committee Report on P.L. 96-471.
[79] Code Sec. 453(e)(2)(A).

¶ 1407.2

1. The holding of a put on the property or similar property;
2. Another person holding a right to acquire the property; or
3. A short sale or any other transaction.[80]

An option does not significantly reduce the risk of loss if the option price is determined by the fair market value of the property at the time the option is exercised.

Payments After Second Disposition

Under the related party resale rule, the tax treatment of the initial installment seller does not turn on the strict chronological order in which resales or payments are made. If the initial seller must recognize gain as a result of the resale of the property by a related person, subsequent payments actually received by the initial seller as a result of the installment sale are tax-free until they equal the amount realized as a result of the second disposition by the related person.[81]

The following examples illustrate the tax treatment of an installment seller when the sale is made to a related party and the related party resells the property within two years.

Comprehensive Example 1: In 2002, Larry Brown sold farmland to his son Dan for $500,000. The sale price is to be paid in five equal installments over five years, plus adequate stated interest on the unpaid balance. Larry's installment sale basis for the land was $250,000 and the property was not subject to any outstanding liens or mortgages.

Larry's gross profit ratio is 50 percent or $1/2$ ($250,000 gross profit divided by $500,000 contract price). Larry received $100,000 in 2002 and included $50,000 in his income for that year ($100,000 × 50 percent). Dan made no improvements to the property and sold it for $600,000 to the ABC Corporation in 2003. This $600,000 is the amount realized from the second disposition. Larry computes his installment sale income for 2003 as follows:

Lesser of amount realized on land sold by Dan or contract price	$500,000
Minus: Total payments from Dan in 2002 and 2003	200,000
Amount treated as payment because of second disposition	$300,000
Plus: Payment from Dan in 2003	100,000
Total payment received and treated as received for 2003	$400,000
Multiply by gross profit ratio	.50
Installment sale income for 2003	$200,000

---

[80] Code Sec. 453(e)(2)(B).   [81] Code Sec. 453(e)(5).

¶ 1407.2

Larry does not include in income from installment sales any principal payments he receives on Dan's installment obligation for 2004, 2005, and 2006, because Larry has already reported the entire amount of the payments from the first disposition of $500,000 ($100,000 in 2002 and $400,000 in 2003).

Comprehensive Example 2: Assume the same facts as in Example 1, except that Dan resells the farmland for $400,000 rather than $600,000. Larry computes his gain for 2003 as follows:

Lesser of amount realized on land sold by Dan or contract price	$400,000
Minus: Total payments from Dan in 2002 and 2003	200,000
Amount treated as payment because of second disposition	$200,000
Plus: Payment from Dan in 2003	100,000
Total payment received and treated as received for 2003	$300,000
Multiply by gross profit ratio	.50
Installment sale income for 2003	$150,000

In 2004, Larry receives a payment of $100,000 from Dan which is not taxed. It is recovered tax free, because Larry already has reported the payment and gain in 2003 as a result of the $200,000 that he treated as a payment even though he did not actually receive that payment. Larry would apply the $100,000 payment in 2004 against the $200,000 reported in 2003. Larry also is not taxed on the payment he receives in 2005, and he would apply this payment against the $200,000 treated as a payment in 2003. In 2006, Larry receives the final $100,000 payment and computes the amount of gain he must recognize in 2006 from the installment sale as follows:

Total of payments actually received as of the end of 2006 from first disposition		$500,000
Minus the sum of:		
Payment from 2002	$100,000	
Payment from 2003	100,000	
Amount treated as payment in 2003	200,000	
Total of amounts on which gain was previously recognized		400,000
Amount of payment on which gain is recognized for 2006		$100,000
Multiply by gross profit ratio		.50
Installment sale income for 2006		$ 50,000

Exception to Related Party Resale Rule

An installment seller is not treated as receiving a payment on a second disposition of the property by a related person if it is established to the satisfaction of the IRS that neither the first disposition nor the second disposition had as one of its principal purposes the avoidance of federal income taxes.[82] Guidance on when the nonavoidance exception may apply is provided in the Senate Finance Committee Report on P.L. 96-471.

The Senate Finance Committee Report anticipates that regulations and rulings under the nontax avoidance exception will deal with certain tax-free transfers that normally would not be treated as a second disposition of the property, for example, charitable transfers, like-kind exchanges, gift transfers, and transfers to a controlled corporation or partnership. The Finance Committee also intends for a second disposition to qualify under the nontax avoidance exception when it is an involuntary disposition, for example, foreclosure by a creditor of the related purchaser or bankruptcy of the related purchaser. The Finance Committee recommends that the exception also apply in the case of a second disposition that is also an installment sale if the terms of payment under the installment resale are substantially equivalent to, or longer than, those for the first installment sale. The exception would not apply, however, if the resale terms would permit significant deferral of recognition of gain from the initial sale when proceeds from the resale are being collected sooner.

Statute of Limitations Extension

The period for assessing a deficiency in tax attributable to a second disposition by the related purchaser does not expire until the day which is two years after the date the initial installment seller furnishes a notice to the IRS that there was a second disposition of the property. The initial seller provides this notice by answering questions G and H on Form 6252, Installment Sale Income, and attaching this form to the tax return for the year in which the second disposition takes place. A protective notice may be filed to prevent the tolling of the statute of limitations when there are questions as to whether a second disposition has occurred or when there is a principal purpose of tax avoidance.

¶ 1409 Interest on Deferred Tax

In the case of a sale of property on the installment method for more than $150,000 by a non-dealer, the seller must pay interest on the deferred tax attributable to the installment obligation if the aggregate face amount of all the outstanding installment obligations held by the seller as of the end of the year exceeds $5,000,000.[83] Amounts treated as a payment because of a pledge of an installment obligation, as discussed at ¶ 1411, reduce the face amount of outstanding installment obligations for purposes of this rule. If interest must be paid on an

---

[82] Code Sec. 453(e)(7).

[83] Code Sec. 453A.

installment obligation that arises during any year, interest must be paid for any subsequent year as long as any portion of that installment obligation remains outstanding.[84] Interest does not have to be paid on the deferred tax that arises from the installment sale of personal use or farm property.[85]

The amount of interest payable on the deferred tax arising from an installment obligation covered by the interest rules is determined by multiplying the "applicable percentage" of the deferred tax liability by the interest rate applied to tax deficiencies for the month in which the taxable year ends.[86] For any taxable year, the deferred tax liability from an installment obligation equals the amount of gain under the obligation that has not been recognized as of the close of the tax year multiplied by the maximum rate of tax in effect for the year[87] (if gain will be capital gain when recognized, the maximum rate of tax is the maximum rate on net capital gain under Code Sec. 1(h)). This tax rate varies depending on whether the taxpayer is a corporation or is an individual, estate or trust.

The "applicable percentage" for an installment obligation arising in a taxable year is the percentage determined by dividing:

1. The portion of the aggregate face amount of installment obligations outstanding as of the close of the tax year in excess of $5 million, by
2. The aggregate face amount of the installment obligations outstanding as of the close of the tax year.

This applicable percentage does not change as payments are made on the installment obligation in subsequent tax years.[88]

The interest on deferred taxes arising from installment obligations for any tax year is payable as an additional tax.[89] The interest payable, however, is treated as interest that is subject to the general rules regarding the deductibility of interest on an underpayment of tax.[90]

> *Example:* In year 1, the Taxpayer, an individual who is not a dealer, sells property for $250,000, on which gain of $200,000 is realized. The Taxpayer receives $100,000 down and takes back the buyer's note for the $150,000 balance of the purchase price. The Taxpayer makes no other installment sales in year 1 but has $5,350,000 of installment obligations outstanding from sales in prior years. The Taxpayer receives no payments on the $150,000 note during year 1, so that the Taxpayer's outstanding installment

---

[84] Code Sec. 453A(b)(2).
[85] Code Sec. 453A(b)(3).
[86] Code Sec. 453A(c)(2).
[87] Code Sec. 453A(c)(3).
[88] Code Sec. 453A(c)(4).
[89] Code Sec. 453A(c)(1).
[90] Code Sec. 453A(c)(5).

obligations as of the end of year 1 total $5,500,000. Assume that the maximum tax rate imposed on individuals in year 1 is 28 percent and the interest rate on tax deficiencies as of the end of year 1 is 10 percent (also assume simple interest rather than daily compounding for purposes of the example).

As of the end of year 1, the gain still to be reported by the Taxpayer as a result of the year 1 installment sale is $120,000 (the gross profit ratio of 80 percent × $150,000). The deferred tax liability on this gain is $33,600 ($120,000 × 28 percent). The applicable percentage applied to the deferred tax liability is 9.09 percent ($500,000/$5,500,000). Accordingly, the interest on the Taxpayer's deferred tax liability for year 1 arising from the year 1 installment obligations is $303.60, which is the 10 percent interest rate on tax deficiencies applied to the applicable percentage of the Taxpayer's deferred tax liability of $3,036 ($33,600 × 9.09 percent).

In year 2, the Taxpayer receives no payments on the installment obligation from year 1 but receives other payments which reduce the amount of the outstanding installment obligations as of the end of year 2 to $4,800,000. Assume that the interest rate on tax deficiencies as of the end of year 2 is 12 percent (again, assume simple interest), and that the maximum tax rate on individuals remains at 28 percent. Even though the Taxpayer's outstanding installment obligations have fallen below $5 million, the Taxpayer still must pay interest on the deferred tax from the year 1 installment obligation. The amount of this interest is computed in the same fashion as the interest for year 1, with the exception of the interest rate on tax deficiencies. The applicable percentage remains the same, despite the reduction in the Taxpayer's aggregate outstanding installment obligations. Accordingly, the interest on the deferred tax for year 2 stemming from the year 1 installment obligation is $364.32, calculated as follows:

Gain to be reported	$120,000
Maximum tax rate	× .28
Deferred tax	$ 33,600
Applicable percentage	× .0909
	$ 3,036
Rate on deficiencies	× .12
	$ 364.32

¶ 1411 DISPOSITION OR PLEDGE OF INSTALLMENT OBLIGATIONS

If the holder of an installment obligation disposes of that obligation, the holder usually will have a gain or loss to report. The gain or loss is considered to be gain or loss from the sale of the property for which the holder received the installment obligation.[91] Also, if an installment seller uses an installment obligation from a sale of business or rental real property for more than $150,000 to secure any debt, the net proceeds from the debt are treated as a payment on the installment obligation.[92] Repossession of property can also trigger a gain or loss for the installment seller.[93]

¶ 1413 Sale or Satisfaction at Less than Face Value

If an installment obligation is satisfied for an amount other than its face value or if an installment obligation is distributed, transmitted, sold, or otherwise disposed of, gain or loss may result. The gain or loss is measured by the difference between the basis of the obligation and the amount realized, in the case of satisfaction at other than face value or a sale or exchange.[94] In the case of some other disposition of the installment obligation, gain or loss is measured by the difference between basis and the fair market value of the obligation at the time of the disposition.[95]

The basis of an installment obligation is the difference between the face value of the obligation and the amount of income that would be returnable if the obligation were satisfied in full.[96]

Example: Several years ago, the Taxpayer sold some property on the installment method. The buyer still owes the taxpayer $10,000 of the sales price. Assuming the Taxpayer's gross profit ratio is 60 percent, $6,000 (60% × $10,000) is the gain the Taxpayer still has to report. The balance of the unpaid obligation, $4,000, is the Taxpayer's basis in the installment obligation.

Any gain or loss resulting from the sale or disposition of an installment obligation is treated as if it resulted from the sale or exchange of property for which the installment obligation was received.

¶ 1413.1 Exceptions to Rule for Recognition of Gain

Exceptions to the requirement that gain or loss be recognized on the disposition of an installment obligation apply in the case of the transfer of the obligation at death and for transfers as part of the complete liquidation of a subsidiary corporation. Also, the sale or

---

[91] Code Sec. 453B(a).
[92] Code Sec. 453A(d).
[93] Code Sec. 1038.
[94] Code Sec. 453B(a)(1).
[95] Code Sec. 453B(a)(2).
[96] Code Sec. 453B(b).

transfer of an installment obligation to a spouse or incident to a divorce does not result in gain or loss.

Transfer at Death

The transfer of an installment obligation as a result of the death of the seller or other holder of the obligation is not a disposition. Unreported gains from installment obligations are treated as items of gross income in respect of a decedent. This means that whoever receives the installment obligation as a result of the holder's death is taxed on the installment payments in the same way as the holder would have been if the holder had lived to receive the payments.[97] If an installment obligation is cancelled or transferred to the buyer because of the death of the holder of the obligation, however, it is a taxable disposition.

Liquidation of Subsidiary

If a parent corporation receives an installment obligation as part of the tax-free liquidation of its subsidiary corporation under Code Sec. 332 and the basis of the obligation to the parent is the same as the subsidiary's basis, the subsidiary does not recognize gain or loss on the distribution of the installment obligation.[98]

Transfer Between Spouses

No gain or loss is recognized on the transfer of an installment obligation between a husband and wife or former husband and wife if incident to a divorce. Rather, the transferor spouse merely takes the place of the transferee spouse and continues to report gain as payments are received just as the transferor spouse would have done if the obligation had not been transferred. The basis of the obligation to the transferee spouse (or former spouse) is the adjusted basis of the transferor spouse.[99]

A transfer of an installment obligation between former spouses is incident to a divorce if it occurs within one year after the date on which the marriage ends, or is related to the end of the marriage.

The nonrecognition rule does not apply if the spouse receiving the obligation is a nonresident alien.

¶ 1413.2 Cancellation of Installment Obligations

If the holder of an installment obligation cancels the obligation or if the obligation otherwise becomes unenforceable, it is treated as a disposition of the obligation other than a sale or exchange.[100] Gain or loss is the difference between the holder's basis in the obligation and the fair market value of the obligation at the time it is cancelled.

---

[97] Code Sec. 453B(c).
[98] Code Sec. 453B(d).
[99] Code Sec. 453B(g).
[100] Code Sec. 453B(f).

If the holder of the obligation accepts partial payment on the balance of the installment obligation and forgives the rest of the debt, the settlement is a disposition. Gain or loss is the difference between the holder's basis in the obligation and the amount realized on settlement.[101]

¶ 1415 Pledge of Installment Obligations

While an installment sale permits the tax on gain in excess of depreciation recapture to be deferred to future years, it also defers the receipt of the cash payments. At one time, it was possible to borrow against installment obligations to obtain cash without triggering the deferred tax. This strategy, however, was eliminated for pledges of installment obligations arising from the sale of property, other than personal use and farm property, for more than $150,000.[102]

If an installment obligation covered by Code Sec. 453A(d) is pledged by the holder as security for a debt, the net proceeds of the loan are treated as a payment on the installment obligation as of the later of the date that the debt is secured or the date the proceeds are received by the holder.[103] The "net proceeds" are the amount of the loan secured by the installment obligation less the direct expenses of obtaining the loan. To determine the amount of gain the holder must recognize on the pledge of an installment obligation, the gross profit ratio applicable to the installment obligation is applied to the net loan proceeds, just as it is applied to an actual payment to determine taxable gain.

A debt of a holder of an installment obligation is treated as secured by the installment obligation to the extent that the payment of principal or interest on the debt is directly secured, either under the terms of the debt or any other arrangement, by an interest in the installment obligation.[104]

Receipt of payments on an installment obligation after it has been pledged as security for a debt of the holder generally does not result in recognition of additional gain.[105] If gain that otherwise would be recognized on account of the payment exceeds the gain recognized as a result of the pledge, however, this additional gain is recognized. The total amount of gain that can be recognized on an installment obligation as a result of secured loans and the receipt of actual payments can never exceed the total gain from the installment sale.

---

[101] See the discussion of settlement of debt at a discount at ¶ 1201. See also the discussion of reduced selling price under the discussion of the general rules applicable to installment sales at ¶ 1405.1.
[102] Code Sec. 453A(d).
[103] Code Sec. 453A(d)(1).
[104] Code Sec. 453A(d)(4).
[105] Code Sec. 453A(d)(3).

¶ 1417 Repossession of Property

Although the general rule provides that gain or loss is not recognized when seller-financed real property is reacquired by the seller, an exception applies when the seller has received money or other property from the purchaser in excess of gain reported on the sale of the property for periods prior to the reacquisition.[106] This may occur if the seller is reporting the original sale on the installment basis or if the seller elected out of installment reporting.

For a full discussion of the tax effects of the repossession of seller-financed property, see ¶ 1231.

---

[106] Code Sec. 1038(b)(1).

Chapter 15

Casualty, Condemnation, and Demolition

¶ 1500 OVERVIEW OF CHAPTER

Not all real estate dispositions are voluntary. A variety of factors may force the owner of real estate to part with all or a part of his property. These "involuntary conversions," for the most part, arise from some sort of casualty. In other cases, an involuntary conversion may be the result of deliberate government action.

When property is damaged or destroyed by fire, flood, wind, vandalism, or similar events, there is a casualty. A casualty to business or investment property may produce a deductible loss, but not all casualties result in losses. If the owner is reimbursed through insurance or some other arrangement, the casualty can produce a taxable gain, if the reimbursement for the loss exceeds the basis of the property.

When the federal, state, or local government takes business or investment property for public use without the owner's consent, a condemnation of the property occurs. Since the owner of condemned property is compensated for the taking, the owner may realize a taxable gain or loss as a result of the condemnation.

Regardless of the reason for an involuntary conversion of business or investment property, if the conversion results in a gain, the owner may avoid current tax by timely reinvesting the proceeds from the involuntary conversion in qualifying replacement property.

The deduction for casualty losses to personal use property, such as a personal residence, is considered in Chapter 17. Losses from condemnation of property held for personal use, such as a personal residence, are not deductible.

¶ 1501 BUSINESS CASUALTY

Losses to business or investment real estate as a result of a casualty are deductible.[1] Unlike casualty losses to personal use property, discussed at ¶ 1711, the loss deduction for a business casualty is not subject to the "$100 deductible" or gross income limitations.

---

[1] Code Sec. 165(a).

Business casualty gains and losses are subject to the characterization rule of Code Sec. 1231, as discussed at ¶ 1305.2. When property is used partly for business and partly for personal purposes, a casualty loss is treated as two separate casualties—one to business property and one to personal use property.

¶ 1503 Casualty Defined

Generally speaking, a casualty (other than a fire or storm, which are specifically mentioned in Code Sec. 165) is an identifiable event that is sudden, unexpected, or unusual.[2] A "sudden" event is one that is unanticipated and unintentional on the part of the one suffering the casualty, and an "unusual" event is one that is not typical for the property or activity involved. Under this definition, the term casualty embraces hurricanes,[3] floods,[4] vandalism,[5] sonic booms,[6] earthquakes or earthslides.[7]

Generally, there is no casualty when damage or destruction is a result of progressive deterioration, such as from a steadily operating cause or normal process of deterioration. The IRS has ruled that the death of trees caused by a massive attack of insects was sufficiently "sudden," however, when the death occurred within 10 days after the infestation.[8] On the other hand, the loss of trees due to Dutch elm disease spread by insects was held not to be a casualty because of the progressive nature of the disease.[9] Also, in Rev. Rul. 87-59,[10] the IRS ruled that loss of timber over nine months caused by a combination of events, first an attack of pine beetles, followed by wood-destroying organisms to which the timber became susceptible because of the beetle attack, was not sudden enough to be labeled a casualty.

The loss of shoreline buildings from battering by waves and winds or flooding of buildings is a casualty, but damage from gradual erosion or inundation is not.[11] Damage or loss to property from an unusual and unprecedented drought also may be a casualty.[12]

---

[2] Rev. Rul. 76-134, 1976-1 CB 54.

[3] *Western Products Co.*, 28 TC 1196, CCH Dec. 22,582, Acq. 1958-1 CB 6; Rev. Rul. 70-164, 1970-1 CB 37.

[4] *W.M. Ferguson Jr.*, CA-10, 3 USTC ¶ 975, 59 F.2d 893.

[5] *B.E. Davis*, 34 TC 586, CCH Dec. 24,246, Acq. 1963-2 CB 4; *C. Gutwirth*, 40 TC 666, CCH Dec. 26,198, Acq. 1966-2 CB 5.

[6] Rev. Rul. 60-329, 1960-2 CB 67.

[7] *P. Abrams*, 41 TCM 1459, CCH Dec. 37,892(M), T.C. Memo. 1981-231 (earthquake); *R. Tank*, CA-6, 59-2 USTC ¶ 9673, 270 F.2d 477 (earthslide).

[8] Rev. Rul. 79-174, 1979-1 CB 99.

[9] *H.F. Burns*, CA-6, 61-1 USTC ¶ 9127; 284 F.2d 436; see also *W.R. Miller*, 29 TCM 741, CCH Dec. 30,196(M), T.C. Memo. 1970-167, and *D.W. Forrest*, 45 TCM 1156, CCH Dec. 40,006(M), T.C. Memo. 1983-177, in which losses to trees from root suffocation and rain and snow damage were not sudden enough to qualify as casualties.

[10] 1987-2 CB 59.

[11] Rev. Rul. 76-134, 1976-1 CB 54.

[12] Rev. Rul. 76-521, 1976-2 CB 44; Rev. Rul. 77-490, 1977-2 CB 64.

¶ 1505 Casualty Gains and Losses

In the absence of insurance or other reimbursement, a casualty to business or other income-producing property will result in a deductible loss. How this loss is measured depends on whether there was a complete or total destruction of property or only a partial loss. Reimbursements, whether through insurance or other means, reduce the amount of the deductible loss or, if they exceed the basis of the property suffering the casualty, produce a gain.

¶ 1505.1 *Casualty Losses*

A taxpayer whose business or income-producing property is totally destroyed as a result of a casualty has a deductible loss equal to the adjusted basis of the property minus any salvage value and any insurance or other reimbursement. A taxpayer whose business or income-producing property is damaged but not completely destroyed as a result of a casualty has a deductible loss equal to the lesser of the adjusted basis of the property or the decrease in the fair market value of the property as a result of the casualty, less any insurance or other reimbursement.[13]

Example: The Taxpayer owned a building that was used in a trade or business and was worth $100,000 when a fire totally destroyed the building. At the time of the fire, the Taxpayer's adjusted basis for the building was $40,000. The building was not insured and the Taxpayer expects no other reimbursement for the loss. The Taxpayer's deductible casualty loss is $40,000, the adjusted basis for the building at the time of its complete destruction.

Suppose, however, that the Taxpayer's building was not completely destroyed but only partially damaged by the fire. Further suppose that after the fire, the building was worth $80,000. In this case, the Taxpayer's casualty loss is $20,000, the difference between the fair market value of the building before the casualty and its fair market value after the casualty ($100,000 − $80,000 = $20,000). If the building were worth only $50,000 after the fire, the Taxpayer's casualty loss would be limited to $40,000, the lesser of the adjusted basis of the building ($40,000) or the decline in fair market value ($100,000 − $50,000 = $50,000) as a result of the casualty.

Measuring the Decline in Fair Market Value

According to the IRS, the difference between the fair market value of property immediately before and immediately after a casualty should be determined by a "competent appraisal."[14] Competent ap-

---

[13] Reg. § 1.165-7(b)(1). [14] Reg. § 1.165-7(a)(2)(i).

praisal means that the appraiser should have knowledge of sales of comparable property and conditions in the area and knowledge of the specific property involved, both before and after the casualty. The cost of cleaning up or repairing damaged property after a casualty may be used as a measure of the loss of value if:

1. The repairs are needed to bring the property back to its condition before the casualty,
2. The cost of repairs is not excessive,
3. The repairs do no more than take care of the damage, and
4. The value of the property after the repairs is no more than its value before the casualty.[15]

Separate Components

The casualty loss to business or income-producing property must be computed separately for each item that is damaged or destroyed.[16] Separate items in the case of business or income-producing real estate might include a building, the land under the building, and landscaping or other improvements to the land separate and apart from the building.

Example: The Taxpayer owned rental property for which the Taxpayer paid $45,000. Of the total cost, $8,000 was allocated to the land, $35,000 to the building, and $2,000 to the landscaping. Before the building and landscaping were badly damaged by a fire, the Taxpayer had taken depreciation deductions for the building of $18,550.

After the fire, competent appraisers determined that the building was worth $43,500 before the fire and only $13,000 after the fire. They also said that the landscaping (trees and shrubs) were worth $2,500 before the fire and only $1,500 after the fire. The landscaping was not covered by the Taxpayer's insurance, but the insurance company did pay the Taxpayer $30,500 for the damage to the building.

The Taxpayer has a deductible casualty loss as a result of the damage to the landscaping. This loss is $1,000, the lesser of the basis of the landscaping ($2,000) or the decrease in the landscaping's fair market value ($2,500 − $1,500 = $1,000) as a result of the casualty.

The Taxpayer does not have a deductible casualty loss because of the fire damage to the building. In the absence of insurance reimbursement, the Taxpayer's loss would be limited to the ad-

---

[15] Reg. § 1.165-7(a)(2)(ii).   [16] Reg. § 1.165-7(b)(2)(i).

¶ 1505.1

justed basis for the building or $16,450 ($35,000 original cost less $18,550 depreciation). Since the insurance reimbursement exceeds the Taxpayer's basis for the building, the Taxpayer has a casualty gain of $14,050 ($30,500 amount realized less $16,450 adjusted basis) as a result of the fire damage to the building.

¶ 1505.2 Casualty Gains

Reimbursement for a casualty that exceeds the adjusted basis of the damaged or destroyed property results in a gain equal to the difference between the adjusted basis of the property and the reimbursement.[17] This rule applies even if the decrease in value to the property is more than its adjusted basis. Also, while the intentional destruction of property, such as by arson, cannot produce a casualty loss, it can produce a casualty gain. The IRS has ruled that insurance proceeds received by a taxpayer who paid a third party to burn down a building represent gain includible as ordinary income in the taxpayer's gross income.[18]

A taxpayer can postpone recognition of gain realized as a result of a casualty to business or income-producing real estate by replacing the damaged or destroyed property with property that is similar or related in service or use (see ¶ 1523.1). Gain realized as a result of a casualty is characterized as ordinary or capital under the rules of Code Sec. 1231, as discussed at ¶ 1305.2.

¶ 1505.3 Insurance and Other Reimbursements

Insurance or other types of reimbursement for a casualty reduce the amount of deductible casualty loss. No deduction is allowed to the extent a casualty loss is compensated for by insurance or otherwise.[19] Also, if a claim for reimbursement exists and the taxpayer reasonably expects to recover on the claim, the casualty loss is reduced by the expected recovery, even though the taxpayer has not actually received payment. If the taxpayer later determines with reasonable certainty that there will be no reimbursement, the taxpayer takes the casualty loss at that time for the amount of the loss that is not reimbursed.[20]

Example: The Taxpayer owned business property with an adjusted basis of $100,000 which was completely destroyed by a fire in 2002. In 2002, the Taxpayer had a claim for insurance against the loss in the amount of $80,000 but did not receive any payment from the insurance in 2002. The Taxpayer's casualty loss deduction from this casualty for 2002 is $20,000.

---

[17] Code Sec. 1001.
[18] Rev. Rul. 82-74, 1982-1 CB 110.
[19] Code Sec. 165(a).
[20] Reg. § 1.165-1(d)(2).

In 2003, the insurance company offered to settle the Taxpayer's claim for $70,000, and the Taxpayer accepted this offer. The Taxpayer may take a casualty loss deduction of $10,000 for 2003 as a result of the 2002 fire. This amount is the Taxpayer's loss of $30,000 ($100,000 basis − $70,000 insurance reimbursement) less the $20,000 the Taxpayer deducted for 2002.

Although insurance is the most common reimbursement for a casualty, reimbursement may come in other forms. For example, the following have been held reimbursement that reduces the amount of an otherwise deductible casualty loss:

1. If part of a federal disaster loan under the Disaster Relief Act is forgiven, the forgiven amount is a reimbursement.[21]
2. If a lessee must make repairs or repay the lessor for any part of the loss, the repayment and cost of repairs are considered a reimbursement to the lessor of the property.[22]
3. Court awards for damage or theft loss, less attorneys' fees and other necessary expenses, are reimbursements.[23]
4. Repairs, restoration, or cleanup services provided by a relief agency, such as the Red Cross, are reimbursements, but not food, medical supplies and similar items.[24]

¶ 1505.4 Basis After Casualty

A casualty loss deduction reduces the basis of the property damaged or destroyed by the casualty. Insurance or other reimbursements also reduce basis.[25]

Example: Before being partly destroyed by a fire, the Taxpayer's building had an adjusted basis of $150,000. Just before the fire, the building was worth $300,000. After the fire, the building was worth $200,000. The Taxpayer collected $100,000 from insurance on the building as a result of the fire. Since the insurance fully compensated the Taxpayer for the loss, the Taxpayer has no casualty loss deduction. The $100,000 insurance recovery reduces the Taxpayer's adjusted basis for the building from $150,000 to $50,000.

If the Taxpayer's building was not insured, the $100,000 loss would be deductible as a casualty loss. If this were the case, the $100,000 casualty loss would reduce the adjusted basis of the building by $100,000, from $150,000 to $50,000.

---

[21] Rev. Rul. 71-160, 1971-1 CB 75.
[22] J.R. Hamilton, 29 TCM 97, CCH Dec. 29,949(M), T.C. Memo. 1970-34.
[23] H.L. Jackson, 29 TCM 980, CCH Dec. 30,281(M), T.C. Memo. 1970-227.
[24] Special Ruling, May 11, 1952, 525 CCH ¶ 6196.
[25] Code Sec. 1016(a).

¶ 1507 Disaster Area Losses

A taxpayer that suffers a deductible loss from a disaster in an area declared a federal disaster area by the President may elect to deduct that loss on the tax return for the year immediately preceding the tax year of the disaster.[26] If a taxpayer makes this election, the loss is treated as if it occurred in the preceding year.[27] The purpose of this election is to provide taxpayers who are affected by a major disaster immediate relief in the form of a tax refund or reduced tax liability. An affected taxpayer who chooses not to make the election simply deducts any casualty loss under the normal rule, that is, on the return for the tax year in which the loss actually occurs.

> *Example:* A calendar year Taxpayer's office building is damaged by a flood in June of 2003, and the town in which the flood occurred is declared a federal disaster area. The Taxpayer may deduct the casualty loss as a result of the flood for the 2002 tax year.

¶ 1507.1 Method of Taking Earlier Deduction

A taxpayer who wants to deduct a disaster area loss for the preceding year must write and sign a statement saying that this is what the taxpayer wants to do. The statement should specify the date or dates of the disaster and the city, town, county, and state where the damaged or destroyed property was located. This statement must be filed with the taxpayer's return or amended return for the year in which the taxpayer is taking the deduction.[28] Generally, an affected taxpayer must file the required statement by the due date, without extensions, for filing the tax return for the year in which the disaster actually occurred or the due date, with extensions, for the return for the preceding tax year.

¶ 1507.2 Revocation of Election

Under the regulations, a taxpayer may revoke an election to claim a disaster area loss for the preceding tax year within 90 days of making the election by returning any refund or credit received as a result of the election to the IRS. If the taxpayer revokes the election before receiving a refund, the refund must be returned within 30 days following its receipt.[29] However, a taxpayer who claimed a 1976 disaster loss on the 1975 return, subsequently revoked the election on an amended 1975 return, and took the loss on a timely filed 1976 return was permitted to claim the loss on his 1976 return. The Tax Court held that Reg. § 1.165-11(e) was invalid to the extent it imposed the 90-day period for

---

[26] Code Sec. 165(i)(1).
[27] Code Sec. 165(i)(2).
[28] Reg. § 1.165-11(e).
[29] Reg. § 1.165-11(e).

revoking an election under these circumstances. According to the Court, although the intent of the legislature was to give taxpayers immediate help, a comparison of the relative tax benefits might not be possible until the time arrives for filing their return for the year of the loss.[30]

¶ 1511 CONDEMNATIONS

The condemnation of property by federal, state or local government is, essentially, a forced sale of the condemned property. As a sale, gain or loss, generally must be recognized for tax purposes in the same fashion as any other sale. As with other involuntary conversions, however, a taxpayer may postpone recognition of gain from a condemnation by the timely replacement of the condemned property (see ¶ 1519).

¶ 1513 Condemnation Defined

Condemnation is the process by which private property is legally taken, without the owner's consent, for public use. Since the owner receives money or property in exchange for the taken property, a condemnation is like a forced sale by the owner to the condemning authority.

In addition to actual condemnation, an involuntary conversion also occurs if property is sold under the threat or imminence of condemnation.[31] A taxpayer is under threat of condemnation if a representative of a government body or a public official authorized to acquire property for public use tells the taxpayer that the government body or official has decided to acquire the taxpayer's property. From this communication, the taxpayer would have reasonable grounds to believe that if the taxpayer did not sell voluntarily the property would be condemned.[32] Also, a taxpayer is under threat of condemnation if the taxpayer sells the property to someone other than the condemning authority and the taxpayer has reasonable grounds to believe that the property will be condemned. If the buyer of the property knows it is under threat of condemnation in this situation and sells the property to the condemning authority, the buyer's sale also is a condemnation.[33]

The IRS also has ruled that a taxpayer is under threat of condemnation if the taxpayer learns of a decision to acquire the property for public use through newspaper reports or other news media and this report is confirmed by a representative of the government body or public official involved. The taxpayer must have reasonable grounds to believe that the property will be condemned if the taxpayer does not

---

[30] *C. Matheson*, 74 TC 836, CCH Dec. 37,093, Acq. 1981-2 CB 2.
[31] Reg. § 1.1033(a)-2(a).
[32] Rev. Rul. 74-532, 1974-2 CB 270.
[33] Rev. Rul. 81-181, 1981-2 CB 162.

sell voluntarily. If the taxpayer relies on oral statements by government representatives or officials, the IRS may ask for written confirmation of the statements.[34]

¶ 1515 Gain or Loss from Condemnation

A taxpayer whose business or income-producing property is condemned, or sold under threat of condemnation, computes the gain or loss in a fashion similar to the computation of gain or loss in the case of an ordinary sale. Gain or loss is the net condemnation award (the condemnation award minus the expenses of obtaining the award), less the adjusted basis of the condemned property.

Example: The Taxpayer owned property with an adjusted basis of $87,000. The state highway authority acquired the property under threat of condemnation. The Taxpayer received $94,000 for the property and spent $2,000 to obtain the award. The Taxpayer realized a gain of $5,000 as a result of the involuntary conversion of the property ($94,000 award − $2,000 expenses = $92,000 − $87,000 adjusted basis = $5,000 gain).

Gain or loss from a condemnation is characterized under the rules of Code Sec. 1231, as discussed at ¶ 1305.2. Recognition of gain from a condemnation may be postponed, as discussed below, if the condemned property is replaced with like-kind property. The condemnation of property that is used partly for business purposes and partly for personal purposes is treated as the condemnation of separate properties. Note that unlike casualty losses, no deduction is allowed for losses resulting from the condemnation of personal-use property.

¶ 1517 Determination of the Condemnation Award

A condemnation award is the money or value of other property given to a taxpayer for the taxpayer's condemned property or the proceeds from the sale of property under threat of condemnation. Amounts withheld from the award by the government to pay off liens against the property, such as a mortgage, or other debts of the property owner are part of the amount realized by the owner. This is the rule even if the owner of the property is not personally liable for a mortgage debt against the property.[35] For instance, if a taxpayer has acquired property worth $100,000 subject to a $50,000 mortgage (regardless of whether or not the taxpayer was personally liable for the mortgage debt) and, in a condemnation proceeding, the government awards the taxpayer $60,000 and awards the mortgagee $50,000 in satisfaction of the mortgage, the entire $110,000 is considered to be the condemnation award and the amount realized by the taxpayer.

---

[34] Rev. Rul. 63-221, 1963-2 CB 332.   [35] Reg. § 1.1033(a)-2(c)(11).

Before determination of the amount of gain or loss from a condemnation, the gross amount of the award is reduced by the expenses of obtaining the award. Also, if only part of a taxpayer's property is taken, the gross award is reduced by any severance damages and any special assessments levied against the property.[36] Interest paid on an award for a delay in payment is, of course, interest income and is not treated as part of the condemnation award itself.

¶ 1517.1   Severance Damages

Severance damages are compensation paid to a taxpayer when part of the property is condemned and the value of the remaining property is decreased as a result of the condemnation. For example, a taxpayer may receive severance damages if the property retained after the condemnation is subject to flooding, or if the taxpayer must replace fences, dig new wells or ditches, or plant trees to restore the remaining property to the same usefulness it had before the condemnation.

Severance damages are distinct from the condemnation award. The condemnation award is compensation for the property taken, and severance damages are compensation for the injury to the property retained. The IRS has ruled that severance damages exist only when the designation has been stipulated by both contracting parties.[37] The amount of severance damages paid in connection with the purchase of property by a condemning authority is considered stipulated between the parties and clearly shown, although the contract executed by the parties does not refer to severance damages as such, if the property owner is furnished an itemized statement or closing sheet at settlement and payment by the condemning authority, which indicates the specific amount allocable for severance damages.[38] At the least, the owner of the condemned property must be able to show that a portion of the payment received represents severance damages to remaining property or the entire payment will be treated as a condemnation award paid for the condemned property.[39]

A taxpayer who receives severance damages in connection with the condemnation of a portion of the property reduces the severance damages by the expenses of obtaining the damages and then by any special assessment levied against the remaining part of the property if the assessment was withheld from the award by the condemning authority.[40] The taxpayer then applies the remaining net severance

---

[36] Reg. § 1.1033(a)-2(c)(10).
[37] Rev. Rul. 59-173, 1959-1 CB 201.
[38] Rev. Rul. 64-183, 1964-1 CB (Part 1) 297.
[39] *L.A. Beeghly*, 36 TC 154, CCH Dec. 24,797, Acq. 1962-1 CB 3; *A.B. Johnson*, 42 TC 880, CCH Dec. 26,920, Acq. VII-1 CB 24..

[40] *C.C. Green*, 37 BTA 25, CCH Dec. 9905, Acq. 1938-2 CB 13; *Pioneer Real Estate Co.*, 47 BTA 886, CCH Dec. 12,854, Acq. 1943 CB 18.

damages against the basis of the remaining property. If the severance damages are based on damage to a specific part of the remaining property, only the basis of that portion of the retained property damaged as a result of the condemnation is reduced by the net severance damages.[41]

If net severance damages exceed the basis of the property damaged and retained by the owner, the owner has a taxable gain. Recognition of this gain may be postponed by the purchase of replacement property.[42] If the owner restores the remaining property to its former use, the owner may treat the restoration cost as the cost of replacement property. The owner also may elect to postpone gain if the severance damages, together with the money received for the condemned property, are used to acquire nearby property so that the owner can continue the business, even if the owner retains the damaged property for which the owner received the severance damages.[43] (See the discussion of the tax-free replacement of property at ¶ 1519.)

The expenses of obtaining a condemnation award and severance damages must be allocated between the two when the expenses cannot be specifically allocated to one or the other.

Example: The Taxpayer receives a condemnation award. One-fourth of it was stated in the award as severance damages. The Taxpayer incurred legal expenses in connection with the entire condemnation proceeding. The Taxpayer must allocate one-fourth of the legal expenses to the severance damages and the other three-fourths to the award for the condemned property. On the other hand, if the Taxpayer incurred the legal expenses only to collect the severance damages, the legal expenses would reduce the amount of the severance damages. In this case, the Taxpayer could not use the legal expenses to reduce the amount of the condemnation award.

¶ 1517.2 *Special Assessments*

A special assessment may be levied against the remaining property when only part of an owner's property is taken in a condemnation and the remaining portion of the property is benefited by the improvement resulting from the condemnation. Examples of such improvements may be a widening of a street or the installation of a sewer. Special assessments levied against the remaining property and withheld from the condemnation award are not treated as part of the condemnation award and so reduce the gain or increase the loss that the owner

---

[41] Rev. Rul. 68-37, 1968-1 CB 359.
[42] Rev. Rul. 73-35, 1973-1 CB 367.
[43] Rev. Rul. 80-184, 1980-2 CB 232.

realizes as a result of the condemnation.[44] The assessment must be withheld from the award.[45] If severance damages are included in the award, special assessments must be used first to reduce the severance damages before applying any excess to the condemnation award.

Example: The city acquired 25 feet of the Taxpayer's land in order to widen the street in front of the property. The Taxpayer was awarded $5,000 for this and spent $300 to obtain the award. The city levied a special assessment against the Taxpayer's remaining property for the street improvement and then paid the Taxpayer $4,200. The Taxpayer's net award is $3,900 ($5,000 gross award − $300 expenses = $4,700 − $800 special assessment = $3,900). If the $800 special assessment were not withheld from the award and the Taxpayer were paid $5,000, the net award would be $4,700, even if the Taxpayer later paid the special assessment of $800.

Suppose, however, that the $5,000 awarded to the Taxpayer was divided, $4,000 for the condemned property and $1,000 for severance damages, and the Taxpayer's expenses were solely allocable to obtaining the severance damages. In this case, the $1,000 in severance damages are reduced to zero by first subtracting the $300 expenses and then $700 of the special assessment. The Taxpayer's award for the condemned property, $4,000, is reduced by the $100 balance of the special assessment, leaving a net condemnation award of $3,900.

The following examples were prepared by the IRS to illustrate how severance damages and special assessments affect gain or loss from a condemnation. In all of the following examples, these facts are assumed.

Comprehensive Examples—Facts:

The Taxpayer bought 640 acres of farmland for $128,000 ($200 per acre). The land has a grove of trees and a natural spring that livestock use for shade and water. There were no improvements on the land when the Taxpayer bought it, but the Taxpayer later built storage sheds on the land at a cost of $3,000.

The city condemned a 10-acre strip of land through the property. The condemned strip included the land on which the Taxpayer built the sheds and keeps the livestock from using the grove of trees or the spring on the other side of the property. Before the condemnation, the Taxpayer took $400 depreciation on the sheds

---

[44] *C.C. Green,* 37 BTA 25, CCH Dec. 9905, Acq. 1938-2 CB 13; *Pioneer Real Estate Co.,* 47 BTA 886, CCH Dec. 12,854, Acq. 1943 CB 18.

[45] Reg. § 1.1033(a)-2(c)(10).

¶ 1517.2

and had deducted a $250 casualty loss for fire damage to one of the sheds in the previous year. The Taxpayer's total condemnation award was $12,000, and the Taxpayer spent $600 for legal and appraisal fees to obtain the award.

Comprehensive Example 1—No special assessment or severance damages: No special assessment was levied against the Taxpayer's remaining property and the Taxpayer did not receive any severance damages. The Taxpayer's gain from the condemnation is $7,050, computed as follows:

Total award		$12,000
Less: Legal and appraisal fees		600
Net condemnation award		$11,400
Less:		
10 acres @ $200	$2,000	
Cost of sheds	3,000	
	$5,000	
Less: Depreciation and casualty loss deduction	650	
Adjusted basis of condemned property		4,350
Gain realized...................................		$ 7,050

Comprehensive Example 2—Special assessment but no severance damages: Before paying the Taxpayer the award, the city levied an assessment of $1,600 against the property the Taxpayer retained for benefits received from the public improvement fund. The city withheld the assessment from the Taxpayer's award, and the Taxpayer received only $10,400. The Taxpayer's gain is $5,450, computed as follows:

Total award....................................		$12,000
Less: Legal and appraisal fees		600
		$11,400
Less: Special assessment		1,600
Net condemnation award		$ 9,800
Less:		
10 acres @ $200	$2,000	
Cost of sheds	3,000	
	$5,000	
Less: Depreciation and casualty loss deduction	650	
Adjusted basis of condemned property		4,350
Gain realized...................................		$ 5,450

Comprehensive Example 3—Severance damages but no special assessment: Of the Taxpayer's $12,000 award, $2,000 was stated in the award as severance damages and $10,000 for the

¶ 1517.2

condemned property. No special assessment was levied against the retained property. The Taxpayer's $600 expense for obtaining the award applies to the entire $12,000. The Taxpayer's gain is $5,150, computed as follows:

Severance damages	$ 2,000	
Condemnation award		$10,000
Less: Legal and appraisal fees		
$600 × ($2,000/$12,000)	100	
$600 × ($10,000/$12,000)		500
Net severance damages	$ 1,900	
Basis of remaining property		
(630 acres @ $200)	$126,000	
Less: Net severance damages	1,900	
New basis of remaining property	$124,100	
Net condemnation award		$ 9,500
Less:		
10 acres @ $200	$ 2,000	
Cost of sheds	3,000	
	$ 5,000	
Less: Depreciation and casualty loss deduction	650	
Adjusted basis of condemned property		4,350
Gain realized		$ 5,150

Comprehensive Example 4—Severance damages and special assessment: Of the Taxpayer's $12,000 award, $2,000 was stated in the award as severance damages and $10,000 for the condemned property. The city levied a special assessment of $1,600 against the remaining property. The city withheld the $1,600 from the award paid the Taxpayer. The Taxpayer's $600 expense of obtaining the award applies to the entire $12,000. The Taxpayer's gain is $5,150, computed as follows:

Severance damages	$ 2,000	
Condemnation award		$10,000
Less: Legal and appraisal fees		
$600 × ($2,000/$12,000)	100	
$600 × ($10,000/$12,000)		500
	$ 1,900	
Less: Special assessment	1,600	
Net severance damages	$ 300	
Basis of remaining property		
(630 acres @ $200)	$126,000	
Less: Net severance damages	300	
New basis of remaining property	$125,700	

¶ 1517.2

Casualty, Condemnation, and Demolition

Net condemnation award..........................		$ 9,500
Less:		
10 acres @ $200	$ 2,000	
Cost of sheds...............................	3,000	
	$ 5,000	
Less: Depreciation and casualty loss deduction	650	
Adjusted basis of condemned property		4,350
Gain realized..		$ 5,150

Comprehensive Example 5—Special assessment exceeds severance damages: Of the Taxpayer's $12,000 award, $2,000 was stated in the award as severance damages and $10,000 for the condemned property. The city levied a special assessment of $2,250 against the remaining property. The city withheld the $2,250 from the award paid the Taxpayer. The Taxpayer's $600 expense of obtaining the award applies to the entire $12,000. The Taxpayer's gain is $4,800, computed as follows:

Severance damages	$ 2,000	
Condemnation award		$10,000
Less: Legal and appraisal fees		
$600 × ($2,000/$12,000)	100	
$600 × ($10,000/$12,000)		500
Severance damages minus expenses	$ 1,900	
Condemnation award minus expenses		$ 9,500
Less: Special assessment:		
Subtracted from severance damages............	1,900	
Subtracted from condemnation award		350
Net severance damages	$ -0-	
Net condemnation award..........................		$ 9,150
Less:		
10 acres @ $200	$ 2,000	
Cost of sheds...............................	3,000	
	$ 5,000	
Less: Depreciation and casualty loss deduction	650	
Adjusted basis of condemned property		4,350
Gain realized..		$ 4,800

If the Taxpayer's net severance damages exceeded the basis in the remaining property, the new basis of the remaining property would be reduced to zero.

¶ 1519   TAX-FREE REPLACEMENT OF PROPERTY

The involuntary conversion of property through casualty, theft, condemnation or threat of condemnation may result in either gain or loss, as discussed at ¶ 1505 and ¶ 1515. A loss from an involuntary

¶ 1519

conversion of real estate used for a business or income-producing activity is deductible under the usual rules that apply to business losses.[46] When an involuntary conversion results in a gain, the usual rules affecting the sale or exchange of property generally would require that the owner recognize the gain and pay a tax. Involuntary conversion gains, however, may escape current tax under the nonrecognition provision contained in Code Sec. 1033.

The taxpayer who receives insurance or other compensation for the involuntary conversion of the property in excess of the basis of the property realizes a gain. This gain is not recognized if the property is directly replaced, for example, by the insurer, with property that is "similar or related in service or use" to the converted property.[47] In this case, the nonrecognition treatment is mandatory and the replacement property simply takes as its basis the adjusted basis of the involuntarily converted property.[48]

Direct conversion into similar property, however, is unusual. In the usual case, the owner of involuntarily converted property will receive cash compensation, through insurance in the case of a casualty, the condemnation award in the case of an actual condemnation, or sales proceeds in the case of a sale under threat of condemnation. The owner of property that is involuntarily converted at a gain into money or dissimilar property must recognize that gain unless the owner replaces the property with similar property within a specified period and elects not to recognize the gain.[49]

¶ 1521 Election to Postpone Gain

The owner of involuntarily converted property can elect to postpone reporting the gain from the conversion if the owner purchases property that is similar or related in service or use to the condemned, damaged, destroyed, or stolen property. Nonrecognition also applies if the owner purchases a controlling interest in a corporation that owns similar property.[50] The cost of replacement property must at least equal the proceeds from the involuntary conversion for complete nonrecognition. The owner must recognize gain to the extent the amount realized from the involuntary conversion exceeds the cost of the replacement property.[51]

In order for the nonrecognition provision to apply, it must be the owner of the property who replaces the converted property and takes ownership of the replacement property. For instance, when a corporation's property is condemned, the corporation is the taxpayer that must

---

[46] Code Sec. 165.
[47] Code Sec. 1033(a)(1).
[48] Reg. § 1.1033(a)-2(b).
[49] Code Sec. 1033(a)(2).
[50] Code Sec. 1033(a)(2)(A).
[51] Reg. § 1.1033(a)-2(c)(7).

Casualty, Condemnation, and Demolition

make the replacement. A sole shareholder to whom all the corporate assets are distributed in complete liquidation following the condemnation is not entitled to purchase replacement property.[52] Similarly, a wife who purchases replacement property, after her husband's death, from funds that pass to her absolutely under state law upon his death is not a taxpayer who can replace condemned property owned solely by the husband during his lifetime.[53]

In a private letter ruling,[54] a wife was required to recognize gain from real estate held by her and her husband as tenants by the entirety when real estate was sold under threat of condemnation and the proceeds were reinvested in replacement property with the title held solely in the husband's name.

Grantors and grantor trusts, however, may be treated as the same taxpayer for the tax-free replacement of involuntarily converted property. For instance, the grantor of a trust, the corpus of which would revert to the grantor at a later date, was the taxpayer who could elect nonrecognition of gain from the sale of condemned trust property that was required to be added to the trust corpus.[55] Also, if a taxpayer's grantor trust purchases replacement property for property of the taxpayer that has been involuntarily converted into money, the purchase can qualify the taxpayer's gain for nonrecognition under Code Sec. 1033.[56]

It had been the position of the IRS that there had to be an actual reimbursement in order for the owner of damaged or destroyed property to obtain nonrecognition benefits. For instance, if a hurricane uprooted trees and the timber were not insured, the sale of the downed or damaged timber and the use of the proceeds to buy replacement timber would not be eligible for nonrecognition.[57] The IRS later reversed itself, however, and now holds that the nonrecognition of gain provision of Code Sec. 1033 is applicable to proceeds received from the voluntary sale of timber downed by high winds, earthquake, or volcanic eruption when the proceeds are used to purchase other standing timber.[58]

¶ 1521.1 Advantages and Disadvantages of the Election

Because of the preferential treatment afforded capital gain, the decision on whether to elect nonrecognition requires some careful calculations.

---

[52] Rev. Rul. 73-72, 1973-1 CB 368.
[53] *G.W. Jayne Est.*, 61 TC 744, CCH Dec. 32,497.
[54] IRS Letter Ruling 8429004, March 22, 1984.
[55] Rev. Rul. 70-376, 1970-2 CB 164.
[56] Rev. Rul. 88-103, 1988-2 CB 304.
[57] Rev. Rul. 72-372, 1972-2 CB 471.
[58] Rev. Rul. 80-175, 1980-2 CB 230, revoking Rev. Rul. 73-372, 1972-2 CB 471.

Gain recognized on involuntary conversions is subject to the characterization rules of Code Sec. 1231, as discussed at ¶ 1305.2. Gain from involuntary conversions is also subject to the recapture rules, also discussed at ¶ 1307. This means that gain from an involuntary conversion may qualify as capital gain. If gain is recognized and replacement property is purchased, the replacement property has a basis equal to its full cost.

On the other hand, if gain is not recognized, the basis of the replacement property is the adjusted basis of the involuntarily converted property, as discussed at ¶ 1525. A lower basis, in turn, means lower or reduced depreciation deductions. In short, increased depreciation deductions are purchased at the cost of a current tax if the taxpayer chooses not to elect the tax-free replacement provision. This can be a benefit when capital gain generated on an involuntary conversion is subject to a lower tax rate than the income that will be offset by future depreciation deductions.

¶ 1521.2 *Method of Election*

A taxpayer elects not to recognize gain on an involuntary conversion under Code Sec. 1033 by not reporting the gain for the year in which it is realized. In addition, the taxpayer must file a statement that supports nonrecognition with the tax return for each year gain is realized as a result of the involuntary conversion. This statement should contain all of the details of the involuntary conversion at a gain, including the details that relate to the replacement of the property, such as a description of the property, date and type of conversion, computation of the gain, and decision to replace.

If a taxpayer makes the election not to recognize gain from an involuntary conversion and does not acquire replacement property within the required time period, spends less on the replacement property than was realized from the involuntary conversion, or decides not to replace the converted property, the taxpayer must file an amended return for the year in which the election was made not to recognize gain and must recompute the tax liability for that year.[59]

If a taxpayer who realizes a gain from an involuntary conversion does not elect nonrecognition on the return for the year in which the taxpayer realizes the gain, and subsequently purchases replacement property within the required replacement period, the taxpayer may file a claim for a credit or refund.[60]

---

[59] Reg. § 1.1033(a)-2(c)(2).

[60] Rev. Rul. 63-127, 1963-2 CB 333.

¶ 1521.3 *Replacement Period*

The replacement period for property damaged or destroyed by a casualty begins on the date the property is damaged or destroyed.[61] The replacement period ends two years after the close of the tax year in which the taxpayer realized any part of the gain on the casualty.[62]

In the case of a condemnation, the replacement period begins on the earliest of:

1. Actual condemnation or seizure of the property;
2. Threat or imminence of condemnation or seizure; or
3. Sale or exchange of the property under threat or imminence of condemnation or seizure.[63]

The replacement period ends three years after the close of the first tax year in which the taxpayer realizes any part of the gain on the condemnation, if the property condemned or sold under threat of condemnation is real property held for use in a trade or business or for investment (but not property held primarily for sale).[64] For any property other than real property held for use in a trade or business or investment, the replacement period following an involuntary conversion as a result of condemnation or threat of condemnation is two years.[65]

As discussed at ¶ 1513, a threat or imminence of condemnation occurs when the owner of the property is informed by a public official or government body that is authorized to acquire the property that a decision has been made to acquire the property and it is reasonable to believe that the property will be taken. The communication may be either oral or written.

Example: A calendar-year Taxpayer is notified on August 2, 2002, by the city in which the business is located that the city intends to acquire the Taxpayer's business real property by negotiation or by condemnation. On May 5, 2003, the city condemns the property and pays the Taxpayer $110,000 for the property, which had an adjusted basis at that time of $85,000. The replacement period for this property began on August 2, 2002, the date the Taxpayer was notified of the intent to condemn the property, and the replacement period ends on December 31, 2006, three years after the last day of the year in which the taxpayer realized gain from the condemnation.

---

[61] Code Sec. 1033(a)(2)(B).
[62] Code Sec. 1033(a)(2)(B)(i).
[63] Code Sec. 1033(a)(2)(B).
[64] Code Sec. 1033(g)(4).
[65] Code Sec. 1033(a)(2)(B)(i).

Once the threat or imminence of condemnation exists, the owner may purchase replacement property, as long as the owner continues to hold the replacement property at the time of the actual conversion.[66] Property acquired before there is a threat of condemnation does not qualify as replacement property because it is not property that is acquired during the replacement period.

The replacement property actually must be acquired during the replacement period in order for the nonrecognition provision to apply. For instance, an advance payment from the proceeds of property that is involuntarily converted to a contractor for the construction of replacement property is not a purchase of replacement property when the replacement property actually does not exist prior to the end of the replacement period.[67]

Extension of Replacement Period

Code Sec. 1400L(g) extends the replacement period under Code Sec. 1033 for involuntarily converted property to five years for property that was involuntarily converted within the New York Liberty Zone as a result of the terrorist attacks on September 11, 2001. The five-year period is available only if substantially all of the use of the replacement property is in New York City. The New York Liberty Zone includes the area on or south of Canal Street, East Broadway (east of its intersection with Canal Street), or Grand Street (east of its intersection with East Broadway) in the Borough of Manhattan in the City of New York, New York.

In the case of other property, the replacement period may be extended if the owner of involuntarily converted property can show reasonable cause for not being able to make the replacement within the normal replacement period. A taxpayer in need of an extension should apply to the District Director for the IRS district in which the taxpayer filed the return containing the election to postpone the gain. The application should contain all the details about the need for the extension and should be filed before the end of the replacement period, although a taxpayer may file an application within a reasonable time after the replacement period if the taxpayer can show reasonable cause for the delay.[68]

Ordinarily, the IRS grants requests for extensions near the end of the replacement period or the extended replacement period. The IRS usually limits extensions to a period of one year or less. The high market value or scarcity of replacement property is not a sufficient reason for granting an extension. If a taxpayer's replacement property

---

[66] *Real Estate Corp., Inc.*, 22 TCM 654, CCH Dec. 26,135(M), T.C. Memo. 1963-138.

[67] Rev. Rul. 56-543, 1956-2 CB 521.

[68] Code Sec. 1033(a)(2)(B)(ii); Reg. § 1.1033(a)-2(c)(3).

¶ 1521.3

Casualty, Condemnation, and Demolition

is under construction and the taxpayer can clearly show that the replacement or restoration cannot be made within the replacement period, the IRS generally will grant an extension of the replacement period.

Deficiency Assessments

If a taxpayer elects not to recognize gain from an involuntary conversion, the IRS may assess a deficiency for any tax year in which the taxpayer realizes any part of the gain within three years of the date the taxpayer notifies the District Director that the taxpayer is replacing the involuntarily converted property, or intends not to replace, within the replacement period.[69]

¶ 1523 Replacement Property

Generally, involuntarily converted property must be replaced with property that is similar or related in service or use to the converted property in order for the nonrecognition provision of Code Sec. 1033 to apply.[70] A special rule, however, applies to condemned business or investment real property (see ¶ 1523.3).[71] Other special rules apply to property damaged by presidentially declared disasters (see ¶ 1523.4).[72] There is also a requirement that replacement property be acquired from an unrelated person in several situations (see ¶ 1523.2).[73]

¶ 1523.1 Similar Property

The only statement in the regulations regarding what constitutes similar property is the following:[74]

There is no investment in property similar in character and devoted to a similar use if—

(i) The proceeds of unimproved real estate, taken upon condemnation proceedings, are invested in improved real estate.

(ii) The proceeds of conversion of real property are applied in reduction of indebtedness previously incurred in the purchase of a leasehold.

(iii) The owner of a requisitioned tug uses the proceeds to buy barges.

The IRS had applied a very strict test to determine whether replacement property was similar or related in service or use for all property. Under this test, the replacement property had to be functionally the same as the converted property. A series of appellate court decisions, however, held that this test was not correct when applied to

---

[69] Code Sec. 1033(a)(2)(C).
[70] Code Sec. 1033(a)(2)(A).
[71] Code Sec. 1033(g).
[72] Code Sec. 1033(h).
[73] Code Sec. 1033(i).
[74] Reg. § 1.1033(a)-2(c)(9).

owner-investors rather than owner-users.[75] Accordingly, the meaning of similar or related in service or use depends on whether the taxpayer is an owner-user or an owner-investor.[76]

Owner-User

For property used by the owner, replacement property is similar or related in service or use only if it is functionally the same as the converted property. Property is not considered similar or related in service or use to the converted property unless the physical characteristics and end uses of the replacement and converted properties are closely related. Under this strict function test, the IRS has ruled that a recreational billiards center is not sufficiently similar to bowling alleys destroyed by fire.[77] Also, a floating seafood processing plant in which the taxpayer invested insurance proceeds from a land-based seafood processing plant that was destroyed by fire is not similar or related in service or use and does not qualify as replacement property.[78]

Although it did not specifically state, the IRS also followed the stricter test imposed on owner-users in a ruling involving a bank that had a building destroyed by a tornado. Before it was destroyed, the bank's building was leased for the production of rental income. The replacement building, in addition to being leased, was used by the bank for its banking operations. The part of the replacement building occupied by the bank was not similar or related in service or use to the converted property, and only the tenant-occupied part of the building qualified as replacement property.[79]

Owner-Investor

In considering whether replacement property acquired by an investor is similar or related in service or use, the IRS looks to the similarity in the relationship of the services or uses that the converted and replacement properties have to the owner. Whether replacement property has the same relationship of services or uses as the property it replaces is determined by the following factors:

1. Whether the properties are of similar service to the taxpayer;

2. The nature of the business risks connected with the properties; and

3. What the properties demand of the taxpayer in the way of management, service, and relations to the owner's tenants.

---

[75] *Liant Record, Inc.*, CA-2, 62-1 USTC ¶ 9494, 303 F.2d 326; *Capitol Motor Car Co.*, CA-6, 63-1 USTC ¶ 9344, 314 F.2d 469; *Steuart Bros., Inc.*, CA-4, 59-1 USTC ¶ 9143, 261 F.2d 580.
[76] Rev. Rul. 64-237, 1964-2 CB 319.
[77] Rev. Rul. 76-319, 1976-2 CB 242.
[78] Rev. Rul. 77-192, 1977-1 CB 249.
[79] Rev. Rul. 79-261, 1979-2 CB 295.

¶ 1523.1

Under this test, the IRS has ruled that the investment of proceeds from condemnation of land and a warehouse held for rental purposes in constructing, on other land owned by the taxpayer, a gas station held for rental purposes was a replacement of property similar or related in service or use.[80] On the other hand, a hotel of which the taxpayer was the owner-lessor under a net lease was not similar to a hotel of which the taxpayer was owner-operator. As lessor, the taxpayer had a fixed return not dependent on economic fluctuations and risks of liability to guests. As operator, the taxpayer had to deal directly with guests. Thus, the nature of the taxpayer's relationship to the property was substantially changed.[81]

¶ 1523.2 Required Replacement from Unrelated Person

Some taxpayers cannot take advantage of the nonrecognition provisions of Code Sec. 1033 if they acquire the replacement property from related persons (as defined in Code Secs. 267(b) or 707(b)(1)). The rule does not apply if the related person acquired the property from an unrelated person within the replacement period.[82] The taxpayers affected by this rule are:

1. C corporations;
2. Partnerships in which one or more C corporations own more than 50 percent of the capital or profits interest at the time of the involuntary conversion; and
3. Any other taxpayer if the aggregate amount of realized gain on involuntarily converted property during the year exceeds $100,000.

¶ 1523.3 Special Rule for Condemned Property

A special rule applies to the replacement of real property used in a trade or business or held for investment if the property is condemned or sold under threat of condemnation. This special rule does not apply to real property held for sale. Under the special rule, nonrecognition of gain is available if the taxpayer replaces the condemned property, or property sold under threat of condemnation, with like-kind property.[83] This is the same like-kind test that applies to tax-free exchanges under Code Sec. 1031 as discussed at ¶ 1311. The like-kind test for replacement of condemned realty applies only to direct replacement and not to replacement through acquisition of corporate control, as discussed at ¶ 1523.4.[84]

---

[80] Rev. Rul. 71-41, 1971-1 CB 223.
[81] Rev. Rul. 70-399, 1970-2 CB 164.
[82] Code Sec. 1033(i).
[83] Code Sec. 1033(g).
[84] Code Sec. 1033(g)(2).

Replacement of condemned property that does not qualify under the like-kind test of Code Sec. 1033(g) may still qualify for nonrecognition under Code Sec. 1033(a), if the replacement property is similar or related in service or use to the condemned property.[85] The IRS has ruled that condemnation proceeds received for property containing both the taxpayer's residence and business qualified for nonrecognition when similar amounts were spent to purchase new residential property and an apartment building. The new residential property was similar or related in service or use to the replaced residence, while the apartment building was like-kind property as to the converted business property.[86]

Replacement of Leased Property

Under the like-kind test, a leasehold of 30-year duration is of like-kind to a fee interest. When property under a lease is condemned, the lessee cannot rely on the like-kind test if the lessee replaces a leasehold of less than 30 years with a fee interest. The IRS has indicated, however, that a leasehold interest may be similar or related in service or use to a fee interest.[87] Accordingly, a lessee who receives payment when the leased property is condemned may purchase replacement property in fee under the stricter similar or related in service or use test and avoid recognition of income as a result of the payment. As long as the property purchased will be used for the identical purpose for which the converted leasehold was used, the former lessee does not have to recognize gain under Code Sec. 1033.

Severance Damages

Severance damages are compensation for the reduced value of remaining property after a portion of the owner's property is taken in condemnation. Severance damages are payments in addition to the condemnation award, and, as discussed above, the usual way to handle severance damages is to treat them as a reduction in the basis of the remaining property. If severance damages exceed remaining basis, the excess is a taxable gain.

Gain from severance damages may be reinvested under Code Sec. 1033 to avoid current tax on the gain.[88] At one time, the IRS asserted that the reinvestment had to be in property similar or related in service or use, rather than like-kind property, which allows nonrecognition in the case of a condemnation award. For instance, in Rev. Rul. 80-184,[89] part of a severance damage award was used to demolish a building

---

[85] Rev. Rul. 71-41, 1971-1 CB 223; *Westchester Development Co.*, 63 TC 198, CCH Dec. 32,843, Acq. 1975-2 CB 2.
[86] Rev. Rul. 72-424, 1972-2 CB 469.
[87] GCM 38975, June 15, 1982.
[88] Rev. Rul. 72-433, 1972-2 CB 470; Rev. Rul. 72-549, 1972-2 CB 472.
[89] 1980-2 CB 232.

¶ 1523.3

leased to retail stores and to construct a warehouse for lease in its place. The remaining part of the award was used to purchase another parcel of land and construct an office building. The IRS ruled that the reinvestments were in property similar or related in service or use, and the taxpayer could defer the recognition of gain realized as a result of the severance damage award. Later, however, the IRS recognized that severance damages and condemnation awards should be treated in the same fashion and ruled that severance damages may be accorded nonrecognition treatment under Code Sec. 1033(g)(1), even though the taxpayer reinvests the severance damages in property that is not similar or related in service or use to the condemned property.[90]

¶ 1523.4 *Presidentially Declared Disasters*

If property held for productive use in a trade or business or for the production of income is involuntarily converted as a result of a presidentially declared disaster, tangible property of a type held for productive use in a trade or business is treated as property that is similar or related in service or use.[91] In the case of the loss of a principal residence, no gain is recognized on insurance proceeds received for unscheduled property and other insurance proceeds are treated as received for a single item of property. Any property that is similar or related in service or use to the converted residence is treated as similar or related in service or use to the single item of property.[92]

¶ 1523.5 *Outdoor Advertising Displays*

A taxpayer may elect to treat a qualifying outdoor advertising display as real property if the taxpayer did not claim a Code Sec. 179 deduction for the display or take an investment credit in a previous year.[93] An outdoor advertising display is a sign or device that is rigidly assembled and permanently attached to the ground, a building, or any other permanent structure that is used for commercial or other advertisement to the public.[94]

An election to treat an outdoor advertising display as real property for purposes of tax-free replacement under Code Sec. 1033 cannot be revoked without the consent of the IRS.[95] If a taxpayer makes this election and replaces an involuntarily converted outdoor advertising display with real property in which the taxpayer holds a different kind of interest, the replacement property may qualify as like-kind property.[96] For instance, real property purchased to replace a destroyed

---

[90] Rev. Rul. 83-49, 1983-1 CB 191, modifying Rev. Rul. 80-184, 1980-2 CB 232.
[91] Code Sec. 1033(h)(2).
[92] Code Sec. 1033(h)(1).
[93] Code Sec. 1033(g)(3)(A).
[94] Code Sec. 1033(g)(3)(C).
[95] Code Sec. 1033(g)(3)(B).
[96] Code Sec. 1033(g)(3)(D).

billboard and leased property on which the billboard was located qualify as property of a like kind.

¶ 1523.6 *Acquisition of Corporate Control*

A taxpayer may replace property by acquiring control of a corporation that owns property that is similar or related in service or use to the involuntarily converted property.[97] If the owner of involuntarily converted property does this, gain is recognized only to the extent it exceeds the cost of the stock of the corporation. Control is defined as stock having at least 80 percent of the combined voting power of all classes of voting stock and at least 80 percent of the total number of shares of all other classes of stock.[98]

> **Example:** The Taxpayer owned property with an adjusted basis of $175,000 that the Taxpayer used in the business. The property was destroyed by fire and the taxpayer received $200,000 from the insurer. The Taxpayer was unable to find suitable replacement property, but did buy, for $200,000, control of a corporation that owns property similar or related in service or use to the destroyed property. If the Taxpayer purchased the stock within the replacement period, the Taxpayer can postpone the tax on the $25,000 gain realized as a result of the involuntary conversion.

It is the position of the IRS that the corporation must own the similar or related in service or use property at the time the taxpayer acquires control in order for Code Sec. 1033 to apply.[99] In other words, the taxpayer cannot use the proceeds of an involuntary conversion to acquire control of a corporation by transferring the proceeds to the corporation and then having the corporation purchase the replacement property. The Tax Court, however, has held otherwise.

In *John Richard Corp.*,[100] the taxpayer purchased control of a newly formed corporation in order to replace involuntarily converted property. On the following day, the corporation purchased property similar or related in service or use to the taxpayer's converted property. The Tax Court ruled that the taxpayer was entitled to the nonrecognition of gain provision when the organization of the new corporation, the taxpayer's acquisition of its stock and the purchase of replacement property by the corporation were merely steps in an integrated transaction designed to replace the taxpayer's involuntarily converted property. The Court went on to say that any distinction in the application of Code Sec. 1033 under these circumstances and in the case of a

---

[97] Code Sec. 1033(a)(2)(A).
[98] Code Sec. 1033(a)(2)(E)(i).
[99] Rev. Rul. 77-422, 1977-2 CB 307.
[100] 46 TC 41, CCH Dec. 27,915, Nonacq., 1974-2 CB 5 and Acq. 1967-2 CB 3.

purchase of stock in a corporation that previously owned the property was not justified.

Although the IRS does not approve, the use of a newly formed corporation to acquire replacement property may offer substantial tax savings. As discussed below, replacement property generally takes the same basis as the involuntarily converted property. The owner of involuntarily converted property who acquires stock of a new corporation with the proceeds of an involuntary conversion has a basis for the stock equal to the basis of the converted property. When the new corporation uses the proceeds of the involuntary conversion to purchase replacement property, the corporation's basis is the cost of the property. The new corporation, therefore, may have substantially larger depreciation deductions than would be available to the owner if he had directly purchased the replacement property.

¶ 1525   Basis of Replacement Property

The basis of property acquired as replacement property following an involuntary conversion into money is its cost, decreased by the amount of gain that is not recognized on the conversion.[101]

Example 1: The Taxpayer's store was destroyed by a fire. At the time of the casualty, the Taxpayer's adjusted basis for the store was $126,000. The Taxpayer's fire insurer paid the Taxpayer $136,000 as compensation for the loss and the Taxpayer spent $132,000 to build a new store on the land. The Taxpayer's gain as a result of the involuntary conversion of the store is $10,000, but the Taxpayer reports only $4,000, the amount of gain that was not reinvested in the new store. The Taxpayer's basis for the new store is $126,000, the $132,000 cost less the $6,000 of gain that was not recognized following the involuntary conversion. If the Taxpayer had spent the entire $136,000 to rebuild, the basis would still be $126,000 ($136,000 − $10,000 gain not recognized).

If the replacement property consists of more than one piece of property, the basis must be allocated to the properties in proportion to their costs.[102] This allocation rule also applies to the allocation of basis between land and improvements.[103]

Example 2: The Taxpayer owned land on which a warehouse had been built for use in the Taxpayer's business. When the Taxpayer's basis for the land and building was $500,000, the city condemned the property for public purposes and paid the Taxpayer $800,000 as a condemnation award. The Taxpayer used the $800,000 award

---

[101] Code Sec. 1033(b).
[102] *Ibid.*
[103] Rev. Rul. 73-18, 1973-1 CB 368.

to purchase new land for $200,000 and to construct a new warehouse for $600,000.

The Taxpayer's gain from the involuntary conversion of the land and warehouse is $300,000. This gain is not recognized, however, since the Taxpayer purchased replacement property within the required time period. The Taxpayer's basis for the new land and warehouse is $500,000, the $800,000 cost decreased by the $300,000 of gain that was not recognized. This $500,000 basis is apportioned between the land and warehouse according to cost as follows:

Basis of land: $500,000 × $200,000/$800,000 = $125,000.

Basis of warehouse: $500,000 × $600,000/$800,000 = $375,000.

Gain that is not recognized following the involuntary conversion and replacement of property must be used to reduce the basis of replacement property as a whole. When a taxpayer who elected not to recognize the gain realized on the involuntary conversion of unimproved land subsequently acquired improved land, he selected only the land as replacement property so that the unrecognized gain would only reduce the basis of the land and the taxpayer would have a higher basis for the improvements. The IRS, however, ruled that the taxpayer must apply the unrecognized gain to reduce the basis of the replacement property as a whole, and the remaining basis must be allocated to the land and improvements in proportion to their costs.[104]

¶ 1525.1 Replacement with Corporate Stock

If the basis of corporate stock acquired as replacement property (see ¶ 1523.6) is reduced by unrecognized gain, an equal amount also must be applied to reduce the basis of property held by the corporation at the time the taxpayer acquired control of the corporation. The reduction is limited so as not to reduce the basis of the corporation's property below the taxpayer's adjusted basis for the corporation stock. The decrease in the basis of the corporation's property is applied first to property that is similar or related in service or use to the converted property, then to depreciable property, and finally to any other corporate property.[105]

¶ 1525.2 Direct Conversion to Replacement Property

If property is involuntarily converted directly into other property, the basis of the replacement property is the same as that of the converted property, decreased by any money received and not ex-

---

[104] Rev. Rul. 79-402, 1979-2 CB 297.   [105] Code Sec. 1033(b)(3).

pended for replacement property, and increased by any gain or decreased by any loss recognized on the conversion.[106]

¶ 1531 DEMOLITION AND ABANDONMENT

At times, a taxpayer may dispose of real property by demolishing the property in order to clear the land on which it stands for other uses. In rare cases, a taxpayer may decide to simply walk away from real property and abandon it. While demolition cannot produce a loss deduction, abandonment may.

¶ 1535 Demolition

Before 1984, the costs of demolishing an historic structure and the adjusted basis of the structure at the time of demolition had to be added to the basis of the land on which the structure was located. For all other improvements, however, the tax treatment of demolition depended on whether the property was acquired with an intent to demolish it. If the owner acquired property with an intent to demolish it, costs and other losses were added to the basis of the land. If the owner did not have the intent to demolish at the time of purchase, the owner could deduct the cost and other losses as a result of a later demolition. Needless to say, the question of intent led to a great deal of litigation.

Since 1984, however, the Internal Revenue Code has eliminated all controversy. The owner of property must add the costs and other losses incurred in connection with the demolition of all buildings, including certified historic structures, to the basis of the land on which the demolished buildings were located.[107] A current deduction is not permitted for demolition losses.

¶ 1537 Abandonment

If nondepreciable property, such as land, is permanently retired from use in business or a transaction entered into for profit and physically abandoned, an abandonment loss deduction may be available under Code Sec. 165(a).[108] The deduction is the adjusted basis of the nondepreciable property when abandoned. Similarly, an abandonment loss deduction may be available when depreciable property is abandoned. The regulations provide:

> Where an asset is retired by actual physical abandonment (as, for example, in the case of a building condemned as unfit for further occupancy or other use), loss will be recognized measured by the amount of the adjusted basis of the asset abandoned at the time of such abandonment. In order to qualify for the recognition of loss

---

[106] Code Sec. 1033(b)(1).
[107] Code Sec. 280B.
[108] Reg. § 1.165-2(a).

from physical abandonment, the intent of the taxpayer must be irrevocably to discard the asset so that it will neither be used again by him nor retrieved by him for sale, exchange, or other disposition.[109]

¶ 1537.1 Abandonment of Land

Since land cannot be physically picked up and tossed away, proving an actual physical abandonment of land may be a difficult task. Generally, nonpayment of taxes is an important factor in proving the abandonment of land, especially when supported by other factors. In *Enid Ice & Fuel Co.*,[110] the Court sustained an abandonment loss when, in addition to not paying real estate taxes, the corporate owner charged the property off on its books, had no intent to claim a right of redemption against the property, and held a worthless redemption right because the property was worth less than the unpaid taxes.[111]

¶ 1537.2 Abandonment of Improvements

An interesting question is whether improvements or buildings can be abandoned without also abandoning the land on which they sit. The Tax Court has allowed an abandonment loss for a building, even though the owner retained the land. In *H.R. Hanover*,[112] a partnership claimed an abandonment loss for a hotel equal to its adjusted basis of $260,000. The Court looked for three points to sustain an abandonment loss:

1. The intent to irrevocably discard the property so that it would be neither reused nor retrieved;
2. An affirmative act that establishes this intent; and
3. The complete elimination of all value of the property and recognition by the owner that the property no longer possesses any utility.

The Tax Court held that these conditions were met and that it was not impossible for an owner to physically abandon improvements to land and claim a loss deduction, even though the underlying land is retained. Once the owner established that the building had no value to it, based on the cost involved in reopening the hotel, the Tax Court saw the following as indicating an intent to abandon as well as affirmative acts of abandonment:

1. Business records stated that economic conditions required abandoning the hotel;

---

[109] Reg. § 1.167(a)-8(a)(4).
[110] DC Okla., 56-2 USTC ¶ 9665, 142 F.Supp. 486.
[111] See also *J.R. Hopkins*, 15 TC 160, CCH Dec. 17,811, Acq. 1951-1 CB 2, in which it was held that the existence of back taxes equal to market value of property does not prove that all equity has been lost, but when tax arrearages greatly exceed the value and the owner recognizes loss of his equity, a deductible loss is sustained.

[112] 38 TCM 1281, CCH Dec. 36,262(M), T.C. Memo. 1979-332.

2. Building was locked and boarded;
3. Barricade was placed around the building to protect passers-by from falling masonry and stone;
4. Utilities were terminated;
5. Insurance was terminated;
6. Maintenance was discontinued;
7. Building was not held for sale.

The hotel in the *Hanover* case would have been demolished had it not been for the cost involved. Under current law, if a building is abandoned and then demolished, Code Sec. 280B, as discussed at ¶ 1535, would require that the basis of the building and the cost of demolition be added to the basis of the land.

Chapter 16

Contributions and Gifts

¶ 1600 OVERVIEW OF CHAPTER

In addition to a sale, exchange, involuntary conversion, or abandonment of property, the owner of real estate may make a gift of the property to family, friends, charities, government, or other entities. Obviously, family and charitable giving have many estate planning implications that are beyond the scope of this work. Also, lifetime gifts may produce gift tax consequences and affect future estate taxes. Neither gift nor estate taxes are properly the subject of this chapter or, for that matter, this book. Rather, the focus here is on the income tax consequences of gratuitous real estate transfers.

¶ 1601 CHARITABLE GIFTS

Real estate donated to charity or governmental units may provide the donor with a charitable deduction, subject to the limits on charitable deductions contained in Code Sec. 170. To qualify as a charitable contribution, the donor must transfer the property without receiving or expecting financial or economic benefit equal to the value of the property transferred. If the donor does receive, or can reasonably expect to receive, "substantial benefits" that are greater than those that would inure to the general public from a transfer for charitable purposes, a charitable deduction is not allowed.[1]

Generally speaking, an individual's deduction for charitable contributions in any one year is limited to 50 percent of the individual's adjusted gross income for the year.[2] A 30 percent limit may apply to gifts of certain capital gain property,[3] and also to gifts of ordinary income property to nonoperating foundations and certain other organizations.[4] A corporation's deduction is generally limited to 10 percent of its taxable income for the year.[5] A five-year carryover period is provided for contributions in excess of these limits.[6] The special rules that affect charitable gifts of appreciated property are discussed at ¶ 1607.

---

[1] Rev. Rul. 76-185, 1976-1 CB 60. See the discussion of gifts with mixed motives at ¶ 1605.

[2] Code Sec. 170(b)(1)(A).

[3] Code Sec. 170(b)(1)(C).

[4] Code Sec. 170(b)(1)(D).

[5] Code Sec. 170(b)(2).

[6] Code Sec 170(d).

¶ 1603 Valuation of Real Estate Gifts

The first step in determining the charitable contribution deduction for gifts of real property is to determine the fair market value of the property on the date of the contribution. Fair market value is defined as the price at which a willing buyer and a willing seller agree, neither being under any compulsion to buy or sell, and both having reasonable knowledge of the relevant facts.[7] If there is a restriction on the use of the donated property, the fair market value must reflect that restriction. For example, if a taxpayer donates land and restricts its use to agricultural uses, the taxpayer must value the land at its value for agricultural purposes, even if it would have a higher fair market value if it were not restricted.

Because each piece of real estate is unique and its valuation is complicated, a detailed appraisal by a professional appraiser is usually necessary to establish fair market value. A qualified appraisal is required, as discussed at ¶ 1603.2, for gifts of property that exceed $5,000. The weight given an appraisal depends on the completeness of the report, the qualifications of the appraiser, and the appraiser's demonstrated knowledge of the donated property. An appraisal must give all the facts on which to base an intelligent judgment of the value of the property. An appraiser's opinion is never more valid than the facts on which it is based.

¶ 1603.1 Types of Appraisals

In general, there are three main approaches to the valuation of real estate. An appraisal may involve the combined use of two or three methods rather than only one method.

Comparable Sales

The best indicator of value is, of course, an actual sale of the property on the date it is being valued. The next best indicator is a sale of the property reasonably close to the valuation date. Intervening factors which would affect value and which occur between the sale date and the valuation date must be identified and considered. Examples of such factors include a change in zoning, eminent domain, improvements built near the property, or a change in the neighborhood.

Absent a recent sale of the property being valued, the next best indicator of value is comparable sales. The comparable sales method of

---

[7] See the IRS Valuation Guide for Income, Estate and Gift Taxes. The Guide is designed primarily to benefit IRS officials who negotiate settlements of income, estate and gift tax cases in which valuation of real or personal property is necessary, but it also gives taxpayers and tax advisors insight into the major valuation problems and the accepted methods and approaches applied by IRS Appeals Officers in considering valuation questions. The material here on valuing real estate is based on this Guide and IRS Publication 561, "Determining the Value of Donated Property."

valuing property compares the donated property with several similar properties that have been sold. The selling prices, after adjustments for differences in date of sale, size, condition, and location, indicate the estimated fair market value of the donated property. If the comparable sales method is being applied to unimproved real estate, the appraiser should consider the following factors when comparing the potential comparable property and the donated property:

1. Location, size, and zoning use or restrictions;
2. Accessibility and road frontage, and available utilities and water rights;
3. Riparian rights and existing easements, rights-of-way, leases, etc.;
4. Soil characteristics, vegetative cover, and status of mineral rights; and
5. Any other factors affecting value.

Comparable selling prices must be adjusted to reflect any differences between the sale property and the donated property. Because differences of opinion may arise between appraisers as to the degree of comparability and the amount of adjustment considered necessary for comparison purposes, an appraiser should document each item of adjustment. Only comparable sales having the least adjustments in terms of items and/or total dollar adjustments should be considered as comparable to the donated property.

Capitalization of Income

The capitalization of income method of valuing donated property capitalizes the net income from the property at a rate that represents a fair return on the particular investment at the particular time, considering the risks involved. This method is particularly useful for the appraisal of business or rental properties. The income flow should take into account the future demand for space, the vacancy rate, the cost of labor, maintenance, real estate taxes, and utilities. The key elements in this approach to valuing real estate are the determination of the income to be capitalized and the rate of capitalization.

In determining the income to be capitalized, the appraiser should consider actual income from the property, as well as potential income from the property's highest and best use. The usual method of determining income is to reduce gross income by certain expenses, including interest, because of the different financing choices that are available, and depreciation, which can be accounted for in the capitalization rate. Generally, a reduction for prospective income taxes is not taken because it is too speculative.

¶ 1603.1

There are several methods for determining a proper capitalization rate to apply to the income stream in order to determine value. One is the direct capitalization rate, which is the rate derived by dividing the selling price into net income for comparable properties. With the residual method, a capitalization rate is built based on what a hypothetical willing buyer would want as a rate of return, considering liquidity, risk, safety, and depreciation. Since a common problem in real estate valuation is the allocation of cost to land and buildings, the method often used to separate land and building value is the building residual method. The building residual method is considered the most helpful of the several methods of determining a capitalization rate because it uses land, which can be valued more accurately in most cases, as a basis for the first step in the valuation process.

Still another method of determining a capitalization rate is the band of investment method. Under this method, a capitalization rate is derived by considering the rate for financing, the rate for equity, and the rate for depreciation.

Replacement Cost

This method of real estate valuation, used alone, usually does not result in a determination of fair market value, unless the property has only a special or limited use. Rather, replacement cost generally sets the upper limit of value, particularly in periods of rising costs, because it is reasonable to assume that an informed buyer will not pay more for the real estate than it would cost to reproduce a similar property. Of course, this reasoning does not apply if a similar property cannot be created because of location, unusual construction, or some other reason. Generally, this method of valuation serves to support the value determined from other methods. When the replacement cost method is applied to improved real estate, the land and improvements are valued separately.

The replacement cost of a building is determined from the materials, quality of workmanship, and the number of square or cubic feet in the building. This cost represents the total cost of labor and materials, overhead, and profit. After the replacement cost is determined, the following factors must be considered:

1. Physical deterioration—the wear and tear on the building itself;
2. Functional obsolescence—usually in older buildings with, for example, inadequate lighting, plumbing, or heating, small rooms, or a poor floor plan; and
3. Economic obsolescence—outside forces causing the whole area to become less desirable.

¶ 1603.1

¶ 1603.2　*Required Appraisal*

Generally, if a claimed deduction for an item of donated property is more than $5,000, the taxpayer must obtain a qualified appraisal made by a qualified appraiser and must attach an appraisal summary (Section B, Form 8283) to the tax return.[8] This rule applies to charitable contributions made by individuals, closely held corporations, personal service corporations, partnerships, and S corporations. It also applies to C corporations making contributions of inventory and scientific equipment.[9]

A qualified appraisal is an appraisal document that:

1. Relates to an appraisal made not earlier than 60 days before the contribution of the appraised property;
2. Does not involve a prohibited appraisal fee;
3. Includes certain information (detailed below); and
4. Is prepared, signed, and dated by a qualified appraiser.[10]

The taxpayer must receive the qualified appraisal before the due date, including extensions, of the return on which a charitable contribution deduction is first claimed for the donated property. If the taxpayer first claims the deduction on an amended return, the qualified appraisal must be received before the date on which the return is filed.[11]

Prohibited Appraisal Fee

No part of the fee arrangement for a qualified appraisal can be based on a percentage of the appraised value of the property.[12] This rule does not apply to a fee paid to a generally recognized association that regulates appraisers if:

1. The association is not organized for profit and no part of the net earnings benefits any private shareholder or individual;
2. The appraiser does not receive any compensation from the association or any other persons for making the appraisal; and
3. The fee arrangement is not based in whole or in part on the amount of the appraised value that is allowed as a deduction after an IRS examination or otherwise.

A fee arrangement based on what is allowed as a deduction, after IRS examination or otherwise, generally is treated as a fee based on a percentage of appraised value.

---

[8] Reg. § 1.170A-13(c)(2).
[9] Reg. § 1.170A-13(c)(1).
[10] Reg. § 1.170A-13(c)(3).
[11] Reg. § 1.170A-13(c)(3)(iv)(B).
[12] Reg. § 1.170A-13(c)(6).

Required Information

A qualified appraisal must include the following information: [13]

1. A description of the property in sufficient detail for a person who is not generally familiar with the type of property to determine that the property appraised is the property that was or will be contributed;
2. The physical condition of the property;
3. The date or expected date of contribution;
4. The terms of any agreement or understanding entered into (or expected to be entered into) by or on behalf of the donor;
5. The name, address, and taxpayer identification number of the qualified appraiser and, if the appraiser is a partner, an employee, or an independent contractor engaged by a person other than the donor, the name, address, and taxpayer identification number of the partnership or the person who employs or engages the appraiser;
6. The qualifications of the qualified appraiser who signs the appraisal, including the appraiser's background, experience, education, and any membership in professional appraisal associations;
7. A statement that the appraisal was prepared for income tax purposes;
8. The date or dates on which the property was valued;
9. The appraised fair market value on the date or expected date of contribution;
10. The method of valuation used to determine fair market value, such as the capitalization of income approach, the comparable sales or market data approach, or the replacement cost less depreciation approach;
11. The specific basis for the valuation, such as any specific comparable sales transaction; and
12. A description of the fee arrangement between the donor and appraiser.

Qualified Appraiser

A qualified appraiser is an individual who declares on the appraisal summary (Section B, Form 8283) that he or she:

1. Is publicly acknowledged as an appraiser or performs appraisals on a regular basis;

---

[13] Reg. § 1.170A-13(c)(3)(ii).

¶ 1603.2

2. Is qualified to make appraisals of the type of property being valued;

3. Is not an excluded individual; and

4. Understands the penalty for aiding and abetting an understatement of tax liability.[14]

An appraiser must complete Part IV of Section B, Form 8283 to be considered a qualified appraiser. More than one appraiser may appraise the property, provided that each complies with the requirements, including signing the qualified appraisal and appraisal summary.

The following persons cannot be qualified appraisers with respect to particular property: [15]

1. The donor of the property.

2. The donee of the property.

3. A party to the transaction in which the donor acquired the property being appraised, unless the property is donated within two months of the date of acquisition and its appraised value does not exceed its acquisition price. This applies to the person who sold, exchanged, or gave the property to the donor, or any person who acted as an agent for the transferor or donor in the transaction.

4. Any person employed by, or related (or married to a person who is related) under Code Sec. 267(b) to, any of the above persons. For example, if the donor acquired property from a dealer, neither the dealer nor persons employed by the dealer can be qualified appraisers for that property.

5. An appraiser who is regularly used by a person in 1, 2, or 3 and who does not perform a majority of the appraisals made during the tax year for other persons.

In addition, a person is not a qualified appraiser for a particular donation if the donor had knowledge of facts that would cause a reasonable person to expect the appraiser to falsely overstate the value of the donated property.[16] For example, if a donor makes an agreement with the appraiser that the property will be valued at more than its fair market value, the appraiser is not a qualified appraiser for the donation.

---

[14] Reg. § 1.170A-13(c)(5).
[15] Reg. § 1.170A-13(c)(5)(iv).
[16] Reg. § 1.170A-13(c)(5)(ii).

¶ 1603.2

¶ 1605   Gifts with Mixed Motives

As noted at ¶ 1601, if the donor of property receives or expects to receive substantial benefits that are greater than those than inure to the general public as a result of the contribution, a charitable deduction is not allowed. When the donor is a business, however, the donor may be entitled to a business expense deduction when it expects a benefit in return for its "contribution." The best treatment depends on the property involved and the various limitations on charitable and business expense deductions. A gift that would exceed the charitable contribution limit may have a business seeking an expense deduction. On the other hand, since the applicable business expense deduction for appreciated property is its cost, a charitable deduction measured by fair market value may be preferred. Also, if the expected benefit has a long life or adds to the value of other property, the cost of the benefit may have to be capitalized.

A charitable deduction was disallowed for the contribution of a school site located on a large tract of land that the taxpayer intended to develop when the school site became accessible after construction by the government of two new access roads. The taxpayer's remaining property was also relatively inaccessible and would have benefitted greatly from the construction of the new roads. The contribution of the school site was made with the expectation of receiving "a significant economic benefit." [17]

In another case, however, the taxpayer obtained a charitable deduction for land donated as a school site as a condition of obtaining a zoning change.[18] The taxpayer was under no obligation to make the contribution gratuitously and the local government would have had to purchase or condemn the land if the taxpayer had not donated it.

In a private letter ruling, the IRS allowed a company a charitable contribution deduction for an overpass and a private frontage road donated to local government.[19] The company was located on a limited access highway and could be reached from either of two interchanges along a private frontage road that it owned or from a private overpass that it owned. The company built an interchange to connect with its overpass and then donated the new interchange and its frontage roads to the local government. The IRS concluded that the company would not receive "a substantial benefit," even though the interchange would make it easier for employees, visitors, and others to reach the company. These were incidental benefits in light of the improved traffic patterns

---

[17] *Ottawa Silica Co.*, CA FC, 83-1 USTC ¶ 9169, 699 F.2d 1124.

[18] *J. Scheffres*, 28 TCM 234, CCH Dec. 29,472(M), T.C. Memo. 1969-41.

[19] IRS Letter Ruling 8421018, February 15, 1984.

that would be of public benefit. The "incidental benefits" realized by the company included improved road connections for access to its facilities, an immediate deduction for the cost of improvements that would otherwise be recoverable through depreciation, and removal of the donated property from the tax roles and the expense of local property taxes.

¶ 1607 Gifts of Appreciated Property

As noted above, the deduction for charitable gifts of property generally is measured by the fair market value of the property. There are, however, limitations that may apply in the case of a contribution of appreciated property, and the amount of the charitable deduction for gifts of such property may have to be reduced.[20] Whether a reduction is necessary and the amount of the reduction depends on the type of property given, the recipient of the property, and the use to which the recipient puts the property. Any reduction in the contribution of appreciated property is applied before the percentage of income limitations contained in Code Sec. 170(b).

¶ 1607.1 *Ordinary Income Property*

In the case of a contribution by an individual or by a corporation of ordinary income property, the charitable contribution deduction must be reduced by the amount of gain that would not have been long-term capital gain if the property had been sold by the donor at its fair market value at the time of its contribution.[21] "Ordinary income property" is property that would produce gain that is not long-term capital gain if sold at its fair market value.[22] In short, the charitable contribution deduction for ordinary income property is limited to the adjusted basis of the property at the time of the gift. The nature of the recipient has no effect on the amount of the allowable deduction.

In the case of real property, ordinary income property would include dealer property (see ¶ 1013), depreciable property that is subject to recapture (see ¶ 1307), and any other property subject to various recapture provisions, including mining and farm property. A real estate broker's charitable contribution deduction for parcels of real estate donated to churches was disallowed because the broker failed to prove the basis in the parcels. The broker's deduction, if allowed, would have been limited to the basis in the parcels because they were part of the real estate business and, if sold at the time of the contribution, would have produced ordinary income as dealer property.[23]

---

[20] Code Sec. 170(e).
[21] Code Sec. 170(e)(1)(A).
[22] Reg. § 1.170A-4(b)(1).
[23] *E.B. Lindsley, Jr.*, 47 TCM 540, CCH Dec. 40,652(M), T.C. Memo. 1983-729.

¶ 1607.2 Capital Gain Property

Capital gain property includes any property on which the taxpayer would realize long-term capital gain if the taxpayer sold the property for its fair market value on the date of the contribution. It also includes property used in a trade or business under Code Sec. 1231(b), to the extent recapture provisions do not apply to convert otherwise capital gain into ordinary income.[24] As a general rule, a taxpayer's deduction for a charitable gift of capital gain property is equal to the property's fair market value. An individual, however, must reduce the charitable contribution deduction for capital gain real property by the amount that would be long-term gain if the real property were sold if:

1. The individual contributes the property to certain private nonoperating foundations,[25] or
2. The individual elects to disregard the special 30 percent of adjusted gross income limitation for capital gain property in favor of the 50 percent limitation.[26]

A corporation that makes a charitable gift of real property to a private nonoperating foundation also must reduce its deduction by the amount that would be long-term gain if the property were sold.

Private nonoperating foundations that require a reduction of charitable gifts of capital gain property by the amount of appreciation include any organization, other than a public charity or a private operating foundation, exempt from tax under Code Sec. 501(c)(3).[27]

¶ 1607.3 Mixed Property

If a taxpayer gives property to charity that would produce both ordinary income and long-term capital gain if sold, then both rules affecting the charitable contribution of appreciated property apply. To determine the deduction, the taxpayer must first reduce the fair market value of the property by the amount that would be ordinary income, then apply the capital gain appreciated property rule.

Example: The Taxpayer, an individual, donates a building with a fair market value of $100,000 to a private nonoperating foundation. At the time of the contribution, the Taxpayer's adjusted basis for the building is $40,000, and there is $12,000 in prior depreciation deductions subject to recapture as ordinary income. The Taxpayer figures the amount of the contribution as follows:

---

[24] Code Sec. 170(e)(1)(B).
[25] Code Sec. 170(e)(1)(B)(ii).
[26] Code Sec. 170(b)(1)(C)(iii).
[27] Code Sec. 170(b)(1)(B).

Fair market value		$100,000
Less:		
Ordinary income	$12,000	
Capital gain	48,000	60,000
Contribution		$ 40,000

The capital gain portion of the contribution equals the fair market value of the property less the Taxpayer's adjusted basis and gain subject to recapture ($100,000 − $40,000 − $12,000 = $48,000). Since the Taxpayer's contribution is of capital gain property to a private nonoperating foundation, the Taxpayer could deduct the $40,000 contribution for the current year only to the extent that it did not exceed 20 percent of adjusted gross income,[28] rather than the 50 percent of adjusted gross income limitation that generally applies to individual charitable contributions.

¶ 1609 Gifts of Partial Interests

If a taxpayer gives less than the entire interest in property to charity, the taxpayer generally is not entitled to a charitable deduction for the contribution.[29] Exceptions apply to transfers in trust that meet special requirements,[30] and to transfers not in trust to the extent that the value of the interest would be deductible if the interest had been transferred in trust.[31] A contribution of the right to use property that the taxpayer owns, for instance, the rent-free use of an office, is treated as a contribution of less than the taxpayer's entire interest in property.[32]

The purpose of the rule is to prevent a double tax benefit that might occur in certain situations when a taxpayer gives less than the entire interest in property. For instance, if a taxpayer let a charity use an office in a building rent free, the taxpayer's gross income would be reduced by the rent the taxpayer does not collect on the office and, if a charitable deduction were allowed, by the charitable deduction for the value of the office. Compare this to a cash contribution equal to the value of the rental which produces but a single tax benefit.

There are, however, exceptions to the general rule that denies a charitable deduction for gifts of partial interests not in trust.[33] Specifically, a charitable deduction is allowed for contributions of:

1. An undivided portion of an entire interest in property;
2. A remainder interest in a personal residence or farm; and
3. Qualified real property interests for conservation purposes.

---

[28] Code Sec. 170(b)(1)(D).
[29] Code Sec. 170(f)(3).
[30] Code Sec. 170(f)(2); Reg. § 1.170A-6.
[31] Code Sec. 170(f)(3)(A).
[32] Reg. § 1.170A-7(a)(1).
[33] Code Sec. 170(f)(3)(B).

Each of these exceptions is discussed further below.

The deduction for a charitable contribution of a partial interest in property covered by the exceptions is the fair market value of the partial interest at the time of the contribution.[34] If the contribution is of a remainder interest in real property, straight-line depreciation and depletion must be taken into account in determining value, and the value must be discounted at a rate of 10 percent per annum.[35]

¶ 1609.1   Undivided Portion

A charitable deduction is allowed for contributions not in trust of an undivided portion of the donor's entire interest in property. An undivided portion of a donor's entire interest in property must consist of a fraction or percentage of each and every substantial interest or right owned by the donor in the property and must extend over the entire term of the donor's interest.[36]

Example: The Taxpayer contributes to a charitable organization an undivided one-half interest in 100 acres of land, whereby as tenants in common they share in the economic benefits from the property. The present value of the contributed property is $50,000. The Taxpayer's contribution consists of an undivided portion of the entire interest in the property and, therefore, the Taxpayer is entitled to a charitable deduction of $50,000.

If the Taxpayer had given the charity 50 of the 100 acres instead of an undivided interest in the entire 100 acres, the Taxpayer also would be entitled to a charitable deduction.

Suppose, however, that the Taxpayer only had a life estate in the 100 acres rather than owning the 100 acres outright. In this case, a gift of a one-half interest in the life estate would also qualify for a charitable contribution deduction since the Taxpayer would be giving a undivided portion of the entire interest (a life estate) in the property.

¶ 1609.2   Remainder Interest

The Internal Revenue Code generally does not permit a charitable contribution deduction for remainder interests unless a charitable deduction would be allowed if the charitable gift were given in trust. The only transfers of remainder interests in trust that qualify for a charitable contribution deduction are those in which the annual dollar-amount income interest is payable as a fixed annuity or payable under a trust instrument that provides for the income beneficiaries to receive payments annually, based on a fixed percentage of the net fair market

---

[34] Reg. § 1.170A-7(c).
[35] Reg. § 1.170A-12.
[36] Reg. § 1.170A-7(b)(1)(i).

value of the trust's assets—a charitable remainder annuity trust, a unitrust, or a pooled income fund.[37] Charitable gifts of remainder interests in personal residences and farms, however, are specifically excluded from this rule and a charitable deduction is available for gifts of remainder interests in these properties.[38]

Personal Residence

A charitable deduction is allowed for the value of a charitable contribution of an irrevocable remainder interest in a personal residence that is not the donor's entire interest in the property. For example, if a taxpayer contributes a remainder interest in a personal residence to a charitable organization and retains an estate for life or for a term of years in the residence, the taxpayer may take a charitable deduction for the value of the remainder interest.[39]

A "personal residence" is any property used by the taxpayer as a personal residence, even if it is not used as the taxpayer's principal residence. A contribution of a remainder interest in a vacation home qualifies for a charitable deduction. The term "personal residence" also includes stock owned by a taxpayer as a tenant-stockholder in a cooperative housing corporation if the dwelling which the taxpayer is entitled to occupy as such stockholder is used by the taxpayer as a personal residence.

Farm

A "farm" is any land used by the taxpayer or a tenant for the production of crops, fruits, or other agricultural products or for the sustenance of livestock. Livestock includes cattle, hogs, horses, mules, donkeys, sheep, goats, captive fur-bearing animals, chickens, turkeys, pigeons, and other poultry. A farm also includes the improvements located on the land.[40]

A charitable deduction is allowed for the value of a charitable contribution of an irrevocable remainder interest in a farm that is not the donor's entire interest in the property. For example, if a taxpayer contributes a remainder interest in a farm to a charitable organization and retains an estate for life or for a term of years in the farm, the taxpayer may take a charitable deduction for the value of the remainder interest. The remainder interest does not have to be in the entire farm. The IRS has ruled that a charitable deduction is allowed for a charitable transfer of a remainder interest in part of the donor's pastureland leased to a tenant farmer, even though the donor retained

---

[37] Code Sec. 170(f)(2)(A); Reg. § 1.170A-6.
[38] Code Sec. 170(f)(3)(B)(i).
[39] Reg. § 1.170A-7(b)(3).
[40] Reg. § 1.170A-7(e)(4).

a life interest in the portion donated and in the entire balance of the farm property.[41]

¶ 1609.3 *Conservation Purposes*

A taxpayer who contributes a qualified real property interest to a qualified organization exclusively for a conservation purpose may take a charitable contribution deduction for the interest.[42] Qualified real property interests include:

1. The entire interest of the donor other than a qualified mineral interest,
2. A remainder interest, and
3. A restriction, granted in perpetuity, on the use which may be made of the real property.[43]

If a donor transfers part of an interest in the property to a related person in order to reduce the interest donated or to retain control over more than a qualified mineral interest, the transfer does not qualify as a transfer of the entire interest.[44] Easements and other interests in real property that, under state laws, have similar attributes, such as restrictive covenants, may qualify as restrictions on the use which may be made of the property. The IRS has recognized that a property right exists in air space adjacent to real property. A restrictive easement that limits the height of buildings, if granted in perpetuity and for conservation purposes to a qualified organization, may qualify for a charitable deduction.[45]

The charitable deduction for contributions of real property interests for conservation purposes is limited to contributions to governments and publicly supported charities. Also, an organization that is not itself publicly supported is an eligible recipient if the organization is controlled by a government or publicly supported organization.[46] Generally, the recipient must have a commitment to protect the conservation purposes of the donation and have the resources to enforce the restrictions. Later transfers of the property interest must be to qualified organizations and must be conditioned on the continued use of the property interest for conservation purposes as originally intended.[47]

A contribution made for any one of the following four purposes is made for a conservation purpose:[48]

1. The preservation of land areas for outdoor recreation by, or the education of, the general public. Property that is pre-

---

[41] Rev. Rul. 78-303, 1978-2 CB 122.
[42] Code Secs. 170(f)(3)(B)(iii), 170(h).
[43] Code Sec. 170(h)(2).
[44] Reg. § 1.170A-14(b).
[45] Rev. Rul. 64-205, 1964-2 CB 62.
[46] Code Sec. 170(h)(3).
[47] Reg. § 1.170A-14(c).
[48] Code Sec. 170(h)(4).

served for a water area, boating or fishing, or a nature or hiking trail for use by the public qualifies. The preservation of the area does not meet this test, however, unless the recreation or education is for the substantial and regular use of the general public.[49]

2. The protection of a relatively natural habitat of fish, wildlife, or plants, or similar ecosystem. A contribution qualifies if it operates to protect or enhance the viability of an area or environment in which a fish, wildlife, or plant community normally lives or occurs. This includes areas that have been somewhat altered by human activities if the fish, wildlife, or plants exist there in a relatively natural state. Limitations on public access to the habitat of a threatened species are permissible.[50]

3. The preservation of open space, including farmland and forest land, if the preservation is for the scenic enjoyment of the general public, or made under a clearly delineated federal, state, or local governmental conservation policy, and will yield a significant public benefit. Visual access is sufficient to satisfy the scenic enjoyment requirement. In determining whether the preservation of the open space will yield a significant public benefit, all relevant factors are considered, including: the uniqueness of the property; the intensity of past, present, and projected land development in the area; the consistency of the proposed open space use with public and private conservation programs in the area; the likelihood that development of the property would lead or contribute to degradation of the scenic, natural, or historic character of the area; and the opportunity for the general public to enjoy the use of the property or to appreciate its scenic values.[51]

4. The preservation of a historically important land area or certified historic structure. Historically important land areas include independently significant land areas, such as a Civil War battlefield, and historic sites and related land areas whose physical or environmental features contribute to the historic or cultural importance and continuing integrity of historic structures or districts. In order to deduct a contribution in this category, some visual public access is required. If it is not visible from a public way, the terms of an easement must be such that the general public is given the opportunity on a

---

[49] Reg. § 1.170A-14(d)(3).
[50] *Ibid.*
[51] Reg. § 1.170A-14(d)(4).

regular basis to view the property preserved by the easement.[52]

A contribution for conservation purposes must be *exclusively* for conservation purposes.[53] The conservation purpose must be protected in perpetuity and the contribution must involve legally enforceable restrictions on the interest in the property retained by the donor that would prevent uses inconsistent with the conservation purposes. In the case of remainder interests, a contribution does not qualify if the beneficiary-tenants can use the property in a manner that diminishes the conservation values that are intended to be protected by the contribution.[54] Also, the exclusive conservation purpose requirement is not met if the contribution accomplishes one of the four purposes but also allows uses of the property that would be destructive of other significant conservation purposes.[55]

A taxpayer may not take a deduction for a property interest contributed for conservation purposes if the property is subject to a mortgage, unless the mortgagee subordinates its rights in the property to the right of the charitable organization to enforce the conservation purposes of the gift in perpetuity.[56] Retention of mineral rights, if surface mining may be permitted at any time, defeats the charitable deduction for conservation purposes, unless the method of mining has limited impact on the property and is not irremediably destructive of the conservation purpose.[57] A special rule applies, however, to allow a deduction for a contribution of property in which the ownership of the surface estate and mineral interests has been and remains separated, if the probability of surface mining occurring on the property is so remote as to be negligible.[58]

¶ 1615 GIFTS AND CONTRIBUTIONS OF MORTGAGED PROPERTY

When property subject to a mortgage or other liability is sold, the amount of the debt is treated as part of the amount realized, as discussed at ¶ 1303.2. But what if the property subject to the mortgage or debt is given away to a family member or to charity? Does the amount of the mortgage constitute an amount realized that could trigger a tax on the donor if the debt exceeds the basis for the property? The answer is yes. When property subject to a debt is given away, the transaction is split for tax purposes into a sale part and a gift part.

---

[52] Reg. § 1.170A-14(d)(5).
[53] Code Sec. 170(h)(5).
[54] Reg. § 1.170A-14(g).
[55] Reg. § 1.170A-14(e).

[56] Reg. § 1.170A-14(g)(2).
[57] Code Sec. 170(h)(5)(B); Reg. § 1.170A-14(g)(4).
[58] Code Sec. 170(h)(5)(B)(ii).

The regulations provide that the amount realized from a sale or other disposition of property includes the amount of liabilities from which the transferor is discharged as a result of the sale or disposition.[59] Further, according to the regulations, a disposition of property includes a gift of the property or a transfer of the property in satisfaction of liabilities to which it is subject.[60] The same rationale has been applied in other situations involving the transfer of property without apparent consideration. For instance, a stockholder who conveyed a building to the corporation without consideration but subject to a mortgage in excess of the adjusted basis for the property realized a taxable gain. The mortgaging of the property and its conveyance to the corporation, taken together, constituted a sale.[61]

While gifts of mortgaged property to family and gifts of mortgaged property to charity both can trigger taxable gain, calculation of that gain differs in each case. The difference turns on how basis is applied to reduce the amount realized as a result of the transfer of the mortgaged property.

¶ 1617 Gifts to Family

When the owner of real estate transfers that property subject to a debt, the IRS has substantial authority, in addition to the regulations cited above, for taxing the donor on the difference between the amount of the debts that are assumed by the donee and the donor's adjusted basis for the property, whether or not the donor is personally liable for the debts.

A donor mortgaged farm real estate, used the mortgage proceeds for other business purposes, then transferred the encumbered property to a trust for the benefit of the grandchildren, and the trust assumed primary liability for the unpaid mortgage at a time when the mortgage liability exceeded the donor's basis in the property. The transfer was held to be a gift to the extent of the difference between the value of the property and the amount of the debt, and a taxable sale to the extent of the difference between the mortgage debt and the donor's adjusted basis in the property. According to the court, a part-sale resulted because the donor received valuable consideration, that is, relief from the primary liability for the debt assumed by the trust.[62]

The same rule applies to transfers subject to nonrecourse liabilities. A donor transferred mortgaged real property to a trust as a gift for the benefit of the grandchildren. The Second Circuit ruled that the donor

---

[59] Reg. § 1.1001-2(a)(1).
[60] Reg. § 1.1001-2(a)(4)(iii).
[61] *J.B. Simon*, CA-3, 61-1 USTC ¶ 9136, 285 F.2d 422.
[62] *R.C. Malone*, DC Miss., 71-1 USTC ¶ 9475, 326 F.Supp. 106, aff'd per curiam, CA-5, 72-1 USTC ¶ 9217, 455 F.2d 502.

realized taxable income on the transfer. The taxable income was the difference between the taxpayer's adjusted basis for the real estate and the amount of the nonrecourse mortgages on the property that were transferred to the trust and the amount of liabilities attributable to the property for which the donor was personally liable. The income derived from the nonrecourse loans was taxable under the principles laid down by the Supreme Court in *B.B. Crane*.[63]

Example: The Taxpayer owns real estate that is worth $90,000, but the real estate is subject to a $75,000 mortgage. The Taxpayer gives this property to a son when the adjusted basis for the property is $45,000. This "gift" is, in fact, treated as a part sale and a part gift for income tax purposes. The Taxpayer recognizes income to the extent the liability exceeds the adjusted basis:

Sale Portion:

Amount realized (amount of mortgage)	$75,000
Less adjusted basis	45,000
Gain realized	$30,000

In addition to the taxable gain, the Taxpayer has made a gift equal to the amount by which the value of the property exceeds the liability:

Gift Portion:

Fair market value	$90,000
Less mortgage	75,000
Gift for gift tax purposes	$15,000

Whether the Taxpayer would incur a gift tax liability depends, of course, on the annual and lifetime exclusions still available to the Taxpayer.

If the liability exceeded the value of the property, there would be no "gift" portion of the transfer. Taxpayer would still have taxable income measured by the difference between the adjusted basis and the amount of the liability.

¶ 1619 Charitable Gifts

A transfer of appreciated real property subject to nonrecourse liabilities to a charitable organization was in part a charitable contribution and in part a taxable sale of capital assets. Accordingly, the taxpayer was entitled to a charitable contribution deduction to the extent that the fair market value of the properties exceeded the

---

[63] *B.B. Crane,* S.Ct. 47-1 USTC ¶ 9217, 331 U.S. 1, 67 S.Ct. 1047. *A. Levine, Est.,* CA-2, 80-2 USTC ¶ 9549, 634 F.2d 12; see also the discussion of *Crane* and the discussion of mortgage and basis at ¶ 105.

Contributions and Gifts 571

remaining mortgage indebtedness, but was required to report as capital gain resulting from a bargain sale the amount by which the mortgage indebtedness exceeded the bases in the properties.[64]

The IRS has ruled that a bargain sale to charity occurred when a limited partner donated a partnership interest to charity. The value of the partnership assets at the time of donation exceeded the partner's share of partnership liabilities and a charitable contribution deduction was allowable. Under Code Sec. 1011(b), the amount of the partnership liabilities at the time of transfer constituted an amount realized by the partner. Thus, the partner had a recognized gain on the transfer equal to the excess of the amount realized over that portion of the adjusted basis of the interest allocable to the sale.[65]

Since the charitable donation of property subject to a mortgage or other debt is a bargain sale, the provisions of Code Sec. 1011(b) relating to bargain sales to charitable organizations apply. Under these rules, the donor's basis for the property must be allocated between the gift portion and the sale portion. The IRS explained the rationale in Rev. Rul. 81-163.[66] If property is transferred subject to an indebtedness, the amount of the indebtedness must be treated as an amount realized for determining whether there is a sale or exchange to which Code Sec. 1011(b) applies, even though the transferee does not agree to assume or pay the indebtedness. If a charitable deduction is allowed by reason of a sale, the adjusted basis for determining the gain from the sale is the portion of the adjusted basis of the entire property that bears the same ratio to the adjusted basis as the amount realized bears to the fair market value of the entire property.[67]

> **Example:** The Taxpayer owns real estate that is worth $90,000, but the real estate is subject to a $75,000 mortgage. The Taxpayer gives this property to a charitable organization when the adjusted basis for the property is $45,000. This charitable gift is treated as a part sale and a part gift, but the Taxpayer must allocate the $45,000 basis between the gift portion and the sale portion, based on the value of each. In this case, the gift portion is the $15,000 excess of the value of the property over the mortgage, and the sale portion is the amount of the mortgage, or $75,000. Accordingly, 1/6th of the basis is allocated to the gift portion ($15,000/$90,000

---

[64] *W.F.C. Guest*, 77 TC 9, CCH Dec. 38,037, Acq. 1982-1 CB 1; see also *L.G. Ebben*, CA-9, 86-1 USTC ¶ 9250, 783 F.2d 906, in which a partnership that transferred encumbered appreciated property to a charitable organization was held to realize capital gain from the transaction equal to the amount by which the mortgage indebtedness exceeded the partnership's adjusted basis in the property. The Court held that, based on *Guest*, such a charitable contribution, which entailed relief from nonrecourse indebtedness, constituted a sale.

[65] Rev. Rul. 75-194, 1975-1 CB 80.
[66] 1981-1 CB 43.
[67] Code Sec. 1011(b); Reg. § 1.1011-2(b).

¶ 1619

× $45,000 basis = $7,500), and 5/6ths of the basis is allocated to the sale portion ($75,000/$90,000 × $45,000 = $37,500).

The Taxpayer's income from this charitable gift of mortgaged property is, therefore, $37,500 ($75,000 amount realized − $37,500 adjusted basis = $37,500). The gift portion, valued at $15,000 with a basis of $7,500, may result in a charitable contribution deduction. The amount of the deduction depends on the type of property, the type of charity, and the Taxpayer's income and other charitable gifts. In other words, the deduction is subject to the charitable deduction rules discussed at ¶ 1613 for charitable contributions that do not involve a bargain sale.

Formerly, the regulations required that the charitable deduction be reduced by 100 percent of the unrealized appreciation inherent in the entire property following a bargain sale when the rules applicable to charitable contributions of appreciated property, as discussed above, required such a reduction. The Tax Court, however, ruled that taxpayers who sold their interest in a medical center for less than its fair market value, and who applied the "appreciation reduction rules" with respect to the portion of the capital gain property contributed in the bargain sale, properly reduced their contribution deduction by the unrealized appreciation of only the contributed portion of the property.[68] According to the Court, the regulations, as they existed at that time, led to inequitable results. Not only did the regulations improperly reduce the contribution by 100 percent of the gain on the contributed property, but they put the taxpayer in a less favorable position than if the taxpayer had sold the property and then donated a portion of the proceeds. The regulations were amended as a result of the Tax Court decision.[69]

¶ 1625   GIFTS OF LOSS PROPERTY

Generally speaking, the Internal Revenue Code prevents taxpayers from making a gift of a loss to another taxpayer. Under the basis rules discussed at ¶ 101, the basis of property acquired by gift is generally the same basis that the property had in the hands of the donor immediately before the gift. This general rule, however, does not apply to gifts of property when the fair market value of the property is less than the donor's basis for the property. If the donor's basis is greater than the fair market value of the property at the time of the gift, then for the purpose of determining loss, the basis is the fair market value.[70]

---

[68] *P.E. Bullard Est.*, 87 TC 261, CCH Dec. 43,227.
[69] Reg. § 1.170-A, amended by T.D. 8176, 1988-1 CB 94.
[70] Code Sec. 1015.

As a result of this basis rule, a gift of loss property can be very costly from a taxpayer's point of view. Since the donee cannot benefit from the potential loss on the property in the hands of the donor, the gift of loss property results in the potential loss deduction simply vanishing. If a donor gives property worth less than its basis to a donee, the potential loss cannot be taken by the donor or the donee. A donor considering a gift of loss property should consider a sale of the property and a gift of the proceeds rather than a gift of the property. The sale of the property at a loss would allow the donor to benefit from the loss deduction. At the same time, the donee would receive the same benefit as if the donee had received the property and then sold it for its fair market value.

Example: The Taxpayer owns land and a building in a declining part of town. The land and building are worth only $50,000, although the Taxpayer's adjusted basis for the property is $75,000. If the Taxpayer gives the property to a son and the son sells it for its fair market value of $50,000, the son has neither a gain nor a loss on the sale. Under the usual basis rule, the son's basis for the property would be $75,000, the same basis the Taxpayer had immediately before the gift. Use of this basis by the son would result in a loss, however, so the son must use the fair market value of the property on the date of the gift, or $50,000, as the basis. The Taxpayer's $25,000 potential loss on the building simply disappears when the Taxpayer makes a gift of the property to the son.

On the other hand, if the Taxpayer sells the property for $50,000 and gives the proceeds of the sale to the son, the Taxpayer may benefit from the $25,000 loss. If the property qualifies as Code Sec. 1231 property, the Taxpayer may use the loss to offset ordinary income without limitation. Meanwhile, the son receives the same $50,000 he would get if the Taxpayer made a gift of the building rather than the proceeds of the sale of the building.

¶ 1625

Part V

Personal Residences

Introduction to Part V

Ownership of a personal residence is favored by the tax law. The owner of a home is afforded advantages not given to the occupant of a rented residential apartment. For example, the owner of a home may deduct property taxes and mortgage interest on the personal income tax return. The renter, however, may not deduct any portion of the rental payments, even though some of the rent is used by the landlord to pay property taxes and interest on a mortgage.

The various itemized deductions to which a homeowner is entitled, however, are only one way in which a taxpayer's ownership of a personal residence affects taxes. The sale of a personal residence may produce gain. In most cases, however, the tax on all or part of this gain may be avoided altogether.

These, then, are the primary topics of the following four chapters of Part V. Chapter 17 examines the deductions available to all homeowners. Chapter 18 looks at the additional deductions available when a homeowner uses a personal residence in part for business. Special considerations for cooperative and condominium ownership are found in Chapter 19. Finally, the sale of a personal residence, including the avoidance or postponement of tax, is the topic of Chapter 20.

Chapter 17

Deductions for Homeowners

¶ 1700 OVERVIEW OF CHAPTER

Many homeowners find that it is advantageous to itemize deductions rather than to take the standard deduction. In most cases, the largest deductions occur in the early years of ownership, when the bulk of each mortgage payment is attributable to interest. Most homeowners may deduct for federal income tax purposes the full amount of interest on their home mortgages paid during the year. Also, local property tax on a personal residence is deductible; but if it is paid through an escrow or similar arrangement, it is deductible only when the money is actually turned over to the taxing authority. Homeowners also may deduct, within certain limitations, casualty losses to their homes.

¶ 1701 MORTGAGE INTEREST

Generally, a noncorporate taxpayer may not deduct personal interest.[1] Personal interest does not include any of the following:

1. Interest paid or accrued on debt allocable to a trade or business, other than performing services as an employee;
2. Investment interest;
3. Interest taken into account in computing income or loss from a passive activity;
4. Qualified residence interest; and
5. Interest on the unpaid portion of the estate tax for the period during which there is an extension of time for payment on the value of a reversionary or remainder interest in property or when the estate consists largely of an interest in a closely held business.[2]

The deduction of interest in connection with real estate other than a qualified personal residence is considered at ¶ 321. Also, interest on a personal residence that exceeds the limitations discussed at ¶ 1703.2 may be subject to the tracing rules discussed at ¶ 325.3 to determine whether or not it is deductible as some other category of interest.

---

[1] Code Sec. 163(h)(1). [2] Code Sec. 163(h)(2).

¶ 1703 Qualified Residence Interest

In most cases, homeowners may deduct all of their home mortgage interest. Specifically, a homeowner may deduct interest on a home mortgage that falls within one or more of the following categories:[3]

1. Acquisition debt that does not exceed $1 million, including pre-October 14, 1987 debt ($500,000 in the case of married taxpayers filing separate returns);

2. Home equity debt, other than acquisition debt, that does not exceed $100,000 ($50,000 in the case of married taxpayers filing separate returns); and

3. Mortgages taken before October 14, 1987.

All of these categories are specifically discussed below.

¶ 1703.1 *Qualified Residence Defined*

A taxpayer may deduct interest on a mortgage on a personal residence which falls within the three categories set out above only if the personal residence is a "qualified residence." A qualified residence is the taxpayer's principal residence and one other residence, such as a vacation home, selected by the taxpayer. The home that the taxpayer selects to treat as a second residence must be used by the taxpayer for personal purposes for 14 days during the year or, if greater, 10 percent of the number of days that the second residence is rented.[4] If the taxpayer does not rent a dwelling unit at any time during the year, the unit may be treated as a residence even if it is not used by the taxpayer for 14 days.[5]

A taxpayer cannot have more than one principal residence and more than one second residence which qualifies for the interest deduction at one time.[6] Residence is broadly defined to include much more than the traditional single family home or condominium. According to the regulations, whether property is a residence is determined based on all the facts and circumstances, including the good faith of the taxpayer. A residence may be a house, condominium, mobile home, boat, or house trailer that contains sleeping space and toilet and cooking facilities.[7] Under this provision, many taxpayers are able to deduct interest paid on a boat loan or recreational vehicle loan.

---

[3] Code Sec. 163(h)(3).
[4] Code Sec. 163(h)(4)(A).
[5] Code Sec. 163(h)(4)(A)(iii).
[6] Temp. Reg. § 1.163-10T(p)(1).
[7] Temp. Reg. § 1.163-10T(p)(3)(ii).

Residence Under Construction

A taxpayer may treat a residence under construction as a qualified residence for up to 24 months, but only if the residence becomes a qualified residence once it is ready for occupancy.[8]

Example: The Taxpayer owns a residential lot on which a vacation home will be built. On April 20, 2002, the Taxpayer obtained a mortgage secured by the lot and the property to be constructed on the lot and began construction of the vacation home on August 9, 2002. The residence will be ready for occupancy on November 9, 2004, and the Taxpayer elects to treat this vacation home as a second qualified residence for the period November 9, 2004, through December 31, 2004.

Since the residence under construction is a qualified residence as of the first day that it is ready for occupancy, the Taxpayer may treat the residence as a second residence for up to 24 months of the period during which the residence is under construction. If the Taxpayer treats the residence under construction as a qualified residence beginning with the date construction was started, August 9, 2002, the residence under construction would cease to be a qualified residence on August 8, 2004, until construction is complete and the Taxpayer elects to treat the completed vacation home as a qualified residence.

Married Individuals

If a married couple files separate returns, the couple is treated as one taxpayer for determining whether a residence is a qualified residence. Each may take into account only one of the two qualified residences permitted, unless both consent in writing to allow one spouse to take both the principal and the second residence into account.[9]

¶ 1703.2 *Acquisition Indebtedness*

Acquisition indebtedness is debt that is incurred to acquire, construct, or substantially improve a qualified residence and that is secured by the qualified residence.[10] The aggregate amount of acquisition indebtedness for which a taxpayer may take an interest deduction is limited to $1,000,000 ($500,000 in the case of a married individual filing a separate return).[11] As discussed at ¶ 1703.4, debt incurred and secured by a qualified residence before October 14, 1987, is not subject to the $1,000,000 limitation, but the debt does reduce the amount of the $1,000,000 limitation allowed for other acquisition debt.

---

[8] Temp. Reg. § 1.163-10T(p)(5).
[9] Code Sec. 163(h)(4)(ii).
[10] Code Sec. 163(h)(3)(B)(i).
[11] Code Sec. 163(h)(3)(B)(ii).

In Notice 88-74,[12] the IRS has provided guidance on the home mortgage interest deduction for acquisition indebtedness. According to the IRS, regulations will provide two tests to determine if debt qualifies as acquisition indebtedness. First, debt may qualify as acquisition indebtedness to the extent that the proceeds are used, within the meaning of the tracing rules of Temp. Reg. § 1.163-8T, to acquire, construct, or substantially improve the residence.[13] Secondly, a debt may qualify as acquisition indebtedness if it is incurred within a prescribed time period, that is, it meets the 90-day rules.[14]

Tracing Rules

In general, interest expense is allocated in the same manner in which the debt that gave rise to the payment or accrual of interest is allocated. Debt is allocated under a tracing method that links the debt proceeds to the types of expenditures for which the proceeds are used.[15]

90-Day Rules

Regardless of the tracing rules, debt may be treated as incurred to acquire a residence to the extent of expenditures to acquire the residence made within 90 days before or after the date that the debt is incurred.

In the case of construction or substantial improvement of a residence, debt incurred prior to the time the residence or improvements are complete may be treated as being incurred to construct or improve the residence to the extent that the expenditures were made no more than 24 months prior to the date that the debt is incurred. Debt incurred no later than the date 90 days after the residence or improvements are complete may be treated as qualified debt to the extent of any expenditures made within the 24-month period prior to the date of completion and ending on the date the debt is incurred.[16]

Debt is incurred on the date that the loan proceeds are disbursed to, or for the benefit of, the taxpayer, that is, generally on the loan closing date. A taxpayer, however, may treat the debt as incurred when written application is made to incur the debt, but only to the extent that the debt proceeds are actually disbursed within a reasonable time after approval of the application. Debt proceeds disbursed within 30 days after approval of the application are disbursed within a reasonable time. Regulations will provide that if a written application is made for a debt within the requisite time period and the application is rejected, a reasonable additional time period will be allowed to make a new application for the debt. The rule that a taxpayer may treat debt

---

[12] 1988-2 CB 385.
[13] Temp. Reg. § 1.163-8T, is discussed in detail at ¶ 325.3.
[14] Notice 88-74, 1988-2 CB 385.
[15] The tracing rules are discussed at ¶ 325.3.
[16] Notice 88-74, 1988-2 CB 385.

¶ 1703.2

as incurred on the date that a written application for the loan is made does not apply, however, when determining whether a debt was incurred before October 13, 1987.

Refinancing

If a taxpayer incurs a debt that is treated as incurred to acquire, construct or substantially improve a residence under either the tracing rules or the 90-day rules, and later incurs a second debt, the second debt may be treated as incurred to acquire, construct or substantially improve the residence if the proceeds of the second debt are used to refinance the first debt. Whether the second debt is used to refinance the first debt is determined under the tracing rules of Temp. Reg. § 1.163-8T.

Debt Partially Acquisition and Indebtedness

Regulations will provide that a single debt may qualify as partially acquisition and partially home equity indebtedness. For example, if a taxpayer incurs a debt secured by a qualified residence, uses a portion of the debt proceeds to refinance an existing acquisition indebtedness, and uses the remaining portion for purposes other than home improvement, the portion of the debt used to refinance the acquisition indebtedness will qualify as acquisition indebtedness, and the portion of the debt used for other purposes will generally qualify as home equity debt. The limitation on home equity debt is discussed at ¶ 1703.3.

The following examples illustrate the application of the rules on acquisition indebtedness.

Comprehensive Example 1: The Taxpayer incurs a debt of $100,000 and uses the proceeds under the tracing rules to purchase a residential lot on January 15, 2002. The debt is secured by the lot. On January 1, 2003, the Taxpayer begins construction of a residence on the lot and uses $250,000 of unborrowed funds to construct the residence. The residence is complete on December 31, 2004, and becomes the Taxpayer's principal residence at that time. On March 15, 2005, the Taxpayer incurs a debt of $300,000 secured by the residence. The lender on the second debt disburses $100,000 to pay off the existing debt and disburses the remaining $200,000 directly to the Taxpayer.

The $100,000 debt the Taxpayer incurred in 2002 was incurred to construct the residence because the proceeds of the debt are directly traceable to expenditures to construct the residence, that is, the purchase of the lot. From January 15, 2002, through December 31, 2002, the Taxpayer may not treat the debt as acquisition indebtedness because it is not secured by a qualified

¶ 1703.2

residence. From January 1, 2003, through December 30, 2004, the Taxpayer may treat the residence under construction as a qualified residence, and, therefore, the debt may qualify as acquisition indebtedness. From December 31, 2004, through March 15, 2005, the residence is a qualified residence and the debt qualifies as acquisition indebtedness.

The Taxpayer also incurred the $300,000 debt to construct the residence—$100,000 because the Taxpayer used this amount to refinance debt incurred to construct the residence, and the remaining $200,000 because the Taxpayer incurred the debt within 90 days after the residence was complete and incurred construction expenditures of at least this amount within the period beginning 24 months before the residence was complete and ending when the debt was incurred. The entire $300,000 debt is acquisition indebtedness because it is also secured by a qualified residence. Therefore, the Taxpayer may deduct all of the interest on the debt as qualified residence interest.

Comprehensive Example 2: Assume the same facts as in Example 1, except that rather than borrowing to purchase the lot, the Taxpayer uses cash to purchase the lot. In this case, since the Taxpayer did not use any of the $300,000 debt to refinance a debt incurred to construct a qualified residence, the Taxpayer may treat the debt as incurred to construct a qualified residence only to the extent of the $250,000 in expenditures incurred during the period beginning 24 months before the residence was complete and ending when the debt was incurred. The Taxpayer spent the $100,000 to purchase the lot before this period and, therefore, cannot treat the debt as incurred for this purpose.

Accordingly, the Taxpayer may treat $250,000 of the March 15, 2005, debt as incurred to construct the residence and as acquisition debt. Because the debt is secured by a qualified residence, the remaining $50,000 of the debt qualifies as home equity indebtedness. Therefore, the Taxpayer may deduct all of the interest on the $300,000 debt as qualified residence interest.

¶ 1703.3 Home Equity Debt

Home equity indebtedness is debt, other than acquisition indebtedness, that is secured by a taxpayer's qualified residence. Interest on qualifying home equity indebtedness is deductible regardless of the use made of the proceeds. Qualifying home equity indebtedness may not exceed the fair market value of the residence securing the debt reduced by any acquisition indebtedness on the residence.[17] Also, the aggregate

---

[17] Code Sec. 163(h)(3)(C)(i).

amount of home equity indebtedness for which interest is deductible as qualified residence interest is limited to $100,000 ($50,000 in the case of married taxpayers filing separate returns).[18]

¶ 1703.4 *Pre-1987 Indebtedness*

Debt that a taxpayer incurred before October 14, 1987, and that is secured by a qualified residence is treated as acquisition indebtedness that is not subject to the $1,000,000 limitation. Interest on these loans is deductible regardless of the amount of the loan.[19] The amount of pre-October 14, 1987 indebtedness, however, does reduce the amount of the $1,000,000 limitation on new acquisition debt.[20] Pre-October 14, 1987 debt includes debt incurred before that date that is secured by a qualified residence on October 13, 1987, and at all times thereafter before interest is paid or accrued.[21] It also includes debt incurred after October 13, 1987, that is used to refinance pre-October 14, 1987 debt.[22]

Refinancing

If a taxpayer had a mortgage on a qualified residence on October 13, 1987, and refinances it after that date for no more than the balance of the existing mortgage, the taxpayer may continue to treat all of the new mortgage as pre-October 14, 1987 indebtedness. However, if the refinancing is for more than the balance of the existing mortgage, only the part of the new mortgage equal to the balance of the old mortgage at the time of refinancing is treated as pre-October 14, 1987 debt. The amount of the new mortgage that is in excess of the balance of the existing mortgage is either acquisition indebtedness or home equity indebtedness, or a combination of the two, and subject to the limitations that apply to post-October 13, 1987 debt.

Any refinancing may not extend the term of the debt beyond the term of the debt immediately before the refinancing. If the principal amount of the old debt was amortized over its life, the taxpayer may deduct all of the interest paid during what would have been the life of the old debt. Any interest the taxpayer pays after this period is personal interest.[23] If the principal amount of the old debt was not amortized over the life of the debt (for example, a balloon mortgage) the taxpayer may deduct the interest paid during the life of the new debt, up to a maximum of 30 years.[24]

---

[18] Code Sec. 163(h)(3)(C)(ii).
[19] Code Sec. 163(h)(3)(D)(i).
[20] Code Sec. 163(h)(3)(D)(ii).
[21] Code Sec. 163(h)(3)(D)(iii)(I).
[22] Code Sec. 163(h)(3)(D)(iii)(II).
[23] Code Sec. 163(h)(3)(D)(iv)(I).
[24] Code Sec. 163(h)(3)(D)(iv)(II).

Line of Credit

A taxpayer who had a line-of-credit mortgage on a qualified residence on October 13, 1987, and who borrows additional amounts on the line of credit after that date, cannot treat the new amounts borrowed as pre-October 14, 1987 debt. The additional amounts borrowed against the line of credit are treated as debts incurred after October 13, 1987, and are subject to the $1,000,000 limitation on acquisition indebtedness and the $100,000 limitation on home equity indebtedness.

¶ 1705 Points

"Points" is the term generally applied to charges paid by a borrower at the inception of a loan. These charges may also be called loan origination fees, maximum loan charges, or premium charges. If the payment of points is only for the use of money, it is interest and is treated as such for federal tax purposes. Note that the term "points" also may be applied to fees that a seller of property must pay to arrange financing for a buyer. The seller does not treat these points as interest, but rather treats them as a selling expense that reduces the amount realized from the sale.[25]

When points qualify as interest, the amount is prepaid interest. As a general rule, prepaid interest may not be deducted in the year paid, but must be deducted over the life of the loan.[26] There is an exception, however, for points paid by a taxpayer in connection with a loan to buy or improve his principal residence.[27] In order for the exception to apply and for points to be currently deductible in full, all of the following conditions must be met:

1. The payment of points must be an established business practice in the area where the loan is made;

2. The points paid must not exceed the amount generally charged in the area where the loan is made; and

3. The funds provided by the buyer, plus any points the seller paid, are at least as much as the points charged. (The buyer's funds do not have to be applied to the points, but the buyer cannot borrow the funds from the lender.)

The exception does not apply to points paid in connection with a loan on a second or vacation home.

---

[25] Rev. Rul. 68-650, 1968-2 CB 78.
[26] Code Sec. 461(g)(1).
[27] Code Sec. 461(g)(2).

¶ 1705.1 Points Charged for Services

Points charged for specific services by the lender for the borrower's account are not interest. To be deductible as interest, points must be paid as compensation to the lender solely for the use or forbearance of money.[28] Examples of fees for services not considered interest are the lender's appraisal fee, preparation costs for the mortgage note or deed of trust, settlement fees, and notary fees.[29] Points paid by the borrower to obtain a VA mortgage is a service charge and is not interest.[30]

Example: The Taxpayer borrowed $96,000 to buy a $120,000 principal residence. The Taxpayer paid the lender, in addition to interest on the loan at 10.75 percent, a loan processing fee of $2,880 (three points). No portion of the fee was for specific services, charging points was an established local business practice, and the amount paid was not more than the fee customarily charged. If the Taxpayer paid the points from separate funds, $2,880 may be deducted as interest on the residence for the year of payment.

¶ 1705.2 Refinancing

Points paid in refinancing a mortgage are not deductible in full in the year paid, regardless of how the taxpayer arranges to pay them. According to the IRS, points paid to refinance an existing home mortgage are for repaying the taxpayer's existing indebtedness and are not paid in connection with the purchase or improvement of the home. Points paid on refinancing generally must be deducted ratably over the period of the loan.[31] The IRS has spelled out the method of ratable allocation of points over the life of a loan in Rev. Proc. 87-15.[32]

If part of the proceeds from a refinancing are used to improve a taxpayer's principal residence, the taxpayer may deduct a portion of the points for the tax year paid.[33]

Example 1: In 1996, the Taxpayer secured a mortgage for the purchase of a home. On July 1, 2002, the Taxpayer, who uses the cash method of accounting, refinanced this mortgage with a 15-year $100,000 mortgage loan. In order to obtain this loan, the Taxpayer was required to pay four points ($4,000), consisting of three points ($3,000) for prepaid interest and one point ($1,000) for fees charged for the lender's services. The Taxpayer paid the

---

[28] Rev. Rul. 69-188, 1969-1 CB 54, as amended by Rev. Rul. 69-0582, 1969-2 CB 29.
[29] *L.E. Lay,* 69 TC 421, CCH Dec. 34,782; *R.C. Goodwin,* 75 TC 424, CCH Dec. 37,502; *D.L. Wilkerson,* 70 TC 240, CCH Dec. 35,156, Acq. 1982-2 CB 2 and Nonacq. 1982-2 CB 2, rev'd and rem'd on another issue 81-2 USTC ¶ 9657, 655 F.2d 980.
[30] Rev. Rul. 67-297, 1967-2 CB 87.
[31] IR-News Release 86-68, May 13, 1986.
[32] 1987-1 CB 248.
[33] Rev. Rul. 87-22, 1987-1 CB 196.

$4,000 out of private funds. Payment of points was an established practice, and four points were generally charged in the area. The Taxpayer made six payments on the loan in 2002.

The Taxpayer used the funds obtained from the new mortgage to repay an existing indebtedness. Although the new mortgage loan was incurred in connection with the Taxpayer's continued ownership of a principal residence, the new mortgage was not incurred in connection with the purchase or improvement of that residence. Therefore, the Taxpayer cannot deduct all of the points for 2002. The Taxpayer can deduct three points ($3,000) ratably over the life of the loan, which works out to $100 for 2002 ($3,000 divided by 180 payments over the life of the loan times six payments in 2002). The other point ($1,000) is not deductible as a fee for services.

Example 2: Assume the same facts as in Example 1, except that the Taxpayer used $25,000 of the loan proceeds to improve the home. Because the Taxpayer paid the points in 2002, the Taxpayer is allowed to deduct 25 percent of the three points that represent prepaid interest attributable to the portion of the loan used for home improvement for 2002. This amount is $750 ($3,000 prepaid interest × $25,000/$100,000 = $750).

In addition, the Taxpayer can deduct for 2002 the ratable part of the $2,250 ($3,000 prepaid interest − $750 attributable to home improvement) that must be spread over the life of the loan. This amount is $75 (($2,250/180) × 6 = $75).

Example 3: Assume the same facts as in Example 2, except that the Taxpayer did not pay the points out of private funds. Rather, the lender deducted the points from the loan proceeds. Since the Taxpayer did not actually pay the points, the Taxpayer cannot deduct for 2002 the portion of the three points that is attributable to the part of the loan used for home improvement. The Taxpayer can deduct the entire amount of the three points ratably over the 15-year life of the loan.

¶ 1707 Special Mortgage Situations

Financing for a residence may take forms other than fixed or variable rate loans. Also, a homeowner may receive payments from others toward mortgage costs. These special situations may affect the amount and timing of the deduction for qualified residence interest.

¶ 1707.1 Redeemable Ground Rents

A redeemable ground rent is treated by the Internal Revenue Code as in the nature of a mortgage and real property held subject to liabilities under a redeemable ground rent is treated as held subject to liabilities under a mortgage.[34] Taxpayers who make annual or periodic payments on a redeemable ground rent treat those payments as interest.[35] Accordingly, the payments under a redeemable ground rent are subject to the rules on qualified residence interest.

A ground rent is a redeemable ground rent if:

1. There is a lease of land for a term of more than 15 years, including renewal periods, and the lease is assignable by the lessee without the consent of the lessor;
2. The lessee has a present or future right to, under state or local law, terminate the lease and buy the lessor's entire interest in the land by paying a specific amount; and
3. The lessor's interest in the land is primarily a security interest to protect the rental payments to which the lessor is entitled.[36]

The lessee's right to terminate the lease and acquire the lessor's interest must be granted by state or local law. If the right exists solely by virtue of a private agreement or privately created condition, the ground rent is not a "redeemable ground rent." Payments made by the lessee to terminate the lease and to actually acquire the land are not ground rents, and the lessee may not deduct them as interest.

Payments on a nonredeemable ground rent are not interest and are not deductible unless the rent is for property used in a trade or business or held for the production of income.

¶ 1707.2 Shared Appreciation Mortgage (SAM)

Under a shared appreciation mortgage, SAM for short, the borrower pays a fixed rate of interest plus contingent interest to the lender. The contingent interest is a percentage of any appreciation in the value of the property that secures the loan and is due when the SAM terminates. Generally, monthly payments under a SAM include interest at a fixed rate. The fixed interest portion is deductible when paid by a cash basis taxpayer, subject to the limitations on qualified residence interest. The contingent interest portion is also deductible for the year paid, again subject to the qualified residence limitations.[37]

If a cash basis borrower refinances a SAM with the same lender and the face amount of the new loan includes contingent interest, the contingent interest is not deductible at that time. Rather, the borrower may deduct the contingent interest as it is paid over the term of the new mortgage.

---

[34] Code Sec. 1055(a).
[35] Code Sec. 163(c).
[36] Code Sec. 1055(c); Reg. § 1.1055-1(b).
[37] Rev. Rul. 83-51, 1983-1 CB 48.

Example: In 1997, the Taxpayer purchased a principal residence for $125,000 and financed the purchase with a 30-year, $100,000 SAM. Under the terms of the SAM, the Taxpayer must pay the lender 40 percent of the appreciation on the residence when the Taxpayer pays off the loan or sells the home, or in 10 years, if earlier. The Taxpayer sells the residence in 2003 for $155,000 and pays off the principal on the mortgage plus $12,000 contingent interest (40 percent of the $30,000 appreciation). The Taxpayer may deduct the $12,000 paid in 2003 as qualified residence interest. The result is the same if the Taxpayer pays off the SAM with funds obtained from a source other than the original SAM lender. If the Taxpayer simply refinanced the SAM through the same lender, the contingent interest would not be deductible in 2003, but only as the new mortgage is paid off.

¶ 1707.3 Mortgage Interest Credit

Low-income homeowners who obtained qualified mortgage credit certificates from state or local government may claim a tax credit during any year for which the certificate is in effect for a portion of the interest paid on the mortgage. A mortgage credit certificate is in effect for interest from the date a certificate is issued until it is either revoked by the issuing authority or until the taxpayer sells the residence or stops using it as a personal residence.[38] If a taxpayer takes this credit, the taxpayer must reduce the deduction for mortgage interest by the amount of the credit.[39]

¶ 1707.4 Housing Allowances and Assistance Payments

Ministers and military personnel may deduct home mortgage interest on their homes, subject to the limitations on qualified residence interest, even though they receive a parsonage or military allowance that they may exclude from gross income.[40] Military personnel include all branches of the armed forces, the National Oceanic and Atmospheric Administration, and the Public Health Service. Eligible members of these services are entitled to receive tax-free housing and subsistence allowances if they do not reside on a federal base.[41]

On the other hand, recipients of mortgage assistance payments under Section 235 of the National Housing Act do not include the payments in income,[42] and may not deduct interest on their mortgages to the extent it is paid for them.[43] These payments, however, do not reduce other deductions, such as for real estate taxes.

---

[38] Code Sec. 25.
[39] Code Sec. 163(g).
[40] Code Sec. 265(a)(6).
[41] Reg. § 1.61-2(b).
[42] Rev. Rul. 75-271, 1975-2 CB 23.
[43] Reg. § 1.163-1(d).

¶ 1707.5 Payment Penalties

A taxpayer who pays off a mortgage early may have to pay a prepayment penalty. Such a penalty is deductible as home mortgage interest if it otherwise qualifies.[44]

A taxpayer may deduct a late payment charge or penalty on a home mortgage as mortgage interest, provided the charge is not for specific services performed by the lender.[45]

¶ 1709 REAL ESTATE TAXES

Homeowners may deduct state and local real property taxes as an itemized deduction on their personal tax returns.[46] The term "real property taxes" means taxes imposed on interests in real property and levied for the general public welfare, but it does not include taxes assessed against local benefits or payments for specific services.[47] For a complete discussion of the differences between deductible real property taxes and assessments against local benefits, see ¶ 741. For the apportionment of real estate taxes on the purchase or sale of real estate, see ¶ 119.

Many homeowners pay their real property taxes through an escrow arrangement with their mortgage lender, that is, they make monthly payments to their lender that represent about 1/12th of the annual real estate taxes. The payment of these amounts in escrow is not the payment of the taxes themselves since the mortgagee is acting as the agent of the homeowner. The deduction for real estate taxes for a cash basis homeowner arises only when the mortgagee pays the money over to the taxing authority from the escrow account.[48]

Annual assessments paid to homeowners' associations to maintain common areas and to promote the welfare of residents are not deductible as real estate taxes.[49]

¶ 1711 CASUALTY LOSSES

Losses to a taxpayer's home, household goods, and personal property generally are deductible for federal tax purposes. For the most part, the rules that apply to business casualties as discussed at ¶ 1501 apply to nonbusiness casualties as well. These rules include those concerning:

1. The definition of a casualty loss;

---

[44] Rev. Rul. 57-198, 1957-1 CB 97.
[45] Rev. Rul. 74-187, 1974-1 CB 48; Rev. Rul. 67-297, 1967-2 CB 87.
[46] Code Sec. 164(a)(1).
[47] Reg. § 1.164-3(b).
[48] Rev. Rul. 78-103, 1978-1 CB 58; see also *United Mercantile Agencies, Inc.*, 23 TC 1105, CCH Dec. 20,940, Acq. 1955-2 CB 9, rem'd sub nom *F.W. Drybrough*, CA-6, 57-1 USTC ¶ 9212, 238 F.2d 735; *F.J. Hradesky*, 65 TC 87, CCH Dec. 33,461, aff'd CA-5, 76-2 USTC ¶ 9703, 540 F.2d 821.
[49] Rev. Rul. 76-495, 1976-2 CB 43.

2. The effect of a casualty loss on basis;
3. The determination of the amount of a casualty loss or gain;
4. The postponement of a taxable casualty gain through the purchase of replacement property; and
5. The early deduction of disaster area losses.

The nonbusiness casualty loss deduction, however, is subject to a $100 "deductible" and is further limited to 10 percent of a taxpayer's adjusted gross income.[50]

¶ 1713 Limitations

The deduction of nonbusiness casualty and theft losses is subject to two limitations. The first $100 of a casualty or theft loss is not allowable as a deduction. A separate $100 reduction applies to each individual casualty. After the $100 reduction for each casualty, total nonbusiness casualty losses may be deducted only to the extent they exceed 10 percent of the taxpayer's adjusted gross income.

¶ 1713.1 Deductible for Losses

The first $100 of a casualty or theft loss on nonbusiness property is not deductible.[51] This $100 reduction for each casualty applies after any reimbursement for the loss, such as from insurance, is taken into account.[52]

Example 1: The Taxpayer has a $250 deductible insurance policy on a home. The home is damaged in a windstorm and the insurance company pays the Taxpayer for the damage, less the $250 deductible. The Taxpayer's casualty loss deduction following the windstorm and insurance reimbursement is limited to $150 (before applying the 10 percent of adjusted gross income limitation discussed at ¶ 1713.2). The first $100 of unreimbursed casualty loss on nonbusiness property is not deductible.

The $100 reduction applies to each individual casualty or theft, regardless of the number of items or parcels of property damaged or lost through the same casualty or theft. According to the regulations, events closely related in origin are considered a single event. There is a single casualty when the damage is from two or more closely related causes, such as wind and flood damage from the same hurricane. A single casualty may also damage two or more widely separated pieces of property, for instance, the same severe storm may damage a taxpayer's home and a personal auto that is parked at the taxpayer's place of employment many miles away.[53]

---

[50] Code Sec. 165(h).
[51] Code Sec. 165(h)(1).
[52] Reg. § 1.165-7(b)(4)(i).
[53] Reg. § 1.165-7(b)(4)(ii).

Example 2: Hurricane Donna damages the Taxpayer's home, which is located about 20 miles from the coast. The hurricane also destroys the Taxpayer's pleasure boat, which is kept at a marina in a resort town on the coast. The damage to the Taxpayer's home is $6,700, and insurance covers $5,100 of this loss. The boat cost $12,000 when it was purchased several years ago, but the fair market value was $7,000 when it was destroyed. The Taxpayer carried no insurance on the boat. The Taxpayer's total casualty loss from hurricane Donna is $8,600 ($1,600 unreimbursed damage to the home and the $7,000 loss on the boat). The Taxpayer's deductible casualty loss before application of the 10 percent of adjusted gross income limitation is $8,500. The $100 reduction applies to the Taxpayer's total loss from the single casualty.

If a taxpayer suffers more than one casualty or theft during the year, the taxpayer must reduce each loss by $100.[54]

Example 3: Assume the same facts as in Example 1, except that only the Taxpayer's boat is damaged by hurricane Donna. Four months before hurricane Donna, the Taxpayer's home was damaged by an early summer lightning storm. In this case, the Taxpayer's loss deduction before application of the 10 percent of adjusted gross income limitation is $8,400. The $1,600 unreimbursed loss to the home must be reduced by $100 and the separate $7,000 casualty loss to the boat also must be reduced by $100.

Multiple Owners

If two or more individuals, other than a husband and wife filing a joint return, have losses from the same casualty, the $100 reduction applies separately to each. The same rule applies when two or more individuals, other than a husband and wife filing a joint return, have a loss on property that they own jointly.[55] For instance, if two sisters live in a home that they own jointly and that home is damaged by a fire, each must reduce her casualty loss by $100.

Married Couples

If a husband and wife suffer a casualty loss and they file a joint return, they are treated as one taxpayer in applying the $100 reduction, regardless of whether they own the property separately or jointly. If they file separate returns, however, each must reduce his or her casualty loss by $100, even if they own the property jointly.

If the damaged property is owned separately by one spouse, only that spouse can take the casualty loss on a separate return. If the

---

[54] *Ibid.* [55] Reg. § 1.165-7(b)(4)(iii).

damaged property is owned as tenants by the entirety, each spouse may deduct only one half of the loss on a separate return, neither spouse may deduct the entire loss on a separate return, and each must reduce his or her loss by $100.[56]

¶ 1713.2   Adjusted Gross Income Limitation

A taxpayer may deduct a casualty loss to nonbusiness property only to the extent the loss is more than 10 percent of the taxpayer's adjusted gross income.[57] This adjusted gross income limitation applies after any casualty loss is reduced by any reimbursements and by $100. A taxpayer with more than one casualty loss during the year reduces the total of all losses by 10 percent of adjusted gross income, after reducing each unreimbursed loss by $100.

If a taxpayer has casualty gains in addition to casualty losses, the taxpayer must compare total casualty gains to total casualty losses, after reducing each loss by $100 but before applying the 10 percent of adjusted gross income limitation. If the losses exceed the gains, the casualty gains reduce the casualty losses before applying the 10 percent of adjusted gross income limitation.[58] If the recognized casualty gains exceed the casualty losses, the difference is treated as a capital gain.[59] The 10 percent of adjusted gross income limitation does not apply when a taxpayer's casualty gains exceed casualty losses.

Multiple Owners

When two or more individuals, other than a husband and wife filing a joint return, have a casualty loss on property that they own jointly, the 10 percent of adjusted gross income limitation applies separately to each.

A husband and wife who file a joint return and have a loss from the same casualty are treated as one individual for purposes of the 10 percent of adjusted gross income limitation, regardless of whether they own the property jointly or separately.

¶ 1715   Calculation of the Casualty Deduction

A taxpayer who suffers a casualty generally must determine the loss separately for each item or parcel of property lost or damaged by the casualty. Real estate that is not used for business or investment, however, is considered one item of property.

¶ 1715.1   *Real Estate*

To determine the loss on real estate that a taxpayer uses for personal purposes, all improvements, such as buildings, landscaping,

---

[56] Code Sec. 165(h).
[57] Code Sec. 165(h)(2).
[58] Code Sec. 165(h)(2)(A)(i).
[59] Code Sec. 165(h)(2)(B) and (h)(4)(A).

etc., are considered together. The amount of the loss is the lesser of the decrease in value of the entire property or the adjusted basis of the property.[60] From this loss amount, the taxpayer must subtract insurance or other reimbursements received or expected and the $100 reduction required by Code Sec. 165. If this is the taxpayer's only casualty or theft loss, the taxpayer would also subtract 10 percent of adjusted gross income. If the taxpayer had other casualty or theft losses, the 10 percent of adjusted gross income would reduce the total of all losses. Any amount remaining after these reductions is the casualty loss deduction.

Example 1: The Taxpayer purchased a cottage several years ago for $44,800, including $4,500 for the land. During the current year, the cottage is damaged by a fire, resulting in the Taxpayer's only casualty or theft loss during the year. Immediately before the fire, the fair market value of the cottage and land was $50,000. After the fire, the fair market value of the property is $35,000. As a result of the fire, the Taxpayer collected $10,000 from the insurance company. Assuming that the Taxpayer's adjusted gross income for the current year is $40,000, the Taxpayer's casualty loss deduction as a result of the fire is $900, calculated as follows:

1.	Adjusted basis of property	$44,800
2.	Value before fire	$50,000
3.	Value after fire	35,000
4.	Decrease in value	$15,000
5.	Amount of loss (lesser of 1 or 4)	$15,000
6.	Less: Insurance reimbursement	10,000
7.	Loss after reimbursement	$ 5,000
8.	Less: $100 reduction	100
9.	Loss after $100 rule	$ 4,900
10.	Less: 10% of adjusted gross income	4,000
11.	Casualty loss deduction	$ 900

Example 2: The Taxpayer purchased a personal residence several years ago for $50,000—$10,000 for the land and $40,000 for the house. The Taxpayer also spent $2,000 for landscaping. During the current year, the Taxpayer's home is totally destroyed by fire. The fire also damaged the shrubbery and trees on the property. This was the Taxpayer's only casualty or theft loss during the year. Appraisals valued the property at $75,000 before the fire but at only $15,000 after the fire. An insurance company paid the Taxpayer $45,000 as a result of the loss. Assuming the Taxpayer's

---

[60] Reg. § 1.165-7(b)(2)(ii).

adjusted gross income for the current year is $48,000, the Taxpayer's casualty loss deduction is $2,100, calculated as follows:

1.	Adjusted basis of property	$52,000
2.	Value before fire	$75,000
3.	Value after fire	15,000
4.	Decrease in value	$60,000
5.	Amount of loss (lesser of 1 or 4)	$52,000
6.	Less: Insurance reimbursement	45,000
7.	Loss after reimbursement	$ 7,000
8.	Less: $100 reduction	100
9.	Loss after $100 rule	$ 6,900
10.	Less: 10% of adjusted gross income	4,800
11.	Casualty loss deduction	$ 2,100

¶ 1715.2 Personal Property

Personal property includes any property that is not real property. When personal property is damaged or destroyed by a casualty, taxpayers must compute their loss separately for each item of property.[61]

The amount of the loss is the lesser of the decrease in fair market value or the adjusted basis of the property. From this amount, the taxpayer subtracts insurance or other reimbursements and the $100 reduction required by Code Sec. 165. The loss is further reduced by 10 percent of adjusted gross income, if the loss is the only loss during the year. If the taxpayer suffered several losses during the year, the 10 percent of adjusted gross income limitation, of course, would apply to the total of all the losses. Any amount remaining after these reductions is the taxpayer's personal casualty loss deduction.

Example 1: The Taxpayer's pleasure boat, which cost $8,500, was lost in a storm in August of the current year. This was the Taxpayer's only casualty or theft loss during the year. The value of the boat before the storm was $7,000. The Taxpayer had no insurance on the boat but was able to salvage the outboard motor and sell it for $200. Assuming the Taxpayer's adjusted gross income is $52,000, the Taxpayer's casualty loss deduction is $1,500, computed as follows:

1.	Adjusted basis of property	$ 8,500
2.	Value before storm	$ 7,000
3.	Value after storm	200
4.	Decrease in value	$ 6,800

---

[61] Reg. § 1.165-7(b)(2)(i).

Deductions for Homeowners

5.	Amount of loss (lesser of 1 or 4)	$ 6,800
6.	Less: Insurance reimbursement	–0–
7.	Loss after reimbursement	$ 6,800
8.	Less: $100 reduction	100
9.	Loss after $100 rule	$ 6,700
10.	Less: 10% of adjusted gross income	5,200
11.	Casualty loss deduction	$ 1,500

Example 2: During the year, the Taxpayer was involved in an auto accident that totally destroyed the family auto, purchased two years before for $10,000. Also lost in the accident was the Taxpayer's watch, purchased one month before the accident for $250. The value of the car just before the accident was $7,500, and its value after the accident was $80 (scrap). Insurance reimbursed the Taxpayer $6,000 for the car, but the watch was not insured. Assuming the Taxpayer's adjusted gross income for the year is $31,000, the Taxpayer's casualty loss deduction is zero, calculated as follows:

Car:

1.	Adjusted basis of property	$10,000
2.	Value before accident	$ 7,500
3.	Value after accident	80
4.	Decrease in value	$ 7,420
5.	Amount of loss (lesser of 1 or 4)	$ 7,420
6.	Less: Insurance reimbursement	6,000
7.	Loss after reimbursement	$ 1,420

Watch:

1.	Adjusted basis of property	$ 250
2.	Value before accident	$ 250
3.	Value after accident	–0–
4.	Decrease in value	$ 250
5.	Amount of loss (lesser of 1 or 4)	$ 250
6.	Less: Insurance reimbursement	–0–
7.	Loss after reimbursement	$ 250

Total casualty loss:

1.	Total loss (watch + car)	$ 1,670
2.	Less: $100 reduction	100
3.	Loss after $100 rule	$ 1,570
4.	Less: 10% of adjusted gross income	3,100
5.	Casualty loss deduction	$ –0–

¶ 1715.2

¶ 1715.3 Loss to Real and Personal Property

If a single casualty causes a loss to both real and personal property, the taxpayer must figure the loss separately for each type of property, as discussed above, but the $100 reduction is applied to the total loss, before the 10 percent of adjusted gross income limitation is applied.

Example: The Taxpayer's home, which cost $64,000 including land, was partially damaged by a hurricane in August of the current year. The value of the property before the storm was $70,000, and its value after the storm was $60,000. The Taxpayer's household furnishings were also damaged. The Taxpayer separately figured the loss on each damaged household item and arrived at a total of $600. The Taxpayer collected $5,000 from the insurance company for damage to the home, but nothing for the household items. Assuming the Taxpayer's adjusted gross income for the year is $44,000, the Taxpayer's casualty loss deduction as a result of the hurricane is $1,100, calculated as follows:

1.	Adjusted basis of real property	$64,000
2.	Value before storm	$70,000
3.	Value after storm	60,000
4.	Decrease in value	$10,000
5.	Loss on real estate (lesser 1 or 4)	$10,000
6.	Less: Insurance reimbursement	5,000
7.	Loss after reimbursement	$ 5,000
8.	Loss on furnishings	$ 600
9.	Less: Insurance reimbursement	–0–
10.	Loss after reimbursement	$ 600
11.	Total loss (7 plus 10)	$ 5,600
12.	Less: $100 reduction	100
13.	Loss after $100 rule	$ 5,500
14.	Less: 10% of adjusted gross income	4,400
15.	Casualty loss deduction	$ 1,100

¶ 1717 Part Business and Part Personal-Use Property

If property is used partly for business purposes and partly for personal purposes, any casualty or theft loss deduction to that property must be calculated as though there were two separate casualties or thefts, that is, one affecting the personal-use property and one affecting the business property.[62] The reason for this is simply that the casualty loss to personal-use property must be reduced by the $100 reduction

---

[62] Reg. § 1.165-7(b)(4)(iv).

and 10 percent of adjusted gross income limitation, while casualty losses to business property are deductible in full, as discussed at ¶ 1505.1.

Example: The Taxpayer owns a three-story building that was built on leased land. The Taxpayer uses two floors (2/3 of the building) in the business and lives on the third floor (1/3 of the building). The cost of the building was $140,000, and the Taxpayer made no additions or improvements to it since it was built. A flood during the current year damaged the entire building. The fair market value of the building was $133,000 immediately before the flood and $120,000 after the flood. The Taxpayer collected $9,000 from the insurance company as a result of the flood damage. Before the flood, the Taxpayer had taken $8,400 in depreciation deductions for the business portion of the building. The Taxpayer has a business casualty loss for the current year of $2,267, and, assuming the Taxpayer's adjusted gross income is $50,000, no personal casualty loss deduction is available because of the $100 rule and 10 percent of adjusted gross income limitation. These deductions are computed as follows:

Business Loss:
1. Adjusted basis (2/3 total cost of $140,000 less $8,400 depreciation) $84,933
2. Value before flood (2/3 total) $88,667
3. Value after flood (2/3 total) 80,000
4. Decrease in value .... $ 8,667
5. Amount of loss (lesser of 1 or 4) .... $ 8,667
6. Less: Insurance reimbursement (2/3 total) 6,000
7. Loss after reimbursement .... $ 2,667
8. Deductible business casualty .... $ 2,667

Personal Loss:
1. Adjusted basis (1/3 total cost of $140,000) $46,667
2. Value before flood (1/3 total) $44,333
3. Value after flood (1/3 total) 40,000
4. Decrease in value .... $ 4,333
5. Amount of loss (lesser of 1 or 4) .... $ 4,333
6. Less: Insurance reimbursement (1/3 total) 3,000
7. Loss after reimbursement .... $ 1,333
8. Less: $100 reduction 100
9. Loss after $100 rule .... $ 1,233
10. Less: 10% adjusted gross income 5,000
11. Deductible personal casualty .... $ —0—

¶ 1717

¶ 1721 MOVING EXPENSES

An employee or self-employed person may deduct the expenses of moving from one location to another, provided the move is related to starting work at a new principal place of employment. The deduction is a deduction from gross income.[63]

¶ 1723 Qualification for the Deduction

Generally, taxpayers may deduct moving expenses only if the expenses are related to the start of work at a new location. Moving expenses incurred within one year from the time a taxpayer first reports to work at the new location are considered closely related. If a taxpayer does not move within one year of starting work at a new location, moving expenses are not deductible unless circumstances existed which prevented the taxpayer from moving within the year.[64] For example, taxpayers may delay a move to allow a child to finish high school in the same school and deduct moving expenses incurred after the one-year period.

In addition to meeting the requirement that a move be job related, a taxpayer must also satisfy specific distance and length-of-employment tests to deduct moving expenses.

¶ 1723.1 *Distance*

To deduct moving expenses, a taxpayer must show that the new principal place of work is at least 50 miles farther from the old residence than the old residence was from the old place of work.[65] Note that the distance test does not apply to the location of the taxpayer's new home. Also, distance is measured by the shortest commonly traveled routes.

> ***Example:*** The Taxpayer moved to a new home that was 30 miles from the old home. The distance from the old residence to the new place of work is 52 miles. The distance from the old residence to the old place of work is one mile. Since the distance from the Taxpayer's old residence to the new place of work is at least 50 miles farther than the distance from the old residence to the old place of work, the Taxpayer may deduct moving expenses.

In the case of a taxpayer returning to full-time work after a period of unemployment or part-time work, or in the case of a taxpayer beginning a first full-time job, the taxpayer's place of work must be at least

---

[63] Code Sec. 217.
[64] Reg. § 1.217-2(a)(3).
[65] Code Sec. 217(c)(1).

50 miles from the taxpayer's old home in order for the taxpayer to deduct moving expenses.

The new job must be the taxpayer's principal or main job, that is, the place where the taxpayer spends the most working time. An employee who works for several employers through a union hall treats the union hall as the main job location. A taxpayer with more than one job determines the main job based on the time spent at the different locations, the amount of work done at each place, and the money earned at each job location.

¶ 1723.2 Length of Employment

If the taxpayer is an employee, the taxpayer must be employed full time at least 39 weeks during the first 12 months after his move in order to qualify for the moving expense deduction. The employee does not have to work for the same employer for those 39 weeks, nor does the employee have to work for 39 consecutive weeks. If the taxpayer is self-employed, the taxpayer must be employed full time for at least 78 weeks during the 24 months following the move, in addition to meeting the 39 weeks/12 months test.[66] The full-time work requirement is waived, however, if death, disability, involuntary separation from work (other than for misconduct), or transfer to another location for the benefit of the employer occurs.[67]

A taxpayer who moves during the year and deducts the expenses for the year of the move on the assumption that the taxpayer will meet the length-of-employment test and then fails the test must either report the previously deducted expenses as income for the year following the move or amend the earlier return.

¶ 1727 Deductible Costs

Only those expenses that are reasonable for the circumstances of the move are deductible. A taxpayer who meets the requirements for deducting moving expenses may deduct the following:[68]

1. The cost of packing, crating, and transporting household goods and personal effects from the taxpayer's former home to the taxpayer's new home. The cost of storing and insuring household goods and personal effects within any period of 30 consecutive days after things are moved from the former home and before they are delivered to the new home are deductible.

2. Any costs of connecting or disconnecting utilities required because the taxpayer is moving household goods, appliances, or personal effects.

---

[66] Code Sec. 217(c)(2).
[67] Code Sec. 217(d).
[68] Code Sec. 217(b).

3. The cost of shipping a car and household pets to the taxpayer's new home.
4. The cost of moving household goods and personal effects from a place other than the taxpayer's former home. The deduction is limited to the amount it would have cost to move them from the former home.
5. The cost of transportation and lodging for the taxpayer and members of the taxpayer's household while traveling from the former home to the new home.

The following items are not deductible as moving expenses (many of these items were deductible under the moving expense deduction rules in effect before 1994):

- Premove househunting expenses,
- Temporary living expenses,
- Meal expenses,
- Expenses of buying or selling a home,
- Expenses of getting or breaking a lease,
- Security deposits,
- Home improvements to sell the old home,
- Loss on the sale of a home,
- Mortgage penalties,
- Losses from disposing of club memberships,
- Any part of the purchase price of a new home,
- Real estate taxes,
- Car tags and driver's license fees,
- Storage charges except for foreign moves.

¶ 1727.2 Reimbursements

A taxpayer reimbursed for moving expenses by the employer reports the payments as income.[69] These reimbursements are subject to withholding and information reporting requirements unless the taxpayer is entitled to a moving expense deduction for the amounts.[70]

¶ 1727.3 Foreign Moves

The moving expense deduction relating to the commencement of work outside the United States and its possessions is similar to the deduction for moves within the United States.

---

[69] Code Sec. 82.

[70] Reg. § 31.3401(a)(15)-1.

In addition, deductible amounts include the reasonable expenses of moving household goods and personal effects to and from storage, and of storing goods and effects for part or all of the period during which the new place of work continues to be the taxpayer's principal place of work.[71]

¶ 1727.4   Armed Forces Members

Members of the armed forces on active duty who move because of a permanent change in station do not have to meet the distance and length-of-employment tests discussed at ¶ 1723.1 and 1723.2 in order to deduct unreimbursed moving expenses. Moving and storage expenses that are furnished in kind by the military, or cash reimbursements or allowances to the extent actually paid or incurred incident to a permanent change of station, are not includible in income.[72]

¶ 1731   DISTRICT OF COLUMBIA HOMEBUYER CREDIT

For property purchased after August 4, 1997, and before January 1, 2004, a first-time homebuyer in the District of Columbia may be entitled to a tax credit of up to $5,000.[73]

The amount allowable as a credit is reduced by the amount that bears the same ratio to the credit allowable as the excess of the taxpayer's modified adjusted gross income for the tax year over $70,000 ($110,000 in the case of a joint return) bears to $20,000. Modified adjusted gross income is adjusted gross income increased by any amount excluded from gross income under Code Sec. 911 (foreign earned income exclusion), Code Sec. 931 (exclusion for possessions income), or Code Sec. 933 (exclusion for Puerto Rico income).

A first-time homebuyer is an individual who had no present ownership interest in a principal residence in the District of Columbia during the one-year period ending on the date of the purchase of the principal residence. If an individual is treated as a first-time homebuyer for any principal residence, that individual may not be treated as a first-time homebuyer for any other principal residence.

---

[71] Code Sec. 217(h).
[72] Code Sec. 217(g).
[73] Code Sec. 1400C.

Chapter 18

Mixed-Use Residences

¶ 1800 OVERVIEW OF CHAPTER

Not every taxpayer limits the use of a personal residence to purely personal purposes. Frequently, a taxpayer will use a portion of the residence for income-producing activities or convert all or part of the residence to business or investment use. When this occurs, the taxpayer may take business expense deductions for some costs associated with the home that, if the home were used solely as a personal residence, would not be deductible.

Obviously, the benefit of converting otherwise nondeductible expenses into deductible ones has often led to disputes between the IRS and taxpayers who sought to deduct expenses far in excess of any income produced by the business use of the home. Also, the possible tax deductions have led other taxpayers to claim a "home office" even when they had a regular place of business outside the home and actually conducted very little business from the home. In response to the problem, Congress enacted a special set of rules that govern the business use of a taxpayer's residence and the rental of a taxpayer's personal residence on a part-time basis. These rules, which essentially limit deductions from the business use of the home to income produced by the business activity, are the primary focus of this chapter. Also considered is the effect of converting a personal residence to investment or income-producing property.

¶ 1801 BUSINESS USE OF HOME

Generally, Code Sec. 280A denies an individual or S corporation deductions for the business use of a dwelling that is used by the taxpayer as a residence, unless the deductions are allowed without regard to their connection with the taxpayer's trade or business or income-producing activities.[1] After setting the general rule, the statute goes on to provide the exceptions.

A taxpayer may be able to deduct some of the expenses of using part of a home for business, if specific tests are met. Also, the deduction must be limited to the income produced by the at-home business

---

[1] Code Sec. 280A(a) and (b).

activity.[2] The home to which the tests apply is the taxpayer's dwelling unit, which may be a house, apartment, condominium, mobile home, boat, or similar property, and all appurtenant property.[3] The tests and limitation do not apply, however, to any part of a home that is used exclusively as a hotel, motel, inn, or similar establishment.[4]

¶ 1803   Exclusive Use for Business Test

In order for a taxpayer to take a deduction for using part of a home in business, the taxpayer must use that part *exclusively* and *regularly* for one of the following:

1. As the principal place of business for any trade or business of the taxpayer;
2. As a place to meet or deal with patients, clients, or customers in the normal course of the taxpayer's trade or business; or
3. In connection with the taxpayer's trade or business if the taxpayer is using a separate structure that is not attached to the taxpayer's house or residence.[5]

The requirement that business use must be exclusive generally bars a deduction when the same space is used both for business and personal living purposes. While this does not require a separate room or other segregated area for business, showing exclusive business use for only part of a room is difficult.[6] The requirement that business use be regular means that the part of the home used for business must be used on a continuing basis. Occasional or incidental use does not qualify for the deduction, even if the part of the home is used for no other purposes.

In the case of an employee, business use of part of the employee's home for one of the three purposes listed above must be for the convenience of the employer, in addition to meeting the exclusive use test.[7]

¶ 1803.1   *Exceptions to Exclusive Use Test*

There are two exceptions to the exclusive use test for a home office or other business use of part of a taxpayer's personal residence. The use of part of the home as a day-care center, discussed at ¶ 1809, does not have to meet the exclusive test. Also, use of part of a home for the storage of inventory or product samples may not be subject to the exclusive use test, if several requirements are met.[8]

---

[2] Code Sec. 280A(c)(5).
[3] Code Sec. 280A(f)(1)(A).
[4] Code Sec. 280A(f)(1)(B).
[5] Code Sec. 280A(c)(1).

[6] See, for example, *G.H. Weightman*, 42 TCM 104, CCH Dec. 37,986(M), T.C. Memo. 1981-301.
[7] Code Sec. 280A(c)(1); Prop. Reg. § 1.280A-2(g)(2).
[8] Code Sec. 280A(c)(2).

A taxpayer may deduct expenses that relate to the use of part of his home for the storage of inventory if:
1. The taxpayer keeps the inventory for use in his trade or business;
2. The trade or business is the wholesale or retail sale of products;
3. The home is the only fixed location of the trade or business;
4. The taxpayer uses the storage space on a regular basis; and
5. The storage space comprises a separately identifiable space suitable for storage.[9]

¶ 1803.2 *Principal Place of Business*

Deductions for business use of the home are allowed for that part of the home used exclusively and regularly as the principal place of business of the taxpayer. Generally speaking, each trade or business may have a principal place of business. The deduction is permitted as long as the business part of the home is the principal place of business for any trade or business of the taxpayer.[10]

A taxpayer may have more than one business location, including the home, for a single trade or business. To deduct expenses for the business use of the home in this case, the taxpayer must show that the home is the principal place of business for that trade or business. Factors to consider in determining the principal place of business include:
1. The total time spent doing work at each location;
2. The facilities for doing the work at each location; and
3. The relative amount of income derived from each location.[11]

The IRS withdrew the proposed regulations relating to determining a taxpayer's principal place of business discussed above following the 1993 Supreme Court decision in *Soliman*.[12] In that decision, the Court restricted a taxpayer's ability to deduct home office expenses. Taxpayers who may have used the home office only for administrative or management functions and spent considerable time away from the home office were denied deductions because the home office was not the "principal place of business."

In response to the *Soliman* decision, Congress, in the Taxpayer Relief Act of 1997, amended Code Sec. 280A(c)(1) to define principal place of business to include a place of business that is used by the taxpayer for the administrative or management activities of any trade or business of the taxpayer if there is no other fixed location of the

---

[9] Prop. Reg. § 1.280A-2(e).
[10] Code Sec. 280A(c)(1)(A).
[11] Prop. Reg. 1.280A-2(b)(3).
[12] 93-1 USTC ¶ 50,014, 113 S.Ct. 701.

business where the taxpayer conducts substantial administrative or management activities. Amended Code Sec. 280A(c)(1) is effective for tax years beginning after 1998.

Example: The Taxpayer is an outside salesperson and has no office space except at home. The Taxpayer spends a substantial amount of time on paperwork at home. If the Taxpayer maintains an office in his home, the home may qualify as the Taxpayer's principal place of business under Code Sec. 280A(c)(1) as amended and effective after 1998.

¶ 1803.3 Place to Meet Patients, Clients, or Customers

If a taxpayer meets or deals with patients, clients, or customers in the home in the normal course of business, even though the taxpayer also carries on business at another location, the taxpayer may deduct expenses for the part of the home that is used exclusively and regularly for this purpose. The home office must be visited by clients. The deduction is not permitted if the only client contact is by telephone.

The part of the home the taxpayer uses for meeting patients, clients, or customers does not have to be the taxpayer's principal place of business. The use of the home by the patients, clients, or customers, however, must be substantial and integral to the conduct of the taxpayer's business. Occasional meetings are not sufficient to justify a deduction.[13] Taxpayers who generally meet this requirement are doctors, dentists, attorneys, and other professionals who maintain offices in their homes.

¶ 1803.4 Separate Structures

The expenses for a separate free-standing structure that is next to the taxpayer's home are deductible if the taxpayer uses the structure exclusively and regularly for a business. The structure does not have to be the taxpayer's principal place of business or the place where the taxpayer meets patients, clients, or customers. An artist's studio, a florist's greenhouse, and a carpenter's workshop are examples of structures that may qualify for the deduction under this provision.[14]

¶ 1805 Allocation of Deductions

A taxpayer who qualifies for deductions relating to the business use of a home must divide the expenses of operating the home between personal (nondeductible) and business (deductible) use. A taxpayer may use any method that is reasonable under the circumstances to make this allocation.[15] Generally, some expenses will be directly related to the business use of the home, some will be indirectly related, and still

---

[13] Prop. Reg. § 1.280A-2(c).
[14] Prop. Reg. § 1.280A-2(d).
[15] Prop. Reg. § 1.280A-2(i)(3).

others will be completely unrelated. Expenses that are attributable only to certain portions of the home must be allocated in full to those portions. Expenses that are not related to the use of the residence for business purposes (for example, the cost of lawn care or repairs to personal areas of the home) are not deductible.

¶ 1805.1 Direct Expenses

Direct expenses that benefit only the business part of the home, such as the cost of painting or repairs to the specific area or room that the taxpayer uses for business purposes, are deductible without further allocation, subject to the limitation discussed at ¶ 1807.

¶ 1805.2 Indirect Expenses

Indirect expenses are those that relate to maintaining and running the taxpayer's entire home; that is, they benefit both the business and personal parts of the home. A taxpayer must allocate these expenses between the business and personal uses of the home. Only the percentage that relates to the business portion is deductible.

If the rooms in the taxpayer's home are of approximately equal size, the taxpayer ordinarily may allocate the general indirect expenses of the home between business and personal uses according to the number of rooms used for business purposes. The taxpayer may also allocate indirect expenses according to the total floor space in the home that is used for business purposes.[16]

Example: The Taxpayer's home is 2,400 square feet and the Taxpayer uses a portion of the home that measures 12 feet by 20 feet for business purposes. Since the Taxpayer is using 10 percent (240/2,400) of the total area of the home for business purposes, the Taxpayer may deduct 10 percent of the indirect expenses of the home as a business expenses, subject to the limitation on the deduction discussed at ¶ 1807.

If the rooms in the Taxpayer's home were about equal in size, the Taxpayer could allocate indirect expenses on the basis of the number of rooms. If the Taxpayer's home were a nine-room home and the Taxpayer used one room for business, the Taxpayer could deduct 1/9th of the indirect expenses. The Taxpayer should determine the proportion of the home used for business purposes under both methods, then use the method that produces the higher deductions.

Some examples of indirect expenses include:

---

[16] Prop. Reg. § 1.280A-2(i)(3).

Real Estate Taxes: The portion of real estate taxes paid allocated to the percentage of the home used for business is deductible as a business expense.

Deductible Mortgage Interest: The portion of any deductible mortgage interest allocated to the business portion of the home is deductible as a business expense.

Casualty Losses: A casualty loss may be an unrelated expense, direct expense, or indirect expense. If the loss does not affect the business portion of the home, there is no business deduction. If the loss only affects the business portion, the entire loss is a business deduction. If the loss affects both portions of the home the loss must be allocated between personal expenses and business expenses.

Rent: A taxpayer who rents rather than owns the home and uses a portion of the home for business purposes may deduct a portion of the rent as a business expense. The allocation is made based on the percentage of the rented property used for business purposes.

Utilities: The business portion of utilities paid are deductible. While the allocation between business and personal expenses generally may be made on the basis of the percentage of the home used for business purposes, this may not always be the case. In Publication 587, "Business Use of Your Home," the IRS gives the following example.

> **Example:** The Taxpayer's electric bill is $400 for lighting, cooking, laundry, and television. Only the lighting was used for business. If $250 of the Taxpayer's electric bill is for lighting and the Taxpayer uses 10 percent of the home for business, then $25 is deductible as a business expenses. (Note that the IRS does not make clear how such a breakdown in a utility bill may be done.)

Telephone: The basic local telephone service charge, including taxes, for the first telephone line into a home is a nondeductible personal expense.[17] Long-distance business phone calls, however, are direct expenses.

Insurance: The cost of insurance that covers the business portion of the home is deductible.

Repairs: Repairs and supplies that relate to the business are deductible. For instance, if a central air conditioning unit is repaired and 10 percent of the taxpayer's home is used for business, the taxpayer may deduct 10 percent of the cost of the repair.

Depreciation: When the taxpayer uses the home partly for business purposes and otherwise meets the requirements for deducting business

---

[17] Code Sec. 262(b).

¶ 1805.2

expenses relating to that use, the portion of the home used for business may be depreciated as nonresidential real property under the depreciation rules as discussed at ¶ 903. Other business property used in the home is also subject to depreciation allowances or a deduction under Code Sec. 179.

Note that when property is converted from personal to business use, the basis for depreciation is the lower of the adjusted basis of the property or its fair market value on the date the property is converted to business use.

¶ 1807 Limitation on Deductions

Generally, the deductions for the business use of a home are limited to the gross income derived from the business use of the home.[18] There is no limit on the expenses a taxpayer may deduct for the business use of a home if the total expenses are less than or equal to the taxpayer's gross income from that business use. Any amount otherwise deductible that is disallowed because of the gross income limitation may be carried over and deducted in the following year, subject to the gross income limitation, whether or not the taxpayer continues to use the home as a residence.

¶ 1807.1 Determination of Gross Income from Business Use of Home

In determining gross income from a business use of the home in order to apply the limitation on deductions relating to that use, a taxpayer may take into account only gross income from a business use that gives rise to deductions under the rules discussed at ¶ 1803.[19]

Example: The Taxpayer is a teacher at a public school and also is engaged in a retail sales business. The Taxpayer uses a home office on a regular basis as the principal place of business for the retail sales business (a use that permits deductions) and makes no non-business use of the home office. In applying the limitation on deductions, the Taxpayer takes into account the gross income from the use of the home office for the retail sales business. Even if the Taxpayer also corrects student papers and prepares class presentations in the home office (a business use that does not permit deductions), the Taxpayer cannot take into account any portion of the gross income from teaching in applying the limitation on deductions for the business use of the home.

---

[18] Code Sec. 280A(c)(5).

[19] Prop. Reg. § 1.280A-2(i)(2).

Multiple Locations

If part of the gross income from a taxpayer's trade or business is from the business use of part of the home and part is from the use of another place of business, the taxpayer must determine the part of the gross income that is attributable to the home in order to apply the limitation. The regulations provide that a taxpayer must allocate the gross income from the business to the different locations on a reasonable basis.[20] The regulations further provide that the taxpayer, in making this allocation, must take into account the amount of time that the taxpayer engages in activity related to the business at each location, the capital investment related to the business at each location, and any other facts and circumstances that may be relevant.

Business Expenses Unrelated to Use of Home

In determining gross income derived from the business use of a home, a taxpayer must reduce the gross income from the business activity in the home by expenditures required for the activity but not allocable to the use of the home itself, such as expenditures for supplies and compensation paid to employees.[21]

Example: The Taxpayer, a physician, uses a portion of the home for treating patients. In computing gross income derived from the business use of the home, the Taxpayer must subtract from the gross income attributable to the business activity in the home any expenditures for nursing, secretarial services, supplies, and similar items.

¶ 1807.2 Order of Deductions

Business deductions for the business use of a taxpayer's home are allowed in the following order and only to the following extent: [22]

1. The portions of amounts allowable as deductions for the home without regard to any use of the home in a trade or business are allowable as business deductions to the extent of the gross income derived from the business use of the home. For example, mortgage interest (within limits) and real estate taxes are deductible whether the home is used for business or not. Therefore, the portion of these items allocable to the business use of the home are business deductions and are applied first against gross income from the business use of the home. The balance of any deductible mortgage interest and real estate taxes are taken as itemized deductions.

---

[20] Prop. Reg. § 1.280A-2(i)(2)(ii).
[21] Prop. Reg. § 1.280A-2(i)(2)(iii).
[22] Prop. Reg. § 1.280A-2(i)(5).

2. Amounts otherwise allowable as deductions for the business use of the home, other than those that would result in an adjustment to the basis of the property, are allowable to the extent the gross income derived from the business use of the home exceeds the deductions under Category 1.

3. Amounts otherwise allowable as deductions for the business use of the home and which would result in an adjustment to the basis of the property are allowable to the extent the gross income derived from the business use of the home exceeds the deductions under Category 1 and Category 2.

Example: The Taxpayer uses an office in the home on a regular basis in order to meet with clients of the Taxpayer's consulting service. The Taxpayer makes no other use of this office, which is 10 percent of the area of the home, and has no other location for the consulting business. The Taxpayer has a special telephone line for the office at a cost of $150 for the year. The Taxpayer also employs a secretary on an "as-needed" basis and a gardener to take care of the lawn. The Taxpayer paid the secretary $500 during the year and the gardener $720. Also during the year, the Taxpayer incurred and paid the following expenses: $200 for business supplies, $5,000 in mortgage interest, $2,000 for real estate taxes, $600 for insurance on the home, and $900 for utilities. If the Taxpayer's home were entirely business real estate, the Taxpayer would be entitled to a $3,200 deduction for depreciation for the year. The Taxpayer's gross income from the consulting service was $1,900 for the year. Under the limitation on the deduction of expenses relating to the business use of a home, the Taxpayer's allowable business deductions for the use of the home office cannot exceed $1,050, calculated as follows:

Gross income from consulting		$1,900
Less: Deductions unrelated to home:		
Secretary expense	$500	
Business telephone	150	
Supplies	200	850
Gross income attributable to use of home office		$1,050

The Taxpayer then takes additional deductions for the business use of the home in the following order:

1. Mortgage interest	$500
Real estate taxes	200
	$700

This leaves $350 available for deductions in Category 2:

¶ 1807.2

2. Insurance	$ 60
Utilities	90
	$150

This now leaves the Taxpayer with $200 available for deduction under Category 3. The Taxpayer's deduction for depreciation, if there were no gross income limitation, would be $320. However, since only $200 of the Taxpayer's gross income from the use of the home for the consulting business remains after all other deductions, the Taxpayer's depreciation deduction is limited to $200. The remaining amount of this deduction ($120) is a carryover to the following year and the Taxpayer may deduct this amount in the following year, subject to the gross income limitation for that year.

No portion of the Taxpayer's lawn care expense is allocable to the business use of the home and no deduction is permitted for this expense. The Taxpayer may claim the remaining $4,500 paid for mortgage interest and $1,800 for real estate taxes as itemized deductions.

¶ 1809 Use of Home as Day-Care Facility

A taxpayer may deduct expenses for using part of the home on a regular basis to provide day-care services, if the taxpayer meets the following requirements: [23]

1. The taxpayer must be in the trade or business of providing day care for children, for persons 65 or older, or for persons who are physically or mentally unable to care for themselves; and

2. The taxpayer must have applied for, been granted, or be exempt from having a license, certification, registration, or approval as a day-care center or as a family or group day-care home under any applicable state law.

The second requirement is not met if the application has been rejected or the license or other authorization has been revoked.[24]

A taxpayer who uses part of the personal residence as a day-care facility must compute the portion of the home used for the day-care business as discussed above for the business use of a home in general. If the part used for the day-care business is used exclusively for that purpose, the taxpayer may deduct all allocable expenses, subject to the gross income limitation discussed above. Unlike other business use of the home, however, use of part of the home as a day-care facility need not be exclusive in order for the taxpayer to deduct related expenses. When the use is not exclusive, an additional allocation of expenses must

---

[23] Code Sec. 280A(c)(4). [24] Code Sec. 280A(c)(4)(B).

be made on the basis of the amount of time that part of the home is used in the day-care business.

¶ 1809.1   Allocation Formula

If a portion of a taxpayer's home used for providing day-care services is not used exclusively for that purpose, the amount of expenses attributable to that portion "shall not exceed an amount which bears the same ratio to the total amount of the items allocable to such portion as the number of hours the portion is used for such purpose bears to the number of hours the portion is available for use." [25] In other words, the taxpayer compares the total time of business use as a day-care facility to the total time that that portion of the home can be used for all purposes.

¶ 1809.2   Application of Formula

The taxpayer may make this comparison based on the number of hours the space is used for day care in a week with the number of hours in a week (168), or the hours used for day care during the year with the number of hours in the taxpayer's tax year (8,760 in the case of a 365-day year). The taxpayer then determines the amount deductible, before applying the gross income limitation, by multiplying the expenses allocable based on the amount of space used by the fraction of hours used for day care versus total hours available for use.[26]

> ***Example:*** The Taxpayer uses the basement to care for children an average of 12 hours per day, five days per week, for 50 weeks. The Taxpayer's family may use the basement at other times. During the year, the Taxpayer uses the basement as a day-care center for a total of 3,000 hours (5 days per week × 50 weeks = 250 days × 12 hours = 3,000 hours). Since the basement is available for use for 8,760 hours during the year, only 34.25 percent (3,000/8,760) of the expenses of the Taxpayer's basement are business expenses. The Taxpayer may deduct 34.25 percent of any direct expenses for the basement, but only 34.25 percent of the basement portion of indirect expenses. If the Taxpayer's basement is 20 percent of the total area of the Taxpayer's home, the Taxpayer may deduct 6.85 percent (34.25% × 20% = 6.85%) of the indirect expenses. (Direct and indirect expenses are discussed above at ¶ 1805.1 and ¶ 1805.2.)

¶ 1811   RENTAL OF PART OF HOME

When a taxpayer rents part of the property, the rent received is generally taxable income. As for expenses, the taxpayer generally must divide expenses between the part of the property that is rented and the

---

[25] Code Sec. 280A(c)(4)(C).   [26] Prop. Reg. § 1.280A-2(i)(4).

part that is used for personal purposes as if the taxpayer owned two separate parcels of property. Further, whenever real property is used for personal purposes, in addition to being rented out, there may be limits on the deduction for rental expenses.

¶ 1813   Rental Income

Rental income is any payment a taxpayer receives for the use or occupancy of property and, generally, is included in gross income. In addition to regular, periodic rents, rental income may include advance rents, security deposits retained by the landlord, payments for cancelling a lease, expenses paid by the tenant on behalf of the landlord, payments in property or services, and payments under a lease with an option to buy until the option is exercised by the tenant. These topics are all discussed in some detail in Part II, "Rental and Leasing Arrangements."

A taxpayer that rents property for a period of less than 15 days during the tax year and also uses that property as a residence during the year does not have to include the rent in income.[27]

¶ 1815   Allocation of Expenses

Taxpayers generally may deduct the expenses of renting property from the gross rental income from the property. In certain cases, deductions may exceed rental income. Expenses of operating rental property are discussed in some detail in Part III, "Real Estate Operation."

If the taxpayer rents part of the property, the taxpayer must divide expenses between the part that is rented and the part that is used for personal or other purposes. This division is made in the same fashion as the division of expenses when a taxpayer uses part of the home for business purposes, as discussed at ¶ 1805. The taxpayer does not have to divide expenses that relate only to the rented portion of the property. These items are rental expenses in full. For expenses that must be divided, the division usually also follows the methods used for dividing expenses when part of a home is used for business purposes, that is, by area or number of rooms.

In some cases, there may be other more appropriate methods of dividing expenses relating to the rental of part of a home between rental and personal expenses. For instance, in some cases, the number of people involved may be more appropriate, such as when tenants are provided board in addition to rooms. In such a case, the number of

---

[27] Code Sec. 280A(g); see also the discussion at ¶ 1821.

people may be an appropriate way to divide food costs between rental expense and personal expense.

The same provision that allows a taxpayer to avoid reporting rental income when property used as a residence by the taxpayer is rented for less than 15 days during the tax year also prohibits the taxpayer from taking any deductions for expenses relating to the production of that income.[28] Also, any time a taxpayer rents a residence that the taxpayer also uses for personal purposes during the year, the taxpayer's deductions for rental expenses are subject to the limitation discussed at ¶ 1825.2 in connection with the rental of vacation homes and other residences.

¶ 1821 RENTAL OF VACATION OR OTHER RESIDENCE

If a taxpayer rents out part or all of a vacation home or other dwelling unit and also uses any part of the dwelling for personal purposes, the taxpayer must divide expenses between rental use and personal use.[29] The taxpayer may then be able to deduct some or all of the rental expenses, or the taxpayer may find that none of the rental expenses are deductible, depending on how the dwelling was used during the year.

¶ 1823 Dwelling Unit Classification

For purposes of the rules that apply to vacation homes and other dwelling units under Code Sec. 280A, a dwelling unit includes a house, apartment, condominium, mobile home, boat, or similar property.[30] The key to classification as a dwelling unit is whether the property provides basic living accommodations, which the regulations define to include sleeping space, toilet, and cooking facilities.[31] A single structure may contain more than one dwelling unit, such as is the case in an apartment building. Similarly, if the basement of a home contains basic living accommodations, the basement is a separate dwelling unit. Structures and property appurtenant to a dwelling which do not constitute a dwelling unit are considered part of the unit.

> ***Example:*** The Taxpayer rents space in a garage to another individual. The garage is appurtenant to the house which the Taxpayer owns and in which the Taxpayer lives. The Taxpayer may take deductions related to his rental of the garage only to the extent permitted by the provisions of Code Sec. 280A.

Dwelling units not covered by the rules of Code Sec. 280A are those used exclusively as a hotel, motel, inn, or similar establishment.[32]

---

[28] Code Sec. 280A(g).
[29] Code Sec. 280A(e).
[30] Code Sec. 280A(f)(1)(A).
[31] Prop. Reg. § 1.280A-1(c)(1).
[32] Code Sec. 280A(f)(1)(B).

Property is used for these purposes only if it is regularly available for occupancy by paying customers and only if no person having an interest in the property is considered to have used the unit as a residence during the year.[33] This exception from the Code Sec. 280A rules may apply to a portion of a home used to furnish lodging to tourists or long-term boarders. The exception may also apply to a dwelling unit entered into a rental pool if the owner of the unit does not use it as a residence at any time during the year.[34]

¶ 1823.1 Use as a Residence

If a taxpayer does not use a dwelling unit as a residence at any time during the year, the taxpayer's deductible rental expense can be more than gross rental income from the property. On the other hand, if a taxpayer rents a dwelling unit and also uses the dwelling unit as a residence during the year, deductions for rental expenses are limited under Code Sec. 280A, as at ¶ 1825.

A taxpayer uses a dwelling unit as a residence during the tax year if the taxpayer uses it for personal purposes for more than 14 days and more than 10 percent of the number of days during the year that it is rented at a fair rental price. A unit is not treated as rented at a fair rental for any day on which it is used for personal purposes.[35]

> **Example:** The Taxpayer owns a boat equipped with sleeping space, toilet, and cooking facilities. The Taxpayer uses the boat for personal purposes for 16 days during the year and rents the boat at fair rental for 163 days during the year. Since personal use does not exceed 14 days and 10 percent of the days rented at fair rental (10 percent of 163 days is 16.3 days and the Taxpayer's personal use was for only 16 days), the Taxpayer has not used the boat as a residence for the year.
>
> Suppose, however, that five of the days that the Taxpayer used the boat for personal purposes were included in the 163 days that the boat was rented at fair rental. In this case, those five days are not treated as part of the rental period, and only 158 days are counted. Since 10 percent of 158 days is 15.8 days, the Taxpayer would be treated as using the boat as a residence during the year because personal use exceeded 14 days and 10 percent of the days rented.

---

[33] Prop. Reg. § 1.280A-1(c)(2).
[34] Prop. Reg. § 1.280A-3(e).
[35] Code Sec. 280A(d)(1).

¶ 1823.2 Personal Use

In determining the days of personal use in order to determine whether a taxpayer used a dwelling unit as a residence during the year, count as personal use any day that:[36]

1. The taxpayer or any other person who has an interest in the unit uses the unit, unless the unit is rented at fair rental under a shared equity financing agreement for use as the person's principal residence;[37]

2. A brother, sister, spouse, ancestor, or lineal descendant of the taxpayer or any person who has an interest in the unit uses the unit, unless the rental to the family member is at a fair rental and the family member uses the unit as a principal residence;[38]

3. Anyone uses the unit under an arrangement that allows the taxpayer to use some other dwelling unit, whether or not a rental is charged for the use of the other unit and regardless of the length of time that the taxpayer uses the other unit;[39] and

4. Any individual uses the unit, other than an employee whose use is for the convenience of the employer under Code Sec. 119, unless the unit is rented for that day for a rental which, under the facts and circumstances, is fair rental.[40]

A shared equity financing agreement is any written agreement under which two or more persons acquire undivided interests for more than 50 years in an entire dwelling unit, including the land, and one or more of the co-owners are entitled to occupy the unit as their principal residence upon payment of rent to the other co-owner or owners.[41]

Example: The Taxpayer owns a vacation home which is rented to the Taxpayer's sister at a fair rental for 10 days. The Taxpayer also rents the home to an unrelated individual for 11 days as part of an arrangement under which the Taxpayer is allowed to use another vacation home for six days. As a favor, the Taxpayer rents the vacation home to a friend for 15 days at a discount rate. Based on this rental activity, the Taxpayer has used the vacation home for personal purposes for a period of 36 days.

Maintenance and Repairs

A taxpayer is not treated as using a dwelling unit for personal purposes on any day on which the taxpayer's principal purpose for

---

[36] Code Sec. 280A(d)(2).
[37] Code Sec. 280A(d)(3)(B).
[38] Code Sec. 280A(d)(3)(A).
[39] Prop. Reg. § 1.280A-1(e)(1)(iii).
[40] Prop. Reg. § 1.280A-1(e)(1)(iv).
[41] Code Sec. 280A(d)(3)(C); see also Prop. Reg. § 1.280A-1(e)(3)(ii) and (iv).

using the unit is to perform repair or maintenance work on the unit.[42] Factors that IRS considers in determining whether the principal purpose of use is maintenance or repairs include, but are not limited to, the amount of time devoted to repair and maintenance work, the frequency of the use for repair and maintenance purposes during a taxable year, and the presence and activities of companions. In no case, however, is a day on which a taxpayer engages in full-time repair or maintenance considered a day of personal use.[43]

> *Example:* The Taxpayer owns a lakefront vacation home that the Taxpayer rents during the summer season. The Taxpayer and spouse arrive at the home late on a Thursday evening before the start of the rental season to prepare the home. The couple do no work on the home on Thursday, but the Taxpayer does put in a normal work day on Friday and Saturday, performing necessary maintenance chores. The Taxpayer's spouse spends some time helping, but spends most of the time relaxing and enjoying the lake. The work is completed by Saturday night, so the couple do not work on the home on Sunday, but leave for their principal residence about noon on Sunday.
>
> The principal reason for this use of the Taxpayer's vacation home is maintenance. Therefore, the use of the vacation home during this period is not considered personal use by the Taxpayer.[44]

Rental of Principal Residence

A taxpayer who uses a dwelling unit as a principal residence before or after renting it, or trying to rent it, may not have to count the days the dwelling is used as the principal residence as days of personal use for determining whether the limitation on the deduction of rental expenses applies.[45]

If a taxpayer rents or tries to rent a dwelling unit at a fair rental for 12 or more consecutive months, the taxpayer need not count as personal use the days the dwelling is used as the taxpayer's principal residence during the year in which the taxpayer began renting it or trying to rent it, and which occur before the taxpayer began renting it or trying to rent it. Also, if a taxpayer rents or tries to rent a dwelling unit at a fair rental for 12 or more consecutive months, the taxpayer need not count as personal use the days the dwelling is used as the taxpayer's principal residence during the year in which the taxpayer

---

[42] Code Sec. 280A(d)(2).
[43] Prop. Reg. § 1.280A-1(e)(6).
[44] Prop. Reg. § 1.280A-1(e)(7), Example (3).
[45] Code Sec. 280A(d)(4).

¶ 1823.2

stopped renting it or trying to rent it, and which occur after the taxpayer stopped renting it or trying to rent it.[46]

Example: On February 28, 2003, the Taxpayer, who uses the calendar year as the tax year, moves out of the house that the Taxpayer had lived in for six years in order to take a job in another town. The Taxpayer rents the home at a fair rental from March 15, 2003, until May 14, 2004. On June 1, 2004, the Taxpayer moves back into the old house. The Taxpayer's use of the house as the principal residence from January 1 to February 28, 2003, and from June 1 to December 31, 2004, is not counted as personal use by the Taxpayer.

A taxpayer who sells or exchanges a home after renting it or trying to rent it does not count as personal use the days the home is used as the taxpayer's principal residence during the year the taxpayer rented or tried to rent it and which occur before the taxpayer rented it or tried to rent it.[47]

Example: On January 31 of the current year, the Taxpayer moved out of a principal residence. The Taxpayer offered the old home for rent at a fair rental beginning on February 1. The Taxpayer did not find a tenant until April 1, and then sold the old home on September 15. The Taxpayer's use of the home from January 1 until January 31 is not counted as personal use.

¶ 1825 Determination of Income and Deductions

When a taxpayer rents a dwelling that is also used as a residence during the year, as discussed at ¶ 1823.1, specific limitations apply to the expense deductions that the taxpayer may claim in regard to the rental of the dwelling unit.[48] The limitations are aimed at reducing the tax benefits available to taxpayers who rent out vacation and other homes in order to minimize personal expenses rather than to make a profit from the rental activity.

¶ 1825.1 *Rental for Less Than 15 Days*

If a taxpayer uses a home as a residence during the year and also rents out that home for less than 15 days during the year, the taxpayer does not include in income any of the rental income produced by this minimal rental. Also, the taxpayer may not take any deductions attributable to the rental, but may take deductions otherwise allowable in connection with ownership of the home, including mortgage interest, real estate taxes, and casualty losses.[49]

---

[46] Code Sec. 280A(d)(4)(B)(i); Reg. § 1.280A-1(e)(4)(i).
[47] Code Sec. 280A(d)(4)(B)(ii); Prop. Reg. § 1.280A-1(e)(4)(ii).
[48] Code Sec. 280A(e).
[49] Code Sec. 280A(g).

¶ 1825.2 Rental for 15 Days or More

If a taxpayer uses a home as a residence during the year and also rents out that home for 15 days or more during the year, and the taxpayer's use meets the personal use requirements discussed at ¶ 1823.2, the taxpayer's deductions attributable to the rental activity may not exceed the amount by which the gross income from the rental activity exceeds the deductions otherwise allowable for the property, such as mortgage interest and taxes.[50]

Gross income from rental of a dwelling unit equals the gross receipts from the rental of the unit reduced by expenses to obtain a tenant, such as realtor's fees and advertising expenses. Gross rental income includes rental income from periods during which a unit is rented at less than fair rental, as well as periods during which the unit is rented at fair rental.[51]

Deductions relating to the rental are taken in the following order and only to the following extent: [52]

1. The portions of amounts allowable as deductions for the home without regard to any rental of the home are deductible as rental expenses to the extent of the gross rental income derived from the rental of the home. For example, mortgage interest (within limits) and real estate taxes are deductible whether the home is rented or not. Therefore, the portions of these items allocable to the rental of the home are rental expense deductions and are applied first against gross rental income. The balances of any deductible mortgage interest and real estate taxes are taken as itemized deductions.

2. Amounts otherwise allowable as deductions because of the rental of the home, other than those that would result in an adjustment to the basis of the property, are allowable to the extent the gross rental income exceeds the deductions under Category 1.

3. Amounts otherwise allowable as deductions because of the rental of the home and which would result in an adjustment to the basis of the property are allowable to the extent the gross rental income exceeds the deductions under Category 1 and Category 2.

IRS Allocation Formula

In Prop. Reg. § 1.280A-3(d)(2), the IRS specifies that the portion of any item which is allocable to the rental use of a dwelling unit during

---

[50] Code Sec. 280A(e).
[51] Prop. Reg. § 1.280A-3(d)(2).
[52] Prop. Reg. § 1.280A-3(d)(3).

a taxable year is that amount which bears the same relationship to the total amount of the item as the number of days on which the unit is rented at a fair rental during the taxable year bears to the number of days on which the unit is used for any purpose, other than repair or maintenance, during the taxable year. In other words, the IRS allocation formula for all expenses is based on the ratio between the number of days rented at fair rental and the number of days used for any purpose other than repairs or maintenance, regardless of the number of days the unit is used during the year.

Example 1: The Taxpayer owns a lakeside home that the Taxpayer rents at a fair rental for 90 days during the year. The Taxpayer uses the home for personal purposes on 20 other days during the year and also rents the home to a friend at a discount for 10 days. The home, therefore, is used for some purpose other than repair or maintenance on 120 days during the year and the rental expense allocation fraction is 90/120, or 75 percent. That is, 75 percent of the expenses attributable to the home are rental expenses.

Assume the Taxpayer's gross receipts from the rental of the home, including receipts from the rental at a discount, are $2,400, and that the Taxpayer incurred $200 in advertising expenses relating to the rental. Further assume that the Taxpayer's expenses for the home include $1,000 in mortgage interest, $800 in real estate taxes, $400 for insurance, $600 in utilities, and $1,500 for depreciation. Of these expenses, 75 percent are attributable to generating the rental income and may be taken up to the gross income limitation, or $2,200 ($2,400 receipts − $200 advertising). Applying this allocation in the order in which the deductions must be taken produces the following results:

Deductions permitted by Code Sec. 280A	$2,200
Otherwise allowable deductions:	
Mortgage interest ($1,000 × 90/120)	750
	$1,450
Real estate taxes ($800 × 90/120)	600
	$ 850
Other expenses that do not reduce basis:	
Insurance ($400 × 90/120)	300
	$ 550
Utilities ($600 × 90/120)	450
	$ 100

Expenses that reduce basis:

Depreciation ($1,500 × 90/120 = $1,125)

Since only $100 is left, the Taxpayer's depreciation deduction is limited to $100. The remaining $1,025 of depreciation expense attributable to generating the rental income may not be taken as a deduction under the limitation. The balance of the mortgage interest ($250) and real estate taxes ($200) may be taken as itemized deductions by the Taxpayer.[53]

Tax Court Allocation Formula

The Tax Court takes the position that in determining the amount of interest and real estate taxes allocable to the rental use of a vacation or other home, taxpayers are entitled to allocate an amount based on the approximate percentage of days during the year that the property was rented compared to the number of days in the year rather than the number of days that the home was occupied or used. The rationale for this position is that, unlike other expenses, interest and property taxes are assessed on a yearly basis. This position has been sustained by two Circuit Courts of Appeals.[54] This can make a substantial difference in the total deductions a taxpayer may take.

Example 2: Assume the same facts as in Example 1 demonstrating the IRS allocation formula, except that mortgage interest and real estate taxes allocable to the rental of the home will be based on 90 days of rental out of a 360-day year. Using this allocation formula produces the following results:

Deductions permitted by Code Sec. 280A	$2,200
Otherwise allowable deductions:	
Mortgage interest ($1,000 × 90/360)	250
	$1,950
Real estate taxes ($800 × 90/360)	200
	$1,750
Other expenses that do not reduce basis:	
Insurance ($400 × 90/120)	300
	$1,450
Utilities ($600 × 90/120)	450
	$1,000

Expenses that reduce basis:

Depreciation ($1,500 × 90/120 = $1,125)

Since $1,000 is left, the Taxpayer's depreciation deduction is limited to $1,000, as compared to $100 using the IRS allocation formula. The balance of the mortgage interest ($750) and real estate taxes ($600) may be taken as itemized deductions by the

---

[53] Prop. Reg. § 1.280A-3(d)(4).

[54] *D.D. Bolton*, CA-9, 82-2 USTC ¶ 9699, 694 F.2d 556; *E.G. McKinney*, CA FC, 83-2 USTC ¶ 9698, 721 F.2d 163.

Taxpayer. The overall result to the Taxpayer using the Tax Court allocation formula is deductions totaling $3,550 ($2,200 for rental expense and $1,350 in itemized deductions for mortgage interest and taxes). Under the IRS allocation formula, the Taxpayer's total deductions were only $2,650 ($2,200 for rental expense and $450 in itemized deductions for mortgage interest and taxes).

¶ 1827 Other Limitations on Rental Losses

In addition to the limitation on deducting expenses relating to the rental of vacation or other dwelling units contained in Code Sec. 280A, two other limitations may affect deductions attributable to rental property. The at-risk rules limit deductible losses to the amount a taxpayer has at risk in the activity producing the deductions. Also, taxpayers generally may not deduct losses from passive activities. The at-risk rules are treated in detail at ¶ 311, as are the passive activity loss rules at ¶ 1103.

It should also be noted that any rental that avoids the Code Sec. 280A limitations may be subject to the "hobby loss" rules of Code Sec. 183. Rentals subject to Code Sec. 280A, however, are not also subject to Code Sec. 183.[55]

¶ 1835 RESIDENCE CONVERTED TO INVESTMENT

If a taxpayer converts a personal residence to rental use, the taxpayer becomes entitled to treat the property as investment property and is entitled to all the deductions relating to the operation of real estate, as discussed in Part III. The conversion must be actual and there must be a genuine holding out of the property for rental. The effort to rent need not be successful, but it must be bona fide.[56]

If a residence is converted to rental use, depreciation is based on the adjusted basis of the property or its fair market value at the time of the conversion, whichever is lower.[57]

A taxpayer who converts property to rental use at any time other than at the beginning of the tax year must divide any annual expenses between the portion of the year the property was held for rental and the portion of the year held for personal or other purposes. Only the part of the expense attributable to the part of the year the property is held for rental may be deducted and, of course, the amount may be limited under the rules discussed at ¶ 1807.

---

[55] Code Sec. 280A(f)(3).
[56] See, for example, *I. Meredith*, 65 TC 34, CCH Dec. 33,457; *D.L. Henry*, 46 TCM 186, CCH Dec. 40131(M), T.C. Memo. 1983-277.
[57] Reg. § 1.167(g)-1. See Chapter 9 for detailed discussion on depreciation.

¶ 1835

Chapter 19

Cooperatives, Condominiums, and Associations

¶ 1900 OVERVIEW OF CHAPTER

A personal residence may include a condominium or cooperative apartment. The tax treatment of these units is generally the same as that of any other type of home ownership.

In a condominium, the taxpayer owns outright a dwelling unit in a multi-unit structure. Each unit owner also owns a share of the common elements, such as land, lobbies, elevators, and service areas. Unit owners usually pay assessments or dues to an association or service corporation which is organized to take care of the common elements.

In a cooperative apartment, the taxpayer owns shares of stock in a corporation that owns or leases housing facilities. As a shareholder, the taxpayer is entitled to occupy a dwelling unit in the housing controlled by the corporation. The dwelling unit may be a house, an apartment, or a house trailer, but it must have the three facilities necessary to be classed as a dwelling—that is, cooking, sleeping, and toilet facilities.

Condominium management associations and residential real estate management associations are homeowners associations. Both may elect to be treated as associations that are exempt from tax on their exempt function income. Cooperative housing corporations may not qualify as homeowners associations.

¶ 1901 COOPERATIVE HOUSING CORPORATIONS

Generally speaking, shareholders in a cooperative housing arrangement enjoy the same tax benefits as any other homeowner; that is, they may deduct mortgage interest and real property taxes, as discussed at ¶ 1701 and ¶ 1709, and they may benefit from the provision to exclude gain on the sale of their homes, as discussed at ¶ 2015. The major difference is in the need for the cooperative housing corporation and the tenant stockholders to comply with the provisions of Code Sec. 216.

¶ 1903 Qualification as a Cooperative Housing Corporation

In order for a corporation to qualify as a cooperative housing corporation so that its tenant-stockholders may derive the tax benefits of home ownership, the corporation must meet the following requirements: [1]

1. The corporation must have one and only one class of stock;
2. Each of the stockholders of the corporation must be entitled, solely by reason of ownership of stock in the corporation, to occupy for dwelling purposes a house, or an apartment in a building, owned or leased by the corporation;
3. No stockholder of the corporation may be entitled, either conditionally or unconditionally, to receive any distribution not out of earnings and profits of the corporation except on a complete or partial liquidation of the corporation; and
4. 80 percent or more of the gross income of the corporation must be derived from tenant-stockholders.

A tenant-stockholder is a person who is a stockholder in a cooperative housing corporation, and whose stock is fully paid up in an amount that the IRS considers reasonably related to the portion of the value of the corporation's equity in the houses or apartment building and the land that is attributable to the house or apartment that the person is entitled to occupy.[2]

¶ 1903.1 One Class of Stock Requirement

There is a limited exception to the one class of stock requirement that permits certain stock to be issued to government units for financing and other purposes.[3] Also, the rights of some tenant-stockholders to larger apartments or additional parking spaces under their proprietary leases does not create more than one class of stock.[4] However, debt issued by the corporation that takes on too many of the characteristics of stock may become a second class of stock that could disqualify the corporation.[5]

¶ 1903.2 Right of Occupancy

Each stockholder of a cooperative must be entitled to occupy for dwelling purposes an apartment in a building or unit in a development owned or leased by the corporation, regardless of whether the stockholder qualifies as a tenant-stockholder. The stockholder does not have to actually occupy a unit, but only needs to have the right to occupy the premises as against the corporation. This right must be conferred on each stockholder because the stockholder's ownership of stock in the

---

[1] Code Sec. 216(b)(1).
[2] Code Sec. 216(b)(2).
[3] Reg. § 1.216-1(d)(1) and (f).
[4] Rev. Rul. 87-130, 1987-2 CB 68.
[5] See Code Sec. 385; but see also Rev. Rul. 72-404, 1972-2 CB 180, in which the IRS ruled that a purchase-money debt that carried no voting rights was treated as debt eventhough the debt was secured by the outstanding stock of the corporation.

corporation. The right to actually occupy the unit may be conditioned on the payment of rentals or assessments to the corporation.[6]

The inability of a purchaser of stock in a cooperative housing corporation to obtain occupancy because an existing tenant is protected by local rent control laws does not end the corporation's qualification as a cooperative housing corporation.[7]

In three cases, occupancy may be conditioned on approval by the corporation without jeopardizing the corporation's status as a cooperative housing corporation:[8]

1. When a person acquires stock of the cooperative by operation of law, by inheritance, or by foreclosure;
2. When a person other than an individual acquires stock in the cooperative; and
3. When the person from whom the corporation has acquired the apartments or houses acquires any stock of the cooperative from the cooperative not later than one year after the date on which the apartments or houses are transferred to the cooperative by that person.

¶ 1903.3 Distributions

No distributions may be made to stockholders of a cooperative housing corporation other than out of earnings and profits except on the complete or partial liquidation of the corporation. A refund of an overassessment, however, is not considered a "distribution."[9]

Under the normal rules of corporate taxation, gain is recognized by a corporation when it distributes appreciated property to shareholders in a liquidating distribution. A special provision allows a cooperative housing corporation to escape recognition of this gain when property that qualifies as a principal residence is distributed to a tenant-stockholder in exchange for the tenant-stockholder's stock.[10] This special nonrecognition rule facilitates the conversion of a cooperative into a condominium.

¶ 1903.4 Gross Income of Cooperative Housing Corporation

Eighty percent or more of the gross income of the corporation for the taxable year of the corporation in which the taxes and interest are paid or incurred must be derived from the tenant-stockholders in order for the stockholder to claim deductions for these items. Gross income

---

[6] Reg. § 1.216-1(d)(2).
[7] Rev. Rul. 80-299, 1980-2 CB 82.
[8] Prop. Reg. § 1.216-1(e)(2).
[9] Rev. Rul. 56-225, 1956-1 CB 58.
[10] Code Sec. 216(e); the dwelling must be the stockholder's principal residence as defined in Code Sec. 121, which provides for the exclusion of gain on the sale of a principal residence. Code Sec. 121 is discussed at ¶ 2007.

attributable to any house or apartment that a government unit is entitled to occupy under a lease or stock ownership is disregarded.[11]

Qualifying income includes amounts paid by tenant-stockholders for maid and secretarial services, parking or garage space, utilities, recreational facilities, cleaning, and any related services.[12] On the other hand, qualifying income does not include any rent received for the lease of commercial space within a building owned by the cooperative housing corporation. The cooperative must use care to restrict commercial rents so as not to endanger its status as a cooperative housing corporation and lose the tax benefits of home ownership for its tenant-stockholders.

¶ 1905 Deductions by Tenant-Stockholders

A tenant-stockholder is entitled to deductions for real property taxes and mortgage interest.[13] Also, if the tenant-stockholder uses a unit in a trade or business or for the production of income, the stockholder is entitled to deduct depreciation on the unit, in addition to other business expenses.

¶ 1905.1 Interest and Taxes

A taxpayer who qualifies as a tenant-stockholder of a cooperative housing corporation may deduct from gross income amounts paid or accrued within the tenant-stockholder's taxable year to the cooperative which represent the tenant-stockholder's proportionate share of:

1. The real estate taxes allowable as a deduction to the corporation which are paid or incurred by the corporation during the tenant-stockholder's taxable year on the houses or apartment building and the land on which the houses or apartment building are situated, and

2. The interest allowable as a deduction to the corporation which is paid or incurred by the corporation during the tenant-stockholder's taxable year on its indebtedness contracted in the acquisition, construction, alteration, rehabilitation, or maintenance of the houses or apartment building, or in the acquisition of the land on which the units are situated.[14]

A tenant-stockholder's proportionate share of interest and taxes is calculated by the proportion of the stock owned by the tenant-stockholder in relation to all outstanding stock, including stock held by the corporation.[15]

---

[11] Reg. § 1.216-1(d)(4).
[12] Rev. Rul. 68-387, 1968-2 CB 112.
[13] Code Sec. 216(a).
[14] Reg. § 1.216-1(a).
[15] Reg. § 1.216-1(b).

In order to more accurately reflect the relative burdens of interest and taxes born by different tenant-stockholders, however, a cooperative housing corporation may elect to allocate interest and taxes to its tenant-stockholders in a manner that departs from strict proportionality, if two conditions are met. First, each dwelling unit must be separately allocated a share of the cooperative's interest or taxes. Second, the allocation must reasonably reflect the cost to the cooperative of the interest and taxes attributable to the tenant-stockholder's unit and the unit's share of common areas.[16]

Example 1: MM Corporation is a cooperative housing corporation. MM purchases a site and constructs a building with 10 apartments of equal value at a total cost of $2,000,000. On completion, the fair market value of the land and building is $2,000,000. MM mortgages the property for $1,000,000 and sells 1,000 shares of stock, its total authorized stock, for $1,000,000. Ten individuals purchased this stock, with each person buying 100 shares for $100,000. Each 100 share certificate entitles the holder to lease a particular apartment in the building for a specified number of years. Each lease provides that the lessee must pay a proportionate part of the corporation's expenses.

During the current year (both the corporation and its stockholders use the calendar year), MM incurred expenses totalling $138,000, including $40,000 for real estate taxes, $50,000 for interest on the mortgage, $30,000 for maintenance, and $18,000 for other expenses. Each tenant-stockholder pays MM $13,800 during the year as his or her proportionate part of the expenses of the corporation. The entire gross income of MM during the year was from tenant-stockholders. Each tenant-stockholder is entitled to a deduction of $9,000 in computing taxable income for the current year, calculated as follows:

Shares of stock owned by tenant-stockholder	100
Shares owned by other tenant-stockholders	900
Total shares outstanding	1,000
Proportion of outstanding stock held by tenant-stockholder = 1/10	
Expenses of MM:	
Real estate taxes	$ 40,000
Interest	50,000
Maintenance	30,000
Other	18,000
Total expenses	$138,000

---

[16] Code Sec. 216(b)(3); Reg. § 1.216-1(d)(2).

Amount paid by tenant-stockholder equal to a proportionate part (1/10 × $138,000)	$ 13,800
Tenant's proportionate part of real estate taxes and interest (1/10 × $90,000)	$ 9,000
Tenant's proportionate part of total expenses based on stock ownership (1/10 × $138,000)	$ 13,800
Amount of tenant's payment representing real estate taxes and interest (9,000/13,800 × $13,800)	$ 9,000
Tenant's allowable deduction	$ 9,000

Example 2: The facts are the same as in Example 1, except that the building MM constructs has business space on the ground floor in addition to the 10 apartments. During the current year, MM rented the business space for $24,000 and deducted the $24,000 from its expenses in determining the amount of the expenses to be prorated among its tenant-stockholders. Each tenant-stockholder paid $11,400 instead of $13,800. More than 80 percent of MM's gross income for the current year is derived from tenant-stockholders. Each tenant-stockholder is entitled to a deduction under Code Sec. 216 for the current year of $7,434.80, computed as follows:

Total expenses of MM	$138,000.00
Less rent from business space	24,000.00
Expenses to be prorated	$114,000.00
Amount paid by tenant-stockholder equal to a proportionate part (1/10 × $114,000)	$ 11,400.00
Tenant's proportionate part of real estate taxes and interest (1/10 × $90,000)	$ 9,000.00
Tenant's proportionate part of total expenses based on stock ownership (1/10 × $138,000)	$ 13,800.00
Amount of tenant's payment representing real estate taxes and interest (9,000/13,800 × $11,400)	$ 7,434.80
Tenant's allowable deduction	$ 7,434.80

Tenant-stockholders may not be entitled to a deduction for real estate taxes paid by a cooperative on a building that it leases from another because the payment of those taxes may be considered rent.[17] Similarly, if a cooperative constructs a building on leased land, taxes on the land may not be deductible by the tenant-stockholders, but the taxes on the building owned by the cooperative would be deductible by the tenant-stockholders.[18] Also, tenant-stockholders may not deduct their share of real estate taxes on recreational facilities that are available for their use but are owned by a corporation other than the cooperative.[19]

---

[17] Rev. Rul. 62-177, 1962-2 CB 89.
[18] Rev. Rul. 62-178, 1962-2 CB 91.
[19] Rev. Rul. 69-76, 1969-1 CB 56.

¶ 1905.1

¶ 1905.2 *Depreciation*

Stock in a cooperative housing corporation owned by a tenant-stockholder who uses the proprietary lease or right of tenancy in a trade or business or for the production of income is treated as depreciable property.[20] Depreciation deductions cannot exceed the tenant-stockholder's basis in his or her stock.[21] Any depreciation deduction disallowed because it exceeds the tenant-stockholder's basis may be carried over as a deduction for depreciation in the following year.[22]

A tenant-stockholder's depreciation deduction when the unit is used in a trade or business or for the production of income is determined as follows:[23]

1. Compute the amount of depreciation allowable on the depreciable property owned by the cooperative in which the tenant-stockholder has a proprietary lease or right of tenancy;

2. Reduce the amount computed in Step 1 in the same ratio as the rentable space in the property which is not subject to a proprietary lease or right of tenancy by reason of stock ownership but which is held for rental purposes bears to the total rentable space in the property; and

3. Compute the tenant-stockholder's proportionate share of the depreciation deduction as adjusted in Step 2.[24]

The depreciation deduction determined in the manner set out above must be adjusted when only a portion of the property occupied under a proprietary lease or right of tenancy is used in a trade or business or for the production of income.[25]

¶ 1909 CONDOMINIUMS

A condominium is an interest in real property that consists of an undivided interest in common in a portion of a parcel of real property, which may be a fee interest or an estate for years, together with a separate interest in space in a building located on this parcel. The undivided interests in the common elements must be vested in the unit holders.[26] In other words, the owner of a condominium unit owns a cube of space within a building and shares common property with other unit owners.

---

[20] Code Sec. 216(c)(1).
[21] Code Sec. 216(c)(2)(A).
[22] Code Sec. 216(c)(2)(B).
[23] Reg. § 1.216-2(b)(1).
[24] Examples of the depreciation calculation may be found in Reg. § 1.216-2(d).
[25] Reg. § 1.216-2(b)(1). The allocation of deductions when only part of a taxpayer's home is used for business purposes is covered at ¶ 1805.
[26] Reg. § 1.528-1(b).

¶ 1911 Tax Treatment of Unit Owner

Essentially, the owner of a condominium unit is treated as any other homeowner for tax purposes since the owner owns the unit outright and not indirectly through shares in a corporation. The condominium owner may deduct real estate taxes on the unit, and mortgage interest if the unit is mortgaged, to the same extent as the owner of a single family home (see ¶ 1701 and 1709).[27] If a condominium is damaged by fire, storm or other casualty, the owner may take a casualty loss deduction for the unreimbursed loss.[28] If a condominium owner uses part of the unit for business purposes, or rents the unit to others, the unit owner is entitled to related business or rental expense deductions (see ¶ 1805). Finally, at a sale, the condominium unit owner is entitled to the special tax breaks available to other homeowners (see ¶ 2007-2015).

Occasionally, condominium unit owners are assessed for repairs or replacement. Capital assessments against unit owners for repairs or replacements and proceeds from a suit for defective construction used for repairs, replacements, or improvements are added to the unit owners' bases for their units. Recovery in a suit for defective construction of common elements reduces unit owners' bases proportionately and is not income to either unit owners or the condominium association.[29]

¶ 1913 Tax Treatment of Condominium Association

A condominium management association may elect to be treated as a tax-exempt homeowners association. If this election is made, the association is not taxed on exempt function income.[30] The tax treatment of homeowners associations, including condominium associations, is considered at ¶ 1915.

¶ 1915 HOMEOWNERS ASSOCIATIONS

Under Code Sec. 528, a qualified homeowners association, which may be a condominium management association, a residential real estate management association, or a timeshare association, may elect to be treated as a tax-exempt organization. If an association makes this election, it is not taxed on its exempt function income, that is, membership dues, fees, and other assessments collected from persons who own units and who are members of the association. The association does pay

---

[27] See Rev. Rul. 64-31, 1964-1 CB 300, dealing with the deduction of real estate taxes by condominium owners.

[28] The limitations on and method of calculating a casualty loss on a personal residence are also considered at ¶ 1713 and 1715.

[29] Rev. Rul. 81-152, 1981-1 CB 433.

[30] Code Sec. 528.

a tax at a flat rate of 30 percent (32 percent in the case of a timeshare association) on any income that is not exempt function income.

A condominium management association is any organization that is organized and operated to provide for the acquisition, construction, management, maintenance, and care of a condominium project if substantially all of the units in the project are used by individuals as residences.[31] A residential real estate management association is any organization organized and operated to provide for the acquisition, construction, management, maintenance, and care of a subdivision, development, or similar area if substantially all of the lots or buildings within the area are used by individuals for residences.[32] A timeshare association is any organization, other than a condominium management association, that is organized and operated to provide for the acquisition, construction, management, maintenance, and care of association property, if any member holds a timeshare right to use, or a timeshare ownership interest in, association real property.[33]

¶ 1917 Qualification for Tax-Exempt Status

If an association elects to be taxed as a homeowners association, it is not taxed on its exempt function income. To qualify for this election, a homeowners association must:[34]

1. Be organized and operated to provide for the acquisition, construction, management, maintenance, and care of association property;

2. Obtain 60 percent or more of its gross income from exempt function income;

3. Have at least 90 percent of its expenses be for the acquisition, construction, management, maintenance, and care of association property and, in the case of a timeshare association, for activities provided to or on behalf of association members; and

4. Ensure that no part of its net earnings will be used to benefit any private shareholder or individual, except through the acquisition, construction, management, maintenance, or care of association property or through the rebate of excess membership dues, fees, or assessments.

These requirements are explored in more detail in the following paragraphs.

---

[31] Code Sec. 528(c)(2).
[32] Code Sec. 528(c)(3).
[33] Code Sec. 528(c)(4).
[34] Code Sec. 528(c)(1).

¶ 1917.1 *Association Property*

Association property includes property held by the organization, property held in common by the members of the organization, property within the organization held privately by its members, and property owned by a governmental unit and used for the benefit of residents of the unit. In the case of a timeshare association, association property includes property in which the association or members have rights from recorded easements, covenants, or other recorded instruments, to use property related to the timeshare project.[35]

Property held by the organization or held in common by the organization is association property if it is available for the common benefit of all organization members and tends to increase the enjoyment of the private residences by their owners. This type of association property might include swimming pools and tennis courts. Facilities or areas set aside for nonmembers, or used primarily by nonmembers, however, are not association property. For example, property that is owned by the association for the purpose of leasing it to groups of nonmembers for use as a meeting place is not association property.[36]

Property normally owned by a governmental unit is association property if it includes areas and facilities traditionally recognized as part of a governmental function. These areas and facilities include roads, parks, sidewalks, streetlights, and fire stations. This type of property is association property whether it is owned by the organization, by its members as tenants in common, or by a governmental unit and used for the benefit of the residents of the unit as well as members of the organization.[37]

Property held privately by members of the association is association property if:[38]

1. It affects the overall appearance or structure of the residential units;
2. There is an agreement relating to the appearance or maintenance that applies on the same basis to all such property in the project;
3. There are annual assessments on all members of the association for maintaining this property; and
4. Membership in the association is a condition of every person's ownership of such property in the project.

Example: A condominium association enforces covenants that affect the appearance of individual units and maintains the exte-

---

[35] Code Sec. 528(c)(4).
[36] Reg. § 1.528-3(a).
[37] Reg. § 1.528-3(b).
[38] Reg. § 1.528-3(c).

rior walls and roofs of the individual units. Although the property the association maintains is private, its appearance may directly affect the condition of the entire condominium project. The exterior walls and roof are association property as long as requirements 3 and 4 described above are also met.

¶ 1917.2 *Use as Residences*

"Substantially all" the units within a condominium project, or lots or buildings within a subdivision or development, must be used as residences for a condominium management or residential real estate management association to qualify for tax-exempt status.

Substantially all of the units within a condominium are used by individuals for residences if at least 85 percent of the total square footage of the units in the project is used by individuals for residential purposes.[39] Areas used for residential purposes include the following:

1. A unit constructed for use as a residence but never occupied;
2. A unit that is not occupied but has been in the past, if it was constructed for use as a residence and the last individual to occupy it did use it as a residence; and
3. Units that are used for purposes that are auxiliary to residential use, such as laundry areas, swimming pools, tennis courts, storage rooms, and areas used by maintenance personnel.

Substantially all of the lots or buildings within a subdivision or development, including unimproved lots, are used by individuals for residences if at least 85 percent of the lots are zoned for residential purposes. Lots are considered zoned for residential purposes even if used for parking spaces, swimming pools, tennis courts, schools, fire stations, libraries, and churches. Commercial shopping areas and their parking spaces, however, are not lots zoned for residential purposes.[40]

A unit or building is not used for residential purposes for purposes of qualifying a homeowners association for tax-exempt status if it is occupied for over half of the days in the association's tax year by a person or series of persons who occupy the unit or building for less than 30 days each.[41]

¶ 1917.3 *Exempt Function Income*

At least 60 percent of an association's income must be exempt function income in order for the homeowners association to qualify for tax-exempt status. Exempt function income is any amount received by the association as membership dues, fees, or assessments from owners of

---

[39] Reg. § 1.528-4(b).
[40] Reg. § 1.528-4(c).
[41] Reg. § 1.528-4(d).

condominium housing units in the case of a condominium management association, from owners of residential real property in the case of a residential real estate management association, or from owners of timeshare rights to use, or timeshare ownership interests in, real property in the case of a timeshare association.[42] This income does not have to be labeled as membership dues, fees, or assessments, but it must come from members as owners, not as customers, of the association's services.[43]

Dues, fees, or assessments paid by a developer on unfinished or finished units or lots that remain unsold are exempt function income, even though the developer does not use the units or lots for residential purposes. Dues, fees, or assessments are not exempt function income unless each member's liability for payment arises solely from membership in the association. Amounts based on the value or size of property are considered a result of membership in the association, but amounts based on the extent to which a member makes use of any facility are not exempt function income.[44]

Excess assessments during a tax year that are rebated to members or applied to their future assessments are not exempt function income for that year, but if the excess assessments are applied to a future year's assessments, they are exempt function income in that future year.

Examples of exempt function income are assessments to:

1. Pay principal, interest, and real estate taxes on association property;
2. Maintain association property; and
3. Clean snow from public areas and remove trash.[45]

Examples of income that is not exempt function income are:

1. Amounts that are not includible in the association's gross income other than under Code Sec. 528 (for instance, tax-exempt interest);
2. Amounts received from nonmembers;
3. Amounts received from members for special use of the association's facilities which are not available to all members from paying dues, fees, or assessments required from all members;
4. Interest earned on amounts set aside in a sinking fund;
5. Amounts received for work done on privately owned property that is not association property; and

---

[42] Code Sec. 528(d)(3).
[43] Reg. § 1.528-9(a).
[44] Reg. § 1.528-9(a).
[45] Reg. § 1.528-9(b).

6. Amounts received from members in return for their transportation to or from shopping, work, etc.[46]

Amounts received from members or tenants of residential units owned by members for special use of an association's facilities are considered exempt function income if:
1. The amounts paid by members are not paid more than once in any 12-month period; and
2. The privilege obtained from the payment lasts for the entire 12-month period or portion of the period in which the facility is commonly in use.[47]

For example, amounts received from members for a yearly fee for use of tennis courts or a swimming pool are exempt function income. Amounts received for the use of a building for an evening, weekend, week, etc., however, are not considered exempt function income.

¶ 1917.4 *Expenditures*

An association cannot exclude exempt function income from gross income unless 90 percent or more of its expenditures for the tax year are for the acquisition, construction, management, maintenance, and care of association property or for activities provided to members of a timeshare association. The determination of whether an association meets this expenditure test is made after the close of the association's tax year. Investments or transfers of funds held to meet future costs are not treated as expenditures. For example, transfers to a sinking fund to replace a roof are not considered expenditures, even if the roof is association property. Also, excess assessments that are rebated to members or applied against future assessments are not considered expenditures.[48]

Expenditures counted in the 90-percent test are those to acquire, construct, manage, maintain, and care for association property. They include current operating and capital expenditures. They also include expenditures on association property, even if the property produces income that is not exempt function income.[49] For example, expenditures on a swimming pool are qualifying expenditures even though guests' fees are not exempt function income. Expenditures that apply to both association property and other property must be allocated on a reasonable basis.

Here are some examples of expenditures that are counted for purposes of the 90-percent test:
1. Salaries of an association manager and secretary;

---

[46] Reg. § 1.528-9(c).
[47] Reg. § 1.528-9(d).
[48] Reg. § 1.528-6(a).
[49] Reg. § 1.528-6(b).

2. Paving of streets;
3. Street signs;
4. Security personnel;
5. Legal and accounting fees;
6. Upkeep of tennis courts, swimming pools, and recreation halls;
7. Replacement of common buildings, facilities, and air conditioning;
8. Insurance premiums on association property; and
9. Real estate and personal property taxes imposed on association property.[50]

¶ 1917.5   Inurement

An organization cannot qualify as a homeowners association if any part of its net earnings inures (other than as a direct result of its engaging in one or more exempt functions) to the benefit of a private person. To the extent members receive a benefit from the general maintenance of association property, this benefit is not an inurement. If an organization pays rebates from amounts other than exempt function income, however, the rebates are inurements. In general, in determining whether an organization is in violation of the restriction on inurements, the IRS applies the principles used in making similar determinations for charities and other Code Sec. 501(c)(3) organizations.[51]

¶ 1921   Taxation of Homeowners Association

If a homeowners association elects to exclude exempt function income, it must pay a tax at a flat rate of 30 percent (32 percent in the case of a timeshare association) on its taxable income.[52] Taxable income is the association's gross income for the tax year, other than its exempt function income, reduced by any deductions directly connected with the production of the gross income subject to tax.[53] Deductions are directly connected with the production of gross income if they have both proximate and primary relationship to the production of the income. Deductions attributable solely to items of taxable gross income are proximately and primarily related to that income.[54]

In computing taxable income, the association may not deduct net operating losses, special deductions for corporations, such as the dividends received deduction, or expenses connected with the production of exempt function income. The association is allowed a specific deduction

---

[50] Reg. § 1.528-6(c).
[51] Reg. § 1.528-7.
[52] Code Sec. 528(b).
[53] Code Sec. 528(d)(1).
[54] Reg. § 1.528-10(c)(1).

of $100 so that associations with only a minimal amount of nonexempt income are not subject to tax.[55]

If facilities or personnel are used both for exempt functions of the association and for the production of nonexempt gross income, the expenses attributable to the facilities or personnel must be allocated between the two activities on a reasonable basis. The portion of the expenses allocated to the production of nonexempt gross income is directly connected with that income and is deductible in figuring the association's taxable income.[56]

Example: The Homeowners Association pays its manager a salary of $20,000 per year, and it does realize income other than exempt function income. If 10 percent of the manager's time during the year is devoted to activities generating nonexempt income, a deduction of $2,000 (10% × $20,000) generally would be permitted in computing the Homeowners Association's taxable income.

Note that a homeowners association does not have to elect exempt status under Code Sec. 528. A homeowners association should compute its tax using the regular corporate rates and tax return. Although, as a regular corporation, the association is not eligible to exclude income, the tax may be lower because of the lower regular corporate rates and deductions, which reduce income that would be exempt under Code Sec. 528.

¶ 1923 Election of Exempt Status

A homeowners association must elect the exclusion for exempt function income each year. The election is made by filing a properly completed Form 1120-H. Once made, the election is binding and may not be revoked without the consent of the IRS.[57] The IRS has indicated, however, that it will permit a revocation of the election when the election is made as a result of incorrect tax advice on the part of a professional tax advisor, if the revocation is requested promptly after the error is discovered.[58]

¶ 1925 Nonexempt Associations

If an association is not a tax-exempt organization or cannot exclude exempt function income from gross income, the association must file tax returns in the same manner as other corporations. Even if it is an unincorporated association, it is treated as a corporation for tax purposes.

---

[55] Code Sec. 528(d)(2).
[56] Reg. § 1.528-10(c)(2).
[57] Reg. § 1.528-8.
[58] Rev. Rul. 83-74, 1983-1 CB 112.

¶ 1925.1 Tax-Exempt Status

A homeowners association formed to administer and enforce covenants for preserving the architecture and appearance of a development and to own and maintain common green areas, streets, and sidewalks that cannot exclude exempt function income from gross income under Code Sec. 528 generally cannot qualify as a tax-exempt organization (that is, as a civic league or social welfare organization).[59] It may qualify for that tax-exempt status, however, if it can show that the following conditions apply:

1. The community served by the association is a geographical unit reasonably related to a governmental subdivision;
2. The association does not maintain the exterior of private residences;
3. The association owns and maintains only areas and facilities of direct governmental concern, such as roads, parks, sidewalks, and streetlights which are available to the general public; and
4. The association owns and maintains recreational areas and facilities for the use and enjoyment of the general public (the association may not qualify if it owns and maintains parking facilities only for its members).[60]

If an association establishes a separate organization to own and maintain recreational facilities and restricts their use to members, and no part of its earnings benefits any member, it may be able to qualify for tax-exempt status as a social club. But a club that provides social and recreational facilities and limits their use to members is precluded from qualifying for tax-exempt status as a social club by owning and maintaining residential streets, enforcing restrictive covenants, or providing residential fire and police protection and trash collection.[61]

¶ 1925.2 Cooperative Organization

A condominium management corporation that cannot exclude exempt function income from gross income may operate in such a way as to qualify as a cooperative.[62] This would permit the corporation to retain for reasonable business purposes up to 80 percent of its otherwise taxable income received from unit owner-stockholders as regular assessments. This is done by distributing qualified patronage dividends for which the cooperative receives a deduction. The patronage dividends may be paid 20 percent in cash and 80 percent in qualified written notices of allocation. Therefore, up to 80 percent of otherwise taxable income accumulated from the regular assessments may be retained by

---

[59] Rev. Rul. 74-17, 1974-1 CB 130.
[60] Rev. Rul. 74-99, 1974-1 CB 131.
[61] Rev. Rul. 75-494, 1975-2 CB 214.
[62] Code Secs. 1381—1388.

the cooperative corporation for its reasonable business needs. Owner-stockholders who do not use their condominium units in their trade or business or for the production of income may exclude patronage dividends from their income under this arrangement.[63]

¶ 1925.3 Assessments

Regular assessments paid by condominium owners are income to the corporation for services rendered. The excess of this income over expenses is subject to tax. Excess assessments over the expenses for the year do not result in taxable income to the corporation if they are either refunded to the owner-stockholders or applied to the following year's regular assessments because of a specific vote of the membership at a membership meeting.[64]

A special assessment is not included in the gross income of a condominium management corporation that cannot exclude exempt function income from gross income under Code Sec. 528 if the assessment has been specifically voted on and approved by the stockholders, designated for specific capital expense, set aside in a special bank account, and not committed with the regular assessments of the management corporation. If the special assessment is to pay for services rendered by the corporation to the owner-stockholders, however, the funds collected from the special assessment are included in the gross income of the management association.[65]

Example: A special assessment of $100 is levied and collected from the owner-stockholders of a condominium to pay for the unexpected cost of repairing the condominium's swimming pool filter and for the increased cost of maintaining the lawns of the condominium. Because the special assessment in this case is for services rendered by the management corporation to the owner-stockholders, it is included in the corporation's gross income.

A special assessment that owner-stockholders vote on and designate for the replacement of personal property in the common elements of the condominium is treated as a contribution to the capital of the management corporation. It is not included in gross income, provided that the funds collected are designated for a specific capital expense and kept in a separate bank account.

Example: The owner-stockholders in a condominium levy and collect a special assessment to be used exclusively to replace outdoor lawn furniture owned by the condominium management corporation. The money collected is deposited in a separate bank account specifically designated for this purpose. The special assess-

---

[63] Rev. Rul. 75-371, 1975-2 CB 52.
[64] Rev. Rul. 70-604, 1970-2 CB 9.
[65] Rev. Rul. 75-371, 1975-2 CB 52.

ment is not included in the gross income of the condominium management association.

If the owner-stockholders of a condominium management corporation vote to levy and collect a special assessment for a specific capital expense in the common elements of the condominium's real property, the corporation does not include the assessment in gross income because it owns none of the property benefited. Each owner-stockholder owns an undivided interest in the common elements of the condominium's real property. If the funds are deposited in a separate bank account earmarked for a specific capital expense and may only be spent for that designated purpose, the management corporation is acting as an agent for the owner-stockholders because it may not use these funds to benefit any property that it owns.[66]

Example: The owner-stockholders of a condominium decide to levy and collect from each owner a special assessment of $25 per month for 24 months. The condominium management corporation is directed to deposit these assessments into two separate bank accounts and not to combine these assessments with any regular assessment funds. The special assessments will pay for the replacement of the roof and elevator located in the common elements of the property. The special assessments are not included in the management corporation's gross income because the corporation is collecting these funds as an agent, for the benefit of the owner-stockholders who own undivided interests in the common elements of the property.

---

[66] Rev. Rul. 75-370, 1975-2 CB 25.

Chapter 20

Sale of Residence

¶ 2000 OVERVIEW OF CHAPTER

The sale of a taxpayer's residence is generally a taxable transaction. A residence is a capital asset and its sale at a gain produces capital gain. There are, however, special provisions in the tax law that allow the tax to be avoided or postponed if specified requirements are met. Generally, for home sales on or after May 7, 1997, gain of up to $250,000 ($500,000 for married taxpayers filing jointly) is not subject to tax. For home sales before May 7, 1997, the replacement of a principal residence with a new principal residence allowed the tax on any gain to be postponed until the new residence is ultimately sold. Also, again for sales before May 7, 1997, taxpayers over the age of 55 who sold their homes could exclude a portion of their gain from income.

¶ 2001 GAIN OR LOSS ON SALE OF RESIDENCE

A taxpayer's home is a capital asset; thus, any gain on the sale is a capital gain, and, unless the special provisions discussed beginning at ¶ 2007 apply, the gain is subject to current tax. While any gain is subject to tax, a loss on the sale of a personal residence is generally not deductible. Personal, living, or family expenses are not deductible, and a loss on the sale of a personal residence falls into this category.[1]

The general rules for the calculation of gain and loss on the sale of real property are discussed at ¶ 1303. Of course, to calculate gain or loss, a taxpayer must know his or her adjusted basis.[2] Oftentimes, taxpayers are lax in keeping records to establish the adjusted basis of a personal residence which includes capital improvements and additions. The Tax Court has indicated that it will consider a taxpayer's estimates of such costs based on recollection, but the better course is to maintain receipts and other documentation. The amount of weight the Tax Court gives to recollection will bear heavily against the taxpayer whose own fault is the reason for any "inexactitude."[3]

---

[1] Code Sec. 262(a); Reg. § 1.262-1(b)(4); see also Code Sec. 165(c) and (f), which limit the losses allowed to individuals and for capital losses.

[2] Basis rules are covered in detail at ¶ 101.

[3] *R.C. Bayly*, 42 TCM 1216, CCH Dec. 38,291(M), T.C. Memo. 1981-549.

¶ 2003 Business or Rental Use

While the loss from the sale of a residence is generally not deductible, this is not the case if the residence was used as rental property or in a trade or business of the taxpayer. Even if a house was originally purchased as a personal residence, a loss on its sale is deductible if the house was converted to rental or business use before the sale. The basis for determining any loss in this situation is, of course, the cost of the property or its fair market value on the date of conversion, whichever is less.[4] When a residence was used partly as a personal residence and partly for business or rental, gain or loss is apportioned between the two uses. Any loss on the business or rental portion is deductible, while loss on the part used as a personal residence is not.[5]

¶ 2005 Residence Held for Gain

In rare cases, the holding of a residence, even though it is not held for rental, may be considered as the holding of property for the production of income so as to allow any loss on the sale to be deductible.

In *E.G. Lowry, Jr.*,[6] a taxpayer had stopped using a summer home that was offered for sale at a price in excess of the market value in the area. The taxpayer held out for six years until appreciation finally brought the asking price. While the taxpayer did not rent the property during the six years, maintenance costs were deducted by the taxpayer. The court ruled that these expenses were deductible because the taxpayer had converted the property into property held for the production of income (the appreciation) under Reg. § 1.212-1(b).

In another case,[7] a taxpayer was entitled to deduct a loss on a residence that was inherited from a spouse even though the taxpayer occupied it for a short period of time. The taxpayer was able to convince the court that from the moment the property was acquired the taxpayer never intended to occupy the house as a residence and that the ownership of the property was for the production of income, not for residence purposes.

¶ 2007 TAX EXCLUSION FOR PRINCIPAL RESIDENCE

Individuals can exclude from income up to $250,000 ($500,000 for married couples filing jointly) in gain from the sale or exchange of their principal residence on or after May 7, 1997.[8] Gain excluded under this provision is never subject to tax. This exclusion replaced the tax-free rollover provision (¶ 2011) and the exclusion for taxpayers over 55 (¶ 2021). Any gain in excess of the $250,000 or $500,000 exclusion is

---

[4] Reg. § 1.165-9(b).
[5] Rev. Rul. 286, 1953-2 CB 20.
[6] DC NH, 74-2 USTC ¶ 9821, 384 F. Supp. 257.
[7] *H.V. Watkins*, 32 TCM 809, CCH Dec. 32,070(M), T.C. Memo. 1973-167.
[8] Code Sec. 121.

subject to tax as capital gain regardless of whether proceeds are reinvested in another residence or not.

Although the exclusion generally applies to sales or exchanges after May 6, 1997, homeowners may elect the old tax-free rollover and exclusion for taxpayers over 55 for sales:

1. After May 6, 1997, and before August 5, 1997;
2. After August 5, 1997, if subject to a binding contract in effect on August 5, 1997;
3. After August 5, 1997, if a replacement residence under the tax-free rollover provision was acquired before August 6, 1997, either outright or under a binding contract, and the rollover provision would have applied under prior law.[9]

¶ 2009 Qualifications for Exclusion

To qualify for the $250,000 ($500,000 for joint returns) exclusion on the sale of a home, the taxpayer must have owned and used the home as a principal residence for at least two years out of the five years immediately preceding the sale.[10] Further, the exclusion does not apply to any sale or exchange if the taxpayer took advantage of the exclusion for another residence within the two years preceding the current home sale.[11] Under the latter rule, no sale before May 7, 1997, is taken into account.[12]

If a taxpayer cannot meet the requirements for the exclusion because of a job change or health reasons, or other unforeseen circumstances allowed by the IRS, a reduced exclusion is available. The reduced exclusion also is available if the requirements are not met for any reason if the sale occurs before August 5, 1999, and the taxpayer owned the residence on August 5, 1997.[13] The reduced exclusion is determined by the ratio of the period of use as a personal residence during the previous five years (or the period since the last sale subject to the exclusion, if less) to two years.[14] For instance, if a single taxpayer fails to qualify because he lived in the residence only one year before being relocated by his employer, the ratio would be ½ (one year to two years). His exclusion would be limited to $125,000 (½ × $250,000).

¶ 2009.3 Joint Returns

For a married couple to claim the $500,000 exclusion, the following requirements must be met:

1. They must file a joint return for the year of sale;

---

[9] Taxpayer Relief Act of 1997, Sec. 312(d).
[10] Code Sec. 121(a).
[11] Code Sec. 121(b)(3).
[12] Code Sec. 121(b)(3)(B).
[13] Taxpayer Relief Act of 1997, Sec. 312(d)(3).
[14] Code Sec. 121(c).

2. Either spouse may have owned the home in two out of five of the previous years;
3. Both spouses must have used the home as their principal residence in two out of five of the previous years; and
4. Neither spouse must have taken advantage of the exclusion in the previous two years.[15]

In the Conference Report to the Taxpayer Relief Act of 1997, the conferees clarified that "the provision limiting the exclusion to only one sale every two years by the taxpayer does not prevent a husband and wife filing a joint return from each excluding up to $250,000 of gain from the sale or exchange of each spouse's principal residence provided that each spouse would be permitted to exclude up to $250,000 of gain if they filed separate returns."

¶ 2009.5 Special Situations

Cooperative Housing

A taxpayer who is a tenant-stockholder in a cooperative housing corporation can qualify to exclude gain on the sale of his co-op. The two-out-of-five-years ownership requirement is applied to the cooperative stock, and the two-out-of-five-years use requirement is applied to the house or apartment that the taxpayer occupied as the tenant-stockholder.[16]

Deceased and Former Spouses

An unmarried individual whose spouse is deceased at the time of the sale or exchange can include the period the deceased spouse owned and used the property before death in the period the unmarried individual owned and used the property.[17]

A divorced individual who received the property from the former spouse in the divorce can include in the ownership period the period the former spouse owned the property. Also, an individual is treated as using property as a principal residence during any period of ownership while the spouse or former spouse is granted use of the property under a divorce or separation agreement.[18]

Prior Tax-Free Rollover

Individuals who rolled over gain into a replacement residence under Code Sec. 1034 (see ¶ 2011) can count the time they owned and used the former residence toward the ownership and use requirements for the $250,000 ($500,000) exclusion.[19]

---

[15] Code Sec. 121(b)(2).
[16] Code Sec. 121(d)(4).
[17] Code Sec. 121(d)(2).
[18] Code Sec. 112(d)(3).
[19] Code Sec. 121(g).

Business Use

If a person used a personal residence for business purposes and claimed depreciation deductions for the residence, gain attributable to the depreciation deductions cannot be excluded from income.[20]

¶ 2011 TAX-FREE ROLLOVER OF GAIN

Before passage in 1997 of the $250,000 exclusion for gain on the sale of a principal residence (¶ 2007), a taxpayer could postpone the tax on the gain from the sale of a principal residence by buying a new principal residence that cost as much as the adjusted sales price of the old home.[21] The gain rollover provisions, however, may still apply if the taxpayer sold his principal residence after August 5, 1997, but had acquired a replacement property within the replacement period (¶ 2013.3) before August 6, 1997. Also, the old rollover provisions still determine the basis of a residence that is sold under the new rules if it was purchased as replacement property under the old rollover provisions.

¶ 2013 Postponement of Tax Requirements

In order to postpone the tax on the sale of a residence, the residence must have been the taxpayer's principal residence. Also, the replacement home, which must have been the taxpayer's principal residence, must have been acquired within two years of the sale of the old residence.[22]

¶ 2013.3 *Replacement Period*

The replacement period under Code Sec. 1034 was 48 months. The taxpayer who sold a principal residence must have bought or built and lived in the replacement house within two years before or two years after the date of sale to postpone tax on the gain from the sale of the old residence. The taxpayer must have physically lived in the replacement home as the principal residence within the required period.[23]

The replacement period was suspended for a taxpayer while the taxpayer serves on extended active duty in the armed forces. The replacement period also was suspended while a taxpayer was stationed outside the United States by the military.

If the taxpayer's spouse was in the armed forces and the taxpayer was not, the suspension for military service also applied to the taxpayer if the old home was jointly owned. Both individuals must have used the old home as their principal residence.

---

[20] Code Sec. 121(d)(6).
[21] Code Sec. 1034 as in effect before its repeal in the Taxpayer Relief Act of 1997.
[22] Code Sec. 1034(a).
[23] *E.L. Sheahan*, CA-5, 63-2 USTC ¶ 9720, 323 F.2d 383.

The replacement period after the sale of a taxpayer's old residence was suspended while the taxpayer had a tax home outside the United States. The suspension applied only if the taxpayer's stay overseas began before the end of the two-year replacement period following the sale of the old residence. The replacement period plus period of suspension was limited to four years.[24]

¶ 2015 Tax Treatment

A taxpayer who sold a principal residence and purchased a new principal residence within the replacement period postponed paying tax on some or all of the gain realized on the sale of the old residence.[25] The provision was not elective. The taxpayer, in effect, rolled over the gain into the new residence and had the untaxed gain reflected in the adjusted basis of the new residence.

If the purchase price of the taxpayer's new residence was at least as much as the adjusted sales price of the old residence, no gain was taxed. If the purchase price of the new residence was less than the adjusted sales price of the old residence, the gain taxed in the year of sale was the lesser of the gain on the sale of the old home or the excess of the adjusted sales price of the old residence over the purchase price of the new residence.[26]

¶ 2015.1 Gain on Old Residence

When a taxpayer sold a principal residence, the gain realized was calculated in the usual fashion, that is, amount realized less adjusted basis.[27] The adjusted sales price of the old residence was used to compute the part of the gain that was not recognized and that was rolled over into the new residence as mentioned above. Adjusted sales price is the amount realized less fixing-up expenses.[28]

Fixing-up expenses are decorating and repair expenses paid in order to sell the old residence. To qualify, the expenses must:

1. Be for work done during the 90-day period ending on the day the contract for the sale of the old home is signed;
2. Be paid within 30 days after the sale;
3. Not be deductible in computing taxable income;
4. Not be taken into account in determining the amount realized on the sale; and
5. Not be for capital improvements or additions (which, of course, are added to the basis of the property).

---

[24] Code Sec. 1034(k).
[25] Code Sec. 1034(a).
[26] Reg. § 1.1034-1(a).
[27] For the general rules on the computation of gain or loss on the sale of real estate, see ¶ 1301.
[28] Code Sec. 1034(b)(1).

Fixing up expenses were used only to determine the gain on which the tax was postponed. They did not enter into the computation of the actual gain on the sale.[29]

A taxpayer who traded the old residence for a new residence treated the trade as a sale and purchase for purposes of Code Sec. 1034.[30]

¶ 2015.2 Gain on New Residence and Basis

The purchase price of a taxpayer's replacement home was used to find the amount of gain subject to tax and the amount of gain on which the tax was postponed following the sale of a principal residence under Code Sec. 1034. Purchase price included costs incurred within the 48-month replacement period for:

1. Buying or building the home;
2. Rebuilding the home; and
3. Capital improvements or additions.

The taxpayer could not consider any costs incurred before or after the 48-month period, other than those incurred during a suspension of the replacement period for service in the armed forces.[31]

If a taxpayer sold a principal residence and purchased a new one within the replacement period, the taxpayer's basis for the new residence was its cost reduced by the gain not recognized under Code Sec. 1034 on the sale of the old residence.[32]

Application of the rules under Code Sec. 1034 for the calculation of the amount of gain not recognized and the basis of the new residence is illustrated in the following examples based on Reg. § 1.1034-1(c)(2). Assume the transactions all took place before May 7, 1997.

Comprehensive Example 1: The Taxpayer sold a residence, which had a basis of $17,500. To make it more attractive to buyers, the Taxpayer painted the outside at a cost of $300 in April. The Taxpayer paid for the painting when the work was finished. In May, the house was sold for $20,000. Brokers' commissions and other selling expenses were $1,000. In October, the Taxpayer bought a new residence for $18,000. The amount realized, the gain realized, the adjusted sales price, and the gain recognized are computed as follows:

Selling price	$20,000
Less: Commissions and selling expenses	1,000
Amount realized	$19,000

---

[29] Reg. § 1.1034-1(b)(6).
[30] Code Sec. 1034(c)(1).
[31] Reg. § 1.1034-4.
[32] Code Sec. 1034(e).

Less: Basis	17,500
Gain realized	$ 1,500
Amount realized	$19,000
Less: Fixing-up expenses	300
Adjusted sales price	$18,700
Less: Cost of new residence	18,000
Gain recognized	$ 700
Cost of new residence	$18,000
Less: Gain not recognized ($1,500 − $700)	800
Adjusted basis of new residence	$17,200

Comprehensive Example 2: The facts are the same as in Example 1, except that the selling price of the old residence was $18,500. The computations are as follows:

Selling price	$18,500
Less: Commissions and selling expenses	1,000
Amount realized	$17,500
Less: Basis	17,500
Gain realized	$ -0-

Since no gain was realized, Code Sec. 1034 did not apply. It was unnecessary to compute the adjusted sales price of the old residence. No adjustment to the basis of the new residence was made.

Comprehensive Example 3: The facts are the same as in Example 1, except that the cost of purchasing the new residence was $17,000. The computations are as follows:

Selling price	$20,000
Less: Commissions and selling expenses	1,000
Amount realized	$19,000
Less: Basis	17,500
Gain realized	$ 1,500
Amount realized	$19,000
Less: Fixing-up expenses	300
Adjusted sales price	$18,700
Cost of new residence	17,000
Difference	$ 1,700

Since the adjusted sales price of the old residence exceeded the cost of purchasing the new residence by $1,700, which is more than the gain realized, all of the gain realized ($1,500) was recognized. Since none of the gain goes unrecognized, no adjustment to the basis of the new residence was made and its basis was its cost of $17,000.

¶ 2015.2

Comprehensive Example 4: The facts are the same as in Example 1, except that fixing-up expenses were $1,100. The computations are as follows:

Selling price	$20,000
Less: Commissions and selling expenses	1,000
Amount realized	$19,000
Less: Basis	17,500
Gain realized	$ 1,500
Amount realized	$19,000
Less: Fixing-up expenses	1,100
Adjusted sales price	$17,900
Less: Cost of new residence	18,000
Gain recognized	$ -0-
Cost of new residence	$18,000
Less: Gain not recognized	1,500
Adjusted basis of new residence	$16,500

¶ 2015.3 Joint Ownership

A taxpayer and spouse may have owned a residence separately but have taken title to a replacement residence jointly. Or, they may have owned the old residence jointly but taken title to the replacement separately. The postponed gain that reduces the basis of the new home could be divided between taxpayer and spouse if both met the following requirements:

1. They used the old residence and new residence as their principal residences; and
2. They signed a statement that said: "We agree to reduce the basis of the new home(s) by the gain from selling the old home." The statement may be on Form 2119 or a separate sheet attached to the tax return.[33]

Example: The Taxpayer sold a home that was separately owned by the Taxpayer, but both the Taxpayer and spouse used the home as their principal residence. The adjusted sales price was $48,000, its adjusted basis was $36,000, and the gain realized was $12,000. The Taxpayer and spouse bought a replacement home within the replacement period for $50,000. Each contributed $25,000 from separate funds, and the couple took title jointly. If they consented to reduce the basis of the new home, the Taxpayer's gain on the sale of the old residence was postponed as if they had owned both homes jointly. Each spouse has a basis of $19,000 in the new

---

[33] Code Sec. 1034(g); Reg. § 1.1034-1(f).

residence, that is, $25,000 less $6,000 postponed gain. If they did not sign the consent, the Taxpayer's entire $12,000 was subject to tax because the adjusted sales price of the old home of $48,000 was greater than the Taxpayer's share of the cost of the new residence, and each spouse would have a basis of $25,000 in the new residence.

Suppose, however, that the Taxpayer and spouse owned the old residence jointly, but the spouse used separate funds to purchase the new house and took title individually. In this case, signing the consent meant that the $12,000 gain was postponed and the spouse has an adjusted basis of $38,000 in the new home. If they did not sign the consent, the Taxpayer was taxed on the Taxpayer's share of the gain from the sale of the old residence ($6,000), but the spouse postponed tax on the spouse's share of the gain because it was reinvested in a new principal residence. The spouse's basis for the home in this case would be $44,000.

¶ 2017 Partial Business Use

If a taxpayer sold property that was used partly as a principal residence and partly for business or rental purposes, the transaction was treated as the sale of two properties. Under Code Sec. 1034, the tax on the gain attributable to the residence could have been postponed by reinvesting an equal amount in a new principal residence. Tax on the gain attributable to the business portion of the home could not have been postponed under Code Sec. 1034.

A similar rule applied if a replacement residence was used partly for residential and partly for business or rental use. Only the part of the purchase price allocable to the principal residence portion of the home could be counted as the cost of purchasing the replacement home under Code Sec. 1034.[34]

¶ 2021 EXCLUSION OF GAIN FOR TAXPAYER OVER 55

Under Code Sec. 121 before its amendment by the Taxpayer Relief Act of 1997 to provide for the exclusion discussed at ¶ 2007, a taxpayer could exclude from gross income part or all of the gain on the sale of a principal residence, up to $125,000, if the taxpayer met the age, ownership, and use tests at the time of the sale. (Note: References to Code Sec. 121 in this ¶ 2021 are to that Code Sec. as in effect prior to its amendment by the Taxpayer Relief Act of 1997.)

---

[34] Reg. § 1.1034-1(c)(3)(ii). For further discussion on homes used partly for business or rental purposes, see ¶ 1801.

¶ 2023 Exclusion Amount and Qualification Requirements

A taxpayer could elect to exclude from income $125,000 ($62,500 in the case of a married individual filing a separate return) [35] on the sale of the taxpayer's principal residence if:

1. The taxpayer was 55 or older on the date of the sale;[36]
2. The taxpayer owned and lived in the home for at least three years out of the five-year period ending on the date of sale;[37] and
3. The taxpayer or the taxpayer's spouse never excluded gain on the sale of a home under Code Sec. 121 after July 26, 1978.[38]

The taxpayer must have been 55 by the time the home was sold to qualify for the exclusion. A sale in the year the taxpayer turns 55, but before the taxpayer's birthday, did not qualify.[39]

¶ 2023.1 *Ownership and Use Requirements*

The required three years of ownership and use during the five years before the sale did not have to be continuous. The test was met if the taxpayer owned and lived in the property as a principal residence for either 36 full months or 1,095 days during the five-year period. Short, temporary absences for vacations or other seasonal absences, even if the taxpayer rents the property while away, counted as periods of use.[40]

The ownership and use tests could have been met during different three-year periods, as long as both tests were met during the five years before the sale.[41]

Example: In 1985, the Taxpayer was 50 years old and lived in a rented apartment. The apartment building was later changed to a condominium and the Taxpayer bought the apartment on December 1, 1988. In 1990, the Taxpayer became ill and, on April 15 of that year, moved to a daughter's home. On February 17, 1992, while still living in the daughter's home, the Taxpayer sold the apartment.

The Taxpayer can exclude the gain on the sale of the apartment under Code Sec. 121 because the age, ownership, and use tests were met. The Taxpayer was over 55 at the time of the sale. The five-year period is from February 18, 1987, to February 17, 1992, the date the Taxpayer sold the apartment. The Taxpayer owned the apartment from December 1, 1988, to February 17,

---

[35] Code Sec. 121(b)(1).
[36] Code Sec. 121(a)(1).
[37] Code Sec. 121(a)(2).
[38] Code Sec. 121(b)(2) and (3).
[39] Reg. § 1.121-a(1).
[40] Reg. § 1.121-1(c).
[41] Rev. Rul. 80-172, 1980-2 CB 56.

1992 (over three years). The Taxpayer lived in the apartment from February 18, 1987, to April 15, 1990 (over three years).

¶ 2023.2 Purchase of New Principal Residence

If a taxpayer had gain remaining after the application of the $125,000 exclusion under Code Sec. 121, the taxpayer may have been able to postpone the tax on this gain by purchasing a new principal residence as discussed above.[42] The amount that must have been invested in a new residence in order to fully satisfy the nonrecognition provision of Code Sec. 1034 was reduced by the amount of gain excluded by the election under Code Sec. 121.

Example: The Taxpayers, a married couple, sold their home on June 14, 1991, for $250,000. Both were 60 years old and had lived in the home as their principal residence for 20 years. The adjusted basis of their old home was $75,000 and they had selling expenses of $15,000. They bought a new principal residence for $110,000 and moved into it on July 20, 1991. Neither spouse has excluded gain on the sale of a home before, and they elected to exclude gain on the sale of their old home under Code Sec. 121.

Their gain was greater than $125,000, but because they purchased a new home that cost as much as the difference between the adjusted sales price of their old home and the exclusion claimed, they postponed the tax on part of the gain not excluded under Code Sec. 121. They figured the gain excluded and postponed as follows:

Gain realized:

Selling price of old home	$250,000
Less: Selling expenses	15,000
Amount realized	$235,000
Less: Adjusted basis of old home	75,000
Gain realized	$160,000

Gain after exclusion:

Gain realized	$160,000
Less: Exclusion (lesser of gain realized or $125,000)	125,000
Gain after exclusion	$ 35,000

Gain taxed in 1991:

Amount realized	$235,000
Less: Cost of new home	110,000
	$125,000
Less: Exclusion	125,000
Gain taxed in 1991	$ –0–

---

[42] Code Sec. 121(d)(7).

Gain postponed:
Gain after exclusion	$ 35,000
Less: Gain taxed in 1991	0
Gain postponed	$ 35,000

Adjusted basis of new home:
Cost of new home	$110,000
Less: Gain postponed	35,000
Adjusted basis of new home	$ 75,000

¶ 2025 Election and Revocation of Election

The election, or revocation of the election, to exclude gain under Code Sec. 121 had to be made before the latest of the following dates:

1. Three years from the due date of the return for the year of sale;
2. Three years from the date the return was filed; or
3. Two years from the date the tax was paid.[43]

¶ 2025.1 *Election of the Exclusion*

The election to exclude gain under Code Sec. 121 was made by attaching a filled-in Form 2119 to the income tax return for the year of sale or by attaching a signed statement to the return. The statement must have stated that the taxpayer was choosing to exclude from income gain from the sale and must have also included: [44]

1. The taxpayer's name, age, social security number, and marital status on the date of sale. If jointly owned, this information must be supplied for each owner.
2. The date home was bought and sold.
3. The adjusted sales price and the adjusted basis of the property on the date of sale.
4. The length of time taxpayer was away from the home during the five years before the sale, not including vacations and other seasonal absences even if the home was rented.
5. Whether the taxpayer or a joint owner ever elected to exclude gain under Code Sec. 121, and if so, when and where. If the election was revoked, give date of revocation.

The election could have been made even if the taxpayer originally included it on the tax return for the year of sale by filing an amended return.

---

[43] Reg. § 1.121-4(a).   [44] Reg. § 1.121-4(b).

¶ 2025.2 *Revocation of the Election*

A spouse (or personal representative of a deceased spouse) who joined in making an election must join in revoking the election. The revocation is made in a signed statement showing the taxpayer's name and social security number and identifying the year in which the election was made. The statement is sent to the appropriate IRS service center. If less than one year is left in the assessment period for the return on which the election was made, the taxpayer must consent to extend the assessment period until one year after the statement of revocation is filed.[45]

---

[45] Reg. § 1.121-4(c).

Part VI

Securitized Real Estate Investments

Introduction to Part VI

The three chapters that follow (21-23) take a brief look at ownership interests in real estate that are indirect and mass-marketed. All three, real estate limited partnerships, real estate investment trusts (REITs), and real estate mortgage investment conduits (REMICs), offer interests that are securities under federal securities laws.

According to the Supreme Court, in *United Housing Foundation, Inc. v. Forman,* 421 U.S. 837, 95 S.Ct. 2051 (1975) and *Securities and Exchange Commission v. W.J. Howey Co.,* 328 U.S. 293, 66 S.Ct. 1100 (1946), an investment contract embodies the essential attributes that define a security, namely, the presence of an investment in a common venture premised on a reasonable expectation of profits to be derived from the entrepreneurial or managerial efforts of others. A limited partnership, REIT, or REMIC investment clearly meets this definition. Once an interest is classified as a security, the underlying entity, its sponsors and promoters, and everyone who has a part in organizing the entity and selling interests in it, as well as the interests themselves, become subject to the securities laws, including the Securities Act of 1933, the Securities Exchange Act of 1934, and the Investment Advisors Act of 1940. These laws and the many court decisions interpreting them are quite complex and are a very specialized area of law.

The treatment of these entities under the tax law also may be special. The chapters that follow are not detailed discussions of the tax provisions that govern the operation of these entities, but rather a summary of how the tax law treats investors in these entities. At best, however, the discussion merely skims the surface of these complex laws.

Chapter 21

Real Estate Limited Partnerships

¶ 2100 OVERVIEW OF CHAPTER

As its name implies, a limited partnership is first and foremost a *partnership*. This concept of "partnership" is extremely important, and, for the most part, limited partnerships are subject to the same tax rules as any other partnership. (The general tax rules affecting partnerships are considered in Chapter 2.) In a limited partnership, there must be at least one general partner. The general partner or partners manage the business and are personally liable for the obligations of the partnership. The rights and obligations of the general partners in a limited partnership are the same as those of the partners in a general partnership. The limited partners in a limited partnership are exempt from partnership liability for the debts, obligations, and losses of the partnership as long as they do not participate in the management of the partnership. In other words, the most a limited partner can lose in a partnership is the investment, just like a shareholder in a corporation. This limited liability is what makes the limited partnership attractive as an investment vehicle.

The growth and development of the limited partnership investment vehicle can be traced back to the first real mass marketing of tax shelters that occurred in the early 1970s. In a real sense, the early history of limited partnership investments is the history of tax shelters. Today, limited partnerships may still offer tax advantages in the right situations, but, due to voluminous tax reform legislation enacted in recent years, the main emphasis of partnerships has shifted away from tax shelter and toward enhanced investment return in the form of current cash flow.

A relatively recent development in the limited partnership field has been the formation of what are termed "master limited partnerships." Essentially, a master limited partnership is a limited partnership in which interests are publicly traded through listings on a stock exchange or in the over-the-counter market. Investor interest in master limited partnerships skyrocketed following passage of the Tax Reform Act of 1986, and many new businesses were being formed as publicly traded limited partnerships rather than corporations. The tax incentives appeared very attractive. However, tax legislation at the end of

1987 took away the advantages for many newly formed master limited partnerships. A ten-year grace period was provided for existing partnerships, and certain partnerships, specifically those investing in real estate or oil and gas, were exempted from the new provisions. In any event, with the loss of tax benefits, interest in the formation of new businesses (other than those excepted) as master limited partnerships waned. (The special rules for publicly traded partnerships are considered at ¶ 1151.)

¶ 2101 DEVELOPMENT OF LIMITED PARTNERSHIPS

Many factors influence investments of all types. These factors include economic conditions, the rate of inflation, interest rates, and the tax rates applied by federal, state and local government on income of different types. Investors, of course, respond to the changes and seek investments that offer what they perceive to be the most advantageous benefits in light of existing economic conditions and their own personal financial situations.

The period encompassing the last half of the 1970s and the first half of the 1980s was a time of generally high tax rates and high inflation. It was during this time that tax shelters and tax-advantaged investments experienced explosive growth. Battered by high taxes and high inflation, investors naturally sought out those investments that promised them either tax savings or exceptionally high returns. In this environment, the limited partnership became the investment vehicle of choice. With the election of this form of business organization, the limited partnership could be used to acquire and operate those assets that were perceived (rightly or wrongly) to offer high returns in a period of high inflation, assets such as real estate. Further, since this form of business organization is considered a partnership under the tax law, the limited partnership could be used to pass tax benefits on to investors which they could not obtain through the corporate form of business organization.

¶ 2103 Limited Partnerships as Tax Shelters

Most tax shelters took the form of limited partnerships because this form of organization provided the combination of the tax benefits of a partnership and limited liability for investors. This was the right combination for an investor in a mass-marketed investment in which other participants were total strangers. As a partnership, the limited partnership could bring together an individual (or a corporation) that has expertise in a specific industry and investors seeking specific tax benefits or specific returns. The partner supplying the expertise would act as general partner, and the investors would be limited partners.

In a tax shelter limited partnership, the general partner would manage the business and assume general liability for the partnership's obligations. Of course, this general liability of the general partner was often more illusory than real since the general partner was more often than not a corporate entity. The general partner, as manager of the tax shelter activity, would gather the investors' capital, make investments, keep the partnership books, report results, and distribute any partnership profits to the limited partners. Note that while the general partner would make all decisions regarding partnership capital, the general partner itself would contribute little or none of the partnership's capital. Investors, as limited partners in a tax shelter limited partnership, would provide the necessary capital to acquire and operate the underlying assets of the partnership and, to the extent available, would receive the bulk of cash distributions from profits generated by the partnership. While supplying most, if not all, of the limited partnership's capital, the limited partners surrendered any right to participate in the management of the underlying assets of the partnership.

Tax shelter limited partnerships would provide tax benefits to investors because profits and losses arising from the operation of partnership assets would flow through to the individual limited partners. The activities of the limited partnership would be reflected on the personal returns of the limited partners in proportion to their interests in the partnership. In short, tax shelter limited partnerships permitted investors to share in tax benefits as well as profits generated by the underlying assets of the partnership, while allowing the investors to retain the limited liability enjoyed by corporate shareholders.

Like corporate shareholders, limited partners could realize any income generated by the assets and operations of the business entity, with one additional advantage. Income from the partnership would retain the character of that income when reported on the partner's tax return. For instance, if the partnership realized capital gain or tax-exempt income, the individual partners would report their share of that capital gain or tax-exempt income. If a corporation earned tax-exempt income, that income would lose its character as tax-exempt income and would be taxable as a dividend when distributed to the shareholders.

In most cases, however, the primary goal of a tax shelter limited partnership was not to generate taxable income from the outset of its operations. Rather, tax shelters generally would look to generate tax or paper losses (tax deductions) and various tax credits early in their operations. These tax deductions and credits would be available to the limited partners for use on their personal tax returns to offset highly taxed income from other sources and to reduce their individual income tax bills. The same underlying assets producing tax deductions or

¶ 2103

credits would not provide a direct tax benefit to investors if the assets were held by a corporate entity. Such tax deductions and credits would remain locked in the corporation and could be used only on the corporation's tax return.

The advantages offered by tax shelter limited partnerships, however, unfortunately led to abuses in two respects. Some promoters would misrepresent the value or extent of the underlying assets that would be acquired by a tax shelter limited partnership. Others would misrepresent or overstate the tax benefits that would be available to the investors. It was these abuses that, in large measure, finally influenced Congress to pass the legislation that severely curtailed the tax shelters available to passive investors.

¶ 2105 Real Estate Tax Shelters

Over time, real estate has proved to be an excellent investment. Continuing inflation and the pressure of demand have pushed up values for real estate of all types, albeit to varying degrees and at different times. Widespread home ownership also has made real estate an investment that more people are comfortable with, since they already have some familiarity with its potential advantages and disadvantages.

The major tax shelter aspect of real estate is that rents may be sheltered from taxation by deductions for depreciation and, to some extent, by interest and other expense deductions attributable to the purchase and operation of a real estate investment. Since depreciation does not require a cash expenditure to produce a tax deduction, rents may produce a positive cash flow without a corresponding amount of taxable income.

In the heyday of tax shelters, another feature of real estate was its ability to produce significant tax losses in conjunction with a positive cash flow. These tax losses could be used to shelter an investor's income from other sources which might otherwise be taxed at rates as high as 70 percent on the federal level alone. Now, of course, this feature of real estate is generally not available through public partnerships. Now, if deductions exceed rents so that a tax loss is created by a real estate investment, the excess loss may not be used to shelter income from non-passive activities or income from portfolio investments such as stocks and bonds. Nevertheless, real estate remains an attractive investment in the right situations, and tax benefits may still enhance the return an investor receives from income-producing real estate.

¶ 2105

¶ 2107 Real Estate Limited Partnerships

As noted above, most tax shelters took the form of limited partnerships because of the combination of the tax benefits of a partnership and limited liability for investors. As Congress has passed laws to curtail the effectiveness of tax shelters, the importance of tax shelter limited partnerships to investors, of course, has declined. This has not meant, however, that the limited partnership itself has disappeared as an attractive investment vehicle. The flexibility of this form of business organization permits investments to be structured to provide investors with the best possible return in the face of changing conditions.

The return from a limited partnership investment comes in three forms: cash flow, tax benefits, and appreciation. All successful limited partnership investments provide some combination of these three forms of investment return.

Cash flow is the actual after-tax cash distributed to or realized by the limited partner while holding the interest and upon its liquidation. Tax benefits are the tax savings generated by the underlying investment and passed through to the investor by the limited partnership. These tax benefits flow from initial deductions provided by many underlying investments and deductions generated over the life of the investment. Finally, appreciation is the actual rise in the value of an investment because of an increase in value over time, such as has occurred with real estate; because of growth, such as the increase in the value of a stand of timber; or because of the actual activity of the limited partnership, such as the collection of rents in a real estate limited partnership investing in rental property.

Although all limited partnership investments produce some combination of cash flow, tax benefits, and appreciation, they may not do so equally. The three forms of return are interrelated, so that an increase in one form of return is usually achieved to the detriment of the other two. For example, the tax benefits (deductions) from an investment may be increased through leverage (borrowing) or a higher purchase price. To the extent tax benefits are increased through borrowing, cash flow from the investment is reduced. More borrowing means higher payments of both principal and interest on the debt. Cash that would otherwise flow to the limited partners must be diverted to service the debt. To the extent tax benefits are increased through a higher purchase price, there is obviously less potential for appreciation.

Similarly, cash flow from an investment can be increased by reduced borrowing or reduced equity buildup in an investment. To the extent cash flow is increased by reduced borrowing, tax benefits are reduced. The lower debt service means lower deductions for interest payments and smaller "paper loss" deductions. To the extent cash flow is increased by reducing equity buildup, that is, by drawing out cash that would otherwise be working in the investment, the ultimate value of the investment is reduced. Finally, appreciation, or the buildup in value of a limited partnership investment, may be increased by sacrificing early tax benefits or by drawing less cash out during the course of an investment.

Essentially, the structure and type of a limited partnership investment determines the nature of the return to the investor. Accordingly, limited partnerships may be structured to yield greater cash flow with reduced tax benefits and appreciation; greater tax benefits with reduced cash flow and appreciation; or greater appreciation potential with reduced cash flow and tax benefits.

If a limited partnership is to attract investors, its structure, of course, must be responsive to investors' needs and the existing tax and economic conditions. The shift from a high tax rate, high-inflation environment to a lower tax rate, lower-inflation environment saw a corresponding shift in the structure of limited partnership investments. Instead of structuring investments for maximum tax benefits through artificial or paper losses created by large borrowing, sponsors shifted to investments with reduced borrowing that offered less in the way of tax benefits and appreciation potential, but much more in the way of immediate tax-sheltered cash flow.

¶ 2111 TAX TREATMENT OF REAL ESTATE LIMITED PARTNERSHIPS

The subject of the taxation of partners and partnerships, in general, is discussed in Chapter 2. Recall that the key feature of a partnership for federal income tax purposes is that it is not, in the usual case, a taxpaying entity. Rather, the nature of a partnership for tax purposes is one of a conduit through which tax consequences flow to the individual partners, and this is true regardless of whether the partnership in question is a general partnership or a limited partnership. It is around this core concept that the partnership tax rules are built.

¶ 2113 Restrictions on Partnership-Generated Tax Losses

While the government is more than willing to allow investors in limited partnerships to report and pay taxes on as much income from their investments as possible, it is somewhat stingy in allowing investor use of deductions or losses generated by limited partnerships. The use of tax deductions or losses flowing through the conduit of a limited partnership may be restricted or limited by three different tax rules.

¶ 2111

One of the limitations was discussed in Chapter 2 in connection with the role of a partner's basis in the partnership interest. A tax loss generated by a partnership is deductible by a partner only to the extent of the partner's tax basis for the partnership interest as of the end of the tax year in which the loss arose. A loss that exceeds basis may be deducted to the extent of the basis, and the excess loss may be carried over to future years and deducted against any future increase in basis. If there is an unused loss at the time a partner disposes of his partnership interest through a sale, exchange, or liquidation, the loss may be deducted at that time. The loss in this latter case generally is considered a capital loss.

In addition to the basis limitation on the use of losses or deductions generated by a limited partnership, there are two other rules that may come into play. In both cases, the rules are not directed solely to limited partnerships but apply generally to many investment activities. Limited partnerships, however, are often especially vulnerable to their application.

¶ 2113.1 *At-Risk Rules*

Congress enacted the "at-risk" provisions to curb what were perceived to be abuses in the use of nonrecourse financing. In a nonrecourse loan, the lender can look only to the financed asset for repayment. Before the at-risk rule was enacted, an investor could purchase an asset with nonrecourse financing, or through a limited partnership in which the investor was shielded from liability for partnership borrowings, and still take deductions based on the amount the investor put up in cash plus the amount of the debt (for which the investor had no real liability), that is, the tax basis.

Now, under the at-risk provisions, deductions from an activity may be taken to the extent of income from the activity. Income includes gain on sale of assets used in the activity as well as gain from a sale of the investment itself. In other words, to the extent an activity produces income, there is no at-risk limit on the deductions generated by that activity which may be used to offset that income.

In addition to deductions equal to income from an activity, an investor may take deductions in excess of income to the extent the investor is at risk. Amounts at risk in an activity include the amount of money invested, the adjusted basis of any property contributed to the activity, and borrowed amounts for which the borrower is personally liable for repayment or has pledged property other than the property in the activity to secure payment. The amount considered at risk for subsequent years is reduced by any allowable loss for the current year.

Prior loss deductions are recaptured, that is, are reportable as income, if an amount formerly at risk in an activity becomes nonrecourse.

The at-risk rules are considered in detail at ¶ 311.

¶ 2113.2 *Passive Loss Rule*

The Tax Reform Act of 1986 placed a major restriction on the use of certain types of investments as a means to defer tax on income from sources other than these investments. The passive loss rule essentially provides that losses from "passive activities" can be used only to offset income from passive activities. Similarly, a tax credit generated by a passive activity can be used only to offset tax liability attributable to a passive activity.

Generally speaking, a passive activity is any activity that involves the conduct of a trade or business in which the taxpayer does not materially participate. Also included are most activities involving the rental of real or personal property. Portfolio income, such as dividends, interest, and royalties, is not considered income from passive activities under the rule. Any loss or credit that cannot be used because of the rule may be carried over to future years and applied to passive income or tax liability attributable to passive income in subsequent years.

The passive loss rules are treated in detail in Chapter 11.

¶ 2115 Limited Partnership Interests

In the case of a limited partnership interest, special considerations apply in the application of the passive loss rule. Since a limited partner generally is precluded from participating in the partnership's business if the partner is to retain limited liability status, material participation is not possible and a limited partnership interest is automatically passive. This means that income, deductions, and tax credits passed through to a limited partner generally are considered passive income, deductions, and credits, subject to these important exceptions:

1. Portfolio income (dividends, interest, etc.) earned by a limited partnership and passed through to the partners is not passive income under the passive loss rule. Rather, this income remains portfolio income to the limited partners.

2. The IRS has been given the power to issue regulations permitting or requiring income from certain limited partnership interests to be classified as passive income, portfolio income, or income not arising from a passive activity. Exercise of this authority could affect the classification of income passed through to limited partners by a limited partnership.

3. The Revenue Act of 1987 provides special rules for "publicly traded partnerships." Net income from a publicly traded

partnership that is not subject to corporate taxation is treated as portfolio income and net losses from a publicly traded partnership can be used only to offset future income from that partnership. These special rules for publicly traded partnerships are discussed in further detail at ¶ 1151.

¶ 2121 MASTER LIMITED PARTNERSHIPS

Just what is a Master Limited Partnership (or MLP)? The easy answer is simply that an MLP is a "publicly traded limited partnership," that is, a partnership that has ownership interests, generally referred to as "units," which are traded on a recognized securities exchange or in the over-the-counter market. In reality, the MLP is not a legally defined entity and the term may be a misnomer. Regardless, it is a useful shorthand reference to an entire special class of limited partnership investments.

¶ 2123 Origins of Master Limited Partnerships

The beginnings of the MLP investment vehicle can be found in the explosive growth of tax shelters and tax-advantaged investments during the late 1970s and early 1980s. For various reasons, but most importantly for the tax advantage, these investments, as discussed above, usually were structured as limited partnerships. In most cases, these investments offered little in the way of liquidity, and investors were locked-in for a period of years.

Of all the many different investments packaged in limited partnership form and offered to investors as tax shelters during this period, one of the most popular was certainly oil and gas. As the price of oil shot from little more than $2 per barrel to well over $30 per barrel, oil and gas seemed like the sure ticket to riches. Even better, the tax advantages available to oil and gas investments meant that investors could make relatively sizable investments at little or no immediate out-of-pocket cash cost.

Oil exploration companies and other sponsors of oil and gas programs saw a virtually unlimited supply of capital and launched one program after another in seemingly endless succession. Some of the programs were good, others not so good, and still others were outright frauds. Nevertheless, they all had one thing in common: there was no real secondary market for the interests in the various programs acquired by the investors.

One approach tried early on in the boom of syndicated oil and gas investments as a means of achieving liquidity for investors in oil and gas programs was to have the investors contribute their various limited partnership interests to a corporation. A corporation would be formed so that investors in oil and gas properties could transfer their interests to the corporation in a "tax-free" incorporation transaction. These corporations would provide liquidity because investors who took advantage of the swap opportunity would end up owning shares in a publicly traded corporation, rather than holding limited partnership interests.

Although the corporation could provide liquidity, it defeated the primary reasons for using the limited partnership form in the first place. Any deductions generated by the oil and gas investment that could provide a tax benefit to the investors were locked in the corporation. Moreover, to the extent oil and gas income was produced, it was subject to a double tax, that is, once when earned by the corporation as corporate income, and again as individual income when distributed to the investor-shareholders as dividends. The need for liquidity on the part of oil and gas investors, combined with the desire to retain to whatever extent possible the tax advantages of the partnership form of organization, led one sponsor, Apache Petroleum Company, to form one of the first, if not the first, investment packages that would later fall under the heading of "Master Limited Partnership."

In 1981, Apache Petroleum Company offered to exchange units in Apache Partners (an MLP) for the limited partnership interests held by investors in the various oil and gas programs sponsored by Apache Petroleum Company the past 20 years. About 85 percent of the investors accepted the offer.

The Apache MLP thus became an early illustration of one way in which a master limited partnership may be formed: a promoter may gather together units from various partnerships under one roof. This new entity, organized as a limited partnership, continues the benefits of the limited partnership form of organization. Interests in the new partnership, however, are listed on a stock exchange and the investors achieve a degree of liquidity that they did not have prior to the formation of the master limited partnership. This type of MLP is generally referred to today as a *roll-up* master limited partnership, since smaller existing partnerships are "rolled up" into one large partnership.

It is these roll-up MLPs that probably account for the use of the word "Master" in the term "Master Limited Partnership." The concept underlying the term being simply that a number of smaller partnerships have been combined into one "master" partnership. The publicly traded limited partnership form, however, soon was adopted for many uses beyond that of a mere vehicle to house other partnership entities and provide investors with liquidity. But the MLP name stuck and is now applied to any publicly traded limited partnership, even those that do not involve the combination of many sub-partnerships.

¶ 2123

¶ 2125 Evolution and Growth of the MLP Concept

Once the idea of the publicly traded limited partnership was accepted, it was not long before promoters, sponsors, corporate finance experts, investment bankers, and others found many different ways to employ the concept. Although uses for MLPs other than roll-ups were emerging before the Tax Reform Act of 1986, it was this legislation, even before its passage and while it was under discussion in Congress, that spurred many to act. For the first time, individual tax rates would be below corporate tax rates, thus providing an incentive for moving income off a corporate tax return and onto an individual tax return. Also, the restrictions on passive losses would create a demand for income generated by MLPs, which was thought at the time to be passive income that could be offset by passive losses from other partnership investments.

In addition to the roll-up MLPs, new MLPs were formed in a variety of ways. A corporation with substantial assets, especially real estate assets, would spin off those assets to an MLP. Shareholders who then became partners in the MLP would realize the yield from the assets in the partnership without the layer of corporate taxation that existed when the assets were held within the corporation. These MLPs, formed by a corporation transferring some of its assets to a limited partnership, are referred to as *roll-out* MLPs. In some cases, a corporation might sell units in the roll-out MLP in addition to distributing the MLP units to its shareholders.

Mature companies, those generating substantial cash income without a need to reinvest a substantial portion of that income in operations, also looked to the MLP for its potential as a tax saver. A corporation, by converting entirely to partnership form, could eliminate the corporate tax and provide its shareholders with the benefit of the lower individual tax rates on former corporate income as well. MLPs formed as a result of an existing corporation transferring all of its assets to a limited partnership are called *roll-over* MLPs.

In addition to roll-ups, roll-outs and roll-overs, still other MLPs were formed: first, to attract investor dollars, and second, to acquire assets for the partnership. These MLPs formed, as it were, from scratch are often called *roll-in* MLPs to distinguish them from the MLPs formed by existing entities for purposes other than attracting new investors.

¶ 2127 Impact of Tax Legislation on MLPs

As discussed at ¶ 1153, tax legislation enacted at the end of 1987 was directed at "publicly traded limited partnerships." MLPs are just that—limited partnerships in which interests are traded on a recognized stock exchange or in the over-the-counter market. Although the tax definition of "publicly traded limited partnership" encompasses more than MLPs, it is without question that MLPs are subject to the 1987 legislation.

As a result of the tax changes, some MLPs are or will be treated as corporations for tax purposes, and those MLPs that are not so treated are subject to a special passive loss rule that prevents losses generated by an MLP from being used to offset income from sources other than that particular MLP. Also, income from MLPs that are not treated as corporations is considered portfolio income under the passive loss rules so that losses from nonpublicly traded limited partnerships and various tax shelters cannot be used to offset the MLP income (see ¶ 1159).

While the 1987 tax changes certainly had an effect on MLPs, it by no means meant the end of the MLP as an attractive investment in the right circumstances. The law, perhaps, is more important in what it does not do than in what it does. The law does not treat as corporations a wide range of MLPs, especially those engaged in real estate operations or natural resource operations (primarily oil and gas, although others are covered). Moreover, any MLP in existence on December 17, 1987, cannot be treated as a corporation if it elects to continue its partnership status and consents to pay a tax of 3.5 percent of its gross income from the active conduct of trades or businesses for tax years after 1997 (see Code Sec. 7704(g)).

As for the MLPs that are not treated as corporations, the special passive loss rule should have a limited impact. Most MLPs were designed as income generators rather than as vehicles for creating tax losses.

In the long run, the economics of the investments that may be packaged as MLPs will outweigh whatever negative influence the tax law has. Of course, the conversion of operating corporations to MLPs to avoid the corporate tax is no longer a viable proposition. However, the transfer of real estate and natural resource assets to MLPs as a means to enhance asset values and eliminate the potential double tax of corporate operation should continue, provided the underlying economics of the specific situation warrant it. Existing partnerships that will be treated as corporations down the line may have prices depressed by this fact. Some investors may find bargains among these issues in this environment.

¶ 2129 Real Estate MLPs

As an investment, real estate generally has performed well over the years, offering competitive returns and a hedge against inflation unmatched by most other assets. Although most real estate limited partnerships are not publicly traded and therefore are not within our definition of an MLP, many real estate MLPs have been formed as either roll-in or roll-out partnerships. On some limited occasions, existing real estate limited partnership units have been rolled-up into an MLP, but roll-ups are unusual.

For the most part, a real estate MLP must invest in or own mature properties, that is, properties that are already fully developed and producing steady rental income. A steady and consistent cash flow is a prerequisite if the market is to fully value the partnership units to reflect the value of the underlying real estate. This applies to MLPs of both the roll-out and the roll-in variety. As an inducement to investors, the sponsor of a roll-in MLP may set some minimum cash return to investors and agree to forgo management and other fees if it is not met. The corporate sponsor of a roll-out MLP may offer a similar deal, at least for some limited period of time, in order to support the post-roll-out market value of the MLP units.

A roll-up real estate MLP may end up with mature properties, but very real problems associated with rolling-up existing real estate partnerships are usually too much to overcome. It is extremely difficult, if not well nigh impossible, to value different properties in different markets with different rental rates in order to set a fair exchange rate for investors who swap their existing partnership units for new MLP units. In addition, there are extremely complex tax and accounting issues that must be addressed and overcome. When a sponsor does attempt to roll-up existing partnership units, it is likely to be a last-ditch effort to save partnerships with troubled or distressed properties by combining them with healthy partnerships.

Still another type of real estate MLP is one formed to invest in real estate mortgages rather than in the actual real estate. Mortgage MLPs either buy existing mortgages or provide new financing to other real estate partnerships or other investors. Since the underlying assets of a mortgage MLP are mortgages and the income is derived from interest on the mortgages, the stability and safety of cash flow is usually greater than in a partnership investing in the real estate directly. Of course, this greater stability and safety should be reflected in somewhat lower returns to investors.

Mortgage MLPs, as well as other real estate MLPs, should avoid classification as corporations under the tax rules that treat many publicly traded partnerships as corporations because of the exceptions which treat interest income and any gains from the sale of assets held for the production of interest income, as well as real estate rentals and gains from real estate sales, as qualifying income. Recall that a publicly traded partnership is not treated as a corporation and that partnership tax rules apply, if 90 percent or more of the partnership's gross income is "qualifying income."

¶ 2129

Chapter 22

Real Estate Investment Trusts

¶ 2200 OVERVIEW OF CHAPTER

In general, an entity (corporation, trust, or association) may qualify as a real estate investment trust if it is a trust or corporation with at least 100 different freely transferable interests and if it would be taxed as an ordinary domestic corporation if it did not meet the REIT requirements.[1] These requirements relate to the composition of the entity's assets, which must be substantially real estate assets, and the entity's income, which must be realized in a substantial part from certain real estate and real estate-related sources.[2]

Also, a 100 percent tax is imposed on income from the sale of property held for sale to customers in the ordinary course of trade or business, other than foreclosure property.[3]

¶ 2201 TAX TREATMENT OF REITS

An entity that meets the requirements and elects to be treated as a REIT generally is treated as a partial conduit. A REIT is generally subject to the regular corporate tax[4] but receives a deduction for dividends paid provided that the amount of the dividends paid is not less than 90 percent of its ordinary income.[5] These dividends must be paid within a short period following the end of the REIT's tax year and are generally taxed as ordinary income to the shareholders. A REIT may be subject to tax on capital gains, but to the extent the REIT pays dividends out of capital gains, the dividends are deductible and taxed to the shareholders as capital gains.[6] To the extent a REIT retains and pays tax on capital gains, the shareholders include a proportionate amount of the capital gain in income and receive a credit for the tax paid by the REIT.[7]

Note that unlike a partnership, a REIT cannot serve as a conduit for losses. Losses suffered by a REIT are not passed through to shareholders to be deducted by them as is the case for partnership losses, which are passed through to partners and deducted by partners

---

[1] Code Sec. 856(a).
[2] Code Sec. 856(c).
[3] Code Sec. 857(b)(6).
[4] Code Sec. 857(b)(1).
[5] Code Sec. 857(a)(1).
[6] Code Sec. 857(b)(3)(B).
[7] Code Sec. 857(b)(3)(D).

on their own tax returns (subject to the various limits on passive activity loss deductions discussed at ¶ 1107.1).

¶ 2205 Management and Control

In order to act as a conduit for income from real estate investments, a REIT must comply with the technical requirements of Code Secs. 856-859. In addition, guidelines issued by the North American Securities Administrators Association must be followed. Essentially, the tax code and NASAA requirements impose restrictions on the sources of income, the composition of assets, the interests that may be held by the sponsor, the concentration of ownership, and the independence of a REIT's board of trustees.

A REIT cannot directly manage the properties that it owns rather, it must employ independent contractors. Operations of the REIT must be overseen by a board of trustees, of which a majority must be "outside" trustees under the NASAA guidelines. These restrictions may help in protecting the interests of investors (who have ultimate control to the same extent as shareholders of a corporation), but they greatly limit the operating flexibility of a REIT.

¶ 2207 Liquidity and Marketability

Interests in REITs may be freely traded without impact on the REIT. Owners are free to buy and sell REIT interests without restrictions. REITs, however, have gone through several periods in which their liquidity was more apparent than real. Troubled real estate investments by some REITs in the past have made interests virtually untradeable (since nobody wanted to buy) at one time or another.

¶ 2215 INCOME RESTRICTIONS

A REIT may serve as a conduit for income from real estate, but it must distribute 90 percent of its income to shareholders. Furthermore, a REIT cannot reinvest earnings and still retain its status as a REIT. This limits the capital growth potential of a REIT. Also, as a partial conduit, a REIT serves as a conduit for income, but losses and deductions realized by a REIT do not flow through to provide a tax benefit to investors.

Income from a REIT is considered portfolio income under the restrictions on the use of passive losses, so passive losses cannot be used to offset income from a REIT. Tax-exempt institutions may realize income from a REIT without the imposition of the unrelated business income tax.

Chapter 23

Real Estate Mortgage Investment Conduits

¶ 2300 OVERVIEW OF CHAPTER

In the Tax Reform Act of 1986, Congress provided special tax rules[1] for what it dubbed "real estate mortgage investment conduits" or "REMICs." In general, a REMIC is a fixed pool of mortgages with multiple classes of interests held by investors. Any entity, whether a corporation, partnership, or trust, that meets specified requirements may elect to be treated as a REMIC.[2] Also, a segregated pool of assets may qualify as a REMIC as if it were a legal entity, provided the necessary requirements are met. In short, the REMIC is a replacement entity for limited partnerships, REITS, and mutual funds that in the past have invested in real estate mortgages.

¶ 2301 INVESTOR INTERESTS

As long as the requirements now specified in the Internal Revenue Code for qualification as a REMIC are met, the REMIC is not treated as a separate taxable entity.[3] Rather, the income of the REMIC is allocated to, and taken into account by, the holders of interests in the REMIC.[4] These interests are divided into "regular interests," which can be further divided into more than one class, and the single class of "residual interests."

The terms of a regular interest in a REMIC must be fixed and unconditionally entitle the holder to receive a specified principal or similar amount and base interest or similar payments, if any, at or before maturity on a fixed rate. (A variable rate may be used under regulations specified by the Internal Revenue Service.) These regular interests may be issued in the form of debt, stock, partnership interests, interests in a trust, or any form of legal organization permissible under state law.[5]

A residual interest is any interest in the REMIC other than a regular interest, and which is so designated by the REMIC. There can

---

[1] Code Secs. 860A–860G.
[2] Code Sec. 860D(a).
[3] Code Sec. 860A(a).
[4] Code Sec. 860A(b).
[5] Code Sec. 860G(a)(1).

be only one class of residual interests, and all distributions, if any, made to holders of residual interests must be made on a pro rata basis.[6]

¶ 2305 TAX TREATMENT OF REMICS

A REMIC is not a taxable entity for federal income tax purposes.[7] The income of a REMIC generally is taken into account by holders of regular and residual interests as briefly described below.[8] This conduit feature of the REMIC applies regardless of whether the REMIC otherwise would be treated as a corporation, partnership, trust, or any other legal entity. In enacting the REMIC provisions into the tax law, Congress wanted them to be the exclusive set of rules for the treatment of all transactions relating to the REMIC and holders of REMIC interests, if the requirements for REMIC status are met by the entity. For instance, a REMIC that is organized as a partnership and that would be treated as a partnership under the tax law if there were no special REMIC provisions is not treated as a partnership if the REMIC requirements are met and an election under Code Sec. 860D(b) is made for its first taxable year. In such a case, the partnership tax rules do not apply to any transaction involving the REMIC or to any holders of interests in the REMIC.

¶ 2309 Regular Interests

The holder of a regular interest generally is taxed as if the regular interest were a debt instrument to which the rules of taxation applicable to debt instruments apply,[9] except that the holder is required to report income attributable to the regular interest on the accrual method of accounting regardless of his regular method of accounting.[10] In the case of a regular interest that is not an actual debt instrument, the amount of the fixed unconditional payment is treated as the stated principal amount of the instrument, and the periodic payments, if any, that are based on the amount of the fixed unconditional payment are treated as stated interest payments.[11] In other words, consistent with the conduit nature of the REMIC, the holders of regular interests generally take into account that portion of the REMIC's income that would be taken into account by an accrual method holder of a debt instrument with terms equivalent to the terms of the regular interest.

¶ 2315 Residual Interests

The holder of a residual interest in a REMIC takes into account as ordinary income the daily portion of the taxable income or net loss of the REMIC for each day during the taxable year in which the interest

---

[6] Code Sec. 860G(a)(2).
[7] Code Sec. 860A(a).
[8] Code Sec. 860A(b).
[9] Code Sec. 860B(a).
[10] Code Sec. 860B(b).
[11] Code Sec. 860B(c).

was held.[12] The taxable income or net loss of the REMIC for determining this pass through is figured in the same way that a calendar year individual using accrual accounting would figure taxable income, but with certain modifications.[13] The most important modification is that the REMIC deducts amounts that would be deductible as interest if the regular interests were treated as indebtedness of the REMIC. This provision, in effect, prevents the holders of residual interests from being taxed on income allocable to the regular interests.

¶ 2315.1 *Distributions*

Actual distributions from the REMIC are not included in the income of a residual holder to the extent that distributions do not exceed the holder's adjusted basis for the interest.[14] Distributions in excess of basis are treated as income from the sale of the residual interest.[15] The amount of any net loss of the REMIC that may be taken into account by the holder of a residual interest is limited to the holder's adjusted basis. Any loss disallowed as a deduction because of this provision may be carried over and used in the future, but only to offset future income generated by the same REMIC.[16]

¶ 2315.2 *Income and Basis*

These rules on the treatment of the income and loss of a REMIC allocable to residual interests closely parallel those applicable to partnerships, as discussed at ¶ 229. The method of determining the adjusted basis of a residual interest is also similar to the method of determining the basis of a partnership interest. A holder's initial basis (cost) is increased by the amount of taxable income of the REMIC that is taken into account by the holder. The basis is decreased, but not below zero, by the amount of any distributions received from the REMIC and by the amount of any net loss of the REMIC that is taken into account by the holder.[17]

Essentially, what Congress said in passing the REMIC provisions is that, no matter how an investor makes an indirect investment in a pool of mortgages, the tax treatment will be the same. Regardless of whether an investor acquires an interest in a pool of mortgages through a real estate limited partnership, a REIT, or a mutual fund, if the investor's interest has the characteristics of debt, it will be treated as debt for tax purposes. On the other hand, if the investor's interest has the characteristics of a sharing of profits and losses, that is, an investment in which the investor is assuming a position closely akin to that of a limited partner, the interest in the REMIC will be treated in the same fashion as a partnership interest for tax purposes.

---

[12] Code Sec. 860C(a).
[13] Code Sec. 860C(b).
[14] Code Sec. 860C(c)(1).
[15] Code Sec. 860C(c)(2).
[16] Code Sec. 860C(e)(2).
[17] Code Sec. 860C(d).

Case Table

References are to paragraph (¶) numbers.

A

Aberle, H.C. . . . 1225
Abrams, P. . . . 1503
Abramson, J.G. . . . 1213
Akers, L.R. . . . 117.1
Alabama-Georgia Syrup Co. . . . 723.2
Alaska Realty Co. . . . 603
Alderson, J. . . . 1317.1
Allen, A.L. . . . 723.2
Allen, E.H. . . . 317.1
Allen, G.P. . . . 1315.2
Almac's, Inc. . . . 723.1
American Dental Co. . . . 1203.1
American Spring & Wire Specialty Co. . . . 515.1
Ames, L.S. . . . 605
Amey, E.S. . . . 405
Anderson, P.C. . . . 705.2
Anderson-Trully Co. . . . 735
Anover Realty Corp. . . . 303.1
Arkin, L.J. . . . 1225
Astor Holding Co. . . . 453
Atmore Realty Co. . . . 1213.1
Au, C.T. . . . 1013.1
Ayling, W.A. . . . 1003.2

B

Bachman, C.F. . . . 503.1
Baird & Son, Inc., D. . . . 725
Baldwin, C.A. . . . 743.2
Bank of Houston . . . 723.1
Bardes, O.L. . . . 615
Baron Est., S. . . . 105.1
Baton Coal Co. . . . 413
Baumann & Co. . . . 513.1
Bayley, J.F. . . . 2009.3
Bayly, R.C. . . . 2001
Beck, J.C. . . . 105.3
Bee Holding Co. . . . 723.2
Beecham, Inc. . . . 605
Beecham, Inc. . . . 613
Beeghly, L.A. . . . 1517.1
Bell Electric Co. . . . 615.1

Bell, I.L. . . . 731
Bellingham Cold Storage Co. . . . 415.1
Bender, H.G. . . . 409
Berberovich, T. . . . 1013.2
Berliner, H.A. . . . 1213.2
Berry, M. . . . 349
Best, L.J. . . . 723.1
Beus, E.H. . . . 443
Bev Anderson Chevrolet, Inc. . . . 727.1
Bidart Bros. . . . 1305.2
Biedenharn Realty Co. . . . 1013.1
Biggs, F.B. . . . 1317.1; 1317.2
Bingham, H.P. . . . 1223.2
Biscayne Bay Island, Co. . . . 1003.1
Bjerke, L.A. . . . 317.1
Bjornsen Investment Corp. . . . 323
Black, L.C. . . . 747
Blake, Jr., T.W. . . . 201
Blatt Co., M.E. . . . 613; 615
Bliss, A. . . . 735
Bloomington Coca-Cola Bottling Co. . . . 1313
Blum, A. . . . 1225
Boddie, C.A. . . . 723.2
Boland, J.L. . . . 723.1
Bolker, J.R. . . . 1313.1
Bollinger, Jr., J.C. . . . 205
Bolton, D.D. . . . 1825.2
Bonwit Teller & Co. . . . 501
Bosch Est., H.J. . . . 221
Boss, H. . . . 517
Boston Fish Market Corp. . . . 615.2
Boston Fish Market . . . 513.2
Botany Worsted Mills . . . 727.1
Boyd Est., E.B. . . . 215
Boylston Market Assn. . . . 731
Bradford Hotel Operating Co. . . . 513.2
Brauer, A.E. . . . 1317.1
Brown Printing Co. . . . 403; 409; 409.2
Brown, A.M. . . . 705.2
Brown, I. . . . 613
Brown, K.A. . . . 803
Bryce's Mountain Resort, Inc. . . . 1005.1
Bullard Est., P.E. . . . 1619

Case Table

References are to paragraph (¶) numbers.

Burden, I.T. . . . 803
Burgess Poultry Market, Inc. . . . 705
Burnet, D. . . . 1405.5
Burns, H.F. . . . 1503
Bush Terminal Buildings Co. . . . 735
Byram, J.D. . . . 1003.1

C

Calcasieu Paper Co., Inc. . . . 349
Caldwell Milling Co. . . . 743.2
California Delta Farms, Inc. . . . 1313
Campbel, T.O. . . . 723.1
Capitol Motor Car Co. . . . 1523.1
Car-Ron Asphalt Paving Co. . . . 729.2
Casalina Corp. . . . 735
Casey, G.B. . . . 743.1
Cedar Park Cemetery Assn., Inc. . . . 1003
Century Electric Co. . . . 343.2
Chevy Chase Land Co. of Montogomery County, Md. . . . 807
Chevy Chase Motor Co., Inc. . . . 727.1
City National Bank . . . 723.1
Clapham, R.G. . . . 2009.1
Clarkston, J.M. . . . 1205.2
Clayton, Jr., C.W. . . . 727.1
Clayton, R.M. . . . 1003.2
Clem, J.R. . . . 807
Click, D.H. . . . 1313
Clinton Hotel Realty Corp. . . . 453
Coastal Terminals, Inc. . . . 1317.1
Cohn, B.W. . . . 723.2
Collins Est., M.A. . . . 1005
Colony, Inc. . . . 1003
Colony, Inc. . . . 1005.1
Colston, W.A. . . . 743.1
Comdisco, Inc. . . . 625.1
Community Bank . . . 1215.3
Conners, R.R. . . . 1233
Conte, J. . . . 215
Cooke, C.C. . . . 1205.2
Cooper, R.D. . . . 409.2
Cooperative Publishing Co. . . . 1213
Corley, D.J. . . . 1303.2
Cothran, J.D. . . . 735
Country Club Estates, Inc. . . . 1005
Coupe, L.Q. . . . 735
Coupe, L.Q. . . . 1317.1; 1317.2
Crane, B.B. . . . 105
Crane, B.B. . . . 1213
Crane, B.B. . . . 1303.2
Crane, B.B. . . . 1617
Creston Corp. . . . 117.1
Critzer Est., W. . . . 1013.2
Crowley, Milner & Co. . . . 343.2

Cullinan, J.S. . . . 1003.2
Cunningham, G.H. . . . 615

D

D'Alonzo, N. . . . 1205.2
Dallas Transfer & Terminal Warehouse Co. . . . 1203.2
David & Sons, Inc. . . . 409.2
Davis, B.E. . . . 1503
Davis, B. . . . 805
Dawson-Spatz Packing Co. . . . 615.1
Dean Est., W.K. . . . 1013
Delaney, D.W. . . . 105
DeMatteo Construction Co., M. . . . 607
Detroit Consolidated Theatres, Inc. . . . 303.1
Diamond, S. . . . 229.3
DiLaura, W. . . . 307.2
DiLaura, W. . . . 1203.1
Divine, Jr., T.M. . . . 1005
Dixie Manor, Inc. . . . 117.3
Drive-In Theatre, Inc. . . . 607
Duaine, L.A. . . . 117.3
Dumble, E. . . . 803

E

Ebben, L.G. . . . 1619
Edwards Industries, Inc. . . . 1305.3
Ehlers, W.A. . . . 1303.2
Electro-Chemical Engraving Co. . . . 1213.2
Eller, W.E. . . . 727.2
Endres Floral Co. . . . 117.3
Enid Ice & Fuel Co. . . . 1537.1
Ennis, N.J. . . . 1303.2
Enright, J.M. . . . 705.2
Equitable Publishing Co. . . . 409.2
Ettle Co., Inc. . . . 727.1
Evans, S.C. . . . 723.1
Ewing, R.W. . . . 1003.2
Ewing, R.W. . . . 1303.2

F

Farmers Creamery Corp. of Fredericksburg, Va. . . . 723.1
Fegan, T.B. . . . 409.2
Ferguson, Jr., W.M. . . . 1503
Fieland, L.C. . . . 605
Fifth Avenue-14th Street Corp. . . . 307.2
Film N' Photo, Inc. . . . 117.3
First American National Bank Of Nashville . . . 723.2
Fleming, J.E. . . . 117.3
Fleming, W. . . . 1313.1
Follender, D.B. . . . 317.1

Case Table

References are to paragraph (¶) numbers.

Forrest, D.W. . . . 1503
Foster, W.N. . . . 1013.2
Franklin Est., C.T. . . . 105.3
Freeland Est., E.L. . . . 1011
Freeland, E.L. . . . 1225
Frick, C.F. . . . 729.1
Frishkorn Real Estate Co. . . . 1003
Furmanski, A.R. . . . 727.2

G

Galt, A.T. . . . 503.3
Gem, Inc. . . . 415.1
General American Life Insurance Co. . . . 307.2; 323
Gentsch, F.F. . . . 405
Georgia Ry. & Electric Co. . . . 603
Gersten, A. . . . 1005
Gibbons, J.M. . . . 747
Giffin, E.A. . . . 729.1
Gilbert, A.J. . . . 201
Gilbert, A.J. . . . 743.1
Gladding Dry Goods Co. . . . 201
Goodman, D.B. . . . 1013.1
Goodwin, R.C. . . . 1705.1
Gordy, R.E. . . . 1023
Gorod, G.C. . . . 721
Gorod, G. . . . 721
Grannemann, E. . . . 1403.2
Gray, A.J. . . . 515.2
Green, C.C. . . . 1517.1; 1517.2
Green, P. . . . 1225
Grodt & McKay Realty, Inc. . . . 201
Guelph Hotel Corp. . . . 517
Guenther, H.W. . . . 731
Guest, W.F.C. . . . 1619
Gutwirth, C. . . . 1503

H

Haag, W.J. . . . 407
Haggard, D.M. . . . 443
Hahn, L. . . . 213
Hamilton & Main, Inc. . . . 513.2
Hamilton, J.R. . . . 1505.3
Hammel, G. . . . 1213; 1213.1; 1213.2
Handlery Hotels, Inc. . . . 515.1
Hanover, H.R. . . . 1537.2
Harcum, R.L. . . . 453
Harcum, R.L. . . . 1013.2
Harris, A.F. . . . 805
Harris, E. . . . 1213.1
Haspel, R.B. . . . 807
Haverty Furniture Co. . . . 723.1
Hawkins, J.C. . . . 1213.1
Heath, C.J. . . . 1215.3

Heer-Andres Investment Co. . . . 421
Heininger, S.B. . . . 729.2
Held, E.R. . . . 1233
Henry, D.L. . . . 1835
Hensel Phelps Construction Co. . . . 229.3
Herndon, R. . . . 1013.2
Hibernia National Bank . . . 603
Higgins, E. . . . 1205.3
Hill Admr., S.H. . . . 1213.1
Hill, Jr., C.M. . . . 805
Hirsch, K. . . . 307.2
Hirschel, J. . . . 721
Hoffman, R.C. . . . 705
Hoffman, W.W. . . . 1225
Home Agency Co. . . . 1205.2
Home Trust Co. . . . 513.1
Hoopengarner, H.H. . . . 413
Hooper, H.M. . . . 1305.3
Hopkins, J.R. . . . 1537.1
Hopkins, J.R. . . . 743.2
Hort, W.M. . . . 513.2
Houston Chronicle Publishing Co. . . . 515.1
Hoven, V. . . . 1305.3
Hradesky, F.J. . . . 1709
Huber, P.O. . . . 803
Hudlow, W.C. . . . 723.1
Hudson, L. . . . 721
Hughes, P.C. . . . 1205.2
Human Engineering Institute . . . 723.2
Hurd, P. . . . 117.1
Hurlburt Est., C. . . . 1302.2
Hyde Park Realty, Inc. . . . 423

I

Idaho Power Co. . . . 127.1
Imerman, S. . . . 409
International building Co. . . . 723.1
Iske, J. . . . 735

J

J. & E. Enterprises, Inc. . . . 423; 453
Jackson, H.L. . . . 1005.3
Jacobson, R.V. . . . 729.1
Jacobson, R.V. . . . 731
James, E.C. . . . 105.2
James, W.A. . . . 235.1
Jayne Est., G.W. . . . 1521
John Richard Corp. . . . 1523.4
Johnson & Co., I.G. . . . 735
Johnson, A.B. . . . 1517.1
Johnson, J.A. . . . 1405.3
Jones, A.R. . . . 723.1
Jordan Marsh Co. . . . 343.2
Journal-Tribune Publishing Co. . . . 603

Juister, Jr., M.H. . . . 1201.1

K

Kauai Terminal, Ltd. . . . 731
Kaufman, A.A. . . . 1223.1
Keeling, G.W. . . . 413
Keiler, II, J.W. . . . 515.1
Keller, R.E. . . . 1205.3
Kelley, J.W. . . . 1013.2
Kelller Street Development Co. . . . 727.1
King Radio Corp. Inc. . . . 117.3
Knoxville Iron Co. . . . 723.1
Koch, C.E. . . . 1313.1
Kohler-Campbell Corp. . . . 423
Kolowich, G.J. . . . 1213.1
Kummer Realty Co., P.E. . . . 727.1

L

La France Wine Co. . . . 805
Laguna Land & Water Co. . . . 1005
Lakeland Grocery Co. . . . 1203.2
Land Dynamics . . . 1313
Lang Chevrolet Co. . . . 733
Langley Park Apartments, Sec. C., Inc. . . . 727.1
Lansburgh, L. . . . 317.3
LaPort, F.L. . . . 1225
Latter, H. . . . 515.1
Lay, L.E. . . . 1705.1
Lazarus & Co. . . . 201
Leslie Co. . . . 343.2
Levenson & Klein, Inc. . . . 503.3
Levine Est., A. . . . 1617
Lewis, S.R. . . . 307.2
Liant Record, Inc. . . . 1523.1
Limericks, Inc. . . . 409.2
Lindsley, Jr., E.B. . . . 1607.1
Logan, E.A. . . . 1405.5
Longview Hilton Hotel Co. . . . 303.1
Louisiana Land & Exploration Co. . . . 735
Lovejoy, J.S. . . . 303.1
Lowry, Jr., E.G. . . . 2005
Lutz & Schramm Co. . . . 1223.1
Lyon Co., F. . . . 345.1
Lyon, B.D. . . . 423

M

M&W Gear Co. . . . 349
Main & McKinney Bldg. Co. of Houston, Texas . . . 415.1
Mallat, W. . . . 1013
Mallinckrodt, Inc. . . . 117.3
Malone, R.C. . . . 1617

Mantell, J. . . . 453
Marcus, S. . . . 735
Margolis, B.B. . . . 1013.1
Markovitz, M. . . . 723.1
Marks, D.N. . . . 117.1
Marlo Coil Co. . . . 727.1
Martin, F.T.B. . . . 613
Martin, H.C. . . . 1013.1
Matheson, C. . . . 1507.2
Mathews, C.J. . . . 347.2
McBride, B.E. . . . 613
McKinney, E.G. . . . 1825.2
McLaughlin, E.F. . . . 1213
Meiers, S.A. . . . 117.1
Mele, J.A. . . . 323
Meredith, I. . . . 1835
Metropolitan Building Co. . . . 521
Michaels, J.A. . . . 307.2
Mid-State Products Co. . . . 515.1
Middleton, M.L. . . . 1225
Miller, P.A. . . . 1013
Miller, S.D. . . . 521
Miller, W.R. . . . 1503
Millinery Center Building Corp. . . . 513.1
Millinery Center Building Corp. . . . 615.1
Minor, W.T. . . . 1013.2
Minot Federal Savings & Loan Assn. . . . 117.3
Mitchell, G.W. . . . 1013.1
Moline Properties, Inc. . . . 203
Montgomery Co. . . . 515.1
Moore, A. . . . 1013.2
Moss, J.S. . . . 723.2
Moss, J.S. . . . 803
Moss, S.J. . . . 615.1
Mountain Fuel Supply Co. . . . 723.2
Mountain State Steel Foundries, Inc. . . . 723.1
Mozayeny, M. . . . 805
Mt. Morris Drive-In Theatre Co. . . . 723.1
Municipal Bond Corp. . . . 1013.1
Murray, J.S. . . . 1013
Murray, R.J. . . . 1403.2

N

N.W. Pugh Co., Inc. . . . 503.2
Narver, Jr., D.L. . . . 105.3
National Bank of Commerce of San Antonio . . . 1223.2
National Builders, Inc. . . . 705
National Carbide Corp. . . . 205
New Capital Hotel, Inc. . . . 423
Nicoll Co., R.J. . . . 727.1
Nieman, M.A. . . . 1013.2
Noell, M.J. . . . 1005.1

Case Table

References are to paragraph (¶) numbers.

North Carolina Midland Ry. Co. . . . 603
North Texas Lumber Co. . . . 1303.2
Nutt Est., J.F. . . . 1305.2

O

Oberman Mfg. Co. . . . 723.1
Ockles, T.S. . . . 317.1
Ockrant, W. . . . 1205.2
Oden, J.E. . . . 1403.2
Odom, Jr., F.L. . . . 743
Oesterreich, W. . . . 443
Offshore Operations Trust . . . 117.1
Offutt, G.W. . . . 1003; 1005
Ohio Cloverleaf Dairy Co. . . . 603
Oliver Iron Mining Co. . . . 517
Oriole Homes Corp. . . . 749
Otis, J.J. . . . 805
Ottawa Silica Co. . . . 1605
Ourisman, F.R. . . . 205

P

Parker, P.S. . . . 105
Patrick, O. . . . 1013.2
Paul, M.A. . . . 1305.3
Peabody, S. . . . 513.1
Pearson, H.B. . . . 607
Peerless Steel Equipment Co. . . . 515.2
Peerless Weighing & Vending Corp. . . . 515.1
Pensacola Greyhound Racing, Inc. . . . 117.1
Perimutter, B. . . . 727.1
Peterson Co., G.C. . . . 1205.1
Phil Gluckstern's, Inc. . . . 513.1
Phil Gluckstern's, Inc. . . . 517
Phillips & Easton Supply Co. . . . 723.2
Pickard, A. . . . 729.1
Pig & Whistle Co. . . . 517
Pioneer Real Estate Co. . . . 1517.1; 1517.2
Plainfield-Union Water Co. . . . 723.1
Poe, B. . . . 221
Ponderosa Mouldings, Inc. . . . 117.3
Porreca, J. . . . 317.2
Post, R.H. . . . 517
Powell, L.L. . . . 213
Pozzi, E. . . . 1403.2
Pratt, E.T. . . . 727.5
Price, J.D. . . . 521
Professional Equities, Inc. . . . 1405.2

R

Raffold Process Corp. . . . 1205.1
Ray, L.W. . . . 515.2
Raymond Bertolini Trucking Co. . . . 729.2
Real Estate Cop., Inc. . . . 1521.3

Realty Operators, Inc. . . . 1225
Reisinger, C.H. . . . 601
Renwick, E.A. . . . 501
Riddell, R.A. . . . 1013
Ritholz, S.J. . . . 201
Roberts, W.M. . . . 325.1
Roccaforte, Jr., J.A. . . . 205
Rod Realty Co. . . . 421
Rogers, M.S. . . . 1215.1
Rose, J.T. . . . 723.1
Roth Properties Co. . . . 727.1
Rothschild, H. . . . 1213.2
Roux Laboratories, Inc. . . . 807
Royal St. Louis, Inc. . . . 603
Rush, G.S. . . . 503.1
Rutland, H. . . . 1317.2
Ruttenberg, D.C. . . . 803
Rutter, J.H. . . . 723.2

S

S & L Building Corp. . . . 303.1
S. & B. Realty Co. . . . 727.1
Sabinske, R.J. . . . 1005.1
Safway Steel Scaffolds Co. of Georgia . . . 409.2
Sanders, L. . . . 225
Satterfield, D.G. . . . 605; 613
Scheffres, J. . . . 1605
Scheuber. W.A. . . . 1013
Schieffelin Est., L.S. . . . 1215.1
Schubel, R.A. . . . 1705
Scott, E.V. . . . 807
Seaborn, H.G. . . . 221
Serbousek, R.A. . . . 347.2
Sevier Terrace Realty Co. . . . 1005
Shainberg, H. . . . 731
Sheahan, J.F. . . . 2009.3
Shirley Hill Coal Co. . . . 515.1
Shoney's South, Inc. . . . 117.3
Sickle, B.V. . . . 735
Sieber, R.J. . . . 733
Simmons & Hammond Mfg. Co. . . . 803
Simon, J.B. . . . 1615
Sirbo Holdings, Inc. . . . 513.2
Skinner, F. . . . 1003
Smith Leasing Co., Inc. . . . 725
Smith, J.M. . . . 1303.2
Smith, N.B. . . . 413
Soelling, W.M. . . . 735
Soliman . . . 1803.2
Sorrell, Jr., G.S. . . . 413
South Texas Properties Co. . . . 1013.1
Spain, F.K. . . . 725
Spiegel, May, Stern Co. . . . 725

Case Table

References are to paragraph (¶) numbers.

Spitzer, S. . . . 303.1
Spreckles, A.B. . . . 1223.2
Standart Fruit Product Co. . . . 805
Starke, W.E. . . . 1013.1
Starker, T.J. . . . 1313.1
Steele-Wedeles Co. . . . 515.1
Steinway & Sons . . . 407
Steuart Bros., Inc. . . . 1523.1
Stewart Supply Co., Inc. . . . 723.1
Stickles, S.E. . . . 735
Stokes, T. . . . 1225
Stolk, W.C. . . . 2009.1
Suburban Realty Co. . . . 1013.1
Sutphin, J.H. . . . 307.2
Sutphin, J.H. . . . 1201.1
Swoby Corp. . . . 603

T

Tank, R. . . . 1503
Tennyson, M.L. . . . 117.3
Terre Haute Electric Co. . . . 603
Terry, K.R. . . . 1213.2
Theodore Gutman Est. . . . 1205.3
Thielking, P.W. . . . 501
Third National Bank in Nashville . . . 515.1
Thomas, O.L. . . . 805
Thornbrough, M. . . . 743
379 Madison Ave., Inc. . . . 503.1
Tracy, W.R. . . . 743.1
Tschupp, C. . . . 727.2
12701 Shaker Blvd. Co. . . . 307.1
1220 Realty Co. . . . 507

U

Union Pacific Co., R.R. . . . 723
United Mercantile Agencies, Inc. . . . 1709
United States—See name of other party

V

Veneer & Panel Co. . . . 349
Vinal, R.P. . . . 1303.2
Voloudakis, S. . . . 521

W

Wacker, O.C. . . . 303.1
Wallace, J.D. . . . 735
Warren Service Corp. . . . 513.2
Washington Package Store, Inc. . . . 503.2
Watkins, H.V. . . . 2005
Watson Land Co. . . . 603
Watts, R.O. . . . 723.1
Watts, R.O. . . . 805
Wauwatosa Colony, Inc. . . . 807
WBSR, Inc. . . . 349
Weightman, G.H. . . . 1803
Weiss, G. . . . 807
Weiss, H.W. . . . 603
Wells Fargo Bank & Union Trust Co., Trustee . . . 515.1
Wentz, L.P. . . . 405
Westall, D.W. . . . 1315.2
Westchester Development Co. . . . 1523.2
Western Products Co. . . . 1503
Western Wheeled Scraper Co. . . . 807
Whitman, C. . . . 729.1
Wiener, J.H. . . . 603
Wilensky & Sons Co. . . . 115
Wilkerson, D.L. . . . 1705.1
Williams, W.B. . . . 425
Wilshire Holding Corp. . . . 443
Wilshire Medical Properties, Inc. . . . 615.1
Wilson, P. . . . 601
Wolfsen Land & Cattle Co. . . . 723.2
Wood, H.L. . . . 413
Woodbury, L.A. . . . 1317.1
Woodsam Associates, Inc. . . . 1213.1
Woolf, J.A. . . . 1213
World Publishing Co. . . . 607
Wright, Inc., B.T. . . . 805

Y

Yarbo, J.W. . . . 1225
Yates Holding Corp. . . . 1205.1
Young, M.C. . . . 501
Your Health Club, Inc. . . . 613

Z

Zaninovich, M.J. . . . 413

Index

References are to paragraph (¶) numbers.

A

Abandonment of land and improvements
. . . 1539.1; 1539.2

Accelerated cost recovery system (ACRS)
. computation of deduction . . . 923
. improvements and additions . . . 925
. optional straight-line schedules . . . 923.2
. pre-1987 property . . . 921
. schedules . . . 923.2
. straight-line election . . . 923.1

Accounting methods
. accelerating income and deferring deductions . . . 707.2
. accrual method, operating expenses for real property . . . 705.2
. cash method, operating expenses for real property . . . 705.1
. deferring income and accelerating deductions . . . 707.1
. economic performance requirement . . . 705.2
. home construction contracts . . . 705.3
. long-term construction contracts . . . 705.3
. operating expenses for real property . . . 705
. original issue discount, cash method . . . 335.1
. passive activity loss rules . . . 1143.1; 1143.2
. real property operating expenses . . . 701
. real property taxes, accrual method . . . 705.2
. related party transactions . . . 709
. residential construction contracts . . . 705.3

Accounting methods—continued
. small construction contracts . . . 705.3
. timing of income and expense . . . 707

Accounting periods
. election to use other than required tax year . . . 703.2
. operating expenses for real property . . . 703
. partnership tax year . . . 703.1
. personal service corporation tax year . . . 703.1
. S corporation tax year . . . 703.1
. termination of election to use other than required tax year . . . 703.2
. tiered structures . . . 703.2

Accrual accounting method
. economic performance requirement . . . 705.2
. real property taxes . . . 705.2

Accumulated earnings tax . . . 235.2

Acquisition of property transactions—see Construction of real property; Purchase of real property

Additions and improvements to property—see Improvements and additions to property

Adjustments, alternative minimum tax
. . . 1309.2

Advance rents . . . 413; 423

Advertising
. operating expenses for real property . . . 733

ADV

Allocation of costs
. buildings and personal property purchase ... 117.3
. land and buildings purchase ... 117.1
. land improvements and personal property ... 117.2
. real estate purchase as part of going business ... 117.4
. real property purchase ... 117

Alternative minimum tax
. adjustments ... 1309.3
. basic computation ... 1309.1
. credit against tax ... 1309.6
. depreciation ... 915.3
. optional 10-year writeoff ... 1309.5
. small business exception ... 1309.2
. tax preferences ... 1309.4

Amortization
. improvements and additions to real property ... 811
. investigatory expenses ... 713.1
. pollution control facilities ... 813
. pre-opening expenses ... 713.3
. reforestation expenses ... 815
. soil and water conservation expenditures ... 817
. start-up expenses ... 711; 713.2

Apportionment
. development expenses, basis ... 1003.1
. prior deduction of taxes ... 119
. real property taxes ... 119
. reimbursements ... 119

Appraisals ... 1603.1

Appreciated property, gifts ... 1607

Architectural barriers removal costs ... 723.2

Armed forces members
. moving expenses deduction ... 1717.4
. residence sale replacement period ... 2009.3

Assignments, rental arrangements ... 425

At-risk rules
. application of rules ... 313

At-risk rules—continued
. avoidance of rules ... 317.2
. borrowed amounts ... 317.1
. computation of at-risk amount ... 317.3
. deductions under the rules ... 315
. determination of amount at risk ... 317
. discounted loans ... 317.1
. guaranteed loans ... 317.1
. historical background ... 311
. order of deductions ... 315.1
. qualified nonrecourse financing ... 319
. real estate limited partnerships ... 2113.1
. recapture of prior deductions ... 315.2
. recourse liabilities becoming nonrecourse ... 317.2
. related persons, financing ... 319.1
. transfer of property ... 319.2

B

Bankruptcy
. bad debt deduction ... 1205.2
. creditor, tax treatment ... 1205
. debt forgiveness as gift ... 1203.1
. debtor, tax treatment ... 1203
. loss on debt discount ... 1205.1
. nonbusiness bad debts ... 1205.3
. purchase-money mortgage reduction ... 1203.3
. real estate owners ... 1200
. related parties, debt acquisition ... 1203.1
. settlement of debt at discount ... 1201

Basis
. acquisition of real property ... 100
. calculation of basis ... 103
. casualty, condemnation, or other involuntary conversion ... 1501; 1511
. casualty losses ... 1505.4
. construction of real property by owner ... 103.2
. contingent or speculative obligations ... 105.1
. debt used to artificially inflate purchase price ... 105.3
. development expenses, apportionment ... 1003.1
. exchange acquisition of property ... 103.3

ALL

Index

References are to paragraph (¶) numbers.

Basis—continued
. foreclosure or repossession . . . 1211; 1231
. gift acquisition of real property . . . 103.5
. importance of basis . . . 101
. inheritance acquisition of real property . . . 103.6
. loans against previously owned property . . . 105.2
. mortgages . . . 105
. multiple properties . . . 1313.2
. new residence purchase . . . 2011.2
. option acquisition of real property . . . 103.4
. partially tax-free exchanges . . . 1315.3
. partnership interest . . . 229.1
. partnership or corporation contribution of real property . . . 229.2
. property purchase price, artificial inflation . . . 15.3
. purchase of real property . . . 103.1
. real estate mortgage investment conduits . . . 2315.2
. replacement property, involuntary conversion . . . 1525
. repossessed property . . . 1233.3
. rules . . . 103.8
. sale and replacement of principal residence . . . 2013.1
. sale of real estate, adjusted basis . . . 1303.1
. sales and exchanges . . . 1313.2
. special basis rules . . . 103.8
. spousal property acquisition . . . 103.7
. subdivision of tract . . . 1003.2

Building improvements . . . 813

Business expenses deduction . . . 1605

Business use of home
. allocation of deductions . . . 1805
. business expenses unrelated to use of home . . . 1807.2
. day-care facility use of home . . . 1809
. determination of gross income from business use . . . 1807.1
. direct expenses allocation . . . 1805.1
. exceptions to exclusive use test . . . 1803.1
. exclusive use for business test . . . 1803

Business use of home—continued
. indirect expenses allocation . . . 1805.2
. limitation on deduction . . . 1807
. mixed-use residences . . . 1800
. multiple locations . . . 1807.1
. order of deductions . . . 1807.2
. place to meet patients, clients, or customers requirement . . . 1803.3
. principal place of business requirement . . . 1803.2
. separate structures requirement . . . 1803.3
. tax treatment . . . 1801

Buy downs . . . 305

Buying expenses . . . 115

C

Capital expenditures
. carrying charges . . . 135
. construction of real property . . . 127
. improvements and additions to real property . . . 801
. interest allocation . . . 127.2
. leasehold improvements and additions . . . 615

Capital gains and losses
. sales and exchanges . . . 1305.1
. corporations . . . 1305.1
. individuals . . . 1305.1

Capitalization of costs
. carrying charges . . . 135
. construction expenses other than interest . . . 127.1
. construction of real property . . . 127
. interest allocation, construction of real property . . . 127.2

Carrying charges, capitalization . . . 135

Carryovers
. passive activity losses . . . 1147.3
. passive activity suspended loss . . . 1149.2

Cash accounting method
. operating expenses for real property . . . 705.1
. original issue discount . . . 335.1

Casualty losses
- abandonment ... 1537
- abandonment of improvements ... 1539.2
- abandonment of land ... 1539.1
- adjusted gross income limitation ... 1713.2
- basis after casualty ... 1505.4
- business casualty ... 1501
- calculation of casualty deduction ... 715
- casualty defined ... 1503
- casualty gains and losses ... 1505
- condemnations ... 1511-1517
- deductible for losses ... 1713.1
- demolition ... 1535
- demolition and abandonment, tax rules ... 1531
- disaster area losses ... 1507
- fifty-five-year-old taxpayers, residence sale ... 2017.1
- gains ... 1505.2
- homeowners deductions ... 1711
- insurance and other reimbursements ... 1505.3
- involuntary conversion of property ... 1519
- limitations ... 1713
- losses ... 1505.1
- low-income housing credit ... 837.4
- married couples, deduction limitations ... 1713.2
- multiple owners, deduction limitations ... 1713.1
- outdoor advertising displays, involuntary conversion ... 1523.3
- part business and part personal-use property casualty deduction ... 1717
- personal property casualty loss deduction ... 1715.2
- real and personal property casualty loss deduction ... 1715.3
- real estate casualty loss deduction ... 1715.1
- replacement property, acquisition of corporate control ... 1523.4
- replacement property, basis ... 1525
- replacement property, election to postpone gain ... 1521
- severance damages ... 1517.1

Casualty losses—continued
- special assessments ... 1517.2
- tax rules ... 1500

Charitable contributions
- appraisals, required ... 1603.2
- appraisals, types ... 1603.1
- appreciated property ... 1607
- business expenses deduction ... 1605
- capital gain property ... 1607.2
- charitable gifts limitations ... 1601
- conservation purposes ... 1609.3
- farm ... 1609.2
- gifts of partial interests ... 1609
- loss property ... 1625
- mixed property ... 1607.3
- mortgaged property ... 1615
- ordinary income property ... 1607.1
- personal residence ... 1609.1
- remainder interest ... 160.2
- tax treatment ... 1600
- undivided portion ... 1609.1
- valuation of real estate gifts ... 1603.1

Children, family corporation employment ... 727.2

Closely held corporations
- passive activity loss credit ... 1149.1
- passive activity loss rules ... 1105.1; 1145

Commissions and fees
- operating expenses for real property ... .0729
- sales and exchanges ... 1315.4

Community property ... 221

Compensation
- children and spouses as employees ... 727.2
- family members as employees ... 727.2
- independent contractors and employees ... 727.3
- loans as compensation ... 327.2
- partners ... 727.5
- payroll taxes ... 727.2
- real estate agents ... 727.4
- real estate corporation officers ... 727

Condemnations
. condemnation defined . . . 1513
. determination of condemnation award . . . 1517
. fifty-five-year-old taxpayers, residence sale gain exclusion . . . 2017.1
. gains or losses . . . 515
. replacement property, special rule . . . 1523.3
. severance damages . . . 1517.1
. special assessments . . . 1517.2
. tax rules . . . 1511

Conditional sales contract . . . 349

Condominiums
. application of tax rules . . . 1909
. association tax treatment . . . 1913
. unit owner tax treatment . . . 1911

Construction of real property
. basis . . . 103.2
. capitalization of carrying charges . . . 135
. capitalization of costs . . . 127
. constructive ownership rules . . . 1303.3
. expenses other than interest, capitalization . . . 127.1
. interest allocation . . . 127.2
. interest and taxes allocation, pre-1987 construction . . . 131
. low-income housing tax credit . . . 139
. tax treatment . . . 123

Contingent sales, installment reporting
. . . 1405.5

Contributions to partnership . . . 229.2

Controlled corporations, rental arrangements . . . 409.2

Controlled groups, sales and exchanges
. . . 1303.3

Cooperative housing corporations
. depreciation . . . 1905.2
. distributions . . . 1903.3
. gross income of cooperative housing corporation . . . 1903.4
. interest deduction . . . 1905.1
. one class of stock requirement . . . 1903.1

Cooperative housing corporations—continued
. qualification as cooperative housing corporation . . . 1903
. real property taxes . . . 1905.1
. right of occupancy . . . 1903.2
. tax treatment . . . 1900
. tenant-stockholder deductions . . . 1905

Corporations
. accumulated earnings tax . . . 235.2
. choice of business entity, property ownership . . . 263
. controlled corporations, rental arrangements . . . 409.2
. legal characteristics . . . 233
. mortgaged property . . . 235.1
. operation of corporation . . . 235.2
. organization costs . . . 235.1
. organization of corporation . . . 235.1
. ownership of property, agency relationship . . . 205
. partnership incorporation . . . 235.1
. passive activity loss rules . . . 1109.2
. personal holding company tax . . . 235.2
. property acquisition . . . 231
. property distributions and liquidations . . . 235.3
. S corporations . . . 241; 243
. sales and exchanges, capital gains and losses . . . 1305.1
. section 1250 property, depreciation recapture . . . 1307.2
. taxable incorporation . . . 235.1
. taxation . . . 235
. transfer of services . . . 235.1

Cost allocation, purchase of property . . . 117

Creditors
. debt settlement at discount . . . 1205
. foreclosure . . . 1215

Credits against tax
. alternative minimum tax credit . . . 1309.6
. investment credit . . . 621
. low-income housing credit . . . 139; 831
. passive activity losses . . . 1149
. reforestation expenses . . . 815
. rehabilitation of buildings . . . 821

D

Day-care facilities, business use of home ... 1809

Dealers
. characterization of dealer property ... 1013
. dealer installment sales ... 1015.1
. installment sales ... 1403.1
. sales of timeshares and residential lots ... 1015.2
. status as dealer ... 1011
. subdivided realty as dealer property ... 1013.2
. tax treatment ... 1015
. tests for classification of dealer property ... 1013.1

Death transfers ... 1147.4; 1413.1

Debt property purchases ... 105.3

Debt instruments, original issue discount ... 335.2

Debts and debtors
. bad debt deduction ... 1205.2
. creditor, tax treatment ... 1205
. debtor, tax treatment ... 1203
. election to reduce basis ... 120.2
. forgiveness of debt as gift ... 1203.1
. insolvent or bankrupt debtor ... 1203.2
. installment sales, mortgages, and other debts assumed ... 1405.2
. loss on debt discount ... 1205.1
. nonbusiness bad debts ... 205.3
. purchase-money mortgage reduction ... 1203.3
. real estate owners ... 1200
. real property business debt ... 1203.3
. reduction of tax attributes ... 1203.2
. related parties, debt acquisition ... 1203.1
. repayments and refinancing, interest ... 325.3
. settlement of debt at discount ... 1201
. solvent debtor, acquisition of debt ... 1203.1

Deductions
. interest ... 325

Deductions—continued
. passive activity loss rules ... 1143.2

Deferred or stepped rental agreements ... 431

Deferred payment sales ... 331

Deficiency assessments, replacement of condemned property ... 1521.3

Demand payments, installment sales ... 1405.2

Demolition of property ... 1531; 1535

Deposits, rental arrangements ... 451-455

Depreciation
. accelerated cost recovery system (ACRS), pre-1987 property ... 921
. accelerated cost recovery system deduction ... 923
. accelerated cost recovery system schedules ... 923.2
. alternative depreciation calculation ... 913
. alternative depreciation optional tables ... 913.2
. alternative minimum tax ... 915.3
. anti-churning rules ... 935
. application of rules ... 900
. calculation of deduction for real property ... 933
. change of depreciation methods ... 933.
. computation of the deduction ... 903
. construction of property ... 905.2
. cooperative housing corporations, deductions ... 1905.2
. election of alternative depreciation ... 913.1
. general depreciation system ... 901
. improvements and additions to real property ... 905; 923.2
. installment sales, recapture rules ... 1405.1
. land improvements ... 905.1
. methods ... 933.1
. mid-month convention ... 903.3
. modified accelerated cost recovery system (MACRS) ... 901

Index

Depreciation—continued
. nonresidential property . . . 903.3
. optional schedules (ACRS) . . . 923
. optional tables (MACRS) . . . 903.4
. pre-1981 property . . . 931
. real property subject to alternative depreciation . . . 915
. recapture, sales and exchanges . . . 1301
. recovery periods . . . 903.1
. related party transfers . . . 935.2
. residential rental property . . . 903.3
. section 1245 property, depreciation recapture . . . 1307.1
. section 1250 property, depreciation recapture . . . 1307.2
. straight-line method election . . . 923.1
. straight-line method . . . 903
. tax-exempt bond financed property . . . 915.2
. tax-exempt use property . . . 915.1
. tax-free transfers . . . 935.3
. trust held property . . . 255

Development expenses
. apportionment methods . . . 100.2
. basis apportionment . . . 1003.1
. development improvements as separate interest . . . 1005.1
. equitable apportionment rule . . . 1033
. estimated future costs . . . 1005.2
. inclusion of costs in basis . . . 1005
. tax treatment . . . 1001

Disaster area losses . . . 1507

Distributions
. corporations . . . 235.3
. partnerships . . . 229.4
. real estate mortgage investment conduits . . . 2315.1

District of Columbia
. capital gain . . . 1337
. homebuyer credit . . . 1731

E

Easements
. sale of real estate . . . 1303.2

Elections
. depreciation, straight-line method . . . 923.1
. installment reporting . . . 1403.3

Empowerment zones
. D.C. zone capital gain . . . 1337
. rollover of investment . . . 1333

Escrow arrangements . . . 1403.2

Estates, residence sales . . . 2017.1

Exchange of real property, basis . . . 103.3

Exempt organizations
. depreciation, tax-exempt use property . . . 915.1
. sale-leasebacks . . . 347.4

F

Family members
. compensation for family members as employees . . . 727.2
. intra-family leases . . . 409.1
. land sales, imputed interest . . . 333.2

Fifty-five-year-old taxpayers, residence sale gain exclusion
. election of the exclusion . . . 2025.1
. exclusion amount . . . 2023
. multiple owners . . . 2023.1
. ownership and use requirements . . . 2023.1
. purchase of new principal residence . . . 2023.2
. revocation of election . . . 2025
. tax rules . . . 2015

Foreclosure
. creditor, tax treatment . . . 1215
. debtor, tax treatment . . . 1213
. expenses . . . 1215.1
. gain or loss calculation . . . 1213.1
. gain or loss character . . . 1213.2
. mortgagee purchase of property . . . 1215.3
. tax rules . . . 1211
. third party purchases . . . 1215.2

Foreign moves, expenses deduction . . . 1727.3

Foreign persons
. real property sellers . . . 121
. real property transfers . . . 121

G

Gains and losses
. built-in gain, S corporations . . . 247.1
. casualty losses . . . 1505
. condemnations . . . 1515
. controlled groups . . . 1303.3
. disposition of installment obligations . . . 1411
. foreclosure . . . 1213.1
. low-income housing, deferral of gain . . . 1303.5
. partnership built-in gain or loss . . . 229.2
. passive activity loss rules . . . 1143.2
. real estate limited partnerships, restrictions . . . 2113
. repossessions . . . 1233
. repossessions, recognition of gain . . . 1235
. sale of real estate . . . 1303
. sale of residence, exclusion . . . 2007
. sale of residence, tax-free rollover . . . 2011
. sale of residential property . . . 2001
. sales and exchanges . . . 1305
. subdivision of real property . . . 1025

General partnerships . . . 227.1

Gifts
. acquisition of real property, basis . . . 103.5
. appraisals, required . . . 1603.2
. appraisals, types . . . 1603.1
. appreciated property . . . 1607
. business expenses deduction . . . 1605
. capital gain property . . . 1607.2
. charitable gifts of mortgaged property . . . 1619
. charitable gifts, tax treatment . . . 1600; 1601
. conservation purposes . . . 1609.3
. family members, gifts of mortgaged property . . . 1617

Gifts—continued
. farm . . . 1609.2
. loans, gift tax treatment . . . 327.1
. loans, income tax treatment . . . 327.1
. loss property . . . 1625
. mixed property . . . 1607.3
. mortgaged property . . . 1615
. ordinary income property . . . 1607.1
. partial interests . . . 1609
. personal residence . . . 1609.2
. property acquisition, basis . . . 103.5
. remainder interest . . . 1609.2
. undivided portion . . . 1609.1
. valuation of real estate gifts . . . 1603.1

Grantor trusts . . . 257

Gross income, business use of home . . . 1807.1

Guaranteed payments, partnerships . . . 229.5

H

Handicapped persons, architectural barriers removal costs . . . 723.2

Holding periods
. repossessions . . . 1233.2
. sales and exchanges, gains or losses . . . 1305.3
. subdivision of real property . . . 1023.1

Home construction contracts, accounting methods . . . 705.3

Homeowners associations
. assessments . . . 1925.3
. association property . . . 1917.1
. cooperative organization . . . 1925.2
. election of exempt status . . . 1923
. exempt function income . . . 1917.3
. expenditures . . . 1917.4
. inurement . . . 1917.5
. nonexempt associations . . . 1925
. tax-exempt status, nonexempt associations . . . 1925.1
. tax-exempt status qualification . . . 1917
. taxation of association . . . 1921
. use of units as residences requirement . . . 1917.2

GAI

Index

Homeowners deductions
. acquisition indebtedness . . . 1703.2
. casualty deduction calculation . . . 1715
. casualty losses . . . 1711
. casualty losses, limitations . . . 1713
. home equity debt . . . 1703.3
. housing allowances and assistance payments . . . 1707.4
. mortgage interest . . . 1701
. mortgage interest credit . . . 1707.3
. mortgage penalties . . . 1707.5
. mortgage points . . . 1705
. moving expenses . . . 1721-1727
. personal property casualty deduction . . . 1715.2
. qualified residence interest . . . 1703.1
. real and personal property loss deduction . . . 1715..3
. real estate casualty deduction . . . 1715.1
. real estate taxes . . . 1709
. redeemable ground rents . . . 1707.1
. shared appreciation mortgage (SAM) . . . 1707.2

Homes, business use—see Business use of home

I

Impact fees . . . 747

Improvements and additions to property
. abandonment, casualty losses . . . 1539.2
. abandonment of improvement plans . . . 807
. accelerated cost recovery system (ACRS) . . . 925
. amortization, special provisions . . . 811
. application of tax rules . . . 800
. building component replacements . . . 805
. capital expenditure classification of improvements . . . 801
. capital investment classification of lessee improvements . . . 615
. construction of property, depreciation . . . 905.2
. depreciation (ACRS) . . . 905; 923.2
. election to pass investment credit to lessee . . . 625.1

Improvements and additions to property—continued
. historic structures, certified rehabilitations . . . 825
. investment credit . . . 621
. investment credit split on short-term lease property . . . 625.2
. land and buildings improvements . . . 803
. land improvements, depreciation . . . 905.1
. lease termination . . . 615.2
. lessee-improved property purchase . . . 607
. lessee benefits from improvements . . . 605
. lessee improvements . . . 611
. lessor improvements . . . 601
. low-income housing credit . . . 831
. pollution control facilities amortization . . . 813
. pre-1987 lessee improvements . . . 615.1
. qualified rehabilitations by lessee . . . 623
. qualified rehabilitations by lessor . . . 625
. reforestation expenses and tax credit . . . 815
. rehabilitation of buildings, tax credit . . . 821
. rehabilitation of older commercial buildings . . . 823
. rent classification of lessee improvements . . . 613
. restoration or maintenance by lessee . . . 603
. soil and water conservation expenditures . . . 817
. subdivision of real property . . . 1023.2
. substantial improvement qualification . . . 925.2
. substantial improvements as separate property . . . 925.1

Imputed interest
. contingent interest . . . 337.4
. excessive interest . . . 337.5
. family member land sales . . . 333.2
. installment obligations . . . 337.2
. maximum interest rate . . . 337.1
. original issue discount . . . 331
. rates . . . 337
. unstated interest . . . 3331

IMP

Index

Imputed interest—continued
. variable interest rate obligations . . . 337.3

Independent contractors, compensation
. . . 727.3

Individuals, ownership of property . . . 207; 213

Information returns, sales and exchanges . . . 1325

Inherited property, basis . . . 103.6

Installment obligations
. cancellation of installment obligations . . . 1413.2
. death transfers . . . 1413.1
. liquidation of subsidiary . . . 1413.1
. original issue discount . . . 337.2
. pledge of installment obligations . . . 1415
. recognition of gain, exceptions to rule . . . 1413.1
. repossession of property . . . 1417
. sale or satisfaction at less than face value . . . 1413
. spousal transfers . . . 1413.1

Installment sales
. constructive ownership, related party sales . . . 1407.1
. contingent sales . . . 1405.5
. dealer sales . . . 1403.1
. demand payments . . . 1405.2
. depreciable property sales . . . 1407.1
. depreciation recapture . . . 1405.1
. disposition of installment obligations . . . 1411
. election out of installment reporting . . . 1403.3
. escrow arrangements . . . 1403.2
. installment income, general rules . . . 1405.1
. interest on deferred tax . . . 1409
. like-kind exchanges . . . 1405.4
. mortgages and other debts assumed . . . 1405.2
. multiple assets . . . 1405.3
. passive activity loss rules . . . 1147.4
. payments . . . 1405.2
. qualification requirements . . . 1401; 1403
. reduction in selling price . . . 1405.1

Installment sales—continued
. related party resale rule . . . 1407.2
. related party sales . . . 1407
. reporting installment income . . . 1405
. seller-financed sales . . . 1400
. unstated interest . . . 1405.6

Insurance
. casualty losses, reimbursements . . . 1505.3
. operating expenses for real property . . . 731

Interest
. below-market rate loans . . . 327
. capital expenditures allocation . . . 127.2
. compensation loans . . . 327.2
. construction of real property, allocation of interest . . . 127.2
. cooperative housing corporations, deductions . . . 1905.1
. corporation-shareholder loans . . . 327.3
. debt repayments . . . 325.3
. deduction . . . 325
. deferred payment sales . . . 331
. demand loans . . . 327.2
. employee relocation loans . . . 327.2
. family member land sales . . . 333.2
. financing real estate . . . 321
. gift loans . . . 327.1
. imputed interest . . . 333
. imputed interest rates . . . 337.1
. installment sales, deferred tax . . . 1409
. interest-free loans . . . 327
. interest income . . . 323
. investment interest . . . 325.2
. loan proceeds deposited in an account . . . 325.3
. loan proceeds not paid to borrower . . . 325.3
. loan proceeds received in cash . . . 325.3
. operating expenses for real property . . . 737
. original issue discount . . . 331
. phase-in of disallowance . . . 325.2
. pre-1987 construction of real property, allocation of interest . . . 131
. prepaid interest . . . 325.1
. real property interest and taxes, pre-1987 construction . . . 131

Index

References are to paragraph (¶) numbers.

Interest—continued
. reallocation of debt . . . 325.2
. rental real estate . . . 325.2
. reporting requirements . . . 327.4
. term loans . . . 327.2
. tracing debt proceeds . . . 325.3
. unstated interest . . . 333.1
. vacant land . . . 325.2

Investigatory expenses . . . 713.1

Investment credit
. election to pass credit to lessee . . . 625.1
. leasehold improvements and additions . . . 621
. qualified rehabilitations by lessee . . . 623
. qualified rehabilitations by lessor . . . 625
. short-term lease property, credit split . . . 65.2

Involuntary conversion of property
. direct conversion of replacement property . . . 1525.2
. election to postpone gain . . . 1521
. outdoor advertising displays . . . 1523.3
. presidentially declared disasters . . . 1523.4
. related persons . . . 1523.2
. replacement property, acquisition of corporate control . . . 1523.4
. replacement property, basis . . . 125
. replacement with corporate stock . . . 1525.1
. tax rules . . . 1519

J

Joint tenancy
. ownership of property . . . 207; 213
. sale of residence . . . 2015

Joint ventures . . . 227.3

K

Kickbacks . . . 729.2

L

Land improvements . . . 813

Land sales
. vacant land, investment interest . . . 325.2

Landlords and tenants—see Lessors and lessees

Leasebacks, recapture . . . 435.2

Leasehold improvements and additions
. election to pass investment credit to lessee . . . 625.1
. improvements as capital investment . . . 615
. improvements as rent . . . 613
. improvements by lessor . . . 601
. improvements to benefit particular lessee . . . 605
. investment credit . . . 621
. investment credit split on short-term lease property . . . 625.2
. lessee's improvements . . . 611
. pre-1987 improvements . . . 615.1
. purchase of property with lessee improvements . . . 607
. qualified rehabilitations by lessee . . . 623
. qualified rehabilitations by lessor . . . 625
. renewal options . . . 615.1
. restoration or maintenance by lessee . . . 63
. tax treatment . . . 600
. termination of lease . . . 615.2

Leases
. acquisition costs . . . 501
. cancellation of lease . . . 511
. cancellation of lease, lessee's payments . . . 513
. cancellation of lease, lessor's payments . . . 515
. cancellation of lease, unamortized costs . . . 517
. classification of payments . . . 503
. improvements costs . . . 507
. involuntary conversion, replacement property . . . 1523.2
. lease as sales contract . . . 443
. lease or sale distinguished . . . 445
. lessee's acquisition costs . . . 503.2
. lessor's acquisition costs . . . 503.1
. modification of lease . . . 519
. purchase options . . . 441

Leases—continued
- renewal options ... 505; 615.1
- sale of lease ... 521
- tax rules ... 500
- termination of lease ... 615.2
- unsuccessful lease attempt costs ... 503.3

Legal expenses, operating expenses for real property ... 735

Lessors and lessees
- advance rents ... 413; 423
- assignments and loans ... 425
- cancellation of lease ... 511
- cancellation of lease, lessee's payments ... 513
- cancellation of lease, lessor's payments ... 515
- cancellation of lease, unamortized costs ... 517
- classification of lease payments ... 503
- decrease in rents ... 415.1
- deferred or stepped rental agreements ... 431
- deposits ... 451
- deposits, lessee's deduction ... 453
- deposits, lessor's deduction ... 455
- election to pass investment credit to lessee ... 625.1
- expenses payment ... 405
- graduated rents ... 415
- improvements as capital investment ... 615
- improvements as rent ... 613
- improvements by lessee ... 611
- improvements costs ... 507
- improvements to benefit particular lessee ... 605
- intra-family leases ... 409.1
- investment credit ... 621
- investment credit split on short-term lease property ... 625.2
- lease acquisition costs ... 501
- lease as sales contract ... 443
- lease or sale distinguished ... 445
- leases involving more than $250,000 ... 415.1
- leasehold improvements and additions ... 600

Lessors and lessees—continued
- leasehold improvements by lessor ... 601
- lessee's rent deduction ... 411
- lessor's rent income ... 421
- modification of lease ... 519
- pre-1987 improvements ... 615.1
- purchase of property with lessee improvements ... 67
- purchase options ... 441
- qualified rehabilitations by lessee ... 623
- qualified rehabilitations by lessor ... 625
- recapture in leasebacks and long-term agreements ... 435.2
- renewal options ... 415.1; 505; 615.1
- rent increases ... 415.2
- rental agreement rules, exceptions ... 435.1
- restoration or maintenance by lessee ... 603
- sale of lease ... 521
- section 467 rental agreements ... 433
- tax avoidance transactions ... 435
- termination of lease ... 615.2

Like-kind exchanges of property
- installment reporting ... 1405.4
- like-kind real estate defined ... 1313.1
- requirements ... 1311; 1313
- sale-leasebacks ... 343.2

Limited liability companies ... 237
- check-the-box regulations ... 237.1
- entity classification ... 237.1
- partnership conversion to ... 237.3

Limited partnerships ... 227.2

Liquidations
- corporations ... 235.3
- installment obligations disposition ... 1413.1

Loans
- at-risk rules ... 317.1
- borrowing against property previous owned, basis ... 105.2
- compensation loans ... 327.2
- corporation-shareholder loans ... 327.3
- demand loans ... 327.2
- discounted loans ... 317.1
- employee relocation loans ... 327.2
- gift loans ... 327.1

Index 701

References are to paragraph (¶) numbers.

Loans—continued
. guaranteed loans . . . 317.1
. interest-free and below-market rate loans . . . 327
. rental arrangements . . . 425
. term loans . . . 327.2

Long-term construction contracts, accounting methods . . . 705.3

Losses—see Casualty losses; Gains and losses

Low-income housing credit
. calculation of credit . . . 835
. casualty losses . . . 837.4
. certification . . . 833.2
. compliance provisions . . . 837
. increases in tenant income . . . 837.1
. minimum set-aside . . . 833.2
. partnerships . . . 837.2
. purchase or construction of low-income housing . . . 139
. qualification for the credit . . . 833
. qualified basis for determining credit . . . 835.2
. qualified low-income building . . . 833.1
. qualified low-income housing projects . . . 833.2
. rates of credit . . . 835.1
. recapture amount . . . 837.3
. recapture provisions . . . 837
. rehabilitation expenditures . . . 835.3
. rent restriction . . . 833.2
. section 1250 property, depreciation recapture . . . 1307.2
. state credit authority . . . 833.2
. tax rules . . . 831

M

Master limited partnerships
. evolution of the concept . . . 2125
. origins . . . 2123
. real estate MLPs . . . 2129
. tax legislation impact . . . 2127
. tax treatment . . . 2121

Modified accelerated cost recovery system (MACRS)
. alternative depreciation system . . . 911; 915.3
. anti-churning rules . . . 935
. application of depreciation rules . . . 901
. computation of the deduction . . . 903
. recovery periods . . . 903.1
. straight-line method . . . 903.2
. mid-month convention . . . 903.3
. residential rental property . . . 903.3
. nonresidential property . . . 903.3
. improvements and additions . . . 905
. land improvements . . . 905.1
. property under construction . . . 905.2
. real property subject to alternative depreciation . . . 9.5
. tax-exempt bond financed property . . . 915.2
. tax-exempt use property . . . 915.1

Mortgages
. abandonment by mortgagor . . . 1225
. acquisition indebtedness rules . . . 1703.2
. acquisition indebtedness tracing . . . 1703.2
. basis . . . 105
. borrower's costs . . . 303.1
. borrowing against previously owned property . . . 105.2
. buy downs . . . 305
. charitable gifts of mortgaged property . . . 1619
. contingent or speculative obligations . . . 105.1
. conveyance and abandonment of mortgage . . . 1221
. conveyance to mortgagee . . . 1223
. corporations . . . 235.1
. costs . . . 303
. debt partially acquisition and indebtedness . . . 1703.2
. family members, gifts . . . 161
. financing real estate . . . 301
. foreclosure, purchase by mortgagee . . . 1215.3
. gifts of mortgaged property . . . 1615
. home equity debt . . . 1703.3
. homeowners deductions . . . 1700

MOR

Mortgages—continued
. housing allowances and assistance payments . . . 1707.4
. installment sales, debts assumed . . . 1405.2
. interest deduction . . . 1701
. interest deduction, married individuals . . . 1703.2
. lender's costs . . . 303.2
. mortgage interest credit . . . 1707.3
. partnership contributions . . . 229.2
. payment discounts . . . 307.2
. payoff of mortgage . . . 307
. penalties . . . 1707.5
. points . . . 1705
. points charged for services . . . 1705.1
. pre-1987 indebtedness . . . 1703.4
. prepayment penalties . . . 307.1
. property purchase price, artificial inflation . . . 15.3
. purchase-money mortgages . . . 1203.3
. qualified residence interest . . . 1703
. qualified residence interest defined . . . 1703.1
. redeemable ground rents . . . 1707.1
. refinancing acquisition indebtedness . . . 1703.2
. refinancing points . . . 1705.2
. repossessions, third-party mortgages . . . 1235.3
. residence under construction . . . 1703.1
. sales and exchanges . . . 1315.2
. shared appreciation mortgage (SAM) . . . 1707.2
. special mortgage situations . . . 1707
. tax rules . . . 300
. tax treatment of mortgagee . . . 1223.2
. tax treatment of mortgagor . . . 1223.1

Moving expenses
. armed forces members . . . 1727.4
. deductible costs . . . 1727
. distance requirements . . . 1723.1
. foreign moves . . . 1727.3
. length of employment requirement . . . 1723.2
. qualification for deduction . . . 1723
. reimbursements . . . 1727.2
. tax treatment . . . 1721

N

Nominee corporations, ownership of property . . . 203

New York Liberty Zone . . . 841; 845

O

Oil and gas property, passive activity loss rules . . . 1107.2

Operating expenses for real property
. accounting methods . . . 705
. accounting period . . . 703
. accounting procedures for real estate . . . 701
. advertising . . . 733
. architectural barriers removal . . . 723.2
. back taxes payments . . . 743.2
. children as employees, compensation . . . 727.2
. commissions and fees . . . 729
. compensation, real estate corporation officers . . . 727
. family members as employees, compensation . . . 727.2
. impact fees . . . 747
. independent contractors, compensation . . . 727.3
. insurance . . . 731
. interest . . . 737
. kickbacks . . . 729.2
. legal expenses . . . 735
. licensed real estate agents, compensation . . . 727.4
. materials and supplies . . . 725
. partners . . . 727.5
. payroll taxes . . . 727.2
. real estate commissions . . . 729.1
. real estate corporation officers compensation . . . 727.1
. real property taxes . . . 741; 732
. real property taxes deductions . . . 743.1
. repairs or improvements . . . 723
. repairs, classification . . . 723.1
. replacement, renovation, and reconditioning . . . 723.2
. special assessments and local benefit taxes . . . 745

Index

Operating expenses for real property—continued
. spouses as employees, compensation . . . 727.2
. start-up expenses . . . 711; 713.2
. tax rules overview . . . 700; 721
. tax years for business entities . . . 703
. transfer taxes . . . 747

Options
. acquisition of real property, basis . . . 103.4
. lease renewal . . . 505
. lease renewal options . . . 615.1
. purchase of property, basis determination . . . 103.4
. rental arrangements, purchase options . . . 441

Organization and syndication costs
. corporations . . . 235.1
. partnerships . . . 229.3

Original issue discount
. cash accounting method . . . 335.1
. contingent interest . . . 337.4
. debt instruments assumptions and modifications . . . 335.2
. excessive interest . . . 337.5
. historical background . . . 331
. imputed interest . . . 333
. installment obligations . . . 337.2
. interest rates . . . 337
. maximum interest rate . . . 337.1
. tax rules . . . 335
. unstated interest . . . 333.1
. variable interest rate obligations . . . 337.3

Outdoor advertising displays, involuntary conversion . . . 1523.3

Overseas residence, replacement period . . . 2013.4

Ownership of property
. business form selection . . . 261
. business forms, comparison . . . 267
. community property . . . 221
. corporate agency . . . 205
. corporation or partnership as owner . . . 263
. corporations . . . 231

Ownership of property—continued
. individual ownership . . . 207; 211
. joint ownership . . . 207; 213
. partnerships . . . 225
. S corporation or partnership . . . 265
. S corporations . . . 241
. spousal jointly held property . . . 215
. straw or nominee corporations . . . 203
. tax treatment . . . 200; 201
. trusts . . . 251

P

Partnerships
. accounting period, tax year . . . 703.1
. admission of new partners . . . 229.2
. allocations for services . . . 229.3
. basis of partnership interest . . . 229.1
. built-in gain or loss . . . 229.2
. choice of business entity, property ownership . . . 263; 265
. compensation, disguised payments for services . . . 727.5
. compensation for partners . . . 727.5
. contributions as disguised sales of property . . . 29.2
. contributions to partnership . . . 229.2
. distributions . . . 229.4
. electing large partnerships . . . 229.7
. election to use other than required tax year . . . 703.2
. entity classification . . . 237.1
. general partnerships . . . 227.1
. guaranteed payments . . . 229.5; 727.5
. joint ventures . . . 227.3
. legal characteristics . . . 227
. limited partnerships . . . 227.2
. low-income housing credit . . . 837.2
. master limited partnerships . . . 2121-2129
. mortgaged property contribution . . . 229.2
. operation of partnership . . . 229.3
. organization and syndication costs . . . 229.3
. ownership of property . . . 225
. passive activity loss rules . . . 1123.2; 1143.3

Partnerships—continued
. passive activity loss rules, limited partnership interest . . . 1107.1
. property acquisitions . . . 225
. publicly traded partnerships, passive activity losses . . . 1151-1159
. real estate limited partnerships . . . 2100-2115
. services as contribution . . . 229.2
. special allocations . . . 229.3
. syndicates . . . 227.4
. taxation . . . 229

Passive activity loss rules
. active participation in rental real estate . . . 1131
. activities subject to the rules . . . 1107
. activity rule . . . 1113
. allocation of disallowed loss . . . 1147.1
. allocation within loss activities . . . 1147.2
. carryover of suspended credit . . . 1149.2
. carryovers . . . 1147.3
. change of accounting method . . . 1143.1; 1143.2
. closely held corporations . . . 1105.1; 1145
. computation of deductible loss . . . 1143
. credits against tax . . . 1149
. deductions . . . 1143.2
. disallowed losses . . . 1147
. disposition of passive activity . . . 1147.4
. gain on sale or disposition . . . 1143.2
. general provisions . . . 1103
. grouping, limitations . . . 1115
. grouping, rental real estate . . . 1133.1
. identification of separate activities . . . 1111
. installment sales . . . 1147.4
. limit on active participation . . . 1131.1
. limit on participation, filing status . . . 1131.2
. limited partnership interests . . . 1133.3
. loss on sale or disposition . . . 1143.2
. material participation . . . 1109
. material participation, corporation . . . 1109.2
. material participation, individual . . . 1109.1
. modified undertaking rule . . . 1115

Passive activity loss rules—continued
. oil and gas property working interests . . . 1107.2
. partnership property . . . 1123.2
. partnerships . . . 1143.3
. passive activity gross income . . . 1143.1
. personal service corporations . . . 1105.2
. personal service income . . . 1143.1
. phase-out of deduction . . . 1131.3
. portfolio income . . . 1143.1
. publicly traded partnerships . . . 1151-1159
. real estate limited partnership . . . 2113.2
. real property business exception . . . 1133
. regrouping activities . . . 1117
. rental activities limitations . . . 1121
. rental activity defined . . . 1123
. rental incident to development . . . 1127
. rental of nondepreciable property . . . 1129
. rentals incidental to nonrental activities . . . 1123.1
. S corporation shareholders . . . 1143.3
. S corporations . . . 1123.2
. self-rented property . . . 1125
. tax rules . . . 1100
. tax treatment . . . 1141
. taxpayers subject to rules . . . 1105
. transfers at death . . . 1147.4

Payroll taxes . . . 727.2

Penalties
. mortgage prepayments . . . 307.1
. sales and exchanges, reporting requirements . . . 1327

Percentage rents . . . 403

Personal holding company tax . . . 235.2

Personal service corporations
. accounting period, tax year . . . 703.1
. election to use other than required tax year . . . 703.2
. passive activity loss rules . . . 1105.2

Personal service income . . . 1143.1

Pollution control facilities, amortization . . . 813

Index

Prepayments
. interest . . . 325
. mortgages . . . 307

Property additions and improvements--
see Improvements and additions to property

Publicly traded partnerships . . . 1151-1159

Purchase-money mortgages . . . 1203.5

Purchase of real property
. allocation of costs . . . 117
. basis . . . 103.1
. buildings and personal property, allocation of costs . . . 117.3
. buying expenses . . . 115
. foreign person as seller . . . 121
. land and buildings allocation of costs . . . 117.1
. land improvements and personal property, allocation of costs . . . 117.2
. low-income housing tax credit . . . 139
. real estate as part of going business, allocation of costs . . . 117.4
. real property taxes apportionment . . . 119
. reporting requirements . . . 117.5
. tax treatment . . . 111

R

Real estate agents, compensation . . . 727.4

Real estate commissions . . . 729.1

Real estate investment trusts
. income restrictions . . . 2215
. liquidity and marketability . . . 2207
. management and control . . . 2205
. taxation . . . 2200; 2201

Real estate limited partnerships
. at-risk rules . . . 2113.1
. development of business form . . . 2101; 2107
. limited partnership interest . . . 2115
. losses restrictions . . . 2113
. master limited partnerships . . . 2121-2129

Real estate limited partnerships—continued
. passive activity loss rules . . . 2113.2
. tax rules overview . . . 2100
. tax shelters . . . 2103-2107
. tax treatment . . . 2111

Real estate mortgage investment conduits
. basis . . . 2315.2
. distributions . . . 2315.1
. income . . . 2315.2
. investor interests . . . 2301
. regular interests . . . 2309
. residual interests . . . 2315
. tax rules overview . . . 2300
. tax treatment . . . 2305

Real property
. allocation of costs . . . 117
. alternative depreciation . . . 915
. buildings and personal property acquisition, costs allocation . . . 117.3
. buying expenses . . . 115
. carrying charges, capitalization . . . 135
. construction costs, capitalization . . . 12
. construction of real property . . . 123
. financing methods, overview of rules . . . 300
. forms of ownership, overview of rules . . . 200
. foreign-person as transferor . . . 121
. interest and taxes on pre-1987 construction . . . 131
. land and buildings acquisition, costs allocation . . . 117.1
. land improvements and personal property acquisition, costs allocation . . . 117.2
. lessor and lessee rental arrangements, overview of rules . . . 400
. low-income housing tax credit . . . 139
. ownership, tax rules . . . 100
. purchase of real property . . . 111
. real estate as part of going business acquisition, costs allocation . . . 117.4
. real property taxes apportionment . . . 119
. uniform capitalization rules . . . 127

Real property taxes
. accrual accounting method . . . 705.2

REA

Real property taxes—continued
. apportionment on purchase of real property . . . 119
. back taxes payments . . . 743.2
. cooperative housing corporations, deductions . . . 1905.1
. deductions . . . 743.1
. homeowners deductions . . . 1709
. impact fees . . . 747
. operating expenses for real property . . . 741; 743
. special assessments and local benefit taxes . . . 745
. transfer taxes . . . 747

Recapture
. deductions under at-risk rules . . . 315.2
. depreciation, installment sales . . . 1405.1
. depreciation, sales and exchanges . . . 1307
. low-income housing credit . . . 837
. rehabilitation of buildings tax credit . . . 827

Recovery periods, depreciation . . . 903.1

Redeemable ground rents . . . 1707.1

Reforestation expenses and tax credit . . . 815

Rehabilitation of buildings tax credit
. application of tax rules . . . 821
. basis reduction by credit amount . . . 83.5
. historic structures certification requirements . . . 825.1
. historic structures certified rehabilitations . . . 825
. low-income housing credit computation . . . 835.3
. nonqualified buildings credit allowance . . . 825.2
. nonqualifying expenditures . . . 823.4
. older commercial buildings . . . 823
. predecessor's expenditures . . . 823.2
. recapture of rehabilitation credits . . . 827
. substantial rehabilitation test . . . 823.1
. wall test . . . 823.3

Reimbursements, moving expenses . . . 1727.2

Related parties
. debt acquisition, solvent debtor . . . 1203.1
. definition . . . 709.3
. depreciation on real property transfer, anti-churning rules . . . 935.2
. installment sales . . . 1407
. interest deductions . . . 709.2
. like-kind exchanges . . . 1313.1
. operating expenses deductions . . . 709.
. operating expenses for real property, accounting methods . . . 709
. rental arrangements . . . 409
. resale rules, installment sales . . . 1407.2
. sale-leasebacks . . . 347.2
. sales and exchanges, gain . . . 1305.1
. sales and exchanges losses, accounting methods . . . 709

Renewal communities
. capital gain . . . 1335
. commercial revitalization . . . 843

Rental arrangements
. advance rents . . . 413; 423
. assignments and loans . . . 425
. controlled corporations . . . 409.2
. decrease in rents . . . 415.1
. deferred or stepped rental agreements . . . 431
. deposits . . . 451
. deposits, lessee's deduction . . . 453
. deposits, lessor's deduction . . . 455
. exceptions from rental agreement rules . . . 435.1
. graduated rents . . . 415
. increase in rent . . . 415.2
. interest . . . 325.2
. intra-family leases . . . 409.1
. lease as sales contract . . . 443
. lease or sale distinguished . . . 445
. leasehold improvements as rent . . . 613
. leases involving more than $250,000 . . . 415.1
. lessee's rent education . . . 411
. lessor's expenses payment . . . 405
. lessor's rent income . . . 421
. options to purchase in leases . . . 441
. passive activities limitations 1121
. passive activity loss rules . . . 1115; 1117

Index

References are to paragraph (¶) numbers.

Rental arrangements—continued
- percentage rents . . . 403
- property transactions . . . 407
- recapture in leasebacks and long-term agreements . . . 435.2
- related parties . . . 409
- renewal options . . . 415.1
- rent payments, tax concepts . . . 400
- section 467 rental agreements . . . 433
- tax avoidance transactions . . . 435

Rental of residence
- classification of dwelling unit . . . 1823.1
- conversion to investment property . . . 1835
- determination of income and deductions . . . 1825
- expenses allocation . . . 1815
- limitations on rental losses . . . 1827
- part business use and part personal use . . . 1811
- personal use of residence . . . 1823.2
- principal residence . . . 1823.2
- rental income . . . 1813
- rental income, IRS allocation formula . . . 1825.2
- rental income, Tax Court allocation formula . . . 1825.2
- rental for 15 days or more . . . 1825.2
- rental for less than l5 days . . . 1825.1
- repairs and maintenance expenses . . . 1823.2
- use as principal residence . . . 1823.1
- vacation home . . . 1821

Repairs
- classification of repairs . . . 723.1
- improvement or repair . . . 723
- operating expenses for real property . . . 723
- replacement, renovation, and reconditioning expenses . . . 723.2

Repairs and maintenance expenses . . . 1832

Replacement period
- acquisition of corporate control . . . 1523.6
- armed forces members, sale of residence . . . 2009.3

Replacement period—continued
- basis . . . 1525
- condemned property, special rule . . . 1523.3
- deficiency assessments . . . 1521.3
- definition . . . 1523
- election to postpone gain . . . 1521
- extension of replacement period . . . 1521.3
- gain postponement, method of election . . . 1521.1; 1521.2
- involuntary conversion, election to postpone gain . . . 1521.3
- leased property replacement . . . 1523.3
- outdoor advertising displays . . . 1523.5
- overseas residence sale . . . 2009.4
- owner-investor . . . 1523.1
- owner-user property . . . 1523.1
- sale of residence . . . 2009.3
- severance damages . . . 1523.2
- similar property . . . 1523.1

Replacement property, involuntary conversion . . . 1523

Replacement, renovation, and reconditioning expenses . . . 723.2

Reporting requirements
- interest . . . 327.4
- purchase of real property . . . 117.5
- sales and exchanges . . . 1321
- sales and exchanges, penalties . . . 1327

Repossessions
- basis of reacquired property . . . 1233.3
- gain or loss nonrecognition . . . 1233
- gain recognition, character of gain . . . 1235.4
- holding period of reacquired property . . . 1233.2
- installment obligations disposition . . . 1417
- prior bad debt deductions . . . 1233.1
- reacquisition after election out of installment reporting . . . 1235.2
- reacquisition after installment sale . . . 1235.1
- recognition of gain . . . 1235
- seller-financed property . . . 1231
- third-party mortgages . . . 1235.3

REP

Residences—see Business use of home; Sales of residential property

Residential property
. construction contracts, accounting methods . . . 705.3
. business use of home—see Business use of home
. sales—see Sales of residential property

S

S corporations
. accounting period, tax year . . . 703.1
. built-in gain . . . 247.1
. choice of business entity, property ownership . . . 265
. election to use other than required tax year . . . 703.2
. income and loss . . . 247
. losses . . . 247.2
. passive activity loss rules . . . 1123.2; 1143.3
. property acquisitions . . . 241
. qualification for election . . . 243

Sale-leasebacks
. equity participation . . . 347.3
. IRS guidelines . . . 345.2
. lease with option as conditional sales contract . . . 349
. like-kind exchanges . . . 343.2
. recognition for tax purposes . . . 345
. related party sale-leaseback . . . 347.2
. split financing . . . 347.1
. straight sale-leaseback . . . 343
. supreme court guidelines . . . 345.1
. tax benefits . . . 343.1
. tax-exempt organization leasing . . . 347.4
. tax rules . . . 341
. variations on the sale-leaseback . . . 347

Sales and exchanges
. adjusted basis . . . 1303.1
. alternative minimum tax . . . 1309
. amount realized . . . 1303.2
. basis allocation among multiple properties . . . 1313.2
. basis in partially tax-free exchange . . . 1315.3
. basis rules . . . 1313.2

Sales and exchanges—continued
. build-to-suit exchange . . . 1313.1
. cancellation of installment obligations . . . 1413.2; 1415
. capital gains . . . 1305.1
. commissions and other expenses . . . 1315.4
. constructive ownership rules . . . 1303.3
. contingent sales . . . 1405.5
. controlled group loss deferral . . . 1303.3
. corporations, capital gains and losses . . . 1305.1
. corporations, depreciation recapture . . . 1307.2
. dealer sales, installment reporting . . . 1403.1
. delayed exchanges . . . 1313.1
. demand payments . . . 1405.2
. depreciable property sales, installment reporting . . . 1407.1
. depreciation recapture . . . 130
. disallowed losses . . . 1303.3
. disposition of installment obligations . . . 1411
. easement . . . 303.2
. election out of installment reporting . . . 1403.3
. escrow arrangements . . . 1403.2
. exclusion for residence . . . 2007
. fifty-five-year-old taxpayers residence sale gain exclusion . . . 2021-2025
. four-way exchange . . . 1317.2
. gain or loss character . . . 1305
. gain or loss computation . . . 1303
. gains or losses, holding period . . . 1305.3
. individuals, capital gains or losses . . . 1305.1
. information return and statement . . . 1325
. installment sales . . . 1401
. installment sales, depreciation recapture . . . 1405.1
. installment sales, mortgages and other debts assumed . . . 1405.2
. installment sales, qualification requirements . . . 1401; 1403
. interest on deferred tax, installment sales . . . 1409
. like-kind exchange requirements . . . 1313

Index

References are to paragraph (¶) numbers.

Sales and exchanges—continued
. like-kind exchanges, installment reporting . . . 1405.4
. like-kind real estate defined . . . 1313.1
. low-income housing, deferral of gain . . . 1303.5
. low-income housing, depreciation recapture . . . 1307.2
. mortgages and other liabilities . . . 1303.2; 1315.2
. multi-party exchanges . . . 1317
. multiple transferors, reporting requirements . . . 1323.2
. partially tax-free exchange . . . 1315
. penalties, reporting requirements . . . 1327
. property used in trade or business . . . 1305.2
. real estate . . . 1301
. related parties, like-kind exchanges . . . 1313.1
. related parties losses, accounting methods . . . 709.1
. related party installment sales . . . 1407
. related party resale rule . . . 1407.2
. related party sales gain . . . 1305.1
. reporting person . . . 1323.1
. reporting requirements . . . 1321
. residence sale, gains or losses . . . 2001
. residence sale, tax-free rollover of gain . . . 2011
. residence sale, tax treatment . . . 2011
. sale on contract for deed . . . 1303.2
. sales of multiple assets, installment reporting . . . 105.3
. section 1231 assets . . . 1305.2
. section 1245 property, depreciation recapture . . . 1307.1
. section 1250 property, depreciation recapture . . . 1307.2
. seller-financed sales . . . 1400
. selling expenses . . . 1303.2
. spousal transactions . . . 1303.4
. statement for transferor . . . 1325.2
. tax-free exchange of property . . . 1311
. tax rules . . . 1300
. three-way exchange . . . 1317.1
. transactions subject to reporting . . . 1323
. unstated interest . . . 1405.6

Sale of residence
. exclusion, business use . . . 2009.5
. exclusion, cooperative housing . . . 2009.5
. exclusion, gain . . . 2007
. exclusion, joint return . . . 2009.3
. exclusion, qualification . . . 2009

Sales of residential property
. basis in new residence . . . 2015.2
. business or rental use . . . 2003
. elderly taxpayers, ownership and use requirements . . . 2023.1
. elderly taxpayers, tax treatment . . . 2021
. gain on new residence . . . 2015.2
. gain on old residence . . . 2015.1
. gains or losses on sale . . . 2001
. joint ownership . . . 2015.3
. partial business use . . . 2017
. postponement of tax requirements . . . 2013
. replacement period . . . 2013.3
. residence held for gain . . . 2005
. tax-free rollover of gain . . . 2011
. tax rules . . . 2000
. tax treatment . . . 2015

Section 467 rental agreements . . . 433

Section 1231 assets . . . 1305.2

Section 1245 property, depreciation recapture . . . 1307.1

Section 1250 property, depreciation recapture . . . 1307.2

Selling expenses . . . 1303.2

Severance damages . . . 1517.1

Shared appreciation mortgage (SAM) . . . 1707.2

Soil and water conservation expenditures . . . 817

Spousal jointly held property . . . 207; 213

Spousal transfers of real property, basis . . . 103.7

Spouses
. compensation as family member employees . . . 727.2

709

SPO

Spouses—continued
. installment obligations transfers . . . 1413.1
. property acquisition, basis . . . 103.7
. sales of real estate . . . 1303.4

Start-up expenses
. amortization of expenses . . . 713
. investigatory expenses . . . 713.1
. pre-opening expenses . . . 713.3
. trade or business requirement . . . 715

Straight-line depreciation method . . . 903.2

Straw corporations, ownership of property . . . 203

Subdivision of real property
. gain calculation . . . 1025
. holding period rules . . . 1023.1
. improvements to land tracts . . . 102.2
. investors, special tax treatment . . . 1021; 1023
. necessary improvements after 10 years . . . 1023.3

Subsidiaries, liquidation . . . 1413.1

Supplies, operating expenses for real property . . . 725

Syndicates . . . 227.4

T

Tax assessments and local benefit taxes . . . 745

Tax avoidance transactions, rental arrangements . . . 435

Tax credits—see Credits against tax

Tax-exempt organizations—see Exempt organizations

Tax preferences, alternative minimum tax . . . 1309.4

Taxation
. corporations . . . 235
. property acquisitions, ownership requirements . . . 201
. real estate transactions, ownership of property . . . 201
. trusts . . . 253

Tenants—see Lessors and lessees

Transfer taxes . . . 747

Trusts
. depreciation . . . 253
. grantor trusts . . . 257
. ownership of property . . . 253
. taxation . . . 253

U

Uniform capitalization rules . . . 127

V

Vacant land, investment interest . . . 325.2

Valuation
. real estate gifts . . . 1603.1